To
My Dearest Friend
Rosejeanne Slifer

HOLLAND PRESS CARTOGRAPHICA

Volume 1
THE MAPPING OF AUSTRALIA AND ANTARCTICA
Second Revised Edition Edited by R. V. Tooley

Volume 2
THE MAPPING OF AMERICA
Edited by R. V. Tooley

Volume 3
MAPS AND CHARTS PUBLISHED IN AMERICA BEFORE 1800: A BIBLIOGRAPHY.
Second Revised Edition By James Clements Wheat and Christian F. Brun

Volume 4
MAPS AND VIEWS OF THE HOLY LAND
In 3 Parts: A, B & C

Volume 5
EARLY PRINTED MAPS OF THE BRITISH ISLES: A BIBLIOGRAPHY 1477-1650
Second Revised Edition By Rodney W. Shirley

Volume 6
CHRISTOPHER SAXTON Elizabethan Mapmaker
By Ifor M. Evans andHeather Lawrence

Volume 7
MAPS OF THE ENGLISH-SPEAKING WEST INDIES
Edited by R. V. Tooley

Volume 8
MAPS OF MEXICO AND NEW SPAIN
A Cartobibliography of the Hispanic Southwest, California, Texas and New Mexico
By Kit S. Kapp

Volume 9
THE MAPPING OF THE WORLD
Early Printed World Maps 1472-1700 By Rodney W. Shirley

Volume 10
THE MAPPING OF BERMUDA
A Bibliography of Printed Maps & Charts 1548-1970
By Margaret Palmer. Third revised edition by R. V. Tooley

Volume 11
EARLY PRINTED ITALIAN MAPS 1506-1620
A Comparative List of Maps by Bertelli, Duchetti, Forlani,
Gastaldi, Lafreri, Salamanca, Tramezzino and others
By R. V. Tooley

Volume 12
THE MAPPING OF CALIFORNIA AS AN ISLAND
By R. V. Tooley

Volume 13
PRINTED MAPS OF SOUTH AFRICA AND THE AFRICAN CONTINENT 1505-1900
By R. V. Tooley

THE
MAPPING OF
AMERICA

R.V. Tooley

with an index compiled by
DOUGLAS MATTHEWS

First published in 1980 jointly (as Volume 2
in The Holland Press Cartographica series) by

The Holland Press Limited
37 Connaught Street
London W2 2AZ
(Telephone: 01 262 6184)

Second   Impression   1985

Standard Cloth Edition: ISBN 0 900470 91 7
LCC Number: 79-89796

Printed in England by
The Moxon Press Ltd.
Gillroyd Mills, Wide Lane, Morley, Leeds

PREFACE

This second volume in the Holland Press Cartographica follows the style and format of volume 1 but has this difference: several of the articles are contributed by my friends; Coolie Verner with his Yorktown Campaign and Smith's Virginia; Tony Campbell's Jansson–Visscher Maps of New England based on a collection of 14 issues which I had formed at that time; Stevens and Tree's Comparative Geography; and Skelton's Marine Surveys of James Cook in North America, 1758–1768. This contribution was inspired by many of Cook's early surveys that I had in my possession including the rare collection of charts of Newfoundland and Labrador. Most of the articles appeared in the Map Collectors Series. An occasional correction or addition has been added, two new articles included and a comprehensive index to all the numbers supplied.

My thanks as usual are due to my publishers for their pleasant presentation and to those who consult the volume. I hope they may find it useful and enjoy the pleasure that is to be had from the perusal and study of old maps.

R. V. Tooley   London July 1979

LIST OF
PUBLICATIONS
BY R. V. TOOLEY

Some English Books with coloured plates 1970–1860: a bibliographical account.
A Reprint, Dawsons of Pall Mall, 1973. London: Ingpen & Grant, 1935.
— 2nd edition revised, London: Batsford, 1954.
—3rd edition revised and expanded, London: Dawsons of Pall Mall, 1978.
'Maps in Italian Atlases of the Sixteenth Century'. *Imago Mundi,* vol III, 1939, pp 12–47.
Maps and Map-Makers. London: Batsford, 1949.
— 2nd edition revised, 1952.
— 4th edition revised, 1970.
— 5th edition, 1972.
— 6th edition, 1978.
'Map making in France from the sixteenth century to the eighteenth century'.
Proceedings of the Huguenot Society of London, vol XVIII, No 6, 1952, pp 473–479.
Collectors' Guide to Maps of the African Continent and Southern Africa. London: Carta Press, 1967.
(With C. Bricker and G. R. Crone) *Landmarks of Map making.* Amsterdam & Brussels: Elsevier, 1968.
Also published under the title *A History of Cartography.* London: Thames & Hudson, 1969.

The following contributions to the *Map Collectors' Series,* published by the Map Collectors' Circle, founded and edited by R. V. Tooley, London, 1963 onwards.

AFRICA

'Early maps and views of the Cape of Good Hope' No 6, 1963.
'Printed Maps of Africa. Part I, The Continent of Africa, 1500–1600' No 29, 1966.
'Printed Maps of Africa. Part II, Regional maps, 1500–1600' No 30, 1966.
'Maps of Africa, a selection'. Parts I and II Nos 47 and 48, 1968.
'Printed maps of Southern Africa and its parts. Catalogue of a collection'. No 61, 1970.
'A sequence of maps of Africa' No 82, 1972.

AMERICA

'California as an island' No 8, 1964.
'North American city plans – a selection' No 20, 1965.
'French mapping of the Americas, the De l'Isle succession' No 33, 1966.
(With R. A. Skelton) 'The Marine survey of James Cook in North America 1758–1768' No 37, 1967.
'Printed maps of America' Parts I–IV Nos 68, 69, 80, 96. All published.
'A sequence of maps of America' No 92, 1973.
The Mapping of America. Holland Press Cartographica, Volume 2.

AUSTRALASIA

'Maps of Antarctica' No 2, 1963.
'The printed maps of Tasmania' No 5, 1963. Revised and Extended Edition by Francis Edwards Ltd., 1975.
'One hundred foreign maps of Australia 1773–1887' No 12, 1964.
'Early maps of Australia, the Dutch period' No 23, 1965.
'Printed maps of New South Wales' No 44, 1967.
'Printed maps of Australia' Parts I–VII. Nos 60, 64, 66, 72, 79, 85, 93, 1970–73.
The Mapping of Australia. Holland Press Cartographica, Volume 1.

EUROPE

'Leo Belgicus: a list of variants' No 7, 1964.

'The maps of South-West France' No 26, 1966.

'Scandinavian sea charts' Parts I and II, Nos 70, 71, 1971.

WEST INDIES

'Some early printed maps of Trinidad and Tobago' No 10, 1964.

'The printed maps of Antigua 1689–1899' No 55, 1969.

'Printed maps of Dominica and Grenada' No 62, 1970.

Maps of the English-speaking West Indies. Holland Press Cartographica, Volume 7.

OTHERS

'Dictionary of Map-makers, engravers and printers' Parts I–X (A. Powell) 1964–74. All published.

'Geographical oddities'. No 1, 1963.

Some Portraits of Geographers: 2 parts Nos 104 and 105, 1975.

Collecting Antique Maps. Stanley Gibbons, 1976.

Editor and Contributor to The Map Collector journal

Consulting Editor to Holland Press Cartographica series.

CONTENTS

CHAPTER ONE

French Mapping of the Americas
The De l'Isle, Buache, Dezauche Succession (1700-1830)
by R. V. Tooley

FRENCH MAPPING OF THE AMERICAS, THE DE L'ISLE SUCCESSION

Since the printing of this number I have come across a further example of a De l'Isle Atlas.

Without title, the atlas consists of 38 maps and it is the only example I have seen with a uniform imprint. Each map in this series bears the address of the 'Couronne de Diamans' (except three with Latin titles) and each has also the additional imprint 'se trouve a Amsterdam chez L Renard Libraire prez de la Bourse'. They are dated 1700 to April 1707. There are definitely editions of *L'Amerique Septentrionale*, *Carte du Mexique*, *L'Amerique Meridionale*, *Terre Ferme* and *Paraguay etc*. with the 'Couronne de Diamans' imprint in conjunction with Renard's address.

Additional Note: Jean Nicolas Buache de la Neuville revised the maps for the French edition of the 'Life of Washington' published in Paris by Dentu in 1807.

INTRODUCTION

THE 18th century was one of the most brilliant periods in the history of map making in France. French thought, method, and design dominated Europe, and for the greater part of the century her geographers made the most significant and influential contributions to the scientific progress of cartography.

The basis for this leading position had been established in the preceding century. Under Cardinal Richelieu a prime meridian had been established in 1634 through the island of Ferro. Under Colbert, first minister to Louis XIV, the *Académie Royale des Sciences* was founded in Paris in 1666. The foundations laid by the scientists of this " Académie " made possible the careers of two outstanding geographers in the following century, Guillaume De l'Isle and Jean Baptiste Bourguignon d'Anville.

This essay is an attempt to list the maps relating to America, published by De l'Isle and his successors outlined in the following table.

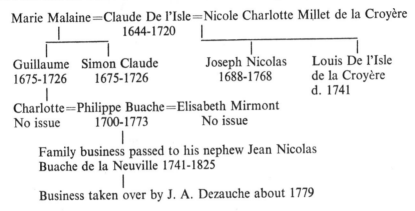

Marie Malaine=Claude De l'Isle=Nicole Charlotte Millet de la Croyère
              1644-1720

Guillaume   Simon Claude   Joseph Nicolas   Louis De l'Isle
1675-1726   1675-1726   1688-1768   de la Croyère
                                                  d. 1741

Charlotte=Philippe Buache=Elisabeth Mirmont
No issue   1700-1773   No issue

Family business passed to his nephew Jean Nicolas
Buache de la Neuville 1741-1825

Business taken over by J. A. Dezauche about 1779

CLAUDE DE L'ISLE

Claude De l'Isle, the founder of the family fortune, was born in Lorraine 5th November 1644 and died in Paris 2nd May 1720. Primarily a historian, and an able teacher, he was tutored in geography by Nicolas Sanson the elder. His own geographical output was small and mostly remained in manuscript. Working in conjunction with the *Académie Royale des Sciences*, he was entrusted with the task of preparing plans and instructions for d'Iberville's celebrated voyage down the Mississippi, and a manuscript map of 1701 is preserved in the Library of the *Service Hydrographique de Paris* based on this information. He produced an " Abrégé de l'Histoire Naturelle " and " Atlas Historique " in 1684.

His second son, Simon Claude, became a historian, and does not come within the scope of this essay. It is his son Guillaume with whom we are primarily concerned.

3

Guillaume De l'Isle [Insulanus] was born in Paris on 28th February 1675 and died in the same city on 25th January 1726. Educated by his father, it is said that at the age of eight or nine years he could draw maps to illustrate ancient history. Later he studied under Jean Dominique Cassini, the astronomer and mathematician, founder of the triangular survey of France.

In 1699, at the age of 24 he compiled a globe. From this manuscript, a printed copy was made in 1700 by J. B. Nolin. De l'Isle obtained an injunction against Nolin with authority to break his plates and burn all examples of printed copies that could be found.

In the same year 1700 De l'Isle himself had his globe printed (Reproduced in part in *Frontières entre le Brésil et la Guyane Française*, Paris 1900), and also separate maps of the continents Europe, Asia, Africa; and America in two sheets, North and South.

These maps were based on observations made in the Royal Observatory of Paris, and inaugurated a new era in cartography. De l'Isle reduced the length of Asia, noting this cartographical effect on other regions and was the first to give the correct measurement of 42° for the Mediterranean.

As a geographer, he must be judged against his background, the methods and information available to him, and his work compared to that of his contemporaries. In this context he was a great map maker, an innovator and a craftsman. His merit was quickly recognised in his own day. Men of science and kings (Louis XIV, Peter the Great, and the King of Sicily) paid him visits.

He raised France from a competitive to a dominating position in geography, and enjoyed an immense reputation throughout the eighteenth and even into the nineteenth century. De l'Isle's name became a hallmark and financial asset to a publisher, and his maps were copied not only in France but in Holland, Germany, Italy and England.

Modern commentators have likewise paid their tribute to his work. Karpinski records his " outstanding prominence as the first scientific cartographer," Carl I. Wheat states " He was a scholar as well as a cartographer." But perhaps the most illuminating comment comes from Lloyd A. Brown who writes " With almost no practical experience behind him [he] undertook a complete reform of a system of geography that had been in force since the second century, and by the time he was twenty five he had very nearly accomplished his purpose."

De l'Isle's maps were of course not without fault. His delineation of part of the coast of Louisiana was defective (Thomassy p. 211) and he was responsible for the incorrect insertion of a high plateau in Michigan (Karpinski p. 134) unfortunately giving credence to some of Lahontan's assertions. He also showed political bias in demarcating boundaries, excusably perhaps in the light of his official position, in extending the areas under French control at the expense of English claims to territory in North America. He particularly enraged the British in his map of Louisiana of 1718 by stating that Carolina was so named after the French King Charles IX and settled by the French. The English retaliated cartographically by extending the boundaries of their colonies westward to the Mississippi.

But his merits far outweigh his faults. His standard was high, his approach in physical geography scientific, and his examination of original sources careful. He was the first to correct the longitudes of America, to discard the well established fallacy of California as an island, to delineate the Mississippi Valley correctly, and to introduce many new place names. For example, in his map of Canada 1703 he records Detroit, founded only two years earlier, and in his map of the northern hemisphere of 1714 he revised place names on the west coast from information obtained from Frondat's voyage of 1709. In his map of Louisiana 1718, he records the travels of M. Denis in 1713 and 1716, names Texas for the first time, and records Natchitoches on the Red River which had been founded only the previous year, 1717.

In only one map, as far as I know, did he actually correct the original copperplate. His map of South America of 1700 gives Magellanica a strong curve westwards. In his second issue of the map still dated 1700, the south-west coast of South America is straightened and Magellanica given an eastwards curve. De l'Isle was continually revising his maps in the light of later knowledge, his normal practice being to issue a new map incorporating the latest information. Thus he compiled three presentations of America, the first in 1700, a second in 1714 corrected by the voyage of de Frondat in the Pacific in 1709, and a third in 1722.

Extremely industrious throughout his working life, from 1700 to 1726, not a year passed without his issuing at least one new map, his total production running to over 100 maps. These maps were sold separately as issued, and sometimes through an agent, e.g. his map of Beauvais 1710 has the additional imprint " Se trouve a Beauvais chez Etienne Aleau Libraire rue S. Pierre " and his maps were sold with the engraved imprint of Renard, bookseller in Amsterdam up to 1708. It is frequently discernible imperfectly erased on later impressions of the plates.

De l'Isle issued atlases, but without titlepages, and with varying contents. The British Museum possesses seven atlases by De l'Isle with different dates and contents; the Library of Congress has four and the Royal Geographical Society one. De l'Isle's atlas was reproduced in Holland by Mortier in 1708 (R.G.S.) and by Covens and Mortier in Amsterdam in 1730 (B.M. and L.C.) and 1733 (L.C. and F.E.) (See Plate 24). After that date Covens and Mortier continued to issue editions of the atlas undated. The L.C. has six examples of the Amsterdam imprint.

De l'Isle, a man of probity, reissued his maps several times in his lifetime, with the same title, and the date unchanged. This was contrary to the commercial practice of some publishers who reissued old plates unchanged except for the addition of the words " A new map &c " to the title. This honesty of De l'Isle creates dating problems for the modern bibliographer. The following information describing his titles may be of assistance.

1700 he is styled simply *Géographe*.

1702 his title is *Géographe de l'Academie Royale des Sciences*.

1718 he is styled *Premier Géographe du Roi* (a title specially created for him). Many of his maps dated before 1718 bear the inscription " Premier Géographe du Roi," but a careful examination of the lettering will reveal that these words have been inserted later. This is usually indicated by the cramped or poor alignment of the additional words (See Plate 17). His changes of address frequently show imperfect erasure of the old address. They were as follows.

1700-[1707] *Rue des Canettes pres de St. Sulpice.*

[1707-1708] *Quai de l'Horloge a la Couronne de Diamans*

[1708 onwards]   *Quai de l'Horloge a l'Aigle d'Or.*
Quai de l'Horloge (only).
Quai de l'Horloge au Palais.

The *Rue des Canettes* address appears on the *original* versions of maps dated 1700-1707. By April 1707 De l'Isle had apparently moved to the *Quai de l'Horloge a la Couronne de Diamans* as this address shows on his map of Piedmont and Montferrat published with that date (See Plate 17). Maps showing this address are rare and all bear the month as well as the year. This address has only been noted on maps dated 1707-1708, the latest seen being dated January 1708. Unfortunately in spite of the number of copies examined, I have been unable to find this address on any of his maps of America. Sometime in 1708, probably before March, De l'Isle altered his shop sign to *a l'Aigle d'Or*, though the address remains the same, *Quai de l'Horloge*. This shop sign, at the Golden Eagle, was to remain for the rest of De l'Isle's life and appears as late as 1732 on a map issued by his widow, but the majority of maps published or reissued after 1708 bear the address only, *Quai de l'Horloge*, without giving any shop sign. Occasionally the variant form, *Quai de l'Horloge au Palais* is used. (For illustration of imprints see Plate 17).

Few maps had as long a life as some of De l'Isle's. His map of America of 1722 was republished until 1830, revised in places but basically unchanged; and his map of Africa first published in 1700 still bears his name in an edition of 1827.

Guillaume died in 1726 and his business was continued by his widow.

PHILIPPE BUACHE

Philippe Buache was born in Paris 7th February 1700 and died on 27th January 1773. He studied drawing under Robert Pitrou, and geography under Guillaume De l'Isle. At the age of 21 he entered the *Dépôt des cartes et plans* where he worked for many years.

Soon after the death of De l'Isle he entered into partnership with the widow, and married her daughter Charlotte in 1729. In the same year he was made *Premier Géographe du Roi* and in the following year 1730, he was elected a member of the *Académie des Sciences*. In 1732 his map of Martinique was published by the widow of De l'Isle, but between 1737 and 1741 he was issuing his own maps from *le Quay de la Mégisserie au St. Esprit près du Pont Neuf.* By 1745 he was issuing maps from the *Quai de l'Horloge* and he was still at the same address in 1763.

In 1755 he was appointed teacher of geography to the Dauphin and the Duke of Burgundy, and later to the young Duke of Berry and the Counts of Provence and Artois.

On the death of his first wife, Charlotte, he married Elizabeth Catherine Mirmont, the sister-in-law of Robert Pitrou his first master. There were no children from either marriage and the inheritance passed to his nephew and assistant Jean Nicolas Buache de la Neuville.

Philippe Buache forms a complete contrast to his predecessor. He was one of the main protagonists of theoretical geography, and in conjunction with Joseph Nicolas De l'Isle produced some of the most fantastic and inaccurate maps of western America ever printed.

Nevertheless Buache made some contribution to the progress of cartography. He was one of the pioneers of physical geography dividing both the earth and the water into mountain chains and basins. He was the first to suggest that America and Asia had once been joined at Bering Straits, and one of the first to take advantage of the technique (devised by Cruquius in 1728) of contours or isobaths in his map of the English Channel in 1737.

JOSEPH NICOLAS DE L'ISLE

Born in 1688, died in 1768, was like his brother Louis De l'Isle de la Croyère, an astronomer. Educated by his father, and later at the *College Mazarin,* he was a pupil of Cassini. In 1724 he made a trip to England, visited Halley and Newton and was made an associate of the Royal Society of London. In 1726 he and his brother Louis took service with the Russian Court, but Louis after making numerous observations during travels in various parts of Russia died in 1741 while accompanying the second expedition of Vitus Bering. Joseph Nicolas who had organised an *Académie des Sciences* on the French model, founded a school of astronomy and created an observatory. In St. Petersburg he issued " Mémoirs pour servir à l'histoire et aux progres de l'astronomie, de la geographie," in 1738. He was a geographer as well as an astronomer and in conjunction with J. K. Kirilov produced the first Russian Atlas. This was printed in St. Petersburg in 1745. Relations between Kirilov and Joseph Nicolas were not always amicable, and though De l'Isle was accused of sending documents to France, he was acquitted of the charge.

Nevertheless, on his return to Paris in 1747 he took with him an immense collection of astronomical notes, manuscript and printed maps which he sold to Louis XV. They were deposited in the *Départment de Marine* and De l'Isle was made custodian of the collection at a salary of 8,000 francs per annum.

Three years later he read a paper before the *Académie des Sciences* embodying his theories about the N.W. coast of America. Together with his nephew by marriage Philippe Buache, he produced a series of maps with an entirely fictitious outline for the north-west coast of America with the so-called discoveries of Amiral de Fonte, Juan de la Fuca, and an enormous Sea of the West. Nicolas De l'Isle and Buache, discredited even in their own day by the more reliable Muller, tried to father their conceptions on the illustrious Guillaume. Nevertheless, as the hope of finding a northwest passage through Hudson's Bay to the Pacific was current at that time, their maps met with a certain amount of credence.

With the death of Buache in 1773, the De l'Isle inheritance with its valuable stock and business passed to his nephew Jean Nicolas Buache de la Neuville.

JEAN NICOLAS BUACHE DE LA NEUVILLE

Born in 1741, died in 1825, he became *Conservator du Dépôt des Cartes de la Marine*. In 1782 on the death of D'Anville he also, like preceding members of the De l'Isle dynasty, succeeded to the title of *Premier Géographe du Roi*. This was annulled during the Revolution.

Buache de la Neuville was a geographer rather than a publisher, and though he issued his own map of Dominica in 1778-9 his later work was published by J. A. Dezauche. He appears to have passed over the family stock and business to the latter about 1779-80.

J. A. DEZAUCHE

Little is known of J. A. Dezauche. He describes himself as *Géographe et Graveur, Successeur et Possesseur du Fond Géographique des Srs. De l'Isle et Phil. Buache et chargés de l'Entrepôt Général de Cartes de la Marine*.

A prolific publisher he issued various atlases reproducing the maps of Guillaume De l'Isle, Philippe Buache and Buache de la Neuville. In some of the later issues of his maps he made corrections and additions to the original maps. All these were issued from the Rue des Noyers.

He was also the publisher of the official charts of the *Hydrographie Francoise*, *Neptune Francois*, and *Neptune Americo-Septentrional*. According to his Catalogue [1782] printed by Morin he likewise acquired the best part of the maps from the stock of Jaillot. He also sold maps by D'Anville and D'Après de Mainvillette's *Neptune Oriental*.

BIBLIOGRAPHY

ADAMS (R. G) Delisle 'Detroit' Maps–editions noted by R. G. Adams. March, 1942.

BREITFUSS (L.) Early maps of N.E. Asia and of the lands round the North Pacific, controversy between G. F. Müller and N. Delisle. Imago Mundi III, 1939.

BROWN (Lloyd A.) Story of Maps. Boston, 1949.

Catalogue of the John Carter Brown Library. Providence, Kraus, 1963.

CUMMING (William P.) The Southeast in Early Maps. Princeton University Press, 1958.

DOUBLET (E.) Une famille de géographes et d'astronomes. De L'Isle. Revue de Geographie Commerciale, 1934.

DRAPEYRON (L.) Les Deux Buaches; & L'éducation géographique des trois princes francais an XVIII Siecle. Revue de Géographie XI, 1887.

FITE (Emerson D.) and FREEMAN (Archibald) A Book of Old Maps, Cambridge. Harvard University Press, 1926.

FORDHAM (Sir H. G.) Studies in Carto Bibliography. Oxford, Clarendon Press, 1914.

ISNARD (A.) Joseph-Nicolas Buache, sa biographie et sa collection des cartes géographiques à la Bibliothèque Nationale. Bull. de la section de Géographie XXX (1915).

KARPINSKI (Louis C.) Bibliography of the Printed Maps of Michigan. Michigan Historical Commission, 1931.

Library of Congress List of Geographical Atlases, 4 vols. by P. Lee Phillips 1909-20, and 2 vols. by Clara Egli Le Gear 1958-1963.

RODGER (Elizabeth) An Eighteenth Century Collection of Maps connected with Philippe Buache. Bodleian Library Record, Vol. VII No. 2, 1963.

SABIN (Joseph) Dictionary of Books relating to America. 29 vols. N.Y., 1868-1936.

THOMASSY (R.) Cartographie de la Louisiane. Chez l'Auteur a la Nouvelle-Orléans, 1859.

WAGNER (H. R.) Cartography of the N.W. Coast of America to 1800. 2 vols. Berkeley, California, 1937.

WHEAT (Carl I.) Mapping of the Transmississippi West. San Francisco, Institute of Historical Cartography, 1957.

EDITIONS OF DE L'ISLE'S WORK

FRENCH

De l'Isle   [Paris 1718]. 40 maps. B.M. 36f4.

          [Paris 1720]. 80 maps. B.M. 37f13.

          [Paris 1720]. 80 maps. B.M. 37f14 (25 additional maps inserted).

          [Paris 1732?]. 90 maps. B.M. 37f15 (published by Philippe Buache).

          [Paris 1732?]. 95 maps. B.M. 37f16 (De l'Isle catalogue inserted).

          [Paris 1732?]. 94 maps. B.M. K.1 Tab 9.

          [Paris 1732]. 95 maps. B.M. 37f18 (maps 50-95 only).

          [Paris 1755?]. 108 maps. B.M. 37f17.

          [Paris 1700-1712]. 59 maps. L.C. 533.

          [Paris 1700-1763]. 94 maps. L.C. 535.

          [Paris 1700-1763]. 97 maps. L.C. 636.

          [Paris 1700-1762]. 98 maps. L.C. 3456.

          [Paris 1700-1718]. 60 maps. F.E.

DUTCH

Amsterdam. Mortier, 1708. R.G.S. 1C59.

Amsterdam. Covens & Mortier, 1730. B.M., L.C. 3486.

Amsterdam. Covens & Mortier, 1733. L.C. 580.

Amsterdam. Covens & Mortier, 1733. L.C. 3487.

Amsterdam. Covens & Mortier, 1733. L.C. 581.

Amsterdam. Covens & Mortier, 1733. F.E.

Amsterdam. Covens & Mortier [1741?]. L.C. 596.

Amsterdam. Covens & Mortier [1741]. R.G.S. 1B14.

ITALIAN

Atlante novissimo, 2 vols. Venice, 1740-50.

Reduced versions of De l'Isle's maps, including North America, Canada, Florida [Louisiana], Mexico, South America and Brasil.

                                  (L.C. 594) (F.E.)

WORKS OF DEZAUCHE

Cartes et Tables de la Géographie Physique ou Naturelle 1780.

                    (R.G.S. 7H20) (B.M. Maps 182M2,

Atlas géographique et universel:

    Paris 1781-[1784]. 156 maps. L.C. 655.

          1789-[1790]. 93 maps. L.C. 3525.

Atlas géographique des quatre parties du Monde:

    Paris [1789?]. 37 maps. L.C. 671.

    Paris [1831?]. 35 maps. L.C. 759.

    Paris [1769-1799]. 34 maps. L.C. 3512.

    Paris [1780-1824]. 37 maps. L.C. 5993.

    Paris [1791]. R.G.S. 14B15.

PRINTED LISTS OF DE L'ISLE'S MAPS

[1712]   Liste des ouvrages géographiques de Guillaume de l'Isle . . . avec le tems auquel ils ont été publiez.   (L.C. 533)

[1732]   Liste des Ouvrages Géographiques de Guillaume delisle . . . A Paris chez l'Auteur, Quay de l'Horloge.   (B.M. 37f16)

[1782]   Catalogue des cartes & ouvrages geographiques de mm. De l'Isle et Buache . . . qui composent le fonds geographique du sieur Dezauche, successeur des sieurs De l'Isle & Buache.   (F.E.)

Supplément au Catalogue [1784].

Liste des Cartes Geographiques de G. De l'Isle. A Amsterdam Chez J. Cóvens & C. Mortier.   [Lists 119 maps].

ABBREVIATIONS

B.M.   = British Museum.
B.N.   = Bibliothèque Nationale Paris.
F.E.   = Francis Edwards Ltd.
H.S.   = Henry Stevens Son & Stiles.
L.C.   = Library of Congress.
R.G.S. = Royal Geographical Society London.

ACKNOWLEDGEMENTS

I wish to acknowledge the assistance of the staffs of the British Museum and the Royal Geographical Society, of Mr. T. Campbell for painstaking checking on my behalf; to Mrs. R. Hyde for care in typing, and in particular to Mlle. de la Roncière, *Conservateur, Départment des Cartes et Plans, Bibliothèque Nationale* Paris for notes on the examples of De l'Isle's maps of the American continent in that Library. I have also to thank the British Museum for permission to illustrate plate 19.

GUILLAUME DE L'ISLE (1675-1726)

The Continent of America

1 **1722** Carte d'Amerique dressée pour l'usage du Roy. Par Guillaume Delisle premier Geographe de Sa Majesté de l'Academie Royale des Sciences. A Paris Chez l'Auteur Sur le Quay de l'Horloge avec Privilege 1722. 61 × 48½ cms. This issue can be distinguished by the ornate lettering of the word *d'Amerique* in the title. The guide lines remain clear e.g. on *Guinée*.

Title within cartouche bottom left surmounted by a crown and the arms of France. Note on the projection used bottom right, headed *Avertissement*, engraved on a draped curtain. Depicts North and South America, the west coast taken north to Cap Mendocin and Cap Blanc with a note, "Entrée decouverte par Martin d'Aguilar". Reproduction in *Venezuela Boundary Arbitration H.M.S.O.* 1898. (F.E.)

There is a Russian version of this map with the title simply, *Amerika* (in Russian script). The *Avertissement* and lettering are also in Russian. It measures 59 × 48 cms. J. N. De l'Isle was in Russia from 1726-47. (Yale)

2 **1722** Another state. *Carte d'Amerique* in the title is now in plain black lettering. The guide lines are faint and the plate shows slight signs of wear, e.g. on inner lines of the title cartouche and the shading on the *Avertissement*.
(B.M. 37f15) (F.E.) (B.N. GeD11618)

The Bibliothèque Nationale possesses another copy of the same edition GeD11619 with a manuscript butterfly in North America and with a new "fleuve de l'Ouest au lac Superieur".

Plates 1 & 2.

3 **[1722]-1730** With the additional imprint: "Se vend a Bruxelles Chéz Eugene Henry Fricx Imprimeur du Roy 1730" between the title cartouche and bottom border. 60 × 48 cms.
Re-engraved with a newly designed though similar title-piece.
(H.S. NS23) (F.E.)

Plate 2.

4 **[1722]-1739** À Amsterdam Chez Jean Cóvens et Corneille Mortier, Geographes 1739. 60 × 48 cms.
Re-engraved though the map remains basically unchanged. The lettering within the title cartouche is copied from the issue of the first edition with the florid lettering for *d'Amerique*. (B.N. GeD11620) (F.E.)

Plate 2.

5 **1722-1745** With the additional imprint in the bottom right margin: "Ph. Buache P.G.d.R.d.l'A.d.S. Gendre de l'Auteur Avec Privilege du 30 Av 1745". An unchanged reissue of the first edition of 1722 apart from the new imprint and

The Continent of America—*continued.*

a foliate garland added to the original title cartouche.   The plate shows signs of having been touched up.

The Bibliothèque Nationale possesses a Spanish edition "Mapa de las Indias Occidentales dedicada al Serenissimo Principe de Asturias Don Fernando, dispuerta por Guillermo Delisle", undated, 60×47 cms.   (GeD 11.628).   A copy of the 1722 map and must be dated before 1746 the date of Ferdinand's accession to the throne of Spain.   (B.N. GeD11622)   (H.S. NS24)   (F.E.)

Plate 2.

6 **[1722-1755]**   A Amsterdam Chez Jean Cóvens et Corneille Mortier, Geographes [1755].

Revised issue of the Amsterdam copper-plate.   The plate for this edition is considerably altered and a Latin title printed in large type above the top border. The west coast is continued northward above Cap Blanc to include a large *Mer de l'Ouest*.   Several legends are expanded, for example, the note on the Papal line of demarcation now occupies three lines.   *Mer Pacifique* is added to *Grande Mer de Sud*.   Other additions include: *Ocean Ethiopien*, a note on the shipping off the Grand Bank of Newfoundland, historical notes in Magellanica &c.   The interior of N. America, to the west of Hudson's Bay and to the north of the Mississippi has been filled in, e.g. Lake Bourbon which in area rivals the Great Lakes replaces Lac du Brochet.   The west end of Hudson's Bay has been closed up and some names added, e.g. C. Churchill, P. Nelson.   Hallifax is shown and, for the first time in this series, Philadelphia.   (F.E.)

Plate 3.

7 **1722-1763**   With altered title: "Carte d'Amérique dressée pour l'usage du Roy en 1722.   Par Guillaume Delisle . . . Et augmentée des Nouvlles Découvertes en 1763 par Phil. Buache son Gendre.   A Paris, Chez l'Auteur, Sur le Quay de l'Horloge avec Privilége". $61\frac{1}{4} \times 49$ cms.

Revised issue of the Paris copperplate.   Title design and *Avertissement* remain the same, but the map is altered.   The west coast of North America is shown as in the preceding with a *Mer de l'Ouest*, and inset in the top left hand corner is an entirely hypothetical continuation of the north west coast with a *Lac de Valasco* &c.   A hypothetical lake is inserted in Labrador.

(L.C. 636)   (B.N. GeD11623)   (F.E.)

Plate 4.

The Continent of America—*continued.*

8 **1722-[1763+]** With the address altered to: "A Paris, Chez l'Auteur Rue des Noyers".

A further revision of the Paris copperplate. The inset map of the continuation of the N.W. coast is completely changed. It shows the Russian discoveries of Cape and Mount St. Elie and the fictitious Mer de l'Ouest and Lake Velasco are discarded. (B.N. GeD11625) (F.E.)

Plate 4.

9 **[1722]-1780** A Paris, Chez l'Auteur Rue des Noyers, avec Privilége 1780. Corrigée et Augmentée par M. Buache [de la Neuville] en 1780.

The plate is again changed, the date 1722 erased and the Marquesas transferred from Longitude 252 to 238 and I.S. Paul from 262 to 252. A note has been added to the islands discovered by Quiros *and recognised by Cook in 1769* and Easter Island now lettered "Terre découverte par Davis nommée auj. I. de Pasques". The N.W. coast of America remains unaltered. The map still bears faint traces of the imprint of Buache. (L.C. 655) (B.N. GeD11626) (F.E.)

10 **[1722]-1785** With new title: "Carte d'Amérique, Dressée pour l'Usage du Roi. Par Guil. Delisle et Phil. Buache, Premiers Géographes du Roi, et de l'Académie Royale des Sciences . . . Par Dezauche Géographe, Successeur des Srs. Delisle et Phil. Buache. A Paris, Chez l'Auteur Rue des Noyers. Avec Privilège du Roi 1785". 60 × 47 cms.

The map is now redrawn and re-engraved with the inset continuation of the N.W. coast corrected according to Capt. Cook's discoveries. California is noticeably different and the names along the west coast are considerably altered, e.g. Monterey is now shown at the head of R. du Carmel. To the north appears *entrée d'Aguilar, entrée du Roi Georges* and *Fousang des Chinois*. The Great Lakes are now more accurately drawn and the huge L. Bourbon compressed. Port Royale, Halifax, Plaisance (Newfoundland) Portsmouth, Philadelphia &c. shown. The Papal line of Demarcation and the Isles de Quiros are erased and the title cartouche has been enlarged. Easter Island now lettered "I. de Pasques vue par Davis".

(R.G.S. 14B15) (B.M. 69810[90]) (B.N. GeCC1238) (F.E.)

11 **[1722]-1790** Unaltered except for the date. (F.E.)

12 **[1722]-1790** The royal arms in the title cartouche are now obliterated and the crown has been transformed into a black cap, though the Republic still pays tribute to De l'Isle. No other change in the map. (F.E.)

Plate 5.

15

GUILLAUME DE L'ISLE

The Continent of America—*continued.*

13 **[1722]-1790** The title changed to: "Carte d'Amérique, Dressée pour l'instruction, Par Guil. Delisle et Phil. Buache . . . Nouvellement Revue . . . Par Dezauche . . . A Paris . . . 1790".

The royal arms erased from the cartouche and replaced by ribbons. The king's name is removed from the title and De l'Isle and Buache referred to as First Geographers to the Academy of Science. The Privilege changed from "du Roi" to "d'Auteur". The watermark shows a revolutionary cap. The monarchy was abolished and the Republic proclaimed September 1792. The King was executed January 1793. South America reproduced in "Frontières entre le Bresil et la Guyane Francaise, Paris 1899". (No. 53).

(B.N. GeC7818) (F.E.)

14 **[1722-1795]** Paris Chez l'Auteur An 7. (H.S. NS33)

15 **[1722]-1800** With addition to title: "Garantie Nationale An 9. 1800".

(B.N. GeC7819) (F.E.)

The plate has been touched up in places, e.g. ice in Det. du Nord, sea hachuring and a river or scratch in Fousang.

[1722-1801] The Bibliothèque Nationale records another issue (Carte muette): "A Paris Chez l'Auteur, rue des Noyers. An 9eme". Lower right, beneath the *Avertissement*, "Garantie Nationale An 9. 1801".

(B.N. GeD15360) (GeC7832)

16 **[1722]-1808** Garantie Nationale An 9. 1808.

The west coast has been redrawn with Vancouver Island and Nootka inserted. Rivers and names in the edition of 1800 have been deleted, both on the main map and inset. S. Part of the map reproduced in "Frontières entre le Bresil et la Guyane Francaise", Paris 1899 (No. 58). (B.N. GeD11627) (F.E.)

17 **[1722]-1809** Date altered to 1809.

18 **[1722]-1822** Garantie Nationale 1822.

The Republican calendar discontinued and the royal reference, "Geographes du Roi", reinserted in the title. (B.N. GeC7820) (F.E.) (L.C. 5993)

Plate 5.

19 **[1722]-1830** Date altered to 1830.

16

The Continent of America—*continued.*

De l'Isle-D'Anville

20 **1774** Carte d'Amerique divisées en ses principales parties, par G. Delisle, premier Geographe du Roy. Rectifiée apres les nouvelles Observations du Sr. D'Anville et autres Geographes. A Amsterdam Chez Cóvens & Mortier & Cóvens Junior. 1774. 59 × 48½ cms.

Though the map is based on De l'Isle and appears under his name it has been redrawn with a redesigned titlepiece. It shows a large sea of the west above C. Blanc and, further north, the Russian discoveries of 1730. Improvements and additions are also made to the islands of the Pacific. (F.E.)

Plate 6.

21 **[1774-1795+]** With altered title: ". . . Rectifiée apres les nouvelles Observations de Cook la Perouse van Couver et Autres Navigateurs et Geographes modernes. A Amsterdam Chez Mortier Covens et Fils".

The N.W. coast is now corrected to show the discoveries up to those of Vancouver (1791-5). There are alterations in the South Pacific, e.g. Pitcairn shown, and Paques (Easter Island) named. (F.E.)

Western Hemisphere

22 **1724** Hemisphere Occidental Dressé en 1720 pour l'usage particulier du Roy sur les Observations Astronomiques et Geographiques raportées la méme année dans l'Histoire et dans les memoires de l'Academie Rle. des Sciences Par Guillaume Del'Isle premier Geographe de Sa Majesté de la méme Academie.

A Paris chez l'Auteur le Sieur Del'Isle sur le Quay de l'Horloge sous le Privilege de l'Académie Royale des Sciences le 15 Septembre 1724. DelaHaye Sculp. Diameter 48½ cms.

Title along the top; imprint along the bottom. Includes the tracks of navigators to 1710. (B.M. 27f15) (F.E.)

Plate 7.

23 **1724-1745** Additional imprint bottom right: "Ph. Buache P.G.d.R; d. l'A.R. d. S. Gendre de l'Auteur. Avec Privilége du 30 Av. 1745".

24 **[1724-1747+]** Added to the title is: "Corrigé suivant les dernières découvertes par Cóvens et Mortier". The imprint reads: "A Amsterdam Chez J. Cóvens et C. Mortier". Diameter 47 cms.

The plate is re-engraved by I. Condet with a number of additions and alterations. The N.W. coast of America, left blank by De l'Isle, is filled in with the Russian

17

Western Hemisphere—*continued.*

discoveries of 1730-41 linked to a ficticious *Mer de l'Ouest.* The Solomon Islands have been moved 10° west, the *I. St. Croix* and *Friesland* have been omitted and various names have been added in the east, e.g. *Philadelphia, Savannah, Mobile, Georgia.* A note to Wager Bay mentions the date 1747. The Hudson's Bay area and Greenland have been corrected, Cap Farwel in the latter changed to Cap Vaarwel.

(F.E.)

25 **1724-1760** Added to the Buache imprint is: "Revu et Augmenté par Ph. Buache en 1760".

A revised version of the original plate. The North West of America redrawn according to the wild fantasies of Nicolas De l'Isle and Philip Buache, with New Zealand forming part of an antarctic continent. The additional tracks of the *Aigle* and *Marie* in 1738 and the Spanish vessel the *Lion* of 1756 are marked. The south polar circle shown according to the members of the Academy in 1754 and 1757.

(L.C. 636) (F.E.)

Plate 8.

26 **[1724]-1782** The title, slightly altered in wording, ends: Revu, Corrigé et Augmenté des Nouvelles Découvertes et des Voyages du Capitaine Cook, avec les Routes de ce Celèbre Navigateur. Par Dezauche Successeur des S$^{rs.}$ De l'Isle et Phil. Buache Premiers Géographes du Roi et de l'Academie R$^{le.}$ des Sciences en 1782.

A Paris Chez Dezauche . . . sous le Privilége de l'Académie Royale des Sciences, et avec Privilege du Roi et seul chargé de l'Entropôt général des Cartes de la Marine du Roi, Rue des Noyers.

Redrawn to show Capt. Cook's discoveries. A key bottom left refers to the tracks of Cook's voyages. A corrected N.W. coast and New Zealand.

(L.C. 655) (F.E.)

27 **[1724-1792]** The map unchanged but references to the King removed from the title and the imprint contracted "sous le Privilege de l'Academie [*Royale* omitted] des Sciences". The Republic was proclaimed September 1792. (F.E.)

North America

28 **1700** L'Amerique Septentionale. Dressée sur les Observations de M$^{rs.}$ de l'Academie Royale des Sciences & quelques autres, & sur les Memoires les plus recens. Par G. De L'Isle Geographe. A Paris Chéz l'Autheur Rue des Canettes préz de St. Sulpice Avec Privilege du Roy pour 20 ans. 1700. $60\frac{1}{2} \times 45\frac{1}{2}$ cms.

Title within cartouche top right with the figures of Neptune and river gods, designed and engraved by N. Guerard. Scale of miles and *Avertissement* top left.

North America—*continued.*

A foundation map. The Great Lakes based on Coronelli showing the French strong points at Tadousac, Quebec, Fort Sorel, Montreal & Fort Frontenac. The English settlements confined to the east of the Alleghenies, with Fort and River Kinibeki as the border between New England and Acadia. The Mississippi valley area is shown well developed with the recent French settlement of d'Iberville at Bilochy and forts at Bon Secours and St. Louis.

In this map De l'Isle corrected longitude positions and was the first to revert to a peninsula form for California. He stops his western coast at Cape Mendocin. The first printed map to show the Saragossa Sea. (F.E.) (H.S. NS33)

There is probably an imprint: "A Paris Chéz l'Autheur sur le Quai de l'Horloge à la Couronne de Diamans", though I have been unable to locate a copy.

Plate 9.

29 **1700-[1708+]** A Paris Chéz l'Autheur sur le Quai de l'Horloge. There is the additional imprint: "se trouve a Amsterdam Chez L Renard Libraire prez de la Bourse". (B.N. GeD11687A)

30 **1700-[1708+]** Quai de l'Horloge. Renard's imprint has been erased. (B.M. 37f14) (F.E.)

31 **1700-[1718+]** "Prem^{r.} Geographe du Roy" added to the title. (B.M. 37f16)

32 **[1700-1708]** L'Amerique Septentrionale . . . Par G. De l'Isle A Amsterdam Chez Pierre Mortier. Avec Privilege. 58 × 45 cms.

The map is re-engraved. In this edition the title cartouche is transferred to the left hand top corner and the scale of miles moved to the top right corner within a new design of a draped curtain. The *Avertissement* is discarded. An additional title in Latin appears above the map.

In, "Atlas Nouveau de diverses cartes choisies des Meilleurs Geographes comme Sanson, G. De l'Isle &c. . . . A Amsterdam Chez Pierre Mortier, Geographe MDCCVIII". (F.E.) (R.G.S. 1C59)

The map also exists ascribed to N. Sanson.

33 **[1700-1730]** A Amsterdam Chez I. Cóvens & C. Mortier. Avec Privilege. In, "Atlas Nouveau . . . Par Guillaume de l'Isle . . . A Amsterdam Chez Jean Covens & Corneille Mortier MDCCXXX". (F.E.)

34 **[1700]-1757** Reissue of above dated 1757.

The map was widely copied, for example, by P. Schenk 1708, J. Wolff (reissued by his successor J. F. Probst), R. & J. Ottens, and Lotter.

Canada

35 **1703** Carte du Canada ou de la Nouvelle France et des Decouvertes qui y ont été faites Dressée sur plusiers Observations et sur un grand nombre de Relations imprimées ou manuscrites Par Guillaume Del'Isle Geographe de l'Academie Royale des Sciences. A Paris, chez l'Auteur Rue des Canettes prez de St. Sulpice avec Privilege de sa Maj^{te} pour 20 ans 1703. 64½ × 49½ cms.

The title is enclosed within an elaborate cartouche with natives, missionaries &c. top left, designed by N. Guerard.

The first issue of the first printed map to show Detroit only two years after the founding of that village by Cadillac. Based on the work of Franquelin Joliet and the Jesuits. In this map he gives a superior rendering of the Great Lakes area than in his map of N. America of 1700.

(B.N. GeDD2987 (No. 8549)) (F.E.) (Yale)

35A With the imprint altered to, "A Paris chez l'Auteur sur le Quai de l'Horloge a la Couronne de Diamans", and with the additional imprint, "et se trouve a Amsterdam chez L. Renard Libraire prez de la Bourse". (Clements Library)

36 **1703-[1708+]** A Paris chez l'Auteur sur le Quai de l'Horloge a l'Aigle d'Or. (B.M. 37f13) (Clements Library)

37 **1703-[1708+]** Renard's imprint has been erased.
Reproduced, "Labrador Boundary Canadian Atlas". (L.C.)

38 **1703-[1718+]** "et Premier Geographe du Roy", added to the title.
(L.C.) (B.M. 37f14) (B.M. 37f15) (B.M. 37f16)

Plate 10.

39 **[1703-1730]** A Amsterdam chez Jean Cóvens et Corneille Mortier Geographes Avec Privilege [1730]. 57 × 48½ cms.

Appears in, "Atlas Nouveau . . . Par Guillaume De l'Isle . . . A Amsterdam chez Jean Covens & Corneille Mortier sur le Vygendam MDCCXXX".

Re-engraved but a close copy of the original. (B.M. 1 Tab. 8)

40 **1703-1745** Reissue of the original edition with an additional imprint in the bottom left corner: "Ph. Buache P.G.d.R.d. l'A.R.d.S. Gendre de l'Auteur Avec Privilege du 30 Av. 1745". (R.G.S. Canada Div. 20) (L.C. 636)

Canada—*continued.*

41 [1703]-1781 Revue et augmentée en 1781 par Dezauche.

Possessions are indicated by coloured boundaries; green for U.S.A., red for English, blue for French and yellow for Spanish.

42 [1703]-1783 With altered title: "Carte du Canada, qui comprend la partie septentrionale des Etats-Unis d'Amérique . . . Revue et augmentée en 1783". A Paris chez Dezauche Successeur des S$^{rs.}$ Del'Isle et Buache, Rue des Noyers pres celle des Anglois. (R.G.S. 14B15) (L.C. 5993)

Louisiana

43 1718 Carte de la Louisiane et du Cours du Mississipi Dressée sur un grand nombre de Memoires entrau^{tres} sur ceux de M$^{r.}$ le Maire Par Guill^{aume} Del'Isle de l'Academie R^{le} des Scien^{ces} A Paris chez l'Auteur le Sr. Delisle sur le Quay de l'Horloge avec Privilege du Roy Juin 1718. $64\frac{1}{2} \times 48\frac{1}{2}$ cms.

The title in one long line within the top border, the imprint bottom centre above the scale. Covers an area from the Great Lakes to New Mexico and south to Florida.

Inset: "Carte Particuliere des Embouchures de la Rivie S Louis et de la Mobile".

"This map is the mother and main source of all the later maps of the Mississipi" —J. G. Kohl.

"One of the most important mother maps of the North American continent"— William P. Cumming.

The first detailed map of the Gulf region and the Mississippi, the first printed map to show Texas [Mission de los Teijas etablie en 1716], the first to show the land routes of earlier centuries—De Soto in 1539 and 1540 and his successor Moscoso in 1542, Cavelier in 1687, Tonty in 1702 and the recent routes of Denis in 1713 and 1716. Two comparatively new settlements in New Mexico, S. Maria de Grado and S. Phelipe d'Albuquerque, both founded in 1705 are indicated as is Natchitoches on the Red River, whose foundation dates from 1717, the year before the map was published. Also marked are the French and English forts and settlements, the situation of mines &c.

The map had political implications and outraged the English by laying claim to Carolina "so named in honour of Charles 9th by the French who discovered it and took possession, and established themselves in 15 . . ." and as a further insult, "Charles Town [Carolina] named by the French Carlefort".

(B.M. 37f14) (H.S. NS23) (F.E.)

Plate 11.

The map was reissued in Nuremburg about 1734 by Christoph Weigel in a reduced format. Lake Michigan, thus named on the original, is now lettered *L. Ilinois.*

Louisiana—*continued.*

44 [**1718-1727**] Reissued on a reduced scale (41 × 35½ cms.) in Vega's "Hist. des Incas . . . Hist. de la Conquête de la Floride", Amsterdam 1727 Vol. II.
(B.N. GeD13657)

45 [**1718-1730**] A Amsterdam Chez Jean Cóvens et Corneille Mortier Géographes [1730]. 59 × 43½ cms.

A re-engraved copy of the original issue.

Appears in "Atlas Nouveau . . . Par Guillaume de l'Isle . . . A Amsterdam Chez Jean Cóvens & Corneille Mortier sur le Vygendam MDCCXXX".

Several later editions were issued of the Cóvens and Mortier Atlas, but the map did not change. (B.M. 1 Tab. 8) (F.E.)

46 1718-1745 Reissue of the original plate with the addition to the imprint: "Ph. Buache P.G. d.R., d. l'A.R.d. S. Gendre de l Auteur. Avec privilege du 30 Av. 1745". (L.C. 3456) (F.E.)

47 [**1718**]**-1782** Title altered: "Carte de la Louisiane et du cours du Mississippi. Avec les Colonies Anglaises. Revue, Corrigée et considérablem^t· Augmentée en 1782 . . . Chez Dezauche . . . Rue des Noyers près la Rue des Anglois".

North and South Carolina, Georgia and Florida are marked and there are many additional names along the east coast. The Buache imprint now ends: "Avec Privilege du Roi". (L.C. 3525) (F.E.)

Mexico & Florida

48 1703 Carte du Mexique et de la Floride des Terres Angloises et des Isles Antilles du Cours et des Environs de la Riviere de Mississipi. Dressée sur un grand nombre de memoires principalem^t· sur ceux de M^{rs}· d'Iberville et le Sueur. Par Guillaume Del'Isle Geographe de l'Academie Royale des Sciëces A Paris Chéz l'Auteur Rue des Canettes pres de St. Sulpice avec Privilege du Roy põ. 20 ans. 1703. 65 × 47½ cms.

Covers an area from the Great Lakes to New Mexico and southwards to Panama and Venezuela, and includes the West Indies. The title within a cartouche bottom left was designed by C. Simonneau; there is a decorated scale of miles top left. The locations of various Indian tribes and villages, French and English forts are shown, but the English possessions are continued to the east of the Alleghenies. Among other sources De l'Isle has drawn on the maps of d'Iberville, Le Sueur, Lederer and Daniel's map of 1679. The map was copied by Homann, Seutter and Lotter in their maps of Mexican Regions. (F.E.)

Mexico & Florida—*continued.*

There is probably an imprint, "A Paris Chez l'Auteur sur le Quai de l'Horloge a la Couronne de Diamans" with Renard's imprint, though I have been unable to locate a copy.

49 **1703-[1708+]** A Paris Chéz l'Auteur sur le Quai de l'Horloge. The *Couronne de Diamans* has been erased. There is the additional imprint: "se trouve a Amsterdam chez L. Renard Libraire prez de la Bourse".

50 **1703-[1708+]** A Paris Chéz l'Auteur sur le Quai de l'Horloge. Renard's imprint has been erased. (B.M. 37f14 and 16) (F.E.)

51 **[1703]-1722** A Amsterdam Chez Jean Covens & Corneille Mortier Avec Privilege 1722. $60\frac{1}{2} \times 47$ cms.

The map is re-engraved with an additional title in Latin along the top margin. The cartouche surrounding the title—a close copy of the original—is signed "I. Stemmers Senior Sculp." Route of the Gallions added to this edition.

Appears in "Atlas Nouveau . . . Par Guillaume de l'Isle . . . A Amsterdam Chez Jean Covens & Corneille Mortier sur le Vygendam MDCCXXX".

(H.S. NS23) (F.E.) (B.M. 1 Tab. 8)

52 **1703-1745** Reissue of the original edition with an additional imprint below the right hand margin: "Ph. Buache P.G.d.R.d. l'A.R.d.S. Gendre de l'Auteur, Avec Privilege du 30 Av. 1745". (F.E.) (L.C. 636)

Plate 12.

53 **[1703]-1783** The title altered: "Carte du Mexique et des États Unis d'Amérique, Partie Méridionale . . . Par Guil. De L'Isle 1ᵉʳˢ Géogr. du Roi. Nouvellement Revuë et Augmentée Par Dezauche Successeur des Sʳˢ Del'Isle et Phil. Buache premiers Géographes du Roi. A Paris Rue des Noyers Année 1783".

The United States are now extended westward to the Mississippi and the boundaries inserted in colour to indicate the different possessions; green for the U.S.A., red for England, blue for France and yellow for Spain.

(R.G.S. 14B15) (L.C. 3525) (F.E.)

Antilles

54 **1717** Carte des Antilles Francoises et des Isles Voisines Dressée sur les memoires manuscrits de Mr. Petit Ingenieur du Roy, et sur quelques observations. Par Guilleaume De l'Isle de l'Academie Rle. des Sciences et Premier Geographe

23

Antilles—*continued.*

du Roy.   A Paris Chez l'Auteur Sur le Quay de l'Horloge avec Privilege du Roy Juillet 1717.

Depicts the islands from Guadeloupe to Grenada.

As this map bears De l'Isle's title of *Premier Géographe du Roi* it must date from 1718 or later, and either there is an earlier edition that I have been unable to trace, or the map was engraved late in 1717 and not published till 1718 when *Premier Géographe* was inserted.

(B.M. 37f14, 15 and 16)   (R.G.S. West Indies D135)

55 **[1717-1730]** A Amsterdam Chez Jean Cóvens et C. Mortier Geographes avec Privilege [1730].   44½ × 59 cms.

The map is re-engraved.   Appeared in, "Atlas Nouveau . . . Par G. De l'Isle.   A Amsterdam Chez Jean Covens & Corneille Mortier sur le Vygendam MDCCXXX".

(L.C. 3486)   (B.M. 1 Tab. 8)   (F.E.)

Plate 13.

56 **1717-1745** Ph. Buache P.G.d.R.d. l'A.R.d.S.Gendre de l'Auteur.   Avec Priv. du 30 Av 1745.

Reissue of the original plate.   The additional imprint appears below the map.

(L.C. 636)

57 **1717-1760** Cette carte a été rectifiée en 1760 par Phil. Buache.

58 **1717-1769** Rectifiée en 1769 par Phil. Buache.   (L.C. 3525)

Santo Domingo

59 **1725** Carte de l'Isle de Saint Domingue, Dressée en 1722 pour l'usage du Roy Sur les memoires de Mr Frezier ingenieur . . . et autres . . . Par G. Delisle premier Géographe du Roy de l'Academie Rle. des Sciences.   A Paris Chez l'Auteur sur le Quai de l'Horloge avec Privilege du Roy Mars 1725.   Marin sculp. 62 × 47½ cms.

On all copies seen the month has been erased, though it is still legible.

(B.M. 37f15)   (B.M. 37f16)

60 **[1722-1730]** A Amsterdam Chez Jean Cóvens et Corneille Mortier Geographes [1730].   61 × 46½ cms.

The map is re-engraved.   Appears in, "Atlas Nouveau . . . Par G. De L'Isle Amsterdam chez Jean Covens & Corneille Mortier sur le Vygendam MDCCXXX".

(B.M. 1 Tab. 8)

Santo Domingo—*continued*.

61 **1722-1745** Ph. Buache P.G.d.R.d.l'A.R.d.S. Gendre de l'Auteur. Avec Privilege du 30 Av. 1745.

Reissue of the original plate. (L.C. 636) (H.S. NS24)

62 **[1722]-1780** Revué et corrigée en 1780 par Dezauche. (L.C. 3525)

S. America

63 **1700** L'Amerique Meridionale Dressée sur les Observations de M$^{rs.}$ de l'Academie Royale des Sciences & quelques autres, & sur les Memoirs les plus recens. Par G. De L'Isle Geographe. A Paris Chéz l'Autheur; Rüe des Canettes préz de St. Sulpice. Avec Privilege du Roy pour 20 ans 1700. 60½ × 46 cms.

The title surround in the bottom left corner, incorporating the figures of Neptune and an Indian, was designed and engraved by N. Guerard. An ornate border encloses the scale beneath. The entire cartouche is printed from a quite separate plate. Top right is an Advertisement: "Je rends raison dans ma Nouvelle Introduction a la Geographie des changemens que jay faits sur cete carte".

Shows the tracks of Drake, Olivier, Mendana, Le Maire, Magellan and Sarmiento in the Pacific.

The southern extremity is shown curving to the west and the land extends to longitude 293°. (F.E.)

Plates 14 & 15.

64 **1700-[1705+]** The imprint remains the same but the map south of 40° is re-engraved. The coast of Magellan now only extends to longitude 304° and the Terre de Feu is re-drawn. Traces of the original version show through, e.g. the tracks of Le Maire at the extreme bottom of the map. This corrected form appears also on the 1703 map of Paraguay &c. (B.M. 37f16) (F.E.)

A note to the I. of Anycon records "decouverte en 1705".

Plate 15.

There is probably an imprint, "A Paris Chéz l'Autheur; sur le Quay de l'Horloge a la Couronne des Diamans", though I have been unable to locate a copy.

65 **1700-[1708+]** A Paris Chéz l'Auteur sur le Quai de l'Horloge a l'Aigle d'or. (B.M. 37f13)

S. America—*continued.*

66 **1700-[1708+]** A Paris Chéz l'Auteur sur le Quay de l'Horloge.

(B.M. 37f14)

67 **1700-[1708]** Amsterdam, P. Mortier. $57\frac{1}{2} \times 45\frac{1}{2}$ cms.

Re-engraved with additional title along the top of the map: *America Meridionalis* &c. It is a close copy of the first, uncorrected version. Appears in "Atlas Nouveau . . . Sanson, G. De L'Isle. A Amsterdam Chez Pierre Mortier, Geographe MDCCVII".

(R.G.S. 1059)

68 **[1700-1730]** A Amsterdam Chez I. Covens & C. Mortier. Avec Privilege. [1730].

Appears in, "Atlas Nouveau . . . Par Guillaume de l'Isle . . . A Amsterdam Chez Jean Covens & Corneille Mortier sur le Vygendam MDCCXXX". In this edition the Amsterdam publishers continue to reproduce the first, uncorrected edition of De l'Isle's South America [No. 63].

(B.M. 1 Tab. 8) (F.E.)

69 **[1700]-1757** Reissue of the above, dated 1757.

De l'Isle's South America was widely copied, for example by Schenk 1708, R. & J. Ottens and Lotter.

Terra Firma etc.

70 **1703** Carte de la Terre Ferme du Perou, du Bresil et du Pays des Amazons Dressée sur les Descriptions de Herrera de Laet, et des P P d Acuna, et M. Rodriguez . . . Par Guillaume Del'Isle Geographe de l'Academie Royale des Sciences. A Paris Chéz l'Auteur Rue des Canettes pres de St. Sulpice avec Privilege du Roy pour 20 ans 1703. $64\frac{1}{2} \times 48$ cms. (F.E.)

There is probably an imprint, "A Paris Chéz l'Auteur sur le Quai de l'Horloge à la C. de Diamants", with Renard's imprint, though I have been unable to locate a copy.

For detail see Plate 17.

71 **1703-[1708+]** A Paris Chez l'Auteur sur le Quai de l'Horloge à l'Aigle d'Or.

There is the additional imprint: "se trouve a Amsterdá chez Louis Renar [*sic*] Libraire prez de la Bourse".

(B.M. 37f15) (B.M. 37f16)

72 **1703-[1708+]** Renard's imprint has been erased.

(B.M. 37f14)

Terra Firma etc.—*continued*.

73 **1703-[1718+]** "Premier Geogra^r· du Roy", inserted in the title.
(B.M. 37f13) (F.E.)

For detail see Plate 17.

74 **[1703-1730]** A Amsterdam Chez Iean Cóvens et Corneille Mortier Geographes Avec Privil. 57×47½ cms.
Re-engraved with an additional title in Latin along the top. The substance of the map is unchanged. Appeared in "Atlas Nouveau . . . Par G De L'Isle. A Amsterdam, chez Jean Covens & Corneille Mortier sur le Vygendam MD-CCXXX".
(B.M. 1 Tab. 8)

75 **1703-1745** Ph. Buache P.G.d.R.d.l'A.d.S. Gendre de l'Auteur Avec Privilege du 30 Av 1745. (L.C. 636)
Reissue of the original plate; the new imprint added in the lower right margin.

76 **[1703]-1782** Revue et augmentée par Dezauche en 1782. (L.C. 3525)

Paraguay etc.

77 **1703** Carte du Paraguay du Chili du Detroit de Magellan &c. Dressée sur les Descriptions des PP Alfonse d'Ovalle, et Nicolas Techo, et sur les Relations et memoires de Brouwer, Narbouroug, M^r· de Beauchesne &c. Par Guillaume De L'Isle Geographe de l'Academie Royale des Sciences A Paris Chéz l'Auteur, Rue des Canettes préz de St. Sulpice avec Privilege du Roi pour 20 ans 1703. Gravée par Liebaux le fils. 64×49 cms. (F.E.)
There is probably an imprint "A Paris Chez l'Auteur sur le Quai de l'Horloge a la Couronne de Diamans", with Renard's imprint, though I have been unable to locate a copy.

78 **1703-[1708+]** A Paris Chéz l'Auteur sur le Quai de l'Horloge. There is the additional imprint: "se trouve a Amsterdam Chez Louis Renard Libraire prez de la Bourse".

79 **1703-[1708+]** Renard's imprint has been erased.

80 **1703-[1718+]** "Premier Geographe du Roy", added to the title.
(F.E.) (B.M. 37f14) (B.M. 37f15)

Plate 16.

Paraguay etc.—*continued.*

81 **[1703-1730]** A Amsterdam, Chez Iean Cóvens et Corneille Mortier Geographes Avec Privil. 57½×48½ cms.

Re-Engraved with a Latin title added along the top. Appears in "Atlas Nouveau . . . Par G De L'Isle. A Amsterdam Chez Jean Covens & Corneille Mortier sur le Vygendam MDCCXXX". (B.M. 1 Tab. 8) (F.E.)

82 **1703-1745** Ph. Buache P.G.d.R.d.l'A.d.S. Gendre de l'Auteur Avec Privilege du 30 Av 1745.

Reissue of the original copper-plate. (H.S. NS24) (L.C. 636)

83 **[1703]-1780** Reissued by Dezauche, annee 1780.

(L.C. 3525) (H.S. NS33)

PHILIPPE BUACHE (1700-1773)

1732 Issued an edition of De l'Isle's Atlas in partnership with the widow of Guillaume, without titlepage, from the Quai de l'Horloge. In this atlas his own map of Martinique listed below was incorporated for the first time.

(B.M. maps 37f15, 16 and 1 Tab. 9)

Martinique

84 **1732** Carte de l'Isle de la Martinique . . . Dressée sur les Plans manuscrits entr'autres sur celui de Mr. Houel . . . et conciliés avec les memoires de feu Mr. Guill. Delisle . . . Par Philippe Buache. Delahaye sculpsit. A Paris chez la Vve. du Sr. Delisle sur le Quay de l'Horloge. Avec Privilege du Roi. MDCCXXXII le 10 Octobr. 60×46½ cms. (B.M. 37f15)

85 **[1732-1733]** Covens & Mortier, Amsterdam [1733]. 59×46 cms.
The map has been re-engraved. (B.M. 82420)

86 **1732-1745** Ph. Buache P.G.d.R.d.l'A.R.d.S. Gendre de l'Auteur avec Privilege du 30 Av. 1745. Added in small letters below right-hand border.

(R.G.S. West Indies D137)

87 **[1732]-1779** Reissued by Dezauche, 1779. (L.C. 3525)

Fernand de Noronha

88　**1737**　Carte de la partie de l'Océan vers l'Équateur entre les côtes d'Afrique et d'Amérique . . . Dressée par Philippe Buache.　Premier Geographe Septembre 1737.　A Paris sur le Quay de la Mégisserie.　63½×48 cms.
The map is divided diagonally, the right half being taken up with the Island of Fernand de Noronha.　　　　　　　　　　　　　　(B.M. K.124.60)
Reissued in the "Cartes et Tables de la Géographie".　(1757) (see no. 99).
　　　　　　　　　　　　　　　　　　　　　　　　　(L.C. 3456)

89　**[1737-1780]**　A Paris chez Dezauche Rue des Noyers près celle des Anglois [1780].
The date has been erased from the title.

Peru

90　**1739**　Carte du Perou.　Pour servir à l'Histoire des Incas et a celle de l'Etat present de cette Province.　Dressée Par Philippe Buache.　A Paris sur le Quay de la Megisserie.　Avec Privilege du Roy 1739.　30½×38½ cms.
　　　　　　　　　　　　　　　　　　　　　　　　(B.M. 84610(6))

Gulf of Mexico

91　**1740**　Carte d'une partie de l'Amerique pour la navigation du Golfe de Mexique avec l'intérieur des Terres depuis la Bermude jusqu'à Cayenne.　Partie Meridionale, Réduite de la carte Angloise en 20 feuilles par Mr Popple avec quelques Corrections et Augmentations par Phil Buache en 1740.　A Paris sur le Quay de la Megisserie prés le Pont Neuf avec Privilege du Roy.　3 sheets.　93×49½ cms.
The title appears in small lettering above the top margin.
　　　　　　　　　　　　(L.C. 636)　(R.G.S. 14C155)
Right half of map reproduced in, "Atlas of Guiana 1898.　Arbitration between Great Britain and Venezuela".

92　**1740-1780**　Reissued with a new title: Carte du Golfe du Mexique et des Isles Antilles Réduite de la grande Carte Angloise de Popple, par Ph. Buache 1er Geographe du Roi.　Corrigée et Augmentée en 1780 par J. N. Buache [de Neuville] Géog ord. du Roi.　A Paris Chez Dezauche Gravr Successeur des Srs De l'Isle et Buache, Rue des Noyers près celle des Anglois.
This new title appears in the bottom left-hand corner of the map.　The old title is left above the top margin but with the date "en 1740" erased.　Also added to the plate is an engraved table of the colours to be used for distinguishing the possessions of the different nationalities, yellow for Spanish, red for English, blue for French, green for Dutch and violet for the Danes.　(B.M. 79435(9))

Gulf of Mexico—*continued.*

93   [1740-1780+]   Another issue, Ph. Buache now described as 1ᵉʳ Geographe de l'Ac., and J. N. Buache as Géog. de l'Academie, i.e. Royal references removed.

Plans, Rades et Ports

94   **1740-1**   [Eight plans on one sheet, on four copperplates numbered 1, 2, 4, 3.] each marked "Desbruslins sculp."

1   [Top left copperplate] Plans des Isles, Rades, et Ports de plusieurs lieux en Amerique Tirés de . . . Popple publiée en 1733 (engraved text and 3 plans). Rade et Port de Plaisance P.B. 1740, Le Port d'Anapolis Royal: Port de Boston. A Paris sur le Quay de la Mégisserie prés le Pt Neuf Avec Priv. du Roy.

Plate 18.

2   [Top right copperplate] Ports de la Nouvelle York et de Pertamboy.   A Paris sur le Quay de la Mégisserie au Sᵗ· Esprit prés le Pont Neuf; Plan de la ville et du Port de Charles Town; I. de la Bermude.
P.B. 1740 in gap between plans.   Numbered outside bottom left corner.

4   [Bottom left copperplate] Cartes des Côtes Meridionales de l'Isle de Terre Neuve . . . Dressée par Philippe Buache sur la Carte . . . du même Auteur . . . A Paris sur le Quay de la Mégisserie . . . le 4 Mars 1741.   Numbered inside bottom right corner.

3   [Bottom right copperplate] Carte de la partie Meridionale de l'Isle de Terre Neuve . . . rectifié Par Philippe Buache Fevrier 1741.   A Paris Sur le Quay de la Mégisserie.   Numbered inside bottom right corner.   (F.E.)   (B.M. 37f17)

95   **1740-1**   Fourteen plans on 1 sheet, on four copperplates numbered 1, 2, 3 unchanged but copperplate 4 [now numbered 3] as 96 (3) below.   (B.M. K118)

96   **1740-1**   [Twelve plans on 1 sheet, on four copperplates].
No. 3   Port de St. Augustin, Port du Providence, La Havane, Baye de Sr. Jago, Port de Kingston dans la Jamaique.   Quay de la Megisserie au St Esprit pres le Pont Neuf.   Plan du Port Antonio, Isle d'Antigoa.   Desbruslins sculpsit.   P.B. 1740.   Numbered bottom left corner.

No. 10   Carte de l'Isle d'Antigoa.   P.B. en 1740.   A Paris Sur le Quay de la Megisserie au St Esprit Avec Privilege du Roi.   Numbered below bottom right corner.

No. 9   Carte de l'Isle de la Jamaique.   Dressée en 1740 par Philippe Buache. A Paris sur le Quay de la Megisserie près le Pont Neuf.   Numbered below bottom right corner.

Plans, Rades et Ports—*continued.*

No. 4 Port, Baye Cul de Sac Royal, Isles des Barbades, Cartagene. Port du Porto Belo. Desbruslins sculp. P.B. 1740. Tirée de la Carte d'Amerique de Mr Popple. Numbered below bottom left corner. (B.M. 37f17)

It is possible that the above copperplates were also published separately or in different combinations, as occasionally they turn up on single sheets.

Slight variations exist in the numbering, e.g. No. 94 (2) also exists with the number in top right corner; 96 (3) numbered either top right or bottom left; 96 (9) also numbered 4; and 96 (10) also numbered 5.

Dezauche offered these plans for sale separately at 12 sous per sheet in his catalogue of [1782].

1745 Philippe Buache issued an edition of maps by G. De l'Isle unchanged except for the addition of his imprint usually below the bottom right-hand corner border as follows: "Ph. Buache P.G. d R.d.l'A.d.S. Gendre de l'Auteur Avec Privilege du 30 Av 1745".

N. W. Passage

97 **1753** Considerations géographiques et physiques sur les nouvelles découvertes au Nord de la Grande Mer, appellée vulgairement la Mer du Sud, avec des cartes qui y sont relatives. Par Philippe Buache, Paris 1753-[1754].

(L.C. 3342) (John Carter Brown Library)

1 prel.+158 pp.+Atlas of 11 maps and 5 plates of coast lines. Liste des Cartes 4 pp., 4to. 1755. Exposé des Decouvertes au Nord de la Grande Mer, 3 pp. Of the eleven maps the following eight refer to America:

1 Carte des nouvelles découvertes entre la partie orientle. de l'Asie et l'occidle. de l'Amérique. A Paris sur le Quay de l'Horloge du Palais. 1752. 31×21 cms. Drawn by Buache and presented to the *Académie des Sciences* who approved it September 6. (Wagner No. 573)

2 Carte des decouvtes, de l'Amal. de Fonte selon la carte angloise donnée par l'écrivain du vaisseau la Californie dans son voyage à la Baye d'Hudson avec les terres vües et reconnues par les Russes et une comparaison du résultat des cartes du 16e et 17e siecle au sujet du Détroit d'Anian. 1752. 31×22 cms. (Wagner No. 572)

3 Carte du géométrique des découvertes de l'Amiral de Fonte et de son Capitaine Bernarda comparee avec le systeme de la carte angloise. 1752. 31×22 cms. (Wagner No. 574)

"Extrait de la Relations de Fonte" down the left of the map. Re-published 1754.

5 Carte d'une Partie de l'Amerique Septentrionale tirée des manuscrits de M. Guill. Del'Isle. 28×25 cms.

Purporting to be a map made by Guillaume De l'Isle in 1695 showing the *Mer de l'Ouest*. It had originally appeared in J. N. De l'Isle's *Nouvelles Cartes*. 1753 (see No. 106). (Wagner No. 577)

N. W. Passage—*continued.*

6   Cartes des terres aux environs du Japon . . . Carte des terres nouvellement connues au nord de la Mer du Sud tant du côté de l'Asie que du côté de l'Amérique. 1752.   2 maps on a plate.   28 × 38 cms.

The map illustrates a supposed expedition to America by the ancient Chinese.
(Wagner No. 576)

7   Carte marine des parties septentrionales de la Grande Mer, et de l'Ocean, 1752.   50 × 21 cms.   (B.M. 37f17)   (Wagner No. 575)
Plate 19.

Copy of note sent out with the map, which was issued later than the others.

La Carte Marine (No. VII) dont it est parlé pag. 136, 142, 143, &c., de la IIIᵉ Partie des Considerations, &c, n'a pu être jointe aux autres, la gravure n'en étant pas encore achevée par un accident imprevu.

On y a reuni diverses Vues Géographiques et Physiques, concernant les parties Septentrionales de l'Océan et de la Grande Mer, aussi bien que les Terres qui les environnent et dont les Eaux s'y dechargent depuis les Chaines de Montagnes, relativement au dernier Article des Considerations.

8   Carte physique des terreins les plus élévés de la partie occidentale du Canada. 1754.   34½ × 24 cms.

9   La Californie d'après une très grande Carte Espagnole M.Ste de L'Amérique Dressée à Florence en 1604 par Mathieu Neron Pecciolen—Carte du Passage par Terre à la Californie découverte en 1701 par le R.P. Kino, Jesuite. [inset] Partie de la Californie tirée de l'Amérique Septˡᵉ· publiée en 1700 par Guillaume Delisle.   Delahaye l'Ainé sculp.   A Paris sur le Quay de l'Horloge . . . 1754. 32½ × 21 cms.   (Wagner No. 580)
Plate 20.

Maps No. 4, 10 and 11 do not relate to America.   They are as follows:

4   Reduction of a map published at Nuremburg showing one of the first ideas that was formed of Kamschatka and its neighbourhood.

10   Map of the Island of Jeso and neighbouring lands.

11   Map of the Kingdom and Islands of Lieou-Kieou.
Plates 12-16.   Plates of the coastline of the Island of Jeso.

The maps originally appeared in the Memoirs of the *Académie des Sciences.* The maps alone were published from the original plates by Dezauche in 1781 with minor changes.   (R.G.S. 9H22)

The Library of Congress (10252) states that Dezauche also reissued the plates in 1761.

N. W. Passage—*continued*.

98 **[1779]** Carte des Nouvelles Découvertes dressée par Phil. Buache Pr.
Géogr. du Roi présentée à l'Acad. des Sciences le 9 Aout 1752. 37½×29 cms.
On a sheet with "Extrait d'une Carte Japonoise de l'Univers". From the
Supplement to Diderot's *Encyclopédie*, 1779, Map No. 6. With the *Mer de
l'Ouest, Lac de Valasco, Lac de Fonte* &c. (F.E.)

Plate 21.

Cartes et Tables

99 **[1757]** Cartes et Tables de la Géographie Physique ou Naturelle Présentées
au Roy le 15 Mai 1757 [followed by a long engraved text of "Avertissement"
terminating] Cet Ouvrage approuvé et Publié sous le Priv.^{ge} de l'Acad^e du
4 Sept^{bre} 1754 se trouve à Paris, sur le Quay de l'Horloge Avec les Cartes de
Guill. De lisle et de Phil Buache.

Title-Avertissement as above, 20 plates in all.

Planisphere Physique.

Carte Physique de l'Ocean où l'on voit des Grandes Chaines de Montagnes . . .
1754.

Carte Physique de la Grande Mer . . . Présentée à l'Acad. des Sc. le 5 Sept^{bre} 1744
Par Philippe Buache. (Wagner No. 550)

For illustration see MCC 23, plate XXIX.

Cartes des Terres Australes (including tip of S. America).

Carte du Globe Terrestre ou les Terres de l'Hemisphere Merid$^{l.}$ sont supposées
éntre vues a travers celles de l'Hemisphere Septent$^{l.}$

[The southern hemisphere superimposed over the northern hemisphere].

Carte des lieux où les differentes longeurs du Pendule à Secondes ont eté
Observées.

[With the Tables of Newton, Bradley & Maupertuis].

Carte de la partie de l'Ocean vers l'Equator entre les Cotes d'Afrique et d'Amerique [with] Plan de l'Isle de Fernand de Noronha. [See No. 88].

The plates are unnumbered (B.M.K.4.37).

100 **[1757-1780]** Reissued by Dezauche.

In the imprint at the end of the Avertissement, the address Quay de l'Horloge is
changed to Rue des Noyers, and below the bottom margin of the plate the imprint
of Dezauche is added: "A Paris Chez Dezauche Graveur Successeur des S^{rs}
De l'Isle et Buache Premier Géographes du Roi, Rue des Noyers près celle des
Anglois".

Cartes et Tables—*continued.*

In this edition the plates are numbered, including the title-advertisement,
Nos. I-XX.   (R.G.S. 7H20)   (B.M. Maps 182M2)

Reissues of De l'Isle's maps published by Buache

America 1745 (See No. 5).

America 1763 revised (See No. 7).

America 1763 revised (See No. 8).

W. Hemisphere 1745 (See No. 23).

W. Hemisphere 1760 revised (See No. 25).

Canada 1745 (See No. 40).

Louisiana 1745 (See No. 46).

Mexico & Florida 1745 (See No. 52).

Antilles 1745 (See No. 56).

Antilles 1760 revised (See No. 57).

Antilles 1769 revised (See No. 58).

St. Domingo 1745 (See No. 61).

Terra Firma 1745 (See No. 75).

Paraguay 1745 (See No. 82).

JOSEPH NICOLAS DE L'ISLE (1688-1768)

N. W. Passage

101 **[1752]** Carte des Nouvelles Découvertes au Nord de la Mer du Sud,
Tant à l'Est de la Siberie et du Kamtchatka, Qu à l'Ouest de la Nouvelle France.
Dressée sur les Mémoires de M^r· Del'Isle Professeur Royal et de l'Académie des
Sciences.   Par Philippe Buache de la même Académie et Présentée à l'Académie
dans son Assemblée publique du 8. Avril 1750.   Par M^r· De l'Isle . . . Se vend à
Paris Quay de l'Horloge du Palais avec les cartes de Guill. Delisle et de Phil.
Buache.   64×45½ cms.

Title as above within rococo cartouche. Broad top border containing an
"Avertissement" and scale with engraving of native of Kamtchatka left corner,
and native of north of Louisiana in right corner.

Shows the discoveries of the Russians 1723, 1732 and 1741, the tracks of Bering's
first and second voyages and of De l'Isle de la Croyère with Capt. Tchirikow 1741;
the track of de Frondat's voyage of 1709, and the route of the Galions in 1743.
Also *Water of Wager* discovered in 1746 and 1747.

N. W. Passage—*continued.*

The west coast of America is fictitious north of Cap Blanc with an enormous Sea of the West, Lac Valasco and Isle of Bernarda.   (B.M. 31d11.2)

——— the British Museum possesses a copy of the above map with a revised form pasted over the upper central part of the map, the cartouche design, broken at foot, being overlaid by a dedication to A. M. Rouillé.

Explication de la Carte des Nouvelles Decouvertes au Nord de la Mer du Sud. Par M. De L'Isle . . . A Paris chez Desaint et Saillant . . . MDCCLII (18 pp.). In this *explication* De l'Isle gives his excuses for the delay in publishing the map shown to the "Académie" in 1750 in manuscript.   The map was engraved for Buache.   (B.M. 31.d.11)   (H.S. NS33)

102 **[1752-1754]** Kaart der Nieuwe Ontdekkingen Benoorden de Zuyd Zee . . . Isaac et Johannes Enschede excuderunt Harlemi 1754.   38 × 32 cms.   (F.E.) Reissue on a much reduced scale.

102A **[1752-1755]** Tabula Geographica partis septentrionalis Maris Pacifici . . . Acad. Reg. scient. et litter: eleg: Borusi. descripta.   Sauerbrey sculps. 37½ × 32½ cms. Similar to the above but with the text in French instead of Dutch.   (F.E.)

103 **[1752-1776]** Carte des Nouvelles Decouvertes au Nord de la Mer du Sud. A Venise Chez François Santini Rue Ste. Justine près de l'Eglise [1776]. (F.E.)

104 **[1752-1784]** Chez M. Remondini added to the Santini imprint.   (F.E.)

105 **[1752-1780]** Se vend à Paris, Chez Dezauche, Rue des Noyers près la Rue des Anglois]1780].   (H.S.) (F.E.) Reissue of the original copper-plate.

Plate 22.

106 **1753** Nouvelles Cartes des découvertes de l'Amiral de Fonte, et autres Navigateurs Espagnols Portugais, Anglois, Hollandois, Francois & Russes, dans les Mers Septentrionales, avec leur Explication qui comprend . . . les Routes de Navigation, les Extraits des Journaux de Marine, les Observations Astronomiques . . . le Commerce que l'on peut faire . . . Paris 1753.

Sabin's Dictionary (No. 35254) and Rich: Bibliotheca Americana 1835 record this 1753 edition as having 60 pp. text and 4 maps. Henry Stevens Catalogue New Series No. 33 (No. 17) records the 1753 edition with 2 preliminary leaves, 76 pages of text and 4 maps.

N. W. Passage—*continued.*

Contains four maps:

I   Carte Génerale des Découvertes de l'Amiral de Fonte et autres Navigateurs Espagnols, Anglois et Russes, pour la recherche du Passage à la Mer du Sud. Par M^r· Del'Isle . . . A Paris Septembre 1752. 42 × 27 cms.

This was probably first issued separately in September 1752 and represents a revised version of the original map [No. 101].   It is reduced in size and there are many alterations to the Fonte geography, e.g. the *Mer de l'Ouest* is diminished.

(Wagner No. 571)

An English Edition was issued in the following year, 1754.

II   Carte dressée sur la lettre de l'Amiral de Fonte, par l'ecrivain de la Californie. Novembre, 1752. 17 × 18½ cms.   (Wagner No. 570)

III   Carte d'une Partie de l'Amerique Septentrionale tirée des manuscrits de M. Guill. Del'Isle. 28 × 25 cms.

Purporting to be a map made by Guillaume De l'Isle in 1695 showing the *Mer de l'Ouest*.   Reissued by Buache in his *Considerations* [see No. 97].

(Wagner No. 568)

IV   Carte dressée par M. Guillaume Del'Isle au commencement de ce siecle, pour servir à ses conjectures sur l'existence de la Mer de l'Ouest.   Novembre 1752. 15 × 18½ cms.   (Sabin A35254)   (H.S. NS33)   (Wagner No. 569)

107   [**1779**]   Carte systématique d'une Partie de l'Amérique du N.O. pour l'intelligence des Découvertes de l'Am$^{al.}$ de Fuente par J. N. Delisle. 1752. Gravé par P. F. Tardieu, Place de l'Estrapade. 15½ × 20 cms.

From the Supplement to Diderot's *Encyclopédie*, 1779. Also appears in Fleurieu's *Voyage autour du monde*, 1798.

108   [**1779**]   Carte Générale des Découvertes de l'Amiral de Fonte . . . Par M. Del'Isle de l'Academie royale des Sciences &c.   Publiée à Paris en Septembre 1752. 38 × 29½ cms.

Inset: Carte dressée sur la lettre de l'Amiral de Fonte par l'Ecrivain de la Californie.

From the Supplement to Diderot's *Encyclopédie*, 1779, Map No. 7.

LOUIS CHARLES BUACHE

Cayenne

109 **1762** Carte géographique de l'Isle de Cayenne et de ses environs . . .
L[ouis] C[harles] Buache et de Préfontaine. 1762.   (L.C. 2720, map 33)

JEAN NICOLAS BUACHE DE LA NEUVILLE (1741-1825)

N. W. Passage

110 **1775** Mémoire sur les pays de l'Asie et de l'Amérique, situés au nord de
la Mer du Sud, accompagné d'une carte de comparaison des plans de MM.
Engel et de Vaugondy, avec le plan des cartes modernes. Par J. N. Buache,
géogr. ord. du Roi. Paris 1775. 22 pp. 4to and folding map. 33 × 25 cms.
                     (Wagner No. 652)   (Eberstadt Cat. 119)

Reproduced in Teleki's Atlas.

111 **1781** Nouvelle Carte de la Partie Septentrionale du Globe, comprise
entre le Kamtchatka et la Californie . . . Par Buache de la Neuville, Géog. Ord.
du Roi Garde-adjoint du Dépôt Gnal. des Cartes et Plans de la Marine. A Paris
chez Dezauche . . . Rue des Noyers, près celle des Anglois. Avec Privilége du
Roi du 15. Novembre 1781. 40 × 26 cms.

Including side panel of engraved text.   (Wagner No. 677)

112 [**1781-82+**] Another issue Géog. Ord., changed to Premier Géog.
Buache de la Neuville was appointed *Premier Géographe* in 1782.
                     (F.E.)   (B.M. maps 970(71))

Plate 23.

Dominica

113 [**1778-9**] Carte de la Dominique prise par les Francois le Septembre 7,
1778. Avec le Plan du Débarquement et de l'Attaque des Forts et Batteries par
les Troupes et les Frégates de sa Majeste . . . Par le S. Buache. A Paris, chez
l'Auteur, Rue des Noyers [1778-9]. 47 × 60 cms.

Inset of the disembarkation of the French troops and the attack on the forts and
batteries at Charlotteville.   (H.S. NS33)   (L.C. 3525)

America

1780 Carte d'Amérique (see No. 9).

Gulf of Mexico

1780 Golfe du Mexique (see No. 92).

Guiana

114 **[1798]** Carte Generale de la Guiane . . . Par N. Buache, Membre de l'Institut National. L'An VI de la Republique. Gravé par P. F. Tardieu, Place de l'Estrapade No. 18. Ecrite par L. Aubert. 69 × 49½ cms.

(B.M. 83955(8))

J. A. DEZAUCHE fl. 1779-1830

Atlases

115 **[1780-91]** Atlas Géographique des quatre parties du monde par Guillaume De l'Isle et Phil. Buache Premiers Géographes du Roi . . . Faits pour les Géographies Elémentaires de Mrs Buache et de l'Abbe Nicolle de la Croix. Revu et augmenté par Dezauche A Paris Chez Dezauche Géographe Successeur et Possesseur du Fond Géographique des Srs De l'Isle et Buache, Et Chargé de l'Entrepôt général des Cartes de la Marine du Roi. Rue de Noyers prés celle des Anglois [1780-91]. The plan of Paris is dated 1791.

Offered for sale in Dezauche's catalogue for 200 Livres.

The following maps relate to America.
Mappemonde 1785.
Planisphere Physique N.D.
Carte D'Amerique 1785.
Carte du Canada Revue et Augmentée en 1783.
Carte du Mexique 1783.
Golfe du Mexique . . . Corrigée et Augmentée en 1780 par J. N. Buache [de Neuville] Géog. ord. du Roi. A Paris chez Dezauche.
For list of examples see page 10.
Another edition of his atlas exists with references to royalty removed.

Plate 25.

REISSUES BY DEZAUCHE

G. De l'Isle's maps

America 1785 (See No. 10).

America 1790 revised (See Nos. 11, 12, 13).

America 1795 (See No. 14).

America 1800 (See No. 15).

America 1808 revised (See No. 16).

America 1809 (See No. 17).

America 1822 (See No. 18).

America 1830 (See No. 19).

W. Hemisphere 1782 (See No. 26).

W. Hemisphere 1792 (See No. 27).

Canada 1781 (See No. 41).

Canada 1783 revised (See No. 42).

Louisiana 1782 revised (See No. 47).

Mexico & Florida 1783 revised (See No. 53).

Santo Domingo 1780 revised (See No. 62).

Terra Firma 1782 revised (See No. 76).

Paraguay 1780 (See No. 83).

The above maps were offered for sale at 1 Livre 5 sous.

Buache's maps

Martinique 1779 (See No. 87).

Fernand de Noronha 1780 (See No. 89).

Gulf of Mexico 1780 (See Nos. 92, 93).

Plans et Rades (See No. 96).

Considerations Géog. 1781 (See No. 97).

Cartes et tables 1780 (See No. 100).

J. N. De l'Isle's map

Carte des Nouvelles Découvertes 1780 (See No. 105).

J. N. Buache de la Neuville map

Partie Sept. du Globe 1781 (See Nos. 111, 112).

CHAPTER TWO

Comparative Cartography

by Henry Stevens and Roland Tree

INTRODUCTION

Comparative Cartography has long been out of print, and it was thought that many new collectors and newly founded libraries would appreciate adding this valuable reference work to their shelves.

Advantage has been taken in this present printing to add additional information that has come to light since its original publication in 1951. For this information, acknowledgment is due to Mr. J. H. Fitch, who suggested this reprint in the first place, to Mr. Roland Tree, to the late Henry Stevens and to Mr. R. V. Tooley, who has added an alphabetical index.

Thanks are also due to Mr. Roland Tree, the co-author, for his good offices in securing permission to reprint, and to the generosity of the owner for the said permission.

ADDENDA

BARBADOS

6 A New Map of the Island of Barbadoes [compiled by Richard Ford, a Quaker]

    [*c*. 1682] (a*) Another Issue. Imprint by Philip Lea . . . and by John Seller [undated]

    [*c*. 1710] (c) Another Issue. Sold by George Willdey at the Great Toy Spectacle, Chinaware and Print Shop, ye corner of Ludgate Street near St Pauls.

BELLE ISLE (Straits of)

7 A Chart of the Straights of Belleisele with Part of . . . Newfoundland and Labradore . . . By James Cook, Surveyor 1766. Size 23½ × 31 inches.

    1766 (a)   Original Issue. No imprint, title within plain oval frame.

    1766 (a*)   Another Issue. Figures of Indians and landscape added to title and imprint. Also to be found with Lords (instead of Lord) Commissioners and a third printing with addition of words 'Price 4 shill^s' added.

    1766 (a**) Another Issue. Cartouche and imprint removed.

    1770 (a***) Another Issue. Michael Lane's name and date 1769 added. Imprint May 1770 by T. Jefferys. 2 sheets 23½ × 14½ inches.

    1770 (b)   Another Issue. Imprint "Sayer & Bennett 1770."

    1794 (c)   Another Issue. Imprint "Laurie & Whittle 1794."

                 Skelton & Tooley "Map Collectors Series" no. 37.

BOSTON

7A Boston, its Environs and Harbour, with the Rebels Works raised against that Town in 1775, from the Observations of Lieut. Page of His Majesty's Corps of Engineers, and from the Plans of Capt. Montresor. Engraved & Publish'd by Wm. Faden . . . 1st October, 1777. Size 24¾ × 17½ inches.

    1777 (a) Original Issue. Title and Imprint as above. Most Easterly point shown is Gallops Island. The top half of a compass is shown just above the bottom border line slightly to the right of the centre but there are no bearing lines radiating from it. The imprint is beneath the bottom border line.

    1778 (b) Another Issue. Title as (a) Imprint (beneath bottom border line) "Engraved & Published by Wm. Faden . . . 1st October 1778". Size 33⅜ × 17½ inches. The right hand border line of

(a) has been cut away and a new half sheet ($9\frac{1}{8} \times 17\frac{1}{2}$ inches) has been added extending the harbour to show Nachant Point, Natasket Head, Broad Sound, and many Islands including the Light House and the Brewsters. A new compass has been added at the extreme right hand side in the centre and bearing lines radiate from it across the plate. Similar bearing lines have been added to the Compass at the bottom of the original plate.

1778 (c) Another Issue. Title altered to read "with Additions from sundry American Plans. Published by Wm. Faden, Charing Cross," in place of "and from the Plans of Capt. Montresor." Immediately below the cartouche is the note "N.B. Some Material Parts were collected from the Observations of Captn. Montresor, His Majesty's Chief Engineer in America." Imprint as (b), beneath the bottom border line.

BRITISH DOMINIONS

7B A New and Accurate Map of the British Dominions in America, according to the Treaty of 1763: divided into the several Provinces and Jurisdictions. Presented upon the best authorities and astronomical observations by Thos. Kitchen, Geographer [London c. 1766]. Size $24\frac{1}{2} \times 20\frac{3}{8}$ inches.

c. 1766 (a) Original Issue. With printed in italics on one long line outside the bottom border line *Printed for And*^w*. Millar opposite Katherine Street in the Strand* Price 2ˢ. 6ᵈ. *Where may be had in Eight Imperial Sheets A Map of the British & French Dominions in N*th *America . . . Price 1 Guinea in Sheets, £1. 5s. 0d. in Boards and £1. 11s. 6d. on Canvass & Rollers.*

1769 (b) Another Issue. With Millar's imprint and advertisement line deleted and with *Engraved for Captn. Knox's History of the War in America* engraved, in the bottom right-hand corner, beneath the border line.

CHARLESTOWN, S.C.

13 A Sketch of the Environs of Charlestown.

1780   (a) Original Issue. See Phillips *Maps*, p. 222 for important note.

[1780 later] (b) Another Issue. No imprint, date, or author's name. Size $21 \times 15\frac{7}{8}$ inches. With references A-L, a-K.

DAWFOSKEE SOUND, S.C.

16   Plan of the River and Sound of Dawfoskee.

  [1773] (a) Cumming gives the date as 1776.

  [1776] (b) Date 1777.

HUDSON'S RIVER

23A   Chart of the Entrance of Hudson's River from Sandy Hook to New York with the Banks, Depths of Water, Sailing marks, &c. London Robt. Sayer & John Bennett, 1st June 1776, 53 Fleet Street.   Size 20½ × 27½ inches.

  1776 (a) Original Issue.

  1794 (b) Another Issue. Imprint "London published 12th May 1794, Laurie & Whittle, 53 Fleet Street".

LAKE CHAMPLAIN

24   The Attack and Defeat of the American Fleet . . . upon Lake Champlain.

  1766 (a*) Another Issue. "Carleton's" name in title replaced by that of Captⁿ Thos. Pringle. No printed account of battle beneath the plan.

LAKE CHAMPLAIN & LAKE GEORGE

25   Coast of West Florida and Louisiana.

  1788 (b*) Another Issue. London, Robert Sayer, 1 Janʸ 1788.

MIDDLE BRITISH COLONIES

29   [Bowles Issue].

  [?1780] (e) Fourth Issue. Title changed to "Bowles's New Pocket Map of the Middle British Colonies in America, viz. Virginia . . . Rhode Island [as (a)]. Comprehending also the Habitations . . . of the Confederate Indians; by Lewis

Evans." Imprint altered to "Printed for the Proprietor Carington Bowles No. 69 in St. Paul's Church Yard, London." The ornamental cartouche of (d) has been removed and a new title without any border has been inserted in its place. The Eastern Shore of Lake Huron has been extended Northwards. New Rivers and Lakes inserted North of Lake Ontario. The long legend to the North of Lake Erie relating to the Confederates has been deleted and the space filled in with Rivers, Trees and Mountains. (Stevens Middle British Colonies 16).

[?1784] (f) Fifth Issue. Title changed to "Bowles's New Pocket Map of the following Independent States of North America . . . as (e). Imprint as (e). The lettering VERMONT has been added. The "Boundary of the United States" (so lettered in Lake Ontario) is shown by a bold dotted line through Lakes Ontario, Erie and Huron. (Stevens 17).

[?1796-1800] (g) Sixth Issue. Title changed to "Bowles's New One-sheet Map of the Independent States of Virginia . . . Rhode Island, &c. . . ." as (e). Imprint altered to "Printed for the Proprietors Bowles & Carver, No. 69 in St. Pauls Church Yard, London." Considerable alterations have again been made. The district South of Lake Erie and North of the Ohio River is now named Western Territory with a similar new lettering on the inset. The new State of Kentucky (admitted 1792) is marked in its proper position south of the Ohio River, Tennessee is also marked. (Stevens 19).

NEW YORK & NEW JERSEY

44 The Provinces of New York and New Jersey.

1776 (e*) August 17. This issue has, in lower sheet, grants in N.E. Penna. now named.

NEWFOUNDLAND

46 Chart of Part of the South Coast of Newfoundland.

[1767] (a*) Another Issue. Carington Bowles' name added to imprint and date 1767. Extended to three sheets, with extension slip pasted on right.

1767   (a**)   Another Issue.   And-Dury and Carington Bowles' names removed from imprint.

1774   (b)   Correct size $67\frac{3}{4} \times 19\frac{3}{4}$.

1794   (c)   Another Issue.   Imprint Laurie & Whittle . . . 12th May 1794.

56   Carte de l'Amerique Septentrionale.

1784   (f)   Same title as (e) with the word *States* added.   Imprint beneath bottom border *Published as the Act directs*, 12 April 1784.

Many additions and alterations in accordance with the Treaty of 1783.

61   [Senex] North America.

1710   (a*)   Another Issue.   "By John Senex F.R.S. 1710."   Price & Maxwell's names deleted from title.   No Imprint beneath the scales in the bottom left corner.

1710   (a**)   Another Issue.   "By John Senex and John Maxwell 1710." No imprint beneath scales in bottom left corner.

[?1760]   (d)   Another Issue.   Imprint changed to T. Bowles, J. Bowles & Son and Robt. Sayer.   [*c*. 1760].

PORT ROYAL, S.C.

71   A Plan of Port Royal.

1773   (a)   Cumming gives date as 1776.

ST. LAWRENCE RIVER

74   A New Chart of the River St. Lawrence.

1777   (e)   Reissued in 1777, 1779, 1799 and 1806 in various editions of North American Pilot.

83   The Courses of the Rivers Rappahannock and Potowmack.

[c. 1752] (e) Another Issue. Published after "Orange County" of (d) had been re-named "Culpeper County" and after the building of Lord Fairfax's house near Winchester. "Frederick County," to the north-west of "The Blew Ridge," is now named. Several forts, houses, rivers, place-names, etc., have been added and numerous roads, shown by means of dotted lines, have been introduced and named, e.g., "Road from the Ohio," "Road to Philadelphia," "Road to Annapolis." Superimposed over the Fairfax Arms a large tract of land is laid out enclosed by dotted lines with a red coloured border line; this is not named but bears the figures 54,000. In all other respects this issue would appear to conform to issue (d).

83A   A Survey of the Northern Neck of Virginia being the Lands belonging to the Rt. Honourable Thomas Lord Fairfax Baron Cameron, bounded by and within the bay of Chesapoyocke and between the River Rappahannock and Potowmack: with the Course of the Rivers Rappahannock and Potowmack, in Virginia, as surveyed according to Order in the Years 1736 & 1737. [London, 1745]. Size $13\frac{3}{4} \times 13\frac{3}{4}$ inches.

This very rare map shows "The boundary Line of the Northern Neck in Virginia from the headspring of the River Conway a Southern Branch of the River Rappahannock to the headspring of the River Potowmack arising in the Allagany Mountains as ordered by his Majesty in Council 11th April 1745 unto the Rt. Hon. Thomas Lord Fairfax the Proprietor thereof".

This boundary decision was the result of a petition made by Thomas Lord Fairfax to the King, in 1733, to have commissioners appointed to run the line between the rivers.

Comparative Cartography

by Henry Stevens and Roland Tree

T HE practice of comparing apparently identical copies of old maps in the hope of discovering hitherto unrecorded variations has so developed during the last half century that it has become, what may be almost termed, a science which has added considerable importance and interest to the collecting of maps, plans, charts, etc. As long ago as the year 1880 the late Henry N. Stevens, F.R.G.S., M.A. (Hon., Mich.), started compiling notes on the variations that had come to light in the maps he was handling, which culminated in the publication in 1905 of his well-known essay on the maps of Lewis Evans which ran into three editions, all of which are out of print and are much sought after. As he had accumulated a mass of information about the maps he had compared, he planned to publish a general work on similar lines but unfortunately the exigencies of his business activities never allowed him to carry out the project. During the twenty years since his death when any new discovery was made it was incorporated into his notes with the result that at the present time a mass of important bibliographical information has been gathered together.

The following descriptions, based on this information, are, generally speaking, confined to maps which were separately issued or are to be found in atlases of the period. We have included maps which occur in books only if they have been separately issued in the first place. Maps in the same category as Capt. John Smith's Map of New England and Map of Virginia, which occur in several states, have been omitted as have also those maps, similar to those of Herman Moll, which were issued, during a period of half a century, without any alterations other than that of the name or names in their undated imprints.

It should be emphasized that the maps here listed are only those which have passed through our hands or which have been brought to our notice and that no attempt has been made to search any of the great map collections for additional information or in the hope of discovering other titles or issues.

The maps have been arranged alphabetically by subject rather than chronologically as by this method the need for an extensive index is obviated.

AMERICA

1. [*Arrowsmith.*] Map of America. *London 4th Sept. 1804, by A. Arrowsmith. No 24 Rathbone Place.* Size, 56½ x 47¼ inches.

    1804 (a) ORIGINAL ISSUE. On Whatman Paper dated 1801.

    1804-[1808] (b) ANOTHER ISSUE. Address in imprint *No. 10, Soho Square.* Paper dated 1808.

    1804-[1811] (c) ANOTHER ISSUE. As (b). Paper dated 1811.

2. [*Faden.*] A Map of America or the New World . . . From the Map of D'Anville with . . . addition of discoveries since 1761. *London W. Faden April 12, 1797.* Size, 22¾ x 20½ inches.

    1797 (a) ? ORIGINAL ISSUE. Title-cartouche with "*O rare Columbus*" engraved in clouds above.

    1819 (b) ANOTHER ISSUE. Title and cartouche as (a). Imprint re-dated "*Augt. 12, 1819.*"

3. [*Gibson.*] A New and Compleat Map of all America . . . with a Copious Table showing the several Possessions of each European Prince & State as settled by the Definitive Treaty concluded at Paris Feby 10th 1763 the Clauses of which relative thereto are inserted. By John Gibson, Geographer. *London: Printed for Rob.t Sayer, Map & Print seller at the Golden Buck near Serjeants Inn Fleet Street* [1763]. Four sheets, size (when joined up), 47 x 41 inches.

    [1763] (a) ? ORIGINAL ISSUE. Handsomely engraved title-cartouche with two parrots at top right corner and basking alligator at its foot. Immediately above are engraved nine of the Articles of the Treaty of Paris of Feby 10th 1763. Scales in top right corner, four only in number, are unenclosed by a border. The colonies of *"Georgia," "S. Carolina," "N. Carolina"* and *"Virginia"* extend from the Atlantic to the Mississippi as also do their names. *"Fort Detroit"* is marked twice on the map (1) at the extreme end of *Lake Erie* (2) *"Ft. Detroit"* on *"L. Pontchartrain"* to the north of No. 1.

1772 (b)   ANOTHER ISSUE. Title-cartouche as (a). Title altered to *"A Map of the Whole Continent of America divided into North and South and West Indies with a . . . as (a) . . . are inserted Compiled from Mr. D'Anville's Maps of that Continent 1772.* Imprint *"London, Publish'd as the Act Directs 1st April 1772 By Robt Sayer . . ."* as (a). Gibson's name has been deleted. The scales have been increased to six and enclosed by a single border. The names of the colonies *Georgia &c* still extend to the Mississippi but their dotted line boundaries terminate at the *Apalachian Mts.* *"Fort Detroit"* is now only marked once (at the northwest corner of *Lake St. Clair*). The two halves of the continent are now lettered *North America* and *South America* respectively.

1777 (c)   ANOTHER ISSUE. Title-cartouche retouched, the two parrots deleted and a large palm tree substituted. Wording of title altered to *"A New Map . . . as (b) . . . Indies. With a descriptive Account of the European Possessions as settled . . . as (a) . . . Feby 10th 1763. Compiled . . . as (b) . . . Continent and Corrected in the Several Parts belonging to Great Britain from the Original Materials of Governor Pownall. M. P. London: Printed for Robt Sayer and John Bennett, No. 53 Fleet Street as the Act directs, 15th Feb^y, 1777."* The imprint has been removed from just inside the bottom border line (traces quite discernible) to form the last four lines of the title. The names of the colonies *Georgia* &c have been much condensed so that they should not extend beyond the *Apalachian Mts.* *"Fort Detroit"* is now located at the southern end of *Lake St. Clair* which has been considerably altered in shape.

1783 (d)   ANOTHER ISSUE. Title-cartouche as (c) but wording altered to read *"A New Map of the Whole Continent . . . as*

(b) ... Indies wherein are exactly described the United States of North America as well as the Several European Possessions according to the Preliminaries of Peace signed at Versailles Jan. 20. 1783. Compiled ... as (b) ... Continent with the addition of the Spanish Discoveries in 1775 to the North of California & Corrected ... as (c) ... as the Act directs 15th. August 1783." The Articles of the Peace of 1763 which had previously surmounted the cartouche have been completely removed. The boundaries of the United States are shewn by dotted lines engraved on the plate and the country so enclosed has been lettered UNITED STATES. The shape of *California* has been considerably amended and new place-names have been inserted northward of it along the Pacific coast.

1786 (e)   ANOTHER ISSUE. As (d) without apparent alteration except that the date in the imprint has been changed to "*15th August 1786.*" Several place-names in *New-Mexico*, which were faintly engraved in the previous issue, would appear to have been retouched.

1794 (f)   ANOTHER ISSUE. As (e) without apparent alteration except for the change of imprint to "*London: Publish'd by Laurie & Whittle, No. 53 Fleet Street, as the Act directs, 12th May 1794.*"

4. [*Green.*] A Chart of North and South America &c. Six sheets of varying size measuring (when joined up) 43½ x 49½ inches.

Each of the six sheets has its own complete border lines all round and its own separate title and imprint, doubtless, so issued in order that it could be sold separately as well as form part of a single large chart. These six sheets bear the following separate titles, which remain intact when the complete chart is found in six separate sheets, but which have to be cut away when the sheets are joined together to form one large single chart.

SHEET I. Chart containing part of the Icy Sea with the adjacent coast of Asia and America. *Publish'd ... Feb. 19, 1753 by T. Jefferys ...* Size, 20½ x 16⅞ inches.

1753 (a)   ORIGINAL ISSUE. Title and imprint as above.

[?1763] (b)   ANOTHER ISSUE. Title and imprint as (a).

[?1768] (c)   ANOTHER ISSUE. Title as (a). Imprint altered to "...
              Robert Sayer ... and Thomas Jefferys ... n.d." No other
              apparent alteration.

1775 (d)   ANOTHER ISSUE. Title as (a). Imprint altered to "*Sayer
           & Bennett, 10 June, 1775.*" Numerous alterations in the
           neighborhood of Behring's Straits including the insertion
           of the track of Lieutenant Sindo in 1764-1767. Alaska ap-
           pears as a large island lettered "*Alaschka.*"

1775-[1783] (e)   ANOTHER ISSUE. Imprint as (d). No further comparison
                  available.

SHEET II. Chart comprising Greenland with the Countries and Islands
about Baffin's and Hudson's Bays. *Publish'd ... Feb^rv 19. 1753 by T. Jefferys ... London.* Size, 23⅞ x 20¾ inches.

1753 (a)   ORIGINAL ISSUE. With title and imprint as above.

[?1763] (b)   ANOTHER ISSUE. Title and imprint as (a).

[?1768] (c)   ANOTHER ISSUE. Title as (a). Imprint as Sheet I (c). No
              other apparent alterations.

1775 (d)   ANOTHER ISSUE. Title as (a). Imprint as Sheet I (d).
           Plate reduced in size by cutting away the 10-degree over-
           lap by which (a), (b), and (c) overlapped the corre-
           sponding issues of Sheet IV. Coast line now shaded and
           small ships inserted in the tracks of the navigators.

1775-[1783] (e)   ANOTHER ISSUE. Imprint as (d). No further comparison
                  available.

SHEET III. Chart containing the coasts of California, New Albion and
Russian discoveries to the North, with the Peninsula of Kamshatka in
Asia, opposite thereto and islands dispersed over the Pacific Ocean to the
north of the line. *Publish'd ... Feb 19 1753 by T. Jefferys ...* Size, 20½
x 16¾ inches.

1753 (a)   ORIGINAL ISSUE with imprint as above. Forms a continu-
           ation to the south of Sheet I. The supposed tracks of the
           early navigators are shown; there is no trace of the "*Is-
           lands of the Northern Archipelago,*" a large tract of land
           marked "*lands of which Capt. Behring found signs in
           1728,*" occupying their position.

[?1763] (b)   ANOTHER ISSUE. Title and imprint as (a).

[?1768] (c)   ANOTHER ISSUE. Title as (a). Imprint as Sheet I (c). No
              apparent alterations.

53

1775 (d)   ANOTHER ISSUE. Title as (a). Imprint as Sheet I (d). Many new tracks of navigators have been laid down, a large number of islands are shown and marked *"Northern Archipelago,"* the coast line of America is much more defined and a number of new place-names have been added including *"Mount St. Elias."*

1775-[1783] (e)   ANOTHER ISSUE. Imprint as Sheet I (d). No further comparison available.

SHEET IV. Chart of the Atlantic Ocean, with the British, French & Spanish Settlements in North America and the West Indies. *Publish'd . . . Feb 19 1753 by T. Jefferys . . .* Size of plate-mark, 24½ x 18½ inches.

1753 (a)   ORIGINAL ISSUE. Title and imprint as above.

[?1763] (b)   ANOTHER ISSUE. Title extended after the words *"West Indies"* to read *". . . as also on the Coast of Africa"* and authorship given as *"By Thoˢ Jefferys, Geographer to His Majesty."* Imprint altered to *"Publish'd according to Act of Parliament by T. Jefferys, the corner of St. Martin's Lane, Charing Cross (n.d.)."* Edged onto the left-hand margin are two overlays (each about 13 x 11 inches) consisting of two pieces of North America cut from duplicate copies of the chart, the main chart and the two overlays being differently colored. In the Table of Contents to Sayer & Jefferys' *"A General Topographer of North America. 1768"* this map is separately priced at *5s.* and described as distinguishing *"1. The Claims of the French in 1756"*; *"2. The French Dominions and Neutral Lands as proposed by M. de Bussy in 1761"*; *"The Dominions ceded by France and Spain to Great Britain in 1762."* In the top left-hand corner of the main chart, in a space previously blank and on to each of the overlays have been pasted separately engraved small descriptive slips. Copies of the main chart with the descriptive matter engraved direct on the plate instead of on the separate pasted-on slip have been observed. This sheet, without the overlays, forms Sheet IV of the Second Issue of Green's complete chart.

For a similar chart *see* No. 56, North America (Palairet) (b).

[?1768] (c)   ANOTHER ISSUE. Title and imprint as (b). No overlays or descriptive slips. No apparent alterations.

1775 (d)   ANOTHER ISSUE. Title altered to *"North America and the West Indies with the opposite Coasts of Europe and Africa."* and centralized in position. Imprint changed to *"Sayer & Bennett 10 June 1775."* Jefferys' name as author has been deleted. The whole coast line is now shaded and many new place-names have been added. A new table entitled *"North Coast of South America Astronomical Observations"* has been inserted at the foot adjacent to Guiana. In its altered state the old plate can only be recognized after minute comparison.

1775-[1783] (e)   ANOTHER ISSUE. Imprint as Sheet I (d). Beyond the fact that the boundaries of the United States are shown by dotted lines and its territory is colored green, no further comparison is available.

SHEET V. Chart containing the greater part of the South Sea to the South of the Line with the Islands dispersed thro' the same. *Publish'd . . . Feb 19 1753 by T. Jefferys . . .* Size, 20½ x 16¾ inches.

1753 (a)   ORIGINAL ISSUE. Title and imprint as above. Tracks of many of the early navigators including Magellan, Quiros, Tasman, Schouten, Le Maire, &c., are laid down.

[?1763] (b)   ANOTHER ISSUE. Title and imprint as (a).

[?1768] (c)   ANOTHER ISSUE. Title as (a). Imprint as Sheet I (c). No apparent alterations.

1775 (d)   ANOTHER ISSUE. Title as (a). Imprint as Sheet I (d). Extensive improvements have been made including the addition of the tracks of later navigators such as Byron, Carteret, Wallis, Bougainville, Cook, &c. The chart has also been embellished with numerous small ships.

1775-[1783] (e)   ANOTHER ISSUE. Imprint as Sheet I (d). No further comparison is available.

SHEET VI. Chart of South America, comprehending the West Indies, with the adjacent Islands in the Southern Ocean and South Sea. *Publish'd . . . Feb 19 1753 by T. Jefferys . . .* Size, 23¾ x 21 inches.

1753 (a)   ORIGINAL ISSUE. Title and imprint as above.

[?1763] (b)   ANOTHER ISSUE. Title and imprint as (a).

[?1768] (c)   ANOTHER ISSUE. Title as (a). Imprint as Sheet I (c). No apparent alteration. Each of the issues (a), (b), and (c) are much larger in size than the other corresponding five sheets. Each overlaps the sheet above it (No. IV) by some 23° which overlapping portion has to be cut away when the six sheets are joined to form one complete chart.

1775 (d)   ANOTHER ISSUE. Imprint as Sheet I (d). Title altered to read *"South America with the adjacent Islands in the Southern Ocean and South Sea."* The overlapping 23° of the previous three issues have been deleted and the top border lowered and re-engraved. Numerous tracks of the more recent navigators such as Cook, Carteret, Byron, &c., have been laid down and the plate embellished with numerous small ships.

1775-[1783] (e)   ANOTHER ISSUE. Imprint as Sheet I (d). No further comparison is available.

Joined together

I	II
III	IV
V	VI

the above six sheets form the large single chart entitled:

COMPLETE CHART. A Chart of North and South America, including the Atlantic and Pacific Oceans with the Nearest Coasts of Europe, Africa and Asia, (London) *Publish'd . . . Feb 19 1753 by T. Jefferys, Geographer . . . St. Martin's Lane, Charing Cross.* Size (when joined), 43½ x 49½ inches.

1753 (a)   ORIGINAL ISSUE. Title and imprint as above. Usually found on thin paper, without watermark.

[?1763] (b)   ANOTHER ISSUE. Title as (a). Imprint of Sheets I, II, III, V and VI as (a) but Sheet IV has undated imprint *"Publish'd . . . by T. Jefferys, the corner of St. Martin's Lane, Charing Cross."* All six sheets of thick paper each with two watermarks. (a) in one half a fleur-de-lys in a large device with the letters "L.G." beneath. (b) in the other half the figure "VI."

[?1768] (c)   ANOTHER ISSUE. Title as (a). Imprint changed to *"Publish'd . . . and printed for Robert Sayer . . . and Thomas Jefferys . . . [n.d.]."* Listed as No. 1 and priced at 12*s.* in the Contents to Sayer & Jefferys' *"General Topography of North America"* published in 1768. This issue may be identified by the one watermark IV found in each sheet of paper.

1775 (d)   ANOTHER ISSUE. Title as (a). Imprint *"Sayer & Bennett, 10 June, 1775."* Numerous alterations in each of the six sheets.

1775-[1783] (e)   ANOTHER ISSUE. Title altered to *"A Chart of North and South America . . . as (a) . . . Asia. According to the Preliminary Articles of Peace signed at Versailles 20 Janᵛ 1783."* Imprint *"Publish'd according . . . 10th June 1775 by R. Sayer and J Bennett . . .* Issued shortly after the signing of the Peace of Versailles without alteration of the imprint as (d) but with a revised title and a dotted line showing the boundary of the United States whose territory was colored green.

ARCTIC

Chart . . . of the Icy Sea with the adjacent coast of Asia and America. 1753. *See* No. 4, America [Green], Sheet I.

ATLANTIC OCEAN

Chart of . . . with British, French & Spanish Settlements in N. America. 1753. *See* No. 4, America [Green], Sheet IV.

5.   A New Chart of the Vast Atlantic or Western Ocean . . . Laid down from the latest Discoveries & regulated by Numerous Astronomical Observations. *London: Printed for Carington Bowles in St Pauls Churchyard* [1762] *Thos. Bowen, Sculp. 1762.* Size, 21¾ x 17½ inches.

1762 (a)   THE ORIGINAL ISSUE. Title and imprint as above.

1779 (b)   ANOTHER ISSUE. Title changed to *"Bowles's New Pocket Map of the Atlantic or Western Ocean."* Imprint as (a) *". . . London. Published 1 Jan. 1779."*

[c1780] (c)   ANOTHER ISSUE. Title as (b). Imprint *"Printed for Carington Bowles [c1780]."*

[c1794] (d)   ANOTHER ISSUE. Title changed to *"Bowles's New One-Sheet Chart of the Atlantic or Western Ocean . . . London: Bowles & Carver, [c1794]."* Title moved from top center to the African Continent in place previously occupied by a note as to the sources of information. *"Thos. Bowen, Sculp. 1762"* has been erased from the plate.

BARBADOS

6. A New Map of the Island of Barbadoes. Size, 21⅞ x 16⅞ inches.

    [c1676] (a)   ORIGINAL ISSUE. Imprint *"to be sold by Mr. Overton . . . Mr. Morden . . . Mr Berry and Mr. Pask."*

    1685 (b)   ANOTHER ISSUE. Numerous alterations. Imprint *"By Philip Lea . . . and by John Seller . . . London 1685."*
See Addenda

BELLE ISLE (Straits of)

7. A Chart of the Straights of Belleisle with Part of . . . Newfoundland and Labradore . . . By James Cook, Surveyor 1766.

    1766 (a)   ORIGINAL ISSUE. Imprint *"I. Mount & T. Page on Tower Hill."* Size, 31¼ x 23¾.

    1770 (b)   ANOTHER ISSUE. *"By James Cook in 1766 and Michael Lane in 1769."* Imprint *"London . . . 10 May 1770 by R. Sayer & I. Bennett . . ."* Size increased to 43¾ x 24 inches. (a) has been widened by a half sheet added to its left-hand edge. See Addenda

BOSTON See Addenda

BRITISH COLONIES

The British Colonies in North America MDCCLXXVII. *See* No. 80 United States [Faden]. BRITISH DOMINIONS See Addenda

CABOTIA

8. Map of Cabotia comprehending the Provinces of Upper and Lower Canada . . . by John Purdy. Four sheets, size (joined), 61½ x 48 inches.

    1814 (a)   ORIGINAL ISSUE. Imprint *"London Jas. Whittle & R. Holmes Laurie 12th October 1814."*

    1821 (b)   ANOTHER ISSUE. Imprint *"London Published 1st Sept 1821 by Richard H Laurie."*

    1821-1825 (c)   ANOTHER ISSUE. Imprint *"London Published 1st Sept 1821 by Richard H Laurie . . . Improved Edn. with Additions 1825."*

CALIFORNIA

Chart containing . . . California, New Albion and Russian Discoveries. 1753. *See* No. 4, America [Green], Sheet III.

CAROLINA

9. [*Thornton & Fisher.*] A New Map of Carolina. *London John Thornton and Will Fisher.* Size, 20⅝ x 15⅝ inches.

  [1689] (a) ORIGINAL ISSUE. Imprint as above.

  [1728] (b) ANOTHER ISSUE. Thornton & Fisher's imprint erased.

10. [*Thornton & Lea.*] A New Map of Carolina. London [c1685]. Size, 17¾ x 21¼ inches.

  [c1685] (a) ORIGINAL ISSUE. With imprint *"John Thornton at the Platt in the Minories, Robert Morden at ye Atlas in Cornhill, and by Philip Lea at the Atlas & Hercules in the Poultry."* With inset map of *"Ashley and Cooper Rivers"* and a *"Table of Settlements on Ashley and Cooper Rivers . . ."*

  [c1690] (b) ANOTHER ISSUE. With imprint *"By Philip Lea, at the Atlas and Hercules in Cheapside"* only.

  [c1695] (c) ANOTHER ISSUE. Imprint altered to *"London: Geo. Willdey."*

CAROLINA (N. & S.)

11. An Accurate Map of North and South Carolina with their Indian Frontiers . . . By Henry Mouzon and others. Size (four sheets when joined up), 56 x 39¾ inches.

  1775 (a) ORIGINAL ISSUE. With imprint *"London: Robt. Sayer and J. Bennett, May 30th, 1775."*

  1794 (b) ANOTHER ISSUE. Imprint altered to *"[London] Laurie & Whittle, 12th May, 1794."*

CAROLINA & GEORGIA

12. A Map of South Carolina and a part of Georgia . . . Composed from Surveys taken by . . . Capt. Gascoygn . . . and William de Brahm, Surveyor General to the Province of South Carolina, one of the Surveyors of Georgia. Four sheets. Size (when joined), 47¾ x 53 inches.

  1757 (a) ORIGINAL ISSUE. Imprint *"London T. Jefferys, Octr 20, 1757."* The survey in this edition is confined almost entirely to the neighborhood of the seacoast and the settlements immediately adjacent.

1780 (b) ANOTHER ISSUE. Title altered to read *"... William de Brahm, Surveyor General of the Southern District of North America. Republished with considerable additions ... By William Faden 1780."* Imprint *"London: Wm. Faden, June 1st 1780."* Those portions of the map which were blank in (a) are now filled in with counties, townships, rivers, &c. The map is now dedicated to the Rt. Hon. Lord George Germaine.

CHARLESTOWN, S. C.

13. A Sketch of the Environs of Charlestown in South Carolina By Captain Geo. Sproule.

1780 (a) ORIGINAL ISSUE. Imprint *"Published 1st June 1780."* With lettered references A-G, a-f.

[1780 later] (b) ANOTHER ISSUE. Imprint erased. With references A-L, a-k. `See Addenda`

CHARLESTOWN, S. C., FORT SULIVAN

14. A Plan of the Attack of Fort Sulivan near Charles Town in South Carolina, by a Squadron of His Majesty's Ships on the 28th June 1776, with the Disposition of the King's Land Forces, and the Encampments and Entrenchments of the Rebels. Engraved by Wm. Faden. *London. Augt. 10th 1776 by Wm. Faden.*

1776 (a) ORIGINAL ISSUE. *(1st State.)* Size, 14⅝ x 11 inches on plate-mark 15⅞ x $11\frac{9}{16}$ on paper 16½ x 22 inches. Immediately below plan on a separate plate (size, 15½ x 1¼ inches) is the dedication *"To Commodore Sir Peter Parker ... by Lt. Colonel Thos. James ... June 30th 1776."* Beneath this again type printed in two columns on the same sheet of paper is *"List of His Majesty's Squadron ..."* and *"The following Account of the Attack of Fort Sulivan ..."* Beneath the printed account is the imprint *"London, Printed and sold by William Faden, Successor to the late Mr. Thomas Jefferys ..."* This issue can be readily distinguished by the absence of the bridge of boats between Sulivan's Island and the mainland and by the British position on Long Island being simply marked *"British Camp."*

(b) ORIGINAL ISSUE. *(2nd State.)* Size, 14⅝ x 11 inches on plate-mark 15 x 11 inches on paper 24½ x 16½ inches. As (a) but printed the reverse way of the paper. Has the dedication to Sir Peter Parker but not the text. The copy from which this note was made had an uncut edge to the paper 2½ inches below the plate-mark of the dedication, proving conclusively that no printed text was issued with it.

(c) ANOTHER ISSUE. Size, 14⅝ x 11 inches on plate-mark 15$\frac{7}{16}$ x 11$\frac{9}{16}$ inches on paper 21¾ x 14¾ inches. Printed the same way of the paper as (b) giving large margins all round, this conclusively proving that no description was intended to be printed beneath the plan. The dedication as in (a) and (b) does not appear, although there is ample room for it. A bridge of boats is now shown connecting Sulivan's Fort with the mainland at its most southerly point now marked "*Hetheral Point*" at which place two positions marked "*Rebel's Camp*" are now shown. The British camp on *Long Island* is now marked "*Encampment of the British Army.*"

(d) ANOTHER ISSUE. Size, 14⅝ x 11 inches on paper 16 x 20¼ inches. The plan printed the narrow way of the paper as in (a). There is no dedication between the plan and the printed description as in the First Issue. The printed description is still in two columns but has been entirely re-set though apparently word for word with that on (a). There are numerous alterations and additions of which the following will be found sufficient for identification. A second bridge of boats has been added to the eastward of that shown in (c), the large sand bank marked "*North Sand*" in previous issues has been altered in shape and re-lettered "*North Breaker*," the "*Ranger Sloop*" which was common to the previous issues has been removed but traces of it are still discernible on the plate in its top right-hand corner.

CHESAPEAKE BAY

15. A New and Accurate Chart of the Bay of Chesapeake . . . Drawn from several draughts . . . chiefly from those of Anthony Smith, Pilot of S. Mary's. Two sheets. Size (when joined) 54 x 37½ inches.

1776 (a) ORIGINAL ISSUE. Imprint "*London: Sayer & Bennett, 1st July 1776. With a Book of Directions.*"

1794 (b)   ANOTHER ISSUE. Imprint *"London: Laurie & Whittle, 12th May, 1794."*

DAWFOSKEE SOUND, S. C.

16. Plan of the River and Sound of Dawfoskee in South Carolina Surveyed by Captain John Gascoigne. Size, 17⅞ x 25¼ inches.

  [1773] (a)   ORIGINAL ISSUE. No imprint or date but [*"London: Jefferys & Faden 1773"*].

  1776 (b)   ANOTHER ISSUE. *"London Printed for R. Sayer & J Bennett . . . 15th May 1776."*

  1794 (c)   ANOTHER ISSUE. *"Published 12 May 1794 by Laurie & Whittle London."* See Addenda

DELAWARE RIVER

17. The Course of the Delaware River from Philadelphia to Chester with the several Forts and Stockadoes raised by the Americans. Size, 27 x 17½ inches.

  1778 (a)   ORIGINAL ISSUE. Imprint *"Engraved by William Faden . . . April 30th 1778."* With inset *"A Sketch of Fort Island."*

  1785 (b)   ANOTHER ISSUE. Imprint altered to *"London: printed for Wm Faden . . . Jan.ʸ 1st 1785. 2nd Edition."* The inset of (a) replaced by *"A Plan of Fort Mifflin on Mud Island."* Numerous alterations and additions.

ENGLISH & FRENCH POSSESSIONS

18. [*Palairet.*] Carte des Possessions Angloises & Francoises du Continent de l'Amerique Septentrionale. *A Londres, 1775, Nourse, Vaillant, Millar, Rocque & Sayer.* Size, 22½ x 16¼ inches.

  1755 (a)   ORIGINAL ISSUE. The *"Explication"* in French only.

  1755 (b)   ANOTHER ISSUE. The *"Explication"* in French and English. Additional dotted boundary lines with titles in French drawn horizontally across the map.

  1756 (c)   ANOTHER ISSUE. Date in title changed to 1756 and *"Par. I Palairet"* added after the date. Bilingual *"Explication"* as (b).

ENGLISH EMPIRE

19. [*Daniel.*] A Map of ye English Empire in ye Continent of America viz. Virginia, Maryland, Carolina, New York, New Jersey, New England. By R. Daniel. W. Binneman sculpsit. *Sold by R. Morden & W. Berry* [1679]. Size, 23⅜ x 19½ inches.

  [1679] (a) ORIGINAL ISSUE. Title and imprint as above. *See* Baer's *Seventeenth Century Maryland*, Baltimore, 1949, for a description of the text which was published to be attached to the map.

  [?1685] (b) ANOTHER ISSUE. Title as (a) except that the author's name "*R. Daniel*" has been erased to make room for the insertion of "*Pennsylvania.*" The imprint has been altered to "*Sold by R. Morden at ye Atlas in Cornhill neer ye Royal-Exchange.*"

20. [*Morden.*] A New Map of the English Empire in America viz Virginia, Maryland, Carolina, New York . . . New France &c. By Rob. Morden. *London: Sold by Rob: Morden and by Christopher Brown* [c1695]. Size, 23¼ x 19¾ inches.

  [c1695] (a) ORIGINAL ISSUE. Inset map in bottom right "*Coasts & Isles of Europe, Africa and America*" with above this, side by side, an inset "*The Harbour of Boston*" and the title surmounted by the royal arms.

  1719 (b) ANOTHER ISSUE. Title as (a) except that "*Revised by Ion Senex 1719*" has been substituted for "*Rob. Morden.*" The Royal Arms surmounting the title in (a) have been replaced by a dedication.

FORTS CLINTON & MONTGOMERY

21. Plan of the Attack of the Forts Clinton & Montgomery upon Hudson River . . . on the 6th of Oct., 1777 drawn . . . by John Hills, Lt. 23d Regt. and Asst. Engineer. *London: Wm. Faden, June 1st 1784.* Size, 20⅜ x 26¼ inches.

  1784 (a) ORIGINAL ISSUE. Title and imprint as above.

  1793 (b) ANOTHER ISSUE. Found in "*Stedman's American War London 1794*" with Lt. Hills' name deleted and imprint altered to "*Published by the Author, April 12th, 1793.*"

GEORGIA

22. Sketch of the Northern Frontiers of Georgia By Archibald Camp-
bell, Lieut? Col!, | 71st Reg? Engraved by Willm Faden. Size, 23⅜
x 37⅜ inches.

> 1780 (a)   ORIGINAL ISSUE. Imprint *"London . . . May 1st 1780 by
> Wm Faden."*
>
> [1794] (b)   ANOTHER ISSUE. Imprint as (a) but printed on wove pa-
> per with watermark *"Whatman 1794."* Probably pub-
> lished by Laurie & Whittle.

GREENLAND

Chart comprising Greenland with . . . Baffin's and Hudson's Bays. 1753.
See No. 4, America [Green], Sheet II.

HUDSON'S RIVER

23. A Topographical Map of Hudson's River . . . from Sandy-Hook
. . . to Fort Edward, also the Communication with Canada by
Lake George and Lake Champlain, as high as Fort Chambly on
Sorel River. By Claude Joseph Sauthier, on the original Scale of
Four Miles to One Inch. Engraved by William Faden, Charing
Cross [*London*] *Octr 1st, 1776 by Wm. Faden.* Size, 20⅞ x 31½
inches.

> 1776 (a)   ORIGINAL ISSUE in which the banks of the river, lakes and
> (*Oct. 1*) islands are shown in outline only. Titles and imprint as
> above.
>
> 1776 (b)   SECOND ISSUE. As (a) but the banks in shaded outline.
> (*Oct. 1*)
>
> 1776 (c)   THIRD ISSUE. Imprint in the title altered to [London] *"En-
> (*Oct. 11*) graved by William Faden, Successor to the late Mr. Jef-
> ferys, Geographer to the King, Charing Cross."* The dated
> imprint at the foot of the map is unaltered. In Lake Cham-
> plain two lettered references "X" and "A" have been add-
> ed corresponding with lettered references engraved on the
> plate. That referring to A is dated *11th Octr. 1776* which
> is later than the dated imprint of the map itself.

1776 (d) FOURTH ISSUE. Imprints as (c). An additional lettered
(Oct. 12) reference "B" has been inserted, on the east shore of Lake
Champlain, to a note "B where the Rebel Fleet was de-
feated & burnt, on the 12 Octr. 1776." See Addenda

LAKE CHAMPLAIN

24. The Attack and Defeat of the American Fleet under Benedict
Arnold by the King's Fleet commanded by Sir Guy Carleton, up-
on Lake Champlain the 11th of October 1776. *London Published
... Decr 3rd 1776 by Wm. Faden.*

1776 (a) ORIGINAL ISSUE. Size, 16⅜ x 10¼ inches. No printed account of the battle beneath the plan.

1776 (b) ANOTHER ISSUE. *"Carleton's"* name replaced by that of
"Captn Thos. Pringle." An account of the battle in three
columns is printed beneath the plan on paper measuring
overall 23⅝ x 19⅜ inches. See Addenda

LAKE CHAMPLAIN & LAKE GEORGE

25. A Survey of Lake Champlain including Lake George, Crown
Point and St. John. Surveyed by William Brassier 1762. Size, 18¾
x 25⅞ inches.

1776 (a) ORIGINAL ISSUE. Imprint *"R. Sayer & J Bennett Augst.
5th 1776."*

1776 (b) ANOTHER ISSUE. Imprint as (a) shows the English and
American fleets off the *Isle de Valcour* on October 11, their
movements down the river and second engagement off
Crown Point on October 13, with lettered references. It
will be observed that both these dates are later than that
in the imprint.

1794 (c) ANOTHER ISSUE as (b). Title enclosed in a cartouche with
note to Lake Champlain added. Imprint altered to *"Laurie
& Whittle, 12th May 1794."* See Addenda

LOUISIANA & FLORIDA

26. (1) The Coast of West Florida and Louisiana (2) The Peninsula
and Gulf of Florida or Channel of Bahama with the Bahama Islands. Two separate Maps each 24⅝ x 19 inches with complete

margins. Size, when joined with centre margins cut away to form one large map, 48¼ x 19 inches.

1775 (a)   ORIGINAL ISSUE. Imprint *"London: Robt. Sayer, 20 Feby ... 1775."* In this issue the bay to the northeast of the mouths of the Mississippi is unnamed but bears the note *"Shallow Water with many small Islands but very little known."*

1775 (b)   ANOTHER ISSUE. Imprint as (a). The bay marked *"Shallow Water"* has now been named *"Bay of Spiritu Santo"* and is carefully charted with many soundings. Many alterations made in the section above New Orleans and in the coast lines of Louisiana, West Florida and on both sides of the Peninsula of East Florida.

1794 (c)   ANOTHER ISSUE. Imprint *"London: Laurie & Whittle, 12th May 1794."*

LOUISBURG

27. A Plan of the City and Fortifications from a Survey made by Richard Gridley 1745—A Plan of the City and Harbour of Louisburg. *T. Jefferys Apl 20. 1757.* Size, 24½ x 15⅛ inches.

1757 (a)   ORIGINAL ISSUE. Title and imprint as above.

1758 (b)   ANOTHER ISSUE. Imprint *"T. Jefferys October 9. 1758."* Much altered.

[?1768] (c)   ANOTHER ISSUE. Imprint *"Printed for Robt. Sayer ... & Thoˢ Jefferys."* Main plan shows both the siege of 1745 and that of 1758.

LOWER CANADA

28. A New Map of the Province of Lower Canada ... By Samuel Holland Esq. Surveyor General ... *London, William Faden, August 12th 1802.* Size, 34¼ x 23¼ inches.

1802 (a)   ORIGINAL ISSUE. Title and imprint as above.

1813 (b)   ANOTHER ISSUE. As (a) except for change in imprint *"... April 12th 1813."*

1829 (c)   ANOTHER ISSUE? from a new plate as size is 34⅛ x 22⅜ inches. Imprint *"James Wyld. Jany. 1. 1829 (Second Edition)."* Many alterations and additions.

1838 (d) ANOTHER ISSUE. As (c). Imprint *"James Wyld, Jany. 1 1838 (Second Edition)."* Notable for the insertion along the *"North Easterly Ridge"* of a new dotted boundary line marked *"Boundary claimed by the United States."*

1840 (e) ANOTHER ISSUE. As (d). Imprint *"James Wyld 1840 (Second Edition)."* Several alterations including a new dotted boundary line.

1843 (f) ANOTHER ISSUE. As (e). Imprint redated *"1843 (Second Edition)"* shows the northeast boundary between Canada and the United States as established by the *Treaty of Washington of 9th August 1842.*

MIDDLE BRITISH COLONIES

29. [*Bowles issue.*] A General Map of the Middle British Colonies in America viz. Virginia, Maryland ... New York, Connecticut, & Rhode Island ... carefully copied from the Original Publish'd at Philadelphia by Mr. Lewis Evans. Size, 25½ x 19⅜ inches within the borders.

   [?1760] (a) ORIGINAL ISSUE. No engraved cartouche frame round title. No imprint. Stevens, *"Lewis Evans, 3rd Edn., 1924,"* 5.

   [?1765] (b) SECOND ISSUE. Title now enclosed in ornamental cartouche. Imprint (in Roman characters) *"London, Printed for John Bowles at the Black Horse in Cornhil & Carington Bowles in St. Pauls Church Yard."* Stevens 7.

   1771 (c) THIRD ISSUE. *(1st State).* Title as (b). Imprint altered to *"Printed for Carington Bowles at No. 69 St. Pauls Church Yard, London, Publish'd Jany 1, 1771."* Stevens 8.

   [?1774] (d) THIRD ISSUE. *(2nd State).* Title and imprint as (c). A long lettering CANADA in large capitals has been added extending diagonally across the map for 16 inches. Stevens 9. See Addenda

30. [*Kitchin issue.*] A General Map of the Middle British Colonies in America viz. Virginia, Maryland ... New York, Connecticut, and Rhode Island ... Publish'd by Lewis Evans. Size, 26¼ x 19 inches.

   1756 (a) ORIGINAL PIRATED ISSUE. Imprint *"Sold by T. Kitchin ... opposite Ely Gate Holborn 1756 Price 2s."* Stevens, *"Lewis Evans, 3rd Edn., 1924,"* 3.

1758 (b)   JEFFERYS' RE-ISSUE of (a). Imprint *"Sold by T. Jefferys, Charing Cross 1758. Price 2s: 6d."* Stevens 4.

1758-[?1768] (c)   SAYER & JEFFERYS' RE-ISSUE of (b). Imprint *"Sold by R. Sayer in Fleet Street & T Jefferys, Charing Cross 1758. Price 2s: 6d."* Apparently no alteration in the wording of the title. Stevens 6.

1775 (d)   SAYER & JEFFERYS' 1ST RE-ISSUE of (c). Imprint *"Sold by R. Sayer in Fleet Street & T Jefferys, Charing Cross 1775 Price 2s: 6d."* Apparently no alteration in the map. Stevens 10.

1775 (e)   SAYER & JEFFERYS' 2ND RE-ISSUE of (c). Imprint *"Sold by R. Sayer in Fleet Street & T Jefferys, Charing Cross. Price 2s: 6d. Publish'd as the Act directs 15 June 1775."* Stevens 11.

1776 (f)   SAYER & BENNETT'S 1ST RE-ISSUE of (e) improved. Imprint *"London. Printed for R. Sayer & J. Bennett, Map, Chart & Printsellers, No 53 Fleet Street, as the Act directs, 15th Oct'. 1776."* Stevens 14.

1776 (g)   SAYER & BENNETT'S 2ND RE-ISSUE of (e). Imprint as (f). The last two lines of the title in the cartouche altered to read *"corrected from Governor Pownall's Late Map 1776."* Stevens 15.

1794 (h)   LAURIE & WHITTLE'S 1ST RE-ISSUE of (g). Imprint *"London: Published by Laurie & Whittle No 53 Fleet Street as the Act directs 12th May 1794."* Title altered to *"A New and General Map."* Pownall's name has been deleted. Stevens 18.

1794-[1796] (i)   As (h) but on thin wove paper watermarked 1796.

1794-[1799] (j)   As (h) but on thin wove paper watermarked 1799.

1794-[1804] (k)   As (h) but on thin wove paper watermarked 1804.

1794-[1807] (l)   As (h) but on thicker wove paper watermarked 1807.

1794-[1808] (m)   As (h) but on Whatman wove paper watermarked 1808.

Cf. Stevens, *"Lewis Evans"* No. 18.

1794-[1812] (n) LAURIE & WHITTLE'S 2ND RE-ISSUE of (g) fully colored on wove paper watermarked *"J. Whatman 1812"* and stamped with the Sheet No. 38. The Upper Canada issue. The *"Province of Canada"* lettering of the previous issues has been deleted and "UPPER CANADA" substituted. The contours of the Great Lakes have been considerably altered. *"Cleveland"* is marked. The boundaries of Pennsylvania and of Vermont have been re-located. Not in Stevens' *"Lewis Evans."*

1794-[?1814] (o) As (n) fully colored on wove paper without watermark and stamped with the Sheet No. 50. Not in Stevens.

1794-[1816] (p) As (n) but outlines only colored; without watermark and stamped with the Sheet No. 72. In this form it occurs in the 1816 edition of Laurie & Whittle's Atlas. Not in Stevens.

MISSISSIPPI RIVER

31. Course of the River Mississippi from the Balise to Fort Chatres; taken on an Expedition to the Illinois in the latter end of the year, 1765. By Lieut. Ross of the 34th Regiment. Size, 13½ x 44¼ inches.

   1772 (a) ORIGINAL ISSUE with imprint *"London: Robert Sayer 1 June 1772."*

   1775 (b) ANOTHER ISSUE with imprint *"London Robert Sayer 1 June 1775"* shewing many alterations in the neighborhood of New Orleans including the addition of *Forts St. Leon* and *St. Mary.*

   1794 (c) ANOTHER ISSUE. As (b) but imprint changed to *"Laurie & Whittle, 12th May, 1794."*

NEW ENGLAND

32. [*Bowles.*] A Map of the Most Inhabited Part of New England containing the Provinces of Massachusetts Bay and New Hampshire with the Colonies of Conecticut and Rhode Island ... *London Printed for John Bowles at the Black Horse in Cornhill & Carington Bowles in St. Pauls Churchyard* [n.d.]. Size, 20⅞ x 25⅛ inches.

   [?1765] (a) ORIGINAL ISSUE of Bowles' one-sheet copy of Jefferys' four-sheet map. Title and imprint as above. The map follows very closely the second issue of Jefferys' first edition of 1755. The cartouche is in the top left corner. Neither of the insets *"Fort Frederick"* or *"Boston Harbour"* is reproduced.

1771 (b)   ANOTHER ISSUE. Title as (a). Imprint changed to *"Printed for Carington Bowles ... London Publish'd 1st Jan.y 1771."*

1776 (c)   ANOTHER ISSUE. Title changed to *"Bowles's Map of the Seat of War in New England ... accurate Plan of the Town, Harbour & Environs of Boston."* Imprint *"London ... Carington Bowles ... 1776."* With inset *"Plan of Boston with its Harbour and Environs 1776."*

[?1776] (d)   ANOTHER ISSUE. Title changed to *"Bowles's New Pocket Map of the Most Inhabited Part of New England ... accurate Plan ... Environs of Boston."* Imprint *"Printed for the Proprietor Carington Bowles ... London [c1776]."* From the same plate as (b) but title and cartouche have been removed from top left corner and the new title without cartouche appears in the sea opposite *Piscataqua Harbour. Dartmouth College* is marked but the old independent state of Vermont is not shown. Many alterations and additions have been made especially around *Lake George* and *Lake Champlain.* In the bottom right corner, previously blank, an inset *"Plan of Boston"* has been inserted.

[c1780] (e)   ANOTHER ISSUE. Title and undated imprint as (d). The country between *Lakes George & Champlain* and the *Connecticut River* is now named VERMONT and a note has been engraved on the plate, beneath the top border, reading *"This State extends Northward to the 45th degree of Latitude."*

[c1796] (f)   ANOTHER ISSUE. Title and imprint altered to *"Bowles's New One Sheet Map of New England comprehending the Provinces of ... as (d) ... Environs of Boston."* Imprint *"Printed for the Proprietors Bowles & Carver, No. 69 in St. Pauls Church Yard [c1796]."* No apparent alteration but for the changes in title and imprint.

33. *[Jefferys.]* A Map of the Most Inhabited Part of New England containing the Provinces of Massachusetts Bay and New Hamp-

shire with the Colonies of Konektikut and Rhode Island . . . [London] *November 29th 1755, Published according to Act by Thos. Jefferys.* Four sheets. Size (when joined), 38¾ x 40¾ inches.

1755 (a)
Streeter Sale 686)
ORIGINAL EDITION, 1ST ISSUE. Title and imprint as above. Inset plan (8⅛ x 5¼ inches) in top left corner entitled *"Fort Frederick, A French incroachment, built 1731 at Crown Point."* In this state *"Connecticut"* is spelled *"Konektikut"* both in the title and on the map and *Newport* and *Providence Counties* are not marked in Rhode Island.

1759 (b)
(Streeter Sale 690)
ORIGINAL EDITION, 2ND ISSUE. Imprint as (a). *"Fort Frederick"* inset, *"Connecticut"* now spelled *"Connecticut."* In Rhode Island colony the counties of *"Providence," "Kings," "Bristol"* and *"Newport"* appear for the first time.

1775-[1764] (c)
(Streeter Sale 688)
SECOND EDITION, 1ST ISSUE. Imprint 1755 but published c1763. The *"Fort Frederick"* inset replaced by *"A Plan of the Town of Boston."* All the country to the north of *"Stephens Fort"* previously marked *"Wilderness"* now laid out in townships.

1755-[c1768] (d)
SECOND EDITION, 2ND ISSUE. Imprint 1755 but published c1768. This state can easily be identified by the note relating to the boundary between New York and New Hampshire which is engraved on the map immediately beneath the inset in the top left corner.

1774 (e)
THIRD EDITION. Imprint altered to *"[London] November 29th 1774 by Thos. Jefferys."* Little apparent alteration from (d).

1794 (f)
ANOTHER EDITION. Imprint altered to *"Laurie & Whittle . . . 1794."*

34. [*Seller.*] A Mapp of New England by John Seller Hydrographer to the King. *And are to bee Sold at his Shop at the Hermitage in Wapping And by John Hills in Exchange Alley in Cornhill London.* Size, 21¼ x 17¼ inches.

[?1675] (a)
ORIGINAL ISSUE. Title in ornamental cartouche near the top left corner, smaller cartouche with blank center on its right. The Royal Arms in a garter surmounted by a crown again to the right. About the dedication cartouche *"A Scale of English Miles" (10-60 miles).*

[?1676] (b) SECOND ISSUE. The blank dedication cartouche of (a) now contains the dedication to Robert Thomson and is surmounted by his arms above which is "*A Scale of English Miles*" *(0-80 miles).*

NEW ENGLAND, NEW YORK &c.

35. A New Map of New England: New York: New Jarsey: Pensilvania: Maryland and Virginia. *Sold by John Thornton at ye Platt in ye Minories. By Robt Morden at the Atlas in Cornhill and by Philip Lea at ye Atlas and Hercules in the Poultry, London.* Size, 21½ x 17 inches.

[?1685] (a) ORIGINAL ISSUE. Philadelphia is shown and New Jersey is divided into East and West. No counties marked in east or west Jersey or on the west side of the Delaware. The British Museum assigns its date as 1685.

[c1686] (b) ANOTHER ISSUE and the first of two issues with Lea's imprint. "*By Philip Lea in Cheap-side London*" added to title and imprint altered to "*By Philip Lea at the Atlas and Hercules in Cheap-side London.*" No other apparent changes.

[c1690] (c) ANOTHER ISSUE. Title and imprint as (b). Exhibits numerous alterations, viz. the "*Provinces of E. & W. Jersey*" now show the five counties; the counties of "*Newcastle*," "*Kent*" and "*Sussex*" are laid down as part of Pensilvania with a dotted line denoting the boundary between Maryland and Pensilvania.

[?1715-20] (d) ANOTHER ISSUE. The words "*in Cheap-side London*" following Philip Lea's name in the title have been deleted. Lea's imprint has been erased and "*Sold by Geo: Willdey at the Great Toy, Spectacle, Chinaware and Print Shop at yᵉ corner of Ludgate Street near Sᵗ· Paul's, London,*" substituted. No other changes apparent.

NEW JERSEY

36. Plan of the Operations of General Washington against the King's Troops in New Jersey from 26th Dec. 1776 to the 3d Jan. 1777 by William Faden. *London: Published 15th April 1777 by Wm. Faden.* Size, 15¼ x 11¼ inches.

1777 (a) ORIGINAL ISSUE. "*Middletown,*" "*Allenstown*" and "*Kingstown*" each in one word and the road above "*Bristol*" unnamed.

1777 (b) SECOND ISSUE. The above mentioned towns each in two words, e.g. "*Middle Town,*" etc., and the road above "*Bristol*" named "*High Road from Philadelphia.*"

37. [*Faden.*] The Province of New Jersey divided into East and West commonly called the Jerseys. [London] *by Wm. Faden, Dec. 1st 1777.* Size, 22¼ x 30¾ inches.

    1777 (a) ORIGINAL ISSUE. Title and imprint as above.

    1778 (b) ANOTHER ISSUE. "*Second Edition with considerable improvements.*" Imprint dated *Dec. 1, 1778.*

1778-[1794] (c) ANOTHER ISSUE. As (b) but on wove paper with watermark "*Whatman 1794.*"

38. [*Seller.*] A Map of New Jersay by John Seller. Ja. Clerk, sculp. [London ?1664.] Size, 21 x 17⅛ inches.

    [?1664] (a) ORIGINAL ISSUE. Title in ornamental cartouche in bottom left, view of New York *(after Visscher)* in top right.

    [?1665] (b) SECOND ISSUE. Title and view as (a). Dedication to Sir Geo. Carteret surmounted by Carteret arms added in center of map. Royal shield and arms added at bottom right just above "*Ja. Clerk, sculp.*"

    [c1670] (c) THIRD ISSUE. Title altered to "*By John Seller and William Fisher.*" Title now in cartouche top center with Royal Arms beneath. Carteret arms deleted and Ja. Clerk, sculp. deleted. Visscher view in top right replaced by another view of New York *(after Allard)* in bottom left.

    1677 (d) FOURTH ISSUE. As (c) but with two side wings, printed from separate plates, added increasing the overall size to 36¾ x 17⅛ inches. Printed text in four columns pasted right across bottom of map "*The Description of West Jersey in America . . .*" Imprint in two lines at foot of fourth column of text "*London. Printed for John Seller at the Hermitage stairs in Wapping, and William Fisher at the Posterngate on Tower Hill 1677.*"

NEW YORK CITY

39. [*Montressor.*] Plan of the City of New York and its Environs to Greenwich . . . Survey'd in the Winter 1766 [London 1766?]. Size, 20⅝ x 25⅝ inches.

> 1766 (a) ORIGINAL ISSUE. Drawn by Capt. John Montressor and dedicated by him "*To the Honble. Thos. Gage, Esqr. . . .*"

> 1775 (b) SECOND ISSUE. Title altered to "*Survey'd in the Winter, 1775*" and an imprint "*Sold by A. Dury, Duke's Court. St. Martin's Lane*" has been added.

40. [*Ratzer.*] Plan of the City of New York in North America surveyed 1766 and 1767 . . . by . . . B. Ratzer, Lieut. in His Majesty's 60th or Royal American Regt. Thomas Kitchin, Sculpt. Size, 35¼ x 47½ inches.

> [?1776] (a) ORIGINAL ISSUE without imprint.

> 1776 (b) SECOND ISSUE. The imprint "*London: Published according to Act of Parliament, Jan. 12, 1776 by Jefferys and Faden, corner of St. Martin's Lane, Charing Cross.*" has been inserted immediately at the right of the title-cartouche and just above the "*South West View of the City of New York.*"

NEW YORK ISLAND

41. A Plan of New York Island with part of Long Island, Staten Island & East New Jersey . . . Engagement on the Woody Heights of Long Island between Flatbush and Brooklyn on the 27th of August 1776 between His Majesty's Forces, commanded by General Howe and the Americans under Major General Putnam, with the subsequent Disposition of both Armies. *Engraved & Publish'd according to Act of Parliament Octr 19th 1776 by Wm. Faden, Successor to the late Mr. Ts. Jefferys, Geographer to the King, Charing Cross, London.*

> *** There are five distinct issues of this plan each in two states. (1) on small-sized paper, 19½ x 24 inches, uncut, bearing a watermark consisting of a rectangular shield crossed by three diagonal lines, surmounted by a fleur-de-lys; beneath the shield are the letters "G. R." and to its left

are the initials "R. G." (2) on larger, thicker paper, 22½ x 30½ inches, having a watermark consisting of the initials "W. F." to the left of a crowned ovalish shield with initials "G. R." beneath. In the center of the shield a large fleur-de-lys. State 1 has no printed text beneath the plan whilst State 2 has text, in each instance, printed in four columns immediately beneath the plan and on the same paper. There being no geographical differences between States 1 and 2 of each issue it has not been thought necessary to make further reference to State 1 in the following descriptions.

1776 (a)   ORIGINAL ISSUE [*2nd State*]. Title and imprint as above. Printed text in four columns beneath the plan, entitled "*An Account of the Proceedings of His Majesty's Forces at the Attack of the Rebels Works on Long Island, on the 27th. of August 1776 . . .*" with last line of imprint reading "*of Mess. Wallis and Stonehouse, Booksellers, Ludgate Street.*" The seacoast, harbor, and rivers in single unshaded outline. The most northerly place marked on Hudson River is "*Tetards Hill.*" The "*Heights of Long Island*" are twice lettered simply "*The Heights.*" The fourth line of the title consists of only four words: "*Disposition of both Armies.*"

1776 (b)   SECOND ISSUE. Title as (a). "*Long Island*" text as (a). The seacoast, harbor and rivers now have their outlines shaded with several lines. Most northerly place on Hudson River is now "*Younker.*" "*The Heights of Long Island*" still marked as in (a).

1776 (c)   THIRD ISSUE. Title as (a) extended after the words "*Major General Putnam*" to read "*Shewing also the Landing of the British Army on New-York Island, and the Taking of the City of New York &c. on the 15 of September following, with the Subsequent Disposition of both Armies.*" Imprint as (a). The fourth line of title now has thirty words, "*British Army . . . Both the Armies.*" Seacoast, &c., shaded as in (b). Most northerly place on Hudson River is still "*Younker.*" "*The Heights of Long Island*" are now lettered (left) "*The Heights of Guana.*" Three lines of lettering, "*Flying Camp | of the Americans | Redoubt with Cannon,*" added on the Jersey shore opposite the head of New-York Island. The text beneath the plan is now entitled *"An Account of the Taking of the City of New York by His Majesty's Forces on the 15th of September 1776 . . ."*

1776 (d) FOURTH ISSUE. Title and imprint as (c). Seacoast, &c., shaded as (b), most northerly place as (b) and (c), *"Heights of Long Island"* as (c). A fourth line of lettering, i.e. *"Fort Independence,"* has been inserted between the lines *"of the Americans"* and *"Redoubt with Cannon"* on the Jersey shore. *"Fort Washington"* is now marked in the river near the head of New-York Island. *Taking of the City of New York* text as in (c).

1776 (e) FIFTH ISSUE. Title and imprint as (c) and (d). Seacoast shaded as in (b). Most northerly place is now *"Fort,"* the *"Younker"* of (b), (c) and (d) having been deleted. *"Heights of Long Island"* as (c) and (d). The four-line lettering on the Jersey shore of (d) has been erased. *"Fort Washington"* is now shown about three inches down from the head of New-York Island and is marked on the island itself and not in the river as in (d). *"Fort Lee or Ft. Constitution"* is now inserted on the Jersey shore a little south of opposite to *"Jefferys Hook."* The text at the foot of the plan reverts to *"The Attack on Long Island"* as in (a) and (b) but in an entirely new set-up. The last line of imprint now reads *"Mr Wallis, Bookseller in Ludgate Street."*

From descriptions I have read it is possible that (c) and (d) were also issued with *"Long Island"* text and (e) with *"New York"* text, but I have not, as yet, come across these variations.

NEW YORK PROVINCE

42. A Map of the Province of New York . . . From an Actual Survey by Captain Montressor, 1775. *London: June 10th 1775 by A. Dury.* Four sheets. Size (when joined up), 36¼ x 56⅝ inches.

1775 (a) ORIGINAL ISSUE. *"Ticonderoga"* marked *"Carillon Fort"* on west bank and *"Tyionderogha or Tienderoga"* on east bank.

1775 (b) SECOND ISSUE. Imprint as (a) *"Carillon Fort"* on west, *"Ticonderoga"* on east.

1775 (c)   THIRD ISSUE. Imprint as (a) "*Ticonderoga* or *Fort Caril-lon*" (in two lines) on west, nothing on east. Many new names and notes in Lake Champlain inset.

1777 (d)   FOURTH ISSUE. Imprint extended to "*Republished with Great Improvements, April 1st 1777.*"

43. The Country Twenty Five Miles round New York. Drawn by a Gentleman from that City. [London] *Published . . . 1st November 1776 by W. Hawkes* . . . Size, 14⅞ x 14⅞ inches on paper 17½ x 24½ inches.

1776 (a)   ORIGINAL ISSUE. "*A Chronological Table of the most in-*
(Nov. 1)   *teresting Occurences since the Commencement of Hos-tilities . . .*" in three columns type printed below the map. Beneath bottom border, one line engraved on the plate commencing "*Sept. 15. 1776 British Forces &c&c.*"

1776 (b)   ANOTHER ISSUE. *Imprint dated 21st Nov 1776.* An extra
(Nov. 21)   line engraved on the plate bringing the information down to November 1, 1776.

1777 (c)   ANOTHER ISSUE. Imprint dated *1st January 1777.*
(Jan. 1)

1777 (d)   ANOTHER ISSUE. Imprint "*R Sayer & J. Bennett 2 June*
(June 2)   *1777.*" Engraved description in two lines bringing infor-mation down to [Nov.] 16.

NEW YORK & NEW JERSEY

44. [*Holland.*] The Provinces of New York and New Jersey . . . and the Governments of Trois Rivieres and Montreal. Drawn by Capt. Holland. Engraved by Thomas Jefferys, Geographer to His Maj-esty. [London] *Printed for Robt. Sayer in Fleet Street, and T. Jef-ferys in the Strand* [1775]. Two sheets. Size (when joined), $26^1/_2 \times 52^3/_4$ inches.

[1775] (a)   ORIGINAL ISSUE. Imprint (undated) as above. Subsidiary title "*A Chorographical Map of the Country Between Al-bany, Oswego . . . exhibiting all the Grants . . . Lake & Montreal. Drawn from Authentic surveys by Thomas Jef-ferys . . .*" in one long line along the top outside the border line.

1775 (b) ANOTHER ISSUE. Imprint (dated) altered to *"Printed for*
(June 15) *Robt. Sayer and T. Jefferys in the Strand, published as the*
Act directs, 15 June 1775." No other apparent alteration.

1775 (c) ANOTHER ISSUE. Title and imprint altered to *"The Prov-*
(Dec. 20) *inces of New York and New Jersey . . . and the Province*
of Quebec, drawn by Capt. Holland Engraved by Thomas
Jefferys . . . and improved from the modern surveys of
those Colonies down to the year 1775. London. Printed
for Robt. Sayer and John Bennett . . . 20 Dec 1775." The
subsidiary *"Chorographical"* title has been removed. Three
insets, *"Mouth of Hudson's River," "City of New York"*
and *"Plan of Amboy,"* have been introduced in the top left
corner of the top sheet.

1776 (d) ANOTHER ISSUE. Title as (c) but altered *"drawn by Ma-*
(Aug. 17) *jor Holland, Engraved by . . . Corrected and improved*
from the original materials by Governr. Pownall, Member
of Parliament, 1776. London R. Sayer and J. Bennett 17
Augt. 1776." Numerous alterations especially in northern
New York, where large tracts of the country have been
laid out in grants.

1776 (e) ANOTHER ISSUE. The second of the two issues dated Au-
(Aug. 17) gust 17, 1776. The title has again been altered, Jefferys'
name as engraver having been deleted. It now reads as
(c) *". . . drawn by Major Holland, Surveyor General of*
the northern District in America. Corrected . . . Governor
Pownall, Member of Parliament 1776. London R. Sayer
and J. Bennett, 17 Augt. 1776." In the sea off Sandy Hook
a four-line note has been engraved reading *"For descrip-*
tion of this Country . . . see Govr. Pownall's Topographl.
Desn. p. 9-14." See Addenda

45. [*Sauthier.*] A Plan of the Operations of the King's Army under
the command of General Sr. William Howe, K.B. . . . against the
American Forces commanded by General Washington . . . wherein is particularly distinguished the Engagement on the White
Plains, the 28th of October [1776] By Claude Joseph Sauthier:
Engraved by Wm. Faden, 1777. [London] *Published Feb. 25th,*
1777 by W. Faden. Size, 19¼ x 28⅝ inches.

1777 (a) ORIGINAL ISSUE. No British ships shown off *"Terry*
Town."

78

1777 (b) SECOND ISSUE. Imprint as (a). British ships lying off "*Terry Town*," three being named "*Tartar*," "*Phoenix*," and "*Roebuck*" with their course up the Hudson shown by a dotted line up the center of the river. Several new place-names are inserted.

NEWFOUNDLAND

46. Chart of Part of the South Coast of Newfoundland ... by James Cook. Two sheets. Size (when joined), 38½ x 27 inches.

    1766 (a) ORIGINAL ISSUE. Imprint "*I. Mount and T. Page . . . Thos. Jefferys . . . and And*ᵂ *Dury . . . London 1766. N.B. With a Book of Directions.*"

    1774 (b) ANOTHER ISSUE. Imprint "*Published . . . by James Cook, Printed for R. Sayer & J. Bennett . . . May 10, 1774. Price six shillings N.B. With a Book of Directions.*" Size increased to three sheets (when joined) 67¾ x 24¾ inches. Only the left-hand sheet of (a) has been retained to form the right-hand sheet of (b) and two new sheets have been added on the left. See Addenda

NORTH AMERICA

47. [*Andrews.*] A New Map of the British Colonies in North America showing the Seat of the Present War ... By John Andrews. London *Published . . . Jan*ʸ *16th 1777 by John Andrews . . . & Andrew Dury. . . .* Size, 31 x 38½ inches.

    1777 (a) ORIGINAL ISSUE. Fifty-four numbered references in three columns in the Atlantic Ocean.

    1781 (b) ANOTHER ISSUE. References as (a). Imprint ". . . *Jan*ʸ *16th 1781 by John Andrews . . . and John Harris . . .*"

48. [*Arrowsmith.*] A Map exhibiting all the New Discoveries in the Interior Parts of North America. Inscribed by Permission to the Honourable Governor and Company of Adventurers of England trading into Hudson's Bay. . . . *A. Arrowsmith, Charles Street, Soho, January 1st 1795.* Size, 66½ x 35¾ inches.

    ** This map was repeatedly re-issued almost year by year as new discoveries came to light. We know of the follow-

79

ing editions: 1795, 1796 (two issues), 1802, 1811, 1814, 1817, 1818, 1819*, 1820*, 1821, 1823, 1824, 1833*, 1838*, 1839, 1850; those marked * we have not seen.

1795 (a) ORIGINAL ISSUE. With overlay over blank space between 60° and 70° Lat. and 95° and 115° Long.

1796 (b) ANOTHER ISSUE. Title and imprint as (a). *"Additions to*
[1st Iss.] *1796"* follows the date. With overlay as (a).

1796 (c) ANOTHER ISSUE. Title as (a) altered to *"A Arrowsmith.*
[2nd Iss.] *No 24 Rathbone Place. January 1st 1795. Additions to 1796."* Imprint *"London, Published Janry. 1st 1795. by A. Arrowsmith, No 24 Rathbone Place."*

1802 (d) ANOTHER ISSUE. Imprint as (c). The plate reduced in width to 56½ inches and increased in height to 48½ inches. The material contained on the overlay in previous issues now engraved, with alterations and additions, on the main map.

1811 (e) ANOTHER ISSUE. Imprint *"Published 1 Jan 1795 by A. Arrowsmith, No 10 Soho Square . . . Additions to 1811."*

1814 (f) ANOTHER ISSUE. Imprint as (e). *"Additions to 1811-June 1814."* Embodies the recent discoveries of Lewis and Clark.

1817 (g) ANOTHER ISSUE. Imprint as (e). *". . . Additions to 1811-1817, Additions to June 1814."*

1818 (h) ANOTHER ISSUE. Imprint as (e). *". . . Additions to 1811-1818, Additions to June 1814."*

1821 (i) ANOTHER ISSUE. *Additions to 1811-1818-1819-1820-1821.* Title moved to extreme left-hand corner.

1823 (j) ANOTHER ISSUE. *Additions to 1811-1818-1819-1820-1823.* Title as (i).

1824 (k) ANOTHER ISSUE. *Additions to 1811-1819-1820-1824.* Title as (i). Space in top center formerly occupied by title now filled with the Arctic discoveries of Captain Ross, Lieutenant Parry, &c. in 1818-1819-1821.

1839 (l) ANOTHER ISSUE. *Additions to 1811-1818-1819-1820-1824-1833-1839.* Interior of Russian America blank.

1850 (m) ANOTHER ISSUE. *Additions to 1811-1818-1819-1820-1824-1833-1839-1850.* Imprint *"London . . . 1 Jan 1850 by J. Arrowsmith, No 10 Soho Square . . . Hydrographer to Her Majesty."* Numerous rivers and places inserted up to 65° in Russian America. *Victoria* now marked on *Vancouver Island.*

49. [*Bowen & Gibson.*] An Accurate Map of North America describing . . . the British, Spanish and French Dominions . . . exhibiting the Present Seat of War and the French Encroachments. Also all the West India Islands . . . by Eman. Bowen, Geogr. to His Majesty, and John Gibson, Engraver. London: *printed for Robt. Sayer, opposite Fetter Lane, Fleet Street* [c1755]. Four sheets. Size (when joined up), 45¼ x 39¾ inches.

[?1755] (a)   ORIGINAL ISSUE. Title and imprint as above.

[?1763] (b)   ANOTHER ISSUE. Title altered to read ". . . *Dominions . . . according to the Definitive Treaty concluded at Paris, 10th Feb, 1763. Also all the West India Islands . . . by Eman. Bowen . . . and John Gibson, Engraver.*" Imprint (undated) as (a). Many engraved notes in (a) erased and others substituted. The XXth Article of the Treaty of 1763 has been inserted in the Atlantic Ocean.

1772 (c)   ANOTHER ISSUE. Title now reads "*British and Spanish Dominions*" (omitting the word French) otherwise as (b). Imprint altered to ". . . *Robert Sayer, No. 53 Fleet Street 2ᵈ July 1772.*" Many alterations in the Hudson's Bay area. "*Lake Ouinipigon or Winipick*" appears for the first time. The title-cartouche which was showing signs of wear in (b) has been retouched.

1775 (d)   ANOTHER ISSUE. Title and imprint as (c) except that the date has been changed to 1775. No other apparent alteration.

1777 (e)   ANOTHER ISSUE. Title altered to "*A New and Correct*
[*1st Iss.*]   *Map of North America with the West India Islands Divided according to the last Treaty of Peace Concluded at Paris Febʸ, 1763 wherein are particularly distinguished the Several Provinces and Colonies which comprise the British Empire. Laid down . . . and corrected from the Original Materials of Goverⁿ Pownall, Membr. of Parliaᵐᵗ· 1777.*" Imprint "*London: Printed for Robert Sayer, No. 53 Fleet Street, as the Act directs. 10th Janʸ 1777.*" Although the title has been completely altered and Gover-

nor Pownall's name appears for the first time, the cartouche, inset maps, general characteristics, Articles of Treaty of 1763 and most of the descriptive notes of the previous issues remain unaltered. The provinces and colonies are outlined by differently colored boundary lines which have been, in many instances, altered in position. *Virginia, N. Carolina, S. Carolina* and *Georgia* which previously extended to the *Mississippi River* are now bounded on the west by the *Apalachian Mts.* The title of *N. Carolina* has been omitted. The sixteen-line note as to the Province of Quebec previously just to the south of Newfoundland has been deleted and does not occur again in any subsequent re-issue.

1777 (f) [2nd Iss.] ANOTHER ISSUE. Title as (e). Imprint altered to ". . . *Printed for Robt Sayer and Jno. Bennett, 15th Feb. 1777."* Follows (e) very closely as to alterations and erasures. The eastern boundary of the Province of New York has been moved from the eastern shores of Lake Champlain and now runs along the *Connecticutt River.* The title of *N. Carolina* has been inserted in two lines.

1779 (g) ANOTHER ISSUE. Title and imprint as (f) except for the alteration of the date in the title to 1779 and in the imprint to *"15th July 1779."* No other apparent alteration.

1783 (h) [1st Iss.] ANOTHER ISSUE. Title of (e) altered to ". . . *Divided according to the Preliminary Articles of Peace signed at Versailles 20 January 1783 . . . distinguished the United States & the several Colonies . . . British Empire . . . Goverr. Pownall . . . 1783."* Imprints as (g) still dated July 15, 1779. The Articles of Peace of Paris, February 10, 1763 have not been deleted but a note has been added in the top left corner. *"The Divisions of this map are coloured according to the Preliminaries signed at Versailles Jan. 20, 1783. The Red indicates the British Possessions: The Green those of the United States: The Blue what belongs to the French and the Yellow what belongs to the Spanish."* This issue consists of the top sheet of the 1779 issue with alteration to the title and date and the addition of a dotted boundary line engraved on the plate, between the United States and the British possessions. The lower sheet of this issue is the lower sheet of the 1779 issue without alteration. It still bears the 1779 imprint.

1783 (i)   ANOTHER ISSUE. Title as (h) but slightly altered to *"A*
[2nd Iss.]   *New Map of North America . . . the United States and the*
Several Provinces, Governments &c which Compose the
British Dominions . . . Gover^n. Pownall . . . 1783." Imprint *"Printed for Robt Sayer and J^no Bennett, No. 53*
Fleet Street, as the Act directs, August 15th. 1783." A
careful scrutiny proves this to be the old plate worked up
despite the numerous alterations. The title cartouche
which had become very much worn has been worked over,
strengthened and altered in a few minor details. All the
Articles of the Peace of 1763 and descriptive notes of previous issues have been entirely removed. In their places a
four-line note re the coast of Labrador and Article III of
the 1783 Treaty have been inserted in the top right corner
of the upper sheet. The boundary line of the United States
shown in (h) has been slightly modified principally between Nova Scotia and New England. The title UNITED
STATES now appears on that portion of North America al-
located by the Treaty. The bottom sheet has undergone
considerable alteration. The XXth Article of the Peace of
1763 and the notes as to east and west Florida have been
removed. The date in the imprint has been altered to *Au-*
gust 15, 1783.

1786 (j)   ANOTHER ISSUE. Title as (i). Imprint altered to *"Lon-*
don: Printed for Robt Sayer, Map, Chart & Printseller . . .
August 15th 1786." Except that the title cartouche has
again been worked up, notably by cross-hatching the Indian figures, there is no apparent alteration from (i) except for the change of imprint.

1794 (k)   ANOTHER ISSUE. Title as (i). Imprint changed to *"Lon-*
[laid paper]   *don: Published by Laurie & Whittle, No 53 Fleet Street,*
12th May 1794." There is no apparent alteration from
the previous issue except for the change of imprint and of
its position from the bottom right corner (just inside the
border) to the title cartouche where it forms the last four
lines of the title. The west coast of Newfoundland is colored red to denote British territory.

1794-[?1798] (1)   ANOTHER ISSUE. Title and imprint as (k). The west coast
[wove paper]   of Newfoundland is colored blue to denote French territory presumably on account of the French fishing rights on
certain parts of the Newfoundland coast. No other ap-

parent alteration. The wove paper has no watermark but Laurie & Whittle published the *"Middle British Colonies"* map on wove paper with a similar texture with watermark dated 1796 or 1798. Either of these dates would be applicable to this issue as on account of both Louisiana and the Floridas being colored yellow, denoting Spanish territory, it must have been published prior to the year 1800.

50. [*Bowles.*] North America and the West Indies: a New Map, wherein the British Empire and its Limits according to the Difinitive Treaty of Peace in 1763 are accurately described ... *London Printed for Carington Bowles Map & Printseller No 69 in St. Pauls Church Yard.* Size, 45 x 39 inches.

    [?1763] (a) PROBABLY THE ORIGINAL ISSUE. Title and imprint as above.

    1783 (b) ANOTHER ISSUE. Title changed to *"Bowles's New Map of North America and the West Indies exhibiting the British Empire therein with the Limits and Boundaries of the United States ... compiled from the best surveys ... to the present year 1783."* Imprint changed to *". . . Carington Bowles . . . London . . . as the Act directs 2 Jan 1783."*

    [?1796] (c) ANOTHER ISSUE. Title changed to *"Bowles's New Four Sheet Map of North America and the West Indies exhibiting the Extent and Boundaries of the United States . . ."* Imprint changed to *"London Printed for the Proprietors Bowles and Carver"* [n.d. ?1796]. Date of 1796 assigned owing to the inclusion of Tennessee which became a territory in 1794 and a state in 1796.

    1808 (d) ANOTHER ISSUE. Title as (c). Imprint altered to *"London: Bowles & Carver 4th Jany 1808."*

51. [*D'Anville.*] North America from the French of Mr. D'Anville improved with the Back Settlements of Virginia and Course of Ohio. Illustrated with Geographical and Historical Remarks. [*London*], *May, 1755. Published . . . by Thos. Jefferys . . . near Charing Cross.* Size 20 x 18 inches.

    1755 (a) ORIGINAL ISSUE. Title and imprint as above. In the top left corner a long note in 2 columns *"French Incroachments."* Beneath the title-cartouche in 3 columns "*English Title to their Settlements on the Continent.*"

[1768] (b)   ANOTHER ISSUE. Title as (a) Imprint "*London. R. Sayer and T. Jefferys . . . [c.1763].*" Added, in 2 lines at the bottom of the 3rd column of the "*English Title . . . Continent*" text, is "*The Boundaries of the Provinces since the Conquest of Canada are laid down in this Map as settled by the King in Council.*" The "*Province of Quebec,*" which was neither named nor laid out in (a), is now named and defined by a dotted line which, on the South, runs from "*Nipi-scrinis L.*" to "*Champlain Lake*" thence to "*Bay Chaleur.*"

1775 (c)   ANOTHER ISSUE. Title altered to "*North America from the French of Mr. D'Anville, Improved with the English Surveys since the Peace.*" Imprint "*Robt. Sayer & J. Bennett, 10 June, 1775.*"

1783 (d)   ANOTHER ISSUE. Title altered to "*The United States of America with the British Possessions . . . Divided with the French . . . according to the Preliminary Articles of Peace signed at Versailles the 20th Jan. 1783.*" Imprint "*London R. Sayer & J. Bennett, 9th February 1783.*" The title of (c) was entirely erased from the cartouche and the new one engraved in its place. Article III of the Treaty was engraved on the plate immediately to the left of the cartouche. The territory allotted to the United States by the Treaty was enclosed by a dotted line and colored green, the rest of the map (coast lines and boundaries excepted) being uncolored.

1794 (e)   ANOTHER ISSUE. Title as (d) with the inclusion of "*New Brunswick*" between "*Nova Scotia*" and "*Newfoundland.*" Imprint "*London Laurie & Whittle, 12th May 1794.*" A flag of the United States now surmounts the cartouche; above this a note in four lines, as to the coloring, has been added.

1794-[1803?] (f)   ANOTHER ISSUE as (e) on paper watermarked 1801. Although Louisiana, according to the title, belongs to Spain, it is shown by the coloring to be part of the United States by whom it was purchased in 1803.

1794-[1808?] (g)   ANOTHER ISSUE as (f) but on paper watermarked 1808.

52. [*De La Rochette.*] A Map of North America and the West Indies. By L. S. De La Rochette. *London . . . 1st March 1781 by Robt. Wilkinson.* Size, 46¾ x 40 inches.

1781 (a)   ?ORIGINAL ISSUE. Boundary between *United States* and *Canada* and also *Florida* by dotted line engraved on map. *United States* territory colored green but not named.

1789 (b)   ANOTHER ISSUE. Apparently as (a) except that imprint is now dated "*1st March 1789.*"

53. [*Dunn.*] A Map of the British Empire in North America by Samuel Dunn, Mathematician. *London Sayer & Bennett 1774.* Size, 12 x 18½ inches.

    1774 (a)   ORIGINAL ISSUE. No cartouche, imprint forms part of title.

    1776 (b)   ANOTHER ISSUE. *"Improved from Surveys of Captain Carver"* added to title. Ornamental cartouche bottom right. Imprint *"Sayer & Bennett Augst. 17th 1776"* beneath bottom border line.

    1783 (c)   ANOTHER ISSUE. Title changed to *"A New Map of the United States . . . by Samuel Dunn, improved from Capt. Carver."* Imprint *"Sayer & Bennett Oct. 9 1783."*

    1786 (d)   ANOTHER ISSUE. Title as (c). Imprint *"Robt. Sayer 10 June 1786."*

54. [*Mitchell.*] A Map of the British and French Dominions in North America with the Roads, Distances, Limits and Extent of the Settlements. Humbly inscribed to the Rt. Hon. the Earl of Halifax . . . by J^{No} MITCHELL. [London]: *Published by the Author Febry 13th 1755 . . . and sold by And. Miller opposite Katherine Street in the Strand. Tho: Kitchin sculp. Clerkenwell Green.* Eight sheets. Size (when joined up), 76 x 53 inches.

    1755 (a)   FIRST EDITION, 1ST ISSUE. With Millar's name and Katharine Street in the imprint, incorrectly spelled "Miller" and "Katherine" respectively.

    1755 (b)   FIRST EDITION, 2ND ISSUE. Title as (a) but Millar's name and Katharine Street in the imprint, correctly spelled "Millar" and "Katharine" respectively.

1755-[1757] (c)   SECOND EDITION. Title and imprint as (b) but, according to the British Museum, published in 1757. Readily distinguishable from (b) by the inclusion, in the sea to the left of cartouche, of two blocks of text, one in three columns and the other in seven. In the sixth line of the first column of the three-column block this issue is referred to as the SECOND EDITION.

   [?1773] (d)   THIRD EDITION. Title as (b). Imprint changed to *"Publish'd by the Author Feb^{ry} 13th 1755. Printed by Jefferys and Faden, St. Martins Lane, Charing Cross, London.*

Tho. Kitchin sculp." As the firm of Jefferys and Faden does not appear in the Rate Book previous to 1773 this edition, although still dated 1755, cannot have appeared before 1773. This edition still contains the words SECOND EDITION in the three-column block of text as in (c). Many variations in contours and boundaries occur and numerous extra place-names have been added. Kitchin's Clerkenwell address has been erased as he had moved to 59 Holborn after 1768.

[?1774] (e) FOURTH EDITION. Title as (b). Imprint changed to "*Publish'd ... Febry 13th 1755. Printed for Jefferys and Faden ... at the corner of St Martin's Lane, Charing Cross, London. Tho: Kitchin, sculp.*" The chief difference between this and (d) lies in the numerous alterations in Sheet 3 in northern and western New York where several new forts have been added, some renamed and others deleted. In (d) there is a dotted line marked "*Limits claimed by New York*" running from Bethlehem, Pennsylvania, to the junction of the Hudson River with the 41° N. Latitude. This line and the relevant lettering have been deleted. Another dotted line, "*Limits claimed by New Jersey,*" has been similarly treated.

1775 (f) FIFTH EDITION. Title as (a) except that the words "*British and French Dominions*" have been altered to "*British Colonies.*" Imprint still dated 1755. In a catalogue issued by Faden in 1778 this edition is described and dated "*A Map of the British Colonies in North America ... on 8 sheets, 1775, Mitchell.*" Except for the change in the wording of the title, this edition would appear to coincide with the fourth edition.

55. [*Moll.*] A New and Exact Map of the Dominions of the King of Great Britain on ye Continent of North America containing Newfoundland ... New York ... Virginia and Carolina ... By Herman Moll, Geographer. Dedication to Walter Dowglass Esq. (in separate ornamental cartouche) dated 1715. Size, 24 x 40 inches.

1715 (a) ORIGINAL ISSUE. Imprint "*Sold by H. Moll, over against Devereux Court without Temple Bar.*" The Carolina inset not divided into parishes and the note in the Louisiana inset undated and reading "*Cherecies 3000 Men.*"

1715-[1726] (b)   ANOTHER ISSUE. Title and dated dedication as (a). Imprint in two lines "*Sold by H. Moll | and by I. King at ye Globe in ye Poultrey near Stock's Market.*" Carolina and Louisiana insets as (a). This state occurs in a collection of Moll's maps with a printed list of contents dated 1726.

1715-[1731] (c)   ANOTHER ISSUE. Title and dated dedication as (a). Imprint in three lines now reads "*Printed and Sold by Thos. Bowles . . . John Bowles . . . and I King.*" Carolina inset divided into counties and the note in the Louisiana inset now reading "*Cherecies 3000 Men, one of the Kings &c of this Nation was in England 1730.*"

1715-[1735] (d)   ANOTHER ISSUE. From an entirely new plate. Dedicated to Luke Gardiner, Deputy Vice Treasurer . . . of His Majesties Revenue in Ireland. Imprint "*Sold by Geo. Grierson, Printer to the King's Most Excellent Majesty, at the King's Arms and Two Bibles in Essex Street*" [Dublin]. Carolina inset divided as (c). "*Cherecies*" note dated 1730 as (c). No subsidiary title to the "*Niagara Falls*" inset as in the London issues.

1715-[1755] (e)   ANOTHER ISSUE. Title and dated dedications as (a). Imprint in three lines now reads "*Printed and Sold by Tho. Bowles . . . John Bowles and Son . . . and by I King.*" Carolina inset divided as (c). "*Cherecies*" note dated 1730 as (c).

56. [*Palairet.*] Carte de l'Amerique Septentrionale 1754.

1754 (a)   THE PARENT MAP. Title as above. Published by Palairet in his "*Atlas Methodique*" in 1755.

[1762/3] (b)   ANOTHER ISSUE. A Map of North America by J. Palairet with considerable Alterations & Improvem^ts from D'Anville, Mitchell, & Bellin, by L. Delarochette. "*London printed for Thos. Bowles in St. Pauls Churchyad*" Size, 23 x 18¾ inches [with two overlays 16¾ x 8½ inches; each of the overlays and the main map have pasted-on descriptive slips].

I. "*Claims of the French in 1756*"; II. "*Partition of N. America proposed by Mnsr Bussy in 1761*"; III. (on main map) "*Dominions . . . ceded to Gt. Britain by France & Spain in 1762.*" For a similar map *see* No. 4, America [Green], Sheet IV (b).

1765 (c)   ANOTHER ISSUE. Title as (b) with date 1765 inserted after Delarochette's name and imprint altered to *"Printed for John Bowles . . . & Carington Bowles."* No overlays or pasted-on descriptive slips. Engraved title cartouche as (a). The new province of West Florida is set out and the peninsula renamed *"East-Florida."* New notes as to Fishing in the Gulf of St. Lawrence and to the Government of Granada have been added.

[c1768] (d)   ANOTHER ISSUE. Title as (c) but date erased beneath Delarochette's name. Imprint altered to *"London Printed for John Bowles at the Black Horse in Cornhill"* and engraved beneath Delarochette's name inside the ornamental cartouche. The John Bowles & Carington Bowles imprint of (c) which was in a long line beneath the cartouche has been erased. No other alterations apparent.

[c1771] (e)   ANOTHER ISSUE. Title altered to *"Bowles's New Pocket Map of North America . . . by J. Palairet . . . with additions . . . by L. Delarochette."* Imprint *Carington Bowles* [c1771]. <small>See Addenda</small>

57. [*Sanson & Berry.*] North America divided into its Principall [*sic*] Parts viz. Arctick Lands, Canaad, New Fpance [*sic*] &c. described by Sanson, Corrected and amended by William Berry. [London] *Sold by William Berry . . . White-Hall 1680.* Size, 35 x 22½ inches.

    1680 (a)   ORIGINAL ISSUE. Title and imprint as above.

    1718 (b)   ANOTHER ISSUE. Imprint changed to *"P. Overton, J. Lenthall & T. Taylor 1718."*

58. [*Sayer & Bennett.*] The Theatre of War in North America with the Roads and a Table of Distances. *London Sayer & Bennett 20th March 1776.* Size, 20 x 16⅛ inches on uncut paper 22¾ x 30½ inches.

1776 (Mar.) (a)   ORIGINAL ISSUE. Below the map type-printed in three columns *"A Compendious Account of the British Colonies . . ."* occupying a space 19½ x 11½ with imprint 7⅜ inches long.

1776 (Mar.) (b)   ANOTHER ISSUE. Printed text 19¾ x 11¾ inches. Imprint 7½ inches long.

1776 (Mar.) (c)   ANOTHER ISSUE. Printed text 19⅜ x 11¾ inches. Imprint 7¾ inches long.

59. [*Sayer & Bennett.*] The Theatre of War in America with the Roads and Tables of ... Distances &c. By an American. London Sayer & Bennett, 20th November 1776. Size, 20¼ x 30½ inches, on uncut paper 22¾ x 30½ inches.

1776 (Nov.) (a)   SECOND EDITION, ORIGINAL ISSUE. From an entirely different plate from the March edition of the same year. Text, *"A Compendious Account ...,"* apparently as (c) of the March issue.

1776 (Nov.) (b)   ANOTHER ISSUE. Title of the text in smaller type 12 inches long. Imprint in large type 10 inches long.

1776 (Nov.) (c)   ANOTHER ISSUE. Title only 11⅛ inches long. Imprint only 7$\frac{5}{16}$ inches long. Different type of rule between the columns.

60. [*Seale & Bell.*] A New and Accurate Map of North America drawn from the famous Mr D'Anville ... engraved by R Seale; Also the New Divisions ... late Treaty of Peace, by Peter Bell, Geoʳ 1768. *Carington Bowles, Map & Printseller, London* [1768]. Size, 20 x 18½ inches.

1768 (a)   ORIGINAL ISSUE. Title and imprint as above.

1771 (b)   ANOTHER ISSUE. Title as (a). Imprint changed to *London: Carington Bowles, 1st Jan. 1771.*

1783 (c)   ANOTHER ISSUE. Title changed to *Bowles's New Pocket Map of the United States of America* and imprint *"Carington Bowles 4 Feb 1783."*

1784 (d)   ANOTHER ISSUE. Title as (c). Imprint *"Carington Bowles, 12 April 1784."*

1795 (e)   ANOTHER ISSUE. Title changed to *Bowles's New One Sheet Map of the United States* and imprint to *London: Bowles & Carver, 12th Jan. 1795.* Printed on laid paper with imprint below bottom border line *"Published as the Act directs 12th Jany. 1795."* One of the few maps published by Bowles & Carver to bear a date.

[?1799] (f)   ANOTHER ISSUE. Title as (d). Imprint *London: Bowles & Carver* [c1799]. Printed on wove paper. Cartouche retouched. Dated imprint of (d) below bottom border erased. Louisiana and Florida colored as Spanish possessions.

[?1819] (g) ANOTHER ISSUE. Title as (d). Imprint *London: Bowles & Carver* [?1799]. South Carolina much reduced in size with corresponding increase in Georgia. The old Mississippi country, now divided by a dotted line and distinctive coloring into Mississippi and Alabama territories, although they are not yet named.

61. [*Senex.*] North America corrected from the Observations ... Royal Society at London ... at Paris. By John Senex, Cha. Price & John Maxwell, Geographers 1710. Size, 25½ x 37½ inches.

1710 (a) ORIGINAL ISSUE. Title as above, no imprint.

1710 (b) ANOTHER ISSUE. "*By John Senex F. R. S. 1710,*" Price & Maxwell's name deleted from title. Imprint added "*Printed for T. Bowles 1710.*"

[?1750] (c) ANOTHER ISSUE. Imprint changed to "*T. Bowles, J. Bowles & Robt. Sayer* [c1750]." The lower part of *Carolina* now marked *Georgia*. See Addenda

62. [*Wilkinson.*] North America *published 12th Aug. 1804 by R. Wilkinson.* Size, 23½ x 20¼ inches.

1804 (a) ORIGINAL EDITION. Title and imprint as above.

1824 (b) ANOTHER ISSUE. Imprint "*12th Aug 1824.*"

1826 (c) ANOTHER ISSUE. Imprint "*Republished by William Darton 13 Jan. 1826.*"

63. [*Wyld.*] Map of North America ... exhibiting the recent Discoveries ... of Humboldt, Pike, Lewis & Clarke, Mackenzie, Hearne &c. ... *London Jas Wyld, May 1, 1824.* Six sheets. Size (when joined), 65 x 57 inches.

1824 (a) ?THE ORIGINAL ISSUE. Title and imprint as above.

1827-8 (b) ANOTHER ISSUE. Imprint "... *Ja^s Wyld ... March 1st 1827. Additions to 1828.*" Height increased to 69 inches between the 77° and 110° of W. Long.

1838 (c) ANOTHER ISSUE. Imprint dated 1838.

1851-56 (d)   ANOTHER ISSUE. Imprint "*. . . Ja^s. Wyld . . . Geographer to Her Majesty [1851-56]*." Size as (b). Although imprint is undated, two sheets bear the date "*May 1, 1851*" and "*1856*" respectively.

NORTHWEST COAST

64. Chart of the N.W. Coast of America and the N. E. Coast of Asia explored in 1778 and 1779. Prepared by Lieut. Henry Roberts under the immediate inspection of Capt. Cook. *London W. Faden July 24 1784.* Size, 27 x 15⅝ inches.

1784 (a)   ORIGINAL ISSUE. Imprint as above.

1794 (b)   ANOTHER ISSUE. Imprint "*W. Faden, Second Edition . . . Jany 1st 1794.*" An "*Advertisement*" dated "*Jan 1st 1794*" added beneath the title.

1808 (c)   ANOTHER ISSUE. Imprint as (b). Advertisement as (b) but now dated "*Jan 1st 1808.*"

NORTHERN BRITISH COLONIES

65. A General Map of the Northern British Colonies in America, which comprehends the Province of Quebec, the Government of Newfoundland, Nova Scotia, New England, & New York . . . Corrected from Governor Pownall's late Map, 1776. *London Sayer & Bennett, 14th August 1776.* Size, 26 x 18⅞ inches.

1776 (a)   ORIGINAL ISSUE. Outside the top border line is a subsidiary title in one long line "*The Seat of the War in the Northern Colonies . . .*" The main title is in the top right corner in an ornamental cartouche surmounted by a beaver.

1788 (b)   ANOTHER ISSUE. Title altered to "*A New and Correct Map of the British colonies in North America comprehending Eastern Canada . . . with the adjacent States of New England, Vermont . . . and New Jersey.*" Imprint "*London: Robert Sayer, 1st Jany. 1788.*" The revised title is contained in the same "*beaver*" cartouche as in (a).

1794 (c)   ANOTHER ISSUE. Title as (b). Imprint altered to "*London: Laurie & Whittle 12th May 1794.*" Re-issued without other alteration. The north and west coasts of Newfoundland are colored blue to indicate French fishing rights by treaty.

1794-[1806] (d) ANOTHER ISSUE. As (c) but printed on wove paper dated 1806. The French fishing rights by treaty are not distinctively colored.

NOVA SCOTIA

66. A New Map of Nova Scotia and Cape Britain [*sic*] with the Adjacent Parts of New England and Canada … with an Explanation. [Imprint] *May 1755 published according to Act of Parliament by Thos. Jefferys, the corner of St Martins Lane, Charing Cross.* Size, 24¼ x 18½ inches.

May 1755 (a) ORIGINAL ISSUE. The boundary between Nova Scotia and New England runs up the "*Pessemiquddi or St Croix River.*" The Penobscot River is named "*Ramassok Penobscot or Pentagoet R.*"

1755 (b) ANOTHER ISSUE. Imprint as (a) except for the deletion of "*May*" from before the date. The boundary between Nova Scotia and New England is moved about two degrees west to the "*Kenebec River.*" The Penobscot River is now named "*Penobscot or Pentagoet R.,*" the name "*Ramassok*" having been deleted.

1775 (c) ANOTHER ISSUE. Title altered to "*A New Map of Nova Scotia and Cape Breton Island.*" Imprint "*Published … Thos. Jefferys, Geographer to the King | London Printed and sold by R. Sayer & J. Bennett No. 53 in Fleet Street, 15 June 1775.*" The words "*with an Explanation*" forming the last line of the title in (a) and (b) have been deleted and "*by Thomas Jefferys, Geographer to the King*" substituted. The boundary between Nova Scotia and New England as in (a) but the boundary along the *Kennebec* as in (b) has not been erased.

1775 (d) ANOTHER ISSUE. Title and imprint as in (c). In this issue the colored boundary line runs up the "*Penobscot River*" to the "*Bic River*" thence east along the "*Risligouche R.*" to "*Chaleur Bay.*" Beneath the coloring is a dotted line along the "*Penobscot R.*" Traces of the old dotted line up the "*St Croix R.*" are still visible and the dotted line along the "*Kenebec R.*" has not been erased.

1775 (e)   ANOTHER ISSUE. Title and imprint as (c). Colored boundary line runs up the "*St Croix R.*" through "*Medarosta Lake*" to "*Bic River*" thence along it to the mouth of the "*St Lawrence River.*"

1775 (f)   ANOTHER ISSUE. Title and imprint as (c). Colored boundary line runs up the "*St Croix R*" to the source of the "*Pistole River*" thence extends eastwards to "*Chaleur Bay.*" The "*Province of Maine*" and "*Territory of Sagadahok*" extend right up to the south bank of the St. Lawrence.

1775 (g)   ANOTHER ISSUE. Title and imprint as (c). Colored boundary reverts to the "*Kenebek R*" as in (b) but instead of following "*Chaudiere R.*" to the St. Lawrence it follows a range of mountains parallel with the St. Lawrence as far as "*Chaleur Bay.*" "*Maine*" still extends to the St. Lawrence but "*Sagadahok*" is here part of Nova Scotia.

1775 (h)   ANOTHER ISSUE. Title and imprint as (c). Colored boundary line runs along the "*Penobscot R.*" to the mountains parallel with the St. Lawrence. "*Maine*" and "*Sagadahok*" are separated from the St. Lawrence by a wide strip of territory.

1775 (i)   ANOTHER ISSUE. Title and imprint as (c). Colored boundary line as (h). The dividing strip of territory is much wider than in (h) and follows a range of mountains from "*Fort Chambly*" to the "*Nipessiguit River*" which it follows until it reaches "*Chaleur Bay.*"

[?1783] (j)   ANOTHER ISSUE. Title and imprint as (c) but probably issued in 1783 as it shows the boundary between Canada and the United States practically in accord with the Treaty of Versailles. Nova Scotia is colored pink, Canada green and the United States (not so named) yellow.

1786 (k)   ANOTHER ISSUE. Title as (c). Imprint as (c) with second line altered to read "*London, printed and sold by R. Sayer, Map-seller, No 53 in Fleet Street, 1 Augt 1786.*" Nova Scotia colored yellow, Canada red and the United States green.

1794 (l)   ANOTHER ISSUE. Title as (c). Imprint as (c) but second line altered to read "*Published 12th May 1794 by Laurie & Whittle, 53 Fleet Street, London.*" Coloring as (k).

PACIFIC OCEAN

67. Chart of the Pacific Ocean ... *by A. Arrowsmith, Geographer, No 24 Rathbone Place, London 1798.* Nine sheets. Size, each 31¾ x 25 inches.

    1798 (a)   ORIGINAL ISSUE. Imprint "... *Octr 1st 1798 ... 24 Rathbone Place.*"

    1798-[1810] (b)   ANOTHER ISSUE. Additions to 1810. Imprint "... *Octr 1st 1798 ... 10 Soho Square.*"

    1798-[1814] (c)   ANOTHER ISSUE. Additions to 1810 and 1814. Imprint as (b).

PENNSYLVANIA

68. A Mapp of ye Improved Part of Pensilvania in America Divided into Countyes, Townships and Lotts. Surveyed by Tho: Holme. [London] *Sold by P. Lea at ye Atlas and Hercules in Cheapside* [c1687]. Size, 21¼ x 15¾ inches.

    [c1687] (a)   ORIGINAL ISSUE. Title and imprint in two lines across top of the map.

    [c1715] (b)   ANOTHER ISSUE. Title as (a) but Lea's imprint erased and that of George Willdey substituted. This latter is in three lines in a rectangle inserted in the bottom left corner in a space previously blank.

    [c1730] (c)   ANOTHER ISSUE. Title as (a). Willdey's imprint, as in (b), erased from the plate although traces of it are still visible. No alterations to the map appear to have been made.

PHILADELPHIA

69. Plan of the City and Environs of Philadelphia survey'd by N. Scull and G. Heap. Engraved by Willm. Faden 1777. *London: March 12th 1777 by W. Faden.* Size, 18 x 24½ inches.

    1777 (a)   ORIGINAL ISSUE. With unnamed island between "*Hog*" and "*Mud*" islands, no soundings in Delaware River and its south bank not completed.

    1777 (b)   SECOND ISSUE. Unnamed island of (a) now named "*Port Island*" and three lettered references to it introduced.

1777 (c) THIRD ISSUE. Below *"Hog Island"* a new one appears, *"Billingsfort Island,"* this being joined by a *"chevaux de frises"* with *"Billingsfort Fort"* on the mainland immediately opposite on the south bank of the river.

PITTSBURGH

70. Plan of Fort le Quesne built by the French at the Fork of the Ohio and Monongahela in 1754.

1755 (a) ORIGINAL ISSUE. Dated imprint in bottom left corner outside the border line *"[London] Published according to the Act by J. Payne in Pater-noster row [sic] July 15 1755."*

[?1756-7] (b) ANOTHER ISSUE. Title as (a). Imprint (undated) altered to *"[London] Printed for Robt. Sayer and Thos. Jefferys."* The imprint is in the same position as that of (a).

PORT ROYAL, S. C.

71. A Plan of Port Royal in South Carolina. Survey'd by Capn. John Gascoigne. *London . . . Jefferys & Faden . . .* [c1773]. Size, 23 x 28 inches.

[1773] (a) ORIGINAL ISSUE. Title and imprint as above.

1776 (b) ANOTHER ISSUE. Imprint altered to *"Sayer & Bennett 15th May 1776."*

1791 (c) ANOTHER ISSUE. Imprint now *"Robert Sayer, 15 Jany. 1791."*

1794 (d) ANOTHER ISSUE. Imprint now *"Laurie & Whittle 1794."*
See Addenda

QUEBEC

72. A Plan of Quebec. [London] *Publish'd . . . Jan, 1759 by E. Oakley.* Size, 19⅞ x 12¼ inches.

1759 [*Jan.*] (a) ORIGINAL ISSUE. Title and imprint as above. No inset plan in top right corner.

1759 [*Oct.*] (b) SECOND ISSUE. Imprint altered to *Publish'd . . . Octbr. 1759 by E. Oakley.* Inset plan of *"A Draught of the River St. Lawrence"* in top right corner.

QUEBEC PROVINCE

73. A New Map of the Province of Quebec according to the Royal Proclamation of the 7th October 1763. From the French Surveys connected with those made after the War by Capt. Carver. *London: Sayer & Bennett, 16th Feb., 1776*. Size, 26⅝ x 19¼ inches.

    1776 (a) ORIGINAL ISSUE. Insets of *"Isles of Montreal," "Plan of Montreal," "City of Quebec"* and *"River of St. Lawrence."*

    1788 (b) ANOTHER ISSUE. Title altered to *"A New and Correct Map of the Province of Quebec with the adjacent States and Provinces . . ."* and imprint changed to *"London: Robert Sayer, 1 Jan. 1788."*

    1794 (c) ANOTHER ISSUE. Title as (b). Imprint changed to *"London: Laurie & Whittle, 12th May, 1794." "Nova Scotia"* of the original edition is now marked *"New Brunswick."*

ST. LAWRENCE RIVER

74. [*Cook.*] A New Chart of the River St. Lawrence from Anticosti to the Falls of Richlieu . . . Engraved by Thomas Jefferys. Twelve sheets. Size (when joined), 91½ x 33½ inches.

    [1760] (a) ORIGINAL ISSUE. *"Published by Command of the Rt. Hon Lords Commissioners of the Admiralty."* Capt. Cook's famous chart.

    1775 (b) ANOTHER ISSUE. *"Published . . . as (a) . . . Admiralty. London Printed for Robt Sayer & Jno. Bennett Map & Sea Chart Sellers . . . 16 Feby. 1775."* See Addenda

75. [*Harwar.*] A New and Exact Draught of the River Canada. Aproved by the Honbl. Sr. Will: Phipps . . . *By George Harwar at his shop at the Long-Cellar nere Hermitage Bridge.* F. Lamb sculp. Size, 29 x 18 inches.

    [?1691] (a) ORIGINAL ISSUE. Imprint as above.

    [?1694] (b) ANOTHER ISSUE. Imprint changed to *"By John Thornton at the England, Scotland & Ireland in ye Minories,"* F. Lamb sculp. Both (a) and (b) are dedicated to King William and Queen Mary and this issue was probably published before December, 1694, when Queen Mary died.

76. [*Jefferys.*] An Exact Chart of the River St Laurence from Fort Frontenac to the Island of Anticosti . . . for navigating that River to Quebec. [London] *Thos. Jefferys at Charing Cross Jan 25, 1757.* Two sheets in one. Size, 37 x 23½ inches.

    1757 (a)   ORIGINAL ISSUE. Dedicated to Richard Earl Temple, &c.

    [?1768] (b)   ANOTHER ISSUE. Title as (a). Imprint (undated) altered to "*. . . Thos. Jefferys the corner of St Martin's Lane, Charing Cross.*"

    1771 (c)   ANOTHER ISSUE. Dedicated to Jn⁰· Montague, Earl of Sandwich. Imprint "*Robert Sayer 25 May 1771.*"

    1775 (d)   ANOTHER ISSUE. Dedication as (c). Imprint ". . . *Robert Sayer 25 May 1775.*"

SOUTH AMERICA

Chart of South America, comprehending the West Indies. 1753. *See* No. 4, America [Green], Sheet VI.

77. Outlines . . . of South America delineated by A. Arrowsmith. *London 10, Soho Square . . . 4th January 1811.* Six sheets. Size (when joined), 78 x 94½ inches.

    1811 (a)   ORIGINAL ISSUE. Title and imprint as above.

    1811-[1814] (b)   ANOTHER ISSUE. Title and imprint as (a). Additions to 1814.

    1811-[1817] (c)   ANOTHER ISSUE. Title and imprint as (a). Additions to 1817.

    1811-[1819] (d)   ANOTHER ISSUE. Title and imprint as (a). Additions to 1819.

SOUTH SEA

Chart . . . the South Sea to the South of the Line. 1753. *See* No. 4, America [Green], Sheet V.

SOUTHERN BRITISH COLONIES

78. A General Map of the Southern British Colonies in America . . . *London R Sayer & J. Bennett . . . 15th Octr 1776.* Size, 25¼ x 19¾ inches.

1776 (a) Original Issue. Insets of *Charleston* and *St. Augustine* above title in ornamental cartouche bottom right. Subsidiary title in one line above top border line *"The Seat of War in the Southern British Colonies . . ."*

1794 (b) Another Issue. Title altered to *"A New and General Map of the Southern Dominions belonging to the United States . . ."* Imprint *"Laurie & Whittle 12th May, 1794."*

1794-[1809] (c) Another Issue. On wove paper watermarked 1809 as (b) except that Louisiana is now colored as part of the United States.

UNITED STATES

79. [*Arrowsmith.*] A Map of the United States of North America, drawn by *A. Arrowsmith, Geographer, Charles Street, Soho Square, Jan. 1st 1796.* Four sheets. Size (when joined), 55½ x 48 inches.

1796 (a) Original Issue. Title and imprint as above. In sheet
[*1st Iss.*] three *"Tennassee Government."* Very few roads shown.

1796 (b) Another Issue. Title as (a). Imprint altered to *"No 24*
[*2nd Iss.*] *Rathbone Place."* *"Tennassee"* only. Numerous roads.

1802 (c) Another Issue. Address in title altered to *"No 24 Rath-*
[*1st Iss.*] *bone Place."* Imprint *"London Jan 1st 1796. Additions to 1802."* Paper watermarked *"J. Whatman 1801."*

1802-[1804] (d) Another Issue. Title and imprint as (c). The twenty-
[*2nd Iss.*] two-line note, *"Boundaries communicated by Geo. Chal-*
Paper watermarked 1804 *mers Esqr.,"* in bottom left corner, common to previous issues, now deleted.

1802-[1808] (e) Another Issue. Address altered to *"10 Soho Square."*
[*3rd Iss.*] Arrowsmith now styled *"Hydrographer to H.R.H. the Prince of Wales."* Arrowsmith moved to Soho Square during the year 1808. Many new place-names and rivers added. A copy of this issue has been observed with paper watermarked 1811.

1815 (f) Another Issue. Title and imprint as (e). Additions to 1802-1815. Paper watermarked *"J. Whatman 1811"* and *"Additions to 1815"* in manuscript.

1818 (g) Another Issue. Title and imprint as (e). Additions to 1802-1818.

1819 (h)   ANOTHER ISSUE. Additions to 1819 [*sic*] *North West*
[*Early Iss.*]   *Territory, States of Indiana & Louisiana*, and *Territories
of Illinois, Missouri* and *Mississippi* now appear.

1819 (i)   ANOTHER ISSUE. As (g) but with wings to top and bot-
[*Later Iss.*]   tom sheets where the map extends through the border lines
to include additional country.

80. [*Faden.*] The British Colonies in North America, engraved by
William Faden MDCCLXXVII. Size, 24¾ x 20¾ inches.

1777 (a)   THE PARENT PLAN. Title and imprint as above.

1783 (b)   ANOTHER ISSUE. Title changed to "*The United States of
[*1st Iss.*]   North America with the British & Spanish Territories according to the Treaty Engrav'd by Wm Faden 1783.*"
The first of two issues in 1783. This has only four color
references and no note beneath them regarding the St.
Croix River. In this state two rivers, running into the Bay
of Fundy, are named "*St. Croix.*"

1783 (c)   ANOTHER ISSUE. Title as (b). The second of two issues
[*2nd Iss.*]   in 1783. Has five color references with a seven-line note
on the St. Croix River beneath. Two rivers are still shown
running into the Bay of Fundy, but only the more easterly
one is named "*St. Croix.*"

1785 (d)   ANOTHER ISSUE. Title as (b) with "*of 1784*" added between the words "*Treaty*" and "*Engraved by Wm. Faden
1785.*" Imprint below bottom border in center. "*Published ... Feb. 11. 1785 by Willm. Faden.*" Four color
references only and a new nine-line note in place of the
seven-line note on (c). Two rivers "*St. Croix*" shown, the
more westerly named "*Green's R. St. Croix*" and the other
"*D'Anville's R. St. Croix.*"

1793 (e)   ANOTHER ISSUE. Title as (d) but altered to "*Engraved
by Wm. Faden 1793.*" Imprint positioned as (d). "*Published Feb 11, 1793 by Wm. Faden ...*" A fifth color reference and a new note (in three lines) as to *Florida* have
been added. Numerous alterations have been made.

1796 (f)   ANOTHER ISSUE. Title as (d) altered to "*Engraved ...
1793.*" Imprint altered to "*... Feb. 11, 1796 by Willm.
Faden.*" A new note (four lines) as to the limits of the Indian land has been added to the right of the color refer-

ences. *"Tannessee Government"* introduced to the south of Kentucky and *"Washington, or the Federal City"* appear for the first time in this series.

1809 (g)   ANOTHER ISSUE. *"According to the Treaty of 1784"* deleted from title. No imprint below bottom border line in center. Imprint (in four lines) changed to *"Published by W. Faden, Charing Cross, Geographer to His Majesty and to His Royal Highness the Prince of Wales, 1809."* Alterations in *Nova Scotia* and *Western Canada.* Size, now 25⅛ x 20¾ inches.

1820 (h)   ANOTHER ISSUE. Imprint *"London. Published by W. Faden, Charing Cross, Geographer to His Majesty April 12th 1820."* Ornamental cartouche removed and title re-engraved. New states of *"Michigan," "Illinois," "Indiana," "Ohio," "Alabama," "Mississippi"* and *"Louisiana"* introduced. *"New Mexico"* now called *"Potosi and Texas."*

1824 (i)   ANOTHER ISSUE. Imprint *"London. Jaˢ· Wyld (Successor to Mʳ Faden) . . . April 1st 1824."* Little or no apparent alteration except the imprint.

1829 (j)   ANOTHER ISSUE. Imprint *"London Jaˢ· Wyld (successor to Mʳ Faden) Geographer to His Majesty 5 Charing Cross, Janʸ· 1st 1829."* Little or no alteration but the six lines of *"Reference to the Colouring"* have been deleted from the Atlantic Ocean.

1832 (k)   ANOTHER ISSUE. Imprint *"Jaˢ· Wyld, Successor to Mʳ Faden . . . 1832."* Some alterations in boundaries of South Carolina and Georgia.

1838 (l)   ANOTHER ISSUE. Imprint altered to *". . . Geographer to Her Majesty, Charing Cross East, 1838."* States of *"Missouri"* and *"Arkansas"* introduced.

1841 (m)   ANOTHER ISSUE. Imprint *". . . Jaˢ Wyld, Successor to Mʳ Faden . . . 1841."* The lettering *"Potosi Texas,"* see (h) above, has been erased and replaced by *"Texas"* with the new towns *"Austin"* and *"Houston"* located.

1843 (n)   ANOTHER ISSUE. Date in imprint altered to 1843. Hatched key pattern border all around the map.

    [*Bowles*]. *See* No. 60 [*Seale & Bell*] (c), (d), (e) & (f).
    [*Dunn*]. *See* No. 53 (c) & (d).
    [*Laurie & Whittle*]. *See* No. 51 (e), (f) & (g).
    [*Sayer & Bennett*]. *See* No. 51 (d) & No. 53 (c)

UPPER CANADA

81. A Map of the Located Districts in the Province of Upper Canada. ... Compiled from Surveys of William Chewitt, Senior Surveyor ... *By William Faden.* [London] *January 1st 1813.* Size, 44¾ x 32¾ inches.

  > 1813 (a) ORIGINAL ISSUE. Title and imprint as above.
  >
  > 1825 (b) ANOTHER ISSUE. Imprint *"London Jas. Wyld (Successor to Mr. Faden) April 5, 1825."* Many additional townships laid out. Several insets inserted.

82. A Map of the Province of Upper Canada ... By David William Smyth Esqr. Surveyor General ... *London W. Faden April 12th 1800.* Size, 33¾ x 22¼ inches.

  > 1800 (a) ORIGINAL ISSUE. Imprint as above.
  >
  > 1818 (b) ANOTHER ISSUE. *"Second Edition 1818."* Imprint as (a). Numerous alterations and additions.
  >
  > 1831 (c) ANOTHER ISSUE. Imprint changed to *"Jas. Wyld April 12th 1831."*
  >
  > 1835 (d) ANOTHER ISSUE. Imprint *"Jas Wyld 1835."* Numerous alterations, &c.
  >
  > 1838 (e) ANOTHER ISSUE. Imprint *"Jas Wyld 1838."* Numerous alterations, &c.
  >
  > 1843 (f) ANOTHER ISSUE. Imprint *"Jas Wyld 1843."* Numerous alterations, &c.
  >
  > [1850] (g) ANOTHER ISSUE. Imprint *"Jas. Wyld, Geographer to Her Majesty."* The first appearance of railroads on this map.

VIRGINIA

83. The Courses of the Rivers Rappahannock and Potowmack in Virginia as surveyed according to Order in the Years 1736 & 1737. Size, 13⅜ x 11¾ inches.

  > [c1737] (a) ORIGINAL ISSUE. (*Cf. William and Mary Quarterly*, 2nd Series, vol. 19 (1939), pp. 82 and 83.)
  >
  > [c1740] (b) ANOTHER ISSUE. Deletions from original issue indicated by text in brackets: "Potowmack *River called* Cohongoronta [*by Colll Lee since the Date of ẏ Patent*]"; "Rapahan-

nock *River S° Branch lately called* Rapidan [by Col. Spots-wood"]; *etc.*

[c1743] (c)   ANOTHER ISSUE. *Fairfax County* appears for first time.

[c1745] (d)   ANOTHER ISSUE. Published after the boundary line be-tween the rivers was ordered by His Majesty in Council, April 11, 1745. This boundary line with four lines of de-scription, the Fairfax arms, the ornamentation of the car-touche and an extension of the title were added to this is-sue. The additional title reads "*A Survey of the Northern Neck of Virginia, being the Lands belonging to the Rt. Honourable Thomas Lord Fairfax Baron Cameron, bound-ed by & within the Bay of Chesapoyocke and between the Rivers Rappahannock and Potowmack with the Courses of the Rivers* . . . (as above)." See Addenda

84. [*Farrer.*] A Mapp of Virginia discovered to ye Falls and in its Latt from 35 deg. & ½ neer Florida to 41 deg: bounds of New Eng-land. John Farrer, Esq. Collegit. *Are sold by J. Stephenson at ye sunn below Ludgate, 1651.* John Goddard Sculp. Size, 13¾ x 10½ inches.

1651 (a)   ORIGINAL ISSUE. Without portrait of Sir Francis Drake at top and without words "*Fort Orang*" on the right bor-der above "*Septen.*"

1651 (b)   ANOTHER ISSUE. Same as (a) but with the addition of place-name "*Fort Orang.*"

[1652?] (c)   ANOTHER ISSUE. Imprint changed "*Domina Virginia Farrer Collegit. Are sold by . . . Ludgate 1651.*" Portrait of Drake added, "*Canada flu*" connected with "*Sea of China,*" many place-names added.

[1652?] (d)   ANOTHER ISSUE. Title changed "A MAPP OF VIRGINIA TO YE HILLS" . . . Imprint as in (c). "*Canada flue*" sep-arated by an isthmus from "*Sea of China.*"

[1667?] (e)   ANOTHER ISSUE. Imprint altered . . . "*Are Sold by John Overton without Newgate at the corner of little Old Baly,*" and the date dropped. "*Canada flu*" as (d), "*Hills*" in title as (d).

85. [*Senex.*] A Map of Virginia according to Captain John Smith's Map published Anno 1606. Also of the Adjacent Country called

103

by the Dutch Niew Nederlant Anno 1630. By John Senex 1735. Size, 19⅝ x 14¾ inches.

- 1735 (a) ? ORIGINAL ISSUE. Title and imprint as above.

- 1735 (b) ANOTHER ISSUE. Found in *"A Short Account of the First Settlement of . . . Virginia 1735"* and has printed along the 39° N. Lat., in two lines, *"The True Bounds of Pensilvania . . ."* and along the 40°, also in two lines, *"Hitherto Lord Baltimore claims . . ."*

VIRGINIA AND MARYLAND

86. A New Map of Virginia, Maryland and the Improved Parts of Penn-sylvania & New Jersey. Size, 22 x 19¼ inches.

- [c1685] (a) ORIGINAL ISSUE. Imprint *"Sold by Christopher Browne at the Globe near the West End of St. Paul's Church."*

- [c1700] (b) ANOTHER ISSUE. As (a) without apparent alteration except for the erasure of Browne's imprint from the plate.

- 1719 (c) ANOTHER ISSUE. The title amplified by *"Most humbly inscrib'd to the Right Honble the Earl of Orkney &ct. Knight of ye most noble and Anciet [sic] Order of ye Thistle 1719. Revised by I. Senex."*

87. [*Fry & Jefferson.*] A Map of the [Most] Inhabited Part of Virginia . . . Province of Maryland &c. Drawn by Joshua Fry and Peter Jefferson in 1751. *Engrav'd and published according to Act of Parliament by Thos. Jefferys Geographer to His Royal Highness the Prince of Wales at the Corner of St. Martins Lane, Charing Cross, London.* Four sheets. Size (when joined up), 48½ x 30½ inches.

- 1751 (a) ORIGINAL EDITION. The word *"Most"* is not used in the title. No table of distances, neither *"Fort du Quesne,"* *"Fort Necessity,"* *"Wills' Creek,"* *"Great Meadows,"* nor *"Gists' Settlement"* are marked. No "degree marks" inside the upper and lower borders.

- 1751 (b) ANOTHER ISSUE. Title as (a) *Prince of Wales* in imprint, "degree marks" (incorrect) *65° 19' to 72° 19' West of London* inserted inside the upper and lower borders.

1751 (c)   ANOTHER ISSUE. As (b) except "degree marks" corrected to *75° 19' to 82° 19'.*

1755 (d)   ANOTHER ISSUE. Title as (a) with the word *"Most"* in-
2nd EDITION   serted in the title. Table of distances dated *"J. Dalrymple,
London, Jany ye 1st 1755"* added in the top left corner.

[176–?] (e)   ANOTHER ISSUE. Title as (d) only change being imprint
altered to *Printed for Robert Sayer at no 53 in Fleet Street
& Thos. Jefferys at the Corner of St. Martins Lane, Charing Cross, London.*

1775 (f)   ANOTHER ISSUE. Title as (d) except date 1751 has been
altered to 1775. Imprint same as (e).

1794 (g)   ANOTHER ISSUE. Title as (f). Imprint altered to *"Laurie
& Whittle 1794."*

VIRGINIA, MARYLAND, NEW JERSEY &c.

88. A Mapp of Virginia, Mary-Land, New Jarsey, New York & New
England. *By John Thornton at the Sundy-all in the Minories and
by Robert Greene at ye Rose and Crowne in Budg-rowe, London.*
Size, 17½ x 20¾ inches.

[?1673-1680] (a)   ORIGINAL ISSUE. *"Delaware River"* shown but not named
but the *"Schuylkill River"* is named *"Hore Kill or Dille-
ware R."* There is no sign of *Pennsylvania,* so called, and
all the country north of *Virginia* and west of the *Delaware
River* is marked *"Maryland." New Jersey* exhibits the partition line dividing it into east and west.

[?1673-1680] (b)   ANOTHER ISSUE. *"Schuylkill R"* now named *"Skoole Kill
or Dillewar R."* Two new place-names have been added
to the north of the *"Schuylkill"* on the west bank of the
real *"Delaware R,"* viz. *"Shakamaxon"* and *"George Heath-
nut's Land."*

[?1685] (c)   ANOTHER ISSUE. Considerably altered to show the new
Province of Pennsylvania. The *upper part of Maryland*
is now lettered *"Part of Pennsylvania."* The *"Delaware R"*
not named in the previous issues is now so named and the
lettering *"Skoole Kill or Dillewar R"* of (b) still remains.
Both *"Philadelphia"* and *"Chester"* are marked.

WEST INDIES

89. Chart of the West Indies and Spanish Dominions in North America, by A. Arrowsmith 1803. *London . . . June 1st 1803 . . . 24 Rathbone Place.* Four sheets. Size (when joined), 75 x 47½ inches.

    1803 (a)   ORIGINAL ISSUE. Title and imprint as above.

    1810 (b)   ANOTHER ISSUE. Address in imprint altered to *"10 Soho Square"* and size reduced to 56 x 47½ inches. Additions to 1810.

WORLD

90. [*Arrowsmith.*] Chart of the World on Mercator's Projection . . . by A. Arrowsmith, Geographer. *London . . . April 1st 1790 . . . Castle Street, Long Acre.* Size, 79½ x 56 inches, made up of eleven sheets joined together.

    1790 (a)   ORIGINAL ISSUE. Title in rectangle bottom right. Imprint as above.

    1790 (b)   ANOTHER ISSUE. Imprint as (a). Title now in top left without rectangle. Without the three-line note re *"Wake I"* dated 1794 at 166° E. Long. and 19° N. Lat.

    1790 (c)   ANOTHER ISSUE. Address in imprint changed to *"Charles Street, Soho Square,"* title position as (b). Without three-line note dated 1794.

    1790-94 (d)   ANOTHER ISSUE. Imprint and title position as (b). Has the three-line note re *"Wake I"* dated 1794 and a four-line note between 225° & 240° E. Long. just above 70° N. Lat.

    1790-1803 (e)   ANOTHER ISSUE. Imprint and title as (b). Has both notes as (d) and an overlay 8¼ inches wide over the bottom right (Australian) sheet showing Van Dieman's Land disconnected from the mainland. This sheet marked in contemporary Ms. *"Improvements to 1803."*

    [1790-?1805] (f)   ANOTHER ISSUE. Address in imprint changed to *"No 24 Rathbone Place."* Embodies the overlay of (e).

    1790-[?1808] (g)   ANOTHER ISSUE. Address in imprint altered to *"10 Soho Square"* where Arrowsmith moved in 1808 or early 1809. We have no notes of comparison regarding this issue.

91. [*Arrowsmith.*] Map of the World on a Globular Projection ...
Researches of Capt. James Cook F.R.S. ... by A. Arrowsmith.
London, Jany 1st 1794 ... Charles Street, Soho Square. Size, 73½
x 38 inches.

  1794 (a) ORIGINAL ISSUE. Title and imprint as above.

  1799 (b) ANOTHER ISSUE. Title and imprint as (a). Additions to
    1799.

  1808 (c) ANOTHER ISSUE. Address altered to "*10 Soho Square.*"
    Additions to 1799-1808.

  1814 (d) ANOTHER ISSUE. Address as (c). Additions to 1799-
    1808-1814.

92. [*Molyneux-Wright.*] Thou hast here (gentle reader) a true hy-
drographical description of so much of the world as hath beene
hetherto discouered ... Two sheets. Size (joined), 25 x 16⅞
inches.

  1600 (a) ORIGINAL ISSUE. No note re Magellan's Straits.

  1600 (b) SECOND ISSUE. A long inscription added, concerning Ma-
    gellan's Straits, in the bottom center of the left-hand sheet.

93. [*Purdy.*] A Chart of the World on Mercator's Projection with the
Tracks of the more Distinguished Navigators. By John Purdy.
*Published Dec. 12th 1810 by Robt. Laurie & Jas Whittle ... Lon-
don.* Four sheets. Size (when joined), 73 x 48¾ inches.

  1810 (a) ORIGINAL ISSUE. Title and imprint as above.

  1815 (b) ANOTHER ISSUE. Imprint as (a). *Additions to 1815.*

  1818 (c) ANOTHER ISSUE. Imprint as (a). "*3rd Edition improved
    1815 additions to 1818.*"

  1828 (d) ANOTHER ISSUE. Imprint "*London, Richard Holmes Lau-
    rie Aug. 14 1828.*"

  1829 (e) ANOTHER ISSUE. Imprint as (d) extended by "*New Edi-
    tion, Materially improved, 1829.*"

CHAPTER THREE

California as an Island

A Geographical misconception
illustrated by 100 examples from 1625 to 1770

by R. V. Tooley

The following small essay concerns itself with a comparatively short period of history and is restricted to a particular manifestation of the mapping of the West Coast of North America: the geographic delineation of California as an island.

There are already two great standard works on the mapping of the West, H. R. Wagner's *Cartography of the North West Coast of America* (1937) and Carl I. Wheat's *Mapping of the Transmississippi West* (1957), but neither covers this particular field except in passing reference, and rightly so, for their concern was the geographic development of the West. Wheat correctly states that " the 17th century was almost wholly barren of cartographic progress with respect to the American West ".

But the subject matter of this article, if of small value to historians dealing with the broader scope of geographic advance, can be nevertheless of considerable interest to bibliographers, and a just delight to collectors who have the taste to appreciate the minor vagaries, and leisure to enjoy the frequent beauty of the maps of the 17th and early 18th centuries.

One hundred maps have been chosen to illustrate this geographical misconception. This number, of course, is not exhaustive. World maps have been excluded for in general they merely give, on a smaller scale, the same representation as the general map of America if they come from the same atlas.

Nevertheless, this list does contain many maps, not noted by either Wagner or Wheat, that merit attention for their scarcity or beauty.

The earliest printed maps of America all show a continuous western coastline from the far south to the far north. Mercator 1531, Ortelius 1570 and Wyfliet 1597 all show California correctly as a peninsula.

The idea of California as an island is supposed to have originated with a Carmelite Friar, Father Antonio Ascension, possibly on a misconception of the reports of the Spanish navigators Juan de la Fuca 1592 and Martin d'Aguilar 1602, one of whom reported a great opening in the west coast and the other a vast inland sea north of Cape Medocin. Father Ascencion about 1620 drew up a map of his idea of California as an island and dispatched it by ship to Spain. The ship was captured by the Dutch and the chart taken to Amsterdam.

The earliest representation of California as an island known to me is a small map on the engraved title of the 1622 edition of Herrera's Description of the Indies, though in the same work the general map of America shows California as a peninsula. It was, however, in England that the mapping of California as an island was first popularised. The first in the field was Henry Briggs with his map of North America engraved by Elstracke in 1625. This was copied by John Speed in 1626-7. Holland for a time resisted the innovation; Hondius 1631, De Laet 1633, Blaeu 1635, and Visscher 1636 still followed the Mercator-Ortelius tradition. The Hondius and Blaeu plates, reprinted many times, Blaeu as late as 1667, remained unchanged, but the Visscher redrew his map and became one of the main supporters of the Island theory. Jansson adopted the island form in

1638 and his influence and Visscher's was sufficient to swing the whole of European geography behind them. California was almost invariably depicted as an island till well into the 18th century.

One of the first to correct the misconception was Guillaume de Lisle in the commencement of the 18th century. This great French geographer was among the first to discard theoretical geography. Where real knowledge ceased, De Lisle had the courage to stop and was content to leave a blank in his map.

A Jesuit, Father Eusebio Kino, was the first European to cross from the mainland to the peninsula of California, and to point out the fallacy of the island theory. His map, compiled in 1698, was printed in 1705. This map, however, was not generally accepted: in fact it provoked a fairly strong reaction. Herman Moll in 1711 wrote indignantly that California was undoubtedly an island. "Why," he said," I have had in my office mariners who have sailed round it." Moll's view was followed by Senex and Overton in England, by De Fer and Chatelain in France, Keulen in Holland, and by the great German firms of Homann and Seutter up to about 1750. Van der Aa 1715-30 tried to have the best of both worlds, issuing maps of America with California both as an island and as a peninsula so that his patrons could take their choice.

Finally in 1746 Father Consag sailed completely round the Gulf of California and at last settled the vexed question. Ferdinand VII in 1747 in a royal decree, stated: " California is not an Island ".

ABBREVIATIONS

BM = British Museum

M = Muller (F.) Catalogue Part III, Amsterdam 1875

T = Tiele (P. A.) Nederlandshe Bib. van Landten Volkenkunde Amsterdam 1884

Wa = Wagner (H. R.) Cartography of N.W. Coast of America, Univ. of California Press, Berkeley. Cal. 1937

Wh = Wheat (C. I.) Mapping the Transmississippi West. San Francisco 1957

DATING

Few maps were issued dated, for obvious commercial reasons, and those that were are sometimes misleading (for example, Speed's map published in 1676 still bears the 1626 date which was not erased from the copperplate). Some atlases had a printed title from which an individual map can be dated, but many atlases, particularly those of a later date bear no year of publication. These are perforce dated approximately, and even experts frequently differ as to the dates assigned (see no. 68 Valk).

1 **1625** [BRIGGS (HENRY)] The North part of America conteyning Newfoundland, new England, Virginia, Florida, new Spaine, and Nova Francia . . . and
upon ye West the large and goodly Iland of California . . . R. Elstracke sculpsit
[1625].   28½×35½ cms.

The first printed map in English to show California as an island. It appeared in
Samuel Purchas's Hakluytus Posthumous or Purchas His Pilgrimes' London
1625.

A nicely balanced map, it is finely engraved by R. Elstracke with beautiful clear
lettering with three long " legends " (passages of text). One, bottom left, reads
" California sometymes supposed to be a part of ye westerne continent, but since
by a Spanish Charte taken by ye Hollanders it is found to be a goodly Ilande:
the length of the west shoare beeing about 500 leagues from Cape Mendocino to
the South Cape thereof called Cape St Lucas as appeareth both by that Spanish
chart and by relation of Francis Gaule whereas in the ordinarie charts it is set
downe to be 1700 leagues ".

Two notes, one on Sr. Thomas Button, the other on Mr. Baffin are engraved in
the top centre. The aim of the map was to emphasise the probability of a North-
West Passage and to minimise the distance from Port Nelson to northern
California providing an easy south-westward voyage by open seaway to the
rich trade of the East Indies.

Two large towns are shown in New Mexico " Pueblos de Moqui " and "Real de
Nveva Mexico." Costa del Perles is shown both sides of the Gulf. California is
shown as an island with a flat northern coast and contains the following names
reading downwards:

C Blanco	P de S Diego	B de St Symon
C de St Sebastian	St Clement	I. de la Carr
C Mendocino	I. St Martin	P de St Bartolome
P° Sr Francisco Draco	St Martin	Sierra Pintado
Punta de los Reyes	B de Todos Santos	P de Roqui
P° de Monte Rey	B de St Quinten	B de las arenas
P de Carinde	I. de Pararos	R de St Cristoual
Punta de la Conception	B d Virgines	Punta de St Apalmat
Canal de St Barbaria	C de Engano	B de Martin
Punta de la Conception	St Marco	P de la Magdale
(second time)	B de Francisco	P de la Marquena
St Catalina	Is de Ceintas	P de Cenous
		P de la Paz
		C de St Lucas

Plate 26.

Wa *295   Wh p. 37.

112

2 **1626-7** SPEED (J.) America with those known parts in that unknowne worlde both people and manner of buildings Discribed and inlarged by I. S. Ano 1626 Are to be sold in pops head alley against the Exchange by G. Humble Engraved Abraham Goos $51\frac{1}{2} \times 39\frac{1}{2}$ cms.

Issued in the "Prospect of the World", published by Humble for John Speed in 1627, the first general atlas of the World published in Britain. This charming map has side borders of single costume figures and top border of birds-eye plans of the principal towns.

This first edition may be recognised by the date 1626, by the imprint " pops head alley G. Humble," and by the fact that Boston and Long Island are not marked on the map, and by the pagination numbers 9 and 10.

California is shown as an island based on the Briggs's map with the same names, but omits B. de S Quintin and the last four names in the southern tip.

Wa *3016. Wh 39.

3 —— —— Reissued in 1631 by G. Humble, the map unchanged and the text on reverse the same as to content but the first page unnumbered, the fleuron heading being continued into the outside ruled column taking the place of the figure 9.

4 —— —— Again reissued in 1662 by new publishers " Are to be sold by Roger Rea ye Elder and younger at ye Golden Cross in Cornhill against ye Exchange." In this issue the town of Boston in New England, Connecticut, Maryland and Long Island are added to the plate and a dotted boundary placed round Delaware and Hudsons Rio. The text on reverse is again the same as to content but the type is reset and now commences with a historiated capital A, a new fleuron heading and the page number 9 restored top right.

5 —— —— It was again reissued in 1676 by new publishers "are to be sold by Thomas Bassett in Fleet Street, and by Richard Chiswell in St. Paul's Churchyard."

In this last issue of Speed's map, the copperplate is unchanged but the text on the reverse is not only reset but rewritten. There is no fleuron heading, New York and Maryland are mentioned for the first time in the text to Virginia (section 14) and Hochelaga, Quebec and Tadusac added to the description of Canada.
The representation of California is unchanged.

Plate 27.

6 [**1638**] JANSSON (J.) America Septentrionalis. $55 \times 46\frac{1}{2}$ cms.
California shown as an island on the Briggs's model.

Reissued many times 1639, 1641, 1642, 1645, 1646, 1652, 1662, 1666, etc.
Wa 330 Wh 45 (gives first date of 1640, and a second issue of 1652) M 1875 (1887)

Plate 28.

7 **1650** SANSON (N.) Amerique Septentrionale Par N Sanson d'Abbcville Geog. du Roy A Paris Chez l'Auteur et chez Pierre Mariette rue S. Jaques a l'Esperance 1650. $54\frac{1}{2} \times 38\frac{1}{2}$ cms.

California as an island with a flat northern coast unnamed, with 41 place names. Four names shown on Sanson's map C de Fortune, C de Pinos, C de S Martin and C de Galera do not appear on Briggs, and one of Briggs's names, Sierra Pintado is not engraved on Sanson's.

Wa *360. Wh 47.

Wagner speaks disparagingly of Sanson's maps but Wheat more discerningly calls this, and the map of 1656, by far the most interesting and important maps since the manuscript map of Oñate route of 1602.

Sanson inserts Santa Fe capital of New Mexico, introduces the word Apaches and for the first time, Navajo.

Plate 29.

8 ———-**1669** ——— Amerique Septentrionale Par N Sanson . . . Revue et changee en plusieurs endroits . . . Par G. Sanson . . . A Paris Chez Pierre Mariette 1669. 55×39 cms.

A re-drawn and corrected edition of the preceding. The title cartouche is now on left instead of the right. The island of California now has an indented northern coast with two extra names Talago and R de Eslite on this coast. On West side C de Fortune and C de Pinas are omitted. C de S Martin changed to Pta de MonteRey and Port de Monterey, and B de Francisque omitted. Gotheburg is now inserted in New Sweden, and Mon Royal changed to Mont Real.

Wa 699.

9 ———-**1690** ——— Amerique Septentrionale Par N Sanson . . . Reveuë . . . G. Sanson A Paris Chez Pierre Mariette . . . 1690.

A reissue of the preceding but re-engraved and with minor alterations Terre de Jesso and Conibas inserted but without a coastline. Detroit d'Anian placed immediately above California and a few changes in spelling (I. de Pararos from I. de Para). New Albion is inserted in the north of the island, and New York replaces Amsterdam.

10 **[1650]** JANSSON (J.) Mar del Zur Hispanis Mare Pacificum $54\frac{1}{2} \times 44$ cms.

Map of the Pacific showing the west coast of America from Cape Horn to Straits of Anian, with California shown as an island immediately below the latter. First appeared in the Marine Atlas of Janson, Waterwereld 1650. Reissued 1652 and 1657 and later.

Title within ornamental cartouche with cherubs and figures of orientals and decorated scale of miles of cherubs with surveying instruments.

California as an island with a flat northern coastline from C. Blanco to C de S. Lucas with the Vermillion Sea and Coast of Pearls. It has 28 place names.

Wa *359 T 533.

Plate 30.

11 **1652** SEILE (H.) Americae Descriptio Nova. Impensis Henrici Seile. Will: Trevethen sculp 1652. 42×34 cms.

Based on Speed's map of 1627, the only change in California being the insertion of the words Nova Albion in large type in the north of the island. Issued in Heylin's Cosmography 1652.

Wa *368.

12 ——-**1663** —— Another issue published by the widow of H. Seile "Impensīs Añae Seile" 1663. Rob. Vaughan sculp. 42×34 cms.

A reissue of preceding re-engraved. Cape Mendocin is now placed below the island of St. Clement and C Martin inserted between C de St. Sebastian and Po S Fra Drake. I Hatorash is omitted on the east coast.

Wa 368.

13 ——-**1666** —— Americae Descriptio Nova Impensis Philippi Chetwind. Will Trevethen sculp 1666. 42×34 cms.

In spite of the title "newly described" this map is a further copy of Seile's map of 1652, without the changes of the 1663 edition.

Wh 56.

14 **1656** SANSON (N.) Le Nouveau Mexique, et la Floride; Tirées de diverses Cartes, et Relations. Par N. Sanson d'Abbeville Geogr. ordre du Roy A Paris Chez Pierre Mariette. Rue S Jacque a l'Esperance 1656. Engraved Somer. 54½×31 cms.

An important map, the first in a printed atlas to put the greatest emphasis on California and New Mexico. A map of great influence, it became the model for the delineation of California for the next fifty years. In this map Sanson changed the place names from French into Spanish, and altered the shape of the island giving it an indented Northern Coastline.

The place names, running from North to South are:

R. de Estiete	I. S. Cathalina	I de Ceintas
Talaago	B de Todos los Santos	Sierra Pintado
C. Blanco	S Clement	B de les Arenas
C de Sebastian	I S Martin	I de la Carre
C de Mendocino	B de S Quintin	Pta de Roqui
Pto de los Reyes	B de las Virgines	R de S Cristoval
Pto de Monte Rey	C de Engamo	Punta de S Apollinat
Pto de Francisco Draco	I d e Parraros	B de S Martin
Pto de Carinda	B de S Francisco	Pto de la Magdalena
P de la Conception	I. S. Marco	P de la Marque
Canal de S Barbara	B de S. Simon	P de Cenou
B de la Conversion	P de S Bartolomeo	P de la Pas
P de S Diego		B Bernabe
		C de S Lucas

Wa *374   Wh 50

Plate 31.

115

15 **1656** SANSON (N.) Audience de Guadalajara, Nouveau Mexique, Californie &c. Par N Sanson . . . A Paris chez P Mariette. $23\frac{1}{2} \times 20$ cms.

A reduced version of the left half of preceding with the same names except that B. Bernabe is omitted.

The reduction of Sanson's maps to a convenient small 4to size, included, besides the above, a general map of N. America showing California as an island but with few names. His work was reissued in 1657, 1662 and 1676, 1683, 1696 and 1699, and Dutch editions 1683, 1705 and 1715.

Wh only cites a Dutch edition of *c*. 1665.

16 **[1656]** COLOM (J.) Zuyd-Zee. t'Amsterdam by Iacob Colom op 't Water 55×43 cms.

Map of the Pacific showing California as an island as in the second Sanson model, but without B de S Francisco and Pto de la Magdalena. Point Sir Francis Drake is inserted below C Mendocino and P de Cenou changed to P de Canons. P. S. Juan is added to the East Coast.

M. 1931 (1875)

Plate 32.

17 **[1659]** DONCKER (H.) Pascaart vertoonende de Zeecusten van Chili, Peru, Hispania Nova, Nova Granada, en California. 't Amsterdam. By Hendrick Doncker Boeckverkooper inde Nieuwe brugh steegh in't Stuiermans gereedt schap. 54×43 cms.

West coast of America from Chili to New Granada with California as an island after the 2nd Sanson model.

With insets of New Zealand, Ladrones area, and Jedso.

Appeared in Doncker's Zee Atlas Amstd 1659. Reissued 1665, 1666 and 1672.

Wa * 382   M 1875 (1934)

Plate 33.

18 **[1660]** WIT (F de) Nova totius Americae descriptio Auct. F. de Wit 1660. $55\frac{1}{2} \times 44$ cms.

Based on the Kaerius map of 1614 and Visscher map of 1636, it is entirely revised for the west coast, the two former showing California as a peninsula, but De Wit in this map changes California into an island on the second Sanson model of 1656. Being on a smaller scale he omits some of the Sanson names including Pto de Francisco Draco.

The map is decorated with side borders of costume figures and top border of birds-eye views of principal towns based on the designs of Kaerius, with a charming titlepiece including a native sitting on an armadillo copied from the Visscher map.

Plate 34.

19 **[1661]** VAN LOON (JOH) Pascaerte van Nova Granada en t'Eylandt California t Amsterdam by Joh van Loon Plaetsnyder, en Ioh van Waesberge. $54\frac{1}{2} \times 42\frac{1}{2}$ cms.

Van Loon puts Port Sir Francis Drake above Port of MonteRey, and Canal de S. Barbara below P. de la Conversion.

Appeared in " Klaeɪ Lichtende noort ster ofte zee atlas." Amsterdam 1661. It was reissued in 1666 and 1668.

Wa 388 T 696.

Plate 35.

20 **1664** DU VAL (P.) L'Amerique autrement le Nouveau Monde et Indes Occidentales Par P. Du Val d'Abbeville Geographe Ordinaire du Roy. A Paris chez l'Autheur proche le For l'Evesque 1664. Engraved Lhulier. $38 \times 36\frac{1}{2}$ cms. Based on Sanson's map with five Great Lakes, last two open at their western ends. Shows New Sweden, and New York as New Amsterdam.

California as an island with 12 place names and a flat northern coast.

Plate 36.

21 —— **-84** ——— Another edition, A Paris Chez Madlle DuVal Fille de l'Auteur. Sur le Quay de l'Orloge du Palais 1684 [engraver's name erased]. $38 \times 36\frac{1}{2}$ cms.

A reissue of DuVal's map by his daughter, with a Table of Signs within an ornamented frame added above the original titlepiece and " Partie de la grande Terre Australe " added in bottom right-hand corner and the islands of Tristan de Cunha and Goncal Alvares.

Otherwise, the map is unchanged, California retaining the same shape and names as in the earlier edition.

22 **1666** GOOS (PIETER) Paskaerte van Nova Granada en t'Eylandt California. t'Amsterdam by Pieter Goos op't Waater inde Vergulde Zeespiegel Ao 1666. $54\frac{1}{2} \times 44$ cms.

Perhaps the most attractive and certainly the most definite representation of California as an island. California is the centre and " raison d'etre" of the map, immediately to its north is the Strait of Anian with a large unknown land at the top of the map.

The title and scale of miles are decorated with winged cherubs and ships sail off the coast.

Reissued in 1668, 1669, 1670, 1672, 1675 and 1676 by the widow of Goos, and a French edition in 1679 and 1697, Spanish 1669 and English 1669. In shape it follows the Sanson map of 1656 except that it omits Pta de Roqui, and adds Bay of S. Juan and Coast of Perles on the east side of the island.

Wa 394 T 399 M 1875 (1944).

Plate 37.

23 **1666** HOLLAR (W.) A New and Exact Map of America and Ilands thereunto belonging. Published and are to be Sold by Thomas Jenner, at the South Entrance into Royal Exchange of London 1666. W. Hollar fecit 1666. 48×37 cms.

" This California was in times past thought to [have] beene a part of ye continent and so made in all maps, but by further discoveries was found to be an Iland long 1700 legues."

Briggs' shape with flat northern coast to California with following names in Iland of California:

C Blanco	B de Francisco
C de S. Sebastian	I S Marco
C Mendocino	B de Simon
Po Sr Francisco Draco	I de Ceintas
Punta de los Reges (sic)	Punta de Bartholome
Pt de monte Rey	I de la Carre
P de Carinde	P de Roqui
Punta de la Conception	B de la arenas
Canal de S Barbara	R de S Cristoval
I S Catharine	Coast of Pearles
P de S Diego	Punta de S Apalmat
S Clement	P de la Marque
I S Martin	P de St Martin
Baia de Todos Santos	P de Cenou
B de St Quintin	P de la Magdalena
I de Parraras	P de la Paz
B de la Virgines	C de S Lucas

A curious representation of the Great Lakes, the St. Laurence into one large lake the Iroquois (after Jansson) this connected to one larger lake unnamed and open at its western end.

Plate 38.

24 **1668** OVERTON (JOHN) A New and Most Exact map of America described by N. I. Visscher and don into English Enlarged and Corrected according to I Blaeu and others with the Habits of ye people and ye manner of ye Cheife Sitties ye like never before. London Printed Colloured and are to be sould by John Overton at ye White horse in Little Brittaine neare the Hospitall 1668. 54×32½ cms.

A rare and attractive map with its side borders of costume figures and top and bottom borders of views of cities and portraits of navigators. Originally drawn and issued by Petrus Kaerius in 1614 it was reissued by Visscher in 1636, by De Wit in 1660 and again by Overton as above.

It is more rare than the De Wit map of 1660 and far more decorative, following the Kaerius model in having a bottom as well as a top border of town plans interspersed with portraits of navigators, the sea covered with ships and a large inset of Polar Regions.

California follows the Speed, not the Sanson, model with a flat northern coast.

Plate 39.

25 **1668-1670** WALTON (R.) A New Plaine, and Exact Map of America; described by N. I. Visscher, and don into English, enlarged and corrected according to I Blaeu . . . Printed, Colered, and are to be sold by Ro. Walton at ye Globe and Compass in St Paules Churchyard between ye two north doores. 52½ × 41½ cms.

This is an extremely interesting and uncommon map being an intermediate state in the geographical conception of the West Coast, the only map I know to show this compromise solution in the controversy as to whether California was an island or a peninsula.

California is shown as an island on the revised Sanson model but the coast is continued north-westwards in the old Mercator-Ortelius tradition. New Albion is shown on the mainland coast far to the north of the island, and the island itself is named California.

The map forms one of the series Kaerius, Visscher, De Wit, Overton.
It is sometimes found in editions of Heylin's Cosmography, inserted instead of the normal Seile maps. Also occasionally in Varenius.

26 **1669** BLOME (RICHARD) A New Mapp of America Septentrionale Designed by Monsieur Sanson Geographer to the French King and Rendred into English and Illustrated by Richard Blome . . . London Printed for Richard Blome 1669. Engraved Francis Lamb. 54½ × 38 cms.

An exact copy of Sanson's map of N. America of 1650 as regards California, except that a tiny vignette of a deer is shown in the north of the island. The title cartouche is redesigned with cherubs and ribbons &c. and is placed in top left-hand corner. Top right a dedication to the Rt. Hon. Caecilius Calvert Baron Baltimore.

Plate 40.

27 —— —— Another issue, undated and unchanged save for a new dedication to Rt. Hon. Anthony Earle of Shaftesbury.

28 —— —— Another issue, undated, and unchanged save for a new dedication to Jeffery Jefferys of the Priory in Brecknockshire pasted over the dedication to the Earl of Shaftesbury.

Wa 400.

29 **[1670]** VISSCHER (N.) Novissima et Accuratissima totius Americae descriptio per N. Visscher. 53½ × 43 cms.

A handsome and important map that was copied many times. Dedicated to Cornelius Witsen, his arms are shown on a shield supported by angels and a female figure holding aloft a cross, a falling devil at her feet. Title on a stone block with two snakes above and figures of natives either side, one a chief under an umbrella. The St. Laurence is shown entering a large lake open at its western end.

California is shown as an island with a flat northern coast with the following names from north to south:

C Mendocino	S Clement	P de S Bartelome
C de Forturas	Baia d Todos Santos	Sierra Pintado
Nova Albion	I S Martin	P de Roqui
P de los Reyes	I de Parraros	B de las Arenas
P de Monterey	B St Quintin	R de Cristoval
P de Carinde	B de las Virgines	P de S Apolinas
P de la Conception	C Engano	B S Martin
Canal de S Barbara	I S Marco	P de Marquez
P de la Conversion	B Francisco	P Canous
I. S. Catalina	B S Simon	P de la Paz
P S Diego	I de Ceinta	I de S. Lucas

T 1161   M 1875 (1899)

Plate 41.

30 **[1670]** DE WIT (F.) Novissima et Accuratissima totius Americae Descriptio per F de Wit Amstelodami. F de Wit excudit. 57×49 cms.

A revised edition of the Visscher map. Witsen's arms are removed, the same cartouche with the figures reversed now contains a descriptive text on America. The title cartouche also uses the same native figures again mostly reversed, and more ships are added in the sea.

The single lake is now changed into the five Great Lakes, two still open, and California still shown as an island now has an indented northern coastline based on the second form of G. Sanson, and follows the same nomenclature in general, with a few omissions.

T 1217   M 1910 (309) gives date *c.* 1680.

31 ——— **-1680** ——— Novissima et Accuratissima Totius Americae Descriptio per F de Wit Amstelodami. 58×49 cms.

A revised edition of the preceding, titlepiece and plaque remain the same, but all the vignettes of small ships are removed from the sea. New Guinea, Solomon Islands and Land of Quiros are added to the plate (above the titlepiece) and Fretum Aniani and Terra Esonis inserted north of California.

California remains exactly the same except for one important addition, the words Nova Albion being inserted in the north of the island.

32 ——— ——— Copies exist of this map with a printed Alphabetical Table of Names as a paste on each side of the map, making the overall size 83×49 cms. They are rare.

33 ——— ——— Another edition with an amended title Novissima et Accuratissima Septentrionalis et Meridionalis Americae Descriptio multis Locis recentibus aucta . . . per Fredericum de Witt Amstelodami. 58½×49 cms. Apart from the title, a reissue of preceding.

M 1910 (310)

34 **[1671]** SCHAGEN (GERARDUS A). Novissima et Accuratissima totius Americae Descriptio per Gerardum a Schagen. 54 × 43½ cms.

Issued in Montanus " De nieuwe en onbekende weereld of beschrijving van America 't Amsterdam Anno 1671 " (By Jacob Meurs). A copy of the Visscher map with the same title cartouche, but without the cartouche and dedication to Witsen in top left.

I have also seen it occasionally in Ogilby's America in place of the similar map by Ogilby.

California is on the English-Dutch model with the flat northern coastline.

Wa *405   T 763.   Wh 56.   M 1872 (1012)

35 **[1671]** OGILBY (J.) Novissima et Accuratissima totius Americae Descriptio per Johanem Ogiluium Cosmographum Regium. 54½ × 43½ cms.

Based on the Visscher map with the same figured titlepiece bottom left, the cartouche top left now enfolds the arms of Anthony Ashley.

As regards California, Ogilby follows Visscher's outline but has some variation in nomenclature. As regards the East coast and the English colonies in particular, Ogilby makes many improvements, inserting the towns of Boston, N. London and Milford and changes New Amsterdam to New York. Maryland and Carolina are added with the James, Barkly and Ashley rivers.

Wa *404

Plate 42.

36 **1671-73** MEURSIUS (JACOBUS) Novissima et Accuratissima totius Americæ Descriptio. 54 × 43 cms.

Yet another copy of Visscher, the map unchanged but with a newly-designed titlepiece and a large emblematic vignette of Neptune top left.

California shown as an island on the Briggs-Speed model with flat northern coast. Appeared in German edition of Montanus " Die unbekante newe Welt " Amsterdam 1673.

Wh 57.

Plate 43.

37 **1674** SANSON-JAILLOT. Amerique Septentrionale divisee en ses principales parties ou sont distingues . . . les Estats . . . Francois, Castillans, Anglois, Suedois, Danois, Hollandois . . . Par le Sr Sanson . . . A Paris Chez H. Jaillot joignant les grands Augustins, aux deux globes . . . 1674. Cordier sculp. 87 × 56 cms.

Jaillot who succeeded to Sanson's business makes a rehash of his maps. California is copied from Sanson's map of 1656. The remainder of the map is based on that of 1669. Jaillot retains the 5 lakes with two open at their western ends. He shows New Sweden and New Amsterdam. Curiously he omits Montreal, but does insert a few French missions round the Great Lakes; S. Simon Jude, S. Pierre, S. Pol, S. Alexis, S. Joseph at Lake Erie.

Large handsome titlepiece with arms of the Dauphin, natives and indigenous fauna.

Plate 44.

Jaillot reissued the Sanson maps on a much larger scale. This plate of America was reissued in 1685, 1690, 1692, 1695, [1700 Pierre Mortier] again undated Covens and Mortier, and in Paris 1719 where the plate is changed, no northern coast being shown, and the question as to whether California is an island or peninsula left undecided. An English edition was issued in 1680 by William Berry.

Its long life was due in part to the expense of production, for it continued in use long after its geographical information became out of date.

Wa 4096   Wh 58

38   —— -1679   ——   Reissued on a smaller scale.   64 × 54½ cms.

With a new titlepiece and scale of miles but the representation of California is unchanged.

Editions are as follows 169-, 1694, and in Amsterdam by R & J Ottens.

39   1675   SELLER (JOHN). A Chart of the South-Sea by John Seller Hydro-grapher to the Kings most Excellent Majestie. [London 1675] Dundee sculp. 53 × 42½ cms.

Sea chart of the Pacific showing the West coast of America from Magellan Straits to Anian.

California as an island on the 2nd Sanson model.

Wa 410

Plate 45.

40   [1675]   DE WIT (F.) Magnum Mare del Zur cum Insula California. Gedruckt't Amsterdam by Frederick de Wit inde Calverstraet 57 × 49½ cms.

Map of the Pacific with title in Latin and Dutch within cartouche with figures of Neptune and winged cherubs and portrait of Magellan above.

California is shown as an island with indented northern coast and is copied from Goos's map of 1666 but being on a smaller scale omits some names.

It was reissued by L. Renard in Amsterdam in 1715 and 1739 unchanged.

41   —— -1745   It was again reissued by R & I Ottens also in Amsterdam in 1745.   As regards California, the map was unchanged but the remainder of the map was revised.   The Solomon Islands and the Land of the Holy Ghost etc. are added.

Wa 411   M 1875 (1950)

42   1677   ROSSI (G.) L'America Settentrionale Nuouamente corretta et accresciuta . . . da Guglielmo Sansone . . . E data in luce da Gio Giacomo de Rossi in Roma nella sua Stamperia alla Pace l'anno 1677. Giorgio Widman Sculp.   54½ × 39 cms.

An Italian copy of G. Sanson's map of 1669 with a newly designed titlepiece of acanthus leaf decoration with landscape scenery and small figures of natives below. Reissued in 1687 with some additions.

Wh 59

43　**1679**　Du Val (P.)　L'Amerique suivant les dernieres Relations avec les Routes que l'on tient pour Les Indes Occidentales par P. DuVal Geographe Ordinaire du Roy A Paris Chez l'Auteur en l'Isle du Palais Sur le Quay de l'Orloge, proche le coin de la rue de Harley 1679.

Large scale map or 4 sheets. Title within cartouche with native supporters California shown as an island with 17 place names on Sanson's model.

Wa 414　Wh 60 a one sheet edition

Plate 46.

44　——　——　Another edition but the imprint changed to A Paris Chez Melle Du Val Fille de l'Auteur Sur le Quay de l'Orloge proche le coin de la rue de Harley a l'ancien Buis 1679　　M 1910(306)

45　**1680**　Keulen (J. van)　Pascaert vande Zuyd Zee en een gedeelte van Brasil van Ilhas de Ladronos tot R de la Plata 't Amsterdam By Joannes van Keulen een de Nieuwe brugh in de Gekroonde Lootsman.　$60 \times 51\frac{1}{2}$ cms.

Sea chart of the Pacific showing America from New Granada to Cape Horn with California as an island on the 2nd Sanson model.

Reissued 1681, 1683, 1685, 1688 and later.

T 593

46　**1683**　Hennepin (L. de)　Carte de la Nouvelle France et de la Louisiane nouvellement decouverte dediée au Roy l'an 1683. Par le Reverend Pere Louis Hennepin Missionaire Recollet et Notaire Apostolique.　46×29 cms.

Issued in Hennepin's Description de la Louisiane Paris 1683.

Wa 421

47　**[1685]**　De Ram (J.)　Novissima et Accuratissima Totius Americae descriptio per Joannem de Ram.　56×44 cms.

A reissue of the first De Wit map with the same decorative plaque and the same figured titlepiece with a bull's hide and tobacco roll added at foot.

No lakes at all are shown. California as an island in the second Sanson shape.

Wa 437　T 898

Plate 47.

48　**[1688]**　Morden (R.)　New Mexico vel New Granada et Marata et California.　$12\frac{1}{2} \times 11$ cms.

A curious small map showing California as an island on the second Sanson model but with 2 new names in the southern tip C de la Trinidad and B California. It is also of interest as showing Santa Fe on East bank of the Rio del Norte, which continuing as the Rio Bravo debouches into the Gulf of Mexico, whereas most contemporary maps show it flowing into the Gulf of California.

It appears in a small 4to volume " Geography rectified or a Description of the World 1768." California is also shown consistently as an island in the same work in the General Map of the World and the General Map of America.

123

49 **1689** CORONELLI (LE P.) L'Amerique Septentrionale ou la Partie Septentrionale des Indes Occidentales . . . Par le P. Coronelli Cosmographe de la Serme. Republique de Venise. A Paris Chez I. B. Nolin sur le Quay de l'Horloge du Palais, proche la Rue de Harley, a l'Enseigne de la Place des Victoires 1689. 59 × 43 cms.

Decorative title cartouche with urns and cornucopias supported by native and European. Dedicated to Pierre Venier with coat of arms above.

California shown as a large island after the version of N. Sanson of 1656 but with the addition of several mountains in northern California and three in the Southern tip.

Wa 431   Wh No. 70

Plate 48.

50 **1689-1704** ———— Another edition unchanged except for the title, the Dedication to Pierre Venier and acknowledgement to P. Coronelli omitted and the date changed to 1704.

51 **1690** SANSON (G.) Atlantis Insula a Nicolao Sanson Antiquitati Restituta . . . ex conatibus Geographicis Gulielmi Sanson Nicolai Filii 1669 Lutetiae Parisiorum 1690. 56 × 40 cms.

An attempt by Sanson to show ancient North and South America on a contemporary outline.

California is shown as an island without nomenclature.

52 **1690-[1730]** ———— Another edition published in Amsterdam by Covens & Mortier. Unchanged.

53 **[1690]** DANCKERTS (I.) Recentissima Novi Orbis sive America Septentrionalis et Meridionalis Tabula. Per I Danckerts Amst. 58 × 49 cms.

A reissue of the Visscher-De Wit map, showing California as an island with a Terra Esonis stretching from there to a Terre de Yedso. With the same title vignette as in the Visscher and De Wit maps.

54 **1690** LEA (PHILIP). A New Mapp of America devided according to the Best and latest Observations and Discoveries wherein are discribed . . . the seaverall Countries that Belonge to ye English which are wholly left out in all French and Dutch Maps . . . New Scotland, Long Island, N. York, N. Jarsey, Mary Land, Pensilvania, Carrolina, etc. by Philip Lea at ye Atlas and Hercules in Cheapside=and by I Overton at the White Horse without Newgat London. Engraved J. Moxon Philip Lea excudit 56½ × 48 cms.

Title within cartouche with figures of natives either side copied from Blaeu, inset of Polar Regions, and dedication on a draped curtain to the Duke of Beaufort. California is shown as an island in the Sanson manner.

55 **1690** LEA (PHILIP). North America divided into III Principall Parts I English Part viz English Empire containing ye Articklands near Hudsons Bay, New North and South Wales, New Britain N Foundland N Scotland N England N York N Jarsey Pensylvania, Maryland, Virginia, Carolina, Carolinia or Florida California Sommer Is. Bahama Is. Jamaica & ye Caryby Is. II Spanish Pt. viz N Spain pt of ye Antilles III French pt. viz N France & pt. of ye Cariby Is. 57 × 51 cms.

An uncommon and interesting map. California shown as an extremely large and bold island off west coast with nothing to the north of it. In shape it is based on the Sanson model but has a chain of mountains running right down the island from North to South and contains two new names on northern shores St Pedro, B Arnas, St Jago and P Matayo. The West is marked " Tract of Land full of Wild Bulls."

Plate 49.

56 [**1695**] SCHENK (P.) America Septentrionalis Novissima (and Meridionalis accuratissima). 56½ × 48 cms.

A slightly unusual feature of this map is the double title, one for North and one for South America each within a decorative cartouche.

California shown as an island on the second Sanson model.

M 1910 (315)

57 **1696** CORONELLI (P.) America Settentrionale colle Nuoue Scoperte sin all Anno 1688 . . . del P. Mro Coronelli [Venice] 2 sheets each 45 × 61 cms.

California as an island after 2nd Sanson model, but with heavy mountain range along the east coast.

Plate 50.

58 —— —— Mare del Sud detto altrimenti Mare Pacifico Auttore Il P. M. Coronelli M. C. Cosmografo della serenissima Republica di Venetia. 61 × 44 cms.

Map of the Pacific, title on a shell with supporting nereids and fruits of the sea below.

California as an island shown on the G. Sanson model.

Wa *436

59 **1698** HENNEPIN (L DE). Amerique Septentrionalis. Carte d'un tres grand Pays entre le Nouveau Mexique et la Mer Glaciale Dediée a Guillaume III Roy de la Grand Bretagne Par le R. P. Louis de Hennepin Mission Recol: et Not: Apost: Chez C. Specht a Utrecht 1698 J V Vianen del et fecit. 52 × 43 cms.

California is shown as an island on the G. Sanson model with a few place names and a large landmass Terre de Iesso immediately to the North. The map is of course more famous for its rendering of the Great Lakes and the Mississippi areas. It has a decorative figured titlepiece surmounted by the arms of William III of Great Britain.

Wa 452

60 **1699** DE FER (N.) L'Amerique, Meridionale, et Septrentrionale Dressée selon les derniers Relations et suivant les Nouvelles Decouvertes dont les points principaux sont placez sur les Observations de Mrs de l'Academie Royale des Sciences. A Paris. Chez l'Autheur dans l'Isle du Palais sur le Quay de l'Horloge a la Sphere Royale 1699. H van Loon fecit. 60 × 46½ cms.

De Fer's map of America engraved with several " legends ", for example, by the Solomon Islands is a note " the Spaniards have suppressed these Islands in their new maps to deprive a knowledge of them to Strangers." A note is given on the discovery of Captain David (Davis) of 1685 of land thought to be Antarctica. California is shown as an island on the Sanson model.

Reissued 1705 unchanged, and in 1717 with new imprint " A Paris Chez I. F. Bernard dans l'Isle du Palais sur le Quay de l'Orloge a la Sphere Royale," and again in 1726 with new descriptive text within cartouche top right-hand corner, otherwise unchanged.

Wa apparently unaware of this edition as he only cites the edition of 1705 (No. 482). Wh 96 cites the map of 1717.

Plate 51.

61 ———— -**1700** ———— L'Amerique Meridionale et Septentrionale Dressée selon les derniers Relations et suivant les Nouvelles Decouvertes . . . A Paris. Chez l'Autheur dans l'Isle du Palais sur le Quay de l'Orloge a la Sphere Royale . . . 1700 with a scale of miles in elaborate penmanship by C Inselin. 33½ × 22¼ cms. De Fer's small map of America dedicated to " Nosseigneurs les Enfans de France " by de Fer Geographer to the Dauphin.

California shown as an island with a few coastal names only.

Reissued in 1705, 1717 without change, and again in 1740 with new imprint " A Paris Chez G. Danet sur le Pont de Notre Dame a la Sphere Royale," otherwise unchanged.

62 ———— ———— Cette Carte de Californie et du Nouveau Mexique est tiree de celle qui a ete envoyee par un grand d'Espagne pour etre communiquée a Mrs de l'Academie Royale des Sciences. Par N. de Fer Geographe de Monseigneur le Dauphin. A Paris dans l'Isle du Palais Sur le quay de l'Orloge a la Sphere Royale 1700. Engraved Inselin. 34 × 22½ cms.

A small but highly important map. California as an island lettered " Californias o Carolinas " with 50 place names.

A very unusual map. New Mexico is shown covered with engraved numbers from 1 to 314 with an engraved key above giving the names of these 314 places. Thus a great amount of information is given on a small map.

According to Wagner, this is the first map known to show the discoveries of Father Eusebio Kino:

New names: Co S. Franco Xavier   S. Juan
           Rio de Carmelo   S. Ant.
           Po de S Lucia   Virgines
           B de Balenas   Po Matanza
           Rio de S Thomas descubierto 1684   Na S^{a}dl Carmen
           Po de Anno Nuevo descubierto 1685   Ba Darate
           Sierra Carmelo   S. Joseph
           Sierra Ensado   Spu Sto
           S. Marcos   B d la Paz
           S. Matheo   Serubbo
           S. Rosalia   Co d la Porfia
           and Gimies and Edues and Guaicures.

Wa *462   Wh 78

63 [1700] DE LA FEUILLE. Novissima et Accuratissima totius Americae Descriptio per Jacobum de la Feuille. $56\frac{1}{2} \times 44\frac{1}{2}$ cms.

A close copy of the De Ram map, titlepiece and decorative plaque remaining the same, but Terra Esonis inserted north of California and one or two ocean names engraved in Roman type added to the plate Mare Californiae, Mar de Zur, Mare Magellanicum, Mare Paraguayae etc.

Wa 437

64 1700 MORTIER (P.) Mer du Sud du Pacific contenant L'Isle de Californe les Costes de Mexique du Perou, Chili, et le Destroit de Magellanique etc. . . . A Amsterdam Chez Pierre Mortier. $74 \times 59\frac{1}{2}$ cms.

65 [1700] ALLARD (C.) Recentissima Novi Orbis sive Americae Septentrionalis et Meridionalis Tabula ex officina Caroli Allard. 58×49 cms.

California as an island on the G. Sanson model with the same nomenclature except that Nova Albion is inserted in the North, P de Cenou omitted and B. S. Simon inserted from N. Sanson. Immediately to the north of California is a large land mass stretching north westwards "Terra Essonis." Large titlepiece of natives and sugar cane and small inset map of New Zealand.

66 1700 PETRINI (PAOLO). America Settentrionale . . . Corretta, et aumentata . . . da N. Sanson d'Abbevile . . . l'an 1700. In Pariggi A spese di Paolo Petrini e da lui si vendono in Napoli a S. Biaggio de Librari. Antonius Donzel Gallus sculpsit. $53\frac{1}{2} \times 39$ cms.

A late Italian version of the G. Sanson map of 1669 (not of N. Sanson of 1656) with a new titlepiece of acanthus leaves and ribbons.

Wa *468 cites 2 wall maps of this date by Petrini viz. World and America 118×92 *c.*1700 each showing California as an island.

67 **[1700]** Schenk (P.) Americae tam Septentrionalis quam Meridionalis in Mappa Geographica Delineatio . . . opera A. F. Zurneri . . . ex Officina Petri Schenkii in platea vulgo de Warmoes Straat sub signo N Visschers athlas. $57\frac{1}{2} \times 49\frac{1}{2}$ cms.

California as an island on the Sanson model but with 3 place names inserted in Southern California, S Isidoro, Gigante and N S de la Guadalupe.

M 1875 (1976)

Plate 52.

68 **[1690-1700]** Valk (G. & L.) America aurea Pars Altera Mundi Auctoribus Gerardo et Leonardo Valk. $59\frac{1}{2} \times 48\frac{1}{2}$ cms.

Largely a copy of Allard's maps of c. 1700 with the same titlepiece except that the inset of New Zealand has been removed. California bears the same names but the outlines of its coasts are far more indented and the interior is filled with mountains and forests.

There is considerable discrepancy between various authorities as to the date of this map. The B.M. lists it as 1690?, Wagner c. 1710, Muller 1740, Wheat while not mentioning this map in particular gives a date of 1653 for a Valk map, and the Library of Congress mention Valk in various atlases from 1695 to 1756. According to Nagler, Valk was born in 1626 and died in 1720. Waller states that he flourished 1670-1726. Wurzbach, that he produced maps in conjunction with Schenk from 1683.

69 **[1700]** Wells (E.) A New Map of North America Shewing its Principal Divisions Chief Cities, Townes, Rivers, Mountains etc. Delin M Burg. sculpt., Univ. Oxon. 49×36 cms.

Compiled for and dedicated to William Duke of Glocester. Intended as a school map, its detail is slight. California is shown in the Sanson form of island but with only two names, C. St. Lucas and " New Albion discovered by Sir Francis Drake Anno 1577."

Wa 466

Plate 53.

70 **1705** De Fer (N.) L'Amerique divisée selon l'etendue de ses principales parties et dont les points principaux sont placez sur les observations de Messieurs de l'Academie Royale des Sciences. Dressée Par N De Fer, Geographe de monseigneur le Dauphin. A Paris, Chez l'Autheur dans l'Isle du Palais sur le Quay de l'Horloge a la Sphere Royale 1705. 117×106 cms.

Large-scale map in 4 sheets each $58\frac{1}{2} \times 45$ cms. (excluding title printed above and text below the map).

Fine handsome map with numerous large vignettes; the Beavers in Canada and Cod Fishery in Newfoundland, later used by Herman Moll, and other vignettes of the inhabitants of Illinois, Louisiana, Virginia, Brasil, Chili, Peru, La Plata, Mexico and new Mexico, also of the Buccaneers.

California shown as an island after Sanson.

[1706-1728] AA (P. VANDER) the prolific publisher of Leiden bought or pirated other cartographers' work and issued many atlases and collections in large, medium and small size. With impartiality he issued maps of America showing California as an island, at other times as a peninsula. The following maps all show California as an island.

71 —— L'Amerique Selon les nouvelles Observations de Messrs de l'Academie des Sciences, etc. A Leide Chez Pierre vander Aa. 66½ × 47 cms.

Finely designed and engraved title cartouche by J. Baptist after J. Goeree.

California shown as an island on the second Sanson model.

Plate 54.

72 —— Nouvelle Carte de l'Amerique . . . Pierre vander Aa Marchand Libraire a Leide. 53 × 43 cms.

Charming titlepiece with figures of natives and traders. California as an island on the earlier Sanson model, but with the insertion " Nova Albion " in the North of the island.

Apart from being highly decorative it is of interest for an innovation " Village des Canots' inserted between P. de Carinde and P de la Conception.

Plate 55.

73 —— America of Nieuw-Ondekte Weereld tot de Beschryving van Joseph D'Acosta afgebakend. 29 × 21½ cms.

74 —— Amerika of de Nieuwe Weereld aller eerst door C Kolumbus ondekt. 28½ × 21½ cms.

Plate 56.

75 —— Noorder Deel van Amerika. 30 × 20 cms.

76 —— Zee-Togten door Thomas Candys na de West Indien. 23 × 15 cms.

77 —— F. Draakx Schip-Vaart door de Straat en Zuyd Zee. 22½ × 15 cms.

78 [1709] MOLL (H.) The Isle of California New Mexico Louisiane the River Misisipi (sic) and the Lakes of Canada. Herman Moll Fecit. 18½ × 16 cms.
California shown on second Sanson model. It appears in Herman Moll's Atlas Manuale: or New Sett of Mapps London 1709.

Wa 487   Wh 81 cites edition of 1701

79 [1710] HOMANN (J. B.) Totius Americae Septentrionalis et Meridionalis novissima repraesentio . . . Johannes Baptista Homann Norimbergae. 56½ × 48½ cms.

California as an island after the Sanson model but with the addition of the towns of S Isidoro, Gigante and N S de la Guadalupe inserted in the south of the island.

The large title cartouche is copied from De Fer's map of 1699 and the cartouche top left containing descriptive text is in part copied from the design used in De Lisle's map of Canada of 1703.

Plate 57.

80 **[1719]** CHATELAIN-GUEDEVILLE. Carte tres curieuse de la Mer du Sud, contenant des remarques nouvelles et tres utiles non seulement sur les ports et iles de cette mer . . . les Noms & la Route des Voyageurs . . . [Amsterdam 1732]. Large-scale map on 4 sheets of North and South America. One of the most decorative maps of North America of the 18th century, with numerous vignettes within rococo framework, beavers, cod fishery, customs of the Canadians & Mexicans, animals, sugarmill, turtle fishing, town plans, portraits etc.

In the North of the Island it is written " The Californias or Carolines that some moderns believe is attached to the Continent of America by its northern part." Some mountains are inserted in the south and south-east and a few new place names added.

Based partly on the De Fer map of 1700 it is of interest as showing some of the missions established in Southern California marking S. Jacques, S. Innocents, S. Etienne, S. Leon, Bonnenuit, S. Juan, S. Bruno and Gigante. It also marks the Bay of S. Simon & S. Jude.

It appeared in Atlas historique published in 7 volumes in Amsterdam by Chatelain with text by Guedeville 1705-1720, the above map being in volume 6 published in 1719 and was reissued in 1732.

81 **[1719]** SENEX (G.) A New Map of America from the latest Observations Revis'd by I. Senex. $55\frac{1}{2} \times 48$ cms.

Dedicated to the Earl of Berkshire, Deputy Earl Marshal of England.

California as an island after Sanson. Reissued 1721.

Wa 520

82 **(1720)** MOLL (H.) To the Right Honourable John Lord Sommers . . . This map of North America according to ye Newest and most Exact Observations is most humbly Dedicated by . . . Herman Moll Geographer. 97×58 cms.

California as an island on the Sanson shape but with one or two extra names, Mounts Nevada & St. Martin, P de Sardines, and 4 towns in the South, La Conception, St. Nicholas, St. Isidore and Gigante.

Wa 514   Wh 105

83 **1720** FER (N. DE). La Californie ou Nouvelle Caroline teatro de los Trabajos Apostolicos de la Compa. e Jesus en la America, Septe. Dressée sur celle que le Viceroy de la Nouvelle Espagne envoya il y a peu d'Années a Mrs de l'Academie des Sciences Par N. de Fer Geographe de sa Majeste Catolique. 66×45 cms.

A Paris dans l'Isle du Palais a la Sphere Royale 1720

This fine rare map is a reissue of de Fer's map of 1705 but on a larger scale and with some notable additions. In the tip of California, the Rio Madelena is now named and several settlements along the R. de S. Thomas discovered 1684,

S. Tiago, SS. Inocentes, S. Juan, S. Estavan, Los Reyes, la Thebayda, S. Domingo, S. Nicolas, S. Isidoro, S. Juan and S. Bruno.

In New Mexico the names given in the key in the map of 1705 are now engraved on the map.

The scale of miles is within a light cartouche decorated with birds, a sloth, and an armadillo, title and text contained within scroll with vignettes of natives.

Below the title is a lengthy engraved text giving the early history of California.

1533   Discovered by Fernand Cortez who landed Port de Notre Dame, 1535
1535   General Francois de Alarcon at his own expense.
1602   Returned at expense of Phillip III of Spain and landed opposite coast of California in 1608. Ordered to found colony at Monterey.
1615   Jean Eyturbie visited California twice.
1632-4 Capt Francois Ortegay three visits Capt Carbonelly shortly after.
1642   Governor de Cinalea called Cestin de Cana's to California with the P. Jacinte Cortez.
1644   Amiral Pierre Porter Casanaty landed Bay of St. Barnabas.
1648-9 Two further visits by Admiral Casanaty
1664   Admiral Don Bernard de Bernal de Pinandero.
1672   Second visit of Pinandero.
1668   Capt Francois Lucenilla
1681-5 Amiral Isidra de Atondo et Antillon fitted out 3 vessels at Cinaloa for Charles II of Spain and named the county New Carolina after his master.
1694   Capt Francois Ytamara.
1695   Discovery of Riviere du Coral.

Wa 517 Wh 102

Plate 58.

84 [1720] KEULEN (GERARD VAN). [Sea Chart of Pacific without title]. Tot Amsterdam by Gerard van Keulen Aan de Nieuwe Brig California as an island on the Sanson model.   60 × 50 cms.

T 593

85 [1720] SCHERER. America Borealis 1699.   35 × 22½ cms.

California as an island after the G. Sanson model. The interior shown as mountainous and wooded. Coastal names only, save in the south where three towns are marked, St. Jago, S. Bruno and N.S. de Guadeloupe.

86 ———— ———— Provinciae Borealis Americae non ita pridem detectae aut magis ab Europae is excultae.   35 × 23 cms.

The following towns shown in Southern California, S. Jacob, S. Delphin, S. Nicholas, S. Bruno and S. Maria de Quadlupe (sic).

In right-hand lower corner a vignette depicts a Frenchman, Spaniard and an Englishman holding small maps of their respective territories supported on one side by an Iroquois the other by a Huron.

Plate 59.

87 **[1720]** SCHERER. Religionis Catholicæ in America Boreali Disseminatae Representatio Geographica. 34×21½ cms.

California as an island with one name only, the town of S. Bruno, but the locations of 3 Missions in the south are indicated by Crosses. The large titlepiece shows representative figures of the four continents bowing before the crucifix.

88 ——— ——— Repraesentatio Americae Borealis cuius provinciae vera fide illuminatae umbram non Habent, reliquae umbris immersae sunt. 33×23½ cms.

California with two names only, S. Jago and S. Bruno. A large vignette bottom left shows Christ in a cornfield with six followers with sickles.

Plate 60.

89 ——— ——— Idea naturalis Americae Borealis digito dei formata Geographice proposita   An MDCC.

California as an island wooded and mountainous, but without names save for 3 Capes in the north.   Designed to show the fauna of America small vignettes of animals are scattered about the map.   The sea is full of fish and unnatural monsters, an unusual one being an octopus or cuttlefish. The title-piece depicts not only birds, leopard and cattle, but also a lion and a rhinoceros.

90 **[1725]** WEIGEL. Novi Orbis sive Totius Americae cum adiacentibus Insulis Nova exhibitio. 34½×27½ cms.

Small decorative map with California as an island, with mountain chains in the North.

91 **[c 1730]** SEUTTER (M.) Novus Orbis sive America Meridionalis et Septentrionalis . . . cura et opera Matth. Seutter . . . Aug. Vind. [Augsburg]. 57½×49½ cms.

California as an island based on the Sanson-Homann formula but with additions, several rivers are inserted on the west coast and two mountains in the north M. Neges and M.S Martin and C de Fortuna, C & R de Pins, C de S Martin, I Barbades, I de St. Nicholas, I Cenica, I de S. Augustin, C de la Trinite, Canots, P des Sardines, Seyo, P de S Martin but omits Pta de Monte Rey, B de las Virgines, Pta de Roqui and Pta de la Conversion.

The tracks of the early navigators are shown in the Pacific. Large title cartouche of natives and another cartouche round descriptive account.

M 1910 (317)

Plate 61.

92 **[1730]** OVERTON (HENRY). America [Dedicated to Queen Caroline reigned 1727-1737]. 96×57 cms.

Long folding map of North and South America with large figured dedication title with broad right hand border of 8 engravings " Representations of ye remarkable Customs of ye Natives of America " copied from De Bry and a larger engraving of the cod fishery, copied from Moll. On left hand side is a large circular inset of North Polar Regions and a copy of Moll's engraving of beavers building a dam.

California is shown as an island on the Briggs model with the same names rather carelessly applied. One name is added, P. S. Juan on S.E. tip of the island.

93 1740 BAKEWELL (T.) America a new and most exact Map laid down according to the observations communicated to the English Royall Society the French Royall Academy of Sciences and those made by the latest Travellers to this present year 1740 Printed and Sold by Tho Bakewell Next to the Horn Tavern in Fleet Street. 60 × 47 cms. (with borders 95 × 59½ cms.).

A rare map. With a large vignette " The Harbour Town and Fort of Porto Bello taken by Admiral Vernon Nov 22nd 1739 " and broad side borders including the Beaver and the Cod Fishery engraving after H. Moll, view of Potosi after Montanus and view of native customs based on De Bry. Also the River Town and Fort of Chagre. These side strips project below the map itself and the intervening space is filled in with engravings and notes of weapons " As this Part of the World is the present Seat of War, we have thought it may be agreeable to exhibit the Chief Instruments of War so as to give an Idea of them to those who are not therewith aquainted.'

California is shown as an island on the G. Sanson model.

Plate 62.

94 [1740] DE LETH (A. AND H.) Carte Nouvelle de la Mer du Sud . . . Donne au Public par And: & Henry de Leth, a Amsterdam sur le Pont de la Bourse au Pescheur. 92 × 58½ cms.

Long folding map covering an area greater than suggested in the title, from the west coast of Africa to the east coast of Asia, America occupying a central position with California prominent as an island.

Based in part on Chatelain's map of 1719 with decorative vignettes inspired from that map but slightly varied. California as in the Chatelain map except that owing to the closeness of a vignette of Havana, no coastal names are shown in Northern California above St. Simon & St. Jude.

95 [1740] SEUTTER (M.)—LOTTER. Nov. Orbis sive America Septentrionalis . . . cura et opera Matth. Seutter SCM Geogr Aug V. A C Seutter delin Tob. Conr. Lotter sculpsit. 26 × 19½ cms.

96 1741 OVERTON (Henry). A New & Correct Map of the Trading Part of the West Indies, including the Seat of War between Gr Britain and Spain; Likewise the British Empire in America with the French and Spanish Settlements adjacent thereto . . . 1741 Dedicated to Honble Edward Vernon Esqr. Vice Admiral . . . Printed for and Sold by Henry Overton at the White House without Newgate London. 99 × 55½ cms.

A rare and decorative map with side panels of 10 engraved views: Havana, Panama, Porto Rico, Cartagena, Porto Bello, Boston, New York, Mexico, Vera Cruz, Chagre.

California is shown as an island in the Sanson style with northern tip marked New Albion, and though it has fewer names some new ones are inserted, Mount Nevada, P de Sardines and in the south, the towns of S. Juan, S. Nicolas, S. Isidore and Giganti.

Plate 63.

97 [1745] SEALE (R. W.) A Map of North America with the European Settlements and whatever else is remarkable in ye West Indies R. W. Seale delin et sculp. 47 × 37½ cms.

California presented as an island with a mountainous chain down the centre with two named M. Nevada and Mt St Martin, and 6 towns marked, Canot, St Nicholas, St Juan, St. Isidore, Gigante, and Na Sa de la Guada.

Seale engraved maps for Tindal's Continuation of Rapin's History of England 1744-1747.

98 1745-[60] KITCHIN (T.) America Sold by T. Kitchin and Co at No 59 Holborn Hill London. 60 × 47 cms.

This map is a copy of the Bakewell map of 1740 with the engraving of the taking of Porto Bello by Admiral Vernon but without the broad side borders of views and bottom border of Instruments of War. I have only come across one copy of this map. It is a very late example of California as an island.

Plate 64.

99 [1754] BOWLES & SON (JOHN). A New and Exact Map of America laid Down from the latest observations & Discoveries. Printed for J Bowles & Son at the Black Horse in Cornhill. 96 × 56½ cms.

Large decorative and uncommon map. The decoration is curious, the title-piece being copied from De Lisle map of 1703. Immediately below this is a large vignette of beavers and below that of the cod fishery, both copied from Moll's map, and on either side is a broad panel each with 6 compartments containing engravings of the " Customs and manners of ye Natives of divers parts of America " based on De Bry. There is an inset map of the North Pole and smaller insets of harbours: New York, Boston, St. Johns, Charlestown, Port Royal, Havana, Acapulco, Cartagena, Porto Bello and Vera Cruz. John Bowles took his son into partnership with him in 1754 and changed his imprint to John Bowles & Son. California is shown as an island in the Sanson manner.

Plate 65.

100 1770 [VAUGONDY]. Carte de la Californie Suivant (I) Carte Manuscrit 1604, (II) Sanson 1656, (III) De Lisle 1700, (IV) Pere Kino 1705, (V) Soc. des Jesuites 1767.

Five representations of California on 1 sheet representing its delineation at various periods. Issued in Diderot, Encyclopedie Paris 1770. 37 × 39 cms.

CHAPTER FOUR

Smith's *Virginia* and its Derivatives

*A Carto-Bibliographical Study of the Diffusion of
Geographical Knowledge*

by Coolie Verner

INTRODUCTION

THE early printed map was the principal instrument for the spread of new geographical information and newer relationships that had been established among already known facts. The process through which this was achieved was simple. The discoverer of new information prepared a map which was then used by a cartographer as the basis for a change to an existing map plate or for the preparation of a new plate. This information would then be accepted by other publishers for their maps until it found its way into all maps in time. If the original explorer's map remained only in manuscript the diffusion process was much slower than if the original was printed and distributed. In some instances, early discoveries did not spread beyond the original manuscript and never actually entered the stream of knowledge.

Samuel Hearne explored the Coppermine River in 1771-1772 and submitted a map with his manuscript journal that was sent to the Hudson's Bay Company. The report was kept secret by the company so that the Coppermine River did not appear on a map until 1784 when it was included in the map of the Pacific prepared by Lt. Roberts for the official edition of Cook's third voyage. Curiously, it appears to have been ignored as the first state of the great Arrowsmith map published in 1795 does not show Hearne's explorations. The Hearne material was finally published in 1795 and was added to the Arrowsmith map on *State* 3 in 1802. The Arrowsmith map was the principal instrument for introducing the Coppermine River into the stream of knowledge; consequently, some thirty years elapsed between the discovery and the diffusion of the information.

The carto-bibliographical description and analysis of an important prototype map will often clarify the way in which geographical information is diffused in the map and chart trade. The study reported here shows something of the sequence through which the first delineation of the Chesapeake Bay became a part of geographical knowledge.

ACKNOWLEDGEMENTS

The plates have been made from originals in the possession of the following, to whom grateful acknowledgement is made for the permission to reproduce: British Museum (Plates 66, 70, & 75); Florida State University (Plate 67); Messrs. Francis Edwards Ltd. (Plates 68, 69, 73, 74, 76, 77, 78 & 79); the Mellon-Verner Collection (Plates 71, 72 & 79).

ORIGIN OF THE MAP

CAPTAIN JOHN SMITH accompanied the party that sailed from England to establish the first permanent English settlement in North America. After sailing into the Chesapeake Bay and up the James River, they landed at Jamestown, Virginia, in the spring of 1607. A set of instructions issued to the party in 1606 noted:

"You must observe, if you can, whether the river on which you plant doth spring out of mountains or out of lakes. If it be out of any lake, the passage to the other sea will be more easy, and is like enough, that out of the same lake you will find some sprint which runs the contrary way towards the East Indian Sea."

These directions illustrate the then prevalent belief that the western ocean was near at hand with only the open passage to it remaining to be discovered. This dream is illustrated in the Ferrar map of 1651 and it accounts for the sea-to-sea grants of the original colonial charters. The first explorations of the bay area tended to support the belief in a westward passage and Smith wrote Henry Hudson that there was a sea leading into the western ocean to the north of the Virginia Colony, which led Hudson to the discovery of the river which bears his name.

The exploration of the area began almost immediately after settling at Jamestown. In May 1607, Captain Newport led the first party of twenty-three men, including Smith, up the James River as far as the fall line. Later that same year in November and December, Smith explored the Chickahominy River, and on June 2, 1608, Smith, with a party of fourteen men, set out to explore the Chesapeake Bay returning to Jamestown on July 21st. During this period of seven weeks they explored and mapped the eastern shore of the bay and the Potomac River to its fall line. From July 24th to September 7th—six weeks this time— Smith, and a party of twelve men, went to the northern tip of the Chesapeake Bay and explored the Susquehanna, Patuxant, Rappahannock and Piankatank Rivers. During the winter of 1608-1609 further explorations were conducted which included the Pamunkey, Mattaponi and Nansemond Rivers.

Manuscript draughts of these explorations were sent to England periodically. Some of these are extant and illustrate the developing knowledge of the cartography of the area. The first draught is believed to be one sent by Robert Tindall to Prince Henry with a letter dated June 22, 1607, in which he writes: "May it therefore please your grace to accepte at the handes of your most humble and dutifull servante a dearnall of our voyage and draughte of our River, hear inclosed . . ."[1] This manuscript is lost.

The next manuscript is another draught by Tindall dated 1608 which is in the British Museum. It was sent to England with Captain Newport who arrived there May 21, 1608. On this manuscript Tindall shows the area of Hampton

---

[1] Alexander Brown, *The Genesis of the United States* (Boston, 1890), p. 109.

Roads from Cape Henry to some distance above Jamestown, and the York River to its origin. The James River is delineated more accurately than the York with shallow water indicated by stippling. Numerous Indian villages are shown along the river and Jamestown is indicated as on a peninsula. The delineation of the York River is less accurate as Tindall depicts two equal size streams coming together at the head of that river. The James and the York are named "King James his River" and "Prince Henneri his River". Cape Henneri and Cape Comfort are also named. Tindall has named two features after himself, one a shoal in the James River east of Jamestown which he calls "Tindalls Shouldes" and the other is on the north bank of the York River (probably at Gloucester) which he calls "Tendales fronte". This latter designation has survived on subsequent printed maps in various forms such as Tindall's fort or Tindall's Creek. The northeast end of the peninsula between the two rivers is depicted as a small bay with eight small islands in it. It is obvious from this manuscript that Tindall had no perception of the Chesapeake Bay as such at the time this chart was drawn.

The third draught was sent to England in 1608 via Captain Francis Nelson who left Virginia on June 2nd. This accompanied Smith's *True Relation . . .* and is known as the Zuniga chart as a copy of it was sent to the King of Spain by his ambassador to London of that name, and it survives in the archives at Simancas, Spain. This chart extends from below Cape Henry to the Potomac River. The relationship between Capes Henry and Charles is quite in error and not depicted as accurately as on Tindall's chart of 1608. The James is delineated much the same as on Tindall except that it extends farther west and its headspring in the mountains is indicated. The Chicohominy River is shown in greater detail and the York is properly delineated from its mouth to the junction of the two rivers which form it. The most curious feature of this chart is the manner in which the west shore of the Del-Mar-Va. peninsula is extended to form the north bank of the Potomac River so that the Chesapeake Bay as now known does not exist. This map was drawn before Smith had explored the bay or the Potomac.

The final extant chart is sometimes known as the *Simancas Map* because it was discovered by Alexander Brown in the archives there; or as the *Velasco Map* because the Spanish Ambassador to London of that name sent a copy of it to Spain in a letter dated March 22, 1611. In the letter Velasco noted: *"This King sent last year a surveyor to survey that Province, and he returned here about three months ago and presented to him King James a plan or map of all that he could discover, A copy of which I send Y.M."*[1] This map includes the east coast from Newfoundland to North Carolina and is a composite of numerous surveys.

On this map the four chief rivers are named: The Kings River, The Princes River, The Queens River, and Elizabeth River.

In the late fall of 1609, Captain John Smith returned to England, where he prepared a draught for his map. Some historians have argued against the

---

[1] Alexander Brown, *The Genesis of the United States* (Boston, 1890), p. 457.

possibility that this map is the work of Captain John Smith, but such a question of origin is academic since historical tradition assigns this map to Smith and there is insufficient evidence at present to resolve the issue either way. The principal arguments against Smith are presented by Alexander Brown[1] and elaborated by Worthington C. Ford.[2] The former is more emphatic in stating: ". . . I do not believe that Smith made the drawing himself". while Ford acknowledges that he is taking a ". . . journey into the realm of hypothesis . . ." and ". . . to advance the claim that Powell, a skilled surveyor, made the platform, or basis, of the Smith map and is entitled to the credit of it".

At the risk of doing them an injustice, their arguments can be summarized and commented upon briefly as follows:

1. The Smith map was engraved from a copy of the Virginia portion of the Velasco map of 1610-1611. Both Velasco and Smith are incorrect which ". . . furnishes quite conclusive proof that the latter was copied from the former". (Brown).

The most that should be said with assurance is that both the Velasco and Smith maps copied the same prototype. Actually, it would appear that the proper sequence places the Smith map before the Velasco. As noted elsewhere, Smith does not delineate the eastern shoreline of the Del-Mar-Va. peninsula but the Velasco map does. Smith had not himself explored that shore by the time of his return to England in 1609. It was not explored and mapped until Argall's voyage along that coast from June to August 1610. The Velasco map more nearly relates Cape Charles to the Delaware Bay correctly while the Smith map by its indefiniteness gave rise to innumerable distortions. Had Smith copied Velasco he surely would have included the eastern line of the peninsula and possibly the Delaware Bay too. Since he relied upon Indians for some of his information it is strange that he would ignore the reports and surveys of his own countrymen. The Velasco map was made early in 1611 by which time Smith may well have had his own map under way or even in print since it was known to be in print by Samuel Purchas when he was writing his *Pilgrimage* which was entered at Stationers' Hall in August 1612. Smith was in disfavour with the London Company at this moment and may never have seen the original Velasco chart, and had he done so he might have added the east coast line at some time when he made numerous other changes to the plate as noted below. It is equally improbable that Velasco copied Smith since it depicts Smith's Isle indefinitely and out of all proportion while Smith shows it as a small island specifically located. Furthermore, Velasco shows the end of the peninsula at Cape Charles as a smoothly rounded point while Smith depicts two protrusions at the point. There are numerous other

[1] Alexander Brown, "Queries: The Map of Virginia", *Magazine of American History* 8:576 (1882).
[2] Worthington C. Ford, "Captain John Smith's Map of Virginia 1612", *Geographical Review* 14:433-443 (1924-5).

delineational differences between the two that would tend to deny that there is as close a relationship between them as Brown assigns.

2.   Distances given in the text of his work do not always correspond with the distance in the map.   (Brown).

Presumably Smith made the rough draught of his map at the time of surveying and exploring the area, in which case his distances would be accurately recorded on the spot.   His description was written some years later and his memory of time and distance would be less exact, which could account for the differences between the work and the map.

3.   There is no real evidence that Smith could draw a map.   (Brown, Ford). As evidence to support this statement Brown cites a sketch of the Roanoke Island area which he ascribes to Smith.   This has since been found to be a rough sketch made by John White in 1585 of the North Carolina coast.[1]

4.   There is no manuscript of the area signed by Smith equivalent to that by Tindall.   (Brown).

Certainly this statement is true so far as present evidence reveals; however, Brown reproduces the Zuniga manuscript—the original for which was sent to England to accompany Smith's *True Relation*.   The original may have been signed and this part omitted by the copyist.   Furthermore, Henry Hudson acknowledges a map from Smith which was probably a copy of the Zuniga chart.   Any manuscript for Smith's map of the Chesapeake Bay would probably be destroyed in the process of engraving.

5.   Smith is not cited by contemporary writers as having actually made the map.   (Ford).

In citing Laet, as he does for evidence of this statement, Ford is using as a point of reference a work published over a decade after the map was in print. Plagiarism was quite common in the 17th century so it is not unusual to find authors failing to credit their sources.   Ford overlooks the reference by Purchas in 1612 which does acknowledge ". . . his mappe. . . " which would appear to be more creditable positive and contemporary evidence of Smith's work than the negative evidence from Laet a decade later.

6.   A tract first published in 1641 and republished in 1648 refers to Captain Smith's book and Captain Powell's map.   Since the only published map of Virginia was Smith's such a reference must indicate that Powell made the map. (Brown).   This point is based on an ambiguous reference which Ford cited in more detail.

---

[1] William P. Cumming, *The Southeast in Early Maps*, (Chapel Hill, 1962).

A tract by Robert Evelyn published in 1641 contains the statement: "But going to *Delaware Bay*, by Cape May, which is 24 miles at most and is as I understand very well set out, and printed in Captain *Powels* Map of *New England*, done as is told me by a draught I gave to M. Daniel the plot-maker, which Sir Edmund Plowden saith you have at home . . ." This tract is reprinted in a book published in 1648 where an additional comment notes: "Which is further witnessed by Captain *Smith* and other books of *Virginia* and by *New Englands* Prospect, new *Canaan*, Captain *Powels* Map, and other descriptions of *New England* and *Virginia*". The validity of this circumstantial evidence is hardly comparable to that offered by Purchas when he credits the map to Smith specifically. It is quite possible that Powell did make a map of the area and it is not inconceivable that it was printed but is now lost, or even that it served as the original source for the Baltimore map of 1635. This latter map is sufficiently unlike Smith to suggest a separate and distinct draft but enough like it to suggest certain similarity in the initial survey.

This digest of Brown and Ford does not do justice to their interesting but uncertain arguments; however, it does summarize their main points. The evidence is inconclusive either that Smith did or did not make this first map of the Chesapeake Bay. The fact that the map is credited to him by Purchas at the time it was published; that it appeared with a pamphlet which he authored; that it bears only his name on the plate; and that it was used by Smith in later works associated with his name would seem to tip the balance in favour of continuing the tradition now firmly established that Smith made the first map of the bay.

Smith appears to have draughted his map to illustrate a pamphlet which he wrote. This pamphlet was printed in 1612 by Joseph Barnes at Oxford University on a small hand press given to the University by the Earl of Leicester in 1585. The map itself appears to have been in print before the pamphlet which it illustrates. Purchas' *Pilgrimage* dated 1613 but entered in Stationers Hall August 7, 1612, notes: ". . . Captain John Smith, partly by word of mouth, partly by his Mappe there of in print, and more fully by a manuscript which hee courteously communicated to mee . . ." and : "Captaine Smith's Mappe may somewhat satisfie the desirous, and his books when it shall be printed, further". This, a small quarto pamphlet *A Map of Virginia . . .*, was intended to supplement and explain the map and the country it depicts. On page ten Smith notes with respect to the Indians: "Their several habitations are more plainly described by this annexed mappe, which will present to the eye the way of the mountains and current of the rivers, with their several turnings, bays, shoules, isles, inlets and creeks, the breadth of the waters, the distances of the places and such like".

After its use with this pamphlet, the map was not used again until Smith published his *History . . .* in 1624 and thereafter. This subsequent use of the map is discussed more fully below.

The plate for the map was engraved by William Hole who was at work in London from about 1607 to his death around 1624. He engaged in all types of engraving on copper including title pages as well as maps. He is particularly noted as the first in England to engrave music on copper in, among other works, Byrd's *Parthenia*. He also engraved Martin Billingsley's *Pens Excellencie* in 1618 which Hind describes as "... the most important as well as one of the earliest, of English engraved copy-books". Among engravers of the period Hole has a distinct place apart. Hind describes his work as "... more congenially allied to the French ..." rather than to the Dutch and Flemish engravers who were exerting a strong influence on others working in England at the time.[1]

The printed map is distinguished by two illustrations that were frequently copied on later versions of the map. Along the right border is a large figure of an Indian holding a bow in his right hand with a pig slung at his hip. This figure is most certainly copied from PLATE 3 of the De Bry engravings which was after White's drawing of "Weroan or great Lorde of Virginia". The Smith illustration follows the engraving rather than the original drawing for De Bry has the bow in the right hand rather than the left as does White. The left hand is holding an arrow on De Bry not included by White and a "bracer" on the right wrist which White placed on the left. While the Smith figure follows De Bry with respect to the bow, arrow and bracer, it adds details not on either. The suspended tail of the animal skin loincloth has been omitted; the necklace is rope rather than beads; the upper part of the body is partially covered by animal skin rather than naked; an animal head hangs from the right hip with arrows in a quiver showing beyond the left hip; and the left arm is extended to hold a club resting on the ground rather than placed on the hip as it is in both White and De Bry. McCary[2] notes that this figure is designed to correspond with the description of the Indian which Smith gives in the pamphlet: "The picture of the greatest of them is signified in the mappe . . . his haire, to one side was long, the other shore close with a ridge over his crown like a cocks combe. His arrows were five quarters of a yard long, headed with flints or splinters of stones, in forme like a heart, an inch broad, an inch and a halfe or more long. These he wore in a wolves skinne at his back for a quiver, his bow in one hand and his clubbe in the other . . ."

The second illustration is in the upper left corner of the map. This depicts an Indian hut which is described as the residence of Powhatan. The prototype of this drawing is not clearly discernible as it is not similar to any of the surviving White drawings or the De Bry engravings. This illustration has certain features similar to De Bry's PLATE 22 "The Tomb of the Weroans" with respect to the background which shows the internal construction of the hut but the figures in the Smith picture are unlike any in De Bry. In all probability this is a composite drawing formed from specific bits and pieces of numerous De Bry pictures.

[1] Arthur M. Hind, *Engraving in England . . . Part II*, (Cambridge, 1955).
[2] Ben C. McCary, *John Smith's Map of Virginia with A Brief Account of Its History*. (Williamsburg, 1957).

GEOGRAPHICAL CONTENT

PRIOR to the settlement at Jamestown the Chesapeake Bay had been depicted by a vague and indefinite indentation on the coast. On Spanish maps and their derivatives this bay was usually designated "B. de St Marie" without any accurate suggestion of its shape or size. The White and De Bry maps depicted it as a somewhat rectangular shape north of the main area which they described. The information they had about the bay was obviously from the Indians and, interestingly enough, showed four major rivers and some lesser ones emptying into it. The De Bry map is the first to attach the name Chesopioc Sinus to the Bay.

In his delineation of the bay, Captain John Smith achieved a factual and amazingly accurate representation of its shape, proportions and orientation. This map, therefore, is the *basic prototype* map of the Chesapeake Bay. In addition to providing the first accurate representation of the bay area, Smith also introduced some distinctive characteristics that were perpetuated and often accentuated on derivative maps. The most conspicuous of these include the overall shape and alignment of the bay, the Del-Mar-Va. Peninsula, the James-York Peninsula, and the Potomac River.

In presenting the Chesapeake Bay Smith drew it on a rather straight line from north to south with a slight angle from southeast to northwest. In the bay toward the north end are a number of large islands and the adjacent shore line is indefinitely drawn to indicate his lack of exploration of that section. The single most conspicuous characteristic of the Smith delineation of the bay is the pronounced turn to the east at the head of the bay. Each of these characteristics of the bay as a whole are perpetuated on the derivatives with varying degrees of deviation. Some maps, like the Visscher, accentuate the slant to the west; while others shorten or lengthen it disproportionately or alter the straight north-south line.

The distinctive shape of the Del-Mar-Va. Peninsula as presented on many derivative maps is due as much to what Smith did not draw as to what he did. He apparently did not explore and map any of the eastern or Atlantic side of this peninsula and stopped his delineation of it at Cape Charles. Hole, in engraving the plate, represented this unknown territory by a vague stippled area leading off indistinctly in a general northeasterly direction which suggested a gradual widening of the peninsula. Subsequent maps made this widening of the peninsula a permanent feature as they joined Cape Charles to the Delaware Bay. A subsidiary characteristic of this peninsula is the shape of the southern tip which Smith depicts with two points that become increasingly exaggerated on many derivative maps.

The peninsula between the James and York Rivers is presented by Smith with two distinctive characteristics: the breadth of the peninsula at the end (i.e., north to south) is greater than in reality, and the northeast end of the peninsula has a large semicircular bay containing five fairly large islands (Gosnold's Bay).   This latter representation is found also on the Tindall and Zuniga charts and implied on the Velasco manuscript.   The former two of these three charts contain a westward hook at Point Comfort which is not on Smith.

In his delineation of the Potomac River Smith introduced a decided pattern similar to a large Z.   From the mouth, the river has a northwest course then turns northeast and finally northwest again.   This is found only on the Velasco chart as none of the earlier manuscripts had included a representation of the Potomac based on actual surveys.

Some of the names Smith attached to geographical features have survived while others have been abandoned or replaced.   Smith himself claims credit for naming Capes Henry and Charles after the 'princes of the day': George Percey in his *Discourse* also mentions the naming of Cape Henry but he neither assumes credit nor assigns it to anyone else.[1]   He does, however, relate substantially the same story as Smith with respect to the naming of Point Comfort as it, in Smith's words, ". . . gave great comfort to his men upon landing at Cape Henry to know there was land accross the way".   Smith named the four major rivers Powhatan (James), Pamunk (York), Tappahonock (Rappahannock) and Patowmec and of these, only the last name has survived.   Other features were assigned the names of members of Smith's surveying party such as *Fetherstone's Baye* after Master Richard Fetherstone who died on the second expedition in August, 1608.   Many names of this sort were not on the original plate and may have been added later by Smith or the printer to favour or honour those after whom features were named.

There are black crosses at various points on the map which Smith explains: ". . . as far as you see the little Crosses on rivers, mountains, or other places, have been discovered the rest was had by information of the savages and are set down according to their instructions".

Last, but by no means least, is the information which Smith provides on his map about the location of Indian Tribes.   Major Jed Hotchkiss, in a letter dated October 5, 1883, published in Arber,[2] notes: "I am sorry to say that about the only information we have concerning the location of Indian Tribes at the time of the settlement of Virginia is to be found on Smith's map".   He remarks further that the map is ". . . a marvel of results in representation of outline compared with the time occupied in procuring information.   Smith had all the important features of our wonderfully developed coast well shown".

---

[1] Alexander Brown, *The Genesis of the United States*, (Boston, 1890), p. 158.

[2] Edward Arber and A. C. Bradley, *Travels and Works of Captain John Smith.* (Edinburgh, 1910)

TOPONOMY

Since it is the first printed map of the Chesapeake Bay, the Smith map is the first to assign names to topographical features. The original map which can be observed in impressions of *State* 1 of the plate assigns thirty-two English names to features and seventeen names to rivers. Later states of the plate contain an additional thirteen names. Only very few of these original names have survived to identify the features named. The map also identifies and names ten Indian tribes and some 166 Indian villages.

The names on the Smith map are transcribed below. In making this transcription the map was enlarged to a size five times that of the original but some of the engraved letters were still difficult to decipher so that error may exist. Those which are most doubtful are indicated by a question mark.

In the list which follows the names are arranged according to geographical area with the rivers acting as boundaries for the areas. The names of Indian tribes are provided first followed by the names of the rivers with the modern equivalent name provided. These are listed in a clockwise direction, beginning with the James River (Powhatan).

Names of Indian Tribes
Powhatan—for the nation or confederation in Virginia
Mangoags—South of the James
Chawons—South of the James
Monocans—Southwest
Mannahoaks—West
Massawomecks—Northwest
Sasquesahanough—North
Atquanachukes—Northeast
Tockwoghs—Eastern Shore
Kuskarawacks—Eastern Shore

Names of Rivers
Powhatan flu—James
    Chickahamama flu—Chickahominy
Pamaunk flu—York
    Youghtanund flu—Pamunkey
    Mattapament flu—Mattaponi
Tappahanock flu—Rappahannock
    Payankatank flu—Piankatank
Patawomeck flu—Potomac
    Quiyough flu—either Occoquan or Potomac Creek
Pawtuxunt flu—Patuxent

145

Bolus flu—either the Severn or the Patapsco
Willowbyes flu—either the Gunpowder or the Bush
Sasqusahanough flu—Susquehanna
Tockwogh flu—Sassafras
Rapahanock flu—Wye East River
Kus flu—probably the Choptank
Wighco flu—Pocomoke

Names between Powhatan flu and Pamaunk flu

Indian		
Kecoughtan	Moysonee	Orapaks
Kiskiack	Mamanahunt	Powhatan
Mattapanient	Potaucat	Monasukapanough
Ozenick	Attamtuck	Paspanegh
Matehut	Wean-ock	
Werawahon	Paspanegh	*English*
Askakep	Righkahauk	Poynt Comfort
Acconoc	Pammcoroy (?)	Poynt Hope
Memascestc (?)	Nechanicok	Gosnolds Baye
	Appecant	Ceader Ile
		James town

Names between Pamaunk flu and Payankatank flu

Indian		
Capahowasick	Cinquateck	Passawikack
Cantaunkack	Menampucun	Cattachiptico
Werowocomoco	Vttamussak	
Mattacock	Kupkicock	*English*
Poruptanck	Accosswinck	Poynt Warde
Pasaughtacock	Matchutt	Wiffins Poynt
Mamanassy	Quackcohowan (?)	Tindals Poynt
	Myghtuckpassu	

Names between Payankatank flu and Toppahanock flu

Indian		
Paranka-tank	Muttanmussinsack	Checkaconia
Opisco-pank	Anaskenoans	Stegara
Anrcuapeugh	Martoughquaimk	
Nandtanghtacund	Secobeck	*English*
Checonissowo	Accoqueck	Stingra Ile
	Uteustank	

Names between Toppahanock flu and Patawomeck flu

Indian		
Cinquack	Noraughtacun	Wingeck (?)
Wighcocomoco	Oquornock	Vttamussamacoma (?)
Cuttatawomen	Pawcomonet	Ouawmament
Chesakawon	Auhonesk	Acquack
Ottuachugh	Menaskunt	Cawwontell (?)
Kapawnich	Povektaunk	Passacoack
Nepawtacum	Toppahanock	Matchipick
Pawcocome (?)	Nawnautaugh (?)	Wecuppom
Cekakawwon	Poykemkack	Mangoraca
	Tinoicquack (?)	Nawacaten

146

Pissaseck
Kerahacak
Papiscone
Assaweska
Monanask
Waconiask
Cuttatawomen

Sockobeck
Massawoteck
Mahaskahod
Hassiuga
Tanxintania
Quiycugh
Patawomeck

Mattacunt
Ozaiawomen (?)
Ouawmament

Added Later
Boolers Bush
Fetherstones Baye
Sparkes Vaylley

Names between Quiyough flu and Patawomeck flu

Indian
Pamacocack
Tauxenent
Namassingakent
Assaomeck

Namoraughquend

Added later
Democrites Tree
Burtons Mount

Names between Patawomeck flu and Bolus flu

Indian
Opament
Quomocac
Pawtusiint (?)
Onacack (?)
Wascocup (?)
Tauskus
Wepanawomen
Quactataugh
Monanauk
Acquintanacsuck
Cecomocomoco

Petapaco
Nushemouck
Mataughqument (?)
Nussamek
Pamacocack
Cinquaeteck
Moyaons (?)
Tessamatuck
Wosameus
Nacotchganck
Mattpament

Quotough
Pocatamaough
Macocunaco
Wasapokent
Aquaskack

English
Richard Cliffes

Added later
Sparkes Poynt
Tauerners Roade

Names between Bolus flu and Sasquasahanough flu

Indian
Attaock
Utchowig
Cepowig

English
Smyths Falls

Powels Iles
Smals Poynt

Added later
Blands C
Downes Dale

Names between Sasquasahanough flu and Cape Charles

Indian
Accowmack
Accohanock
Wighcocomoco
Nause
Nantaquack
Kuskawawack
Ozines
Chickahokin
Macocks
Atquanachuke

Sasquesahanough
Quadroque
Tesinigh

English
Cape Charles
Smyths Iles
Cage harbour
Keales hill
Reades Poynt
Watkin's poynt
Momfords poynt

Borhes poynt
Poynt Pesinge
Peregryns mount
Russels Iles
Limbo
Sandersos Poynt

Added later
Washeborne C
Winstons Iles
Brookes Forest
Gunters Harbour

PLATE 66	1612
Title	VIRGINIA
Imprint	*Difcovered and Difcribed by Captayn John Smith / Grauen by William Hole /* The imprint appears within the secondary cartouche containing the scale in the bottom centre of the map.
Engraver	*Grauen by William Hole.* The plate is signed in the imprint. Plate 66.
Source	Smith, John. *A Map of Virginia . . .* At Oxford, Printed by Joseph Barnes, 1612.
Copy Examined	ICN
Copies	BM; CSmH; MH; MdBJ-G; MiU-C; MWiW-C; N; NN; NjP; RPJCB; ViU The locations of copies are those holding the volume
Size	*Plate* NS 41.4 EW 32.9 *Map* NS 40.6 EW 32.2
Orientation	West
Latitude	37-41
Longitude	310-307 (Added in a later state)
Scale	*Scale of Leagues / and halfe / Leagues* 15=6.8 cm R.F. 1:1,280,000 The scale is located in a separate cartouche in the centre of the map along the bottom border. This houses the scale, the imprint, and the name of the engraver. The scale bar is surmounted by a pair of dividers through which runs a double banner containing the wording of the scale. Beneath the scale is a horizontal rectangle 6.6 by 1 cm. containing the imprint and engraver. This is framed in simple strapwork.
Cartouche	The title is contained on a banner or ribbon cartouche along the top border of the plate extending to the right from the centre. This banner is furled at the left and extending to split ends on the right. The portion containing the title measures 14.0 cm. by 2.2 cm. from the roll to the split.
Border	Incomplete geographical functional on the bottom (east) only with the degree figures outside the border (i.e. no final neat line). The other borders are made of three parallel lines with a greater space between the second and third than between the first and second. The condition of the border is altered in later states. (See Carto-bibliographical note below).
References	Baer 1; Church 359; JCB II, I, 88; Sabin 82832; EBM p. 333; Swem 15; Hind p. 339; Verner, *Va. Mag.* p. 10; Clark I: 149.
Reproductions	The Smith map is one of the most frequently reproduced maps of Virginia. Various reproductions are noted in the Carto-bibliographical Note below for the different states of the plate.
Description	This map is a beautiful example of the engraver's art. The geographical features are clearly drawn yet the illustrative features tend to overpower the geographical representation although they are so placed that they do not

obscure the content of the map itself. At the top centre is the large decorative banner cartouche containing the single word title. Immediately below this to the right of centre is a replica of the Royal Arms surmounted by a crown and circled by the Garter. This measures 8.0 by 4.1 cm. In the upper left corner is an illustration showing Powhatan inside his hut. This measures about 7.8 by 10.0 cm. It depicts the chief and two others on a bench at the end above two double rows of natives beside a fire built in the centre of the hut. Below this picture is the legend: *POWHATAN | Held this state & fashion when Capt. Smith | was delivered to him prisoner. |* In a later state the date 1607 is added on a third line.

Along the right side of the map above centre is a large standing figure of an Indian approximately 13.0 cm. long. At the feet of this figure is the note: *The Sasques=ahanougs | are a Gyant like peo-ple & | thus a-tired |.* In the upper right corner immediately above the figure is a legend: *Signification of these markes, | To the crosses hath bin discouered | what beyond is by relation* (cross) *| Kings houses* (rule-figure of a house) *| Ordinary howses* (rule-period enclosed in a small circle).

A large compass rose is in the bottom left corner. This is about 5.0 cm. in diameter and has thirty-two points with rhumb lines radiating over the water areas. To the right and below this rose is a ship with sails furled. A small boat such as Smith might have used for his exploration is depicted in the upper end of the bay.

On the bottom border slightly to right of centre is the scale cartouche. This is a very decorative example of strap-work design.

The lettering is quite decorative while at the same time consistent in style and clarity. The major words are in large Roman capitals; the names of Indian tribes in upper case italic; the names of villages and geographical features in regular italic; and the principal features in Roman. The major water areas are stippled. Shallow water is indicated by fine lines overlaid on the stippling creating a hatched effect. Mountains are carefully drawn and trees are depicted by different styles of representation to suggest differing species. On the Atlantic Coast north of Cape Charles a black cross indicates the extent of Smith's exploration of the coastline. Beyond this point the coast is not drawn by line, however, the stippling of the ocean area stops abruptly and suggests a delineation of the coast. With this technique the Delaware Bay is also suggested as is another body of water north of that and a lake in the northwest section.

In a later state of the map a small replica of Smith's arms is added to the right of the scale cartouche.

CARTO-BIBLIOGRAPHY

One of the principal tasks encountered in the detailed carto-bibliographical analysis of early printed maps is that of identifying the changes which may have been made to the plate during the time it was in use. In addition, there is the problem of determining the use which was made of each state identified. This problem is particularly complex when reviewing the Smith map and its derivatives.

The publishing sequence of Smith's map has plagued scholars for a century. In 1854, *Norton's Literary Gazette*[1] published an identification of two states of the plate which was followed by Charles Deane's identification of four states in another issue.[2] In 1907, the Church catalogue contained Cole's identification of eight states,[3] Eames,[4] in 1927, listed ten states which were re-examined and extended to eleven by Verner in 1950.[5] In 1955, Hind[6] re-examined the Verner list and settled on nine states. The present re-study of the map isolates twelve distinct states. Although this study does not alter the sequence originally identified by Eames, it does add two additional states at the end. This necessitates a re-examination of all copies heretofore identified as Eames (i.e., Sabin) State 10.

The relationship among these seven studies of this map is identified in the following table. The column on the left contains the plate changes with the state notation of each as recorded in the seven studies.

	Norton's March 1854	Deane May 1854	Church 1907	Eames 1927	Eames-Verner 1950	Hind 1955	Verner 1961
Proof	–	–	–	–	–	–	A
Original Plate ..	–	1	1	1	1	1	1
1606, 1607	–	2	2	2	2	2	2
Smith's Arms ..	1	–		3	3	3	3
Motto	2	–		4	4	4	4
Lat. & Long. ..	–					–	
Taverners Roade ..	–		3			–	
Winstons Isle ..	–	3		5	5	–	5
Brookes forest ..	–					–	
Gunters Harbour ..	–					–	

[1] "Curiosities of American Literature . . . Smith's General History . . ." *Norton's Literary Gazette* NS 1:134-135, 218 (March, 1854)

[2] *Ibid.*, pp. 218-219 (May, 1854)

[3] G. W. Cole, *A Catalogue of Books . . . Library of E. D. Church* (New York, 1907), item 359

[4] Wilberforce Eames, *A Bibliography of Captain John Smith* (New York, 1927) Also Sabin 82823

[5] Coolie Verner, "The First Maps of Virginia, 1590-1673" *Virginia Magazine* 58: 3-15 (January 1950)

[6] Hind, *op. cit.*, p. 340.

	Norton's March 1854	Deane May 1854	Church 1907	Eames 1927	Eames-Verner 1950	Hind 1955	Verner 1961
Sparkes content ..	−					5	
Democrites tree ..	−		4	6	6	−	6
Burtons mount ..	−					−	
1692-1693	−	−	5	7	7	8	7
Sparkes vaylley ..	−					7	
Page 41 / Smith ..	2		6	8	8		8
Sparkes Poynt ..	−	−				−	
Fetherstones Baye..	−					−	
Bollers Bush ..	−	4				−	
Blands C;	−					−	
Downes Dale ..	−		7	9	9	−	9
Washborne C. ..	.−	−				−	
Boolers Bush ..	−					−	
1690 & 1691 ..	2	3	8	10	10	9	10
Indian Hair ..	−	−	−	−	−	−	11
Crack	−	−	−	10a	11	(9)	12

THE STATES OF PLATE 66

In preparing the following delineation of states a minimum of two copies of each state was studied with a total of sixty copies of the map examined. This re-study has resulted in the identification of a hypothetical preliminary proof copy of the plate, the verification of the original ten states determined by Eames, and two supplemental states—one of which Eames noted but had not examined and an additional state not heretofore recorded.

Proof State A

The existence of this state has not been verified by the examination of a copy, therefore it is listed here as a preliminary state preceding those identified by the examination of specific copies. The possible existence of this state is assumed from evidence on later impressions.

The left arm of the large standing Indian figure along the right border of the map is draped with an animal skin which terminates in a claw lying at the elbow. In this preliminary state the claw was engraved so as to stand apart from the arm but this was later removed and the claw engraved to lie against the inner side of the elbow. The ghost print of this prior form of the claw is clearly visible on most subsequent impressions.

This proof state is not identified by any previous study.

State 1

This state of the plate is readily identified by the absence of dates, of longitude figures, and of Smith's Arms in the lower right corner.

The plate is bordered by three parallel lines with the centre line closer to the inner line. The east or bottom border has been segmented for latitude with the inner space divided into twelve segments and the outer space into four. The latitude figures reading from 37 to 41 are engraved outside the final border line.

Copy Described	BM (G7121) *A True Relation*—1608
	CSmH (18537) *History . . . 1624*
Copies Reported	MiU-C *A Map . . . 1612*
	NN (2) *A Map . . . 1612*
	MH *A Map . . . 1612*
	ICN *A Map . . . 1612*
	NjP Strachey manuscript 1612 (coloured)
	BM Separate (Maps C.7.c.18.)
Reproduction	A coloured reproduction of the NjP copy is published in Sotheby's *Catalogue of Exceedingly Rare and Valuable Americana*, London, 1928, pp. 68-69; and by Rand McNally & Co., as its 1961 Christmas card. See also:

	Brown, A.	*Genesis . . .* Vol. 2, p. 596
	Winsor, J.	*Narrative . . .* Vol. 3, p, 167
	Mathews,	*Maps . . .* Vol. 2, Plate LIII
	Hind,	*Engraving . . .* Plate 209

Note	Hind assigns this state to *A True Relation . . .* 1608. This is in error as the map could not have been issued originally with that volume although it may have been added later to late gathered copies.
	The *True Relation . . .* was entered in Stationers Hall on August 13, 1608. The original manuscript had been brought from Virginia by Captain Nelson commanding the *Phoenix* which left Virginia in June and arrived in London in July 1608. The book does not mention the existence or presence of a map. Since the map includes information that was collected by Smith during his three-month exploration of the Chesapeake Bay, from which he returned to Jamestown on September 7, 1608, it could not have been in London in time to be included with the *Relation . . .*
	This is identified as *State* 1 by Deane, Church, Eames, Eames-Verner, and Hind.

State 2

The changes to the plate introduced in this state are bibliographical. The date 1606 has been added to the imprint in the scale cartouche and the date 1607 has been added as a third line to the legend beneath the picture of Powhatan in the upper left corner.

At this state an accidental change occurs which appears on all later impressions. The plate is scratched in the curve formed by the elaborate engraved ending to the letter S in the lower right corner.

Copy Described	CSmH (19883) *A Map . . . 1612*
	MdBJG *A Map . . . 1612*
Copy Reported	MH—*Purchas*, 1625
Reproduction	*The World Encompassed*, Plate LIII

Note	Hind says: "Probably belonged . . . to *A True Relation*, 1608, and later in *A Map of Virginia* . . ." (See note under *State* 1)
	This state is identified by Eames, Eames-Verner, and Hind. Deane and Church combine this with *State* 3.

State 3

The change is bibliographical with the addition of Smith's arms without the motto in the lower right corner. In adding the arms some of the stippling and one tree have been removed. After cutting the arms the stippling was replaced so that it now covers a somewhat larger area and is of coarser grain.

Copy Described	CSmH (17934) *A Map* . . . 1612
	BM (679.h.14) *Purchas* . . . 1625
	NjP (Ex 1230,862.5) *A Map* . . . 1612
	NjP (Kane, copy 1) *History* . . . 1624
Copy Reported	NN *History* . . . 1624; *History* . . . 1627
	NNP *A Map* . . . 1612
Note	This state is identified by Eames, Eames-Verner, and Hind. It is combined with *State* 2 by Deane and Church.

State 4

Changes introduced in this state are both geographical and bibliographical.

Bibliographical	The motto has been added underneath Smith's arms without removing the stippling.
Geographical	Longitude has been added. The north (right) and south (left) borders have been segmented and longitude figures have been added outside the final line of the border. On the south these figures read from 310 to 307, while on the north they read from 311 to 307.
	The west (top) border has been segmented and latitude figures added outside the final line. In adding these figures which read from 37 to 41, the figure for 40 degrees has been reversed.
Copy Described	MWiC-C *A Map* . . . 1612
	NNP *History* . . . 1624
Note	For a second MWiW-C copy usually reported as State 4, see the note under *State* 11. This state is included in the identification of *State* 3 by Church and Deane. It is identified as *State* 4 by Eames and Eames-Verner. Hind's *State* 4 identified only the motto but not the border changes.

State 5

All of the changes introduced in this state are geographical. The following names have been added:

> *Gunters Harbour*—at the casternmost tip of the northern end of the Chesapeake Bay.
>
> *Taverners roade*—just above the word BAY in the centre of the map.
>
> *Winstone Iles*—immediately below the large islands in the centre of the Chesapeake Bay.
>
> *Brookes Forest*—immediately below the preceding name.

Copy Described	CSmH (1947)	*History* . . . 1624
	NjP (Kane, copy 3)	*History* . . . 1624
Copies Reported	NjP (Kane)	*History* . . . 1626
	CSmH (69259)	*A Map* . . . 1612
	(69269)	*History* . . . 1624
	NN (James I)	*History* . . . 1624
Note	This state is identified by Eames, and Eames-Verner. It is not listed by Hind and it is included in the *State* 3 identified by Deane and Church.	

State 6

The changes in this state are again solely geographical with the addition of the following three new names:

> *Sparkes / content*—at the centre of the map to the left of the large Royal Arms.
>
> *Democrites / tree*—to the left and slightly below the large Royal Arms.
>
> *Burtons Mount*—immediately below the preceding name.

Copy Described	CSmH (3341)	*Purchas* . . . 1625
	NjP (Kane-Huth copy)	*History* . . . 1624
Copies Reported	MH	*History* . . . 1624
	MiU-C	*History* . . . 1624
Reproduction	The facsimile reproduction issued by the Library of Congress is of this state, and is, without question, the finest reproduction that has been made of this map to date.	
Note	This state has been identified by Eames and Eames-Verner. It is partially identified by Hind as *State* 5. It is listed as *State* 4 by Church and included in *State* 3 by Deane.	

State 7

The Purchas page numbers 1692 and 1693 have been added in the upper left and right corners.

Copy Described	NjP (Kane copy)	*Purchas . . .* 1625
Copies Reported	PPL	*Purchas . . .* 1625
	NhD	*Purchas . . .* 1625
	MH	*Purchas . . .* 1625
Reproduction	Fite and Freeman, p. 116.	
Note	This state is identified by Eames and Eames-Verner. It is *State* 8 of Hind and *State* 5 of Church. It is included in his *State* 3 by Deane.	

State 8

Many extensive changes have been introduced on the plate in this state. These are both geographical and bibliographical.

Geographical	Three new names have been added:
	Featherstones / Baye—below and to the left of Sparkes Vaylley.
	Bollers bush—immediately below the preceding name.
	Sparkes Poynt—on the peninsula formed by the junction of the Potomac River with the Chesapeake Bay. (The present St. Mary's Point).
Bibliographical	*Page 41 / Smith* has been added in the lower right corner.
	Sparkes / Content added in State 6 has been altered to *Sparkes / Vaylley.* Numerous mountains on the right half of the map have been re-engraved so that the shading on the north side is now formed by closely parallel diagonal lines rather than finely sculptured shading as found in earlier states. Some of the trees in the cluster immediately above Smith's arms have been re-engraved with heavy shading on the north side.
	The scale cartouche has been re-engraved in spots particularly around the scale bar and the frame immediately adjacent to it.

Copy Described	CSmH (99578)	*History . . .* 1627
Copies Reported	ICN	*History . . .* 1624
	ViHi	*History . . .* 1626
	ViHi	*History . . .* 1632
	MH	*Purchas . . .* 1625
	ICN	*Purchas . . .* 1625
Note	This state is identified as such by Eames and Eames-Verner. It is noted as *State* 6 by Church and part of the changes listed as *State* 7 by Hind. Deane notes this as *State* 4. None of the previous studies has noted the re-engraving of portions of the plate.	

State 9

The changes introduced in this state are again both geographical and bibliographical.

Geographical	Three new place names have been added:

Washeborne / C:—near the tip of the Cape Charles peninsula, immediately over the ship.

Blands / C:—above and to the right of Bolus flu on a line and to the left of the feet of the large standing Indian figure.

Downes dale—immediately below the preceding name.

Bibliographical	*Bollers bush*—added in State 8 has been altered to read *Boolers bush*.

Numerous mountains and trees have been re-engraved in the manner described under *State 8*. These are largely in the top centre of the map to the left of the large Royal Arms with a few others scattered elsewhere on the map.

Further re-cutting has been made around the scale bar and the initial A in *Appamatuck* at the bottom right corner of the Powhatan illustration has been extended. The face of the large standing Indian figure has been touched up so that the features are now more pronounced—particularly the eyes, and it now has definite eyebrows which were missing earlier. This has resulted in a more "pleasing", less "worried" expression than previously.

Copy Described	CSmH (3349)	*History* . . . 1625
	NjP (Ex 1230.862.6q)	*History* . . . 1624
Copies Reported	NjP	*A Map* . . . 1612
	RPJCB	*A Map* . . . 1612
	NN (2)	*History* . . . 1624
	CSmH	*History* . . . 1625
	ICN	*History* . . . 1627
	NN	*History* . . . 1632
	ICN	*History* . . . 1632
	CtY	*History* . . . 1632

NNP; NjP; MWiW-C; MiU; NN (3): MH; CtY (3) — *Purchas* . . . 1625

Note	This state is identified by Eames and Eames-Verner but not by Hind. It is included in *State* 4 by Deane and it is listed as *State* 7 by Church.

None of these studies has noted the re-engraving made to certain portions of the plate.

State 10

The changes to the plate in this state are wholly bibliographical with the alteration of the Purchas page numbers added in *State* 7. These are now "corrected" to read 1690 on the left rather than 1692, and 1691 on the right instead of 1693.

Copy Described	CSmH (3346) *History* . . . 1626
Copies Reported	*History* . . . 1624 PPL; NcD; NNP; CtY; ViU; BM; RPJCB; ViNN; WW: InW.
	History . . . 1626 CSmH; NN; RPJCB.
	History . . . 1627 NNP; NjP(2); NN(2); ViWW; ViU; InU; MB.
	History . . . 1631 RPJCB.
	History . . . 1632 NjP; MWiW-C; RPJCB; MiU-C; NN(3); CSmH(2).
	Purchas . . . 1625 MdB-P; PPL; MiU-C; NN(2); InU; RPJCB; MdBJ-G; ViU; NcU; MB.
Reproduction	McCary, *Smith* . . . *Geographical Review* 14 (1924-25) pp. 434-435.
Note	This state is identified by Eames and Eames-Verner. It is listed as *State* 9 by Hind and as *State* 8 by Church. Deane notes the change in his *State* 3. The copies reported above are those which have been identified by the reporting institution as being in *State* 10 (Eames). The following two states are certainly found among some of these copies but the various institutions were not re-circularized for a more specific identification of *States* 10, 11 and 12.

State 11

The change in this state is bibliographical and quite minor. The hair of the standing Indian figure has been re-engraved so that the top-knot is now cross hatched rather messily and the flowing tresses have been extended slightly.

Copy Described	BM (G7120) *A Map* . . . 1612
	MWiW-C (Calthorpe copy) *History* . . . 1624
Note	None of the earlier studies noted any re-engraving of the illustrative features of the plate, therefore, this state was overlooked.
	A copy of this state is in MWiW-C. This is ordinarily reported as being a copy of *State* 4 as almost all of the identifying data added subsequent to *State* 4 has been erased from the impression. The re-engraving of illustrative features, however, was not disturbed so that the copy is easily recognized as being originally from this state. Obviously some one sought to fake a copy of *State* 4 by removing the recognized identifying features. They failed to remove the name *Burtons mount* added in *State* 6 and did not notice the re-engraved features. This has created an anomaly which Eames studied in 1926 and concluded then that the names had been erased from the copy. Mr. H. Richard Archer of the Chaplin Library has been very helpful in clearing up the problem created by the existence of this bastard impression.

State 12

The change occurring in this state is an accidental bibliographical change. Such "accidental" changes to a plate are normally not recorded as a separate state; however, it is significant in identifying the sequence of publication of this plate and is reported here as a separate state.

The accidental change is a conspicuous heavy crack in the plate. It begins at the 38° latitude figure in the bottom border running to the rudder of the ship, thence due west to pass between the E and the continuation marks in CHE (sapeake Bay). From here the crack continues to divide the large O in Powhatan thence to the small r in the name of the Indian town *Orapaks* just above the O. At this point the crack turns sharply to the northeast for a short distance, terminating at the end of a tributary stream at the name *Myghtuckpassu*.

Plate 67.

Copy Described	FTaSU *Purchas . . .* 1625
Note	The crack in the plate was listed by Eames who notes:

"A later impression of the tenth state, printed after the plate had become cracked, and which may be called 10a, was noted by Mr. Henry N. Stevens in 1922. As described by him in a letter of March 1926, the crack extends from the letter "t" in the place-name *Powhatan*, nearly two inches to the right of the picture of the king, downward to the rudder of the ship, and then to the lower border of 38° latitude".

The Eames-Verner list identified this as *State* 11 and Hind noted it in his *State* 9. Neither Deane nor Church mention the crack.

DISTRIBUTION OF STATES

In conducting this re-study of the Smith map the major collections were circularized with the request that they identify the various states of the map (as delineated by Eames) found in each of the appropriate volumes in their collection. From this enquiry reports on 111 copies of the map were received.

These states are found to be distributed among the several volumes as indicated on the following table.

State	Map 1612	1624	1625	History 1626	1627	1631	1632	1625 Purchas	Total	Separates
I	5	1							6	2
II	2							1	3	
III	3	2			1			1	7	
IV	1	1							2	
V	1	4		1					6	
VI		3						1	4	
VII								4	4	
VIII		1		1	1		1	2	6	
IX	2	3	1		1		3	12	22	
X	3	10		3	10	1	9	11	47	1
XI		1						2	3	
XII								1	1	
Total	17	26	1	5	13	1	13	35	111	3

As Hind notes: ". . . the distinction of states, and the books to which the several impressions properly belonged is, in certain cases, difficult to define . . . The maps must frequently have been detached and impressions misplaced, especially if inserted later, so that confusion is difficult to avoid".[1]

The nature of the changes to the plate reported earlier are quixotic. The printer and/or engraver seem almost to have toyed with the plate—pulling several

---

[1] Hind., *op. cit.,* p. 340

158

impressions, making an alteration or addition to the plate, and then pulling several more.

An attempt to test the statistical significance of the frequency distribution of the states proved inconclusive; therefore, any analysis of the distribution must be purely hypothetical. By comparing the nature of the plate changes with the frequency chart certain hypotheses appear justified:

1. *States* 1 *to* 6 are the equivalent of proof copies and belong properly with *A Map of Virginia* . . . 1612. Other states with that volume or other volumes with these states are probably sophisticated copies.

2. *State* 7 belongs only to the earliest gathered copies of *Purchas* . . . 1625, which probably appeared in late 1624 or early 1625. The page numbers 1692 and 1693 are probably "typographical errors". This state has been found only with copies of *Purchas*. A collation of the textual material of this volume may provide an effective test of this hypothesis.

3. *States* 8 *to* 10 inclusive belong properly both to *Purchas* . . . and to the *History* . . .; however, plate changes are made "in press". According to Baer[1] all editions of the *History* . . . are from the same sheets with cancelled title pages and corrected engraved title plates. Thus, one may assume that some impressions were pulled from the plate in *State* 8 and distributed among the sheets, the plate was altered to *State* 9, more impressions were pulled and distributed among the sheets for the *History* . . . but most of them were used for another gathering of *Purchas* . . . This was probably done in late 1624 and early 1625. After this, the plate was altered to *State* 10 with the corrected *Purchas* numbers and more copies were pulled for use with both the *History* and *Purchas*.

4. *States* 11 *and* 12 belong to the latest gathered copies of *Purchas*.

Since *States* 8 and 9 contain the principal re-engraving of portions of the plate this would seem to indicate that numerous copies were pulled from the plate in *States* 1 *to* 7 for use in *A Map* . . . the first gathering of *Purchas* and the *History* . . . 1624, and probably for sale as separates. At the time the printer was preparing to make his major printing from the plate for the *History* . . . he found it advisable to touch-up certain worn parts of the plate. He made his impressions through *State* 10 and then was finished with the plate; however, some remaining sheets of *Purchas* . . . lacked the map so he touched it up again in *State* 11, and pulled a few more impressions during which time the plate cracked and he managed just a few impressions from *State* 12 before abandoning the plate entirely.

On the basis of the frequency distribution of this plate alone it appears that most of the copies for the sheets of the *History* were pulled at about the same time with the earliest copies using impressions remaining from the first pulls from the

---

[1] Elizabeth Baer, *Seventeenth Century Maryland*. (Baltimore, 1949).

plate (*States* 1-6), and most of the copies of all editions using impressions from *States* 9 and 10.

Purchas . . . on the other hand was gathered at least three different times with impressions pulled as needed. The first gathered copies using *State* 7 impressions from the plate. The main gathering of the sheets used impressions from *States* 9 and 10, while late gathered copies used *States* 11 and 12. It is quite likely that this use of the plate occurred from late 1624 to early 1625 when copies were pulled intermittently for both *Purchas* and the *History* simultaneously.

There is very little logic to the alterations made in the plate throughout the twelve states. The introduction of place names probably resulted from whimsey. Discounting these, the functional changes were the dates, the completion of the border, the *Purchas* and Smith page numbers, and the corrected *Purchas* numbers.

States with *A Map* . . . 1612

Copies of *A Map of Virginia* . . . 1612 are found with states of the map other than State I. These are noted as follows:

State 2 CSmH (19883)
          MdBJ-G
State 3 NNW
          NjP (Ex 1230,862.5)
          CSmH (17934)
State 4 MWiW-C (Chaplin-Huth copy)
State 5 CSmH (69259)
State 9 NjP (Kane)
          RPJCB
State 10 NN (Arents)
          InU (Lilly)
          BM

PLATE 67   1819

A reproduction of the map was published in Richmond, Virginia, in 1819 to accompany an edition of Smith's *History* . . . This was copied from *State* 10 and printed from an engraved plate. This map measures NS 40.7 cm. and EW 31.7 cm. The style of engraving is conspicuously different and the name of William Hole has been omitted from the imprint.

In the 1873 *Report of the Commissioners on the Boundary* . . . The Smith map is included among the maps reproduced with the note:

Smith's map is printed from an engraved copper plate, which is the property of a gentleman of this city, who obtained it from a town in Pennsylvania when it was found in a lot of old metal imported from England. An examination of it proves that it is the one which was engraved for and used in the publications of the reprint of Smith's *History* . . . the . . . maps were printed . . . by order of the Senate, by resolution adopted February 28th, 1873.

The reprint edition was produced by Francis Waller Gilmer and John Holt Rice who were both members of the William Wirt Literary Circle in Richmond. It was reviewed in the *North American Review*, April, 1832.

DERIVATIVES

Smith's map of the Chesapeake Bay was the basic prototype until it was supplanted by the large four-sheet map prepared by Augustine Herman and published in London in 1673. There were nine major copies of the Smith map but only one of these was important in the diffusion of the Smith data. The principal derivative maps are as follows:

Derivative 1

1618   HONDIUS-BLAEU

State 1

Title	NOVA VIRGINIÆ TABVLA
Imprint	*Ex officina Judoci Hondij*
Engraver	*D. Grijp. Sculpt*

Plate 68.

The engraver's name is located in the bottom left corner of the scale cartouche.

Source	Separate
Copy Examined	DLC(2), BM
Size	*Plate* NS 48.2 EW 38.0
	Map NS 47.6 EW 37.5
Orientation	West
Scale	*Milliaria Germanica Communia* 15 *pro Uno gradu* 12=7.9 R.F. 1:1,120,000

The scale is with the imprint in a secondary cartouche in the bottom centre. The scale bar is graduated. This cartouche is framed in stylized strapwork.

Cartouche	The title is in a single line along the top centre of the map with the border of the map forming the top frame of the cartouche. The remaining portions of the frame are of simple strapwork.
Border	Geographically functional for latitude only. The entire plate is enclosed by a decorative border composed of a stylized pattern of a dart and two reels.
Description	This plate is copied from *State* 1 of Smith's map lacking longitude and the various names added at various times in the later states of Smith's map. These missing names include: *Blands C., Sparkes Vaylley, Fetherstones Baye, Downes dale, Burtons Mount, Boolers bush, Sparkes Poynt, Washeborne C., Demacrites tree, Gunters Harbour, Taverners roade, Winstons Isles,* and *Brookes Forest.* The inset *Status Regis Powhatan* is in the upper left corner and undated as on the first state of Smith's map. The large standing figure of the Indian is along the right border at the centre. Above this is a tertiary cartouche framed in strapwork containing the *Notarum explicatio.* The royal arms as on Smith is present but the garter belt surrounding it lacks the motto which is present on Smith. This map is larger than its prototype and is a somewhat finer engraving. It was copied, in turn, by Hondius-Jansson in 1633 and by Montanus-Ogilby in 1671.

Jodocus Hondius was the eldest son of the J. Hondius who published Mercator's *Atlas sive Cosmographicae* . . . beginning in 1606 and the *Atlas Minor* . . . beginning in 1607. For many years he was a "phantom", since the firm continued to publish under his father's imprint following the elder Hondius' death in 1612. J. Hondius, Jr., was establishing his own business in addition to continuing his work with the family firm. Among other things he was preparing a new set of folio plates either to augment the family atlas or with the intention of entering into competition with it. Hondius Jr. died in 1629 and Blaeu acquired his plates at that time.

CARTO-BIBLIOGRAPHICAL NOTE

There are two states of this plate.

State 1
(1618-1629)

The map described above with the Hondius imprint. This is known only by the separate copies as indicated above.

State 2
1630-*c.* 1761

The copper plates for a number of maps made originally by Jodocus Hondius Jr. were purchased by Blaeu in 1629 and the imprints were altered to reflect the new ownership. Blaeu used this map first in his *Atlantic Appendix* (1630) and thereafter in virtually all editions of the atlas. The imprint was altered to read: *Ex officina Guiljelmi Blaeuw.*

Plate 69.

The associated letterpress text printed on the reverse of the map can serve as an aid in identifying the proper edition of the atlas to which a copy belongs:

Date	Language	Sig.	Catchword	Page No.	Folio No.
1630	Latin	Blank			
1631	Latin	Nnn			
1631A		C^7			
1634	German	B			
1635	French	C^8	*canards*		
1635	Latin	D			
1635	German	B	*chamins*		
1635	Dutch	F	*defe*		
1640	French	I	*cons*		
1640	Latin				
1642	Dutch				
1642	German	G		7	
1644	French	I	*naux*		9
1645	French	Blank			
1650	Latin	H	*parte*		9
1650	Dutch				
1658	Dutch	G	*ooft*		8
1662	Latin	N	*nor*	39, 40	
1663	French, Dutch, Latin?				
1665	Dutch	G	*ooft*		8
1667	French	H	*hom-*	21	
(1680?)	DeWit	Blank			
(1717?)	Visscher	Blank			
(1761?)	Covens & Mortier	Blank			

162

Derivative 2

1628	MINOR-MERCATOR
Title	NOVA / VIRGINIÆ / TABVLA / Petrus Kœrius / Cœlavit. /

Plate 70.

[Letterpress above plate: VIRGINIA & FLORIDA. 643]

Source	Mercator, G. *Atlas Minor Gerardi a I. Hondio plurimus aeneis tabulis auctus et illustratus: denuo recognito, additilique novis delineationibus emendatus. Amsterodami, ex officina Ioannis Ianssonii*, 1628, p. 643.
Note	For a detailed carto-bibliographical description of this map see: Coolie Verner, "Maps of Virginia in Mercator's Lesser Atlases". *Imago Mundi* XVII (1963): 45-61.

CARTO-BIBLIOGRAPHICAL NOTE

The plate used in this second series of the *Atlas Minor* . . . was unchanged during its use in some twelve editions from 1628 to 1636. The identification of the edition from which a free copy was removed can be facilitated by the associated letterpress on the reverse.

Date	Text	Catchword	Page No.
1628	Latin	*nes*	644
1628	French	unknown	
1629	Dutch	unknown	
1629	German	unknown	
1630	French	*& cruels*	632
1630	Dutch	*doende |*	750
1631	German	*Ca ien*	590
1631	Latin	unknown	
1632	Latin	unknown	
1633	German	unknown	
1634	Latin	*pavo*	640
1636	Dutch	unknown	

Derivative 3

1628	DE BRY
Title	VIRGINIA
Imprint	Erforshet und beschriben durch Capitain Iohan Schmidt.
	The imprint is along the bottom below the scale.

Plate 71.

Source	De Bry, T. *Dreyzehender Theil Americae* . . . Franckfurt, Bay Casper Rotel, 1628.

Copy Examined	CSmH
Size	*Plate* NS 36.6 EW 29.2
	Map NS 35.9 EW 28.5
Orientation	West
Latitude	37-40
Longitude	307-310
Scale	Meylen und halbe Meylen 15=6.8 cm. R.F. 1:1,300,000
	The graduated bar scale is located along the bottom of the map to the right of centre unframed.
Cartouche	None, the title is in the top centre.
Border	Modified geographically functional with final outside neat line wanting.
Description	This copy is from *State* 6 and is somewhat simplified in details and style of engraving. The Smith view of Powhatan is in the upper left with the standing figure and legend on the right.
Note	The map measurements provided above do not include the figures which are outside the final line. The volume in which this map is found is De Bry's *German America*, Part XIII, sole edition, first issue.
1634	The map also appeared in 1634 in De Bry's *Decima Tertia Pars Historia Americanae* . . . , Francforti, Merioni, 1634.
1655	In this year it was used in Gottfreidt's *Newe Welt und Americanische Historien* . . . Franckfort, Merianischen Erben, 1655.

Derivative 4

1630	OBLONG-MERCATOR
Title	NOVA / VIRGINÆ / TABVLA / *Miliaria Germanica com* = / *munia 15 pro uno gradu.* [graduated scale bar] /
Engraver	Petrus Kœrius / Caelavit. The plate is signed in large letters immediately below the cartouche.
Source	Mercator, G. *Atlas Sive Cosmographicae* . . . Amsterdami, Sumptibus Iohannis Cloppenburgij, 1630.
Note	For a detailed description of this map see: Coolie Verner, "Maps of Virginia in Mercator's Lesser Atlases". *Imago Mundi* XVII (1963): 45-61.

CARTO-BIBLIOGRAPHICAL NOTE

The several states of this plate can be differentiated as follows:

State 1	
1630-1636	As described above.
1630	The French edition of the atlas. This map is in an appendix. Above the plate is the letterpress headings: DESCRIPTION DE LA NOUVELLE VIRGIN. 47. On the reverse are two poems with the first headed: AV LECTEVR.
1632	The Latin edition. The letterpress heading above the plate is: NOVÆ VIRGINIÆ DESCRIPTIO 729. On the reverse of the map is a double column Latin text.

1636	This is precisely like the edition of 1630.
State 2 1673-1734	In this state the shot-silk or moire effect used to depict the water area on *State* 1 has been deleted.
1673, 1676	This state is found in editions of the Atlas published under these dates by Jan. Jansson von Waesberge. No reverse material.
1734	The plate was taken over by Du Sauzet and used by him in his *Atlas Portatif* . . . along with a number of other plates. The reverse is blank.
State 3 1734	The plate number 263 has been added within the border in the upper right corner. This is found in an edition of Du Sauzet with the imprint date of 1734.

Plate 72.

Derivative 5

1633	MERCATOR-HONDIUS
Title	NOVA VIRGINIÆ TABVLA
Imprint	Amſtelodami, ex officina Henrici Hondii. The imprint is in the scale cartouche in the bottom centre of the map.

Plate 73.

Source	Mercator, G. *L'Appendice de l'Atlas* . . . A Amsterdam, chez Henry Hondius . . . A.D. 1633.
Copy Examined	BM
Size	*Plate* NS 49.5 EW 39.1 *Map* NS 49.9 EW 38.3
Orientation	West
Latitude	(36°) 40′-41°
Scale	*Millaria Germanica Communa* 12=7.8 cm. R.F. 1:1,140,000. The graduated scale bar is located in a scale cartouche which also contains the imprint on the bottom of the plate to right of centre. This is framed in plasterwork.
Cartouche	The title is in a long horizontal rectangle in the top centre of the plate. The border of the plate forms the top frame of the cartouche and the other three sides are framed in plasterwork.
Border	Geographically functional for latitude only. An incomplete functional border at longitude.
Description	This is a copy of the Hondius-Blaeu plate of 1629. In the upper left corner is a large view of the interior of an Indian house with the legend below "Status Regis Powhatan". On the right border at centre is a standing figure of an Indian holding a bow in the left hand and a club in the right. Above this near the upper right corner is a large coat of arms surmounted by a crown and circled by the symbol of the Garter. To the left of this is a small cartouche containing a "Notar explicatio". This is a beautifully engraved and decorative map.

CARTO-BIBLIOGRAPHICAL NOTE

State 1
1633-1666

The copy described above. This state was used in all editions of the Mercator-Hondius atlas published after 1633. The various impressions can be identified as follows:

Date	Language	Sig.	Page	Catchword
1633	French App.	O⁸2	697	*peu*
1633*	Latin			
1633	French	O⁸2	697	*peu*
1633	German	8G	669	*auch*
1634	Dutch	Not present		
1635*	French			
1636	English	9.Q	437	*hurt*
1636	German App.	Not present		
1636*	German			
1638	English	9.Q	437	*hurt*
1638	Latin	R 4		*fluvio*
1638*	Dutch			
1638*	German			
1639	French	f 5		*n'en*
1640	French	f 5		*n'en*
1641*	German App.	Not present		
1641	French	f 5		*n'en*
1642	French	f 5		*n'en*
1642	Dutch	E		*is*
1644*	Dutch			
1645*	Dutch			
1647*	Dutch			
1647	Latin	D 3		*nient*
1649	German	D 3		*grosser*
1649	Latin	D 3		*nient*
1649	French	e		*ses*
1652	Dutch	D 2		*riviere*
1652	French	F 5, E		*n'en, ses*
1653	Spanish	G		*nave-*
1657	Latin	Blank		
1657*	Dutch			
1657	German	D 3		*grosser*
1658	French	E		*ses*
1658*	German		229	
1658	Latin	D 3	230	*nient*
1666	Latin		256	Maxime
1666*	Spanish			

* Copy not examined.

State 2
(1680-1710)

The original imprint has been changed to read: Amstelodami, ex officina apud (brace) PET: Schenk, et / Ger: Valk. C. Priv: In addition, longitude and latitude lines crossing the map have been added as well as a dotted line indicating the boundary of Virginia.

Derivative 6

1635	HALL
Title	VIRG (arms) INIA
Engraver	*Ralph Hall, Sculpsit.* 1636
	The plate is signed below the scale on the bottom.

Plate 74.

Source	*Historia Mundi: or Mercator's Atlas* . . . Englished by W. S. (Wye Saltenstall) London, Printed by T. Coates for Michael Sparke and Samuel Cartwright, 1635.
Copy Examined	DLC; MdBJ-G; NN; RPJCB.
Size	*Plate* NS 24.1 EW 17.1 *Map* NS 23.3 EW 16.5
Orientation	West
Latitude	37-41
Longitude	307-310
Scale	*Scale of Leagues* 19=2.3 cm. R.F. 1:2,300,000. The graduated bar scale is along the bottom to the right of centre. The bar is surmounted by a fleur-de-lis and dividers.
Cartouche	The title is on a banner with both ends split along the top centre of the plate. There is a large coat of arms surmounted by a crown which interrupts the title.
Border	A modified geographically functional border containing the graduated inner scale but without an outside line so that the longitude and latitude figures are outside the border.
Description	This absurd little map is one of the curiosities of Virginia cartography. It is a copy of the John Smith map, but represents the whim of the engraver rather than any concern for geographical accuracy or even care and attention in copying. There are three illustrations that are bad copies of those found in De Bry. In the upper left corner is the scene of the Indians sitting around a fire before a chief. In the upper right corner is a view of the interior of an Indian hut showing bodies lying side by side. In the bottom right corner is a bird's-eye view of a stockaded village. Animals, Indians, boats, canoes and monsters inhabit the map at will, and houses, huts and castles are shown.
Note	This map was intended for this volume but was not actually ready when the volume was printed. On the errata leaf at the end of the volume is the following note: "In page 905 for the Description of New Spaine read New Virginia, but there is no Map of Virginia in regard there is a more exact map drawing in that Country, whose Platforme is not yet come over, but when it comes, every buyer of the Books shall have it given him gratis". The Hall map may be found in all editions of the atlas published in 1635, 1637 and 1639.

Derivative 7

1648   MINOR-MERCATOR

Title   VIRGI / NIA

Plate 75.

Source   [Mercator, G.] *Atlas Minor, das ist: Eine Kurtze jedoch gruend-*
            liche Beschreibung der gantzen Welt in zwey Theile abgetheilt . . .
            Amstelodami, Ex officina Ioannis Ianssonii.

Note   For a detailed description of this map see: Coolie Verner, "Maps of Virginia
            in Mercator's Lesser Atlases". *Imago Mundi* XVII (1963): 45-61.

CARTO-BIBLIOGRAPHICAL NOTE

The plate was not altered during its period of use. Associated letterpress
identification is as follows:

Date	Language	Catchword	Page No.
1648	German	*auff*	390
1648	Latin*		
1651	German	*auff*	390
1656	Dutch*		
1656	*Latin**		

*Copy not examined.

Derivative 8

1671   MONTANUS-OGILBY

Title   NOVA / VIRGINÆ / TABULA

Plate 76.

Source   Montanus, A. *De Nieuwe en onbekende Weereld* . . . t'Amster-
            dam, J. Meurs, 1671.

Copy Examined   DLC; ICN; MiU-C; NN; RPJCB.

Size   *Plate* NS 35.8   EW 29.4
            Map NS 35.2   EW 29.0

Orientation   West

Latitude   37-41

Scale   *Milliaria Germanica communia.* 12=6.4 cm. R.F. 1:1,400,000
            The scale is on the bottom to the right of centre. The scale bar is on a
            pedestal slab with a single Greek column standing at one end. Three
            cherubs with tape and dividers are on and around the slab.

Cartouche   The title is in the upper left corner on a drapery measuring 3.5 by 5.0 cm.
            This is held up by cherubs.

Border   Geographically functional for latitude only.

Description This is a careful copy of the Hondius-Blaeu version of the Smith map but
            smaller in size and somewhat more decorative. In the upper right corner is
            a "Notarum" on a small panel surrounded by figures of animals including a
            llama and goats and two Indian figures one of which holds a bow.

Note	This plate was prepared by Meurs for the Dutch edition of Montanus and printed on paper watermarked with a jester. The plate was then printed for Ogilby's *America . . .* of 1671 on paper watermarked with a cockatrice. It is not known whether the plate was printed in Amsterdam with the maps sent to London or whether the plate was sent to and printed in London. In 1673 the plate was used in the High German edition of Montanus which is attributed to Olfert Dapper. These copies of the map are also on paper watermarked with a jester. The plates later came into possession of Vander Aa who altered them so thoroughly that they are not normally identified as the original Meurs' plates. These copies of the map were published in 1729 on unwatermarked paper. After Aa's use, the plates passed to Covens and Mortier who added their imprint to the plate after deleting part of the Aa imprint.
State 1 1671-1673	The copy described herein. Impression 1 for Montanus 1671 — jester. Impression 2 for Ogilby 1671 — cockatrice. Impression 3 for Montanus 1673 — jester.
State 2 1729	The Vander Aa version. All of the original cartouches — scale, title, and "Notarum"— were deleted and replaced by a single cartouche. A new scale of German and French leagues is provided. Longitude figures have been added. Some new names — including three counties in eastern Maryland — have been added. In this new form the map description is as follows: VIRGINIE, / *Grande Region del'* / AMERIQUE / SEPTENTRIONALE, / *avec tous ses Bourges, Hameaux, Rivieres / et Bayes, suivant les recherches exactes / de ceux qui l'ont decouverte, et nouvellement / mise au jour par /* PIERRE VAN DER AA, / *Marchand Libraire* A'LEIDE. /

Plate 77.

Source	Aa, P. vander, *La Galerie Agreable du Monde . . .* A Liede, Pierre Vander Aa, 1729 Vol. 63-64.
Copy Examined	DLC; ICN; NN.
Size	*Plate* NS 35.7 EW 29.3 *Map* NS 35.4 EW 28.9
Orientation	West
Latitude	37-41
Longitude	300-302
Scale	*Lieues d'Allemagne de* 15 *au Degre* 30=6.1 cm. *Lieues de France de* 20 *au Degre* 40=6.1 cm. *R.F.* 1:1,430,000 The graduated scale bars are in the base of the cartouche.
Cartouche	The title is transcribed on the face of a monument which is surrounded by a geographically descriptive scene.
State 3 1761	The Van der Aa imprint has been deleted and replaced with the following: *a Amsterdam chez I Covens et C. Mortier.*

Derivative 9

1676	SPEED
Title	A MAP OF / VIRGINIA / AND / MARYLAND. / *Sold by Thomas Basset in Fleet ſtreet, / and Richard Chifwell in St. Pauls / Church yard.*
Engraver	F. Lamb Sculp.

Plates 78 & 79.

Source	Speed, John *The Theatre of the Empire* . . . London, Printed for Thomas Basset . . . and Richard Chiswell . . . 1676.
Copy Examined	DLC; ICN; MdBP; MdBJ-G; RPJCB; ViU.
Size	*Plate* NS 50.6 EW 38.7 *Map* NS 49.4 EW 37.7
Orientation	West
Latitude	37-41
Scale	*A Scale of English Miles* 40=6.5 *R.F.* 1:1,140,000 The graduated scale bar is located in the upper left corner and framed by slightly decorated plasterwork. This is surmounted by the arms of England.
Cartouche	The large title cartouche is in the upper right corner. It is a modified vertical oval measuring 7.8 by 6.9, framed in an elaborately decorated plasterwork with garlands and mythological figures on each side.
Border	A geographically functional border is provided for latitude while the two sides are not completed with respect to degree markings and sub-degree divisions.
Watermark	The primary mark is a small fleur-de-lis and the countermark is an illegible name.
Note	This is the last major derivative of the Smith map and it is unique as an example of the transition from one basic prototype map to another. The delineation of the land area follows Smith while the toponymic prototype was the Herman map of 1673.

CARTO-BIBLIOGRAPHICAL NOTE

Three states of this map have been identified:

State 1   1676   The copy described here.

State 2   *c.* 1680   The Basset and Chiswell imprint has been deleted.

State 3   *c.* 1685   The imprint of Christopher Browne has been added as follows:
Printed & / Sold by Chriſtopher Browne at the Globe / near the Weſt end of S Pauls Church / London. /

Plate 79.

CONCLUSIONS

The manuscript draughts sent to England at the time of the initial explorations of the Chesapeake Bay did not get into the stream of geographical knowledge. The first printed map to picture the bay correctly appears to have been Blaeu's first *Paskaart*, published around 1617. It is probable that Blaeu got his information about the bay from the manuscript which John Smith is known to have sent to Henry Hudson since it showed the Chesapeake Bay as part of the east coast in much the same way as Blaeu used it on his chart. The Smith map itself could have been in Blaeu's hands at the time but there is too little evidence on the *Paskaart* to determine the source precisely.

Although published separately in 1612, the Smith map made no noticeable impact on the cartography of the east coast until several years had elapsed. Jodocus Hondius Jr. made his copy of Smith around 1618 and used the first state of Smith as his model indicating that he had at hand a copy of the map as issued with the pamphlet. This Hondius plate was not widely circulated until after Blaeu acquired the plate in 1629 and published it first in 1630. The reduced version published with the *Atlas Minor* in 1628 was actually the map that first released the Smith delineation of the Bay and it was obviously a reduced copy of the larger Hondius plate. The De Bry plate of 1628 was copied from *State* 6 of Smith and probably got into De Bry's hands through either Purchas or Smith's *History*. Even though it was used until 1655, this version was not copied by others.

The main instrument for the diffusion of the Smith data initially was the Hondius-Blaeu copy which was itself copied by Henricus Hondius. Either of these two folio copies served as the primary source of information about the Chesapeake Bay for all subsequent uses of the data. The Hall map of 1636 and the Farrer map of 1651 were copies of the Smith delineation and in maps of larger areas of the east coast, such as those by Visscher, the Smith data is found. Many of the maps that utilized the Smith delineation added variations of their own that would tend to suggest some other basic source. The Dudley map is such a case in point. Even Hondius and Blaeu themselves were not careful adherents to their own maps. Their maps which relate Virginia to Florida show a distortion of the Del-Mar-Va. peninsula not characteristic of Smith's representation. Blaeu is guilty of a strange anomaly that was obviously an error made by an apprentice, for his world map of 1648 shows the Chesapeake Bay running east to west rather than north to south.[1]

Even though Smith's map was the prototype for the delineation of the Chesapeake Bay, his toponomy did not survive beyond the copies of the map itself. Among the great rivers around the bay, only the name Potomac survives from among those names attached to these features by Smith. The names currently

---

[1] This is reproduced in F. C. Wieder, *Monumenta Cartographia*, Vol. III.

in use are first found on a map published in 1635 with *A Relation to Maryland . . .* by Lord Baltimore.   This particular map presents a delineation of the Chesapeake Bay that differs from Smith materially so that it cannot be considered to have copied the Smith map yet there is enough similarity to suggest that they both have some ancestry in common.   The Baltimore map does not appear to have exerted any material influence on the representation of the Chesapeake Bay comparable to that which resulted from Smith's map.   It was copied precisely by John Ogilby for his *America . . .* in 1671 with some additions.

Although carto-bibliographers attach great importance to place names on maps in the analysis of derivatives, this may be misleading evidence.   In the case of the Virginia rivers, the name James appeared first on the Tindall manuscript and in the Baltimore map in printed form.   Smith attached the name Rappa-hannock to a small river on the Del-Mar-Va. Peninsula while the Baltimore attached it properly to the river which now bears that name.   The survival of place names may depend more upon local usage than in cartographical designa-tion.

In spite of the Baltimore map, the Smith representation of the Chesapeake Bay dominated the cartographical representation of the east coast for much of the seventeenth century.   After the publication of the Herman map in 1673, the Smith data is not again used to any extent except that the Hondius and Blaeu firms continued to print copies from their plates.   The original Smith map disappeared into obscurity.   In 1780, when he was preparing his *Notes on Virginia* for publication, Thomas Jefferson was unsuccessful in his efforts to find a copy of the original Smith map which he wanted to reproduce and include with the book.

CHAPTER FIVE

The Marine Surveys of James Cook in North America 1758-1768

particularly the Survey of Newfoundland

A bibliography of printed charts and sailing-directions

by R. A. Skelton and R. V. Tooley

PREFACE

THIS Bibliography embraces (so far as known to its authors) all editions of the original charts and associated tracts of sailing-directions compiled and printed from the North American surveys made by James Cook between 1758 and 1768, with editions of the collective works—sea-atlases or tract-volumes—in which they were republished from time to time. If it is appreciated that, between the publication-dates of these collective works, sale of the individual items as separate sheets or pamphlets went on continuously, the Bibliography will be seen to illustrate the public interest and use of Cook's hydrographic work in this region up to the end of the 18th century.

The Bibliography has considerably outgrown the form in which it was first conceived by its compilers. The extreme rarity of most of the works described and the diffusion of extant copies through various libraries render collation difficult and suggest that a thorough survey of this virtually unmapped bibliographical country may be helpful to librarians and collectors. Hard wear by practical users has resulted in severe wastage. It is probable that the tally here is incomplete, and the compilers will welcome reports of states of the engraved charts or editions of the printed tracts which have escaped their notice.

In entries for atlases, "Phillips numbers" are given, from Philip L. Phillips (continued by Clara E. LeGear), *List of Geographical Atlases in the Library of Congress* (6 vols., 1909-63). In transcription of titles and imprints (whether of charts, of volumes or of tracts), line-endings are marked; differences of type (capitals, italic, etc.) are not reproduced, and the presence of rules is not indicated. Where the titlepage of an edition is reproduced in facsimile, the title is transcribed in summary form, with a reference to the illustration.

The authors are indebted to Mr. David Magee for permission to use in the Foreword parts of the introduction written by one of them to accompany the facsimile edition of *A Collection of Charts of the Coasts of Newfoundland and Labradore* published by Mr. Magee (San Francisco, Grabhorn Press, 1965).

LIST OF PLATES

ACKNOWLEDGMENTS

Plate 83 is reproduced by gracious permission of Her Majesty the Queen. Other owners by whose courtesy reproductions have been made are the Trustees of the British Museum (Plates 80, 82, 85, 88-91, 95, 97, 100); the Ministry of Defence (Plates 81, 86, 92-94, 98); the Trustees of the John Carter Brown Library (Plate 96); the University of California at Los Angeles (Plates 84, 87); Toronto Public Library (Plate 99); and the Library of Congress (Plate 101).

FOREWORD

ON 19 April 1763 James Cook, Master R.N., was ordered by the Admiralty to proceed to Newfoundland "in order to your taking a Survey of Part of the Coasts and Harbours of that Island". Cook, now in his thirty-sixth year, had seventeen years of experience at sea behind him. Nine of these had been spent in merchant shipping, the other eight in the Royal Navy, with the rating of Master since 1757. For the past five years Cook had served on the North American station, taking part in the operations against the French in Nova Scotia, in the St Lawrence river and gulf, and on the Newfoundland coasts, as master of H.M.S. *Pembroke* (Oct. 1757-Sept. 1759) and of H.M.S. *Northumberland* (Sept. 1759-Nov. 1762). During this period he had learnt the rudiments of surveying from military engineers and, by private study and practical experience, had acquired sufficient technical competence in marine survey to justify his commanding officer in writing to the Admiralty, in December 1762, "that from my experience of Mr. Cook's genius and capacity, I think him well fitted for the work he has undertaken, and for greater undertakings of the same kind". Cook's hydrographic work up to this date comprised manuscript charts and plans, with sailing-directions, of the coasts and harbours of the Gulf of St. Lawrence, Nova Scotia and south-east Newfoundland. Two charts from his surveys had already been printed in London; these were a plan of Gaspé bay and harbour, "taken in 1758" and published by Mount and Page at some date before 1762 (Bibl., No. 1), and a "New Chart of the River St Lawrence", completed from surveys made in 1759-60 by Cook and the military engineer Samuel Holland and engraved by Thomas Jefferys in 1760 (Bibl., No. 2).

By the Treaty of Paris, which in February 1763 ended the Seven Years' War, France was required to evacuate Newfoundland, apart from the two islands of St Pierre and Miquelon off the south coast; but her fishermen were allowed rights of fishing and curing from Cape Bonavista in the north-east to Point Rich in the north-west. But no reliable maps existed and, if disputes between English and French fishermen were to be averted, there must be a survey.

The charting of Newfoundland and southern Labrador by Cook, in the years 1763-7, and by his successor Michael Lane, in 1768-73, was unequalled, for thoroughness and method, by any previous hydrographic work by Englishmen; and it produced the first charts of this extensive and difficult coastline that could (in the words of a later hydrographer) "with any degree of safety be trusted by the seaman". The survey technique adopted by Cook, perhaps under the influence of military engineers such as Holland and J. F. W. DesBarres, can be inferred from his selection of instruments, from scattered references in his ship's log, and from surviving original manuscript charts. The coastal survey was constructed round a network of shore stations, whose positions were fixed by triangulation with the theodolite from a carefully measured base-line; the longshore detail was completed by observing cross-bearings between headlands and islands and by soundings from the ship and from boats; latitudes were determined when possible by meridian observations; and the scale of the chart was derived from the distance between stations, computed from their latitude and true bearing from one another. In addition, Cook seized every opportunity of carrying his survey inland by theodolite observations or by traverses of the courses of rivers; the interior of Newfoundland had been virtually a blank on all earlier maps, and this was the first serious attempt to delineate its topography from survey.

Nearly 50 manuscript charts signed by Cook, or attributed to him, or drawn directly from his surveys in North American waters before 1768, are preserved in various libraries and archives. Between 1766 and 1768, with the permission of the Admiralty, which did not then (or indeed until 1808) undertake chart-publication, Cook had four charts of the Newfoundland coasts engraved (Bibl., Nos. 4, 6, 8, 9) and three tracts of sailing-directions printed (Bibl., Nos. 5, 7, 10), all apparently at his own expense. The bibliographical history of these publications, and of other charts and sailing-directions derived from his hydrographic work, is closely connected with the chronology of the surveys.

In May-July 1763 Cook was surveying the islands of St Pierre and Miquelon in advance of their surrender to the French; and in July-October of the same year, in the *Grenville*, a schooner purchased for his use, he carried out surveys of harbours in northern Newfoundland and along a short stretch of the Labrador coast on the north side of Belleisle Strait. During the next four years Cook's professional life followed a regular pattern. From May or June to September or October he was working along the Newfoundland coasts in the *Grenville*, taking her back to England in the autumn; and from December to April (when he returned to the scene of his surveys) he supervised the refitting of the ship at Deptford dockyard and drew his charts at his home in Mile End Road.

The naval surveys were designed to cover the coasts most frequented by British shipping and those of political concern, particularly the "treaty coast" of northern Newfoundland. For the east coasts of the island, there were French charts, besides an old English survey of 1677 published in editions of *The English Pilot The Fourth Book* since 1689; the south coast was very imperfectly charted; and the west coast and the Labrador shore of Belleisle Strait were practically unmapped. Cook's surveys in 1764-7 were to be supplemented by those made in other ships of the Newfoundland squadron (notably by Joseph Gilbert, master of H.M.S. *Guernsey*) and by those carried out after 1767 by Michael Lane, who had been his mate in the *Grenville* and succeeded him in command of her.

The progress of the surveys is shown below:

Area	Date	Surveyor
St Pierre & Miquelon	1763 (May-July)	Cook
N. E. Newfoundland (Quirpon & Noddy Harbs.) Labrador (York Harb.)	1763 (July-Oct.)	Cook
N.W. Newfoundland (C. Bauld—Pt Ferolle)	1764 (Aug.-Oct.)	Cook
S. Newfoundland (St Laurence Harb.—Despair B.)	1765 (June-Oct.)	Cook

S. Newfoundland (Despair B.—C. Anguille)	1766 (June-Oct.)	Cook
W. Newfoundland (C. Anguille—Pt Ferolle)	1767 (May-Sept.)	Cook
Labrador (St Peter's Bay—C. Bluff)	1767	Gilbert
Labrador (Grand Point—Shecatica)	1768	Lane
S.E. Newfoundland (St Mary's & Placentia Bays)	1768	Gilbert
Labrador (Shecatica—Chateaux B. & York Harb.)	1769	Lane
Labrador (C. St Michael—Spotted I.)	1770	Lane
S.E. Newfoundland, with Placentia B.	1772-3	Lane

In their earlier states, the four charts of the Newfoundland coasts engraved for Cook in 1766-8 were based mainly on his own surveys. In later states, additions and corrections were made on the plates from surveys by Cook himself, by Gilbert (1767-9) and by Lane (1768-9), and there was a good deal of re-working of titles and insets; the dates of publication were altered, and the imprints of successive mapsellers, into whose hands the plates passed, were substituted for those of previous proprietors. No alteration in the hydrographic content of Cook's own charts was made on the plates after 1770; and the final states of the charts bear the date 1794. Their first publication in an atlas was in 1769, their last in 1806; and as loose sheets they were still on sale eighty years later. The peak-periods in the publication of Cook's hydrographic work during the 18th century (1766-70, 1775-9, 1794-1806), as the Bibliography shows, were those in which international tension or warfare created a demand for reliable charts and navigational guides for North American waters. That in each of these periods the chart-plates and copyrights came into the possession of new proprietors is doubtless no more than coincidence.

The early printing- and publication history of Cook's four charts (Bibl., Nos. 4, 6, 8, 9) can be reconstructed from the successive alterations to the plates described in the Bibliography.

In the spring of 1766 Cook, having obtained the Admiralty's approval, sent for engraving by J. Larken, at his own cost, manuscript charts from his surveys in the three seasons of 1763-5, embracing the north coast of Newfoundland (with a short tract of the Labrador coast) and the central section of the south coast (with St Pierre and Miquelon). These provided the materials for the first two charts (Nos. 4 and 6). Cook had made arrangements for their sale by Mount and Page (with whom he had done business before) and also, for No. 6 only, by Thomas Jefferys and Andrew Dury; and the two charts accordingly came out in 1766. Whether the first, and very rare, state of No. 4 was in fact put on sale or must be regarded as a rejected proof, is uncertain; the third state evidently represents a preliminary stage of revision by Jefferys before the results of Lane's 1769 survey became available and enabled him to produce the fourth state. Cook also sent for printing, likewise at his own expense, his sailing-directions to accompany the two charts, and they were put on sale as quarto pamphlets by Mount and Page in 1766 (Nos. 5 and 7). When Cook returned home in the autumn of 1766, he had continued the survey of the south coast westward to Cape Anguille; he once more got the Admiralty's licence and sent his originals to Larken who, incorporating one plate of No. 6, engraved the third chart (No. 8); this was published by Cook in 1767, and sold by the same three firms, with the addition of Carington Bowles. Similarly, the charts of the west coast which Cook brought home from his season's surveys in the autumn of 1767 were engraved by Larken, published by Cook in 1768 and put on sale by Mount and Page, Jefferys, and Dury (No. 9); the accompanying sailing-directions were printed for Cook in the same year and sold by Mount and Page and others (No. 10). In none of the four charts hitherto published by Cook does the imprint state the "day of first publishing", although by an Act of 1734 (8 Geo. II, *c*. 13) this was required if copyright was to be claimed in the plates.

When the fourth chart (No. 9) was published, presumably in the spring of 1768, the copperplates of his engraved charts and the copyright in the printed sailing-directions were (so far as the evidence goes) still Cook's. Early in April 1768 Cook knew that he was to be appointed to command the *Endeavour;* and it appears probable that before he sailed in July he had conveyed his rights in the charts to Thomas Jefferys.

When Cook's last three Newfoundland charts (Nos. 6, 8, 9) next came before the public, it was as Jefferys' property and at a time (very probably in 1769) when Cook was in the Pacific. *A Collection of Charts of the Coasts of Newfoundland and Labradore, &c.* (Bibl., No. 11), bearing Jefferys' imprint on its titlepage, includes the three Cook charts, with seven others from plates in Jefferys' possession. That copies of the *Collection* were on sale in 1769 is suggested by the imprint and advertisement on the titlepage of the accompanying volume of sailing-directions, *The Newfoundland Pilot* (Bibl., No. 12); "Printed for Thomas Jefferys . . . M.DCC. LXIX. Of whom may be had, bound together or seperately, all the Charts belonging to the above Directions". This inference on the date of publication is supported (as will appear) by the contents of surviving copies of the *Collection.*

As Geographer to the King, Thomas Jefferys enjoyed semi-official standing which may have given him access to public documents and map-drafts for engraving and publication. It is a reasonable conjecture that his purchase of Cook's plates prompted him to seek other materials of comparable authority on the hydrography of Newfoundland and the adjoining waters, and to assemble them into a sea-atlas. This was the (now very rare) *Collection of Charts* of 1769-70, a prototype or assay for the celebrated *North-American Pilot* which was to be published in five English editions from 1775 to 1806 and copied in a French version of 1784.

If (as we suggest) Jefferys became the owner of the three Cook charts before July 1768, by purchase of the copperplates from Cook and by taking over the rights of other mapsellers whose names appeared in the imprints, he did not lack materials from which to supplement them. These materials were, without exception "founded on Actual Surveys, taken by Surveyors that have been employed by the Admiralty, and other Officers in the King's Service". Some of them already lay to hand in Jefferys' shop, among his considerable stock of charts of Nova

Scotia and the St Lawrence region; others were to be supplied by the surveyors, principally Lane and Gilbert, who continued Cook's work on the coasts of Labrador and Newfoundland. The charts produced by each summer's surveying were fair drawn and engraved during the winter, for publication in the course of the following year.

It was certainly with authority, and perhaps encouragement, from the Admiralty that Jefferys undertook the publication of the Newfoundland and Labrador survey. Whether his engravers worked from the original charts which are still preserved in the Hydrographic Department or from other manuscript copies taken from them, is uncertain. The Royal Geographical Society possesses a manuscript "Catalogue of Drawings & Engraved Maps, Charts & Plans; the Property of Mr. Thomas Jefferys . . . 1775". In this inventory of the compilation materials left by Jefferys at his death in 1771, and at the later date in the hands of his successor William Faden, we find listed many MS. charts, by Cook, Lane, Gilbert and others, which seem to have served as copy for the engravers of those printed in the *Collection* of 1769-70 and the *North-American Pilot* of 1775. We do not know what happened to the materials listed in this "Catalogue", nor whether the MS. charts in question were subsequently acquired by or returned to the Hydrographic Office (after its establishment in 1795), or were duplicates of those now held by the Hydrographic Department.

Jefferys' undated *Collection* was (as we have seen) advertised in 1769; but, although incomplete advance copies were in circulation in this year, the atlas seems to have been published in its definitive form, corresponding to the contents list on the titlepage, on or after 10 May 1770. Of the four surviving copies of the *Collection*, two are evidently of the preliminary issue; both lack the general chart of Newfoundland (pl. 1), and both have that of Belleisle Strait (pl. 4) in its earlier state, showing the Labrador coast only in outline apart from the short eastern section surveyed by Cook in 1763. In the other two copies of the *Collection*, the general chart is present with the imprint date 10th May 1770, and the chart of Belleisle Strait has been revised by the re-engraving of the whole Labrador coast, to incorporate Lane's surveys to the westward in the summers of 1768 and 1769, and by the addition of a half-sheet extending the north-west coast of Newfoundland from Cook's survey of 1767. Neither of these charts could have been completed by the engraver before the winter of 1769-70, for publication in 1770.

The materials for all the other charts in the *Collection* were available to Jefferys by the end of 1768. They comprised Cook's charts of the south and west coasts of Newfoundland (pl. 2, 3), the plates of which Jefferys had acquired; two charts of the Labrador coast "from Grand Point to Shecatica" (pl. 5), from Lane's survey in 1768, and "from the entrance of the Straights . . . to Cape Bluff" (pl. 6), from Gilbert's survey in 1767; charts of the Magdalen Islands (pl. 7) and Sable Island (pl. 8), the former surveyed by Samuel Holland in 1765, the latter by J. F. W. DesBarres in 1764; and, on two plates, seven plans of harbours in S.E. Newfoundland, apparently from Cook's surveys in August-September 1762, perhaps supplemented by Gilbert in 1768. Manuscripts of all these charts are listed in Jefferys' "Catalogue" of 1775.

The *Newfoundland Pilot* (Bibl., No. 12), issued by Jefferys in 1769, brought together the sailing-directions for use with the charts of the *Collection;* the content of none of these is later than 1768. It was regular practice in the 18th century to issue a quarto tract of sailing-directions with a printed chart. Four tracts by Cook had been published: that for the St Lawrence chart of 1760 (Bibl., No. 3) issued without his name, and the tracts accompanying his three Newfoundland charts of 1766-8 (Bibl., Nos. 5, 7, 10). Similar pamphlets were put on sale with the other charts comprising the *Collection* of 1769-70 and the *North-American Pilot* of 1775. The tracts of sailing-directions could, like the charts, be purchased either separately or in a bound collection. Five such collections are known, dated respectively 1769, 1775, 1778, 1782 and 1794 (Bibl., Nos. 12, 14, 16, 18, 21) and accompanying atlases of the same or near date. Each has a printed titlepage; and in all but the last two (of 1782 and 1794, in which the contents are reset throughout) the component tracts are variously composed of reissues (from an earlier type-setting) and reprints (with the type reset). It is clear that collections were made up from the stocks of the pamphlets available at the time in the mapsellers' shop, supplemented by reprinting where necessary, and it seems probable that, from the bibliographical point of view, such collections were no less unstable than the atlases. It is however rash to generalise because of the extreme rarity of these sailing directions, both separately and collectively. Of each of the collections of 1769 and 1778, only one copy has come to light, of that of 1782 we know three copies, and of that of 1794 two copies, while that of 1775 is little less scarce; and in their separate issues the pamphlets are practically unknown today.

Thomas Jefferys died on 20 November 1771, and his successor in business, William Faden, who was perhaps more interested in topographical maps, does not seem to have taken over his chart plates. Most of these, including the ten plates of the *Collection*, were acquired by Robert Sayer and John Bennett. Sayer had been joined, in 1770, by Bennett as partner in his shop at 53 Fleet Street, about half a mile east of Jefferys' establishment down the Strand at Charing Cross.

The evidence for the date of publication of the *Collection*, in its final form, is provided by the imprint-dates found on its charts, in the states as issued by Jefferys (in the *Collection*, 1770) and by the next owners of the plates, Sayer and Bennett (in *The North-American Pilot*, 1775). Of the ten charts in extant copies of the *Collection* (in its definitive state), one is dated 10 May 1770, one May 1770; three have earlier dates (1767, 1768, 4 April 1769), and five are undated. Of the same ten charts in *The North-American Pilot*, one is dated variously 10 May 1770 and 10 May 1774; no fewer than seven have the date 10 May 1770 (with the imprint of Sayer and Bennett, who at that date presumably did not own the plates); one is dated May 10, 1774; and one (previously dated 4 April 1769) is now undated. It seems clear that, at some stage before Jefferys' death, the plates of nine (of the ten) charts of the *Collection* were dated 10 May 1770 in their imprints, generally with Jefferys' name as publisher, and that a standard copy of the *Collection* of 1770 would have contained the charts in this state. (See Table A.)

As the impressions taken over in Jefferys' stock by Sayer and Bennett were sold out, the new proprietors reprinted the charts after inserting their own names in the imprints on all the plates used in the *Collection* of 1770; on two charts only (pl. 1 and 2) the date of publication was altered, though in rather a slapdash way, the original day and month (10 May) being retained and only the year corrected. By 1774 Sayer and Bennett were projecting a new atlas, some copies of which were on sale by the middle of 1775 (Bibl., No. 13). Of the 20 charts in *The North-American Pilot*, as it was called, with roman plate-numbers from I to XXII, ten were from the plates used in the Collection. The other ten, including Cook's chart of the St Lawrence (pl. XX-XXII) first published in 1760, had also been Jefferys' property, though not included in the *Collection*; each of the first three—the general chart (pl. I), the "Banks of Newfoundland" (pl. II) and the "South East Part of Newfoundland" (pl. III)—was reworked in accordance with Michael Lane's surveys in south-east Newfoundland in the seasons of 1772 and 1773. (It is curious that in the years 1772-6 Faden engraved and published four distinct charts from Lane's surveys in Labrador and Newfoundland; see note to Bibl., No. 12.)

Cook, who returned to England from his second circumnavigation at the end of July 1775, was presented by Sayer and Bennett with a copy of *The North-American Pilot* and persuaded to write a letter of commendation, dated from Mile End, 26 February 1776; and in copies issued after this date the letter was printed on the verso of a leaf which bore on its recto a dedication to Admiral Sir Hugh Palliser, Cook's first commander in the Navy and the director of the Newfoundland surveys. Two further editions of the *Pilot*, with the charts in the same state but the date in the titlepage imprint changed, were published in 1777 and 1779 (Nos. 15, 17); and a second part was added in 1776, embracing the Atlantic coasts from New England to Florida. The charts continued to be sold as loose sheets, without further alteration, so long as Sayer and Bennett remained in business.

Bennett died in 1787, and a year or two before his own death in 1794 Sayer transferred his business and shop to Robert Laurie and James Whittle. The plates of *The North-American Pilot* now underwent their last change, when Laurie and Whittle inserted their names and the date 12 May 1794 in the imprints. In this form the charts appeared in the editions of the *Pilot* published by Laurie and Whittle in 1799 and 1806 (Bibl., Nos. 22, 23), in which two of the old Jefferys plates (pl. VII, IX) were replaced by more recent surveys and three new charts were added. The plates remained in the stock of this firm, which continued to trade until 1895 from the same address in Fleet Street under Robert Laurie's son, Richard Holmes Laurie, and his successors in business; and two of Cook's charts from the *Pilot* were last advertised for sale in its catalogue of 1886. In 1903, when the firm was merged with two other old chart-publishing houses, the plates came into the possession of the amalgamated company thus created, Messrs. Imray, Laurie, Norie & Wilson. The house whose "blue-back charts" now serve yachtsmen in the North Sea waters sailed by James Cook as an apprentice seaman still preserves one of the copperplates recording the survey of Newfoundland by James Cook, Master R.N.

A NOTE ON PUBLISHERS

MOUNT AND PAGE. See Coolie Verner, *A Carto-bibliographical Study of The English Pilot The Fourth Book* (1960), pp. 12-13, 73-77; W. R. Chaplin, "A seventeenth-century chart publisher", *The American Neptune*, VIII (1948), pp. 1-24.

THOMAS JEFFERYS (fl. 1735-1771); business continued by WILLIAM FADEN until his retirement in 1823, then by JAMES WYLD the elder (1790-1836).

ROBERT SAYER (d. 1794), in partnership with PHILIP OVERTON (d. 1751), 1745-51; with JOHN BENNETT (d. 1787), 1770-87. The business was taken over in 1792 or 1793 by ROBERT LAURIE (1750-1836) and JAMES WHITTLE (d. 1818); Laurie retired in 1812, when his son RICHARD HOLMES LAURIE (d. 1858) took his place. The successive imprints used by the firm were Laurie & Whittle (1794-1812), Whittle & Laurie (1812-18), R. H. Laurie (1818-1903). In 1903 the firm was merged with two others, Norie & Wilson and Imray & Son, under the style IMRAY, LAURIE, NORIE & WILSON. See Elena Wilson, *The Story of the Blue Back Chart* (1937).

BIBLIOGRAPHY

[1759?]

1 To the Right Honble / the Master and Wardens / of the Trinity House / of Deptford Strond / This Draught of the Bay and / Harbour of Gaspee in the Gulf of / St Laurence taken in 1758 is humbly / presented by their most obed.^t hum.^{le} Servt / James Cook / Master of his Majesty's Ship the Pembroke. / Sold by W. & I. Mount T. & T. Page on Tower Hill / London.

> 2 sh.; overall $16\frac{1}{4} \times 37$ in. Scale 2 in.=1 mile. Profiles at top and bottom, with a note on the latitude of Pt Gaspee (48° 50'N) and on the tides.

> The survey for this chart, of which no MS. original is known, must have been made on the occasion of General Wolfe's raid on Gaspé in August 1758, in which Cook, as master of H.M.S. *Pembroke*, was engaged. The engraved chart, which is undated, was published while Thomas Page III (who joined the firm in 1755) was in business with his father Thomas Page II (who died in 1762). No later states are known.

[1760]

2 A New Chart / of the River S^t. Laurence, / from the / Island of Anticosti / to the Falls of Richelieu: with all the / Islands, Rocks, Shoals, and Soundings. / Also / Particular Directions / For Navigating the River with Safety. / Taken by Order of / Charles Saunders, Esqr / Vice-Admiral of the Blue, and Commander in Chief / of His Majesty's Ships in the / Expedition against Quebec in 1759. / Engraved by Thomas Jefferys / Geographer to his Royal Highness the Prince of Wales. / Published by Command of / The Right Honourable the Lords Commissioners of the / Admiralty.

> 12 sh.; overall 35×90 in. Scale 1 in.=2 leagues. With insets of the River from Richelieu Falls to I. of Coudres, and from I. of Coudres to Green I., on scale 1 in.=1 league; five inset plans; and a note by Saunders dated Pall Mall, 1 May 1760.

> The origin of this chart is described in a letter of Major Samuel Holland, 11 January 1792, to John Graves Simcoe, Lieutenant-Governor of Upper Canada. The chart was first compiled, mainly from French maps, by Cook and Holland on board H.M.S. *Pembroke* in the winter of 1759-60 at Halifax, where the English fleet was wintering; Captain John Simcoe (father of the governor) commanded the *Pembroke*, and Cook was her master. The chart was completed, corrected and fair-drawn from the surveys made jointly by Holland and Cook "coming up the river" to Quebec in the spring of 1760. It was ready by April, when Admiral Saunders recommended its publication to the Admiralty. Although neither the chart nor the accompanying sailing-directions (Bibl., No. 3) bear Cook's name,

there can be no doubt of his authorship. Three MS. originals are known—two in the Admiralty (one of them signed by Cook), the third in a private collection in Montreal; and one was listed in Jefferys' MS. "Catalogue" of 1775 (see above, p. 181).

The printed chart was issued, in later states (only the imprint being altered and plate-numbers added), in the *North-American Pilot*, editions of 1775, 1777, 1779, 1799 and 1806 (Bibl., Nos. 13, 15, 17, 22, 23).

1760

3   Directions / for / Navigating / the / Gulf and River / of / St. Laurence,/ . . . Printed for Thomas Jefferys, Geographer to his Royal / Highness the Prince of Wales. / M.DCC.LX. [*For full title, see the reproduction*, Plate 88]

4to. B-E⁴; first leaf (title) and last leaf (advertisement) not included in signatures. Sig. B1ᵛ-E4ʳ paginated 2-31

Contents: p. [1] (dropped head), Directions / for / Sailing / in the / Gulf of St. Lawrence.—p. 3, Directions for sailing up the River St. Lawrence.—p. 16, Directions for passing the Traverse.—p. 25 (dropped head), Directions / for / Sailing from Quebec / down the / River St. Lawrence.

1766

4   A Chart / of the / Straights of Belleisle / with part of the coast of / Newfoundland and Labradore / from actual surveys / Taken by Order of / Commodore Pallisser / Governor of Newfoundland, Labradore, &ᶜᵃ. / by / James Cook / Surveyor / 1766.

Of the six states identified, the first three are in one sheet, $23\frac{1}{2} \times 31$ in.; the last three are in two sheets, overall $23\frac{1}{2} \times 43\frac{1}{2}$ in. Scale, 1 in.=1 league. *First state*, in one sheet; perhaps a pre-publication proof.   The title enclosed in a simple oval frame; no imprint. The Labrador coast, from St Peter's Bay to Chateaux Bay, with the inset plans of Red Bay, York or Chateaux Bay, White Cape to Maria Head (with Quirpon Harbour), and Croque Harbour, is from Cook's surveys in the *Grenville*, August-October 1763. (MS. originals: Hydro. Dept., X54, and eight plans: B.M., Add. MS. 31360, two plans.) The Newfoundland coast, from White Cape to Point Ferolle, with the inset plan of Old Ferolle Harbour, was surveyed by him in July-October 1764. (MS. originals: Hydro. Dept., C 54/3, C 54/4, C 54/7, 342; B.M., Add. MS. 31360.11.) The Labrador coast, east and west of the surveyed section, and the east coats of Newfoundland, from White Cape to Croque Harbour, are drawn in outline.—*Second state*. Figures of Indians in a rocky landscape engraved on either side of the frame of the title; imprint inserted below, in a decorative cartouche, "Published by

Permission, / of the Right Honourable the Lord / Commissioners of the Admiralty, by / Iames Cook, and Sold with a Book of Directions, by / I. Mount & T. Page, on Tower Hill, London. / Larken sculp." Two additions were made in the imprint at different stages of printing from this state of the plate: (a) "s" added after "Lord"; (b) "Price 4 Shill." added after "London".—*Third state*. The cartouche and imprint have been deleted, as have the seventh-ninth lines of the title ("Taken by Order of . . . Labradore, &ᶜᵃ."). The title, unframed, now ends: "Published by Permission / of the Right Honourable the / Lords Commissioners of the Admiralty / by / James Cook / Surveyor / 1766'. In this state the chart is found (as pl. 4) in early copies of *A Collection of Charts*, probably those issued in 1769.— *Fourth state*, in two sheets, a narrower sheet being added on the left. The last four lines of the title ("by / James Cook / Surveyor / 1766.") have been deleted, and the following substituted: "Surveyed by / James Cook in 1766/ and / Michael Lane in 1769. / London / Published according to Act of Parliament May 1770 / by T. Jefferys Geographer to the King". The west coast of Newfoundland is completed (on the new sheet) southward to Mal Bay, from Cook's surveys in the *Grenville*, May-September 1767; the whole Labrador coast is re-engraved and continued east to Niger Sound and Cape Charles and west to Shecatica Island, with a new inset of Bradore Harbour, from Lane's surveys in the *Grenville* in 1768-9. (MS. original: Hydro. Dept., C 54/2.) In this state the chart is found in later copies of *A Collection of Charts*, i.e. those issued in 1770.—*Fifth state*. Jefferys' name has been deleted from the imprint at the end of the title, which now reads "London / Published according to Act of Parliament / 10 May 1770 / by R. Sayer & I. Bennett . . ." Plate Number (XVII) inserted. In this state the chart was issued in *The North-American Pilot*, editions of 1775, 1777 and 1779, pl. XVII.—*Sixth state*. Sailing directions have been engraved in the top left-hand corner, and the title and imprint (following the word "Admiralty") are re-engraved to read "and Taken in 1766, by James Cook, / afterwards Capᵗⁿ. Cook, the Celebrated Circumnavigator, / and by / Michael Lane in 1769. / London Published 12ᵗʰ May, 1794, by Laurie & Whittle . . . " In this state the chart was issued in *The North-American Pilot*, edition of 1799, pl. XVII, and edition of 1806, pl. 20.

Plate 85 [State II], Plate 86 [State III], Plate 87 [State V]

1766

5   Directions / for Navigating on Part of the / North East Side of Newfoundland, / and in the Streights of / Bell-Isle, / with / A Chart thereof, / . . . / By James Cook, / Surveyor of Newfoundland. / London: / Printed for the Author and Sold by J. Mount and T. Page on / Tower-Hill, / M.DCC.LXVI. [*For full title, see the reproduction*, Plate 89]

4to. A⁴B². Verso of t.p. blank; sig. A2ʳ-B2ᵛ paginated 3-12.

6   A Chart, / of Part of the South Coast, of / Newfoundland, / including the Islands / S^t. Peters and Miquelon, / from an actual survey / Taken by order of / Commodore Pallisser, / Governor of Newfoundland, Labradore &c. / by / James Cook, / Surveyor.
Larken sc.

Published by Permission, / of the Right Honble. the Lords Commissioners of the Admiralty / by James Cook / and Sold by I. Mount and T. Page on Tower Hill, / Thos. Jefferys the corner of St. Martins Lane in y^e Strand / and And.^{w} Dury, in Dukes Court, near St. Martins Church, / London. / 1766. / NB. With a Book of Directions.

> Scale, 1 in.=1 league. *First state*, in two sheets, overall 27$\frac{1}{4}$×38 in. The Newfoundland coast is charted from Great Jervis Harbour to St Laurence Harbours (Burin Peninsula), from Cook's survey in the *Grenville*, June-October 1765; the three inset plans of St Laurence Harbours, Harbour Breton and Great Jervis Harbour are from the same survey; the coastline east of St Laurence and west of Great Jervis is drawn in outline. (MS. original: Hydro. Dept., C 58.) St Pierre and Miquelon are from Cook's survey in the *Tweed*, June-July 1763. (MS. originals: Hydro. Dept., B. 5299, and one plan; B.M., Add. MS. 31360.21, K. Top. CXIX.111, and four plans.)—*Second state*: not published separately. The left-hand sheet (with corrections and additions) was incorporated in No. 8, below.

7   Directions / for Navigating on Part of the / South Coast of Newfoundland, / with / A Chart thereof, / Including the Islands of / St. Peter's and Miquelon, / . . . / By James Cook, / Surveyor of Newfoundland. / London: / Printed for the Author, and Sold by J. Mount and T. Page on / Tower-Hill, M,DCC,LXVI. [*For full title, see the reproduction*, Plate 90]

> 4to. A-B^{4}C^1. Verso of t.p. blank; sig. A2^r-C1^v paginated 3-18.

8   A / Chart of Part / of the South Coast of / Newfoundland / including the Islands / S^t. Peters and Miquelon / with the Southern Entrance into the Gulph of S^t. Laurence / from actual Surveys Taken by Order of / Commodore Pallisser / Governor of Newfoundland, Labradore, &c. / by / James Cook / Surveyor.
Larken sculp. 1767.

Published by Permission, / of the Right Honble the Lords Commissioners of the Admiralty / by James Cook / and Sold by I. Mount and T. Page on Tower Hill, /

Thos. Jefferys the corner of St. Martins Lane in ye Strand, / And w. Dury in Dukes Court, near St. Martins Church / and Carington Bowles in S.t Pauls Church Yard. / London. / 1767.

> Scale, 1 in.=1 league. *First state*, in three sheets, with an extension slip pasted on at right: overall 25 × 68 in. The right-hand sheet is printed from the left-hand plate of No. 6 (see above), with a good deal of re-engraving: the coast west of Great Jervis Harbour completed (from Cook's 1766 survey), many soundings and a view of Chapeau Rouge added. The cartouche and title are re-engraved, with the same wording. The imprint (worded as above) has been added. The extension slip shows the head of Fortune Bay, copied in crude engraving from the right-hand sheet of No. 6. The two left-hand sheets are new, and show the coast west to Cape Ray and Cape Anguille from Cook's surveys in the *Grenville*, June-October 1766. (MS. originals; Hydro. Dept., C 54/5; B.M., Add. MS. 31360, two plans.) The inset plans of St Laurence Harbours, Harbour Breton and Great Jervis Harbour are re-engraved on a smaller scale; the new one of Port aux Basques is from the 1766 survey. In this state the chart was issued in *A Collection of Charts*, 1769-70 (pl. 2).—*Second state*. The names and addresses of And w Dury and Carington Bowles are deleted from the imprint.—*Third state*. The fifth line of the title ("including the Islands") is re-engraved to read "Including the Islands of Langley"; the imprint is altered to "Printed for R. Sayer and Jno. Bennett / . . . / May 10, 1774"; an inset plan of "St. Peters Island, survey'd by Engineer Fortin, in 1763" is added; and the plate number (VI) inserted. In this state the chart was included in *The North-American Pilot*, editions of 1775, 1777 and 1779, pl. VI.—*Fourth state*. The imprint of Sayer and Bennett is replaced by: "Published by Laurie & Whittle . . . / 12th May 1794". In this state the chart was published in *The North-American Pilot*, edition of 1799, pl. VI, and edition of 1806, pl. 9.

1768

9 A Chart of the West Coast of Newfoundland, / Surveyed by Order of Commodore Pallisser, / Governor of Newfoundland, Labradore &c. &c. / By James Cook, Surveyor.

Larken Sculpt:
Published by Permission, / of the Right Hon.ble the Lords Commissioners / of the Admiralty, By / James Cook, / and Sold with a Book of Directions, / By J. Mount, and T. Page, on Tower-Hill, / Thos. Jefferys, the corner of St. Martin's Lane, in the Strand, / and And w. Dury, in Duke's Court, near St. Martin's Church, / London. / 1768.

> Scale: 1 in.=1 league.—*First state*, in three sheets, overall 20 × 68 in. The chart, which extends from Cape Anguille to Point Ferolle, is from Cook's surveys in the *Grenville*, May-September 1767, as are the two inset plans of Hawkes Harbour, Port Saunders and Keppel Harbour and of York and

Lark Harbours. (MS. originals: Hydro. Dept., C 54/1; B.M., Add. MS. 17693.D.) In this state the chart was issued in *A Collection of Charts*, 1769-70 (pl. 3).—*Second state*. The imprint (following "Directions") is altered to read "Printed for R. Sayer & I. Bennett . . . / . . . 10 May 1770"; and the plate number (XVI) inserted. In this state the chart was issued in *The North-American Pilot*, editions of 1775, 1777 and 1779, pl. XVI.—*Third state*. The imprint of Sayer and Bennett is replaced by "Publish'd by Laurie & Whittle . . . / 12ᵗʰ May, 1794". In this state the chart was issued in *The North-American Pilot*, edition of 1799, pl. XVI, and edition of 1806, pl. 19.

1768

10   Directions / for Navigating the / West-Coast of Newfoundland, / with / A Chart.thereof, / . . . / By James Cook, / Appointed by the Admiralty to Survey the Coast of Newfoundland. / London: / Printed for the Author, and Sold by J. Mount / and T. Page, on Tower-Hill; A. Dury, in Duke's Court, near / St. Martin's Church; and T. Jeffery's, the Corner of / St. Martin's-Lane, and N. Gill, Naval Officer in St. John's / Newfoundland, M,DCC,LXVIII. [*For full title, see the reproduction*, Plate 91]

> 4to. A⁴B². Verso of t.p. blank; sig. A2ʳ-B2ᵛ paginated 3-11; B2ᵛ blank.

Plate 97.

[1769-70]

11   A / Collection of Charts / Of the Coasts of / Newfoundland / and / Labradore, &c. / . . . / London: / Printed according to the Act of Parliament; and sold by Thomas Jefferys, in the Strand. / N.B. Of whom may be had the Newfoundland Pilot, containing a collection of Directions for each of the above Charts. [*For full title, see the reproduction*, Plate 92]

> Folio. 10 charts. (Phillips 1254.) Copies were probably issued in 1769, without the general chart, pl. 1, and with that of Belleisle Strait, pl. 4, in state III (Admiralty Library, L.C.); and in 1770, including the general chart and with that of Belleisle Strait in state IV (N.M.M., U.C.L.A.). See above, pp. 8-10.

> The charts are here listed from the definitive edition of 1770. They have no plate-numbers; the numbers given to them below are derived from those on the titlepage.

> Charts:

> 1   A General Chart of the Island of Newfoundland . . . Drawn from surveys taken by Order of . . . the Lords Commissioners of the Admiralty. By James Cook and Michael Lane Surveyors and Others. London Publish'd . . . 10ᵗʰ May 1770. By Thomas Jefferys . . . [First state; see above, pp. 9, 11.]

Plate 84.

2 A Chart of Part of the South Coast of Newfoundland including the Islands S^t. Peters and Miquelon . . . By James Cook Surveyor. Larken sculp. 1767. Published . . . by James Cook . . . London 1767. [First state of No. 8 above.]

3 A Chart of the West Coast of Newfoundland . . . By James Cook, Surveyor. Larken Sculp^t: Published . . . By James Cook . . . London. 1768. [First state of No. 9 above.]

4 A Chart of the Straights of Bellisle with part of the coast of Newfoundland and Labradore . . . Surveyed by James Cook in 1766 and Michael Lane in 1769. London Published . . . May 1770 by T. Jefferys . . . [Fourth state of No. 4 above. The third state is found in early copies of the *Collection* (1769).]

5 A Chart of Part of the Coast of Labradore, from Grand Point to Shecatica. Surveyed by Michael Lane in 1768. And engraved by Thomas Jefferys . . . [No imprint or date.]

6 A Chart of Part of the Coast of Labradore, from the Straights of Bell Isle, to Cape Bluff. Surveyed by Joseph Gilbert in 1767. And Engraved by Thomas Jefferys . . . [No imprint or date.]

7 A Chart of the Magdalen Islands Surveyed 1765. T. Jefferys Sculp. Published . . . April 4. 1769.

8 [Chart of Sable Island. No imprint or date.]

9 [Four plans.] Trinity Harbour; S^t. Johns Harbour; Carboniere and Harbour Grace; The Harbours of Ferryland and Aquafort with Caplin Bay. [No imprint or date.]

10 [Three plans.] The Harbour of Trepassey; The Road and Harbour of Placentia. By James Cook; S^t. Mary's Harbour. [No imprint or date.]

1769

12 The / Newfoundland Pilot: / . . . / London: / Printed for Thomas Jeffreys . . . / M.DCC.LXIX. / Of whom may be had, bound together or seperately, all the Charts belonging to the above Directions. [*For full title, see the reproduction*, Plate 93]

> 4to. Prelim. leaf (recto, general title; verso, "The Contents", see Plate 94) plus five tracts, each with separate signatures and pagination, as below.

> 1 [*titlepage:*] Directions / for Navigating on Part of the / South Coast of Newfoundland, / with / A Chart thereof, / Including the Islands of / St. Peter's and Miquelon, / . . . / By James Cook, / Surveyor of Newfoundland. / London: / Printed for T. Jefferys, Corner of St. Martin's-Lane, in the /

Strand; and sold by J. Mount and T. Page on Tower-Hill. / MDCCLXIX. A-D⁴. Sig. A2ʳ-D⁴ᵛ paginated 3-32.

Reprint of Cook's edition of 1766 (Bibl., No. 7), reset page-for-page; imprint and date on title-page altered.

2 [*titlepage:*] Directions / for Navigating the / West-Coast of Newfoundland, / with / A Chart thereof, / . . . / By James Cook, / . . . / London:/ Printed for the Author . . ./ . . . / . . . M,DCC,LXVIII.

Reissue of Cook's edition of 1768 (Bibl., No. 10).

3 [*titlepage:*] Directions / for Navigating on Part of the / North East Side of Newfoundland, / And in the Streights of / Bell-Isle, / with/ A Chart thereof, / . . . / By James Cook, Surveyor of Newfoundland. / London: / Printed for the Author; / M.DCC.LXIX.

A-B⁴. Sig. A2ʳ-B4ᵛ paginated 3-16.

Reprint of Cook's edition of 1766 (Bibl., No. 5), reset and augmented by Joseph Gilbert's description (pp. 12-16) of the Labrador coast from St Peter's Bay to Cape Bluff, from his survey in 1767. Date on titlepage altered, but imprint copied from that of 1766 edition.

4 Description / of Part of the / Coast of Labradore, / from / Grand Point of Great Mecatina to Shecatica. [*imprint on last page:*] London: / Published according to Act of Parliament; and sold by Mess. Mount / and Page, on Tower-Hill; and Thomas Jeffery's, Geographer to the / King, at Charing-Cross 1769.

A-B². Sig. A1ᵛ-B2ʳ paginated 2-7.

As stated in "The Contents", this is by Michael Lane, from his survey in 1768. The advertisement above the imprint on the last page lists, as "just published", Cook's three charts and the General Chart of Newfoundland, implying that they were on sale in 1769.

5 [Five items relating to the east and south-east coasts of Newfoundland, without a common title but with continuous signatures.]

A-E⁴. Sig. A1ʳ-E4ᵛ paginated 1-40.

Sig. A1ʳ: Remarks made between the Island of / Groias and Cape Bonavista, / 1768.—sig. B1ᵛ: Directions for Navigating from Cape Race / to Cape Bonavista, made by Capt. South- / wood; with his Remarks upon the Fishing / Banks. [Southwood's survey of 1677; printed in editions of *The English Pilot*, Bk IV, from 1689.]—sig. E1ʳ: Directions for Navigating from Cape Race, / to Cape St. Mary's, made by John Gaudy, in 1718, / with his Remarks on the Banks, and his Directions for / sailing to Newfoundland. [Printed in editions of *The English Pilot*, Bk IV, from 1729.] —sig. E2ʳ: St. Mary's Bay.—sig. E3ʳ; Placentia Bay. [According to "The Contents", both are by Joseph Gilbert, 1768.]

NOTE

The Newfoundland Pilot, "printed for Thomas Jefferys" in 1769, is composed, bibliographically, of five tracts, each with its own signatures, pagination and imprint (except the fifth, which has no imprint). It is evident that, like the charts composing *A Collection of Charts*, the tracts were on sale either "bound together or separately"; in the latter case, a tract of sailing-directions would be bought with its associated chart, in the imprint of which it was often advertised. The division of the contents, in the list (PLATE XV) on the verso of the titlepage of the *Pilot*, does not correspond to the bibliographical division. The list enumerates eight items, giving some information on authorship which is not in the tracts themselves; but since two items are merged in the list (under No. 3), there are in fact nine. As the stock of any tract was exhausted, it was re-set and reprinted; two copies of the *Pilot* may therefore contain a tract or tracts of different editions. (Since only one copy of the *Pilot*—that in the Admiralty Library—has come to light, this surmise cannot be verified; but such variations of contents occur in copies of the *Sailing Directions* of 1775.) In successive editions of the tracts relating to the Labrador coast and to south-east Newfoundland, corrections and additions from more recent surveys were incorporated.

The first edition of each tract may be taken to have been on sale separately from the date of publication. The tracts were gathered into a composite volume, with a general titlepage, five times: by Jefferys in *The Newfoundland Pilot* (1769), by Sayer and Bennett in their three editions of *Sailing Directions for the North American Pilot* (1775, 1778, 1782), and by Laurie and Whittle in their edition (1794). A French edition of the three tracts by Cook, with some supplementary matter, was published in 1784 under the title *Instructions Nautiques, Relatives aux Cartes & Plans du Pilote de Terre-Neuve*.

All editions of these composite volumes are exceedingly rare. The following copies are known to the present authors (1967):

Newfoundland Pilot, 1769: Admiralty Library.

Sailing Directions, 1775: National Maritime Museum, Greenwich; John Carter Brown Library; Harvard College Library; Boston Public Library.

Sailing Directions, 1778: Admiralty Library.

Sailing Directions, 1782: Library of Congress; Toronto Public Library; Historical Society of Pennsylvania.

Instructions Nautiques, 1784: British Museum; Bibliothèque Nationale; John Carter Brown Library; Messrs. Henry Stevens Son & Stiles.

Sailing Directions, 1794: Library of Congress [two copies].

Table B shows the editions of the tracts known, with their occurrence in the composite volumes. It will be noted that no edition of the *Sailing Directions for the North American Pilot* is wholly a reissue of its predecessor. Except for the first three items in *The Newfoundland Pilot* of 1769, none of the separate items in the five composite volumes has its own titlepage, although in several cases the signatures or pagination point to a missing first leaf. If we may judge by the frequency of reprinting, the demand was greatest for the directions for Belleisle Strait and for the South Coast of Newfoundland, and least for those of the West Coast (which were not re-set until 1782).

In addition, four tracts of Lane's sailing-directions with charts, from his surveys in 1770-75, appear to have been printed for Jefferys' successor William Faden. (Manuscript originals of some of these charts and plans are listed in the Jefferys catalogue of 1775; see above, p. 9.) They relate to (a) the Labrador coast from Cape Charles to Sandwich Bay, surveyed 1770-71, published 1772; (b) Placentia Bay with the South Coast from Cape Chapeau Rouge to Cape St Mary, surveyed 1772, published 1773; (c) Point Lance [C. St Mary] to Cape Spear, surveyed 1773, published 1774; and (d) Cape Spear to Cape Bonavista, surveyed 1775, published 1776. The original editions of only charts (b) and (c) and of one tract (Point Lance to Cape Spear, 4to, "published . . . 7th April 1774 by Jefferys and Faden") have been found; but in 1809 Faden issued a second edition of chart (c) revised by J. F. Dessiou, and in 1810 he put out all four pamphlets, 8vo, in a "Second edition. Revised by J. F. Dessiou".

13   The / North-American Pilot / for / Newfoundland, Labradore, / the / Gulf and River St. Laurence: / being a collection of / sixty accurate charts and plans, / . . . / Chiefly engraved by / The Late Mr. Thomas Jefferys, Geographer to the King. / On thirty-six large copper-plates. / London: / Printed according to Act of Parliament, and sold by R. Sayer and J. Bennett, No. 53, in Fleet-Street. / M.DCC.LXXV. / N.B. Of whom may be had, the Sailing Directions for the above Charts. [*For full title, see the reproduction*, Plate 95]

Folio. 2 or 3 or 4 leaves of text plus 22 charts numbered I-XXII.

The preliminary leaves occur in four variant forms, which may be assigned a *terminus post quem* from internal evidence and from the variant imprint-dates of charts associated with them, as below:

State A (2 leaves)—[fol. 1ʳ] title, as above, [1ᵛ] blank; [2ʳ⁻ᵛ] "Index of the Charts, Plans, &c." Latest imprint-date in charts, 25 March 1775.

State B (3 leaves)—[fol. 1ʳ] title, [1ᵛ] blank; [2ʳ] dedication "To Sir Hugh Palliser, Bart. . . . Vice-Admiral of the Blue", signed Robert Sayer, Fleet-Street, 1775, [2ᵛ] blank; [3ʳ⁻ᵛ] "Index of the Charts . . . " Latest imprint-date in charts, 25 March 1775. Palliser was appointed Rear-Admiral (not Vice-Admiral) of the Blue on 31 March 1775; his next promotion was to Rear-Admiral of the White, on 5 February 1776.

State C (3 leaves)—[fol. 1ʳ] title, [1ᵛ] blank; [2ʳ] dedication as in B, [2ᵛ] Cook's letter to Sayer dated 26 February 1776; [3ʳ⁻ᵛ] "Index of the Charts . . . " Latest imprint-date in charts, 15 June 1775.

State D (4 leaves)—[fol. 1ʳ] title, [1ᵛ] blank; [2ʳ] dedication, [2ᵛ] blank; [3ʳ] Cook's letter, [3ᵛ] blank; [4ʳ⁻ᵛ] "Index of the Charts . . . "Latest imprint-date in charts, 15 June 1775. Since this is the form in which the preliminary pages are found in the 1777 edition, we take it to be later than State C.

State A was therefore on sale after 25 March 1775; B after 31 March 1775; C and D after 26 February 1776. In the lists of charts below, their occurrence in *A Collection of Charts*, 1769-70 (Bibl., No. 11), is noted; reference may also be made to Table A and to the Foreword, pp. 10-11].

Charts:

I   A General Chart of the Island of Newfoundland . . . London Published . . . 10ᵗʰ May 1770. By Thomas Jefferys . . . Printed for Rob.ᵗ Sayer & Jn.º Bennett. [Variant imprint, 10ᵗʰ May 1775. *Collection*, pl. 1. Second state, with revision; see above, pp. 9-11.]

II   A Chart of the Banks of Newfoundland. Drawn from . . . surveys, chiefly from those of Chabert, Cook and Fleurieu . . . London. Printed for & Sold by Rob.ᵗ Sayer & Jn.º Bennett . . . 25ᵗʰ March 1775. [Second state, with revision; see above, p. 11.]

III A Chart of the South-East Part of Newfoundland . . . London. Printed for R. Sayer and I. Bennett . . . 10 May 1770. [Second state, with revision; see above, p. 11. The magnetic variation for 1773 is given.]

IV [Four plans.] Trinity Harbour; S^t. Johns Harbour; Carboniere and Harbour Grace; [Ferryland and Aquafort Harbours.] Printed for R. Sayer & I. Bennet . . . 10 May 1770. [*Collection*, pl. 9.]

V [Three plans.]. The Harbour of Trepassey; The Road and Harbour of Placentia. By James Cook; S^t. Mary's Harbour. Printed for R. Sayer & I. Bennet . . . 10th May 1770. [*Collection*, pl. 10.]

VI A Chart of Part of the South Coast of Newfoundland including the Islands of Langley S^t. Peters and Miquelon . . . by James Cook Surveyor. Printed for R. Sayer and J^{no}. Bennett . . . May 10, 1774. [Third state of No. 8, *Collection*, pl. 2.]

VII A New Map of Nova Scotia and Cape Breton Island, with the adjacent parts of New England and Canada, composed . . . by Thomas Jefferys. Published . . . by Thos. Jefferys . . . London, Printed & Sold by R. Sayer & J. Bennett. [No date. Variant imprint, 15 June 1775.]

VIII The Island of Sable. T. Jefferys sculp. Printed for R. Sayer & I. Bennett . . . 10 May 1770. [*Collection*, pl. 8.]

IX A Chart of the Harbour of Halifax in Nova Scotia . . . Survey'd . . . By Charles Morris . . . Engraved by Thomas Jefferys . . . London, Printed for & Sold by Robt Sayer & Jno Bennett . . . 25th March 1775.

X [Three plans.] A Plan of Port Dauphin; A Plan of Murgain or Cow Bay; A Draught of the Gut of Canso. London. Printed for & Sold by Robt Sayer and Jno Bennett . . . 25th March 1775.

XI A Chart of the Gulf of St. Laurence. Printed for & Sold by Robt Sayer & Jno Bennett . . . 25th March 1775.

XII A Chart of the Magdalen Islands . . . surveyed in 1765. T. Jefferys Sculp. [No imprint or date. Variant: imprint of Sayer and Bennett, 15 June 1775. *Collection*, pl. 7.]

XIII A Map of the Island of S^t. John . . . Published . . . April 6, 1774. [No publisher's name. Variant; imprint of Sayer and Bennett, 6 April 1775.]

XIV A Plan of Chaleur Bay . . . surveyed . . . in 1760. London Printed for & Sold by Robt Sayer & J^{no}. Bennett . . . 25th March 1775.

XV A Plan of Ristigouche Harbour in Chaleur Bay, surveyed in 1760 . . . London. Printed for & Sold by Robt Sayer & J^{no}. Bennett . . . 25th March 1775.

XVI A Chart of the West Coast of Newfoundland . . . by James Cook, Surveyor. Printed for R. Sayer & I. Bennett . . . 10 May 1770. [Second state of No. 9, *Collection*, pl. 3.]

XVII   A Chart of the Straights of Bellisle with part of the coast of New-foundland and Labradore . . . Surveyed by James Cook in 1766 and Michael Lane in 1769. London Published . . . 10 May 1770 by R. Sayer & I. Bennett. [Fifth state of No. 4, *Collection*, pl. 4.]

XVIII   A Chart of part of the Coast of Labradore, from the Straights of Bell Isle to Cape Bluff. Surveyed by Joseph Gilbert in 1767. And engraved by Thomas Jefferys . . . London. Printed for R. Sayer & I. Bennett . . . 10 May 1770 [*Collection*, pl. 6.]

XIX   A Chart of part of the Coast of Labradore, from Grand Point to Shecatica. Surveyed by Michael Lane in 1768. And engraved by Thomas Jefferys . . . London. Printed for R. Sayer and I. Bennett . . . 10 May 1770. [*Collection*, pl. 5.]

XX-XXII   A New Chart of the River S^t. Laurence, from the Island of Anticosti to the Falls of Richelieu . . . Engraved by Thomas Jefferys. London. Printed for Robt Sayer & Jno Bennett . . . 16 Feby 1775. [Bibl., No. 2.]

1775

14   Sailing Directions / for the / North-American Pilot: / Containing the / Gulf and River St. Laurence, / the Whole Island of Newfoundland, / including / the Straits of Bell-Isle, / and / the Coast of Labradore. / . . . / London: / Printed for R. Sayer and J. Bennett . . . / MDCCLXXV. / Of whom may be had, bound together or separately, all the Charts belonging to the above Directions. [*For full title, see the reproduction*, Plate 96]

4to. Ten tracts, each with separate signatures and pagination, as below.

1   Directions / for Navigating on Part of the / South Coast of Newfound-land.

A-D^4. Sig. A1^r is the general titlepage of the whole collection; A1^v blank. Sig. A2^r-D4^v paginated 3-32.

Reprint of the edition of 1769 (No. 12 (1)), reset; no titlepage.

2   Direction / for Navigating the West Coast of Newfoundland, / with a Chart thereof.

Reissue of Cook's edition of 1768 (No. 10), without the titlepage leaf (A1).

3   Directions / for / Navigating on Part of the N.E. Side of Newfound-/land, and in the Streights of Bell-Isle.

Reissue of the edition of 1769 (No. 12 (3)), without the titlepage leaf (A1).

4   Description / of Part of the / Coast of Labradore, / from / Grand Point of Great Mecatina to Shecatica.

[A]^4. Sig. [A] 1^v-4^r paginated 2-7; [A]4^v, an advertisement for 28 charts sold by Sayer and Bennett. Without signatures. Reprint of the edition of 1769 (No. 12 (4)), reset.

5   Directions / for / Navigating on that Part / of the / Coast of Labradore, from / Shecatica to Chateaux, in the Straits of Belle-Isle.

[A]². Sig. [A]1ᵛ-2ᵛ paginated 2-4. Without signature.

Not in *Pilot* of 1769. By Lane, from his survey in the summer of 1769; the text gives the magnetic variation for "this present Year 1769".

6   Description / of the / Coast of Labradore, / from / Cape Charles / to Cape Lewis.

[A]². Sig. [A] 1ᵛ-2ʳ paginated 2-3; [A] 2ᵛ blank. Without signatures.

Not in *Pilot* of 1769. By Lane, from his survey in the summer of 1770; the text gives the variation for "this present Year 1770".

7   Description / of the / Coast of Labradore, / from / Cape St. Michael / to / Spotted Island.

[A]². Sig. [A] 1ᵛ-2ʳ paginated 2-3; [A] 2ᵛ blank. Without signatures.

Not in *Pilot* of 1769. By Lane, from his 1770 survey; variation given for "this present Year 1770".

8   [Two items reprinted from the *Pilot* of 1769, without a common title but with continuous signatures.]

A-D⁴. Sig. A1ᵛ-D4ᵛ paginated 2-32. sig. A1ʳ: Remarks / made between / the Island of Groias / and / Cape Bonavista, / 1768. [Reprint of the edition of 1769 (No. 12 (5)), reset.]—sig. B1ʳ: Directions / for Navigating / From Cape Race to Cape Bonavista, / Made by Captain Southwood; / With his Remarks upon the Fishing Banks. [Reprint of the edition of 1769 (No. 12 (5)), reset.]

9   [Two new items, without a common title but with continuous signatures.]

A-B⁴ C³. Sig. A1ᵛ-C3ᵛ paginated 2-22. sig. A1ʳ: Directions / for Navigating the / Bay of Placentia / on the / South Coast of Newfoundland, / from Cape Chapeau Rouge to Cape St. Mary's. / Surveyed . . . / . . . by Michael Lane. [From Lane's 1774 survey. The text gives the magnetic variation for "this present Year 1774", and incorporates Gilbert's description of Placentia Bay (No. 12 (5, fifth item)), with revision.]—sig. B3ʳ: Directions / for Navigating Part of the / Coast of Newfoundland, / from [C]ape St. Mary to Cape Spear, / including / St. Mary's and Trepassey Bays. / Surveyed . . . / . . . by Michael Lane, in 1773. [Incorporates Gilbert's description of St. Mary's Bay (No. 12 (5, fourth item)), with revision.]

10   Sailing Directions / for the Gulf of St. Lawrence. B-C⁴ D². Sig. B1ᵛ-D2ᵛ paginated 2-20. Reprint of Jefferys' tract of 1760 (Bibl., No. 3), reset; no titlepage.

15   The / North American Pilot / for / Newfoundland, Labradore, / the Gulf and River St. Laurence: / . . . London: / Printed . . . and sold by R. Sayer and J. Bennett . . . / M.DCC.LXXVII. / . . .

>   Folio. 4 leaves of text plus 22 charts numbered I–XXII. (Phillips 1209.) Text-leaves: [fol. 1ʳ] title, [1ᵛ] blank; [2ʳ] dedication to Palliser, [2ᵛ] blank; [3ʳ] Cook's letter to Sayer, [3ᵛ] blank; [4ʳ⁻ᵛ] "Index of the Charts . . ." The title is reset line-by-line from that of the 1775 edition (No. 13). The charts are in the latest state found in the 1775 edition.

>   Issued with *The Second Part of The North American Pilot*, 1777 (which was first published in 1776).

16   Sailing Directions. / for the / North American Pilot: / . . . / London: / Printed for R. Sayer and J. Bennett, Map, Chart, and Print Sellers, in Fleet-Street. / MDCCLXXVIII. / Of whom may be had, bound together or separately, all the Charts belonging to the above Directions. [*For full title, see the reproduction*, Plate 98]

>   4to. Nine tracts, each with separate signatures and pagination, as below.

>   1   Directions / for Navigating Part of the / South Coast of Newfoundland. A–D⁴. Sig. A1ʳ is the general titlepage of the whole collection, reset line-by-line from that of the 1775 edition (No. 14); A1ᵛ blank. Sig. A2ʳ–D4ᵛ paginated 3-32.

>   Reprint of the edition of 1775 (No. 14 (1)).

>   2   Directions / for / Navigating the West Coast of Newfoundland, / with a Chart thereof.

>   Reissue of Cook's edition of 1768 (No. 10), without the titlepage leaf (A1).

>   3 Directions / for / Navigating on Part of the N.E. Side of Newfound- / land, and in the Streights of Bell-Islle [*sic*].

>   A⁴ B². Sig. A1ᵛ–B2ᵛ paginated 2-12.

>   Reprint of the edition of 1775 (No. 14 (3)), reset.

>   4   Description / of Part of the / Coast of Labradore, / from / Grand Point of Great Mecatina to Shecatica.

>   Reissue of the edition of 1775 (No. 14 (4)).

>   5   [Three items without a common title but with continuous signatures.] B⁴. Sig. B1ᵛ–B4ᵛ paginated 2-8.

>   Sig. B1ʳ: Directions / for Navigating on that Part of the / Coast of Labra- dore, / from / Shecatica to Chateaux, in the Straits of Belle-Isle. [Reprint of the edition of 1775 (No. 14 (5)), reset.]—sig. B2ᵛ: Description / of the /

Coast of Labradore, / From Cape Charles to Cape Lewis. [Reprint of the edition of 1775 (No. 14 (6)), reset.]—sig. B3ᵛ: Description / of the / Coast of Labradore, / From St. Michael to Spotted Island. [Reprint of the edition of 1775 (No. 14 (7)), reset.]

6 [Two items from the *Sailing Directions* of 1775, without a common title but with continuous signatures.]
Reissue of the edition of 1775 (No. 14 (8)).

7 Directions / for Navigating the / Bay of Placentia / on the / South Coast of Newfoundland, / From Cape Chapeau Rouge to Cape St. Mary's.
A⁴ B². Sig. A1ᵛ-B2ᵛ paginated 2-12.
Reissue of the corresponding pages in the edition of 1775 (No. 14 (9), first item)).

8 Directions / for Navigating Part of the / Coast of Newfoundland; / from Cape St. Mary to Cape Spear, / including / St. Mary's and Trepassey Bays.
A⁴. Sig. A1ᵛ-A4ᵛ paginated 2-8.
Reprint of the edition of 1775 (No. 14 (9, second item)), reset.

9 Sailing Directions / for the / Gulf of St. Laurence.
B-C⁴ D². Sig. B1ᵛ-D2ʳ paginated 2-19; D2ᵛ, an advertisement for 30 charts sold by Sayer and Bennett.
Reprint of the edition of 1775 (No. 14 (10)), reset.

1779

17 The North American Pilot / for / Newfoundland, Labradore, / the Gulf and River St. Laurence: . . . / London: / Printed . . . and sold by R. Sayer and J. Bennett . . . / M.DCC.LXXIX. / . . .

Folio. A reissue of the edition of 1777 (Bibl., No. 15), the title only being reset; the charts are in the same state. (G. R. Dalphin, *Marine Atlases in the Dartmouth College Library* (Hanover, N. H., 1950), No. 15.)

1782

18 Sailing Directions / for the / North American Pilot: / containing the / Gulph and River St. Laurence, / The Whole Island of Newfoundland, / including / the Straits of Bell-Isle, / and / The Coast of Labradore: / . . . / Published by Permission

of the / Right Honourable the Lords Commissioners of the Admiralty. / London: / Printed for R. Sayer and J. Bennett, Map, Chart, and Print-Sellers, in Fleet-Street. / MDCCLXXXII. / Of whom may be had, bound together or separately, all the Charts belonging to the above Directions. [*For full title, see the reproduction*, Plate 99]

4to. A-S⁴ T². Nine tracts, each with separate pagination; the signatures are continuous throughout the volume. The tracts are new editions, reset page-for-page from those in the 1778 collection (Bibl., No. 16).

1 Directions / for Navigating Part of the / South Coast of Newfoundland. A-D⁴. Sig. A2ʳ-D4ᵛ paginated 3-32. Sig. A1ʳ is the general titlepage of the whole collection, reset line-by-line from that of the 1778 edition (No. 16); A1ᵛ blank. Reprint of No. 16 (1).

2 Directions / for / Navigating the West Coast of Newfoundland, / with a Chart thereof.

E⁴. Sig. E1ᵛ-E4ᵛ paginated 4-10. Reprint of No. 16 (2).

3 Directions / for / Navigating on Part of the N.E. Side of Newfound- / land, and in the Streights of Bell-Isle.

F⁴ G². Sig. F1ᵛ-G2ᵛ paginated 2-12. Reprint of No. 16 (3).

4 Description / of Part of the / Coast of Labradore, / from / Grand Point of Great Mecatina to Shecatica.

H⁴. Sig. H1ᵛ-H4ʳ paginated 2-7. Reprint of No. 16 (4).

5 [Three items from the *Sailing Directions* of 1778, without a common title.]

I⁴. Sig. I1ᵛ-I4ᵛ paginated 2-8. Reprint of No. 16 (5).

6 [Two items from the *Sailing Directions* of 1778, without a common title.]

K-N⁴. Sig. K1ᵛ-N4ᵛ paginated 2-32. Reprint of No. 16 (6).

7 Directions / for Navigating Part of the / Coast of Newfoundland, / from Cape St. Mary to Cape Spear, / including / St. Mary's and Trepassey Bays.

O⁴. Sig. O1ᵛ-O4ᵛ paginated 2-8. Reprint of No. 16 (8).

8 Directions / for Navigating the / Bay of Placentia, / on the South Coast of Newfoundland, / From Cape Chapeau Rouge to Cape St. Mary's.

P⁴ Q². Sig. P1ᵛ-Q3ᵛ paginated 2-12. Reprint of No. 16 (7).

9 Sailing Directions / for the / Gulf of St. Lawrence.

R-S⁴ T². Sig. R1ᵛ-T2ʳ paginated 2-19. Reprint of No. 16 (9).

19   Le Pilote de Terre-Neuve / ou / Recueil de Plans / des Côtes et des Ports de cette Île. / Pour l'usage des Vaisseaux du Roi, / et des Navires de Commerce destinés à la Pêche. / D'après les Plans levés par MM. James Cook* et / Michael Lane Ingénieurs Géographes Anglois. / Précédé / De Deux Cartes Réduites, l'une de Terre-neuve avec les Bancs et Côtes voisines, / l'autre de cette Île en particulier; dressées sur les mêmes Plans et assuietties aux Observations Astronomiques / de MM. le Mⁱˢ. de Chabert en 1750 et 1751, J. Cook et autres Officiers Anglois in 1766, / le Mⁱˢ. de Verdun, le Ch.ᵉʳ de Borda et Pingré en 1772. / Publié par Ordre du Roi, / au Dépôt général des Cartes, Plans et Journaux de la Marine. / . . . / 1784. / *James Cook est celui qui s'est rendu depuis si célèbre par ses Voyages et ses Découvertes.

Folio. 11 plates, numbered 1-11. (Phillips 4490.)

The plates were also issued, with different plate-numbers, in the series *Hydrographie Françoise*, both as separate sheets and in the volume entitled *Neptune de l'Amerique Septentrionale* (or *Neptune Americo-Septentrional*). Plates 1-9, all dated 1784, are copied from charts by Cook and Lane in *The North-American Pilot*, Nos. 1 and 2 being drawn as *cartes réduites*, i.e. on the Mercator projection. Plates 10 and 11 are from the survey of St Pierre and Miquelon made by the *ingénieur-géographe* Fortin in 1763. Some copies have a Plate 12 added, though not listed in the "Table" on the titlepage ("Plan de la Baye de S.ᵗ Lunaire . . . Levé . . . en 1784 Par M. de Granchain . . . et Publié . . . en 1785"); cf. also Phillips 4490. (In the list below the plate-numbers of the *Hydrographie Française* and of the corresponding charts in *The North-American Pilot* are given in brackets.)

1   Carte Réduite des Bancs et de l'Île de Terre-neuve . . . Publiée . . . 1784. [*HF*, No. 141; *NAP*, pl. 1.]

2   Carte Réduite de l'Île de Terre-neuve Dressée d'après les Plans Anglois de James Cook et Michael Lane. [*HF*, No. 142; *NAP*, pl. II.]

3   Plan des Côtes de Terre-neuve. 1ᵉʳᵉ Feuille. Contenant la Partie Méridionale depuis le Cap de Raze jusqu'au Cap du Chapeau Rouge. Tiré des Plans Anglois de J. Cook et M. Lane. [*HF*, No. 143; *NAP*, pl. III.]

4   Plan des Côtes de Terre-neuve. IIᵉ. Feuille. Contenant la Partie Méridionale depuis le Cap du Chapeau Rouge jusqu'aux Îles de Burgeo, avec les Îles de Sᵗ. Pierre et Miquelon: Tiré des Plans Anglois de J. Cook et M. Lane. [*HF*, No. 144; *NAP*, pl. VI.]

5   Plan des Côtes de Terre-neuve. IIIᵉ. Feuille. Contenant la Partie Méridionale depuis les Îles de Burgeo jusqu'au Cap de Raze avec l'Entrée du Golfe de S.ᵗ Laurent . . . Tiré des Plans Anglois de J. Cook et M. Lane. [*HF*, No. ?; *NAP*, pl. VI.]

6   Plan des Côtes de Terre-Neuve. IVᵉ. Feuille. Contenant la Partie Occidentale depuis le Cap de Raze jusqu'au Cap de S.ᵗ Gregoire. Tiré des Plans Anglois de J. Cook et M. Lane. [*HF*, No. ?; *NAP*, pl. XVI.]

7 Plan des Côtes de Terre-neuve. V^e. Feuille. Contenant la Partie Occidentale depuis le Cap de St Gregoire jusqu'à la Pointe de Ferolle. Tiré des Plans Anglois de J. Cook et M. Lane. [*HF*, No. ?; *NAP*, pl. XVI.]

8 Plan des Côtes de Terre-Neuve. VIe. Feuille. Contenant la Partie Septentrionale depuis la Pointe de Ferolle jusqu'à l'Île de Quirpon, avec le Détroit de Bell'-Île et les Côtes de Labrador situées sur ce Détroit. Tiré des Plans Anglois de J. Cook et M. Lane. [*HF*, No. 150; *NAP*, pl. XVII.]

9 Plan des Côtes de Terre-neuve. VII. Feuille. Contenant la Partie Orientale depuis l'Île de Quirpon jusques au Cap de St Jean . . . Dressé d'après la Carte Générale de Terre-neuve de J. Cook et M. Lane. [*HF*, No. 152; not separately in *NAP*.]

10 Carte Particulière des Îles de St Pierre et Miquelon. Levé par M. Fortin . . . Rédigée . . . 1784. [*HF*, No. 145.]

11 Plan de l'Île de Saint Pierre . . . Levé en 1763 par le Sr Fortin . . . et Publié . . . 1763. [*HF*, No. 60.]

1784

20 Instructions / Nautiques, / Relatives aux Cartes & Plans / du Pilote de Terre-Neuve / Publié au Dépôt général des Cartes Plans & Journaux / de la Marine, en 1784; / Pour l'usage des Vaisseaux du Roi & des Bâtimens / particuliers employés à la Pêche. / Extraites du Recueil de divers Mémoires anglois, intitulé: / Sailing Directions for the North american Pilot; / Traduites & imprimées par ordre du Roi, / Sous le ministère de M. le Maréchal de Castries, / . . . / A Paris, / de l'Imprimerie Royale. / M.DCCLXXXIV. [*For full title, see the reproduction*, Plate 100]

4to. Five tracts, each with separate signatures, and pagination, as below.

1 Exposé / des / Cartes et Plans / qui composent / Le Pilote de Terreneuve.

*a-c*⁴. Sig. *a2*ʳ-*c4*ᵛ paginated iii-xxiv.

2 Instructions / pour Naviguer / sur la Côte Méridionale / de Terre-neuve. A-K⁴. Sig. A2ᵛ-K4ᵛ paginated 4-80.

Freely translated from Cook's directions for the South Coast, supplemented by those of Lane (No. 14 (1) and (7)).

3 Instructions / pour Naviguer / sur la Côte Occidentale / de Terre-neuve. A-C⁴ D¹. Sig. A2ᵛ-D1ᵛ paginated 4-26.

Translated from Cook's directions for the West Coast (No. 14 (2)).

4 Instructions / pour Naviguer / sur la Côte Septentrionale / de Terreneuve.

A-C⁴ D². Sig. A2ᵛ-D2ᵛ paginated 4-28.

English source unidentified.

21 Sailing Directions / for the / First Part / of the / North American Pilot: / containing the / Gulf and River St. Lawrence, / the whole Island of / Newfoundland, / including the / Straits of Belle-Isle, / and the / coast of Labradore / ... / A new edition. / London: / Printed for Robert Laurie and James Whittle, / No. 53, Fleet Street, / (successors to the late Mr. Robert Sayer.) / 1794. / N.B. This book of directions is sold only with the Pilot, but any of the charts may be had separate. [*For full title, see the reproduction*, Plate 101]

4to. A-P⁴. Sig. A3ʳ-P4ᵛ paginated 1-132.

The contents of the Sailing Directions of 1782 (Bibl., No. 18) are reset in the same order and with continuous pagination throughout, as below:

Directions for Navigating Part of the South Coast of Newfoundland (pp. 1-27).—Directions for Navigating the West Coast of Newfoundland (pp. 28-35).—Directions for Navigating on Part of the N.E. Side of Newfoundland, and in the Streights of Belle-Isle (pp. 36-48).—Description of Part of the Coast of Labradore, from Grand Point of Great Mecatina to Shecatica (pp. 49-55).—Directions for Navigating on that Part of the Coast of Labradore, from Shecatica to Chateaux, in the Straights of Belle-Isle (pp. 56-58).—Description of the Coast of Labradore, from Cape Charles to Cape Lewis (pp. 59-60).—Description of the Coast of Labradore, from St. Michael to Spotted Island (pp. 61-63).—Remarks made between the Island of Groias and Cape Bonavista (pp. 64-71).—Directions for Navigating from Cape Race to Cape Bonavista, made by Captain Southwood; with his Remarks upon the Fishing Banks (pp. 72-93).—Directions for Navigating Part of the Coast of Newfoundland, from Cape St. Mary to Cape Spear, including St. Mary's and Trepassey Bays (pp. 94-100).—Directions for Navigating the Bay of Placentia, on the south coast of Newfoundland, from Cape Chapeau Rouge to Cape St. Mary's (pp. 101-111).—Sailing Directions for the Gulf of St. Lawrence (pp. 112-132).

22 The First Part of / the / North American Pilot / for / Newfoundland, Labradore, / and the / Gulf and River St. Lawrence: / being a collection of / sixty-one accurate charts and plans, / drawn from original surveys: / taken by / Captain James Cook and Michael Lane, surveyor, / Joseph Gilbert, / and other experienced Officers in the King's Service. / ... / On thirty-seven large copperplates. / A new edition. / London: / Printed and published by Robert Laurie and James Whittle, No. 53, Fleet Street. / (Successors to Mr. Robert Sayer.) / 1799. / Price Two Guineas—Half-Bound, with a Quarto Book of Directions / ...

Folio. 3 leaves of text plus 22 charts numbered I-XXII. (Phillips 4476.)

Text leaves: [fol. 1ʳ] title as above, [1ᵛ] advertisement; [2ʳ] dedication to Sir Hugh Palliser, [2ᵛ] blank; [3ʳ] "Index of the Charts, Plans, &c." [3ᵛ] "Index" continued and "Copy of Capt. Cook's Letter".

The imprint of Sayer and Bennett has been deleted from all the original chart-plates except (in some copies of the atlas) pl. VI, X, XV, XIX; and the imprint of Laurie and Whittle is substituted with the date 12 May 1794 (except XVIII, undated).

The original chart VII is replaced by "A New Chart of the Coast of Nova Scotia with the South Coast of New Brunswick . . . By Capt. Holland . . . Published . . . 12th July 1798"; after chart IV is inserted "A Chart of S^t. John's Harbour in Newfoundland. Surveyed in October 1798 by Francis Owen . . . Published . . . 12th Jany 1799; and the "Index of the Charts" is altered accordingly in MS. In later copies of this edition of the atlas, Owen's plans of Trinity Harbour and Great Placentia with the imprint-date 1801 are inserted (see Phillips 4476; and No. 23 below).

1806

23   The First Part of / the / North American Pilot; / for / Newfoundland, Labra-dore, / and the / Gulf and River St. Lawrence: / On thirty-seven large copper-plates. / A new edition. / London: / Printed and Published by Robert Laurie and James Whittle . . . / . . . / 1806. / . . .

Folio. 3 leaves of text plus 25 charts stamped with arabic numbers 1-25. (Phillips 1236.)

Text leaves: as in 1799 edition (Bibl., No. 22), reset. Three new charts have been added (5, 6, 7), and plates V-XXII of the 1799 edition renumbered as 8-25. The original chart IX has been replaced by "The Harbour of Halifax in Nova Scotia. By Thos. Backhouse. Published . . . 1798" (new No. 12). In chart II, the title is altered to end ". . . from those of Cook, Chabert, Fleurieu and recent observations of Fran.^{s} Owen . . . Published . . . 1803", and the hydrography of S.E. Newfoundland corrected accordingly. Other-wise the charts are in the same state as in the 1799 edition.

The three additional charts are:

5   A New Survey of Trinity Harbour in Newfoundland. By Francis Owen . . . Published . . . 1801.

6   A Chart of S^t. John's Harbour in Newfoundland. Surveyed in October 1798 by Francis Owen . . . Published . . . 12th Jany 1799.

7   A Chart of the Road and Harbour of Great Placentia, in Newfound-land. Surveyed in August, 1800, by Francis Owen . . . Published . . . 1801.

TABLE A

The chart-plates of A Collection (1769-70) and of The North American Pilot (1775): sources and publication history

(The states of the three Cook charts, nos. 2-4, are described in the Bibl., Nos. 4, 6, 8, 9. All charts in *NAP* (1775) have the imprint of Sayer and Bennett. Abbrev.: n.i.d. = no imprint or date.)

No.	COLLECTION (1769-70) Short title of chart	Surveyor and date of survey	MS original(s)	Date of first publication	State and imprint-date in Collection — early issue, 1769 (Adm. Lib., L.C.)	State and imprint-date in Collection — later issue, 1770 (N.M.M., U.C.L.A.)	North-American Pilot, 1775 — pl.	North-American Pilot, 1775 — state and imprint-date
1	[1]General chart of Newfoundland	(a) Cook 1763-7, Lane 1768-9; (b) Lane 1772-3	Hydro. Dept., 400 (Lane); 380 (Lane 1774)	10 May 1770 (Jefferys)	[wanting]	state I; 10 May 1770	I	state II; 10 May 1770 or 10 May 1775
2	[2]South Coast of Newfoundland	Cook 1763, 1765-6	H.D., C58 and C54/5; B.M., Add. MS. 31360 (two plans)	1767 (Cook)	state I; 1767	state I; 1767	VI	state III; 10 May 1774
3	West Coast of Newfoundland	Cook 1767	H.D., C54/1; B.M., Add. MS. 17603.d.	1768 (Cook)	state I; 1768	state I; 1768	XVI	state II; 10 May 1770
4	[3]North Coast of Newfoundland with Strait of Belleisle	(a) Cook 1763-4; (b) Cook 1767; Lane 1768-9	H.D., X54, C54/2-4, C54/7, 342, and eight plans; B.M., Add. MS. 31360.11.	(a) 1766 (Cook); (b) 1770 (Jefferys)	state III; 1766	state IV; May 1770	XVII	state V; 10 May 1770
5	Labrador: Grand Point to Shecatica	Lane 1768	H.D., 399	1769 (Jefferys)	state I; n.i.d.	state I; n.i.d.	XIX	state II; 10 May 1770
6	Labrador: entrance of Straits to C. Bluff	Gilbert 1767	H.D., B191	[1769?] (Jefferys)	state I; n.i.d.	state I; n.i.d.	XVIII	state II; 10 May 1770
7	Magdalen Islands	Holland 1765	H.D., B5304	1769? (Jefferys)	state I; 4 April 1769	state I; 4 April 1769	XII	state II; date deleted
8	Sable Island	DesBarres 1764	H.D., Z52	? (Jefferys)	state I; n.i.d.	state I; n.i.d.	VIII	state II; 10 May 1770
[9]	Harbour-plans:							
	Trinity Harbour	Cook? 1762?	?	[1769?] (Jefferys)	state I; n.i.d.	state I; n.i.d.	IV	state II; 10 May 1770
	St John's Harbour	Cook 1762	Adm. Lib., MS. 20	—	—	—	—	—
	Carboniere & Harbour Grace	Cook 1762	Adm. Lib., MS.20; Aust. Nat. Lib.	—	—	—	—	—
	Ferryland & Aquaport	Cook? 1762?	?	—	—	—	—	—
[10]	Harbour-plans:							
	Trepassey	Cook? 1762?	Adm. Lib., MS.20; Whitby Mus.	[1769?] (Jefferys)	state I; n.i.d.	state I; n.i.d.	V	state II; 10 May 1770
	Placentia, 'by James Cook'	Cook 1762	?	—	—	—	—	—
	St Mary's Harbour	Cook? 1762?	?	—	—	—	—	—
[NOT IN A COLLECTION]								
	[4]Banks of Newfoundland	Various; mainly 1750-5, 1765-6, 1769	—	[1775?]	—	—	II	state II; 25 March 1775
	[5]South East Part of Newfoundland, with Bays of Placentia, St Mary Trepassey and Conception	Gilbert? 1768 or 1770?; Lane 1772-3	H.D. x58 (Gilbert, *Pearl*, 1770); H.D. 402, 403, 397 (Lane 1772-4)	—	—	—	III	state II (?); 10 May 1770
	Nova Scotia and Cape Breton I., by T. Jefferys	Various; mainly French	—	[c. 1765]	—	—	VII	No date or 15 June 1775
	Halifax Harbour	C. Morris, before 1761	H.D., E155	[c. 1760]	—	—	IX	25 March 1775
	Harbour-plans:							
	Gut of Canso	1761	—	[c. 1765]	—	—	X	25 March 1775
	Port Dauphin	1743	—	—	—	—	—	—
	Murgain or Cow Bay	1760	—	—	—	—	—	—
	Gulf of St Laurence	Various; c. 1750-65	H.D., 276	[c. 1765]	—	—	XI	25 March 1775
	Island of St John	Holland 1765	—	[c. 1770]	—	—	XIII	6 April 1774 or 6 April 1775
	Chaleur Bay	H.M.S. *Norwich* 1760	—	[c. 1765]	—	—	XIV	25 March 1775
	Ristigouche Harbour	H.M.S. *Norwich* 1760	—	[c. 1765]	—	—	XV	25 March 1775
	River St Lawrence	Cook and Holland, 1759-60	H.D. (two MSS); Pub. Archives of Canada	[1760] (Jefferys)	—	—	XX-XXII	16 February 1775

NOTES.—[1]State II revised from Lane's surveys of 1772-3 (see p. 11). [2]State II revised from states II and III. [3]State II revised from Lane's surveys of 1772-3. [4]The U.C.L.A. copy of A Collection has also impressions of states II and III (apparently inserted in 1962). [5]Revised from Lane's surveys of 1772-3. State I not found.

The extension slip is wanting in all copies of A Collection except U.C.L.A.

TABLE B

Editions of tracts included in The Newfoundland Pilot (NP) *and in* Sailing Directions for the North-American Pilot (SD)

(New editions, with text reset, are distinguished by separate roman numerals. Copies collated: *NP* 1769, Admiralty Library; *SD* 1775, National Maritime Museum; *SD* 1778, Admiralty Library; *SD* 1782, Toronto Public Library; *SD* 1794, Library of Congress. In *SD* 1794, signatures and pagination are continuous through all the tracts comprising the volume; in the earlier editions, wherever signatures and pagination are continuous through adjoining tracts, this is recorded in the last column of the Table.)

Ref.	Short title of tract	Author and date of survey	Date of first publication	Separate publication before 1769	Jefferys NP 1769	Sayer and Bennett SD 1775	Sayer and Bennett SD 1778	Sayer and Bennett SD 1782	Laurie and Whittle SD 1794	Notes (with references to associated charts in *A Collection*, 1769-70, and in *The North-American Pilot*, 1775)
a	Directions for navigating on Part of the South Coast of Newfoundland	Cook 1765-6	I 1766	I (Cook)	II	III	IV	V	VI	*Coll.*, pl. 2; *NAP*, pl. VI.
b	Directions for navigating the West-Coast of Newfoundland	Cook 1767	1768	I (Cook)	I	I	I	II	III	*Coll.*, pl. 3; *NAP*, pl. XVI.
c	Directions for navigating on Part of the North East Side of Newfoundland and in the Streights of Bell-Isle	Cook 1763-4	1766	I (Cook)	II	II	III	IV	V	Editions II-V add, from Gilbert's survey in 1767, the Labrador coast from St Peter's Bay to C. Bluff. *Coll.*, pl. 4; *NAP*, pl. XVII, XVIII.
d	Description of . . . the Coast of Labradore, from Grand Point of Great Mecatina to Shecatica	Lane 1768	1769	—	I	II	II	III	IV	*Coll.*, pl. 5; *NAP*, pl. XIX.
e	Directions for navigating . . . on the Coast of Labradore, from Shecatica to Chateaux	Lane 1769	[1770?]	—	—	I	II	III	IV	In *SD* 1778 and 1782, signatures and pagination are continuous through *e, f* and *g* (so also in J.C.B. copy of *SD* 1775). *Coll.*, pl. 4; *NAP*, pl. XVII.
f	Description of the Coast of Labradore, from Cape Charles to Cape Lewis	Lane 1770-1	[1772?]	—	—	I	II	III	IV	See note under *e*.
g	Description of the Coast of Labradore, from Cape St Michael to Spotted Island	Lane 1770	[1771?]	—	—	I	II	III	IV	See note under *e*.
h	Remarks made between the Island of Groias and Cape Bonavista, 1768	? 1768	[1769]	—	I	II	II	III	IV	In *NP* 1769, signatures and pagination are continuous through *h. i. j. k. l*; in *SD* 1775, 1778 and 1782, through *h* and *i* only.
i	Directions for navigating from Cape Race to Cape Bonavista, made by Capt. Southwood	Hy Southwood 1677	1689	—	I	II	II	III	IV	Reprinted from *The English Pilot*, Bk. IV. See note under *h*.
j	Directions for navigating from Cape Race, to Cape St Mary's, made by John Gaudy, in 1718	John Gaudy 1718	1729	—	I	—	—	—	—	Reprinted from *The English Pilot*, Bk. IV. See note under *h*.
k	St Mary's Bay	Gilbert 1768	[1769]	—	I	—	—	—	—	See notes under *h, n*.
l	Placentia Bay	Gilbert 1768	[1769]	—	I	—	—	—	—	See notes under *h, n*.
m	Directions for navigating the Bay of Placentia	Lane 1772	[1773?]	—	—	I	I	II	III	Incorporates, with correction, Gilbert's text from his 1768 survey (*l*). In *SD* 1775, signatures and pagination are continuous through *m* and *n*. *NAP*, pl. III.
n	Directions for navigating . . . the Coast of Newfoundland, from Cape St Mary to Cape Spear	Lane 1773	[1774]	—	—	I	II	III	IV	Incorporates, with correction, Gilbert's text from his 1768 survey of St Mary's Bay (*k*). For *SD* 1775, see note under *m*.
o	Sailing Directions for the Gulf of St Laurence	[Cook ? 1759]	1760	I (Jefferys)	—	II	III	IV	V	*NAP*, pl. XX-XXII.

CHAPTER SIX

North American City Plans

being a selection of plans of the cities of
Albany, Baltimore, Boston, Charlestown, Cincinnati,
Detroit, Ebenezer, Montreal, Newport,
New Orleans, New York, Philadelphia, Quebec,
Savannah, St. Augustine and Washington

by R. V. Tooley

THIS essay consists of a selection of 42 Town Plans of North America, all described and illustrated, ranging from the middle of the 16th Century to well into the 19th. Some 16 towns are noted.

It is not intended to produce a comprehensive survey of any town or towns: nor to cover systematically any period of history or urban development. The selection here chosen is designed to encourage map-collectors towards a wider interest, in an absorbing, aesthetically pleasing but comparatively neglected aspect of map collecting—Town Plans: an aspect in which the architect and surveyor have perhaps a more important role than the " pure" cartographer, and in which Science plays a growing part.

Many of the Town Plans were integral parts of maps, usually insets. Only with the growth of the City, the Metropolis, has the geography of town and country become less and less integrated. Today the tendency is for a large City to have a life of its own, mechanically dependent, of course, on supplies fiom outside sources but not necessarily, save for the accidents of climate and language, peculiar to the country in which it is sited. The illustrations in this essay are culled from more idyllic times.

Note

The number assigned to each entry in this chapter refers to the appropriate plate number at the end of the book.

102 ALBANY, 1765. A Plan of the City of Albany. 16½ × 12 cms.

There are no direct records of the early life of John Rocque. He was born at the beginning of the 18th century in the south of France and he was of the Reformed faith. Forced to leave France, he settled in England, and became one of the foremost cartographers of his time. He died in 1762 and his business passed to his second wife Ann Bew, whom he had married in 1751. Ann Rocque published the above plan in "A Set of Plans and Forts in America Reduced from Actual Surveys 1765." One of the rarest of Rocque's publications it consisted of a title, 30 plans and an index. (See also Plates 118 & 125).

103 BALTIMORE (Maryland), 1792. Folie, A. P. Plan of the Town of Baltimore and its Environs Dedicated to the Citizens of Baltimore Taken upon the Spot by their most humble Servant A. P. Folie French Geographer 1792. James Poupard sculpsit Philadelphia.

The site for Baltimore was chosen in 1729 but it was not named Baltimore until 1745 and in 1768 it became the county town. In the census of 1790, two years before the printing of this map, there was a population of 13,530 inhabitants.

104 BALTIMORE (Maryland), 1801. Warner & Hanna's Plan of the City and Environs of Baltimore. With inset of the New Assembly Rooms and View of the Market Space Canal.

By 1800 the number of inhabitants increased to 26,514.

105 BOSTON (Mass), 1763-4. [Bellin, S.] Plan de la Ville de Boston. 15¼ × 21 cms.

1st state: the plate, unnumbered, appears in Petit Atlas François, 5 vols., Paris, 1763.

2nd state: the plate numbered above engraved border top right Tome I, No. 31, appears in Petit Atlas Maritime, 5 vols., Paris, 1764.

Boston as it was before Independence.

Jacques Nicolas Bellin was born in Paris in 1703 and died in Versailles in 1772. Educated as an engineer, he was attached to the Dépôt de la Marine, and charged with the task of compiling charts of all the known seas. His main works were the Neptune Français 1753, the Hydrographie Française 1756 and the Petit Atlas Maritime. The last is of particular interest for its detailed plans of maritime towns and harbours. The work was issued in Paris, first under the title Petit Atlas François for vols. 1-4, the title to vol. 5 being changed to Petit Atlas Maritime. This issue is rare.* It was reissued the following year in 5 vols. all with the title Petit Atlas Maritime and all dated 1764. The maps were increased as follows :—

Vol. I   Amérique Septentrionale 1763, 98 maps; 1764, 102 maps

Vol. II   L'Amérique Méridionale, N.D., 86 maps; 1764, 89 maps

BOSTON [Bellin]

Vol. III   L'Asie. L'Afrique 1763, 117 maps; 1764, 126 maps

Vol. IV   L'Europe excepté la France, N.D., 128 maps; 1764, 130 maps

Vol. V   Costes de France 1764, 132 maps; 1764, 132 maps

*And not recorded by Sabin.

106   BOSTON (Mass.), 1775. Dury, A. A Plan of Boston, and its Environs, shewing the true situation of His Majesty's Army and also those of the Rebels. Drawn by an Engineer at Boston Octr 1775. Engrav'd by Jno. Lodge from the late Mr. Jefferys Geographer to the King. London Publish'd as the Act directs 12th March 1776 by Andrew Dury, Duke's Court, St. Martins Lane. Engrav'd by Jno. Lodge from the late Mr. Jefferys, Geographer to the King. 64×45 cms.

Boston during the War of Independence.

This scarce plan on a scale of about 4¼ inches to the mile was compiled mainly by Richard Williams, Lieutenant at Boston. Issued in colour, the American positions are coloured yellow and the British green. A typical example of the excellent work produced by military engineers during the War of Independence.

107   BOSTON (Mass.), 1842. S.D.U.K. Boston with Charlestown and Roxbury. Engraved by B. R. Davies, Under the Superintendence of the Society for the Diffusion of Usefull Knowledge. London. Published for Chapman & Hall, 186 Strand, August 1842. 29½×37 cms.

Showing Boston as an incorporated City.

Later editions by Charles Knight and George Cox.

108   BOSTON (Mass.), 1851. Tallis. Boston. The Plan Drawn & Engraved by J. Rapkin. The Illustrations Drawn & Engraved by J. Watkins. [Published] John Tallis & Company, London & New York.

With three small vignettes, general view of Boston, the State House and Bunkers Hill Monument

Shows following railroads, Old Colony, Worcester, Lowell, Fitchburg, Boston and Maine, and three ferries, Chelsea, East Boston and Eastern Railroad Ferry.

109   CHARLES TOWN (Carolina), 1704. A Plan of Charles Town from a Survey of Edwd. Crisp in 1704. Engraved by James Aikin. 28½×23 cms. Scale 1″=660′.

Charleston or Charlestown is one of the oldest cities of the United States, its foundations being laid in 1672. Named after King Charles, it was first settled in 1680. The first plan of the city was drawn by Edward Crisp in 1704 but no actual copy of this first edition is known at the present time. Crisp's map (as above) probably a fair copy of the original, is found in Ramsey's History of South Carolina, Charleston 1809.

110 CHARLES TOWN (Carolina), 1739. The Ichnography of Charles Town at High Water. G. H. delin. W. H. Toms sculp^t. Published According to Act of Parliament June 9.1739 by B. Roberts and W. H. Toms. 53×44 cms. Scale 1″=300′.

Shows location of each house and street, with alphabetical list below. In 1700 Charlestown contained 600 houses.

"The most important early view of Charleston," Stokes.

111 CHARLES TOWN (Carolina), 1763-4. [Bellin, M.] Port et Ville de Charles Town dans la Caroline. 15×21 cms.

1st state: the plate, unnumbered, appears in Bellin's Petit Atlas François, 5 vols., Paris, 1763.

2nd state: the plate numbered above engraved border Tome I No. 37, appears in Petit Atlas Maritime, 5 vols., Paris, 1764.

See note to Plate 105.

112 CINCINNATI, 1815. Plan of Cincinnati Including All the late Additions & subdivisions Engraved for Drake's Statistical View 1815. J. H. Seymour sc.

The site was visited by explorers for well over 100 years before the first settlement in 1788 and was originally called Losanteville. Until 1795 there was continuous and disruptive warfare with the Indians, and in 1800 Cincinnati had a mere 750 inhabitants.

113 CINCINNATI, 1838. Cincinnati. Entered according to Act of Congress in the year 1838 by T. G. Bradford in the Clerk Office of the District of Mass. 17½×13½ cms.

One of four plans together on one sheet, the others being Washington, New Orleans, Louisville and Jeffersonville. Eighteen years later than the previous plan, the population had increased to about 40,000.

114 DETROIT, 1763-4. [Bellin, S.] La Riviere du Détroit. Depuis le Lac Sainte Claire jusqu'au Lac Erie. [Inset] Plan du Fort du Détroit 31½×20½ cms.

1st state: the plate, unnumbered, appears in Petit Atlas François, 5 vols., Paris, 1763.

2nd state: the plate numbered above engraved border top right Tome I, No. 12, appears in Petit Atlas Maritime, 5 vols., Paris, 1764.

The first engraved plan of Detroit.

Detroit was founded by the French under Antoine de la Motte Cadillac in 1701 but was taken over by the English in 1760.

115 EBENEZER (Georgia), [1747]. Seutter, Matth. Plan von neu Ebenezer verlegt von Matth. Seutter Kayser Geogr. in Augspurg. $49\frac{1}{2} \times 31\frac{1}{2}$ cms. including 4 lines of text below. Scale $1'' = 255'$.

This plan originally appeared in Urlsperger's Ausführliche Nachricht von den Saltzburgischen Emigranten 1735-52 [Vol. III 1747]. It was later issued by Seutter, probably as a separate, though included in some of his atlases, printed on stout paper, and with a map of Eastern Georgia and a water mill added to the plate.

Ebenezer was a German settlement on the Savannah River and the engraved plate shows the town in plan, and the surrounding countryside in perspective. Each building is lettered and a key supplied below. The town is divided into four squares, each surrounding its own market place.

116 MONTREAL (Canada), 1556. [Ramusio] La Terra de Hochelaga nella Nova Francia. $38 \times 27\frac{1}{2}$ cms.

Appears in Delle Navigationi e viaggi . . . raccolti gia da Gio. Bat. Ramusio printed in Venice by Giunta. Various editions from 1550. The above plan, in Vol. III printed 1556, 1565 and 1606, is the earliest printed view of Montreal, woodcut, showing the native village and stockades. Based on the information of Jacques Cartier who visited the Indian village of Hochelaga in 1535 on the site of what is now Montreal.

117 MONTREAL, 1763-4. [Bellin, S.] L'Isle de Montreal et ses Environs [Inset] Plan de la Ville de Montreal ou Ville Marie. $34\frac{1}{2} \times 21\frac{3}{4}$ cms.

1st state: the plate, unnumbered, appears in Petit Atlas François, 5 vols., Paris, 1763.

2nd state: the plate numbered above engraved border top right Tome I, No. 11, appears in Petit Atlas Maritime, 5 vols., Paris, 1764.

Montreal first came under British rule in 1760.

118 MONTREAL, 1765. Plan of the Town and Fortifications of Montreal or Ville Marie in Canada. 16×12 cms.

In A Set of Plans and Forts in America compiled by John Rocque and published by his widow, Mary Ann Rocque, in 1765. (See note Plate 102).

119 NEWPORT (Rhode Is.), 1777. Blaskowitz, Charles. A Plan of the Town of Newport in Rhode Island Surveyed by Charles Blaskowitz, Engraved and Publish'd by Willm. Faden, Charing Cross, Sept. 1st, 1777. $36 \times 33\frac{1}{2}$ cms. $1'' = 500'$.

Newport was first settled by Dissenters in 1639. It became a flourishing commercial centre engaged in a triangular trade; shipping rum to Africa, taking slaves in return to Barbados which in turn were exchanged for sugar and molasses to provide the basis for production of more rum. The city suffered severely under the English occupation.

120 NEW ORLEANS (Louisiana), 1759. Plan of New Orleans the Capital of Louisiana with the Disposition of its Quarters and Canals as they have been traced by Mr de la Tour in the Year 1720 Nov 1759. Published according to Act of Parliament by T. Jefferys at Charing Cross. Price 2s. 48½×33 cms. Scale: approx. 1½″=1 mile.

La Tour's plan was made only 2 years after the first settlement by Jean Baptiste le Moyne.

New Orleans 1838, see Plate 113.

121 NEW ORLEANS (Louisiana), 1845. New Orleans [inset on] Neueste Karte von Louisiana . . . 1845. Meyers Hand Atlas.

122 NEW YORK, 1670. Novum Amsterodamum. 16×12½ cms.

Copperplate illustration in text. This view, which depicts New Amsterdam at about 1650, was published in Montanus De Nieuwe en Onbekende Weereld, Amsterdam 1671, and in Ogilby's translation "America, Being an Accurate Description of the New World," of which editions exist dated 1670 and 1671. Although this suggests that the English preceded the Dutch, other evidence makes it likely that the Dutch edition was first. There was also a German edition of 1673.

The first settlements were made here by the Dutch in the 1620s, during which time the south end of Manhattan Island was chosen as the principal site. In 1626 the Island was bought from the Indians for $24. In 1664 New Amsterdam was captured by the English and named New York after James, Duke of York. So it has remained, except for a short period 1673-4 when the Dutch regained it and called it New Orange.

123 NEW YORK, 1698. Nieu Amsterdam al New York. Carolus Allard excudit cum Privilegio ordinum Hollandiae et Westfrisiae. A Mayer fc. 26½×21 cms. In Allard's Orbis habitabilis oppida [1698].

Based on the Restitutio View made during the brief Dutch re-occupation 1673-4.

124 NEW YORK, 1763-4. [Bellin, S.] Ville de Manathe ou Nouvelle-Yorc. 16×21 cms.

1st state: the plate, unnumbered, appears in Petit Atlas François, 5 vols., Paris, 1763.

2nd state: the plate numbered above engraved border top right Tome I, No. 33, appears in Petit Atlas Maritime, 5 vols., Paris, 1764.

For Bellin see note to Plate 105.

125　NEW YORK, 1763-5.　A Plan of the City of New York, reduced from an actual survey by T. Maerschalckm 1763. P. Andrews sculp. Published according to Act of Parliament by M. A. Rocque near Old Round Court in the Strand.　40×23 cms.

The original of this was published in 1755 and is known as the Maerschalck Plan. The original survey was made by Francis and not T. Maerschalckm. The Terminal "m" appears to stand for maker.

126　NEW YORK, 1775.　Montresor, John.　A Plan of the City of New-York & its Environs to Greenwich, on the North or Hudsons River, and to Crown Point, on the East or Sound River, Shewing the Severall Streets, Publick Buildings, Docks, Fort & Battery . . . Survey'd in the Winter 1775. Sold by A. Dury, Dukes Court, St. Martin's Lane. P. Andrews Sculp.　52×63½ cms.

By the famous English engineer John Montresor born in Gibraltar, wounded at the Battle of Du Quesne, chief engineer in America 1775. Montresor's survey was begun in Dec. 1765 at the time when the hated Stamp Act had brought into being the Sons of Liberty and revolution was imminent. Montresor's survey, described at that time as " extremely uncorrect and full of gross errors " (Du Simitiere 1768) was made hurriedly, and increasingly for military reasons as it became clear that resistance to the English was determined. One can picture the English Captain taking bearings of the land around the town while the crowds were burning Grenville and others in effigy.

127　NEW YORK, 1776.　RATZER, B.　Plan of the City of New York in North America Surveyed in the Years 1766 & 1767. London Published according to Act of Parliament Jan. 12 1776 by Jefferys & Faden, Corner of St. Martin's Lane Charing Cross.

Large-scale plan engraved on 3 sheets 89½×120 cms.　Scale 1″=400′.

Dedication by Lieut. B. Ratzer, H.M. 60th or Royal American Regt. Engraved by Thomas Kitchin. With a broad view of the City below: A South West View of the City of New York taken from the Governour's Island. "One of the most beautiful, important and accurate early plans of New York."—Stokes.

It is the most accurate plan of New York for the last years of colonial rule and was drawn about 1766. It was issued in the year New York was captured by the English and partially destroyed by fire.

128　NEW YORK, 1840.　New York.　Published by the Society for the Diffusion of Useful Knowledge, 59 Lincolns Inn Fields, February 1st, 1840. 37½×30½ cms.

Small vignettes of Broadway from the Park and City Hall.　Engraving on steel.

New York, with its population of 300,000 now moves into the machine age. There was still no proper water supply or fire protection and the sober minded could still bemoan the constant riots that upset business.

129 New York, 1851. New York. The Plan Drawn & Engraved by J. Rapkin, the Illustrations Drawn & Engraved by H. Winkles.

With vignettes of Brooklyn, City Hall, Custom House, New York Steamer, New York from Williamsburg, the Narrows from Port Hamilton.

130 Philadelphia (Penn.), [1687]. The City Philadelphia two miles in Length and one in Breadth. 18 × 7 cms. [Inset on] A Mapp of ye. Improved Part of Pensilvania in America, Divided into Countyes Townships and Lotts. Surveyed by Tho. Holme. Sold by P. Lea at ye Atlas and Hercules in Cheapside. 54 × 40 cms.

Dedication to William Penn with his arms above signed Ino. Harris. Title along top of map. Key reference either side.

Another issue Sold by Geo. Willdey at the Great Toy Spectacle, Chinaware, and Print Shop, at the Corner of Ludgate Street, near St. Paul's London [1715]. The plan of Philadelphia was likewise used with minor alterations on Hendrick Doncker's Chart of Sea Coasts of New Nederland, Virginia, New England and Pennsilvania and Keulen's map of *c.* 1730.

The most important date in Philadelphia's early history is 1681 when William Penn was made full proprietor of the Province. In the following year the city began to be laid out, and this plan shows Penn's house begun in that year.

131 Philadelphia (Penn.), 1776. A Plan of the City of Philadelphia, the Capital of Pennsylvania from an actual survey by Benjamin Easburn Surveyor General 1776 London Published as the Act directs 4th November 1776 By Andrew Dury, Duke's Court, St. Martin's Lane. 67 × 49½ cms.

With inset Chart of Delaware Bay and River.

Published in the year that Philadelphia saw the signing of the Declaration of Independence.

132 Philadelphia (Penn.), 1777. A Plan of the City and Environs of Philadelphia. Engraved and Published by Matthew Albert Lotter 1777 [Augsbourg] 45½ × 59½ cms.

Copied by Lotter from the first issue of Faden's plan 1777.

133 Philadelphia (Penn.), 1802. To the citizens of Philadelphia this New Plan of the City and its Environs Is respectfully dedicated By the Editor 1802.

134 Quebec, 1756. Homann. Plan de la Ville de Quebec. 23 × 21½ cms.

One of four plans together on one sheet with general title Vorstellung einiger Gegenden und Plaetze in Nord-America unter Franzoesisch und Englische Jurisdiction gehoerig zu finden bey den Homaennischen Erben in Nurnberg Ao. 1756.

135 QUEBEC, 1759. A Plan of Quebec. Publish'd according to Act of Parlia-
1759 by E. Oakley & Sold by J. Rocque near Round Court in the Strand.
(January) $50\frac{1}{2} \times 31$ cms.

Second state of the plate (Octob^r. 1759) with " A Draught of the River St.
Lawrence " added in top right-hand corner.

Plan of Quebec as it was at the time of the British attack under General Wolfe.

136 QUEBEC, 1763-4. [Bellin, S.] Plan de la Ville de Quebec. $34\frac{1}{2} \times 21$ cms.

1st state: the plate, unnumbered, appeared in Petit Atlas François, 5 vols.,
       Paris, 1763.

2nd state: the plate numbered above engraved border top right Tome I, No. 9,
       in Petit Atlas Maritime, 5 vols., Paris, 1764.

137 SAVANNAH (Georgia), 1734. A View of Savanah as it stood the 29th of
March 1734. P. Gorden Inv. P. Fourdrinier Sculp. 55×40 cms.

The earliest known view of Savannah. This plan was almost certainly issued in
conjunction with a pamphlet written to attract settlers to the recently-founded
colony of Savannah. A later issue of this print is dedicated to General Ogle-
thorpe who, in February 1733, had founded the colony of Georgia to provide a
settlement for debtors from England. A contemporary account describes the
town " for herewe see Industry honoured and Justice strictly executed, and
Luxury and Idleness banished from this happy Place where Plenty and Brotherly
Love seem to make their Abode."

138 ST. AUGUSTINE (Florida), 1670. [Ogilby, John] Pagus Hispanorum in
Florida. $35 \times 26\frac{1}{2}$ cms.

Reissued by Van der Aa in Galerie Agréable du Monde 1729 unchanged except
for title which now reads La Ville, le Chateau et le Village de St. Augustin en
Amerique.

The oldest city of the U.S.A. first settled in 1565 by the Spaniards. It had a
troubled history; Francis Drake and later (1665) John Davis sacked it.

139 ST. AUGUSTINE (Florida), 1802. Luffman, J. St. Augustine. Engrav'd &
Publish'd Jany. 1, 1802 by J. Luffman, Little Bell Alley, Coleman Street, London.
12×15 cms. (excluding title above and imprint below).

In Select Plans of the Principal Cities . . . of the World By John Luffman
1801-2. Other American plans included in the work are Charleston Harbour,
Philadelphia, Boston and New York.

140 ST. AUGUSTINE (Florida), 1818. Barra y Puerto de Sn. Agustin. $26\frac{1}{2} \times 17\frac{1}{2}$ cms.

Appears in Portulano de la America Setentrional construido en la direccion de trabajos hidrograficos . . . Madrid 1809, Aumentado y corregido en 1818.

Town named Sn. Agustin de la Florida shown as small plan on coastline.

141 WASHINGTON, 1794. Map of the State of Maryland laid down from an actual survey . . . By Dennis Griffith, June 20th 1794. Philad: Published June 6th 1795 by J. Vallance, Engraver, No. 145 Spruce Street.

With large inset Plan of the City of Washington and territory of Colombia.

In 1790 Congress passed an Act for the building of a national capital on the Potomac on the borders of Virginia and Maryland where it was neutral to the north-south rivalry and, after Washington had chosen the actual site, it was surveyed by Andrew Ellicott. Building began in 1791 and Congress first met there in 1800.

142 WASHINGTON, 1800. Plan of the City of Washington in the Territory of Columbia ceded by the States of Virginia and Maryland to the United States of America and by them established as the Seat of Government, after the year 1800. Engraved by Samuel Hill Boston. 51×42 cms.

143 WASHINGTON. A Correct Map of the City of Washington, Capital of the United States of America. Engraved by W. I. Stone. Washn.

CHAPTER SEVEN

Maps of the Yorktown Campaign
1780-1781

A Preliminary Checklist of Printed and Manuscript Maps
Prior to 1800

by Coolie Verner

WHEN Mr. R. V. Tooley indicated that I might prepare a number for the Map Collectors Circle I saw an opportunity to follow a suggestion made to me by the late Randolph G. Adams of the William L. Clements Library that I make a study of the maps relating to the Yorktown Campaign of 1781. Now twenty years later that suggestion is accomplished, albeit imperfectly, in the accompanying list.

In preparing this list I am indebted to a number of individuals and institutions for their never failing response to my request for help: Walter W. Ristow, The Library of Congress; R. A. Skelton, The British Museum; Miss Isabell Fry, The Henry E. Huntington Library; Howard C. Rice, Jr., Princeton University Library; Alexander O. Vietor, Yale University Library; Mrs. Muriel Willing who typed the manuscript; and R. V. Tooley, who saw it into print. The deficiencies of this work are my own in not following adequately every helpful lead these individuals have supplied.

COOLIE VERNER

Vancouver, B.C.

CONTENTS

I

INTRODUCTION

The Revolutionary War in America ended on October 19, 1781 at Yorktown, Virginia with the surrender of the British forces under Lord Cornwallis to the Allied Armies commanded by General Washington. This event terminated a contest between unmatched forces that had lasted five years. During this period the thirteen original and separate colonies became welded into a single unit by a fierce determination to achieve independence from an insensitive and inept British government.

This war remains an anomaly among wars. A relatively small group of dedicated and uncompromising individuals was able to form and coordinate an army composed of citizens often reluctant to serve; which battling sporadically over a long period of time against a generally superior force, operated in a vast country populated by largely indifferent—if not hostile—residents; and which emerged successful with the assistance of an external power that was basically disinterested in the plight of the one combatant although keenly desirous of humbling the other.

THE MAPS

The Yorktown Campaign consisted of four major military operations. It opened with the invasion of Virginia by Lord Cornwallis in a continuation of his *Southern Campaign*. This was followed by a major *Naval Engagement* in which the French Fleet under de Grasse defeated the British and gained mastery of the seas at the entrance to the Chesapeake Bay and of the Bay itself. The third phase involved the arrival of the Allied land forces from the north and the subsequent *Investment* of Yorktown. The final operation was the *Siege* of Yorktown and the ultimate capitulation.

Each of these military operations can be documented by a wealth of cartographic material not usually available so long after the events. These documents are arranged in this list according to the sequential ordering of the events which they illustrate. In addition to the four phases of the Campaign, two additional sections are included in the list. One section accommodates contemporary maps that depict the *Setting* in which the Campaign occurred and the other added section includes those miscellaneous maps of particular interest produced well after the events they illustrate. Each of the six sections in which the maps are arranged lists both printed and manuscript maps appropriate to it.

THE PRINTED MAPS

The printed maps of the Yorktown Campaign are of two types:

1 *Prototype Maps.*

Maps in this category are valid historical documents that can be considered to be primary source material. They are either composite maps formed from a variety of manuscript sources or a printed version of a single manuscript. In some instances the original manuscript from which a printed map was copied is included in the list and this relationship is indicated wherever it can be done on sure grounds. Most of the prototype printed maps are of British origin.

Prototype maps are identified by an asterisk in the chronological list.

2 *Illustrative Maps.*

Maps in this category constitute secondary source material. They are formed from data supplied by prototype maps and are used to illustrate chronicles of the events by various writers. In some cases there may be several versions of the same map or a single map may have been used with more than one account of the events. The relationship among the maps is indicated where this information can be supplied on sure grounds.

The printed maps in the list arranged in the sequential ordering of the events which they depict. In this order they are identified by the use of Roman numerals. The actual date of publication of the particular map does not necessarily follow the sequence of events, therefore, the printed maps are also numbered with Arabic numerals to indicate the sequence of publication in chronological order. An index of printed maps in this order is supplied at the end of the list. Since most of the printed maps are either dated on the plate or found in volumes with dated imprints, the chronological order of publication can be established with some certainty.

Printed maps of the Campaign were generally produced in some quantity either for publication as separate maps or as items included in volumes. Thus, they tend to be more readily available and of primary interest to collectors. Because of this, the printed maps are described with considerable carto-bibliographical detail provided so that collectors can identify a particular copy of a map specifically. In most cases this description is derived from an examination of one or more copies of the map in question. The location of copies in libraries or collections is not indicated in the description since the maps are generally available.

MANUSCRIPT MAPS

Manuscript maps of the Yorktown Campaign are astonishingly numerous and much more difficult to locate than are printed maps. For the most part these constitute the primary cartographic documents of the Campaign and are, therefore, of particular interest to historians. Since each manuscript map is an unique item each one must be located and identified individually. They are generally found with collections of papers of individual persons associated with the events and since calendars of such papers are not always available the maps are difficult to find. It is not possible to circularize every institution that might hold collections of papers relating to the Revolutionary War or to search for such collections personally; consequently, this listing of manuscript maps is not definitive.

The entry for each manuscript map included here provides as much information about the map as was available in the source from which the entry was extracted. At times this source has been a published listing such as Adams or Brun, a microfilm such as Karpinski, or library catalogue card entries studied from xerox copies. The amount of information about a map will, therefore, vary from one entry to another but in every case the location is provided and the origin of the information is indicated where the source is such as to be available to others. In spite of these inherent imperfections this will provide a useful finding list of most of the principal manuscript documents of the Campaign.

The manuscript maps are arranged in the order of the events they illustrate and are listed in each section following the printed maps appropriate to that section. In the section dealing with the Siege itself the maps are grouped by country of origin with the British maps first, followed in turn by the French and American made maps. They are numbered sequentially through the entire list using Arabic numerals prefixed by the letter M to avoid confusion with the chronological numbering of the printed maps.

II

THE SOUTHERN CAMPAIGN IN VIRGINIA

THE Southern Campaign of 1780-1781 was the last major contest in the Revolutionary War. The colonial troops commanded by General Washington had grown from an undisciplined militia to a significant force of trained troops augmented in the latter years by French units under the command of the Count de Rochambeau. Throughout the war, the allied forces had been at a disadvantage by the lack of any significant naval power to impede the free movement of the British forces by their navy. With this naval power the British commander could shift the theatre of war from one place to another at will and with greater speed than the earth bound allied forces could counter. Just such a manoeuvre started the Southern Campaign.

General Sir Henry Clinton was securely seated in New York City when he decided to surround the rebels by an attack on their southern flank. He moved a portion of his forces to South Carolina and occupied Charleston. In the Spring of 1780, Lord Cornwallis arrived to reinforce General Clinton who shortly returned to New York leaving Cornwallis in command of the Southern Campaign. Lord Cornwallis was an unscrupulous enemy who imposed his will upon the residents with vicious intent. Almost immediately he intensified the southern operations and defeated the colonial forces under Gates at Camden in August of 1780 thus opening the way north. From this victory he moved northward through the Carolinas with the intention of taking Virginia. At Guilford Court House he met the forces of General Nathaniel Greene and a major battle ensued which ended in a draw favouring Cornwallis. Greene was able to rally his command and to set out in pursuit of the British. By the end of March, 1781,

221

Cornwallis was moving northward with Greene at his heels. After crossing Deep River at Ramsey's Mill, Cornwallis destroyed the bridge blocking Greene who then decided to abandon the pursuit and turn again to the south in order to liberate the Carolinas.

Free of harassment now, Cornwallis hastened north to attack the soft underside of Virginia and arrived in Petersburg, Virginia, on the 20th of May in 1781. He was joined by reinforcements commanded by Phillips. This force had been sent from New York to strengthen General Arnold, the colonial traitor, who was located in Portsmouth, Virginia. With this added power Cornwallis proceeded to capture Richmond and force Thomas Jefferson and the Virginia legislature to flee westward into the Blue Ridge Mountains followed by Lt. Col. Tarleton's calvary in futile pursuit.

The colonial troops in the Richmond area were commanded by General Lafayette whom Cornwallis viewed with contempt as he was not yet twenty-four years of age. Lafayette had been sent south by Washington to contain Cornwallis until the northern army could arrive as reinforcements. In abandoning Richmond to the British, Lafayette avoided any major engagement but continued to annoy Cornwallis with harassing action and minor conflicts. Among the numerous minor skirmishes were those involving the Queen's Rangers under Lt. Col. John Graves Simcoe at Petersburgh and at other places along the James River.

General Wayne arrived from Pennsylvania with reinforcements for Lafayette. Cornwallis was misinformed about the size of the combined forces facing him and decided it more prudent to evacuate Richmond moving his forces toward Williamsburg with Lafayette in pursuit to prevent his escape south into the Carolinas again. During this period, Cornwallis had some 4,000 trained troops including Tarleton while Lafayette commanded some 3,900 troops of which only 1,500 were well disciplined regulars.

When he arrived in Williamsburg, Cornwallis received orders from General Clinton to rush reinforcements to New York in expectation of an attack on that city. After dispatching these troops, Cornwallis crossed the James River and made his way to Portsmouth which was then the chief seaport of Virginia and headquarters of the British forces in the area. He arrived in July, 1781, only to receive too late an order from Clinton that rescinded the request for reinforcements. Clinton also ordered Cornwallis to fortify stations for the defense and control of the Chesapeake Bay particularly a safe anchorage for the fleet. In this Clinton had in mind a spot such as Point Comfort on the end of the peninsula between the York and James Rivers as the logical location. Point Comfort, which had been named by Captain John Smith some two hundred years earlier because it gave his men great comfort to know there was land across the way, commanded Hampton Roads and the mouth of the James River. Cornwallis, however, was advised by his engineers that this was not a strategic position so he sought another location. He finally selected Yorktown as the place to fortify as well as Gloucester across the York River since these two positions would provide adequate defensive anchorage for the fleet. By controlling the York River and the peninsula, Cornwallis felt that he could then control the Chesapeake Bay.

Unknown to Cornwallis at this time but known to General Washington in the North, was the intelligence that the Count de Grasse with a substantial fleet was enroute to the Chesapeake Bay from the French West Indies. The arrival of a large French naval unit provided the colonists their first opportunity to mount a combined operation against the British. Immediately upon receipt of this intelligence in August, Washington started south to join Lafayette and advised the Count de Barres whose fleet was at anchor in Newport, Rhode Island, to sail south to join de Grasse.

With Lord Cornwallis at Yorktown, Lafayette astride the peninsula to prevent any escape, the French Fleet sealing the entrance to the Chesapeake Bay, the stage was set and most of the actors in the drama were ready for their cues.

PRINTED MAPS

I

4. 1781

A MAP | of the Seat of War *in the |Southern Part of |* VIRGINIA, | NORTH CAROLINA, | *and Northern Part of |* SOUTH CAROLINA, | [rule 3.3 cm] *By Thos. Kitchin Senr. | Hydrographer to his Majesty |*

Imprint	*Published by R. Baldwin at the Rose in Pater Noster Row.* The imprint is below the border in the bottom centre of the plate.
In	*The London Magazine* Vol. 50, p. 291. London, Printed for R. Baldwin . . . June 1781.
Size	Plate NS 28.7. EW 34.6 Map NS 27.2. EW 34.1
Latitude	34-37
Longitude	76-82 West from London
Scale	English Miles. 40=3.6 R.F. 1:1,750,000 The scale bar is located in the bottom right corner. Unframed.
Cartouche	The title is in a flattened shield-shaped cartouche measuring 5.5 cm. by 4,5 cm. in the upper left corner. This is framed with stylized leaves and garlands.
References	Swem 273; Verner 785; VC/p. 60.
Description	This map includes the southern section of Virginia as far north as Henrico County, south to below Cape Fear, and west to the Holstein River. It is a simple undistinguished map with many places, rivers, etc. named. In the upper right corner above the border is the designation " London Mag:June 1781."

II

15. 1787

THE MARCHES | OF | *LORD CORNWALLIS* | IN THE | SOUTHERN PROVINCES, | NOW | STATES OF NORTH AMERICA; | Comprehending | THE TWO CAROLINAS, | WITH | VIRGINIA AND MARYLAND, | and

223

THE DELAWARE COUNTIES. / BY WILLIAM FADEN / Geographer to the King.

Imprint	London, Published Feb.y. 3, 1787, by W.m. Faden, Geographer to the King, Charing Cross. The imprint is below the bottom border in the centre.
In	Tarleton, Lt. Col. *A History of the Campaigns* . . . London, T. Cadell, 1787.
Size	Map NS 64.4 EW 49.0 Plate NS 66.7 EW 51.7
Latitude	32-40
Longitude	75-82
Scale	*Nautic Leagues, 20 to a Degree,* 3 = 11.1 cm. *English Miles about 69½ to a Degree,* 100 = 10.7 cm. R.F. 1:1,550,000 The two scales are immediately below the cartouche.
Cartouche	The title is in the lower right corner in a circle 12.0 cm. enclosed by a single engraved line.
Border	Geographically functional with an extra heavy neat line.
References	Swem 317; Verner 827; VC/p. 59, 64.
Description	The map includes the area from Trenton and Reading on the north to the mouth of the Savanna River and west to the junction of the Kanawha and Ohio Rivers. The Virginia portion is after Fry and Jefferson but the western portion provides more details than is provided on that map.
Note	This map may also be found as a separate with wide paper margins.

III

12. 1784 State 1

SKETCH OF THE SKIRMISH *AT* PETERSBURG, / *between the* Royal Army *under the Command of MAJOR GEN.L. PHILLIPS,* / *and the* American Army *commanded by MAJOR GEN.L. STEWBEN;* / *in which the latter were defeated, April 25th. 1781 copied from a Plan of L.t. Spencers.* / By I. Hills, Lieut. 23.d. Regt. & Asst. Engr. /

Imprint	*London, Published by W.m. Faden Geographer to the King, Charing Cross, May 3.d. 1784.* The imprint is below the bottom border in the centre.
In	Simcoe, Lt. Col. *A Journal of the Operations of the Queens' Rangers,* . . . Exeter: Printed for the Author, 1787.
Size	Plate NS 36.2 EW 28.4 Map NS 34.3 EW 26.1
Orientation	West
Scale	SCALE 1 mile = 11.8 cm. The scale is in the bottom right corner.
Cartouche	None. The unframed title is in the upper left corner.
Border	Single line.
References	Church 1233; Verner 809, 833.
Description	This map shows both sides of the Appomatox River at Petersburgh with roads, woods and positions of the troops shown.
Note	In State 2 several words are deleted from the end of item 7 in the legend. See M 24.

IV

18. 1787

Skirmish at RICHMOND Jan: 5th. 1781

Imprint	*From a Sketch of L^t. Allans of the Queens Rangers.* The imprint is below the bottom border in the left corner.
In	Simcoe, See III.
Size	Plate NS 19.2 EW 20.6 Map NS 15.6 EW 19.6
Cartouche	The title is below the map on the bottom of the plate.
Description	This plate shows the area surrounding Richmond. The map shows fields, woods, roads, houses, etc.
Note	This plate appears between pages 112-113. The original coloured drawing for this is listed in Church 1223. See Manuscript Map M 21.

V

19. 1787

The | *LANDING* | [rule 1.5 cm.] at [rule 1.5 cm.] | BURRELL'S | April 17th. 1781. |

Imprint	*taken on the Spot by G. Spencer L^t. Q. R.* The imprint is below the bottom left corner.
In	Simcoe, see III.
Size	Plate NS 19.3 EW 24.4 Map NS 15.2 EW 20.3
Scale	*Scale of One Mile.* 1=7.3 cm.
Cartouche	The title is in a vertical rectangle measuring 4.7 by 3.8 in the bottom right corner. This is framed by a single line.
Border	The map has a border resembling a picture frame with a heavy neat line outside, a space .3 mm. then a single line, a space 1.1 cm. and finally an inside single line.
Description	This platt shows the James River at Burrell's Landing with ravines, creeks, and fields shown. The batteries are indicated and the map illustrates how the landing was made by small boats. This map appears between pages 132-133. Immediately following the title is a legend in five lines of italics lettered A-E.
Note	The original coloured drawing for this platt is listed in Church 1223. See Manuscript Map M 23.

VI

20. 1787

SKETCH | *of the Action at* | OSBURNS | *April 27th. 1781.* | [rule 3.0 cm.] |

Imprint	*taken on the Spot by G. Spencer L^t. Q. R.* The imprint is below the bottom left corner.
In	Simcoe, see III.
Size	Plate NS 20.4 EW 25.4 Map NS 15.5 EW 20.5
Scale	None.
Cartouche	The title is in a vertical rectangle measuring 8.8 by 5.0 cm. on the right border. This is framed by a single line.
Border	A wide border (2.0 cm.) made of many fine parallel lines.

Description   A detailed platt of the area around Osburns. Immediately following the title is
                   a legend of 8 lines lettered A-H in italics.
                   The map is between pages 140-141.
                   The original coloured drawing for this platt is listed in Church 1223. See
                   Manuscript Map M 25.

                                        VII

21. 1787

ACTION | at | SPENCER'S ORDINARY. | June 26th. 1781. | [legend]

Imprint   *Taken on the Spot by G. Spencer L*ᵗ*. Q. R.*
In   Simcoe, see III.
Size   Plate NS 24.2 EW 26.2
                   Map   NS 19.1 EW 21.0
Scale   None.
Cartouche   The title is in a vertical rectangle measuring 8.9 by 6.9 cm. along the right border
                   at centre and above. It is framed by a single line.
Border   A very wide (1.6 cm.) single line.
Description   This is a detailed platt of the immediate area of Spencer's Ordinary. Below the
                   title is a legend of twelve lines of italics labeled A-N.
                   The map is between pages 166-167.
                   The original coloured drawing for this is listed in Church 1223. See Manuscript
                   Map M 27, M 36.

                              MANUSCRIPT MAPS

M 1

Plan of the Post of Portsmouth as it is occupied by His Majesty's Forces under
the Command of Major General Phillips April 1st 1781. Shewing, in yellow,
the works proposed, in addition to those already constructed by order of
Brigadier General Arnold. Wm. Fyers, Lieutt. & Sub Engineer.

In   Clinton Papers, William L. Clements Library.
Size   25¼ × 19¾ inches.
Scale   1 inch to 500 feet.
Description   A finished, coloured, topographical map showing the town, the defensive works
                   and the soundings in the river.
References   Adams 278; Brun 577.

M 2

Plan of Portsmouth on Elizabeth River from an exact survey made ye.
21st January 1781. By James Straton. 2d 1t. of engineers.

In   Clinton Papers, William L. Clements Library.
Size   19¼ × 24 inches.
Scale   1 inch to 500 feet.
Description   A finished, coloured, topographical map indicating the houses in the town and
                   the proposed defensive works.
                   Enclosed in: Benedict Arnold to Sir Henry Clinton, 23 January, 1781.
References   Adams 277; Brun 575.

M 3

Plan of the Post at Great Bridge, on the South Branch of the Elizabeth River, Virginia, Establish'd the 5th February, 1781. James Stration, Royal Engineer, October 1788.

In   Library of Congress.
Size   18 × 11½ inches.
Description   Coloured.

M 4

[Road from Sleepy Hole by which Col. Simcoe marched to Portsmouth] [By: Brig. General Benedict Arnold. 1781]

In   Simcoe Papers, William L. Clements Library.
Size   8¼ × 9⅜ inches.
Scale   1 inch to approximately two and one-half miles.
Description   An unfinished, pen and ink sketch showing the route between the Nansemond River and Portsmouth on the Elizabeth River near its confluence with the James.
Reference   Brun 582.

M 5

[Portsmouth]

In   Clinton Papers, William L. Clements Library.
Size   7¾ × 11¾ inches.
Scale   1 inch to 3168 feet.
Description   A finished, coloured topographical map of the town and the Elizabeth River from Crany Island to the South Branch. Indicates " ruins of Norfolk " and the roads to Great Bridge and Suffolk.
References   Adams 279; Brun 578.

M 6

[Portsmouth and Norfolk]

In   Clinton Papers, William L. Clements Library.
Size   15¼ × 12¼ inches.
Scale   1 inch to 2⅓ miles.
Description   A finished, coloured topographical map showing the towns of Portsmouth, Suffolk, and Norfolk in ruins. Roads and plantations up the branches are shown as far as Great Bridge.
References   Adams 282; Brun 579.

M 7

A plan of Portsmouth harbour in the province of Virginia: Shewing the work erected by the British forces for its defence. 1781. Copied from the original of Lieut. Stratton, 1782.

In   Faden Collection 92, Library of Congress.
Size   36 × 24½ inches.
Scale   3000 feet to 3⅞ inches.
Description   Shows line of fortifications around Portsmouth.
Reference   Phillips, *Maps of America* . . .; Swem 291.

M 8

Carte de la campagne en Virginie du major général mis de la Fayette ou se trouvent les camps et marches ainsy que ceux du lieuten't général lord Cornwallis en 1781. Par le major capitaine A. d.C. du gl. la Fayette.

In	Yale University. (783hc/1781).
Size	94 × 148 cm.
Scale	Echelle de 15 milles.
Note	Reproduced in collotype in 1951.

M 9

Campagne en Virginie du Major Général Me de la Fayette, ou se trouvent les camps et marches, ainsy que ceux du Lieutenant Général L. Cornwallis par le Major Capitaine. Camp du Gl. La Fayette, en 1781.

In	Colonial Williamsburg, 595.
Scale	1½ inches = 5 miles.
Size	44 × 35 inches.
Description	Coloured.

M 10

[Area around Portsmouth]

In	Guerre, États Majors, L.I.D. No. 117, Paris.
Size	24.0 × 30.0 cm.
Description	An outline map showing the area around Portsmouth. This map is in English.
Reference	Karpinski, II, 184.

M 11

Plan de Portsmouth en Virginie.

In	Dépôt de la Marine, 136-7-4. Paris.
Size	44.3 × 30.6 cm.
Description	A detailed plan of the roads, etc. around Portsmouth. Appears to be a second draught of the preceding map.
Reference	Karpinski, III, 309.

M 12

Plan de Portsmouth en Virginie.

In	Rochambeau Manuscripts 52. Library of Congress.
Size	12 × 17 inches.
Reference	Swem 278; Phillips, *Maps of America* . . .; Winsor VI: 553.

M 13

Plan des ouvrages de Portsmouth en Virginie.

In	Rochambeau Manuscripts 53. Library of Congress.
Size	12½ × 16 inches.
Description	Coloured.
Reference	Swem; Phillips, *Maps of America* . . .; Winsor VI: 553.

M 14
Plan des ouvrages de Portsmouth en Virginie.

In	Library of Congress (G3701 / S331 / 1781 / .Pr).
Size	31 × 41 cm.
Scale	100 toises equals 6.2 cm.
Reference	Henkels, Catalogue 943, Part 2, item 611.

M 15
[Virginia]

In	Guerre, État-Major, L.I.D. No. 171. Paris.
Size	123.0 × 188.0 cm.
Description	Four sheets showing area from Chesapeake Bay to the Blue Ridge Mountains. Copy of Fry and Jefferson map.
Reference	Karpinski II, 192A, 192D.

M 16
Carte de la Virginie.

In	Guerre, État-Major, L I.D. No. 171. Paris.
Size	82.8 × 119.2 cm.
Description	A more carefully drawn copy of the preceding. Long note along left border. Inset map of area around Williamsburg in upper left corner. Shows route of march of French troops. Dated 4 Sept. 1781.
Reference	Karpinski II, 193.

M 17
Affair at Quintin's Bridge: 18th March, 1778.

In	Henry E. Huntington Library.
Size	$6\frac{3}{4} \times 8\frac{3}{8}$ inches.
Description	Original coloured drawing from Simcoe papers.
Reference	Church 1223(1).

M 18
SURPRIZE of the REBELS at HANCOCK'S HOUSE

In	Henry E. Huntington Library.
Size	$6\frac{1}{4} \times 6\frac{11}{16}$ inches.
Description	Original coloured drawing from Simcoe papers.
Reference	Church 1223(2).

M 19
Skirmish at Crosswick's

In	Henry E. Huntington Library.
Size	$6\frac{1}{2} \times 8\frac{5}{16}$ inches.
Description	Original coloured drawing from Simcoe papers.
Reference	Church 1223(3).

M 20

Retreat from Generals Clinton and Morgan by L^t. C: Simcoe from a *Sketch by Lieut^t. Colo: Simcoe, taken on the Spot. Copy. G. Spencer, L^t. Q^s. R^s.*

In   Henry E. Huntington Library.
Size   6 $\frac{13}{16}$ × 8 $\frac{1}{16}$ inches.
Description   Original coloured drawing from Simcoe papers.
Reference   Church 1223(4).

M 21

Skirmish at Richmond, 5th Jany., 1781.

In   Henry E. Huntington Library.
Size   7 $\frac{3}{16}$ × 8 $\frac{1}{8}$ inches.
Description   Original coloured drawing from Simcoe papers. See Printed Map IV (18).

M 22

Plan of the Post at Great Bridge, on the South Branch of Elizabeth River, Virginia: from a Survey by J. Stratton, L^t. Royal Engineers. Copy — G. Spencer L^t. Q^s. R^s.

In   Henry E. Huntington Library.
Size   8 $\frac{7}{16}$ × 6 $\frac{13}{16}$ inches.
Description   Original coloured drawing in Simcoe papers. See also Manuscript Map M3; M31.
Reference   Church 1223(9).

M 23

Sketch of the Landing at Burwell's Ferry April 20th. 1781, from a sketch taken on the spot by Lt. Spencer Q.R.

In   Henry E. Huntington Library.
Size   6 $\frac{3}{8}$ × 8 $\frac{1}{4}$ inches.
Description   Original coloured drawing from Simcoe papers. See Printed Map V (19).
Reference   Church 1223(10).

M 24

SKETCH of Action at Petersburgh, April 25th, 1781.

In   Henry E. Huntington Library.
Size   6 $\frac{3}{4}$ × 8 $\frac{1}{4}$ inches.
Scale   2 $\frac{3}{4}$ inches = 1 mile.
Description   Original coloured drawing from Simcoe papers.
Reference   Church 1223(11).

M 25

SKETCH of Action at Osburns, April 27th 1781, taken on the Spot by G. Spencer Lt. Q.R.

In   Henry E. Huntington Library.
Size   6 $\frac{1}{4}$ × 8 inches.
Description   Original coloured drawing from Simcoe papers.
References   Church 1223(14).

M 26
Point of Fork 4th. June 1781 taken on the Spot by G. Spencer, Lt. Q: Rs.

In	Henry E. Huntington Library.
Size	$6\frac{1}{4} \times 8$ inches.
Description	Original coloured drawing from Simcoe papers.
Reference	Church 1223(14).

M 27
ACTION at SPENCER'S ORDINARY . June 26:1781 . taken on the Spot.
G. Spencer Lt. Queen's Rangers.

In	Henry E. Huntington Library.
Size	$8\frac{3}{16} \times 8\frac{13}{16}$ inches.
Description	Original coloured drawing from Simcoe papers. See Printed Map VII (21).

M 28
[Sketch of Richmond Virginia.]

In	Simcoe papers. Colonial Williamsburg.
Note	This is a rough pen sketch.
Reference	Verner 833.

M 29
[Affair at Osburns, Virginia]

In	Simcoe papers. Colonial Williamsburg.
Note	This is a coloured map.
Reference	Verner 833.

M 30
[Great Bridge on Elizabeth River, Virginia.]

In	Simcoe papers. Colonial Williamsburg.
Note	Coloured map.
Reference	Verner 833.

M 31
Plan of the Post at Great Bridge, on the south branch of the Elizabeth River in Virginia.

In	Simcoe papers. Colonial Williamsburg.
Note	Coloured map.
Reference	Verner 833.

M 32
[James River Action]

In	Simcoe papers. Colonial Williamsburg.
Note	The Simcoe papers contain three different coloured maps of action on the James River.
Reference	Verner 833.

M 33

[Rebels Dislodged from Williamsburg Landing]

In   Simcoe papers. Colonial Williamsburg.
Reference   Verner 833.

M 34

[Map of Attack of the Rebels at the Point Forks]

In   Simcoe papers. Colonial Williamsburg.
Reference   Verner 833.

M 35

[Map of Point Fork Virginia]

In   Simcoe papers. Colonial Williamsburg.
Reference   Verner 833.

M 36-M 40

Maps and sketches of Action at Spencer's Ordinary or Plantation seven miles from Williamsburg between L.Col. Simcoe with Rangers and General Wayne with 2200 Rebels

In   Simcoe papers. Colonial Williamsburg.
Note   This group contains five maps and sketches related to the action at Spencer's Ordinary. The separate items are not titled.
Reference   Verner 833.

III

THE SETTING

Yorktown was a small village of some sixty houses on the south bank of the York River. Surrounding the village were high bluffs with a commanding view of the river. The peninsula on which it is situated is bound by the York River and Chesapeake Bay on the north and east with the James River along the south. It is some twenty-five or so miles in length and varies in width from three to twelve miles. The village itself is the county seat of York County which is one of the earliest units of local government in Virginia having been formed in 1643. Yorktown is eleven miles north of the mouth of York River and but a short distance from Williamsburg and Jamestown. Portsmouth is some thirty-five miles south and east.

Directly across the river from Yorktown was the smaller village of Gloucester situated on a point of land jutting into the river so that the two positions effectively controlled the river at that point. The York River is actually a tidal estuary which is quite broad and deep although short in length. The western end, some twenty miles distant from Yorktown and there, at the junction of two rivers that formed the York, was the village of West Point. This estuary provided an excellent and safe anchorage for a considerable fleet. All things being considered as they were known to Cornwallis at the time, the choice of this setting was, perhaps, not as unwise as Clinton maintained after the event. Had he known that French rather than British fleets were to control the use of surrounding waters, Cornwallis might not have selected this particular setting.

PRINTED MAPS

VIII

3. 1781

A MAP and CHART | of those Parts of the | BAY of CHESAPEAK | YORK and JAMES RIVERS | which are at present | The SEAT of WAR. |

Imprint	London, *Publish'd as the Act directs 30th. Novr. 1781, by J. Bew. Pater Noster Row.* The imprint is below the bottom border in the centre.
Engraver	*Jno. Lodge sc.* The plate is signed in the bottom right corner.
In	*The Political Magazine.* London, J. Bew, November 1781, p. 624. Also issued as a separate.
Size	Plate NS 26.2 EW 37.7 Map NS 25.2 EW 36.9
Latitude	37°-37° 30′
Longitude	76-75
Scale	*Three Sea Leag. or Nine Miles* 3=5.5 cm. The scale is in the bottom right corner without frame.
Cartouche	None. The unframed title is in the upper left corner.
Border	Geographically functional.
References	Swem 272; Verner 784.
Reproduction	A facsimile has been issued by Colonial Williamsburg, Inc.

IX

25. 1788

The Part of | VIRGINIA | which was the | SEAT of ACTION.

Imprint	*Engraved for Dr. Gordon's History of the American War.* The imprint is above the top border in the centre.
Engraver	*T. Conder Sculpt. London.* The plate is signed below the bottom right corner.
In	Gordon, Wm. *History . . . of the Independence of the United States . . .* London, Printed for the Author and sold by Charles Dilly . . . 1788 Vol. IV.
Size	Plate NS 19.8 EW 27.1 Map NS 18.3 EW 26.4
Latitude	37-38
Longitude	76-78
Scale	*British Statute Miles* 30=5.3 cm. R.F. 1:920,000 The scale is on the bottom left to the right of the cartouche.

233

Cartouche	The title is in a rectangle measuring 4.3 by 3.8 cm. in the lower left corner. It is framed on two sides by two parallel lines with the outside heavier. The map border frames the other two sides.
References	Swem 320; Verner 842; Sabin 28011; VC/p. 93.
Description	This map covers an area from the Potomac River to Cape Henry and west to Orange County. It is based on The Fry and Jefferson map and has numerous counties, places and rivers named. The work is a simple line engraving without ornamentation. Above the top left corner is " Plate VIII " and above the top right corner is " To face Page 116, Vol. IV."

MANUSCRIPT MAPS

M 41

[Delaware Bay and Chesapeake]

In	Clinton Papers, William L. Clements Library.
Size	$13\frac{1}{4} \times 7\frac{1}{8}$ inches (overall: $14\frac{7}{8} \times 9\frac{1}{2}$ inches).
Scale	1 inch to 18 miles.
Description	A finished, pen and ink map. In the margin is the following in the hand of Sir Henry Clinton:

> the Plan of operations below was proposed by S[ir] H[enry] C[linton] under Idea that the Campaign 81 would be the last of French assistance and of American resistance. It was proposed under promise of an Early reinforcement, to which S[ir] H[enry] intended to add most of the troops he had sent into Chesapeak & such others as Lord Cornwallis should be able to spare from the defensive which was recommended to him in S. Carolina. If S[ir] H[enry] C[linton] was not reinforced, or till he was, he had proposed to assemble all his force at N. York & S. Carolina convinced if he received no affront that Campaign it would be the last.

The following list of references, also in the hand of Sir Henry Clinton, is given at the bottom of the map:

1. The Posi[tio]n. of the French Fleet.
2. That intended to be taken by the british after they had passed the French Fleet.
C. York & Gloucester.
D. Old Pt. Comfort.
E. The district which S[ir] H[enry] C[linton] had proposed for operation beginning with Philadelphia where the Enemys principal depot was &c &c &c & their new formed bank—Very healthy, safe against naval superiority, perfectly friendly, and from whence the Enemys supplies in great measure come. in short in every particular differing from the plan Cornwallis forced and recommended to the Cabinet, & by the adoption of which we were undone.

References	Adams 259; Brun 555.

M 42

[Virginia]

In	Min War, État-Major, L.I.D. No. 171. Paris.
Size	123.0×188 cm.
Description	Four sheets showing Virginia from the Chesapeake Bay west to the Blue Ridge mountains. Appears to be copy of Fry & Jefferson. Names, etc. in English. Numerous counties named. Shows Potomac River and part of Maryland.

234

M 43
Plan of the peninsula of Chesopeak Bay compiled from actual surveys by Iohn Hills assistant engineer 1781.

In	Germaine Papers, William L. Clements Library.
Reproduced	*The World Encompassed*, Plate LV.
Size	48⅝ × 27¾ inches.
Scale	1 inch to five miles.
Description	A finished, coloured map showing primary roads, streams, and settlements, and including, at the top of the map, a series of profile views of certain parts of the Bay and also some of the streams. Soundings are given on the map for the main channel. The map is dedicated to Lord Germain. A note with the views at the top of the map indicates that they were " taken in the passage up to Elk River in 1777 by John Hills . . ." This indicates that they were drawn at the time General Howe with a fleet of 250 vessels sailed up the Bay and disembarked for Philadelphia as a prelude to the battle of Brandywine.
References	Brun 561; *World Encompassed* . . . 248.

M 44
Plan of the peninsula of Chesopeak Bay compiled from actual surveys by John Hills, assistant engineer, 1781.

In	Ayer Collection, Newberry Library.
Size	63.0 × 15.1 cm. Coloured.
Scale	5 miles to 1 inch.
Note	The soundings up to Turkey Point were taken in 1777.
Reference	Smith 240.

M 45
[A Sketch map of York and Gloucester peninsula, July 20, 1781.]

In	Archives, Colonial Williamsburg.
Size	37.0 × 31.0 cm.
Reference	Leclerq Manuscripts, 197, No. 3.

M 46
Confluence of the James River, York River and Chesapeake Bay

In	Clinton Papers, William L. Clements Library.
Size	14¾ × 8⅞ inches.
Description	A rough, red crayon sketch map indicating primarily roads and distances on the peninsula of York. Map too inaccurate to determine scale.
References	Adams 265; Brun 570.

M 47
The Siege of Yorktown

In	Clinton Papers, William L. Clements Library.
Size	12¾ × 16 inches.
Scale	1 inch to 3 miles.

Description   A map of the confluence of the York and James Rivers, showing the peninsula of York and, very roughly, the relative positions of the American and French forces.   The area included extends from New Point Comfort on the north to Great Bridge and the town of Suffolk on the south, and from the confluence of the Chickahominy and James Rivers on the west to Cape Henry on the East.

References   Adams 275; Brun 583.

M 48
Chart showing the depth of the James and York Rivers as they enter Chesapeake Bay, 1781.

In   Library of Congress.
Size   14 × 18 inches.
Reference   Swem 270; Phillips, *Maps of America* . . .

M 49
Yorktown, Virginia and the surrounding area.

In   Simcoe Papers, William L. Clements Library.
Size   6 × 7¼ inches.
Scale   1 inch to approximately 10 miles.
Description   A finished, pen and ink, drawing showing the principal towns within about a thirty mile radius of Yorktown.
Reference   Brun 590.

M 50
Area around the town of West Point.

In   Clinton Papers, William L. Clements Library.
Size   13½ × 20 inches.
Scale   1 inch to 1760 feet.
Description   Pen and ink topographical sketch of the confluence of the Matapony and Pamunkey Rivers where they join the York River, showing the town of West Point.   Plantations are designated by name.   River soundings given.
References   Adams 266; Brun 571.

M 51
Carte détaillée de West Point sur la rivière d'York au confluent des rivières de Pamunky et Matapony.

In   Rochambeau Mss. 54.   Library of Congress.
Size   13 × 13½ inches.
Description   Coloured.
Reference   Winsor VI: 553.

M 52
Battéries de West-point au haut de la rivière d'York.

In   Rochambeau Mss. 55, Library of Congress.
Size   13 × 16½ inches.
Reference   Winsor VI: 553.

M 53
Battéries / de West point au haut de / La Rivière d'York.

In	Min. War, 15-1-7, 31. Paris.
Size	41.4 × 32.5 cm.
Description	A plan showing the junction of the Pamunky and Mattaponi Rivers above Yorktown with the fortifications and lines of fire.
Reference	Karpinski II, 164.

M 54
Plan de West-Point du Sud.

In	Library of Congress.
Size	15½ × 12½ inches.
Description	Coloured.

M 55
Plan / de / West-Point / du Sud.

In	B.-O-H, 2847. Paris.
Size	37.0 × 40.7 cm.
Description	Detailed map of area around West Point showing soundings in the rivers, terrain, etc.
Reference	Karpinski IV.

M 56
Nôtes sur les environs de York, 1781.

In	Rochambeau Mss. 61, Library of Congress.
Size	13½ × 24 inches.
Reference	Swem 274; Phillips, *Maps of America;* Winsor VI: 553.

M 57
Nôtes sur les environs de York.   Plan donné par des arpenteurs du pays, 1781.

In	Rochambeau Mss. 62, Library of Congress.
Size	13 × 25½ inches.
Reference	Swem 275; Phillips, *Maps of America*.

M 58
[Yorktown Area.]

In	Min. War., 15-3, Sieges, York 5. Paris.
Size	49.4 × 49.2 cm.
Description	Topographical platt of area around Yorktown with numerous notes.
Reference	Karpinski II, 171.

M 59

Carte de l'Entrée de la Baye de Chesapeak / qui Comprend le Cap Charles, le Cap Henry, la Baye de Lynhaven, l'Embouchures / de la Rivière de James, à celle de la Rivière d'York. / 1782.

In	Guerre, 14-7, York. Paris.
Size	101.0 × 101.8 cm.
Description	A draught showing the end of the peninsula between the York and the James Rivers.
Reference	Karpinski, II, 139.

M 60

Cartes des environs d'Hampton, 1781.

In	Rochambeau Mss. 50, Library of Congress.
Size	22 × 36½ inches.
Description	Coloured.
Reference	Winsor, VI: 553.

M 61

[Virginia.]

In	Min. War., 15-1-7, P 8, Paris.
Size	52.4 × 80.3 cm.
Description	A draught of the lower end of the Chesapeake Bay as far as Williamsburg and north to the Rappahannock River.
Reference	Karpinski, II, 143.

M 62

[Courses of the York and James Rivers.]

In	Guerre Etat Major, 70-219. Paris.
Size	75 × 117.4 cm.
Description	A large draught from Capes Henry and Charles west to Turkey Island including both the York and James Rivers and south to Suffolk. Numerous towns and residences are named.
Reference	Karpinski, II, 218.

M 63

[Map showing the coastline from the James River northward to Long Island, 1778].

In	Henry E. Huntington Library (HM3098).
Note	The Huntington Library indicates that this map is by John André.

M 64

Plan d'Hampton pour servir à l'établissement du Quartier d'hiver de la Légion de Lauzun, le 1er novembre, 1781.

In	Berthier papers 28. Princeton University Library.
Note	Town plan for use in assigning billets to the French troops who were quartered here during the winter of 1781-82. This map was probably drawn by Louis-Alexander Berthier.

M 65
Environs de Glocester

In   Princeton University Library.

Note   This map is between pages 90-91 in the manuscript journal of Joachim du Perron, Comte de Revel. A re-drawn version of this map is found in: Joachim du Perron, Comte de Revel, *Journal particulier d'une campagne aux Indes Occidentales.* (Paris, H. Charles-Lavauzelle, 1898), pp. 146-147.

IV

THE NAVAL ENGAGEMENT

Sir Samuel Hood and his units of the British Fleet were en route to New York to join Admiral Graves when he learned of the movement toward the Chesapeake Bay of a large French Fleet. Upon arriving in New York he informed Graves of this and the combined units set sail immediately for the Virginia Capes. Graves wished to intercept the fleet units commanded by de Barras which he knew were leaving Newport to join de Grasse and to prevent de Grasse from sealing the entrance to the Bay. De Grasse, however, had arrived in the Bay before Graves could intervene. Immediately upon arrival, he disembarked at Jamestown on August 27th fresh French troops from the West Indies under command of the Marquis de Saint Simon. These troops joined Lafayette near Williamsburg and provided the necessary reinforcements to prevent any escape by Cornwallis.

On September 1, 1781, a member of Lafayette's army wrote a letter to a friend in Philadelphia which was published in the *Pennsylvania Packet* on September 18th that discusses the situation at this point:

>   . . . let me make you acquainted with Major-General the Marquis de St. Simon and the French army. You have seen the British troops and the troops of other nations, but you have not seen troops so universally well made, so robust, or of such an appearance as those General St. Simon has brought to our assistance. These are all under the command of our General. They now encamp nearly on the ground the British occupied before they evacuated Jamestown. I do not pretend to know the secrets of our Commander, or I would tell you what is to be done; I pretend, however, to see a great general in the Marquis de St. Simon; an affectionate politeness in his officers towards ours, and a general impatience in the French army to complete the gordian knot in which our second Fabius, Fayette, has been entangling his lordship; some of its cords already press him, and, I believe, if there were hopes of succeeding, he would attempt to cut it. But notwithstanding his lordship is, perhaps, the first officer in the British service, yet he may not be in possession of the sword of Alcides.
>
> The light infantry are advanced to Williamsburg. The Pennsylvanians lay near his place, and it is the talk of the camp, that the French troops

will take their position to-morrow in its vicinity. The French ships lay in James river, to prevent a retreat, in York river and at the Capes.

On September 5th, the British Fleet commanded by Admiral Graves was sighted off the Virginia Capes. De Grasse weighed anchor and sailed out immediately to meet them. In the late afternoon on that day the last great naval battle of the Revolutionary War was launched.

The French Fleet consisted of twenty-four ships and two frigates mounting 1,826 guns, while the British numbered twenty-one ships with 1,694 guns. The engagement started at 4 p.m. and lasted some two hours the first day with eighteen officers and two hundred men of the French forces killed or wounded and five British vessels damaged, one of which remained afloat only by dint of superhuman effort. The battle continued for several days during which de Grasse was unable to involve Graves in a head on clash. By September 10th, Graves recognized that the engagement was lost and after setting fire to one crippled vessel he set sail for New York. De Grasse pursued him for a short distance but then returned to the Bay. The seas at the Virginia Capes and the Chesapeake Bay were now effectively controlled by the French.

A Baltimore journal published a contemporary description of the French Fleet under de Grasse:

White and Blue Squadron, commanded by Monsieur de Monteil—La Bourgoyne, 74 guns; le Glorieux, 74 guns; le Vaillant 64; le Destin, 74; le Languedoc, 84 (to repeat signals l'Aigreete, 32), le Sceptre, 74; le Réflechi, 64; le Marceillois, 74; le Diadem, 74.

White Squadron, commanded by Monsier de Grasse—Le Northumberland, 74; le Zèle, 74; le St. Esprit, 86; le Tritton, 54; le Cafare, 74 (to repeat le Serpent, 18) le Ville de Paris, 110 (to repeat l'Amdromaque, 42); la Victorie, 74 (to repeat l'Alerte, 16); le Solataire, 64; l'Experiment, 50; 14 Sovereign, 74.

White Squadron, commanded by Mons. Bougainville—Le Palmier, 74; l'Hector, 78; le Citoine, 74; le Scipeon, 74; l'Auguste, 84 (to repeat la Diligente, 32); le Magnamine, 74; le Gâton, 64; l'Hercule, 74 (to repeat la Raileuse, 40); le Pluton, 74.

Major-Général Baron de Viomenil, with his Suite and many officers of distinction (French and American) are just arrived in town.

The Count de Grasse wrote a letter to the Chevalier de la Luzerner, French Minister to the Colonies, which briefly mentioned the naval engagement:

... Nothing gave me greater pleasure than the approach of the armies under General Washington and Count de Rochambeau. In order to hasten their arrival I had selected out seven vessels that drew the least water to transport them from the mouth of Elk down Chesapeake Bay. But the moment they were ready to sail to execute this service, I was myself obliged to make preparations for repelling the enemy's fleet, which appeared off the entrance of the Bay. I have fought them and their van has been very roughly handled. I returned to the bay on the 10th. In the meantime Count de Barras had arrived and sent up the transports he had with him to bring down the troops, which induced me not to send up the seven vessels above mentioned; and I had only to add to those sent by Count de Barras as many frigates as I could. My putting to sea facilitated the entrance of M. de Barras, and our junction has added much to our strength. I fell in with two of the enemy's frigates—the Iris and the Richmond, of 32 guns each. They had been sent by the English admiral to cut away the buoys of our anchor. They had paid dear for them.

While de Grasse was pursuing the British Fleet, de Barres arrived from Newport on the evening of September 9th. He brought with him the heavy artillery which the northern Allied Army had not been able to transport by land. This added to the forces accumulating on the peninsula for the final acts of the drama.

In addition to the maps listed here, see also printed maps XIV (1) and XX (11), and manuscript maps 83, 95.

PRINTED MAPS

X

2. [1781]
A: REPRESENTATION, | *Of the Sea Fight, on the 5th of Sepr 1781, between Rear* | *Admiral* GRAVES *and the Count* DE GRASSE | [rule 9.7]

In	Separate.
Size	Plate NS — EW 39.6
	Map NS 31.2 EW 38.4
Cartouche	None. The unframed title is to the right above the centre.
Border	Single line.
Description	This map shows the area of Hampton Rhodes with Cape Henry and Cape Charles. It is a battle plan with the positions of the various ships indicated. There are long descriptive legends in the bottom left corner and along the right border under the title. These describe the battle and explain the various symbols used on the plan.

XI

29. 1794
POSITION | [rule 1.5 cm] of the [rule 1.6 cm.] | ENGLISH and FRENCH FLEETS | *Immediately previous to the* | *ACTION.* | *on the 5th Sepr. 1781.* |

Imprint	*Engraved for Stedman's History of the American War.*
	Below the bottom border in the centre of the map.

In	Stedman, C. *The History . . . American War*. London, Printed for the Author; and sold by J. Murray . . . 1794. Vol. II between pp. 400-401.
Size	Plate NS 23.0 EW 28.3
	Map NS 21.2 EW 25.1
Cartouche	None. Title in the lower left.
Border	Single line.
References	Swem 353; Verner 888; VC/p. 62; Sabin 91057.
Reproduction	*Magazine of Amer. Hist.* Vol. 7 (1881), p. 369.
Description	This is a simple engraving employing very few lines to indicate the area and to illustrate the positions of the fleets in the area of the Hampton Roads, including Capes Charles and Henry and Point Comfort. The fleets are represented by small ovals depicting ships. Dotted lines are used to illustrate the line movement of the fleets with explanatory notes along the lines.

MANUSCRIPT MAPS

M 66

Combat naval à la hauteur de la Baye de Chézapeake le 5 7bre.

In	Ayer Collection. Newberry Library.
Size	59.9 × 46.2 cm. Coloured. Oriented with the west at the top.
Scale	2 leagues equal 18.5 cm.
Description	The position of the two fleets at the beginning of the battle is placed just east of Cape Henry.
Reference	Smith 239.

M 67

Position of the French and British fleets at the mouth of the York River on 5 September 1781.

In	Smith Collection. William L. Clements Library.
Size	17⅛ × 13½ inches.
Description	An unfinished, coloured, French naval battle plan. A table of reference identifies the major French vessels.
Reference	Brun 580.

M 68

Expédition de Chesapeack.

In	Princeton University Library.
Note	This map shows the Chesapeake Bay from Cape Henry to the mouth of the Potomac. On the back are four diagrams showing the positions of the ships on the seventh and eighth of September 1781.
	A re-drawn version of this map is reproduced in: Joachim du Perron, Comte de Revel, *Journal particulier d'une campagne aux Indes Occidentales*, (Paris, H. Charles-Lavauzelle, 1898), pp. 120-121.

V

While de Grasse and Graves were fighting off the Virginia Capes Washington and Rochambeau were hastening south in a triumphant march that saw them greeted joyously at Philadelphia and Baltimore among other places along the way. Washington had started the march south on August 16th and by September 14th they were in Williamburg where they joined Lafayette.

After ten days or so in preparation the combined allied forces moved to Yorktown on September 28th. The General Orders issued on the preceding day describe the arrangements for the move:

General Orders
Williamsburg Sept. 27, five o'clock P.M.

The whole Army will march by the right in one column at 5 o'clock to-morrow morning precisely, the particular orders of march for the right wing will be distributed by the Quartermaster General. The General desires that the officers will confine themselves in point of baggage to objects of the first necessity, that the Army may march as light and unencumbered as possible. The Quartermaster General will have directions to appoint a proper deposit for the effects that will be left, from whence they will be transported to the army as soon as permanent position is taken.

The Quartermaster General will allot a proportionate of waggons in his service for the service of the left wing. If the enemy should be tempted to meet the army on its march, the General particularly enjoins his troops to place their principal reliance on the bayonet, that they may prove the vanity of the boast which the British make of their peculiar prowess in deciding battles with that weapon; he trusts that a generous emulation will actuate the allied armies. That the French whose national weapon is that of close fight, and the troops in general that have so often used with success, will distinguish themselves on every occasion that offers.

The *Pennsylvania Packet* for October 9th, 1781, carried a report of the march from Williamsburg to Yorktown which describes the investment of that place in detail:

On Friday, September 28, the whole army marched from Williamsburg to within one mile of the enemy's works at York, and formed the first line of the circumvallation without any loss. On the 29th our troops had a few skirmishes with the enemy, and but little damage done on either side. In the night the British evacuated Pigeon quarter and three other redoubts, which are so high as to be able to command the town. These were taken possession of on Sunday morning at sunrise under a heavy cannonade from York Town. The enemy next fled from a stockade when the French grenadiers had advanced within fifteen yards of it, and retreated, under cover of their shipping, with the loss of ten taken prisoners. It was expected

243

our troops would break ground on the 1st inst. Cornwallis's forces in York are supposed to be 6000 troops, including refugees, besides 1000 armed nigroes. He has possession of the river and Gloucester, strongly fortified and garrisoned by about 1000 men; these are hemmed in by General Wheeden with 1500 men, the Duke de Lucerne with his legion and 2000 marines from the fleet to prevent any escape that way,—one ship of 44 guns, two frigates and a 20 gun packet lie at Burwell's landing in James's river; one of 50, one of 40, two frigates and a store ship in the mouth of that river— five ships of the line off Cape Henry: 32 ships of the line and several frigates are drawn up across the mouth of York river; and three ships of considerable force are in that river below the town, which were to proceed onward with the first fair wind. Gen. Washington sent in a flag to Lord Cornwallis, directing him not to destroy his shipping or warlike stores, as he would answer it at his peril. The easy capture of the outposts will greatly accelerate the future operations of our army. Lieut. col. John Conolly was taken near York-Town by two militia men, and is paroled to Hanover in Virginia.

PRINTED MAPS

XII

22. 1787

[Côte de York-town à Boston.   Marches de l'Armée] [Map of the East Coast of North America from Albemarle to Buzzards Bay]

In	Soules, F. *Histoire des Troubles de l'Amérique* ... A Paris, chez Buisson, 1787.
Size	Plate NS [93.7] EW 28.2
	Map NS [91.2] EW 26.2
Orientation	West.
Scale	*Échelle de 80 Milles* 80=11.4 cm.
	R.F. [about 1:1,000,000].
Cartouche	None. The map is untitled. Both titles provided above are supplied with the French title being that applied to the original manuscript in DLC.
Border	Single line.
Watermark	Three unidentified lines of letters and grapes.
Reference	Rochambeau 65; Verner 840.
Description	This map of the east coast includes the area from Boston Harbour to the Gulf of Albemarle. The map is designed on an oblique so that some coastal areas are not included. Roads are shown with colours to indicate the marches and encampments of the various military forces.
Note	The original manuscript upon which this map is based is M 69. The map is printed on two sheets joined and the NS measurements provided above are for a joined copy.

XIII

6. 1782

The POSITION of the ARMY / between the Ravines / *on the 28th. and 29th. of Sept. 1781*

Size	Plate NS 34.5 EW 26.2

Reference   Swem 266; Verner 789.

Note   This is an overlay intended to be mounted on Des Barres *A Plan of the Posts of York* . . . (5, XV). It should be attached to the bottom border of that map at the place where the "Great South Road from Hampton" which appears on each will overlay. See Manuscript Map M88.

XIV

1. 1781

A PLAN / OF THE ENTRANCE OF CHESAPEAK BAY, / with JAMES and YORK RIVERS; / *wherein are shewn* the Respective Positions (*in the beginning of October*) / 1o. *OF THE BRITISH ARMY* Commanded By *LORD CORNWALLIS,* / *AT GLOUCESTER* and *YORK* in Virginia; / 2o. of the American *and* French Forces *under* General Washington, / 3o. *and* of the French Fleet *under* Count de Grasse. / *By an Officer* / [rule 5.2 cm] / [scale] / [imprint] /

Imprint   LONDON. / *Publish'd by W^m. Faden Charing Cross, Nov^r, 26th, 1781.* /

In   Separate.

Size   Plate   NS 41.3   EW 53.4
        Map   NS 40.4   EW 51.1

Scale   Scale of Miles   10=6.5 cm.

Cartouche   None. The title is in the upper left corner of the plate.

Border   Two parallel lines with the outside line heavier.

References   P/1337; VC/p. 61; Johnston 7; Swem 282; Verner 778.

Reproductions Anderson Sale 2239 (Feb. 1928) p. 31.
        The Pennsylvania Magazine, Vol. 51 (1927), p. 193.

Description   This is a large map of the Hampton Rhodes area extending west to Williamsburg, south to Suffolk, and north to the southern point of the junction of Rappahannock River and the Chesapeake Bay.

Note   This map by Faden was issued first as a separate item which, in 1793, he incorporated in his *Atlas of Battles of the American Revolution* . . . It is listed for sale in the Faden *Catalogue* . . . of 1822 (p. 15) where it is priced at one shilling. The *Atlas* . . . containing this map was re-issued in 1845 in New York by Bartlett & Welford. Sabin (2309) notes: "A New York firm purchased a large remainder of these maps, and issued them with the above title page. Their edition is distinguished by the broad letters with which the title is printed, and the omission of the place and date of publication." See Manuscript Map M 83.

MANUSCRIPT MAPS

M 69

Côte de York-town à Boston. Marches de l'armée, 1781.

In   Rochambeau manuscripts 65, Library of Congress.

Size   17 × 64½ inches. Coloured.

Description   Shows the route of Rochambeau from Boston to Yorktown. This map was published in Soules. See Map XII (22).

Reference   Swem 271; Phillips, *Maps of America*.

M 70

Plans des différents camps occupés par l'armée aux ordres de Mr. le Comte de Rochambeau.

In   Rochambeau Collection, Library of Congress.
Size   12½ × 8 inches.
Description   A volume of plans of various camps made by Rochambeau's army en route to Yorktown. Includes many in Virginia.
Reference   Swem 292.

M 71

Carte de La Campagne Faîte en Virginie en 1781.

In   Guerre, États Majors, L.I.D. 174. Paris.
Size   56.0 × 28.0 cm.
Description   Detailed, carefully drawn map from Green Spring to Yorktown and Gloucester showing the breadth of the peninsula. Fields, woods, streams, roads, etc. shown. The legend is signed: " Levé en Sep^{bre} et Oct^{bre} par Pechon, aide decamp de M^r le M^m de St Simon."
Reference   Karpinski, II, 196.

M 72

Carte de la Virginie / ou précis de la Campagne de 1781.

In   Serv. Hyd. C4044-39. Paris.
Size   116.0 × 83.0 cm.
Description   This map is obviously after Fry & Jefferson. There is a long detailed note on the left border. " Dessiné par Chantavoine."
Reference   Karpinski, IV, 463.

M 73

Plan du débarquement et de la / Marche de la division Commandée parle / Mr. de St. Simon, sa réunion avec le Corps / du Mr. de la Fayette, et celle de l'Armée / combinée de Washington et de / Rochambeau, et le Siège d'Yorck, 1781.

In   Min. War. État-Major, L.I.D. No. 174. Paris.
Size   36.0 × 22.5 cm.
Description   Area of the peninsula around Williamsburg from Green Spring to Yorktown showing both rivers. Inset view of Yorktown bottom right corner. Long explanation along left border.
Reference   Karpinski, II, 197.

M 74

Carte de la campagne de la division aux ordres du Mis. de St. Simon en Virginie dépuis le 2.7bre. 1781, jusqu'à l'rédition d'York le 19.8bre. même année.

In   Ayer Collection, Newberry Library.
Size   67.3 × 44.0 cm. Coloured.
Note   Contains an inset view of Yorktown.
Reference   Smith 238.

M 75

Armée de Rochambeay / 1782 / Carte / des Environs de Williamsburg / en Virginie ou les Armées / France et Américaine / en campes en Septembre 1781.

In	Min. War. 15-1-7, 29 Map. Paris.
Size	76.6 × 64.8 cm.
Description	Large scale plan of area around Williamsburg. Hauchering to show terrain. Small platt of city.
Reference	Karpinski, II, 162.

M 76

Plan du terrain à la rive gauche de la rivière de James vis-à-vis James-town en Virginie ou s'est livré le combat du 6 Juillet 1781, . . .

In	Rochambeau Mss. 51, Library of Congress.
Size	18 × 19 inches. Coloured.

M 77

Carte des environs de Williamsburg en Virginie ou les Armées Francoise et Americaine ont campé's en Septembre 1781. Armée de Rochambeau, 1782.

In	Rochambeau Manuscripts 57, Library of Congress.
Size	26 × 36 inches. Coloured.
Reference	Swem 298; Phillips, *Maps of America;* Winsor VI: 553.

M 78

Plans des environs de Williamsburg, York, Hamton et Portsmouth.

In	Rochambeau Mss. 56, Library of Congress.
Size	12 × 12 inches.
Reference	Swem 298; Phillips, *Maps of America;* Winsor VI: 553.

M 79

[College Creek and Vicinity.]

In	Rochambeau Mss., Library of Congress.
Size	12 × 12 inches.
Reproduced	Lewis & Loomie, Plate XVIII, facing p. 262.

M 80

Williamsburgh and the slip of land between York and James Rivers from thence to Hampton.

In	Clinton Papers, William L. Clements Library.
Size	16 × 12¾ inches.
Scale	1 inch to approximately 2½ miles.
Description	A freehand, pen and ink sketch map indicating roads, distances and water approaches to the town. Title taken from verso of map.
Reference	Adams 264; Brun 589.

M 81

A Sketch of / the East end of / The / Peninsula / Whereon is / Hampton / W.P.M.

In	Clinton Papers, William L. Clements Library.
Size	$19\frac{3}{4} \times 28\frac{1}{4}$ inches.
Scale	1 inch to approximately 4750 feet.
Description	Shows the peninsula including Point Comfort, Hampton, and Newport News.
Reproduced	Lewis & Loomie, Plate XIX, facing p. 266 (partial).
Reference	Adams 263; Brun 584.

M 82

Position of the troops, under Earl Cornwallis, on the 28 and 29 September 1781; when the Enemy first appeared.

In	Clinton Papers. William L. Clements Library.
Size	$30 \times 21\frac{1}{4}$ inches.
Scale	1 inch to approximately 500 feet.
Description	A finished, coloured, topographical map of the area from the outer fortification of Yorktown to the confluence of Wormley's Creek and the York River. The following units are shown in their positions: 17th, 23rd, 33rd, 43rd, 76th, 80th and 71st. Regiments: the Anspach Regiment, the Light Infantry, the Regiment de Bosse, the Guards, the Provincials and the Seamen.
References	Adams 273; Brun 581.

M 83

A Plan of the Entrance of Chesapeak Bay, with James and York Rivers; wherein are shewn the Respective Positions (in the beginning of October.)

> 1º· Of the British Army, commanded by Lord Cornwallis, at Gloucester and York, in Virginia.
>
> 2º· Of the American and French Forces under Gen. Washington.
>
> 3º· And of the French Fleet, under Count de Grasse.

By an Officer, London: Published by William Faden, Charing Cross, Nov. 26, 1781 [added in a different hand.]

In	Library of Congress.
Size	20×16 inches.
Description	This is the original manuscript for Printed Map XIV (1).
Reference	Hale 90.

M 84

Carte des Environs de York en Virginie avec les attaques des Armées François et Americaine devant cette Place, 1781.

In	Henry E. Huntington Library (HM1093).
Note	The Huntington Library notes that this map is by Querenet de la Combe.

M 85

Map of the Encampment of the French and American Armies at Archer's Hope, 25, September 1781.

In   Berthier papers No. 21 (38) Princeton University Library.

Note   A similar map, from another set by Berthier, is reproduced in Jean-Edmond Weelen, *Rochambeau Father and Son*, translated by Lawrence Lee, (NY, 1936), facing p. 218.

M 86

Map of the Encampment of the French and American Armies outside Williamsburg, 26 September 1781.

In   Berthier papers, No. 21 (39), Princeton University Library.

Note   This map is reproduced in *The Papers of Thomas Jefferson*, edited by J. P. Boyd, *et al.*   Vol. II, p. 304.

M 87

Établissement des hussards en correspondence à New-Kent Court House, new-Castle, et Linch Taverne, 1781.

In   Berthier Papers, No. 30.   Princeton University Library.

Note   This is a sketch-map of the communication lines for messengers between Williamsburg, Richmond, and Bowling Green.

M 88

Positions of the Army under the Command of Earl Cornwallis between the Ravines on the 28th and 29th of Sept., 1781.

In   Norfolk (Va.) Museum.

Size $11\frac{5}{8} \times 12\frac{1}{2}$ inches.

Note   This is a pen, ink and water colour sketch.   See Printed Map XIII.   It is not known whether this is the original for that map or a copy of it.

VI

THE SIEGE

The British forces at Yorktown had been busily erecting their defences around the perimeter of their position.   Cornwallis had some 5,000 troops and upwards of 3,000 negro slaves who had joined him at Portsmouth and elsewhere much to the annoyance of their owners.   These slaves provided labour to dig the trenches and redoubts which ringed Yorktown in concentric arcs.   At Gloucester across the river Cornwallis stationed a body of troops commanded by Brigadier General O'Hara and all his cavalry including the troops under Lt. Colonel Tarleton.   Opposing them and preventing any escape was an American unit commanded by General Wiedon which was ultimately augmented by French units and the entire operations commanded by the Marquis de Choisy. The Duc de Lauzun who was with the French forces described de Choisy as

"... an excellent and worthy man, absurdly violent in temper, constantly in a rage, quarelling with everybody, and without common sense". This allied force on the Gloucester peninsula was sufficient to contain the British and save for minor skirmishes they figure no further in the siege of Yorktown.

General Washington, himself, describes the opening of the siege:

> Having debarked all the troops and their baggage, marched and encamped them in front of the city, and having with some difficulty obtained horses and wagons sufficient to move our field artillery, intrenching tools and such other articles as were indispensably necessary, we commenced our march for the investiture of York. The American Continentals and French troops formed one column on the left, the first in advance. The militia composed the right column, and marched by way of Harwood's Mill. Half a mile beyond the Half Way House the French and Americans separated. The former continued on the direct road to York by the Brick House, the latter filed off to the right for Munford's bridge, where a junction with the militia was to be made. About noon the head of each column arrived at its ground, and some of the enemy's picquets were driven in on the left by a corps of French troops advanced for the purpose, which afforded an opportunity of reconnoitering them on their right. The enemy's Horse on the right were also obliged to retire from the ground they had encamped on, and from whence they were employed in reconnoitering the right column. The line being formed, all the Troops, officers and men, lay upon their arms during the night.

The Colonial and French forces surrounding Yorktown numbered some 15,000. By the first of October they were in place and ready to begin the siege. In his General Orders issued on October 6th, Washington listed fifty-four regulations to govern the operation of the siege, that would cover any eventuality. October the 8th found the allied trenches ready and the artillery under General Knox in position. The British outposts had been pushed back to the main defensive positions so the battle was confined to the immediate circumference of Yorktown.

Lafayette's division took over the trenches on the ninth of October and thereafter French and American units alternated this duty. Among the commanders in the trenches were such officers as Steuben, Lincoln, Lamb, Stevens, Carrington, Bauman, St. Simon, Chastellux, and others. That same evening one of the British ships anchored off Yorktown showed signs of belligerent manoeuvres and a French battery opened fire with red-hot shot which set it afire. This spread quickly to other units of the fleet and the night was aglow from the flames which effectively destroyed most of the fleet at anchor. This further diminished Cornwallis's resources and weakened his position still more.

At the perimeter, the allies successfully stormed one position after another forcing the British to retreat into an ever tightening circle. Both American and

French troops fought valiantly and individual or unit heroism was frequently mentioned in orders and dispatches. The allied artillery maintained a continuous barrage into the village so that after the capitulation the town was found to be in a state of almost total destruction. Lord Cornwallis had his headquarters in the large and stately brick mansion which belonged to Secretary Nelson of Virginia which still bears evidence of the shot which maimed the village.

Although the conclusion of the drama was evident at the outset, the British managed to resist until ten o'clock on the morning of the seventeenth of October when Lord Cornwallis sued for an amnesty in order that commissioners for both sides might meet and discuss a surrender. The eighteenth was devoted to a discussion of terms which were as harsh as those Cornwallis himself was accustomed to impose on the foe he vanquished. The agreement of capitulation was signed before eleven on the morning of the nineteenth of October 1781 and the formal surrender took place at two that afternoon with full military formality. The Count de Rochambeau wrote of the event:

> The garrison marched out at two o'clock between the two armies, drums beating, carrying their arms which were stacked, with about twenty flags. Lord Cornwallis being ill, General O'Hara marched out at the head of the garrison. When he approached me he presented his sword. I pointed to General Washington opposite me as the head of the American army, and said to him that as the French army was an auxiliary on this Continent, that it was now from the American General that he must take his orders.

With this event the Revolutionary War in America was terminated whereby those who had been rebels and traitors to one country became patriots and heroes of another.

The Printed Maps of the Siege

The printed maps depicting the siege at Yorktown total fourteen different maps and four copies or later reprints. Only four of the total number are prototype maps of which one is American, one French, and the remaining two of British origin. These maps are grouped by country of origin and described below. Following the detailed description of the prototype maps will be found the description of the illustrative maps produced in each country.

BRITISH PRINTED MAPS

Prototypes

The first British printed prototype to detail the situation around Yorktown at the time of the surrender was that prepared by Joseph F. W. DesBarres in 1782 with the second appearing in 1785 from the shop of William Faden. Each of these two maps is based on an original survey by a British officer on the scene at the time.

XV

5. 1782

A PLAN of the POSTS / of / YORK AND GLOUCESTER / in the / *PROVINCE OF VIRGINIA.* / Established by / His MAJESTY'S ARMY / under the Command of Lieut. General EARL CORNWALLIS, / *together with* / *The Attacks under Operations of the AMERICAN & FRENCH FORCES* / Commanded by / GENERAL WASHINGTON and the COUNT of ROCHAMBEAU, / *which Terminated in the SURRENDER of the said Posts and Army* / on the 17th. of October 1781. *SURVEYED by CAPT^N. FAGE of the ROYAL ARTILLERY.* / *Scale of Feet.* / [graduated scale bar] / *Publish'd according to Act of Parliament, the 4th. June 1782.* /

In	Des Barres, Joseph F. W. *The Atlantic Neptune, published for the use of the royal navy of Great Britain . . .* [London, 1774-1782]
Size	Plate NS 75.8 EW 104.0
	Map NS 75.2 EW 103.3
Scale	*Scale of Feet* 3,000 = 15.8 cm.
	The graduated scale bar is in the title cartouche as indicated above.
Cartouche	The title is in a vertical rectangle measuring 25.8 horizontal by 31.7 vertical set at an oblique angle to the bottom left corner.
Border	A single line, then a space 1.7 cm. wide, and finally a double line outside border.
References	P/1198; VC/p. 62; Johnston 4; Verner 788.
Reproduction	*The Month*, Vol. XXIX (Oct. 1957), pp. 16-17.
Description	This beautiful chart of the Yorktown area includes the tip of Gloucester Point. It shows the configuration of the land by the use of hauchering with woods, fields, marshes, ravines, etc., indicated. The various positions of the military units are indicated along with the ships in the York River.
	In the upper right half of the sheet is an inset map set at an angle so designed as to have the appearance of another sheet laid on top of the original.
Inset	A map of the area of *Hampton Roads.*
Size	NS 28.2 EW 46.3
Border	Two lines 1.0 cm. apart.
Description	This inset shows the relationship of the larger map to the area. All of the counties in the area depicted are named. The inset included the area from the Capes in the east to Williamsburg on the west; from New Point Comfort on the north to Suffolk on the south. This is a simple outline map.

XVI

13. 1785

A PLAN of / YORKTOWN AND GLOUCESTER, / *IN THE PROVINCE OF VIRGINIA,* / Shewing / the WORKS constructed for the defence of these Posts / by the BRITISH ARMY, / under the Command of Lt. Genl. EARL CORNWALLIS: / *together with* / the Attacks and Operations of the American and French Forces, / Commanded by / GEN^L. WASHINGTON and COUNT ROCHAMBEAU, / to whom the said Posts were Surrendered / *on the 17th. October 1781* / from an actual SURVEY in the Possession of / J^No. HILLS, late Lieut. in the 23d. Regt. & Asst. Engr. / [rule 6.1] / LONDON: Printed for W^m. FADEN, Geographer to the KING, Charing Cross, October 7th. 1785. /

In	Separate.
Size	Plate NS 72.5 EW Map NS 70.5 EW 53.5
Scale	2,640 feet=13.7 cm. The double graduated scale bar is in the bottom left corner unframed.
Cartouche	None. The title is in the lower left corner unframed.
Border	The map is framed in two close parallel lines with the outside (neat) line heavier.
Reference	P/1337; VC/p. 62; Johnson 5; Verner 818.
Description	This is a fine platt of the area of Yorktown showing the positions of the armies and the fleets. Roads, houses, troop placements, lines of fire, and the configuration of the land is shown in detail. Hauchering is used to designate elevation.
Note	A manuscript plan similar to this is in the Rochambeau collection. See Manuscript Maps M95. This map was re-issued in 1793 in the Faden, *Atlas of Battles of the American Revolution*, and again in New York in 1845.

Illustrative

Three different maps depicting the situation at Yorktown during the siege and surrender were printed in England. These are found in three different histories or chronicles of events either written by participants or contemporary historians.

XVII

16. 1787

Plan | of the SIEGE of | YORK TOWN | in Virginia [in black letter] | [rule 4.5 cm.]

Imprint	London, Publish'd March 1st., 1787. The imprint is below the bottom border in the centre.
In	Tarleton, Lt. Col. *A History of the Campaigns of 1780 & 1781* . . . London, Printed for T. Cadell, in the Strand 1787, p. 394.
Size	Plate NS 30.6 EW 34.4 Map NS 29.2 EW 32.1
Scale	*SCALE OF FEET* 3500=5.9 cm. The graduated scale bar is in the bottom left corner unframed.
Cartouche	None. The title is in the bottom right corner unframed.
Border	Two fine parallel lines with the neat line heavier.
Reference	Swem 318; P/1337; Sabin 94397; Church 1224; Johnston 6; Verner 828.

XVIII

26. 1788

YORK TOWN, | and | GLOUCESTER POINT. | as besieged by | the ALLIED ARMY, |

Imprint	*Engraved for Dr. Gordon's History of the American War.* The imprint is above the top border in the centre.
Engraver	*T. Conder Schlpt. London.* The plate is signed below the bottom right corner.
In	Gordon, Wm. *History . . . of the Independence of the United States* . . . London, Printed for the Author . . . 1788. Vol. IV.
Size	Plate NS 30.1 EW 22.0 Map NS 28.5 EW 21.2
Orientation	North West.
Scale	*Scale of Yards* 1000=3.0 cm. The scale is in the bottom right corner.

Cartouche	The title is in a rectangle measuring 4.5×3.8 cm. in the upper right corner. It is framed in two parallel lines with the outside line heavier. This is on two sides and the map border on the remaining two sides.
Border	Two parallel lines with the neat line heavier.
Reference	Swem 321; Verner 843; VC/p. 63.
Note	Across the bottom of the map is a compartment 6.0 cm. containing an " Explanation " in four columns. Above the top left corner is Plate LX and above the top right is *To face page 196. Vol. IV.*

XIX

30. 1794

PLAN / *of* / *the* SIEGE *of* / YORK TOWN / *in* / VIRGINIA. / [rule 4.0 cm.] / Engraved for Stedman's History of the American War.

In	Stedman, C. *The History* . . . London, Printed for the Author, 1794.
Size	Plate NS 28.5 EW 34.0 Map NS 27.2 EW 32.3
Scale	*Scale of Feet* 3,500 = 5.9 cm. The graduated scale bar is along the bottom border on the left.
Cartouche	None. The title is in the upper right corner.
Border	Two parallel lines with the neat line heavy.
References	Swem 352; VC/p. 62; Verner 893.
Reproduction	*The Magazine of American History*, Vol. 6 (1881), p. 8.

BRITISH MANUSCRIPT MAPS

M 89

[Position of British Troops before Yorktown.]

In	Clinton Papers, William L. Clements Library.
Size	$7\frac{1}{4} \times 9$ inches.
Description	A pen-and-ink diagrammatic portrayal of the position of the British, probably sometime before the Americans closed in. Defensive works are laid out on the river banks, and redoubts to defend the position against attacks from Williamsburg. The troops total: " G. Leslie 2177 Lord Cornwallis 3484 Leg. Cavy 350."
Reference	Adams 271.

M 90

Sketch of the posts of York Town and Gloucester Point shewing the French and Rebel attacks upon the former in October, 1781. By: Lieut. [Alexander] Sutherland engineer.

In	Clinton Papers. William L. Clements Library.
Size	$18 \times 25\frac{1}{2}$ inches.
Scale	1 inch to 300 yards.
Description	A finished, coloured, topographical map of the area within about a mile and a half radius of the centre of Yorktown. Fortifications are further described in a table of " References." '
Reference	Adams 270; Brun 585.

M 91

The British works at Yorktown and Gloucester.   By: Alexander Sutherland

In   Clinton Papers.   William L. Clements Library.

Size   10½ × 15¾ inches.

Scale   1 inch to approximately 2000 feet.

Description   An unfinished, topographical, pen and ink map showing the two British posts and their immediate area.   On the verso is the following in the hand of Sir Henry Clinton:
> The only plan of York I could obtain from Sutherland[!]   L.C. Chief Engineer and the person he said that had made an Exact Survey and Examination of it.

References   Adams 272; Brun 567.

M 92

[Mouth of the York River, Gloucester and Yorktown]

In   British Museum.   Add. Mss. 15,535.6.

Description   In ink, pen and brush.   A column at right lists French Infantry (by unit), French, American, and British batteries by size and number of guns.   Dated Juliana, 12 June 1782.   Noted as a copy.   Signed John Hayman, Lieut. 17th Inf.

Reference   Survey Report 159.

M 93

A plan of the operations of the French and American forces against the English in York and Gloucester, at the entrance of York River, in Chesapeake Bay, from the 6th to the 15th October, 1777, prior to the capitulation of General Burgoyne; copy from the original; drawn at Juliana, 12th June 1782, by John Hayman, lieut., 17th infantry.

In   British Museum, Add. Mss. 15,535.6.

Size   24 × 13 inches.

References   Hurlburt, Series II, Vol. III, 32; British Museum Catalogue, III, p. 518.

M 94

[Map of the battlefield at Yorktown, Va. 1781]

In   Private collection in 1931.

                  Photostat, Virginia State Library and Virginia Historical Society.

Size   8 × 10 inches.

M 95

Plan of Yorktown and Glocester in Virginia shewing the works constructed for the defence of those posts by the Rt. Honble. Lieut General Earl Cornwallis with the Attacks of the Combined Army of French and Rebels under the Command of the General Count de Rochambaud and Washington which Capitulated October 1781.

In   Faden Collection 91, Library of Congress.

Size   35¾ × 23¼ inches.

Scale   Scale of Furlongs, 4 to 4/8 inches.

Description   This is the original manuscript of Printed Map XVI (13) although the title is slightly different.

Reference   Hale 91.

M 96

[Map of the Siege of Yorktown]

In   Yale University (*783hc/Y82/1781D).

Size   25 × 20 cm.

Description   Yale notes that this map may be by General John Hartwell Locke.

M 97

This Place is what the Enemy had possession of. Within these lines is the Compact part of Little York in Virginia. Griffin Spencer, Lover of Learning and Ingenious Arts.

In   Yale University (*783hc/Y82/1781G).

Size   33 × 41 cm.

M 98

[Sketch of Yorktown Virginia.]

In   Simcoe Papers, Colonial Williamsburg.

Note   This is a water colour sketch.

M 99

[Sketch of roads in Gloucester, Virginia.]

In   Simcoe Papers, Colonial Williamsburg.

FRENCH PRINTED MAPS

Prototypes

Only one map of French origin depicting the situation at Yorktown can be considered a prototype although it does not state specifically the origin of the data utilized. The map is undated. In a dealer's catalogue, Henry Stevens, Son and Stiles, have assigned the date 1782, however, the only known dated imprint of Esnaut and Rapilly dealing with North America is the map of the United States reproduced in *Ultramar*, Volume Two, on which the imprint reads like that on the present map and is dated 1784. In many respects this map is similar to the Faden map of 1781 (1) as it also shows the position of the fleets during the engagement which began September the fifth.

8. 1784

CARTE / DE LA PARTIE DE LA VIRGINIE / ou / L'ARMÉE COMBINÉE
DE FRANCE & / DES ÉTATS — UNIS DE L'AMÉRIQUE / à fait prissonnière
l'Armée Anglaise / commandée par LORD CORNWALLIS le 19 Octbre. 1781.
/ *AVEC LE PLAN DE L'ATTAQUE* / d' York-town & de Glocester. / *Levée
et dessinée sur les Lieux par Ordre des officiers Gen*x. *de l'Armée Francaise &
Americaine.* / *A PARIS, Chez Esnauts et Rapilly, rue St. Jacques à la Ville
de Countances.*

In	Separate.
Size	Plate NS 48.5 EW 62.3
	Map NS 46.3 EW 60.4
Latitude	37º-37º 45′
Longitude	Bottom " 30′-15-79º — 45′-35′-15′ "
Scale	*Lieues Marines d'une heure de 20 au Degré.* 4=10.5 cm.
	The graduated scale bar is to the left of the cartouche along the bottom right border.
Cartouche	The title is in a horizontal rectangle measuring 13.5 by 10.2 in the bottom right corner. It is framed by a double line with the outside line heavier. The border of the plate encloses the cartouche on two sides.
Border	Geographically functional.
References	VC/p. 60; Verner 808.
Reproductions	The Naval Historical Foundation issued a facsimile of the Library of Congress copy in 1945.
Description	This large scale map is of the southern end of the Chesapeake Bay from St. Mary's Point on the north to Norfolk and from the Atlantic to Williamsburg. It is a detailed map with counties and towns named and the positions of the troops shown. The battle lines of the fleets of the several nations are represented by small ships.
	This map is of particular interest because of the emphasis on the naval engagement. From Cape Henry to Cape Charles a double line of ships (30) have sealed the entrance to the bay. A note here says "Armée Navale de France aux Ordres de Cte. De Grasse avant le Victoire remportée sur / l'Amiral Graves saisant le Blocus de la Baye de Chesapeak." In the Atlantic leading north-east is a line of 14 ships with the note "Armée Française en ligne de Bataille." Facing this line is another of about 20 ships labelled "Armée Anglaise saisant l'Echiquier et s'ensuyant après avoir été défaite par M. De Grasse." One ship behind this line is shown afire with the note " le Terrible en fur ne pouvant / plus soutenir / la Mer."
	Other ships are shown particularly in the York River at Yorktown. The battle positions of the troops are also indicated around Yorktown. In the delineation of the bay this map exaggerates the width of the Del-Mar-Va. peninsula along the top of the map so that the Chesapeake Bay above St. Mary's has an inaccurate delineation. Most of the land areas such as the Point Comfort are exaggerated and distorted.

ILLUSTRATIVE

Five printed maps of French origin are identified here as illustrative maps.
One of these is a precise copy of an American map which was issued twice under
two different dates and one is an inset on a large map of North America.

9. 1783

[Baie de Chesapeak. Plan de l'Attaque des Villes Yorck et Gloucester dans lesquelles étoit fortifié le Général Cornwali a fait prisonnier le 19 Octobre 1781. Se Vend à Paris chez Ve de la Gardette, Mde d'Estampes]

Size   7 × 6 inches.

Reference   VC/p. 60; Verner 798.

10. 1783

SUPLEMENT | Qui représente la partie de | la VIRGINIE, ou se trouvent le Théâtre | ou l'Armée Combinée des François et | des États Unies a fait prisonnier | le Général Cornwalis | Le 19 Octobre 1781, et le Plan d'attaque | D'YORCK et de GLOCESTER. | Par les Generaux WASHINGTON et ROCHAMBEAU |
        [This is the primary title at the top of the inset.]

LE DÉTAIL DE LA BAYE DE CHESAPEAKE | Par L Denis Géographe et Auteur du Conducteur François.

        [This second title is above the inset in the centre.]

An Inset on   [Carte générale des Colonies Angloises dans l'Amérique Septentrionale pour l'intélligence de la guerre présent. D'après des manuscripts Anglais par J. B. Nolin, géographe. Corrigée, augmentée des indications des principaux événe-mens de la guerre avec le tracée des limites pour constituer le traité de paix proposé entre la couronne de la Grande Bretagne et les Etats Unis. Par R. Philipeau 1783].

Imprint   *A Paris Chez Basset rue S^t. Jacques au coin de celle des Mathurins à S^t. Généviève.*
        The imprint is below the bottom border in the centre of the main map.

In   Separate.

Size   Main Map: Plate NS 51.7   EW 72.3
                      Map NS 50.7   EW 71.2
         Inset: NS 27.8   EW 28.2

Reference   Verner 802.

23. 1787

PLAN | D'YORK EN VIRGINIE, | avec les attaques et les Campemens | de l'Armée combinée de France | et d'Amérique. | [double rule 4.9 — topline heavy, bottom line light.]

In   Soules, François. *Histoire des Troubles de L'Amérique* . . .
           A Paris, Chez Buisson 1787.

Size   Plate NS 29.8   EW 39.7
         Map NS 28.5   EW 38.0

Scale   *Echelle de 600 Toises* 600 = 4.9 cm.
         The scale is in the bottom left corner unframed.

Cartouche   None. The title is on the left border at the centre without frame.

Border   Two parallel lines with the outside line heavier.

Reference   Swem 277; Sabin 87290; Johnston 8; Verner 839.

Description   This map of the Yorktown area is carefully prepared and provides fine details of the area including roads, houses, etc. Hauchering is used to indicate elevations. A manuscript which may be the original of this is listed below as M 104.

24. 1787   State 1

PLAN / *du Siège* / D'YORK ET DE GLOUCESTER / *par les Armées Alliées, / en Septembre et Octobre 1781.*

Engraver   Picquet, Sculpt.
             This plate is signed below the bottom right corner.

In   Ramsey, David, *Histoire de la Revolution D'Amérique* . . . Vol. II, p. 399.
             Paris, Chez Froullé, 1787.

Size   Plate   NS 22.7   EW 20.8
             Map   NS 21.5   EW 19.5

Scale   *Échelle de Pas Géometriques*   1000=3.1 cm.
             The scale is in the lower left corner unframed.

Cartouche   The title is in the upper right corner in a space measuring 5.2 horizontal by 4.0 vertical. It appears as if printed on a sheet of paper held at the top by a single tack with the ends curled down at an angle and the bottom part of the sheet curled up.

Border   Single line.

Reference   Verner 840.1.
             This is a copy of Printed Map 14. It was re-issued in 1796 under the same title with Chez Moutardier as publisher. This is a second state of the plate with Tom. II, Pl. 4 added on the top left and Pag. 399 added on the right. (33, XXVIII).

25. [1787]

[Carte de la partie de la Virginie, ou l'armée combinée de France et des États-unis de l'Amérique à fait prisonnière l'armée Anglaise commandée par Lord Cornwallis, le 19. 8bre 1781 avec le plan d'attaque d'Yorktown et de Glocester, par M. Brion de la Tour, ingénieur-géographe du roi.]

Size   5¾ × 11½ inches.

Note   This map has not been examined. It is not listed in Swem or Verner. This entry is taken from the catalogue card of the Virginia Historical Society.
             The conjectural date 1787 is assigned from maps of the American Revolution by Brion de la Tour which are dated 1787 in the imprint.

FRENCH MANUSCRIPT MAPS

M 100

Carte des Environs / d'York en Virginie . . . 8be 1781.

In   Min. Colonies, No. 8.   Paris.

Size   54.9 × 45.9 cm.

Description   A detailed map of the Yorktown area showing the nature of the terrain, features and positions of the troops. A legend is along the right border.

Reference   Karpinski, IV, 491.

M 101

Carte des Environs d'York avec les attaques à la position des Armées française et Américaine devant cette place. York en Virginie, 1781.

In   Library of Congress.
Size   18 × 23 inches. Coloured.
Scale   Échelle de 800 Toises.
Reference   Phillips, *Maps of America* . . .

M 102

Carte / des Environs d'York en Virginie / avec les attaques et la position des- / Armées françoise et Américaine / pendant la Siège en 8bre 1781. /

In   Min. War. 15-3. York 3ter, Paris.
Size   61.7 × 47.7 cm.
Description   Area around Yorktown: many topographical features. Shows positions of troops, etc.
Reference   Karpinski, II, 172.

M 103

Plan du siège d'York fait par l'armée combinée de Amérique et de France sous les / ordres du General Washington . . . (28 Oct. 1781).

In   Min. War., 15-3, York 5. Paris.
Size   36.0 × 51.5 cm.
Description   Platt of Yorktown area showing topographical features, position of troops, etc. Has added folding piece of paper on bottom (east) extending the map.
Reference   Karpinski, II, 173.

M 104

Plan d'York en Virginie avec les attaques et les campmens de l'armée combinée de France et d'Amérique. Siège d'York, 1781.

In   Rochambeau Mss. 59, Library of Congress.
Size   17½ × 25 inches. Coloured.
Description   This map was published in Soules. See Printed Map XXIII (22).
Reference   Swem 277; Phillips, *Maps of America* . . .; Winsor VI:553.

M 105

Plan d'York en Virginie avec les attaques faites par les armées française et Américaine en 8bre 1781.

In	Rochambeau Mss. 58, Library of Congress.
Size	$27\frac{1}{2} \times 34\frac{1}{2}$ inches.
Scale	Échelle d'un ponce et demie pour 100 toises.
Description	The Library of Congress notes that this is by Querenet de La Combe.
Reference	Swem 279; Phillips, *Maps of America* . . .; Winsor VI:553.

M 106

Plan du Siège d'York / par L'Armée combinée, commandée par les Généraux / Washington et Cte. de Rochambeau / en 1781.

In	Serv. Hyd. 2897. Paris.
Size	78.8×30.0 cm.
Description	Platt of the area around Yorktown showing terrain and position of the forces. Long detailed explanation along the right border.
Reference	Karpinski IV.

M 107

Plan du siège d'York par l'armée combinée commandée par les Généraux Washington et Cte. de Rochambeau.

In	Clinton Papers, William L. Clements Library.
Size	21×23 inches.
Description	A coloured topographical map of the immediate Yorktown area. The positions of the allied detachments are shown as after the erection of the second parallel, the French troops being indicated in yellow, the American in green. The British detachments are shown in red, but are not designated by name. The accompanying "Legende" gives identifying details of the American and French units. The "Legende" is as follows:

Les trouppes et les ouvrages ou il y a du vert sont Americains.
Les troupes et les ouvrages ou il y a du Jaune sont François.
Les trouppes et les ouvrages ou il y a du rouge sont Anglois.

- 1 Brigade de Bourbonnois avec Royal deux Ponts.
- 2 Brigade de Soisonnois avec Sant Onge.
- 3 Brigade d'Agenois avec Gâtinois.
- 4 Touraine.

Premier Paralelle Batteries Françoises.

- 6 Batteries de Pes. de 12, 3 Mortiers et 4 Obusiers.
- 7 Batteries de 4 Pes. 24.
- 8 Batteries de 8 mortiers, 3 de 12 p. 5 de 8 ps.
- 9 Batteries de 4 pièces de 24.
- 10 Batteries de 4 pièces de 24.
- 11 Batteries de 8 pec. de 16.   4 mortiers et 2 Obusiers.

Séconde Paralelle Batteries Françoises.

- 12 Batteries de 6 pièces de 16.
- 13 Batteries de 2 pièces de 18 et 4 de 34.
- 14 Batteries de 12 mortiers, 5 de 12 pec. et 7 de 8 pouces et 2 Obusiers de 8 pouces.

On augmenta la Batterie No. 6 de 2 pièces de 24 qui tirerent a boules rouges sur le Charron, qui brûla la nuit du 10, au 11.   7bre avec deux autres bâtiments.

Premier Paralelle Batteries Américaines.

16 Batteries de 6 pes. de 18. 1 pce de 24. 2 obusiers.
17 Batteries de 18 pec. de 18. 2 pec. de 24. 2 Obusiers. 4 Mortiers.
18 Il y avoit 2 Mortiers.

Séconde Paralelle Batteries Americaines.

19 Batteries de 6 pec. de 18.
20 Batteries de 12 pièces de 18. 3 de 24. 6 Mortiers.
21 Batteries de 4 Obusiers. 3 Mortiers.
A. Ouvrages abandonnés per les Anglois la nuit du 30me 7bre.
B. Rédoute enlevée L'Epée à la main par les François Commandés par le Brn. de Viomesnil la nuit du 14 au 15me.
C. Rédoubte enlivée l'Epée à la main par l'Infanterie legère Americaines Commandée par le Marquis de la Fayette la nuit du 14 au 15.
D. Maison ou les Commissaires ont arrêtes les Articles de la Capitulation.
A Frégatte la Guadaloupe que la Batterie No. 6 fit rétirer Batteries Angloises à York.

1 Batteries de 26 pièces de 12.
2 Batteries de 12 pièces de 12.
3 Batteries de 4 pièces de 12.
4 Batteries de 7 pièces.
5 Batteries de 6 pièces.
6 Batteries de 4 pièces.
7 Batteries de 6 pièces.
9 Batteries de 4 pièces.
10 Batteries de 4 pièces.

Nta. il y avoit 20 pièces le long de la ligne angloise qui changeoint contenuellement de place selon qui découvroient le nouveaux travaux des François.

Il y avoit petits Mortiers dans lesqu'elles ils tiroient des Grenades Royales.
gros Mortiers.

à Glocester.

11 Batteries de 10 pièces il y avoit 14 pièces des Canons dans les Rédoutes.

Nta. Les Trouppes Américaines occupent un front dans leurs Camps beaucoup plus grand qui celui des François parce qu'ils sont sur deux Rangs et qu'ils n'ont que 4 hommes dans chaque tente.

E Camp de Mr. le Chevalier de Chattelux et du quartier Général."

References   Adams 268; Brun 573.

M 108

Carte des environs de York en Virginie avec les attaques et la position des armées Françoise et Américaine, devant cette place 1781.

In   Clinton Papers. William L. Clements Library.

Size   18¾ × 25⅝ inches.

Scale   1 inch to 180 toises.

Description   A finished, coloured, topographical map of the area surrounding Yorktown for about two miles from the inner British fortifications.   The position of the various allied detachments is indicated.

References   Adams 269; Brun 568.

M 109

Carte des environs de York en Virginie avec les attaques et la position des armées Françoise et Américaine devant cette place en 1781. [By Edouard Colbert, comte de Maulevrier]

In	William L. Clements Library.
Size	18¾ × 26¾ inches.
Scale	1 inch to approximately 190 toises.
Description	A finished, coloured, topographical map of the Yorktown area. A table of references gives further details of the action. A number of the French and American units are identified on the map.
Reference	Brun 569.

M 110

Attaque de la ville d'York en Virginie prise le 19 8bre 1781 par les armées combinées de France et d'Amérique.

In	Clinton Papers. William L. Clements Library.
Size	12⅞ × 20⅛ inches.
Scale	1 inch to approximately 200 toises.
Description	A finished, coloured, topographical map showing the positions of the French and American troops after the capture of the British redoubts on the 14th of October. Army units are further identified in the accompanying " Legende."
References	Adams 274; Brun 566.

M 111

Amérique septentrionale. Yorck. Reconnaissance des ouvrages de cette ville avec le tracé des attaques dirigées contre eux.

In	William L. Clements Library.
Size	23¾ × 29¼ inches.
Scale	1 inch to 67 toises.
Description	A finished, coloured, topographical map showing the British defeat at Yorktown. A number of points on the map are identified in a table of references. The table also gives a listing, by rank, of the number of British troops captured in the battle.
Reference	Brun 565.

M 112

Reconnaissance Des Ouvrages / de la Ville d'York, avec le Tracé des attaques . . .

In	Min. War. 15-1-7, York No. 1. Paris.
Size	67.8 × 45.7 cm.
Description	Sketch of Yorktown area showing placement of troops.
Reference	Karpinski, II, 168.

M 113

Siège d'York / 1781 /

In	Guerre, États-Majors, L.I.D. 174. Paris.
Size	40.0 × 50.0 cm.
Description	Platt of the area of Yorktown showing terrain and fortifications. Legend along left side.
Reference	Karpinski, II, 222.

M 114
Plan du Siège d'York en Virginie . . . October 1781.

In	Guerre, États-Majors, L.I.D. 174. Paris.
Size	40.0 × 50.0 cm.
Description	Large detailed platt of Yorktown area showing terrain, roads, position of the forces, etc. Long note and cross section of fortification on the right border.
Reference	Karpinski, II, 223.

M 115
Plan du Siège d'York, en Virginie . . . en Octobre 1781.

In	Dépôt de Carte de la Marine, Siège 136-7-3. Paris.
Size	30.8 × 47.2 cm.
Description	Detailed plan of Yorktown area showing fields, roads, positions of the troops, etc. Long legend on the bottom including cross section of fortifications. Probably a second draft of the preceding map.
Reference	Karpinski, III, 308.

M 116
Plan des ouvrages faits à Yorktown en Virginie.

In	Rochambeau Mss. 60. Library of Congress.
Size	15½ × 24½ inches.
Reference	Phillips, *Maps of America* . . .; Swem 280; Winsor VI:553.

M 117
Siège d'York / 1781.

In	Min. War 15-3, York 1. Paris.
Size	64.8 × 66.8 cm.
Description	Platt of immediate area of Yorktown showing position of troops.
Reference	Karpinski, II, 169.

M 118
York / 1781

In	Min. War. États-Majors, L.I.D. 174. Paris.
Size	63.0 × 44.5 cm.
Description	A note on the map reads: " Plan régulier, mais levé à hâte par M M les Ingénieurs sur lequel il y aura peut être une correction par le Second envoy."
Reference	Karpinski, II, 198.

M 119
[Yorktown Area]

In	Min. War. 15-3, York 2. Paris.
Size	50.8 × 31.8 cm.
Description	Shows Yorktown area including Gloucester Point, positions of troops, lines of fire, etc. Numerous notes, etc.
Reference	Karpinski, II, 170.

M 120
Plan figure à vue du Siège d'York

In	Guerre, États-Majors, L.I.D. 174. Paris.
Size	53.0 × 51.5 cm.
Description	Platt of Yorktown—Gloucester area showing terrain and position of troops. Numerous notations on the map.
Reference	Karpinski, II, 200.

M 121
[Yorktown Area]

In	Guerre, États-Majors, L.I.D. 174. Paris.
Size	53.0 × 51.5 cm.
Description	Similar to preceding map. Shows placements of troops and lines of fire.
Reference	Karpinski, II, 200B.

M 122
York en Virginie / 6 Octobre 1781[?]

In	Guerre, États-Majors, L.I.D. 174. Paris.
Size	29.0 × 22.0 cm.
Description	Platt of areas of Yorktown and Gloucester showing positions of troops and ships.
Reference	Karpinski, II, 195.

M 123
Plan des postes d'York et Glocester pris sur les Anglais au mois d'octobre 1781.

In	Princeton University Library.
Note	A re-drawn version of this map is reproduced in Joachim du Perron, Comte de Revel, *Journal particulier d'une campagne aux Indes Occidentales* (Paris, 1898), pp. 152-153. A collotype facsimile reproduction was published by Princeton University in 1942—*A Map of Yorktown by Joachim du Perron, Comte de Revel*, with notes by Gilbert Chinard, Robert G. Albion, and Lloyd A. Brown (Princeton, 1942).

M 124
Plan d'York-Town pour servir à l'Etablissement du Quartier d'hiver du Régiment de Soissonnois et des Grenadiers et Chasseurs de St. Onge, le 12 novembre, 1781.

In	Berthier papers, No. 29, Princeton University Library.

M 125
Plan du Siège d'York en Virginie par l'armée alliée d'Amérique et de france, sous les Ordres des Gaux. Washington & Comte de Rochambeau, contre l'Armée Angloise Commandée par Lord Cornwallis, en Octobre 1781.

In	John Carter Brown Library.
Size	79.3 × 69.2 cm.
Note	The map is coloured, sectioned and mounted on linen. In the lower right is an inset: " profiles of fortifications." On verso, in contemporary lettering: " Plan De La Ville Et Du Siège D'York en Virginie sur La Rivière Du même nom."
Reference	John Carter Brown Library, *Report* 1946-1947, p. 31.

M 126

Plan de l'armée de Cornwallis, attaquée et faitte prisonière dans Yorktown, le 19 8bre par l'armée combinée Françoise et Américaine. Dessiné sur les lieux par les Ingénieurs de l'armée à Paris. Chez Le Rouge, Xbre, 1781.

In   Unknown.
Note   This map is listed by Winsor. It is not clear whether this is a printed or manu-
              script map. It is not listed by Phillips in any of the LeRouge atlases in the
              Library of Congress.
Reference   Winsor VI:551.

M 127

Plan de l'Attaque des villes de Yorck et Gloucester dans lesquelles étoit fortifié le Général Cornwallis fait prisonnier le 19 Octobre 1781.

In   Harvard University Library.
Note   This map is listed by Winsor but it is not clear whether it is a printed or manuscript
              map. An earlier search for printed maps did not produce this item. It is not
              listed in Swem or Verner.
Reference   Winsor 6:553.

M 128

Siège d'Yorck | 1781 19 8bre 1781

In   Min. War. 15-3, York 7. Paris.
Size   82.8 × 83.2 cm.
Description   Area of Yorktown and Gloucester Point.
Reference   Karpinski, II, 174.

M 129

Carte des Environs D'York en Virginie avec les Attaques et la Position des Armées Françoise et Américaine pendent la Siège de 8bre 1781. Quernéal de La Combe

In   Guerre, Amér. Guerre de 1775, No. 3. Paris.
Scale   1 inch to 2250 feet.
Reference   Karpinski, IV, 414.

AMERICAN PRINTED MAPS
Prototypes

Only one prototype map of the situation at Yorktown is of American origin. This map was made by Major Sebastian Bauman from a survey he conducted on the spot following the cessation of hostilities. It was published in Philadelphia in 1782 and was the first map to provide the American public a picture of the events and situation at Yorktown. Since this map was published almost simultaneously with that by Des Barres (5) the question of priority is academic but the evidence appears to favour this one.

A prospectus for this map was published in the *New Jersey Journal* in the issue of January 30, 1782 and indicated that the map was to be published " shortly." Among the subscribers who responded to the proposal was General McDougal to whom Bauman wrote about the map indicating that he had not intended to publish it originally and that this was the first map ever made by the engraver.

Major Sebastian Bauman, as the map indicates, was an officer in the " New York or 2nd Regt of Artillery." He was born in Frankfurt-am-Main in 1739, educated at Heidelburg, and served in the Austrian army. Sometime after 1750 he emigrated to America and served in the French and Indian War. At the beginning of the Revolution he was appointed an officer in the New York militia and served in the northern campaigns. Among other notable activities, Bauman was commander of artillery at West Point at the time of the capture of Major Andre, the British spy, and the defection of Benedict Arnold. He was serving under General Knox when his forces were ordered south for the York-town Campaign, and stood duty in the trenches before Yorktown during the siege. After the war Bauman was appointed postmaster for the City of New York and died there in 1803.

XXVI

7. 1782

To *His Excellency* Gen Washington [in Black letter] | *Commander in Chief of the Armies of the | United States of America | This Plan of the investment of York and Gloucester has been sur- | veyed and laid down, and is | Most humbly dedicated by his Excellencys | Obedient and very humble servant, | Sabast*ⁿ*. Bauman Major | of the New York or 2*nd* *Regt* | *of Artillery.* |

Engraver	*R. Scot Sculp Philad. 1782.*
	The plate is signed in the bottom right corner.
In	Separate.
Size	Plate NS 63.5 EW 45.2
Scale	*A Scale of Yards* 1000=6.3
	The graduated bar scale is along the bottom in the centre.
Cartouche	The title is in the top right corner. It has the appearance of an unrolled sheet of paper with the words inscribed on it. This measures 11.0 NS by 12.0 EW.
Border	None.
Reference	VC/p. 63; Stauffer 2970; Johnston 2; Verner 790.
Reproduction	*The Concise Encyclopedia of American Antiques* (N.Y. 1957) Plate 281.
	The Magazine of American History, 6:56 (1881).
	Virginia Magazine of History, 39:104a (1931).
	Yale University Gazette, 21:15 (1946).
Description	A list of references keyed to the map is in a separate cartouche in the upper left corner. Along the bottom of the map is a long horizontal oval cartouche measuring 27.0 by 11.0 cm. framed in plaster work and decorated with flags, cannon, and implements of war on the right and left sides.

Bauman's map was copied and issued under a different title in 1825. See Printed Map XXXIV (39). See also Manuscript Maps M128 & 131.

Illustrative

Three maps of the siege appeared in American publications prior to 1800. One of these is an interesting and minute woodcut which appeared on the cover of an Almanack published in 1783. The other two appeared in accounts of the war, one of these being used to illustrate two different works.

XXVII

11. 1783

[A PLAN of the Investment of / *York-Town* and *Glocester*.] [In letterpress below the block.]

In	Beers, Andrew. *The United States Almanack* 1783. Hartford, Printed and Sold by Nathaniel Patten.
Size	Plate NS 10.8 EW 8.1
Cartouche	The title in letterpress is in two lines as indicated below the block in a space 1.6 cm. wide.
Reverse	On the reverse is an " Explanation of the Plan " keyed by letters to letters which appear on the map.
Reference	Evans 17467; Verner 801.
Description	This is a small woodcut used on the title page. Above the block in letterpress is: AN / *ALMANACK* / For the year of our Lord CHRIST, 1783 / Below the block is the title as given above. The letterpress material above and below the block and the block are framed by a rule giving overall measurements of 14.4 by 8.3 cm.

XXVIII

14. 1785

PLAN | of | the Investment of | YORK & GLOUCESTER, *| by the* Allied Armies: *| in Septr. & Octr.* 1781.

In	Ramsey, David. *The History of the Revolution of South Carolina . . .* Trenton, Isaac Collins, 1785. Vol. II, p. 326.
Size	Plate NS EW 21.2 Map NS 21.5 EW 19.5
Scale	*A Scale of Yards* 1000=3.2 cm. The graduated bar scale is in the lower left corner.
Cartouche	The title is in a horizontal rectangle measuring 5.4 by 4.0 in the upper right corner. The frame represents a sheet of paper on which the title is inscribed which is rolled at the bottom and pinned at the top centre with the top corners curling down.
Border	Single line.
Reference	Verner 819; VC/p. 61.
Description	This is an inferior representation of the Yorktown battle area. A legend is in the top left corner framed as though printed on a sheet of curled paper similar to the title cartouche.
Note	This work was translated and printed in French. See maps 24, 33. (XXIV).

XXIX

32. 1796

a PLAN of | *the INVESTMENT of |* YORK and GLOUCESTER, |
VIRGINIA. | *Tanner scu* | [rule 2.8] | *Published by C. Smith N. York.* |

Imprint	*Published by C. Smith N. York.* The imprint is immediately below the title as indicated above.
Engraver	*Tanner scu* The plate is signed immediately below the title as indicated above.

In	Smith, Charles. *The Monthly Military Repository*. N.Y., Printed by William A. Davis, For the Author, 1796. Vol. 1, p. 186.
Size	Plate Map NS 42.8 EW 38.7
Scale	SCALE of YARDS 1000=6.3 cm. The scale is in the bottom left near the corner.
Cartouche	None. The title is in the upper left corner.
Border	The border is formed of a single engraved line.
Reference	VC/p. 61; Evans 32492; Verner 924; Church 1271.
Note	Parts of this volume—including this map—were re-issued in 1797 under a different title: Smith, Charles. *The American War from 1775 to 1783*, with Plans . . . N.Y. Printed for C. Smith, 1797. In this form the map is 34 in the list.

AMERICAN MANUSCRIPT MAPS

M 130

To His E[xcellency] G[eneral]. Washington commander in chief of the armies of the United States of America this plan of the investement of York and Goucester [!] has been surveyed and laid down, and is most humbly dedicated by His Excellency's obedient and very humble servand [!] Sebastn. Bauman major of the Newyorkor 2nd Regiment of Art. [Signed at bottom: Waldschmidt 1785.]

In	William L. Clements Library.
Size	18¾ × 17½ inches (overall: 23¼ × 17½ inches).
Scale	1 inch to 1200 feet.
Description	A finished, coloured, topographical map which is evidently a copy of the Sebastian Bauman map of the same title, published in Philadelphia in 1782. The numbered " References to the British Lines " (1-22) and the lettered statement appears just beneath the map: This plan was taken between the 22nd and 28th of October 1781. See printed maps XXVI (7).
Reference	Brun 587.

M 131

[Draught of Yorktown]

Description	" The earliest plan or ' draft ' was doubtless the one Washington states, October 26th, 1781, that he transmitted to Congress with the return of prisoners and the captured standards. It is not known to be in existence." This map has been located and is described in the next entry.
Reference	Johnston 1.

M 132

Plan of the Attacks of York in Virginia by the Allied Armies and France Commanded by his Excellency General Washington his Excellency the Count Rochambeau Commanding the French Army.

In	National Archives.
Size	38 × 29 inches. Coloured.
Scale	370 feet to 1 inch.

Note   The map is dated October 29, 1781, and was made by Lt. Col. Jean-Baptiste Gouvion, a French engineer in the service of the Continental army.
This manuscript was sent by Washington to the President of Congress in a letter from Yorktown dated October 27, 1781. This is the lost map noted by Johnston and listed in the preceding entry. This manuscript has been reproduced and published as: *Washington's Official Map of Yorktown.* National Archives Facsimile, No. 21 (Washington, 1952).

M 133

To his E. G. Washington Commander in Chief of the Armies of the United States of America. This Plan of the investment of York and Gloucester has been Surveyed and laid down, and is most humbly dedicated by his Excellency's Obedient and very humble Servant, Sebastian Bauman, Major of the New York or 2nd Regiment of Art. Waldschmid, 1782.

In   Library, Fort Monroe, Virginia.

Note   This is another manuscript copy of Printed Map XXVI (7) similar to manuscript map M128 listed above. There are some slight differences between these copies.

M 134

Plan of Posts of York and Gloucester in Virginia with the attack of the combined forces of France and America and the Defence of Troops under Earl Cornwallis in October 1781.

In   Norfolk (Va.) Museum.

Size $52\frac{1}{4} \times 29\frac{1}{2}$ inches.

Note   The map contains an inset "A Chart of the James and York Rivers in Virginia from Cape Henry to James Island." It is not known whether this is the original manuscript for that map or a copy of it.

M 135

[The route to York in Virginia]

In   New York Historical Society.

Note   This map by Robert Erskine is extracted from a list, preserved in the New York Historical Society, which is in the handwriting of Robert Erskine and S. DeWitt. This map is entry 124 which consists of twenty separate maps identified as A-H and J-U.

Reference   Heusser, p. 200.

M 136

[The route from Virginia]

In   New York Historical Society.

Note   This series of maps consists of ten and one-half sheets and is part of the Erskine-DeWitt series, entry 125.

Reference   Heusser, p. 201.

MISCELLANEOUS

One map of Yorktown is found in German printing. This is in a German edition of Stedman's *History* . . . published in 1795.

XXX

31. 1795

PLAN | der | Belagerung von | YORK-TOWN | in | VIRGINIA. | *zu Stedmans*
Geschickte des Ame- | rikanischen Krieges. |

Maker	*D. E. Sotzmann del.* Signed below the bottom left corner.
Engraver	*A Sander fecit.* Signed below the bottom right corner.
In	Stedman, C. *Carl Stedman's Geschichte* . . . Berlin, Bobischen Buchhandlung, 1795.
Size	Plate NS 15.1 EW 18.5 Map NS 13.7 EW 16.0
Scale	Mass tab von 3500 Fuss 3500=2.9 cm. The scale is in the bottom left corner unframed.
Cartouche	None. The title is in the upper right corner unframed.
Border	The plate is bordered by two parallel lines with the outside line heavier.
Reference	VC/p. 61; Verner 915.
Note	This is a German copy and translation of Printed Map 30 (XIX).

VII

SOME LATER MAPS

Many maps illustrating aspects of the Yorktown Campaign were produced after 1800. Although no attempt is made here to include all such maps there are a few of particular interest that have been identified. These maps are not listed with the same detailed cartobibliographical description provided for those printed prior to 1800 but they are numbered sequentially and chronologically with the preceding maps.

XXXI

36. 1807

A Map of those parts of Virginia, North Carolina, South Carolina, and Georgia which were the scenes of the most important operations of the Southern armies. Compiled by S. Lewis. Engraved by Francis Shallus. Philadelphia, Published by C. P. Wayne.

Scale	60 miles equal 2¼ inches.
Size	14⅜ × 10 3/16 inches.
In	Marshall, John. *Life of George Washington.* Philadelphia: C. P. Wayne, 1807. No. 8.
Reference	Swem 376.

XXXII

37. 1807

Plan of the Investment and Attack of York in Virginia.

In	Marshall, John. *Life of George Washington.* Philadelphia: C. P. Wayne, 1807. Plate IX.
Engraver	Francis Shallus.

Size	$10\frac{3}{4} \times 8\frac{7}{8}$ inches.
Scale	1800 yards to $2\frac{3}{16}$ inches.
Note	Reproduced in Winsor, VI: 552.

XXXIII

38. 1807

Investissement et attaque d'York, dans la Virginie.

In	Marshall, John. *Vie de George Washington.* Paris: Denter, 1807. Plate XIV.
Size	$10 \times 13\frac{3}{4}$ inches.
Scale	Échelle de verges: 1800 to $2\frac{1}{4}$ inches.

XXXIV

39. 1825

Plan of Yorktown in Virginia and adjacent country, exhibiting the operations of the American, French and English armies during the siege of that place in October 1781. Surveyed from the 22nd to the 28th October. Drawn by Jn. F. Renault with a crow-pen and presented to the Marquis de la Fayette.

Engraver	B. Tanner.
Scale	Scale of Yards: 1000 equals $2\frac{1}{2}$ inches.
Size	$29 \times 19\frac{1}{8}$ inches.
References	Swem 284; Johnston 3.
Note	Johnston notes this to be a copy of Bauman.

XXXV

40. 1834

Plan of the Investment and attack of York in Virginia.

In	Marshall, John. *Life of George Washington.* Second Edition. Philadelphia: J. Cressy, 1834. Atlas Plate 8.
Engraver	J. Yeager.
Size	$7\frac{5}{8} \times 9$ inches. Coloured.
Scale	$2\frac{1}{4}$ inches $= 1800$ yards.
Reference	Swem 596.

XXXVI

43. 1880

Yorktown, Virginia and the ground occupied in the siege of 1781. A topographical survey by direction of B'rt Major Gen'l G. W. Getty, U.S. Army, commanding Artillery School, Fort Monroe, 1880. Surveying party commanded by Captain James Chester, 3rd Artillery.

In	Virginia State Library. Blueprint.
Size	$19 \times 15\frac{1}{8}$ inches.
Scale	Scale of Yards: 1760 equals $4\frac{5}{16}$ inches.
Reference	Swem 1380; *Magazine of American History* 7:408 (1881).

XXXVII

44. 1881

The siege of Yorktown 1781, compiled from the Faden (London, 1781) and the Renault (American, 1781) maps by Lieut. L. V. Caziaic, 2nd Artillery, 1881.

In	Patton, J. H. *Yorktown* . . . facing p. 34.
Size	11 × 8 inches.
Scale	1 mile = 3½ inches.
Reference	Swem 1395; *Magazine of American History*, 7:288 (1881).

XXXVIII

45. 1881

Plan of the siege of Yorktown.

In	Johnston, H. P. *Yorktown Campaign* . . . p. 132.
Size	5¼ × 4⅞ inches.
Reference	Swem 1393.

XXXIX

46. 1881

Map of the Vicinity of Yorktown, Virginia, 1881. Published by Smith and Stroup, 52 & 54 North Sixth Street, Philadelphia. Entered according to Act of Congress in the year 1881 by Smith & Stroup in the office of the Librarian of Congress at Washington, D.C.

In	Virginia Historical Society.
Size	29 × 34 inches.
Reference	Swem 1387.
Note	This map contains numerous engravings of people and places prominent in Virginia.

XL

47. 1931

Department of the Interior and U.S. Geological Survey Colonial National Monument Yorktown Battlefield, Virginia. Surveyed in cooperation with the National Park Service, the Conservation and Development Commission of Virginia, and the United States Sesquicentennial Commission, 1931.

In	Virginia Historical Society.
Size	28 × 23½ inches.
Scale	800 feet to 1 inch.
Note	Shows fortifications and positions of the troops, 19th October, 1781.

MANUSCRIPT MAPS

M 137

Yorktown.

In	Library of Congress.
Size	11 × 15½ inches.
Description	Shows position of American and French troops. The Library of Congress notes that this was apparently drawn in the 20th Century.

M 138

The Siege of Yorktown, 1781. Compiled from the Faden (London, 1781) and the Renault, (American, 1781) maps in Congressional Library, by 1st. Lieut. L. V. Caziaic, 2c. Arty. [1881?]

In	Library of Congress.
Size	48 × 35 cm.
Note	The Renault map is the 1825 copy of the Bauman map. See Printed Map XXXVII (44).

CHRONOLOGICAL LIST OF PRINTED MAPS

Number		Date	Maker	Sequence Number
1		1781	Faden	XIV
2*		1781	Anonymous	XI
3		1781	Political Magazine	I
5*		1782	Des Barres	XV
6*		1782	Des Barres—overlay	XIII
7*	A	1782	Bauman	XXVI
8*	F	1783	Esnault & Rapilly	XX
9	F	1783	Estampes	XXI
10	F	1783	Nolin—inset	XXII
11	A	1783	Beers	XXVII
12*		1784	Simcoe-Phillips	III
13*		1785	Faden	XVI
14	A	1785	Ramsey	XXVIII
15*		1787	Tarleton—southern	II
16		1787	Tarleton—siege	XVII
17		1787	Simcoe-Phillips (reprint 12)	(III)
18*		1787	Simcoe	IV
19*		1787	Simcoe	V
20*		1787	Simcoe	VI
21*		1787	Simcoe	VII
22*	F	1787	Soules—marches	XII
23	F	1787	Soules—siege	XXIII

Number		Date	Maker	Sequence Number
24	F	1787	Ramsey (copy of 14)	XXIV
25	F	1787	Brion de la Tour	XXV
26		1788	Gordon—seat of action	IX
27		1788	Gordon—siege	XVIII
28		1793	Faden (reprint of 1)	(XIV)
29		1793	Faden (reprint of 13)	(XVI)
30		1794	Stedman—naval action	XI
31		1794	Stedman—siege	XIX
32	G	1795	Stedman—(copy of 31)	XXX
33	A	1796	Tanner-Smith	XXIX
34	F	1796	Ramsey—(reprint of 24)	(XXIV)
35	A	1797	Tanner-Smith—(reprint of 33)	(XXIX)
36	A	1807	Marshall—southern	XXXI
37	A	1807	Marshall—siege	XXXII
38	F	1807	Marshall—(copy of 37)	XXXIII
39		1825	Tanner—(copy of 7)	XXXIV
40		1834	Marshall—(copy of 37)	XXXV
41		1845	Faden—(reprint of 1)	
42		1845	Faden—(reprint of 13)	
43		1880	Chester	XXXVI
44		1881	Patton	XXXVII
45		1881	Johnston	XXXVIII
46		1881	Smith & Stroup	XXXIX
47		1931	USGS	XL

BIBLIOGRAPHY

Adams, Randolph G. *The Surrender of Cornwallis.* Bulletin 3, The William L. Clements Library (1924).

——— *British Headquarters Maps and Sketches by Sir Henry Clinton While in Command of the British Forces Operating in North America during the War for Independence, 1775-1782.* (Ann Arber: 1928).

Bauman, Sebastian. "Map of the Siege of Yorktown." *The Magazine of American History*, 6: 56 (1881).

Brown, Lloyd A. "Manuscript Maps in the W. L. Clements Library." *The American Neptune*, 1 : 141-148 (1941).

Brun, Christian. *Guide to the Manuscript Maps in the William L. Clements Library.* (Ann Arber: 1959).

Chinard, Gilbert, Robert G. Albion and Lloyd A. Brown. *A Map of Yorktown by Joachim du Perron, Comte de Revel . . .* (Princeton, 1942).

Cole, G. W. *A Catalogue of Books Relating to the Discovery and Early History of North and South America, Forming a Part of the Library of E. D. Church.* (New York: 1907).

Evans, Charles. *American Bibliography.* (New York: 1941-42).

Faden, William. *Catalogue of the Geographical Works* . . . Published by W. Faden . . . (London: 1822).

Hale, Edward E. *Catalogue of a Curious and Valuable Collection of Original Maps and Plans of Military Positions Held in the Old French and Revolutionary Wars* . . . (Boston: 1862).

Heusser, Albert H. *The Forgotten General: Robert Erskine.* (Paterson, 1928).

Hulbert, A. B. *The Crown Collection of Photographs of American Maps.* (Cleveland: 1907-1930).

Johnston, Henry P. "List of Maps and Plans of the Siege of Yorktown, Va." In: *The Yorktown Campaign.* (New York: 1881), p. 198.

Karpinski, Louis C. *Manuscript Maps Prior to 1800* . . . Microfilm.

"Official Map of Yorktown." *Magazine of American History.* 7 : 339 (1881).

Paltsits, Victor H. "A Plan of the Yorktown Campaign." *New York Public Library Bulletin.* 26 : 855-858 (1922).

Phillips, P. L. *A List of Geographical Atlases in the Library of Congress.* (Washington : 1909-1963).

———— *Virginia Cartography.* Smithsonian Miscellaneous Collections, 1039. (Washington: 1896).

Sabin, Joseph *Dictionary of Books Relating to America.* (New York: 1868).

Smith, Clara A. *List of Manuscript Maps in the Edward E. Ayer Collection.* (Chicago: 1927).

Stauffer, David McN. *American Engravers upon Copper and Steel.* (New York: 1907).

Swem, Earl G. *Maps Relating to Virginia. Bulletin, Virginia State Library,* Vol. 7, Nos. 2 and 3. (April, July, 1914).

———— *Views of Yorktown and Gloucester Town,* 1755. Newport News: The Mariners' Museum, 1946. Museum Publication 14. Reprinted from: *The Virginia Magazine,* Vol. 54, No. 2, (1946).

Trimble, K. W. "Some Old Yorktown Maps." *The Military Engineer.* 23 : 438-443 (1931).

Verner, Coolie. *The Printed Maps of Virginia,* 1590-1800. (Richmond: Virginia Historical Society, in press).

Vietor, Alexander O. "The Bauman Map of the Siege of Yorktown." *Yale University Library Gazette,* 21 : 15 (1946).

Washington's Official Map of Yorktown. National Archives Facsimile No. 21 (Washington: 1952).

Winsor, Justin. " Maps of the Revolutionary Period." In: *The Memorial History of Boston,* Vol. 3, pp. i-xii. (Boston: 1881).

——— "Note on the Maps of the Yorktown Campaign." *Narrative and Critical History.* Vol. 6, pp. 551-553 (New York: 1887).

World Encompassed: An Exhibition . . . (Baltimore: 1952).

Wroth, L. C., and Marion W. Adams. *American Woodcuts and Engravings, 1670-1800.* (Providence: 1946).

CHAPTER EIGHT

The Jansson-Visscher Maps
of New England

by Tony Campbell

THE maps which form the so-called Jansson-Visscher series span more than a century. When the prototype was first issued by Jansson at the mid point of the 17th century it was the most up to date and most detailed map of the region available. When it was last issued by Lotter, basically unchanged, it could have been of little practical value as a representation of the then most important part of colonial America.

Old maps, and particularly those of the 17th century, have much of their area given up to decoration and the changing styles of the cartouches form a branch of the history of art. The prototype map represents Dutch elegance at its best and Visscher's view of New Amsterdam is in keeping with this (Plate 167). By the time the Restitutio view appears much of the precision has been lost and it cannot be compared in design or technique with the Visscher. Already the restraint shown by Jansson and Visscher has gone and the map is becoming cluttered. With the new cartouche that appears on Seutter's version the map has moved finally into the 18th century and reflects the German desire for a map both boldly and fully engraved; the decoration threatens to overrun the map. Although Jansson was concerned with the decoration his primary aim was to produce a detailed and informative map of the Dutch province of New Netherland and the surrounding region. The result is a valuable historical source and as evocative a picture as any we have of North America between Jamestown and Quebec. Besides these two towns, the settlements on the Delaware (*Zuydt*), Hudson and Connecticut Rivers, those in the vicinity of Manhattan and Long Island and those along the Massachusetts coast; besides the imperfectly mapped coastline and the conjectured course of rivers lay an almost unknown continent. Indians surrounded them and from the numerous native names on the map one can almost feel the pressure keeping the settlers back.

At the time this map was made the Swedish control of the Delaware River was passing to the Dutch. In 1638 a Swedish expedition had come out, established the province of *New Sweden* and built *Fort Christina* in honour of their queen. The names shown along the Delaware River on all the maps in this series refer to the forts and settlements that were set up by the numerous expeditions that followed. Often the settlers were farmers but many of them were pressed men, offered this as an alternative to prison. In 1651 Peter Stuyvesant built *Fort Kasimier* and although the Swedes occupied it for a short period he re-captured it in 1655 and New Sweden fell to the Dutch.

Though the area changed hands once more, passing to the English in 1664, the Swedish names, *Nieu Vaasa, Nieu Gottenburg, Uplandt,* etc. remain undisturbed. While in this respect the map does not take account of the historical context many of the more important events are reflected on the maps and may themselves have provided the stimulus for re-publication. The capture of Fort Kasimier by the Dutch in 1655 caused the city of Amsterdam to found the colony of *New Amstel* under its protecting walls and it seems likely that four separate copies of the prototype map were made in response to the sudden interest in the region. The English capture of New York in 1664, followed by the surrender of New Netherland and the Dutch settlements on the Delaware River are recorded on the English maps in this series, Speed and Seller, and the Ogilby-Montanus. The creation of New Jersey—named in honour of Carteret's heroic defence of the Island of Jersey against the parliamentary forces in 1649—under the joint proprietorship of Sir George Carteret and Lord John Berkeley, prompted the publication of the first two Seller maps. The third state of the Seller was issued after Berkeley had sold West New Jersey to Penn in 1676. In its complete form the map carries a text along the bottom which encouraged potential settlers to buy land in the proposed Quaker colony.

It was not until 1681 that Penn was granted a charter for his colony of Pennsylvania and early the following year a site was selected for the capital, Philadelphia. In August 1682 the Quakers started laying out the city; a year later there were 80 houses and by the end of 1683 this number had risen to 150. All the later versions of the map show Philadelphia.

Few changes or additions were made to the place names along the coast of Massachusetts. Only a few of the English settlements are marked and one of the more notable omissions is *Boston.* No map in this series shows it in its correct position though it had been made the capital of Massachusetts colony in 1632 and a print of 1739 described it as "the Metropolis of New England, the largest most populous and flourishing town in the British Dominions in America." Two maps in the series show Boston but inaccurately. Speed's map substitutes it for *London* and Lotter's for *Briston* [see Plate 162]. These towns—equidistant from Boston's true position on the River Charles—had never existed except as names on Captain John Smith's map of New England [1616].

Following general usage the series has been called the Jansson-Visscher map of *New England.* Strictly speaking it covers far more than this, including New York, New Jersey, Maryland and part of Virginia. All the maps in direct descent from the prototype show New England as comprising only Rhode Island, Massachusetts and Maine while the bulk of the map is taken up with New Netherland. After the English capture of the province in 1664 several of the English maps treated New England as extending to the Hudson River.

A NOTE ON THE ARRANGEMENT

The 28 states described here should not be treated as an arbitrary figure since two of them are proofs and proofs must have been pulled from most of the plates. The dating is also tentative since none of the maps carry a date and few are known to occur in dated atlases.

The different states of the map have been arranged according to the nine copper-plates from which they are derived and are only in chronological order within those divisions.

The numbers prefixed by a *K* which appear at the end of the entry refer to the list drawn up by Mr. William G. Kelso, Jr. The Kelso Collection is now in the Free Library of Philadelphia.

ACKNOWLEDGEMENTS

This subject has been dealt with before and any research must owe an inevitable debt to previous writers. Asher's *Essay*[1] provided the basis, Stokes' monumental and invaluable six volume work[2] filled in the historical background while Kelso's list[3] suggested the arrangement and supplied the working basis.

Also I should like to thank the staff of the Map Room at the British Library who have, as always, been most helpful and who courteously permitted me to reproduce maps [Plates 153 and 154]; and more especially Mr. R. V. Tooley, who inspired the present work, whose assistance throughout has been invaluable and whose experienced and steadying hand has saved me from many errors. Those that remain are my own.

NOTES TO THIS REVISED EDITION

Since the original publication of this article in 1965, two important works have appeared. The first has added much new information about the Seller map; the second is now the authority on all Dutch maps.

Black (Jeannette D.) The Blathwayt Atlas. Volume II. Providence, Rhode Island, 1975.

Koeman (C.) Atlantes Neerlandici. 5 vols. Amsterdam, 1967-71.

May, 1979   T.C.

[1] Asher (G. M.) A Bibliographical and Historical Essay on the Dutch books and pamphlets relating to New-Netherland . . . as also on the maps, charts, etc., of New Netherland. Amsterdam, 1854-67.

[2] Stokes (I. N. Phelps) The Iconography of Manhattan Island, 6 vols., New York, 1915-28.

[3] *Reproduced in:* Stokes (I. N. Phelps) & Haskell (D. C.) American Historical Prints, New York, 1933.

SELECTED LIST OF DATES

1620   First permanent settlement in New England, at Plymouth.

1623   Dutch colony of New Netherland set up by the Dutch West India Company.

1638   First Swedish settlement on the Delaware River. Fort Christina built, New Sweden founded.

1641   English settlement at Varkens Kil (now Salem Creek, N.J.).

1643   New Gottenburg settled—became the capital of New Sweden.

1651   Stuyvesant builds Fort Kasimier.

1654   Swedes capture Fort Kasimier.

1655   Stuyvesant re-captures Fort Kasimier. Collapse of New Sweden.

1664   New Amsterdam taken by the English and re-named *New York*. The region between the Delaware and Hudson rivers named *New Jersey*. Fort Orange—on the Hudson River—captured and re-named *Albany*.

1673   Dutch re-capture New York.

1674   English retake New York.

1676   Quintipartite deed establishes the division of West and East Jersey.

1681   Penn granted a charter for Pennsylvania.

1682   Philadelphia laid out.

PUBLISHER'S INDEX

1 **[1651]** [JANSSON (Jan)] BELGII NOVI, ANGLIAE NOVAE, ET PARTIS VIRGINIAE Novissima Delineatio [Amsterdam]   52 × 44.5 cms.

First state without the dedicatory cartouche.

Stokes has assigned the date of 1650 or 1651 for this, the plain-back version of the map.

It shows English settlements on the west end of Long Island (*Greenwyck, Gravesant*), along the shore of Long Island Sound (*Stamford, Strotfort, Nieuhaven,* and *Milfort* [though these were wrongly named and were corrected on the other plates]) and up the Connecticut River (*Herfort,* and two references to the English trader *Pinsers*).

Modern towns appear as follows. The dates in brackets refer to their first permanent settlement.

CONNECTICUT

Hartford—*Herfort* (1636)
Middletown—*Kievitshoeck* (settled 1650 and first named Middletown in 1653. Speed used the Indian name *Matabesick*. Both showed it too far to the south)
New Haven—*Nieuhaven* (1637–8)
Stamford—*Stamfort* (1641)

RHODE ISLAND
The island is shown and named but the places are all referred to by their Indian names.

MASSACHUSETTS

Plymouth—*Neu Pleymont* (1620)

NEW YORK
Albany—*t'Fort Orangie* (settled 1624, in 1664 the fort was taken by the English and renamed *Albany*).

VIRGINIA
Jamestown—*Iames Towne* (1607)

—— Copies also appear with text on the verso in Jansson (J.) Atlantis majoris quinta pars. 5 vols., Amsterdam, 1657. [Latin text edition only]   K1

Plates 144 & 162.

2 —— **Second state** with the dedication to De Raet.
In place of the two smaller Indian canoes appears a dedication to Gualthero de Raet within an ornamental cartouche capped with his arms. These include a hand which signifies his title of Knight Baronet [on the map *Equiti Baronetto*]. Jansson's name appears for the first time on this state, at the bottom of the new cartouche.

As De Raet was knighted by Charles II in 1660 and died in 1663 Stokes suggests that this plain-back version was issued between these dates.

—— Copies are also known with text on the verso. These appear in the *Atlas Contractus,* Amsterdam 1666.   K2

Plate 145.

3 —— **Third state** with the Valk and Schenk imprint.

Jansson's name has been erased and replaced with "Petrum Schenk". Beneath "Novissima Delineatio" has been added "Prostant Amstelaedami apud Petrum Schenk, et Gerardum Valk, C. P."

Pieter Schenk the elder and Gerard Valk acquired some of the Jansson plates, possibly in 1694, and worked together in partnership. In 1687 Schenk married Valk's daughter. Schenk appears to have died about 1718 when his son, also Pieter, took over the business.   K3

Plate 146.

4 [**1655**] Visscher (Nicolas Jansz) Novi Belgii Novaeque Angliae Nec Non Partis Virginiae Tabula multis in locis emendata a Nicolao Joannis Visschero [Amsterdam]   55.5 × 46.5 cms.

Proof state without Fort Kasimier.

This is the first appearance of Visscher's view of New York entitled, "Nieuw Amsterdam op t Eylant Manhattans". Stokes notes that this is the third known engraved view of New York probably drawn between 1650 and 1653.

The map is copied from the Jansson but many of the decorative details have been inverted. The fact that Fort Kasimier fell to the Dutch in 1655 may have prompted its publication. The outside date of 1656 has been established since the map has been found attached to a copy of a report on the South (Delaware) River dated January of that year.

There are other differences between this and the Jansson prototype:

1   Addition of *Zuyder-Zee* (below Cape Cod), *t'kocks Rack* (to the left of Manhattan) and "Onjure ofte Assareawe" (beneath the central word in large print, *Quebecq*).

2   On the mainland above Long Island there are three names which on the Jansson read in sequence, *Stamfort, Milfort, Ailfort*. These have been corrected to *Stamfort, Strotfort, Milfort*.

3   The misprint *Pay Baye* (beside the Charles River, Mass.) has been corrected to *Pye Bay*, and Jansson's *Chesapeach Bay* now reads *Chesapeack*.

4   Some animals and birds have been added.

There are apparently only three copies of this state known. It is reproduced in Stokes, *American Historical Prints*, Plate 6.   K4

5 —— **Second state** with Fort Kasimier, but without Philadelphia.

This is found, sometimes as an insert, in atlases by Blaeu and Jansson as well as Visscher's own.   K5

Plates 147 & 151.

5a   ——   **Third state** showing Philadelphia.

There have been the following alterations to the plate:

1   *Philadelphia* is marked and shown in plan.

2   The imprint has been altered to "per Nicolaum Visscher".

3   The lettering on Long Island now has *Jorck Shire* added.

4   Addition of lettering above the circular Indian village, "Alter Modus apud Minneffincos Ander Manier der Minneffincksche Dorpen".

5   Addition of several names in small script around Philadelphia, e.g. *Schoonberg, Cahoos oft Waterval*.

6   To the *Zuydt Rivier* has been added *eertyts toehoorende de Stat Amsterdam*.

7   Pennsylvania and New York provinces marked.

8   Dutch colony of *Nieu Amstel* (beside Fort Kasimier) marked.

9   Addition of several names in small script at the mouth of the Hudson River—*Gomoenipa, Engelsche Plantagie, Quakers hoeck*, etc.

10   Addition of lettered key *a-f* below Long Island. Nicolas Jansz, the elder, died in 1679 and his son of the same Christian names continued the business.

6   ——   **Fourth state** with the Privilege.

The wording "cum Privil. Ordin. General. Belgii Faederati" has been added to left of the view. A modern fake of this state, dated 1659, is known.   K8

Plate 148.

7   ——   **Fifth state** re-issued by Schenk, Junior.

Beneath Visscher's name has been added, "Nunc apud Petr: Schenk Iun:"   K9

Plate 149.

8   [1655]   DANCKERS (Justus)   Novi Belgii Novaeque Angliae Nec Non Partis Virginiae Tabula multis in locis emendata a Iusto Danckers. [Amsterdam]   54·5 × 46·5 cms.

First state without Philadelphia.

A rare state, Stokes cites only his own copy.

Illustrated in *The Iconography of Manhattan Island*, Vol. 1, Plate 7a.   K10

9   ——   **Second state** with Philadelphia.

The Delaware River has been entirely re-drawn. On the prototype map the river had been given two branches of almost equal importance, the westerly called the *Zuydt* River and the easterly passing through a lake before both united and joined the Hudson River. Danckers completely altered the river's course above Philadelphia making it flow in one broad stream due south from a lake which he enlarged for the purpose. In this version there is no connection between the

285

Delaware and Hudson Rivers [for comparison of the two versions see Plate 151]. The following alterations have been made.

1 The Delaware River has been re-drawn.

2 *Philadelphia* added.

3 Pennsylvania is marked and given bounds. Domestic and wild animals are shown in it.

4 New Jersey is named and its bounds shown.

5 Maryland is named.

6 The title of the Visscher view has been altered to "Nieuw Yorck, eertÿs Genaemt Nieuw Amsterdam op't Eylant Manhattans".

7 A number of names have been added, for instance the words *Nieuw Casteel* in front of *Fort Christina* on the Delaware River.

8 Interspersed with the old lettering *Nieuw port May* is *Delaware Bay*.

9 Scale markings appear beneath the words "Miliaria Germanica communia". These do not occur on the first state of the map as reproduced by Stokes though there are evidently traces of engraving along the line of the scale.

10 The third lines of the title now reads, "Pennsylvaniae et Partis".   K11

Plates 150 & 151.

9a — **Third state** with *Niew Castel*. *Niew Castel alias Sandhoeck* (on the west shore of Delaware Bay) and *Yermonton* (above Philadelphia) have been added.

10 **[1656]** [vander DONCK (Adriaen)] NOVA BELGICA sivc (sic) NIEUW NEDERLANDT. E. Nieuwenhff [Amsterdam].   18·5×30·5 cms.

First state with Fort Christina named twice.

This is a small map showing only a portion of the original—from Delaware Bay to the east end of Long Island—though it keeps to the same scale. There is no title as such and the Visscher view appears on the bottom of the map without cartouche, frame or key. *Fort Christina* on the Delaware River appears twice, the lower instance being a misprint for Fort Kasimier. This was not included in the first edition of vander Donck's *Beschryvinge van Nieuw-Nederlant*, Amsterdam 1655 but appears in the second edition of 1656.

Justin Winsor, in his *Narrative and Critical History of America*, Vol. IV, p. 439, reproduces a map which is identical to the above except that it omits the lettering *Pag.* 2 in the very top left corner. This may constitute another state.

Illustrated in Stokes, *Iconography of Manhattan Island*, Vol. 1, Plate 9.   K12

11 — **Second state** with Fort Kasimier but without the scale.

The lower instance of *Fort Christina* has been corrected to *Fort Casamirus*. Kelso notes that this state also occurs in the 1656 edition of the *Beschryvinge*.

K13

Plate 152.

12 —— **Third state** with the scale but without the superior *c*.

There are the following additions according to Stokes:

1 A scale of miles above which appears the lettering "Milliaria Germania Communia".

2 Two stockades one on either side of *Marquaa Kill*.

3 Groups of natives to the west of the Hudson River.

4 Small animals between the Hudson and Varsse (Connecticut) Rivers.

The first two states are known to occur in vander Donck's *Beschryvinge* but it is not established how the third and fourth states were published. Vander Donck died in 1655 and Sabin in his *Dictionary of Books relating to America* only records the two editions of the *Beschryvinge* mentioned above.　　　　　　K14

13 —— **Fourth state** with the addition of the letter *c* above *Germania*. The lettering above the scale of miles now reads *Milliaria Germani*c*a Communia*.　　K15

14 [1656] ALLARD (Hugo) Novi Belgii Novaeque Angliae Nec Non Partis Virginiae Tabula multis in locis emendata a Hugo Allardt [Amsterdam].
54·5 × 46·5 cms.

First state with the Visscher view.　　　　　　　　　　　　　　　　K16

Plate 153.

15 —— **Second state** with the Restitutio view but no imprint.

This is a hitherto apparently unrecorded proof issue of the first map to show the Restitutio view. This view, with the title "Nieuw-Amsterdam onlangs Nieuw Jorck genaemt en nu hernomen bij de Nederlanders op den 24 Aug 1673", was made presumably between August 1673 and November of the following year, the time of the Dutch re-occupation of New York which it celebrates [for comparison of this and the Visscher view see Plate XXIV].

The new title, "TOTIUS NEOBELGII NOVA ET ACCURATISSIMA TABULA" runs in block type along the top of the map. This has meant the loss of the top 2 cms. and Quebec for instance has gone. Fort Orange is now named *Nova Albania* (Albany, N.Y.).

There are the following additions:

1 Cornelius Evertsen's fleet, the one which re-captured New York, is shown with other ships off Long Island.

2 *Graef Hendric, Nieuw Amstel, Maltees hock, Visschers kil*, etc., along the Delaware River. Also a note at the mouth of the river.

3 Many small representations of animals.

4 *Kahoos* and a description of it, near the source of the Hudson River.

5 Soundings for Delaware Bay and to the north.

6   Lettering between the two Indian villages, "Altor Modus apud Minne-ffincos . . .".

7   *Maerbeltoun, Wiltwyck*, etc., to the west of the Hudson River.

8   *Milfort, Bergen, Gomoenipa*, etc., around New York.

9   *Iorck-shire* and *Iamaica* on Long Island.

10   To *Nieuw Nederlandt* is added *Nu Nieuw-Jorck*.

11   New Jersey is named.

12   A key to the lettered references on Manhattan and Long Island appears to the south of Long Island.

On this proof state the reference letters themselves, *a* and *f* on Manhattan and the remainder on the west end of Long Island have not yet been engraved nor has the publisher's name.

Plate 154.

16 —— **Third state** with Hugo Allard's imprint.

The proof state has been completed by the engraving of the letters on Manhattan and the west end of Long Island and the name of the publisher in the lower right-hand corner, "Hugo Allardt Excut.". K17

17 —— **Fourth state** with the imprint of Carolus Allard.

Carolus has been substituted for *Hugo* in the imprint. Karel was the son of Hugo. Illustrated in Stokes, *Iconography of Manhattan Island*, Vol. 1, Plate 16. K18

18 —— **Fifth state** with the imprint of Carolus Allard within the shield. The shield which had been blank on all the previous states is now occupied with the imprint, "Typis Caroli Allard Amstelodami cum privilegio". There is an additional line to the title of the view, "eindelÿk aan de Engelse weder afgestaan", a reference to the second English victory of 1674. K19

19 —— **Sixth state** with the imprint of Joachim Ottens. The imprint within the shield now reads, "Typis Ioachim Ottens Amstelodami". There are various changes on the body of the map:

1   Philadelphia is shown.

2   Pennsylvania is named and given bounds though they are not the same as those shown on Danckers (No. 9).

3   New York is so named on the map (*Nieuw Iork*). This is as an alternative to *Nieuw Amsterdam*.

4   The misprint *Altor* for *Alter*—between the two Indian villages—has been corrected.

5   Various names which had been erased when the title was placed at the top of the map reappear, e.g. *Hochelaga* in the top left corner.

6   A scale of miles has been added. K21

Plate 155.

20 —— **Seventh state** with the imprint of Reinier and Joshua Ottens.

The imprint now reads, "Apud Reinier & Iosua Ottens Amstelodami".

Reinier and Joshua Ottens took over the business after their father's death in 1719. It is possible to make out traces of Joachim's name beneath the new imprint.   K20

Plate 156.

21 **[1670]** OGILBY (John)/MONTANUS (Arnoldus)] NOVI BELGII, Quod nunc NOVI JORCK vocatur, NOVAEꝗ. ANGLIAE & Partis Virginiae Accuratissima et Novissima Delineatio [London/Amsterdam].   36·5 × 29 cms.

This plate while only two-thirds the size of the others in the series is closely copied from Visscher (No. 5) and although not usually considered as forming part of it is in fact an important link between the Visscher and the later states of the Allard. It does not contain any view of New York but has in its place an entirely new cartouche. The other noticeable difference is in the decorative features. The Indian villages and some of the animals have been deleted.

It differs in the following ways from the Visscher (No. 5):

1 New York is thus named, *Nieu Jorck* and there is no mention of the name New Amsterdam. The province is still called *Nieuw Nederlandt*.

2 *Fort Orangie* is now lettered *Nova Albania*. It had been re-named *Albany* in 1664 when captured by the English.

3 The lettering *Nieu-Jarsey*, *Jorck shire* and *Iamaica*—the latter two on Long Island—has been added.

This map appears without text on the back in all the editions of Montanus' *America*. All these issues are taken from the same plate.
Appears in:

Montanus (A.) De Nieuwe en Onbekende Weereld: of Beschryving van America en 't Zuid-Land . . . Door Arnoldus Montanus t'Amsterdam By Jacob Meurs, 1671.

Ogilby (J.) America: being an Accurate Description of the New World . . . By John Ogilby, Esq; . . . London: Printed by Tho. Johnson for the Author . . . 1670.

—— America: being the Latest, and most Accurate Description of the New World . . . By John Ogilby, Esq; . . . London: Printed by the Author, and are to be had at his House in White Fryers. 1671.

D[apper] (Dr. O.) Die Unbekante Neue Welt . . . Durch Dr. O. D. Zu Amsterdam, Bey Jacob von Meurs, 1673.

Plate 157.

22 —— **Second state** re-issued by vander Aa.

The title cartouche has been erased—though traces of the trees remain—and a new one showing settlers engraved in its place. The title now reads, "NOUVELLE HOLLANDE, (à présent NOUVELLE-YORK) NOUVELLE-ANGLETERRE et une partie de la VIRGINIE, dressées sur les propres manuscrits de ceux qui en ont fait la decouverte, et mises en lumiere par PIERRE VANDER AA, Marchand Libraire A LEIDE".

The scale of miles has been moved to the side and the animals erased. Many names have been added:

1 *Canada.* This is the only map in the series to give the modern name.
2 *Providence* (R.I.). The only map in the series to show this town, first settled in 1636.
3 *Philadelphie*—shown far to the south of its correct position.
4 *Pensilvanie.*
5 *Northampton, Dierfeld* and *Windsor*—on the Connecticut River.
6 *Newcastle* and *Antioche*—at the mouth of the Delaware River.
7 *Oxford, Sommerset* and *C. Henry*—along the Chesapeake River.
8 *Algonquins, F. S. Therese, F. Chambly* and many names towards Canada, particularly around Quebec.

Appears in:

Aa (P. vander) Nouvel Atlas, Leiden [1714].

Plate 158.

22a —— **Third state** re-issued by Covens & Mortier [1761].

23 **1676** [SPEED (John)] A Map of NEW ENGLAND AND NEW YORK. F. Lamb Sculp. Sold by Tho. Bassett in Fleet Street, and Richard Chiswell in St. Pauls Church Yard [London]. 50 × 38 cms.

This is smaller than the Jansson prototype but the scale remains the same and the map stops off short to the west and south, mainly affecting Virginia. It is in appearance very similar to the prototype map as it has no view of New York and little decoration.

There are various differences between this and the prototype:

1 The heads of Chesapeake and Delaware Bays have been brought closer together.
2 The Susquehanna River has been re-drawn with many of the bends removed.
3 Many of the places have been given English names, e.g. *London* (New London, Conn.), *Barnstable* (Mass.) and *New Castl* (Del.), in place of *Fort Kasimier. Boston* appears in place of *London* (Mass.).

John Speed died in 1629. The map is first known to have appeared in the 1676 edition of his *A Prospect of the most famous parts of the world.* It is found both

290

with and without text on the back, the last on thicker paper. As the *Prospect* was not issued again after 1676 it is likely that the plain-back version was published as a separate though whether before or after its inclusion in the atlas is not established. If it had been issued before it must have been after 1664 since it shows New York and not New Amsterdam. **K6**

Plates 159 & 162.

24 **[1730]** SEUTTER (Matthias) RECENS EDITA totius NOVI BELGII, in AMERICA SEPTENTRIONALI siti, delineatio cura et sumtibus MATTHAEI SEUTTERI, Chalcographi Augustani [Augsburg]. 57·5 × 49·5 cms.

First state with "Chalcographi Augustani".

The Restitutio cartouche has been replaced by a new one depicting natives and gods presenting tribute to a seated English monarch, probably George II. As Seutter was a draughtsman and engraver this may have been his own work. The view is now entitled, "Neu Jorck sive Neu Amsterdam", and the key is in Latin not Dutch.

This map incorporates the distinctive course of the Delaware River, showing it separate from the Hudson, which had appeared on Danckers (No. 9). The lakes and rivers have been shaded. Some of the names and notes on the map have been translated from Dutch into German and some of the names into Latin.

This is the first map in the series to show by means of printed lines the boundaries of Massachusetts, New England, New York, New Jersey and Pennsylvania. Previously the dividing line had been left to the colourist who tinted the provinces in different colours and improvised boundaries as best he could. A glance through the illustrations will show how varied these could be. Philadelphia had previously been shown as a ground-plan. Now it is shown representationally with five or six houses in relief.

Matthias Seutter set up his own business in Augsburg in 1707 and was producing atlases from about 1728 until his death in 1757. **K22**

Plate 161.

25 —— **Second State** with "Sac. Caes. Maj. Geographi August. Vind". This is in place of "Chalcographi Augustani" at the end of the imprint. A modern fake of this state is known. **K23**

Plates 160 & 161.

26 —— **Third state** with the privilege.

There is the extra line under the imprint, "Cum Gratia et Privil. S.R.I. Vicariat in part, Rheni, Sveviae, et Juris Franconici". **K24**

Plate 161.

26a —— **Fourth state** with the Lotter imprint and *Briston*.

Seutter's name has been replaced by "Tob. Conr. Lotteri". After Seutter's death in 1757 Tobias Conrad Lotter, his son-in-law, was one of those who continued his business. He had apparently been engraving for his father-in-law before this.

27 —— **Fifth state** with *Boston* but before the addition of "S.A.L.A."

Boston has been substituted, as it was on the Speed, this time in place of *Briston*.

K25

Plates 161 & 162.

28 —— **Sixth state** with the addition of "S.A.L.A." after "August. Vind.".

Addenda A **[1674]** SELLER (John) A Mapp of New JARSEY by John Seller. Ja Clerk Sculp: [London]. 53.5 × 43 cms.
First state with the Visscher view.

This map is not strictly in this series since it covers a smaller area, from Delaware Bay to Long Island, and in a larger scale. Also it is oriented with west to the top which exaggerates the difference. However it does incorporate both the views of New York, and many of the decorative details, such as animals, Indian villages and canoes are taken from the Jansson prototype.

The following names appear: *New York* (town and colony), *Delawar Bay*, *New Jarsey* and *Maryland*. Soundings are shown for the entrance to New York harbour as well as Delaware Bay.

For a fuller analysis of this map, and in particular its dating, see: Jeanette D. Black, The Blathwayt Atlas, Volume II, pp. 88-98. Providence, Rhode Island, 1975.

Appears in:

Seller (J) Atlas Maritimus. J. Darby for the Author, 1675.

Plate 163.

Addenda B —— **Second state** with the dedication.

The arms of Sir George Carteret appear centrally above a cartouche containing Seller's dedication to him. A second version of the Stuart arms appears in the bottom right-hand corner.

The whole of the region around New York has been re-engraved radically altering the course of the Hudson River, the form of Long Island Sound and the shapes of Staten and Manhattan Islands. There are other alterations:

1 *Manhattens Island* is written in two lines.

2 *New York* is written in the water and the town is represented by a square and not a circle.

3   Staten Island bears the name of 7 plantations—3 Dutch, a French, a Danish, *Dodelus* and *Lovelace his Pla.*

4   All soundings in the harbour have been deleted.

5   All the names on the mainland of New York Colony and on Long Island have been deleted with the single exception of *Maresipe.*

6   Hudson River is named.

7   *Staten Island* is named thus and not *States Island.*

This, like the first state, appears in Seller's *Atlas Maritimus* 1675. A new intermediate state is described by Black, pp. 92-3.

Plate 164.

Addenda C —— **Third state** with the Restitutio view.

There is a new title and imprint: "A Mapp of NEW JERSEY, in AMERICA, By John Seller, and William Fisher. The Restitutio view appears now in the place formerly occupied by the title cartouche and the title has been moved to the top of the map where it incorporates the Royal arms.

All reference to Carteret has been deleted. The upper branch of the Delaware River, *The River Delawar or South River* fills the gap left by the Visscher view. This state is found in two forms, the central sheet being completed by the addition of two side panels and text along the bottom. It is unfortunately impossible to illustrate the text here. While the side panels are separate and the central sheet has borders around the sides suggesting it is complete in itself much of the lettering in heavy type runs over onto the panels and is only comprehensible in the complete form. Whether these represent one or two states of the map is not clear and for convenience they will be described together in the complete form.

There have been a number of alterations:

1   The heavy lettering *New Jarsey* has been replaced with *West Jersey* and *East New Jersey*. Between them is a dotted line carrying the inscription "This is the Partition Line Between East and West Iersey".

2   The whole Manhattan area has been re-drawn once more, involving Staten Island, Hudson River, Manhattan and Long Island.

3   The lettering of *New York* and *Manhattan Island* has been changed.

4   Numerous soundings have been added for New York harbour and out to sea.

5   The plantation names have been removed from Staten Island.

6   Sandy Hook is now named *Sandy Point.*

7   The engraver's name has been deleted.

The following place names appear:

(a)   *Naraticon, Ermomex, Aquavachuques,* etc. These are all in heavy type.

293

(b) *Varkins Kill* (near to Fort Elsenburgh).

(c) *Fort Nassou*—indicated before but not named.

(d) Various names along the Hudson River and on Long Island and some Indian names to the east of Delaware Bay.

The text along the bottom, which is a slightly altered reprint of a Quaker broad-side of July 1676, is entitled "The Description of the Province of West Jersey in America as also, Proposals to such as desire to have any Propriety therin". It carries the imprint, "London, Printed for John Seller at the Hermitage stairs in Wapping, and William Fisher at the Postern-gate on Tower Hill, 1677".

Plates 165 & 166.

CHAPTER NINE

A Sequence of Maps of America

by R. V. Tooley

THE end of the 15th and beginning of the 16th century was the heyday of Flemish cartography when control of the map trade passed from Italy to the Low Countries. Their style was entirely different. The Italians were restrained, classic in style relying on beauty of lettering and spacing for effect. The Flemings were the exact reverse, exuberant with an intense love of ornament for its own sake, even their lettering flowering into strange twists and complicated twirls. Large wall maps in several sheets were produced by publishers like Plancius, Jodocus Hondius, Visscher and Blaeu, and these were crowded with ornament. Groups of figures in national costumes were used as side borders, and views of Towns portraits &c. along top and bottom borders.

For these maps the French have a happy phrase "cartes à figures". Such maps were issued separately not originally in atlases, which is why owing to their fragile nature so few have survived. Some of the smaller single sheet maps were incorporated into atlases later, the most notable example being Blaeu. The originals of these single sheet maps by Blaeu, Jodocus Hondius, Kaerius, and Visscher the elder are rare, and unrecorded in most library catalogues and books about maps. They were slightly too large for the average size atlas so in some cases the bottom ornamented border was removed. Finally copper being expensive and manners changing, these borders were removed altogether only the original map content being preserved.

The following short list is a record of the maps that I have seen, or noted in various catalogues, to illustrate this particular phase in map production with its relation to America.

1608-c.1673 Blaeu, W. Nova et acurata totius Americae Tabula Auct. [*c.* 1673]   138 × 100 cm

Wall map on four engraved sheets, broad side borders of 16 costume plates bottom border of 12 views of towns, and title in large letters along the top. These borders were separately engraved and pasted onto the main map.

The costume borders have two or three figures to each compartment and depict natives from both North and South America. This also applies to the towns.

Two inset maps, one depicting northern regions, the other the Antarctic. The map itself is profusely decorated with ships and sea monsters, neptunes, mermaids and compass roses. Probably published by Pietro Tedescho in Bologna *c.* 1673.

A damaged but legible example is preserved in the Royal Geographical Society in London, the letterpress signed by Visscher. The inset map of S. Polar regions records Van Diemens Land (discovered 1642) and another part bears the date 1667 detecta possibly a missprint according to RGS Journal (LX, p. 233). Another copy was recorded in Orion Catalogue 10, number 62 and a third is in the Hollandsche Lloyd building in Amsterdam.

The map was first published in 1608 [Wieder Monumenta Cartographica, Vol. III, p. 68] but there is no known surviving copy. It was reissued 1612? [recorded Lasor], 1624 by Henricus Hondius [Breslau Stadtbibliotek] Wieder: 1656 and 1669 by C. V. Visscher [Paris Bib. Nationale], and an undated edition in Amsterdam, Scheepvaart Museum [Wieder].

Plate 168.

1617 Janssonio Guliel [i.e. Wm. Blaeu]. America nova Tabula Auct. Guliel Janssonio [1617]
55.5 × 41 cm

A Terra Australis Incognita runs along bottom left hand side of the map. Terra del Fuego has no southern boundary and does not show Cape Hoorn or Barnevelt Island. Inserted in 1623 edition of Mercator-Hondius Atlas of 1623 [B.M. Maps C3C9]. Rare not mentioned by Koeman.

1630 — America nova Tabula Auct. Guilel Janssonio [1630]   55 × 41 cm

Reissue of the preceding, side borders of double costume figures including natives of Greenland, Virginia, Florida, New Albion, Mexico &c., top border of 9 vignettes of Towns. No decorated bottom border, title within carouche bottom left, ships and seamonsters in the Oceans. Inset map of Greenland. Cape Hoorn is shown and I. Barnevelte. Appears in Atlantis Appendix, Amsterdam apud Guiljelmum Blaeuw, 1630.

The copy in the British Museum has no text on the reverse and the title bears as author Guilel Janssonio not Blaeuw [B.M. Maps C4B1]. This is not recorded by Koeman.

VIRGINIANI

REX et REGINA Florid.

NOVÆ ALBIONIS REX

1630 Blaeu, G. America nova Tabula Auct. Guilel Blaeuw. [1630]

Koeman Atlantes Neerlandici Vol. I, p. 73 records this map as appearing in the Atlantis Appendix 1630, the name Blaeuw replacing that of Jansson. No text on back [B.M. C4b1] Atlantis Appendix 1630.

Plate 169.

1631 — America nova Tabula Auct. Guiljelmo Blaeuw. [1631]   55×41 cm

Blaeu's name now used in the title. Latin text in reverse Sig. H. catchword Ve/neti. The plate beginning to show signs of wear. Appears in Appendix Theatri A. Orteli et Atlantis G. Mercatoris 1631.

The first edition with German text was in 1634 with Dutch text 1635 and French text 1635 and subsequent editions [see Koeman]. There was no edition with English text.

1630 Hondius, Jodocus. America noviter delineata Auct: Jodoco Hondio
Joannes Janssonius excudit   56.5×47 cm

Inset maps of Greenland and Antarctic. Side borders of double costume figures top and bottom border views of Towns. Pomeiooc, Carolina, S. Augustin, Havana, S. Domingo, Cartagena, Olinda, Cusco, Potosi, Mocha, R. Janeiro and Mexico.

This undated map of Jodocus Hondius is the earliest I have seen. According to Koeman Atlantes Neerlandici Vol. II, page 348 this map first appeared in the 1630 edition of the Atlantis Maioris Appendix published by Jansson in that year.

This may be so as regards an atlas but it was possibly issued earlier as a separate as the top right hand corner of the copperplate is broken, evidence of a later printing. Similar maps of Africa were printed in 1606 and 1623 and it is possible that the four continents were printed at these dates. The New York Public Library Dictionary Catalogue, Vol. I, p. 211 cites America Jodocus Hondius 1606 Facsimile No imprint. On the other hand the top centre of the map shows Davis's Strait and to the left the date 1622. Not in the Library of Congress. The British Museum has an example to which they ascribe the date 1635? [K. 118.5]. Not mentioned by Bagrow-Skelton or Keuning.

Plate 170.

1632 Hondius, Jodocus. America noviter delineata. ANOTHER EDITION. [1632]

56 × 41 cm

Without the bottom border of Town views, Dutch text on reverse top right corner of copper-plate still broken [Francis Edwards 1973].

[1633] — America noviter delineata. Auct. Judoco Hondio   54.5 × 41 cm

Geographically a copy of the preceding but re-engraved in a much coarser manner top right hand corner of the plate restored and the skulls deleted from title cartouche and Joannes Janssonius excudit expunged. No text on back [Francis Edwards 1973].

1634 [—] America noviter delineata. [1634]   44.5 × 35.5 cm

A reissue of the Hondius map of 1632 without the decorative borders. The map is re-engraved The same title cartouche is retained but with the name of Hondius removed. The two inset maps of Greenland and Antarctica are also re-engraved but many names are omitted for example Tiera del Fuego & Cape Horn. The shape of Tierra del Fuego is changed and another island inserted further south [B.M. 69810(24)]. Appears in De Bry's Grand Voyages Tom I Pt. I Hist. Americae sive Novis Orbis.

1644 — America noviter delineata Auct. Judoco Hondio, N. Picart excudit acheu au Mois d'aoust l'an. 1644   53.5 × 41 cm

William M. Clements Library Research Catalogue Vol. I, p. 436.

1648 — America noviter delineata Auct. Judoco Hondio H. Picart fecit. [1648]   48 × 37.5 cm

Re-engraved without side, top or bottom borders. No text on back. Terra del Fuego corrected, divided into two islands. Strait of Le Maire & Barnevelt's Island and Wintergat inserted [Francis Edwards 1973]

Plate 171

1659 — America noviter delineata Auct. Judoco Hondio. [1659]

53.5 × 42 cm

Appears in D'Avity's Les Etats, Empires, Royaumes . . . du Monde Lyon 1659 B.M. K.A.R. (7) William M. Clements Library Research Catalogue Vol. I, p. 435.

1631 Hondius, Henricus. America noviter delineata Auct. Henrico Hondio. 1631   50 × 38 cm

A reissue of the map of his father Jodocus but without the top or side borders. With the two inset maps of Greenland and the Antarctic. The other decorations, the ships and sea monsters retained but printed in reverse Terra del Fuego is revised in outline, Barnevelts and Mauritius islands and Waigat strait inserted. Thus giving the Picart version of Tierra del Fuego.

Relatively common [Library of Congress 444]. An Edition with English text appeared in 1636 [Library of Congress 449].

Plate 172.

298

1641 Hondius, H. America noviter delineata. ANOTHER EDITION. 1641

[Library of Congress 449.]
A reissue of the preceding with the addition of an imprint to the left of the titlepiece Amstelodami Excudit Joannes Janssonius.

—— America noviter delineata. ANOTHER EDITION. Undated [1645?].
BM 61890 (24)

1634 Merian, Matthew. America noviter delineata   44 × 33.5 cm

In Historia Americae sive Novis Orbis. Matth. Meriani Francofurti 1634 [B.M. G6633(1)] [and 69810(24)]. A reduced copy of the Hondius map without the decorative borders.

[1640] —— America noviter delineata. M. Merian fecit.   35.5 × 27.5 cm

With the inset map of Greenland but without the inset of Antarctica. Shape of Tierra del Fuego altered I. Barnevelt inserted [B.M. 69810(2)] ascribes imprint Basle? 1640?

Petrus Bertius (1565-1629) was brother-in-law to both Jodocus Hondius and Peter van den Keere [Kaerius] with whom he worked in close contact. He is principally known for his minature atlas the Caert thresoor and his Geographia Veteris. His maps of America appeared as separate or included in the works of other publishers.

1624 [Bertius]. Carte de l'Amerique Corrigée et augmentée dessus toutes les aultres cy devant Faictes L'année. 1624   50 × 38 cm

With insets of Greenland and Antarctic, ships and sea monsters in Ocean. Based on Jodocus Hondius map.

1646 —— ANOTHER EDITION   50 × 38 cm

The N.W. coast of America is shown by a dotted line and marked, "land not yet discovered". Appears in Pierre Davity's Description generale de America, Paris Sonnius & Denis Bechet 1643 [B.M. 568h10].

1648 Bertius, P. Carte de l'Amerique Corrigée et augmentée dessus toutes les aultres cy devant faictes par P. Bertius. [1648] 49 × 37 cm

A copy of the Hondius map without the decorative borders but the inset maps of Greenland and the Antarctic retained, and the ships and seamonsters engraved in reverse and a newly designed titlepiece. No text on reverse.

Terra del Fuego shown as one island is revised, Cape Hoorn and Pais des Estats being added.

Plate 173.

1650 — Carte de l'Amerique Corrigée et augmentée dessus toutes les aultres cy deuant faictes par P. Bertius. [Paris 1650] 50 × 38 cm

A further copy of the Hondius map without the decorative borders but with inset maps of Greenland and Antarctice [B.M. Maps 69810(21)].

The plate is now slightly worn and is corrected in places e g. the word Anian is inserted to the right of C. Mendocino, Nouveau Mexique to north of California, and Margaias in Brasil. Dotted boundary lines are now inserted for English Colonies, Florida, New Granada, Mexico, Brasil, la Plata & Magellanica.

1661 — Carte de l'Amerique Corrigée et augmentée dessus toutes les aultres cy devant faictes par P. Bertius. 1661 36 × 27 cm

A reduced version of the preceding with the two inset maps but without any decoration, except for the titlepiece [Francis Edwards].

Plate 174.

1662 — ANOTHER EDITION. 1662 36 × 27 cm

Reduced copy of the map of Hondius with the insets of Greenland & Antarctic, oceans without decoration. Appears in Pierre D'Avity's Description générale de l'Amerique nouvelle edition [B.M. 10027.1.6. (2)].

1671 [—] Carte de l'Amerique Corrigée et augmentée, dessus toutes les aultres cy deuant. 1671 51 × 40 cm

Another version of the Hondius map without decorative borders and without faictes par P. Bertius but surrounded by a border of engraved French text [B.M. 69810 (31)].

L.C., Vol. V records maps of America by Bertius 1650 (5942), 1618 (5941).

Plate 175.

1614 Kaerius, Petrus. America Nova Descriptio Petrus Kaerius excudit
Amsterodami 1614 Abraham Goos Sculpsit   55.5×43 cm

Side borders of single figures, top and bottom borders of town plans and portraits of navigators
Colombus, Vespucci, Magellan, Drake, Cavendish and VanNoort.   Inset map of Arctic with
strait of Anian.   The B.M. copy has the top and bottom borders cut off.   The oceans are
adorned with native craft including a Kayak, a Florida canoe with fire, sea monsters, and a
flying fish.   A southern Terra Austra is marked embracing Tierra del Fogo.

Lee Philips List of Maps of America, p. 104, [B.M. 69810 (22)].

1616 — Americae Nova Descriptio . . . 1614 [1616]

Second state.   Tierra del Fuogo is now separated from the southern continent, the strait of
Lemaire and Cape Horn being inserted [Francis Edwards 1973].

Plate 176.

1636 Visscher, Nicolaum Jo. America Nova Descriptio Per Nicloaum Io. Visscher Anno 1636 Abraham Goos Sculpsit   56 × 43.5 cm

A reissue of the Kaerius Map of 1614 with changes only to the cartouche [Map Collectors Circle 40, plate 2]. Visscher also produced a 4 sheet map of America.

1636-1652 — America Nova Descriptio Per Nicolaum Visscher Anno 1652

Reissue of preceding.

Plate 177.

[1666-7] Jollain. Americae Descriptio Jollain Excudit   46 × 34 cm

There should be an America by Jollain as above though I have been unable to locate a copy, but Africa exists dated 1666 and Asia dated 1667.

1626-7 Speed, John. America with those known parts in that unknowne worlde both people and manner of buildings Discribed and inlarged by I. S. Ano 1626 Are to be sold in pops head alley against the Exchange by G. Humble Engraved Abraham Goos   51.5 × 39.5 cm

Issued in the "Prospect of the World", published by Humble for John Speed in 1627, the first general atlas of the World published in Britain. Based on Kaerius with side borders of single costume figures and top border of birds-eye plans of the principal towns.

This first edition may be recognised by the date 1626, by the imprint "pops head alley G. Humble", and by the fact that Boston and Long Island are not marked on the map, and by the pagination numbers 9 and 10.

1631 — ANOTHER EDITION

Reissued in 1631 by G. Humble, the map unchanged and the text on reverse the same as to content but the first page unnumbered, the fleuron heading being continued into the outside ruled column taking the place of the figure 9.

1646 — ANOTHER EDITION

Still nears Humble's imprint, Sig. E numbered pp. 9 and 10. Text commencing with capital A on azured arabesque design catchword "covered".

1662 Speed, John. ANOTHER EDITION

Again reissued in 1662 by new publishers "Are to be sold by Roger Rea ye Elder and younger at ye Golden Cross in Cornhill against ye Exchange". In this issue the town of Boston in New England, Connecticut, Maryland and Long Island are added to the plate and a dotted boundary placed round Delaware and Hudson Rio. The text on reverse is again the same as to content but the type is reset and now commences with a historical capital A, a new fleuron heading and the page number 9 restored top right.

1676 — ANOTHER EDITION

It was again reissued in 1676 by new publishers "are to be sold by Thomas Bassett in Fleet Street, and by Richard Chiswell in St. Paul's Churchyard".

In this last issue of Speed's map, the copperplate is unchanged but the text on the reverse is not only reset but rewritten. There is no fleuron heading, New York and Maryland are mentioned for the first time in the text to Virginia (section 14) and Hochelaga, Quebec and Tadusac added to the description of Canada.

Plate 178.

[1660] Wit, F. de. Nova totius Americae descriptio Auct. F. de Wit. 1660
55.5 × 44 cm

Based on the Kaerius map of 1614 and Visscher map of 1636, it is entirely revised for the west coast, the two former showing California as a peninsula, but De Wit in this map changes California into an island in the second Sanson model of 1656. Being on a smaller scale he omits some of the Sanson names including Pto de Francisco Draco.

The map is decorated with side borders of costume figures and top border of birds-eye views of principal towns based on the designs of Kaerius, with a charming titlepiece including a native sitting on an armadillo copied from the Vischer map [Koeman II, p. 212].

Plate 34.

1668 Overton, John. A New and Most Exact map of America described by N. I. Visscher and don into English Enlarged and Corrected according to I. Blaeu and others with the Habits of ye people and ye manner of ye Chiefe Sitties ye like never before. London Printed Colloured and are to be sould by John Overton neere the Fountain & Tavern without Newgate at ye White horse in Little Brittaine neare the Hospitall.   1668   54 × 32.5 cm

With side borders of costume figures and top and bottom borders of views of cities and portraits of navigators.   It is more rare than the De Wit map of 1660 and far more decorative, following the Kaerius model in having a bottom as well as a top border of town plans interspersed with portraits of navigators, the sea covered with ships and a large inset of Polar Regions.

Plate 39.

1668-1670 Walton, R. A New Plaine, and Exact Map of America; described by N. I. Visscher, and don into English, enlarged and corrected according to I. Blaeu . . . Printed, Colored, and are to be sold by Ro. Walton at ye Globe and Compass in St. Paules Churchyard between ye two north doores.

It is sometimes found in editions of Heylin's Cosmography, inserted instead of the normal Seile maps.   Also occasionally in Varenius.

Plate 179.

Based on the Kaerius, Visscher, Overton tradition this map has one peculiar feature, an attempt to harmonise the island of peninsula theory for the west coast.   California is shown as an island but the coast is continued north westward in the Mercator Ortelius tradition.

CHAPTER TEN

The Mapping of the Great Lakes
A Personal View

by R. V. Tooley

MANY years ago I assembled a large collection of maps of the Great Lakes area, including many duplicates and variations. The ease of comparison this gave made it a most interesting and absorbing study, with many geographical variations and contradictions, which lasted even up to the nineteenth century.

I knew and became friends with Louis C. Karpinski when he was beginning to collect material for his *Bibliography of the Printed Maps of Michigan Constituting an Historical Atlas of the Great Lakes and Michigan*, published in 1931.

This great work, essential to all students of the cartographical history of this area, may seem to make further works superfluous, but the region is so important and the subject so vast that it is possible to explore certain byways and view the whole or parts from a different angle.

The following notes record my own personal reaction and delight in comparing some of these maps for their geographical influence or some peculiarity that makes them stand apart from their contemporaries; I have chosen a small selection to show some of the vagaries in the mapping of this area.

The earliest maps of America naturally showed no Great Lakes, the interior not having been explored. As information came back gradually to Europe, right from the beginning two different concepts of the area were published. The Dutch, who were followed by the English, showed no lakes. The French gave the more correct and first indication of lakes in the area.

The Dutch early school, Ortelius, Mercator, Kaerius, Visscher and Blaeu drew the St. Lawrence without lakes, as did Purchas, Speed and Seller in England. Even as late as 1680 Moses Pitt still showed no lakes. Jan Jansson in the fourth decade of the seventeenth century was the first of the Dutch to break new ground. In his map of North America in 1638 he introduced one lake, the "Lac des Iroquois". Typical of the confusion of the period, in his map of New England in the same atlas he gave three lakes linked to the St. Lawrence, one unnamed, a "Lac des Yroquois" and a "Grand Lac". Some years later, about 1680, N. Visscher produced a less correct map showing a single, large, square-shaped lake open at its western end. This retrograde step became the standard for a few years, being copied by De Witt and others in Holland and by Ogilby, Seller, Hollar and Overton in England. The immense investment and business acumen of the Dutch, giving them predominance in the publication of maps, spread their representation of the region for many years beyond the more correct maps of the French school based on actual observation.

The French under Jacques Cartier in 1534 and Samuel de Champlain at the beginning of the seventeenth century laid the foundation of a more correct mapping of the region. Champlain in his map of 1632 showed a "Lac de Champlain", "Lac St. Louis", "Mer Douce" and "Grand Lac". Boisseau copied him in 1640. It was Nicolas Sanson who in his 1650 map of America was the first to show the five Great Lakes, the last two being open at their western ends. In this he was followed by Duval in 1664 and Jaillot in 1674. It was Richard Blome in England who first promoted this French mapping of the five Great Lakes.

An Italian, Coronelli, using Jesuit surveys, made the best map of his time. His map of America, 1688, closed the western ends of lakes Michigan and Superior, but it was the inferior rendering of Hennepin's map of 1683 that had the greatest circulation owing to the popularity of his book, a narrative of his travels in America.

The five Great Lakes, though now definitely established, still bore no fixed titles, but had a fascinating variety of names and no less a variety of shapes.

Lake Ontario was called *Lake Champlain* or *St. Louis* by Champlain in 1632; *Saint Louis* by Sanson in 1656, Duval 1669; *Lake Frontenac* or *Ontario*, Joliet 1673, Hennepin 1698, La Hontan 1703, Moll 1720, Popple 1733; *Lake Frontenac*, Franquelin 1684, Coronelli 1695; *Cataraqui* or *Ontario*, Colden 1747; *Katarakui* or *Ontario*, Washington 1754.

Lake Erie: called *du Chat* by Sanson in 1656, Duval 1678; *Lac du Conti* or *Errie*, Hennepin 1698; *Lake Erie*, Joliet 1673; Lake Errie or du Conti, La Hontan 1703; Lake Erie or Felix, Daniel 1679; Lake Erie or *Teiocherontion, Felix, De Conty, Du Chat* and *Cadaragua*, Keulen 1720; *Lake Erie* or *Duchat*, Moll 1720; *Erie* and *Oswego*, Colden 1750, Washington 1754.

Lake Huron: called *Mer Douce* by Champlain in 1632; *Great Lake of the Hurons*, Duval 1669; *Karegnondi*, Sanson 1656; *Lake Huron*, Joliet 1673; *Lake Huron and Michigan*, Brehaut de Galinee 1670; *Lac des Hurons*, La Hontan 1703; *Hurons, Karegnondi* or *Algonquins, Michigane* or *Lake Orleans*, Keulen 1740; *Quatoghi* or *Hurons*, Washington 1754.

Lake Michigan: called *Lake Illinois* by Marquette in 1674, De L'Isle 1703, Senex 1710, Bellin 1744; *Mitchgangong, Illinois* or *Dauphin*, Franquelin 1682; *Illinois* or *Missiganin*, Joliet 1673/4; *Ilenese Lake* or *Michigan*, Moll 1720; *Illinois, Michigani* or *Dauphin*, Keulen 1720; *Michigan*, Colden 1750, Jefferys 1761, Washington 1754.

Lake Superior: called *Lake Superior* by Sanson in 1650, Jesuit map 1673, Joliet 1673/4, De L'Isle 1703; *Upper Lake*, Hennepin 1698, Moll 1735; *Tracy* or *Upper Lake*, Coronelli 1698, Wells 1700, Colden 1750; *Lake Tracy, Superior* or *Condé*, Keulen 1720.

Ontario was shown alternatively as stretching east and west, or north and south. Erie angled towards the west or horizontal, Michigan, even more confusing, was slanted either to the right or to the left and Lake Superior was drawn with imaginary islands up to the end of the eighteenth century. Lake Michigan was sometimes drawn almost square, and at other times an elongated, pointed shape with unreal mountain chains alongside.

The following short list of maps have been selected to show some of the vagaries and gradual development of the mapping of this area.

ONTARIO

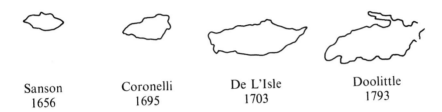

| Sanson | Coronelli | De L'Isle | Doolittle |
| 1656 | 1695 | 1703 | 1793 |

ERIE

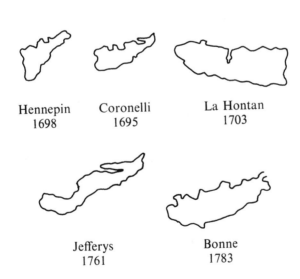

Hennepin   Coronelli   La Hontan
1698   1695   1703

Jefferys   Bonne
1761   1783

HURON

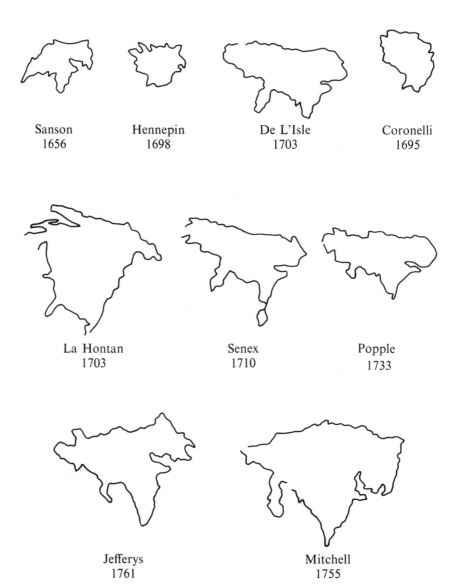

Sanson
1656

Hennepin
1698

De L'Isle
1703

Coronelli
1695

La Hontan
1703

Senex
1710

Popple
1733

Jefferys
1761

Mitchell
1755

MICHIGAN

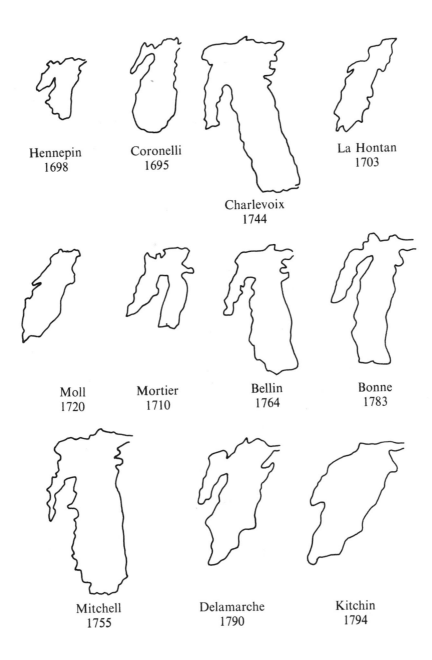

Hennepin
1698

Coronelli
1695

Charlevoix
1744

La Hontan
1703

Moll
1720

Mortier
1710

Bellin
1764

Bonne
1783

Mitchell
1755

Delamarche
1790

Kitchin
1794

SUPERIOR

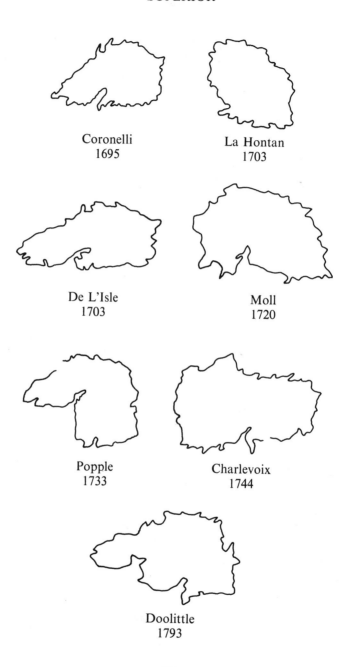

Coronelli
1695

La Hontan
1703

De L'Isle
1703

Moll
1720

Popple
1733

Charlevoix
1744

Doolittle
1793

1613/32 CHAMPLAIN (SAMUEL DE). "Carte geographique de La Nouvelle France". 1613. "Carte de la Nouvelle France, augmentee depuis la derniere". 1632.

The first of these two maps of Canada appeared in *Les Voyages du Sieur de Champlain Xaintongeois* (Paris, 1613) and the *second in Voyages de la Nouvelle France Occidentale, dicte Canada.* (Paris, 1632).

Both these maps are fundamental and essential to any large collection of maps of the Great Lakes, Champlain being the first to give an indication of a chain of Great Lakes connected to the St. Lawrence. Though very approximate in outline they were superior to contemporary Dutch maps, which showed no lakes at all.

The maps can hardly ever be found separately apart from the books, and so popular have maps become today that the price of the maps if found on their own would be not much less than the price of the books themselves.

1636 JANSSON (JOHANNES). America Septentrionalis. "Nova Anglia, Novum Belgium et Virginia". Amsterdam, 1636.

Two important maps, both appearing in the *Appendix Atlantis* published in Amsterdam in 1636. They are important as being the first attempt in Holland to add lakes connected to the St. Lawrence. In his map of North America Jansson shows one large lake, "Iroquois", issuing from the St. Lawrence. In his maps of New England in the same atlas he gives an unnamed lake, a "Lac des Iroquois", and a "Grand Lac" (Superior), the purchasers apparently taking their choice as to which of the two versions to believe.

However Jansson's example was not generally followed: Boisseau in France reverted to the older map of Champlain, and Blaeu, the rival of and in many ways more progressive than Jansson showed no lakes at all at this time. Even as late as 1680 Moses Pitt followed the usual Dutch model of no lakes.

These two Jansson maps are therefore important and valuable as forerunners.

Plate 28.

1650 SANSON (NICOLAS). "Amerique Septentrionale". Paris, 1650.

Sanson, geographer royal to Louis XIII of France, talented and industrious, commenced map making at the age of eighteen. He compiled in all over three hundred maps and became the founder of the French school of geography.

In this map of North America he shows for the first time in a printed map thn five Great Lakes: Lake St. Louis (Ontario), Lake du Chat (Erie), an unnamed lake (Huron), Lake des Puans (Michigan) and Lake Superior, the last two opee at their western ends.

In 1656 he produced a second map, "Le Canada ou Nouvelle France", revising the names of the lakes as follows: Ontario or Lake St. Louis, Lake Erie or Ducaht, the previously unnamed lake he now names "Karegnondi" (Huron), Lake des Puans (Michigan) and Lake Superior.

Sanson revised his map of North America in 1669, calling the third lake "Karegnondi" or "Mer Douce". The map was further reissued by his son in 1690.

Plate 29.

1664 DU VAL (PIERRE). "Le Canada faict par le Sr de Champlain". Paris, 1664.

An example of a retrograde step, typifying the confused state and lack of co-ordination in cartography in France at this period. Few people of leisure were well versed in the topography of America, and a map if well presented and under the aegis of the royal geographer no doubt found ready purchasers.

Du Val in this map ignores Sanson's representation of the Great Lakes published fourteen years earlier and gives the Champlain map of 1632, although as geographer to the King he must have had access to Sanson's work.

In 1677 he reissued the preceding map but with considerable additions, adding Elsenbourg in New Sweden, Tadousac and Montreal to his maps and giving additional information on some Indian tribes, for example the Cat Indians cultivate land, and the Puans are so called because they come from the borders of salt water.

In his 1678 map of Canada Du Val records Sanson's version of the Great Lakes but is still behind the times, ignoring the result of the fine Jesuit map of 1671/2 showing the whole of Lake Superior.

Finally in his map of America, 1684, Du Val has all five lakes completed, their western ends being filled in.

None of the Du Val maps are common today.

1669 BLOME (RICHARD). "A new Map of America Septentrionale designed by Monsieur Sanson rendered into English by Richard Blome". London, 1669.

A map that deserves a place in a Great Lakes collection as it is the first map printed in England to show the five Great Lakes, being copied as the title states from Sanson. Blome not only added his own decorations but also puffed his sales by dedicating his map to different members of the nobility without change in the map.

However his map was better than Speed's map of 1676 or Moses Pitt's maps of 1680, both of which followed the early Dutch tradition of no Great Lakes.

1672 JESUIT MAP. "Lac Superieur et autres lieux ou sont les Missions des peres". Paris, 1672.

Compiled in 1671, this map was printed in the Jesuit *Relations* of 1672 compiled by Father Dablon. Far in advance of any other map of the period, based on physical observation, it did not have the impact its excellence deserved. It was used by Coronelli, a Franciscan, but was not taken up by other geographers, even in France, until the end of the century, when Jaillot made use of this fine survey.

1674 JAILLOT (ALEXIS HUBERT). "Amerique Septentrionale". Engraved Cordier. Paris, 1674.

This map has been chosen as the last to give the Sanson version of the five Great Lakes. It was reissued several times before the end of the century, though geographically it was years out of date. The reason for this was the great capital expenditure in the production of a copperplate. Publishers prolonged the lives of their plate as long as possible and Jaillot had succeeded to the stock and materials of Sanson.

The map itself is extremely handsome, beautifully engraved by Cordier, who was rated by Sir George Fordham as a most skilful engraver, "whose work merits careful study, as a development of the graphic art as applied to the production of maps in a very delicate form".

Jaillot issued a revised map in 1685 based on the Jesuit map of 1672, on Joliet, Franquelin and Hennepin, but in 1690 reverted to the old open-ended lakes of Sanson. "A map maker should not take every map upon trust or conclude that the newest is the best" (John Green, 1717).

Jaillot's maps were issued in three states, the simplest being in black and white with only the boundaries in colour, the second kind fully coloured including the ornamental cartouches, and the most elaborate luxuriously illuminated and heightened with gold. These superb examples of Jaillot's work have been called the first specimens of the decorative map.

In 1923 I sold a copy of Jaillot's *Atlas François* 1695 with 115 maps for £3.00. Today an ordinary copy of his map of America alone fetches around £300 and one of the special copies heightened with gold could be in the £800-£900 bracket.

1679 DANIEL (RICHARD). "A map of ye English Empire in ye Continent of America . . ." sold by R. Morden and W. Berry, 1679.

One of the most curious maps for the Great Lake area, lakes Huron, Ontario and Erie being placed one above the other in a straight line running due north and south. It was reissued later by Robert Morden alone about 1690.

Neither edition is common. Of the first, I have only handled three copies in fifty years.

1680 VISSCHER (N.). "Novissima et Accuratissima totius Americae descriptio". Amsterdam, 1680.

A map of importance, not for its geographic content as regards the Great Lakes but because it became the standard representation of North America for a number of years, copied by other Dutch and English publishers.

Its chief feature is a single large square-shaped lake open at its western end.

Plate 41.

1683 HENNEPIN (REV. PERE LOUIS). "Carte de la Nouvelle France et de la Louisiane". Paris, 1683.

This map and the second edition of 1698 probably had the widest circulation of the many maps showing the Great Lakes area owing to the popularity of Father Hennepin's account of his travels. The book went into many editions and apart from French was printed in Dutch, English, Italian and German editions.

1688 CORONELLI (FATHER VINCENZO MARIA). "Partie Occidentale du Canada ou de la Nouvelle France". Paris: Nolin, 1688. "La Louisiane parte settentrionale". Venice, 1696.

Father Coronelli, a Franciscan friar and finally general of the order, produced over five hundred maps and globes. This fine map of Canada was based on the works of Joliet, Marquette, La Salle, Franquelin and Hennepin. It was the best representation of the Great Lakes, particularly Lake Superior, that was printed up to that date. But though it must have had a wide circulation in his numerous works it was not universally adopted.

It is decorated with small vignettes and an ornamental title-piece. It should be noted that map makers of this period not only attempted to present a map pleasing to the eye, but at the same time used their ornamentation to instruct. Thus Coronelli's map shows the customs and habits of the country, natives hollowing out a canoe by fire, roasting fish, and executing punishments. Even the ornamented title and scale of miles are used to convey information showing Europeans hunting beaver and bear, and a native roasting upon a spit.

The second map, "Louisiana", is almost misnamed, in effect showing mainly the five Great Lakes. A comparatively small map measuring 17 by 10 inches, it appeared in the *Atlante Veneto* in 1696. Unadorned, it nevertheless fetches a high price. The density of population in the area creates a strong demand from would-be possessors.

1700 DE L'ISLE (GUILLAUME). "L'Amerique Septentrionale". A Paris chez l'auteurs, Rue des Canettes, 1700. "Carte du Canada ou de la Nouvelle France". A Paris chez l'auteur, Rue des Canettes, 1703.

Both important and essential maps for any Great Lakes collection. The imprint Rue des Cannettes is rare and was first mentioned to me by the erudite French bookseller the late Maurice Cahmonal, who had a phenomenal collection of French Canadiana which I believe still remains in the family. The second issue, with the address "a la Couronne de Diamans", is also rare.

De L'Isle was easily the outstanding geographer at the turn of the century. His work was copied by many of his contemporaries and his influence lasted throughout the eighteenth century, other publishers seeking to gain success for their own maps by using the phrase "*after Delisle*".

His map of Canada in particular is for me one of the most charming of all the maps of America of this period, with its graceful title cartouche by Guerard, the country typified by its fauna and customs, missionaries and converts, natives scalping, beaver and wild duck.

In the 1920's the map sold for less than £5. By the beginning of the 1970's it had crept up to £60-£80, but the fastest rise has been in the last ten years, the asking price today being around £450.00 and the rare first issue should fetch even more. Strictly speaking the map should not be coloured as it was not the custom at the period, but if it is well done, and I have seen several, it can be attractive.

For details and other maps by De L'Isle, see French Mapping of the Americas, Chapter 1. Map Collectors' Circle No 33, 1967.

1703 LA HONTAN. "Carte Generale de Canada". The Hague, 1703.

La Hontan, like Hennepin, owes his fame to his book of travels, *Nouveaux Voyages de Mr. le Baron de Lahontan dans l'Amerique septentrionale*. An extremely popular work, it went into many editions including an English translation. His Lake Erie is better than Hennepin's but he ignores the better shape of Lake Superior of the Jesuit-Coronelli map of 1688.

1732/3 POPPLE (HENRY). "A Map of the British Empire in America". Engraved W. H. Toms, 1733.

An attractive map and the first large-scale English map of America. Consisting of an index map and twenty sheets, it had considerable influence, editions being printed in Holland and France. Apart from a rather curious Lake Superior, it shows a fair representation of the Great Lakes. There were many issues and reproductions, which are recorded in the *Catalogue of the William L. Clements Library* (Boston: Hall, 1972). The map is usually found with the boundaries alone coloured, but I once had a copy in full contemporary colouring including the views of New York and Quebec, the title and vignettes.

The map is usually found bound flat in a large folio volume. The first copy I had sold for £18 in 1923. A copy bound in red morocco for George II sold in 1930 for £30 and a few years later it still only realised £45. In the early seventies it was on the £1000 mark, in 1974 a copy fetched £1800, and today it is in the £3000 class.

1743 BELLIN (JACQUES NICOLAS)

Bellin, hydrographer to the King of France, was the official cartographer with a prolific output. His first map showing the Great Lakes, "Carte de l'Amerique Septentrionale", was engraved by Dheulland in 1743. This was followed by "Carte des Lacs du Canada", 1744 both being published in works by Charlevoix. Bellin was the first to insert a fictitious Isle Philippeaux in Lake Superior.

His best known work on the Great Lakes appeared in *Le Petit Atlas Maritime*— 5 volumes quarto—published in Paris in 1764. This included the following maps: "La Nouvelle France ou Canada", "Carte des Cinq Grands Lacs du Canada", and, "La Riviere du Detroit depuis le Lac Sainte Claire jusqu'au Lac Erie" (with inset "Plan du Fort du Detroit", the first printed plan of Detroit).

Plate 114.

Bellin's maps from the *Atlas Maritime* used to be fairly common and relatively inexpensive. They are small and charming with the result that so many copies have been broken up that the complete work is now scarce and the first issue of 1763 rare.

For illustrations and other maps by Bellin see *Printed Maps of America*, Part IV. Map Collectors' Circle No 96, 1974.

1746 D'ANVILLE (JEAN-BAPTISTE BOURGUINON). "Amerique Septentrionale". Paris, 1746. "Canada, Louisiane et Terres Angloises". Paris, 1755.

To illustrate the cartography of the second half of the eighteenth century, a d'Anville map is essential. He dominated not only French but all contemporary geographers. He was one of the foremost to leave blank spaces in his maps where knowledge was insufficient. He became First Geographer to the King and was a collector of maps as well as cartographer, starting at the age of fifteen.

His representation of the Great Lakes is superior to that of his contemporary, John Mitchell.

Curiously his maps, being of large size, have never been too popular with collectors and consequently fetch much less than their geographical content merits. For illustrations and other details, see *Printed Maps of America*, Part I.

1755 MITCHELL (JOHN). "A Map of the British and French Dominions in North America". 8 sheets. London, 1755.

This famous map is the second large-scale English map of part of the continent of America. It became the standard map of the area up to the end of the century, being used in international boundary disputes. It was reprinted many times with editions in French, Dutch and Italian; for a list see Chapter Two, *Comparative Cartography*, pp. 86-7. Map Collectors' Circle No 39, 1967. The map has always been a great favourite with collectors and librarians and has always been expensive. Its excellence is no doubt in part due to the fact that Mitchell lived in America for some time though the map was published in England.

The Italian version by Zatta on 12 sheets appears in *Atlante Novissimo*, published in Venice in 1778. Three maps are devoted to the Great Lakes. Sheet I covers Lake Superior, Sheet IV Lake Michigan, and sheet V Lake Erie or Oswego and Ontario. The title of the whole map, *Colonie Unite dell' America Septentrionale*, includes a highly decorative map of Bermuda.

1761 JEFFERYS (THOMAS). "A Map of Canada and North Part of Louisiana". "North America from the French of Mr. D'Anville".

Both the above maps appeared in the *Natural and Civil History of the French Dominions in North America*, by Jefferys. They are an instance of the confused cartography of the region, quite different delineations of the Great Lakes being given in the same volume.

Nevertheless Jeffreys was one of the most able and prolific of map makers in the eighteenth century. He published many excellent maps of America on which he made money but lost it all surveying and publishing large-scale English county maps. Declared bankrupt in 1765, he partially recovered when he was joined by William Faden. His best work, his *American Atlas*, was issued after his death.

1784 BRION DE LA TOUR (LOUIS). "Carte des Etats Unis d'Amerique et du Cours du Mississippi". Paris chez Esnauts et Rapilly, 1784.

Brion de la Tour was Ingenieur géographe du Roi. The map was based on English maps and accounts of operations in the previous war, with boundaries according to the peace treaty of 1783. The population of the United States is given as three million, with the remark that it is possible to bathe in the Mississippi like the Ganges, in full sweat without being incommoded.

Imaginary islands are still shown in Lake Superior, and on Lake Michigan Port Chikago Village and Indian Fort.

The title is·within a decorative cartouche, with foliage and the cap of Liberty on the right and on the left a cannon and two flags, the flag of France and part of a red striped flag. Although the whole flag is not shown, it is probably meant to represent the American flag, and as far as I know is the first printed map to show the Stars and Stripes.

1787-8 Bonne (Rigobert). "Amerique Septentrionale". "Partie Occidentale du Canada Contenant les Cinq Grands Lacs".

Rigobert Bonne was born in the Ardennes and died in Paris. He composed the maps for Raynal's *Histoire Philosophique*, of which there were editions in Dutch, English, French, German and Italian. His maps were also used in Grenet's *Atlas Portatif*, 1781 and later editions. The *Atlas Encyclopédique*, 1787-8, also had Bonne's maps. Thus his maps and representations of the Great Lakes had a greater circulation than any other small maps in the later part of the eighteenth century, all in handy quarto size.

1796 Arrowsmith (Aaron). "A map of the United States of North America". 1796.

This large-scale map was the last important publication on America in the eighteenth century. It had a wide circulation and was reprinted many times, being corrected by Arrowsmith in succeeding editions.

The variety and contradictions in the mapping of the Great Lakes is almost endless; for example Seutter shows Lakes Erie and Illinois of more or less equal size, with Lake Huron quite small; Wells (1700) makes Lake Illinois larger than Lake Superior, and Mortier, about the same date, drew Lac Puans (Green Bay) side by side with and almost as large as the whole of Lake Michigan. Crepy in 1735 obliterates Lake Erie and joins Huron and Michigan into one large lake.

As to Lake Michigan, it is shown sloping south and west by d'Anville, Sayer and Bennett, by Homann and Heirs in 1784 and Lapie in 1812. It is shown sloping south and east by Vaugondy in 1755, Ottens, Brion de la Tour, Laurie and Whittle in 1794.

With the constant decline in the value of money, the price of maps increases. Those who remember the slump of the thirties when items were sold for half of what they cost tend to be cautious but in such a case even if the money is less, in hard times it will buy more. So the map collector is slightly cushioned either way. Apart from their financial value maps of the Great Lakes of America will always intrigue the collector by their diversity, and please by the frequent beauty of their engraving or the quaintness of their presentation.

CHAPTER ELEVEN

Identification of the maps of America in the various editions of the Theatrum of Ortelius

by R. V. Tooley

To date correctly in most cases, and approximately in a few, it is necessary to regard the text on the back of the map. The following list shows the differences in the Maps of America, the Pacific and Tartary (which includes North West America) which were issued in the various editions of the *Theatrum Orbis Terrarum*.

Ortelius America—Latin Text

1570		22 May. *Americae sive Novi Orbis Nova Descriptio*
	Signature 2	Bulge on the South West Coast of South America. Three ships in the Pacific
1570		No change
1570		No change
1570		No change
1571	Signature 2	Second line of text commences "dinem"
1573	Signature 2	Second line of text commences "uus orbis"
1575	Signature 2	Second line of text commences "Nouus Orbis"
1579	Signature 5	Second line of text commences "Orbis Hodie"
		Thirteenth line from bottom commences "ria rerum Atlanticarum"
		The ships are redrawn on the map and are now larger with high poops. The first edition published by Plantin
1584	Signature 5	The thirteenth line from the bottom commences "mentaria rerum"
1589		Quoted by Sabin but no copy apparently known
1591/2	Signature 5	Map corrected and the bulge disappears from the South West coast of South America. Small fleets of ships replace the single ships. The thirteenth line from the bottom commences "rerum Atlanticarum". Fresh names are engraved in Chile
1595	Signature 5	Thirteenth line from the bottom commences "mittet & Postellus Commentaria"

1601	Signature 5	Thirteenth line from bottom commences "Indicis Promittet"
		The last edition published by Ortelius
1603	Signature 5	Thirteenth line from bottom commences "Promittis & Postellus". First line under capital T commences "Atlantis". Published by Vrients
1609		Not seen
1612-1624		Published Moretus. First line under azured T commences "Atlantis descriptam"

Ortelius America—German Text

1572	Signature 2	Die Newe Welt. Text commencing with large white capital D on a black ground. The first German edition
1573	Signature 2	No change
1580	Signature 5	Retains the bulge on South America but the ships are redrawn with high poops, the largest having two pennants. Text commences with a large calligraphic D
1602	Signature 5	Bulge on South America removed. Ships changed from singles to small fleets. Text finishes with 2 columns of names

Ortelius America—English Text

| 1606 | | No signature |
| | | The only edition in English. Text headed "The New World commonly called America" |

Ortelius America—French Text

1572	Signature 2	Text commences with capital letter C with flower motif. Equinoctial line shown in two straight lines. First French edition
1581	Signature 5	Map changed but still retains the bulge in South America. The ships are altered and have high poops. Equinoctial line now marked off in divisions. Text commencing with capital letter C with a design of Cain and Abel. The last line "estant de couleur rousse"
1587	Signature 5	Last line of text "Asne et de la façon bien pres d'un Chameau, estant de couleur rousse"
1598	Signature 5	New map with bulge in South America removed. Fleets of small ships in the Pacific and Atlantic. Text commencing with capital letter C with satyrs. Last line of text commences "nes de la grandeur d'un Asne"

Ortelius America—Dutch Text

1571   Signature 2   South America with bulge. Three ships in Pacific and one in the Atlantic. Last line of text commences "van ghedaente". Though dated 1571 Koeman states that this edition was issued in 1573 or later

1598   Signature 5   New map; bulge removed and names altered. Decorated scale of miles inserted at the top of map. Solomon Islands inserted. Fleets of ships replace single vessels

Ortelius America—Spanish Text

1588   Signature 5   El Orbe Nuevo. South America corrected to have no bulge. Solomon Islands shown and map dated 1587. Second line of text commences "mado"

1593?   Not recorded by Koeman

1602   Signature 5   Second line of text commences "Orbe"

1612   Last Spanish Edition. (Not seen)

Ortelius America—Italian Text

1608   Signature 5   South America has no bulge. The first Italian edition

1612   Signature 5   No change

Ortelius Pacific

1590   Latin Text   First appeared in 1590 Latin Additamentum. "Maris Pacifico (quod vulgo Mar del Zur . . . 1589) (Number 19 in Additamentum but not marked)

1591   German Text

1592   Latin Text
        Signature 6   Last line commences "habitantes mutuo"

1595   Latin Text
        Signature 6   Last line commences "novum ante"

1598   Latin Text   No change

1598   French Text
        Signature 6   Last line commences "peult veoir auxtables icy mises"

1598   Dutch Text

1601   Latin Text
        Signature 6   Last line commences "ex Limano portu"

1602   German Text
        Signature 6   Heading: Das stille Meer oder del Zur. Last line underschendt Orkennen

1603	Latin Text	
	Signature 6	Last line commences "Classe ex Limano" with a footnote on right margin
1606	English Text	
	No signature	The only edition in English
1608	Italian Text	
	Signature 5	
1612	Italian Text	No change
1612	Latin Text	
	Signature 6	No footnote in margin. Last line commences "Habitantes mutuo accepisse"
1612-24	Moretus edition	
	Signature 6	Footnote on righthand margin. Last line commences "classe ex Limano"

Ortelius Tartary

1574	Latin Text	Tartariae sive Magni Chami Regni Typus
	Signature 62	Last line commences "Gregoras alias scriptor Graecus"
1575	Latin Text	
	Signature 62	Last line commences "locis multa"
1579	Latin Text	
	Signature 83	Last line "Scytharium te"
1580	German Text	
1581	French Text	
1584	Latin Text	
	Signature 92	
1587	French Text	
1592	Latin Text	
	Signature 100	Last line "multa ut te"
1595	Latin Text	
	Signature 105	Last line "in Saxoniae Chronico"
1598	French Text	
	Signature 106	Last line "eux memes on lasque Tartariques"
1598	Dutch Text	
1601	Latin Text	
	Signature 105	Last line "ius itinerarum"
1602	Spanish Text	
1602	German Text	Tartaria oder des grossen Chams herzschaft
	Signature 106	Text commencing with calligraphic W. Last line "scher scribent"
1606	English Text	Signature headed Tartaria or the Empire of the Mightie Chams
1612	Latin Text	
	Signature 100	Last line commences "multa ut gregoras alius scriptor Graecus"

1612-24 Latin Text
Signature 108   Last line commences "rarium hic partibus"

THE PLATES

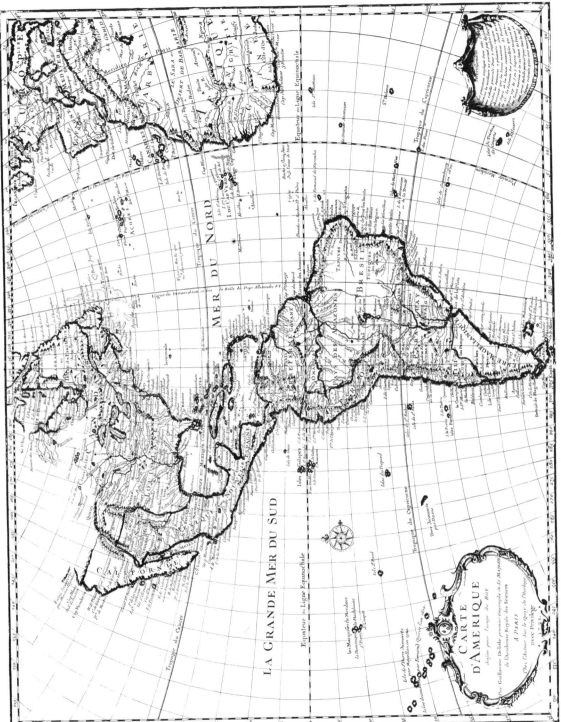

Plate 1   No. 2.   G. De l'Isle, America, 1722.

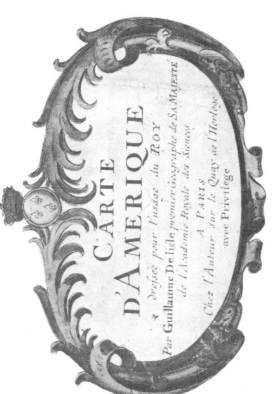

No. 3.

No. 5.

No. 2.

No. 4.

Plate 2   G. De l'Isle, America.
Variations of cartouches.

AMERICA ACCURATE IN IMPERIA, REGNA, STATUS & POPULOS DIVISA, AD USUM LUDOVICI XV. GALLIARUM REGIS.

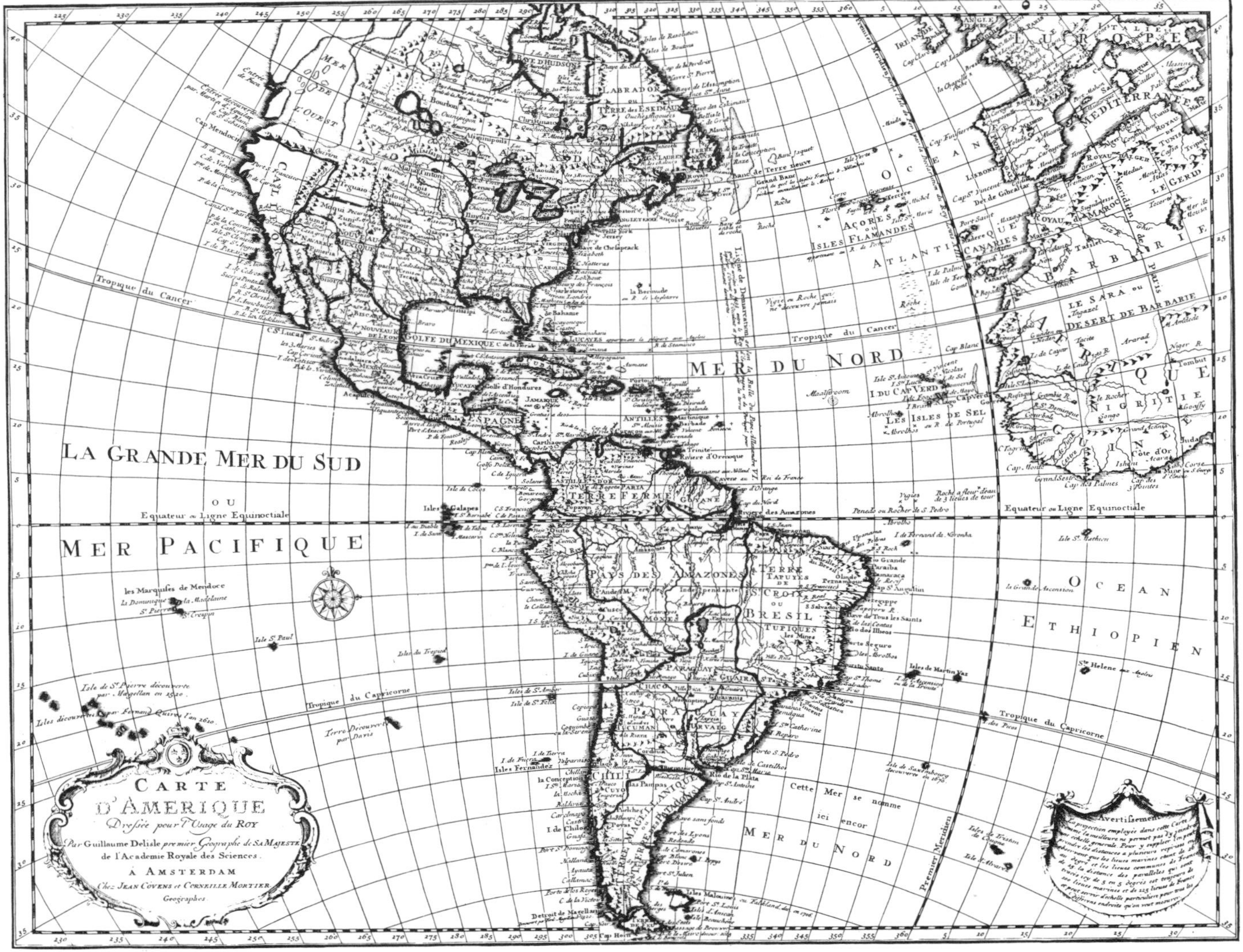

Plate 3 No. 6. G. De l'Isle, America, Covens & Mortier [1755].

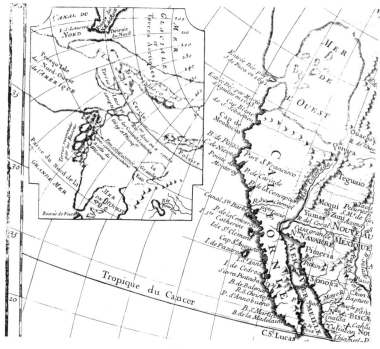

No. 7.

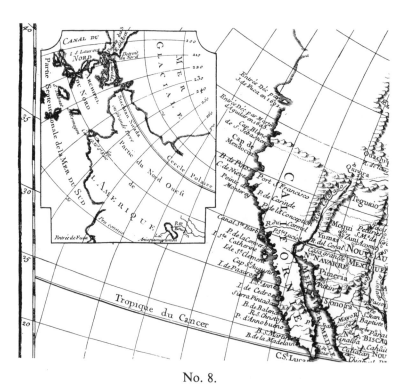

No. 8.

Plate 4   G. De l'Isle, America.   Details of N.W. America.

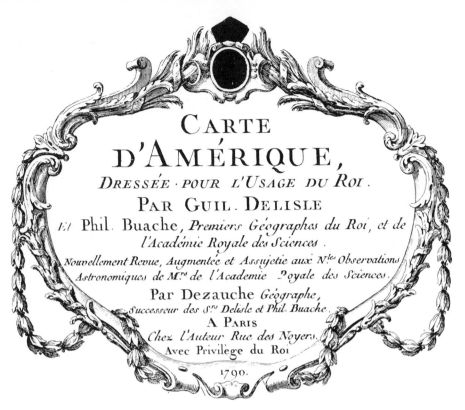

CARTE
D'AMÉRIQUE,
DRESSÉE·POUR L'USAGE DU ROI.
PAR GUIL. DELISLE
Et Phil. Buache, Premiers Géographes du Roi, et de
l'Académie Royale des Sciences.
Nouvellement Revue, Augmentée et Assujetie aux N.les Observations
Astronomiques de M.rs de l'Académie Royale des Sciences.
Par Dezauche Géographe,
Successeur des S.rs Delisle et Phil. Buache.
A PARIS
Chez l'Auteur Rue des Noyers.
Avec Privilège du Roi
1790.

No. 12.

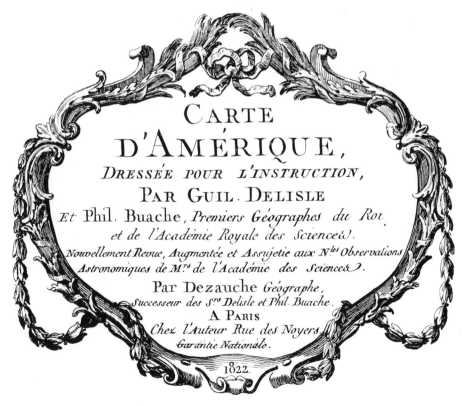

CARTE
D'AMÉRIQUE,
DRESSÉE POUR L'INSTRUCTION,
PAR GUIL. DELISLE
Et Phil. Buache, Premiers Géographes du Roi,
et de l'Académie Royale des Sciences.
Nouvellement Revue, Augmentée et Assujetie aux N.les Observations
Astronomiques de M.rs de l'Académie des Sciences.
Par Dezauche Géographe,
Successeur des S.rs Delisle et Phil. Buache.
A PARIS
Chez l'Auteur Rue des Noyers.
Garantie Nationale.
1822.

No. 18.

Plate 5   G. De l'Isle, America.   Details of the cartouche.

CARTE
D'AMERIQUE
DIVISÉE EN SES PRINCIPALES PARTIES.
par G. DELISLE premier Geographe du Roy.
Rectifiée après les nouvelles Observations
du S.r D'ANVILLE et autres Geographes.
A AMSTERDAM
Chez C.ie COVENS & MORTIER, & COVENS Junior.
1774

Plate 6   No. 20.   De l'Isle-D'Anville, America, 1774.

Plate 7   No. 22.   G. De l'Isle, Western Hemisphere, 1724.

Plate 8   No. 25.   G. De l'Isle, Western Hemisphere, 1760.

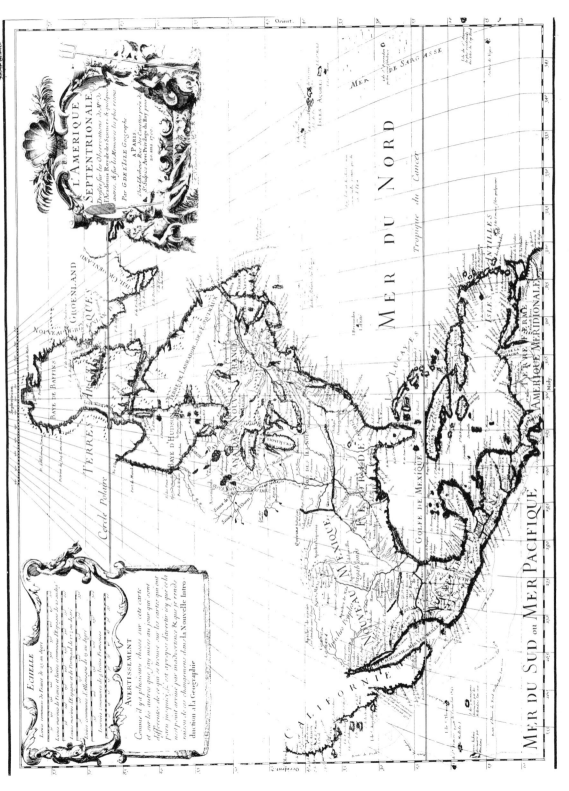

Plate 9   No. 28.   G. De l'Isle, N. America, 1700.

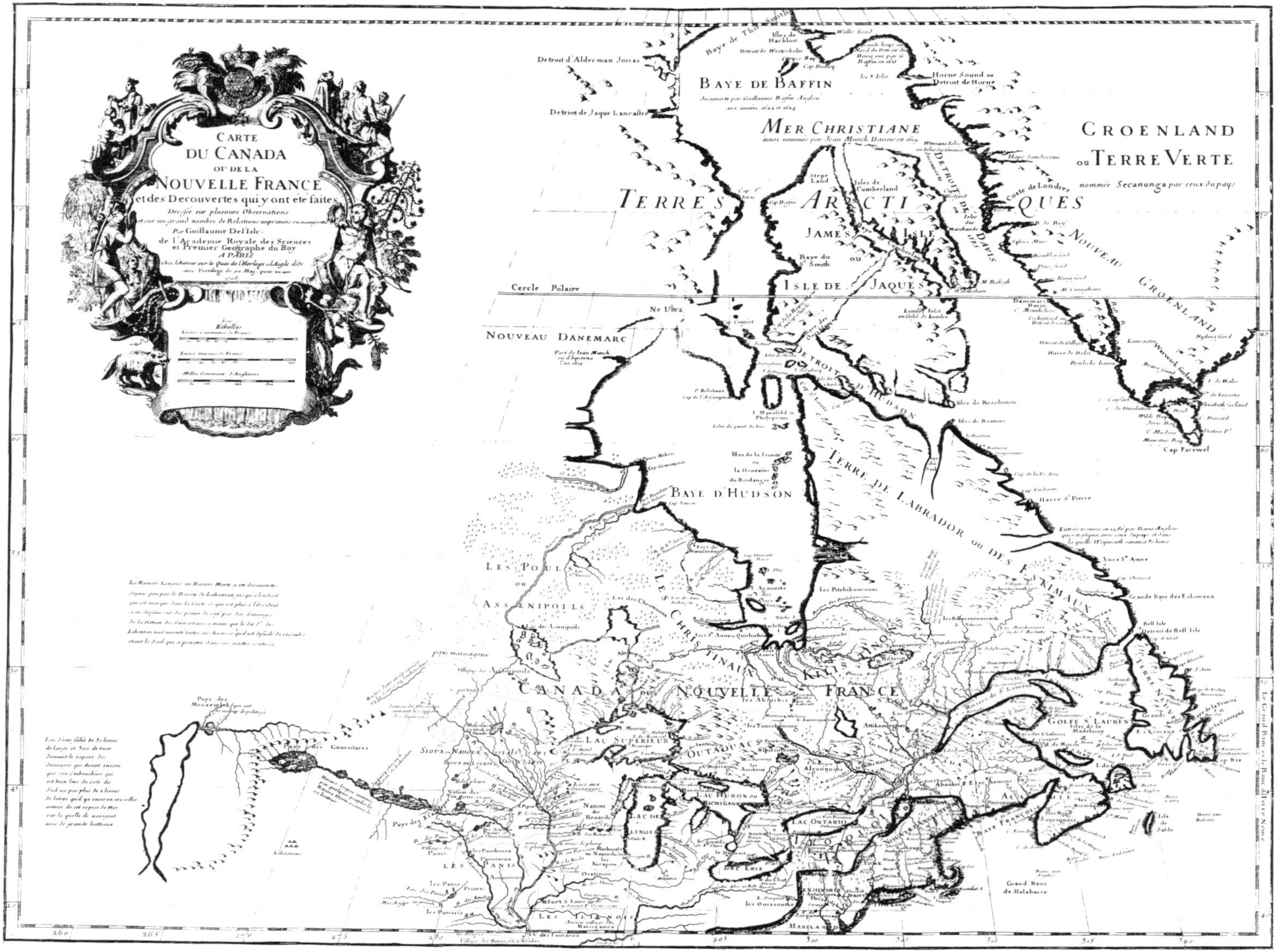

Le Grand Banc ou le Banc deTerre Neuve

GROENLAND
ou TERRE VERTE
ainsi nommée de Leandrs, nommée Secanunga par ceux du pays

MER CHRISTIANE
ainsi nommée par Jean Munck Danois en 1619

ARCTIQUES

TERRES

NOUVEAU DANEMARC

Cercle Polaire

Ne Ultra

BAYE DE BAFFIN

ISLE DE JAQUES

JAMES
ou
Baye du
Sund

DETROIT DE HUDSON

BAYE D'HUDSON

TERRE DE LABRADOR ou DES ESKIMAUX

CANADA

NOUVELLE FRANCE

LES CHRISTINAUX

LES POU

ASSINIPOILS

CARTE
DU CANADA
OU DE LA
NOUVELLE FRANCE
et des Decouvertes qui y ont ete faites
Dressée sur plusieurs Observations
Par Guillaume DeLisle
de l'Academie Royale des Sciences
et Premier Geographe du Roy

Echelle

Plate 10   No. 38.   G. De l'Isle, Canada [1708].

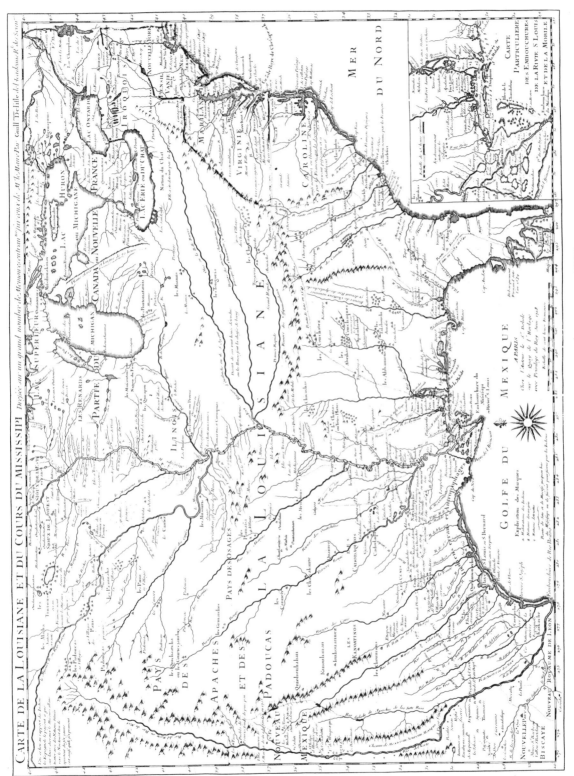

Plate 11   No. 43.   G. De l'Isle, Louisiana, 1718.

Plate 12   No. 52.   G. De l'Isle, Mexico & Florida 1745

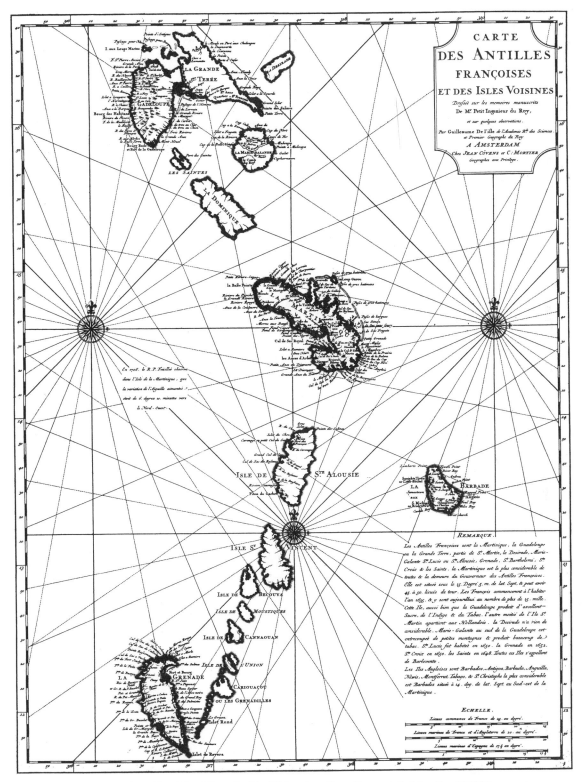

Plate 13   No. 55.   G. De l'Isle, Antilles, Covens & Mortier [1730].

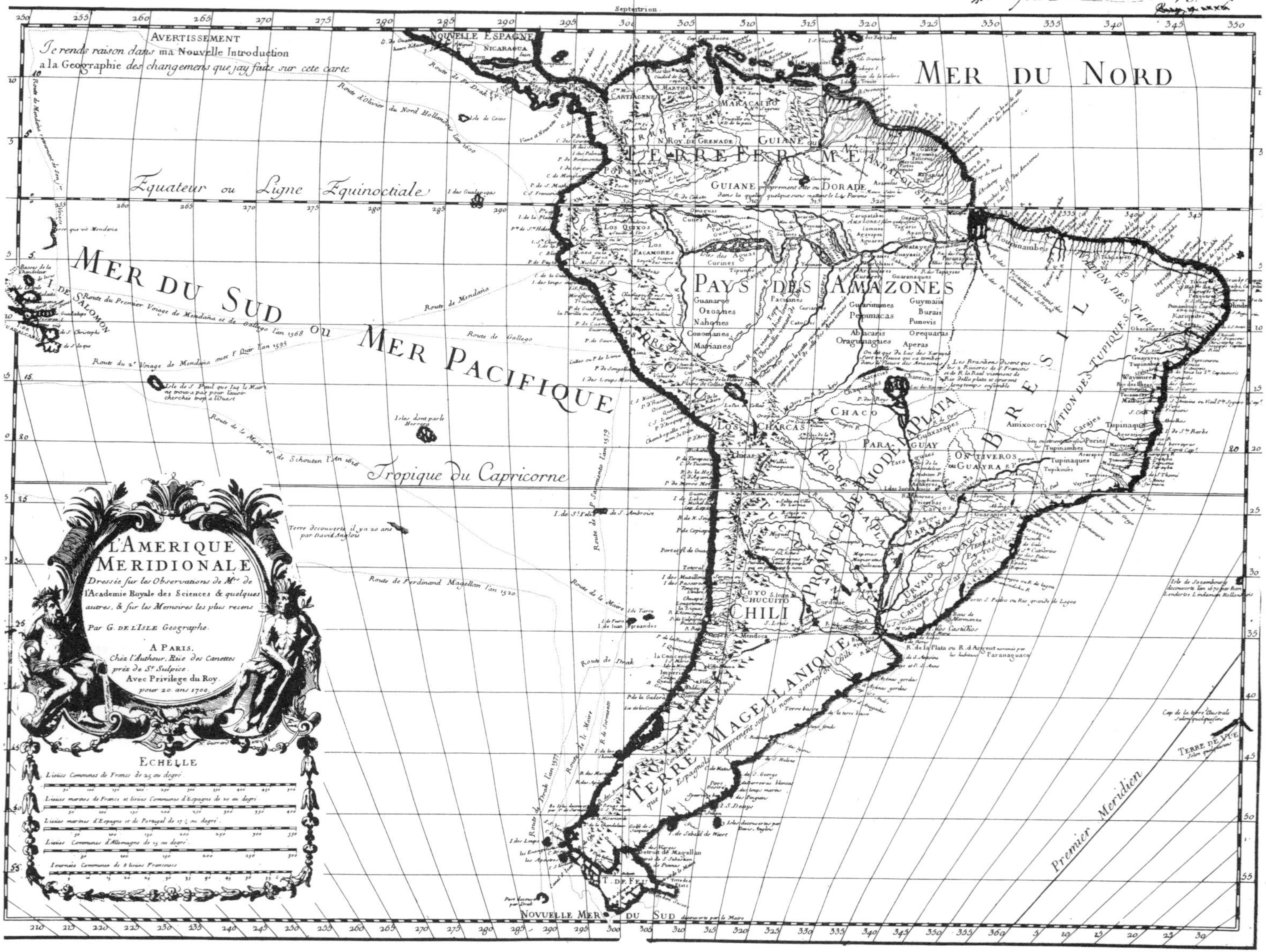

Septentrion
AVERTISSEMENT
Je rends raison dans ma Nouvelle Introduction a la Geographie des changemens que jay faits sur cete carte
MER DU NORD
MER DU SUD ou MER PACIFIQUE
Equateur ou Ligne Equinoctiale
Tropique du Capricorne
Premier Meridien
NOUVELLE ESPAGNE
NICARAGUA
CARTAGENE
MARACAIBO
N. ROY. DE GRENADE
TERRE FERME
GUIANE
GUIANE proprement dite ou DORADE
POPAYAN
LOS QUIXOS
LOS PACAMORES
PAYS DES AMAZONES
BRESIL
NATION DES TAPUIES
NATION DES TUPIQUES
CHACO
LOS CHARCAS
PARAGUAY
PROVINCE DE RIO DE LA PLATA
TUCUMAN
CUYO
CHUCUITO
CHILI
TERRE MAGELLANIQUE
T. DE FEU
NOUVELLE MER DU SUD
I. DE SALOMON
TERRE DE VUE
L'AMERIQUE MERIDIONALE
Dressée sur les Observations de Mrs de l'Academie Royale des Sciences & quelques autres, & sur les Memoires les plus recens
Par G. DE L'ISLE Geographe.
A PARIS,
Chez l'Autheur, Rüe des Canettes prez de St. Sulpice.
Avec Privilege du Roy pour 20. ans 1700.
ECHELLE

Plate 14 No. 63. G. De l'Isle, S. America, 1700.

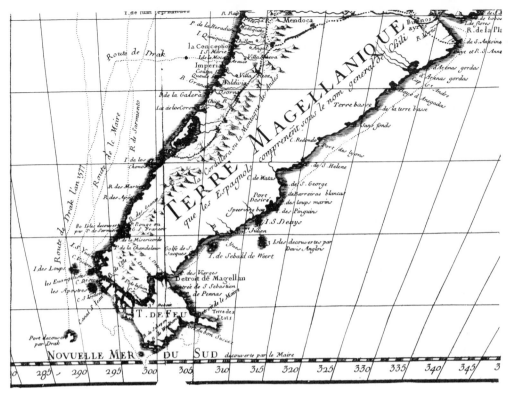

No. 63.

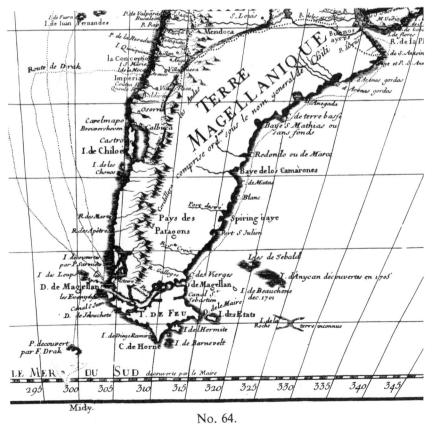

No. 64.

Plate 15   G. De l'Isle, S. America, Details of Magellanica.

Plate 16   No. 80.   G. De l'Isle, Paraguay etc. [1718].

CARTE
DE LA TERRE FERME
DU PEROU, DU BRESIL
ET DU PAYS DES AMAZONES

Dressée sur les Descriptions de Herrera,
de Laet, et des PP. d'Acuña, et M. Rodriguez
et sur plusieurs Relations et
Observations postérieures

Par Guillaume Del'Isle Premier Geogra-
du Roy de l'Academie Royale des Sciences

A PARIS

Chez l'Auteur sur le Quai de l'Horloge
a l'Aigle d'or   avec Privilege du Roy·
pour 20. ans 1703·

No. 73

CARTE
DE LA TERRE FERME
DU PEROU, DU BRESIL
ET DU PAYS DES AMAZONES

Dressée sur les Descriptions de Herrera,
de Laet, et de, PP. d'Acuña, et M. Rodriguez
et sur plusieurs Relations et
Observations postérieures

Par Guillaume Del'Isle Geographe
de l'Academie Royale des Sciences

A PARIS

Chez l'Auteur Rue-des Canettes pres
de S.t Sulpice avec Privilege du Roy
pour 20. ans 1703.

No. 70

CARTE
DU PIEMONT et du MONFERRAT

Dressée sur plusieurs Cartes Manuscrites ou Imprimées

Rectifiées par quelques Observations

Par Guillaume DeL'Isle de l'Academie Royale des Sciences

A Paris

Chez l'Auteur sur le Quai de l'Horloge
a la Couronne de Diamans

avec Privilege
Avril 1707.

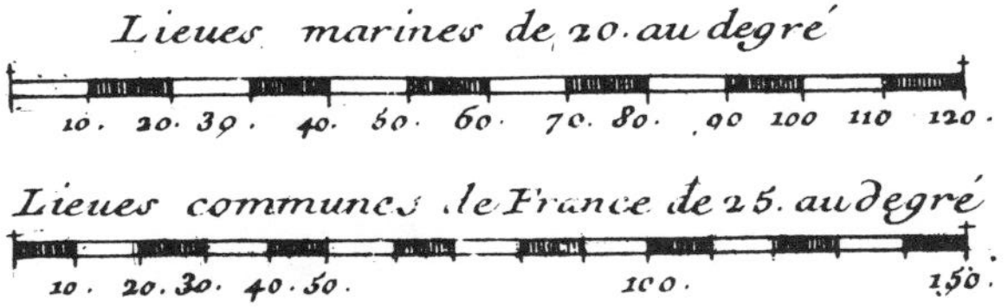

Lieues marines de 20. au degré
10. 20. 30. 40. 50. 60. 70. 80. 90. 100 110 120.

Lieues communes de France de 25. au degré
10. 20. 30. 40. 50.   100.   150.

A Paris Chez l'Auteur sur le Quai de l'Horloge
a la Couronne de Diamans, avec Privilege Aout 1707.
et se trouve a Amsterdam chez L. Renard Libraire
prez de la Bourse

Imprint on map of Guinea.

Plate 17   G. De l'Isle.   Details of imprints.

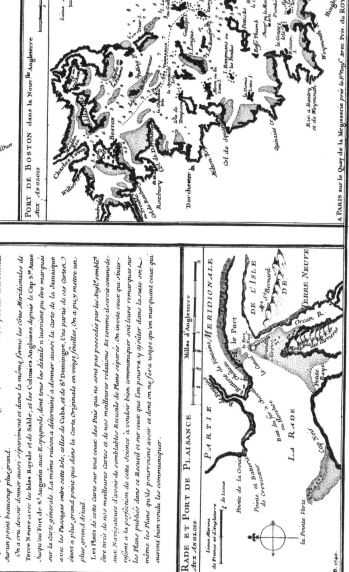

Plate 18   No. 94.   Buache, Plans, Rades et Ports, 1740-1.

Plate 19   No. 97.   Buache, Considerations, map 7.

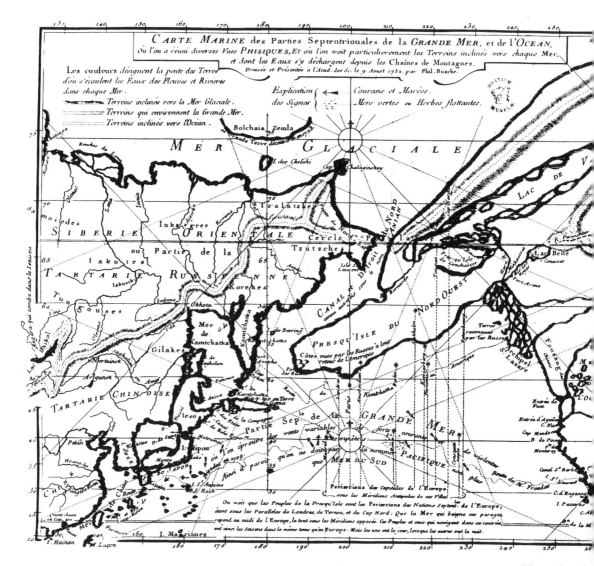

Plate 19 No

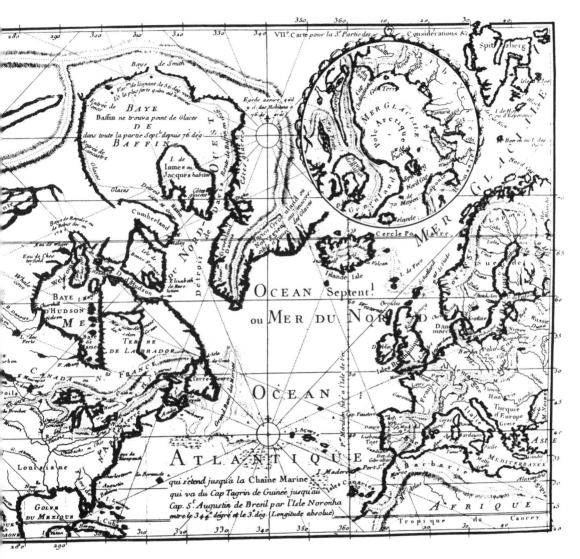

VIIe Carte pour la 3.e Partie des .... Considerations &c^a

MER GLACIALE

Pole Arctique

MER GLACIALE

Spitzberg

Isle de Cloe

Cercle Po. Marc

Baye de Smith

Var.^{on} de l'aymant de 56 deg vers l'O la plus forte qu'on ait ê connue

Entrée de Simon

BAYE

Baffin ne trouva point de Glaces
DE
dans toute la partie Sept.^{le} depuis 76 deg

BAFFIN

E de de nature qu'il y a des Habitans a 76 deg

Espece de Lancastre

I. de Iames ou Jacques habite

Glaces

Cumberland

Détroit de Davis

Côtes glacées

Bayes de Repuls de le Rebut dec en 1743

Islande Isle

OCEAN Septent.

ou **MER DU NORD**

Danemarc

Isles Britanniques

OCEAN

Suede

Lapon

ATLANTIQUE

qui s'etend jusqu'à la Chaine Marine
qui va du Cap Tagrin de Guinée jusqu'au
Cap. St Augustin de Bresil par l'Isle Noronha
entre le 344.e degré et le 3.e deg. (Longitude absolue)

Golfe du Mexique

Louisiane

CANADA

Baye D'Hudson

Terre de Labrador

Nouvelle France

Tropique du Cancer

AFRIQUE

ASIE

che, Considerations, map 7.

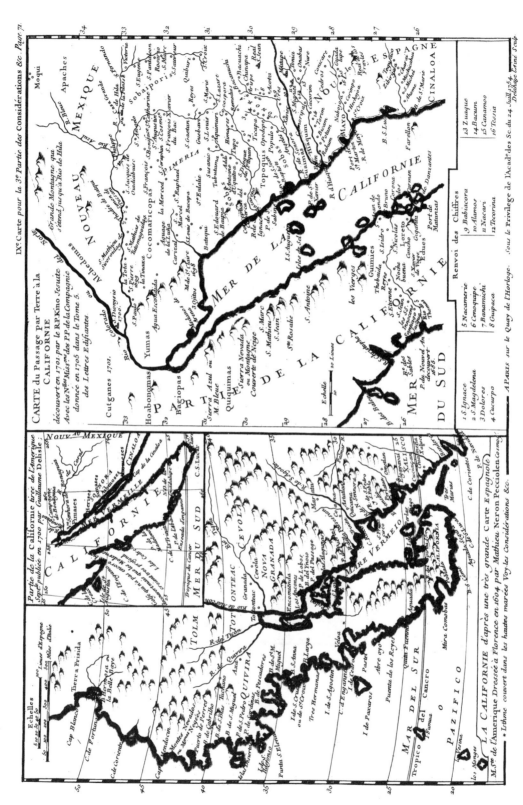

Plate 20   No. 97.   Buache, Considerations, map 9.

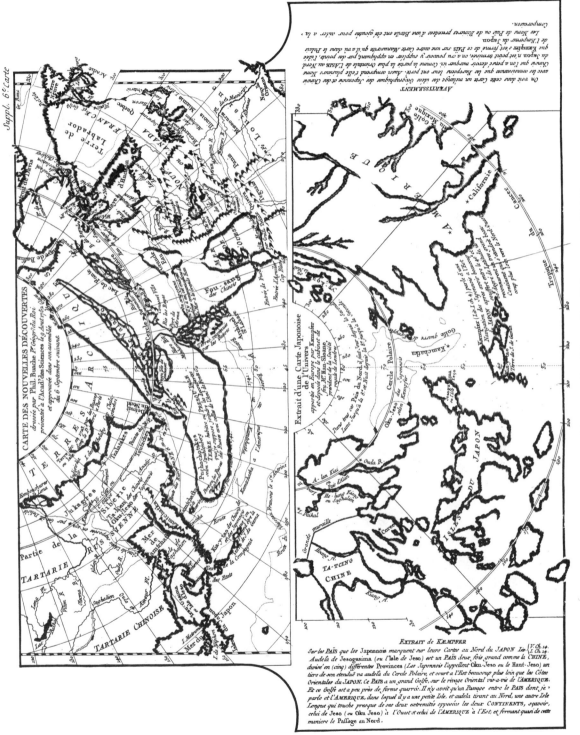

Plate 21 No. 98. Buache, Nouvelles Découvertes [1779].

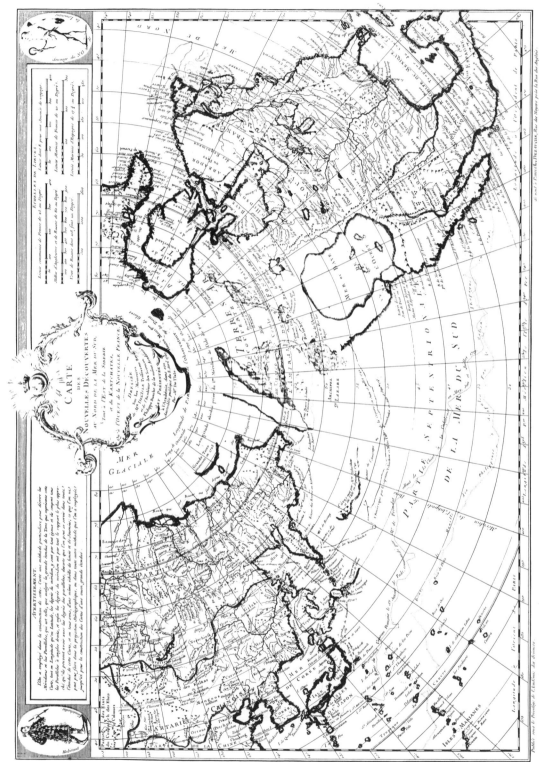

Plate 22   No. 105.   J. N. De l'Isle, Cartes des Nouvelles Découvertes [1780].

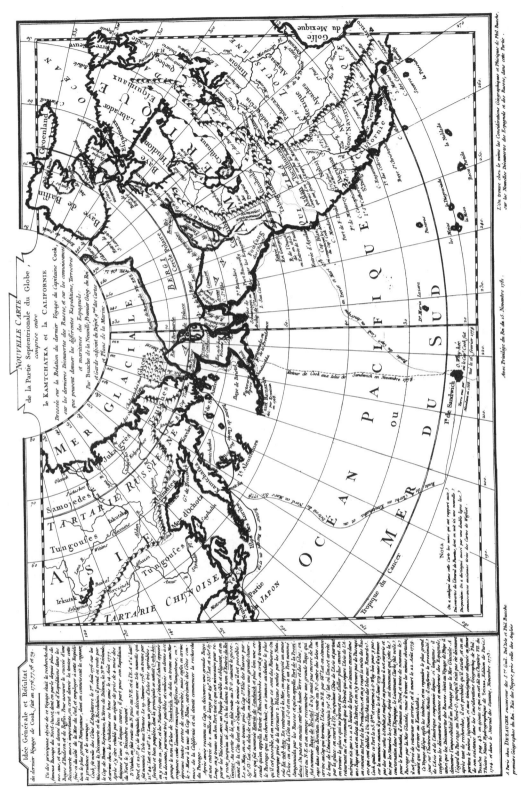

Plate 23   No. 112.   Buache de la Neuville, Partie Sept. du globe, [1782].

ATLAS

NOUVEAU,
CONTENANT TOUTES
LES PARTIES DU
MONDE,

Ou font exactement Remarquées les

EMPIRES,
MONARCHIES,
ROYAUMES,

Etats, Republiques &c.

Par Guillaume de l'Ifle.

Premier Géographe de fa Majefté.

A AMSTERDAM,

Chez JEAN CÔVENS & CORNEILLE MORTIER.
fur le Vygendam.

MDCCXXXIII.

Plate 24 Atlas Nouveau, Amsterdam, 1733.

ATLAS

GÉOGRAPHIQUE

DES QUATRE PARTIES

DU MONDE

PAR

GUILLAUME DE L'ISLE

ET

PHIL. BUACHE

Premiers Géographes

De L'Académie des Sciences

Faits pour les Géographies Elémentaires de M.ʳˢ BUACHE

Et de l'Abbé NICOLLE de la CROIX.

REVU ET AUGMENTÉ PAR DEZAUCHE.

A PARIS,

Chez DEZAUCHE *Géographe Successeur et Possesseur du Fond Géographique des*

S.ʳˢ De l'Isle *et* Buache; *Et Chargé de l'Entrepôt général des* Cartes de la

Marine Nationale

Rue des Noyers près celle des Anglois

AVEC PRIVILEGE D'AUTEUR

Plate 25   Dezauche, Atlas Géographique.

Plate 26   No. 1.   [Briggs], 1625.

OCEANVS IAPONICVS

The North Part of AMERICA

Conteyning Newfoundland new England: Virginia, Florida, new Spaine, and
Noua Fransia, with the Iles of Bermuda: Cuba, Iamaica, and Porto Rico: with the South
land aspers, to the vpp Californ. and further of
of California. The Ilands of the north
Pacifick Ocean: on & South and West Iles: south
and Buttons: haue a faire entrance by North Freten Hudson
and most temperate passage to Iapon & China.

AMERICA SEPTENTRIONALIS

NOVA BRITANNIA

Hudsons bay

BUTTONS BAIE

Canada

Urginia

Florida

GRANADA

NEWE SPAINE

Mexico

CALIFORNIA

PARTE OF GROENLAND

Freten Dauis

Freten Hudson

CUBA

Summers Ilands

California, sometymes suppored to be a part of ye westerne continent,
but since by a Spanish Charte taken by ye Hollanders it is found to be
a goodly Iland: the length of ye west Ilmarck being about 500 leagues
from Cape S. Lucas to the ould Cape called Cape Mendocino
as appeareth both by that Spanish Chart and by the relation of Francis
Gaule, whereas in the ordinarie Charts it is set downe to be 1700 leagues.

R. Elstracke sculpsit.

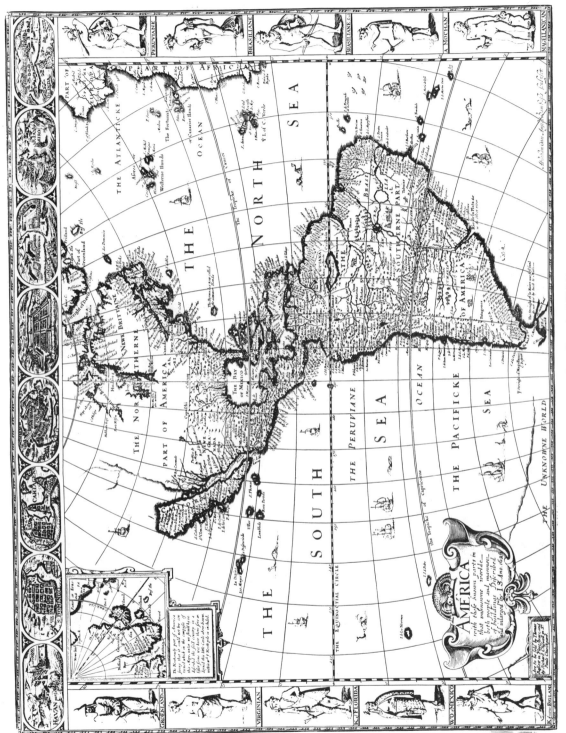

Plate 27   No. 2.   Speed, 1626-7.

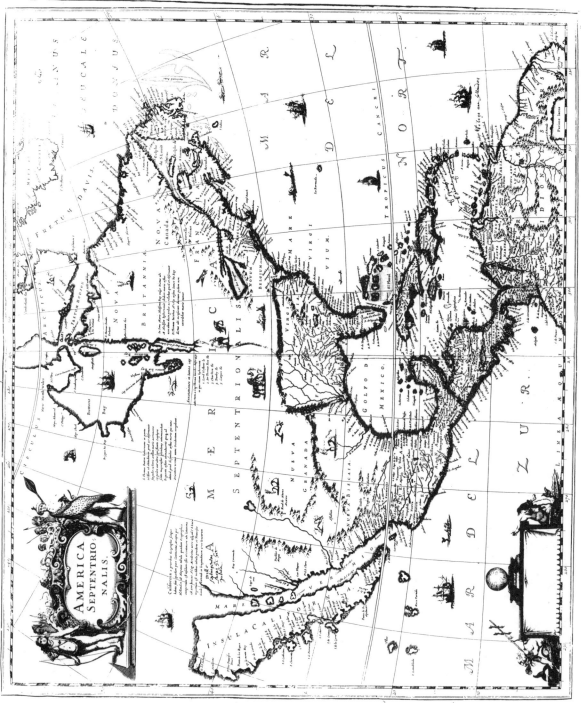

Plate 28 No. 6. Jansson [1638].

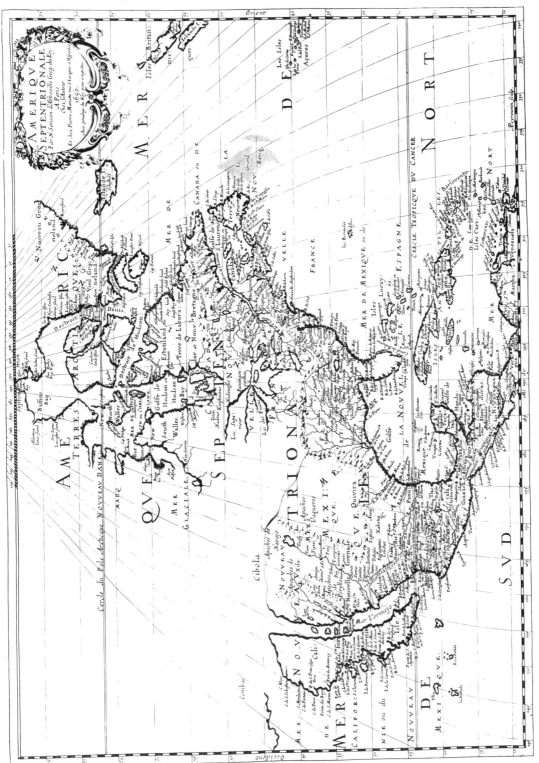

Plate 29   No. 7.   Sanson, 1650.

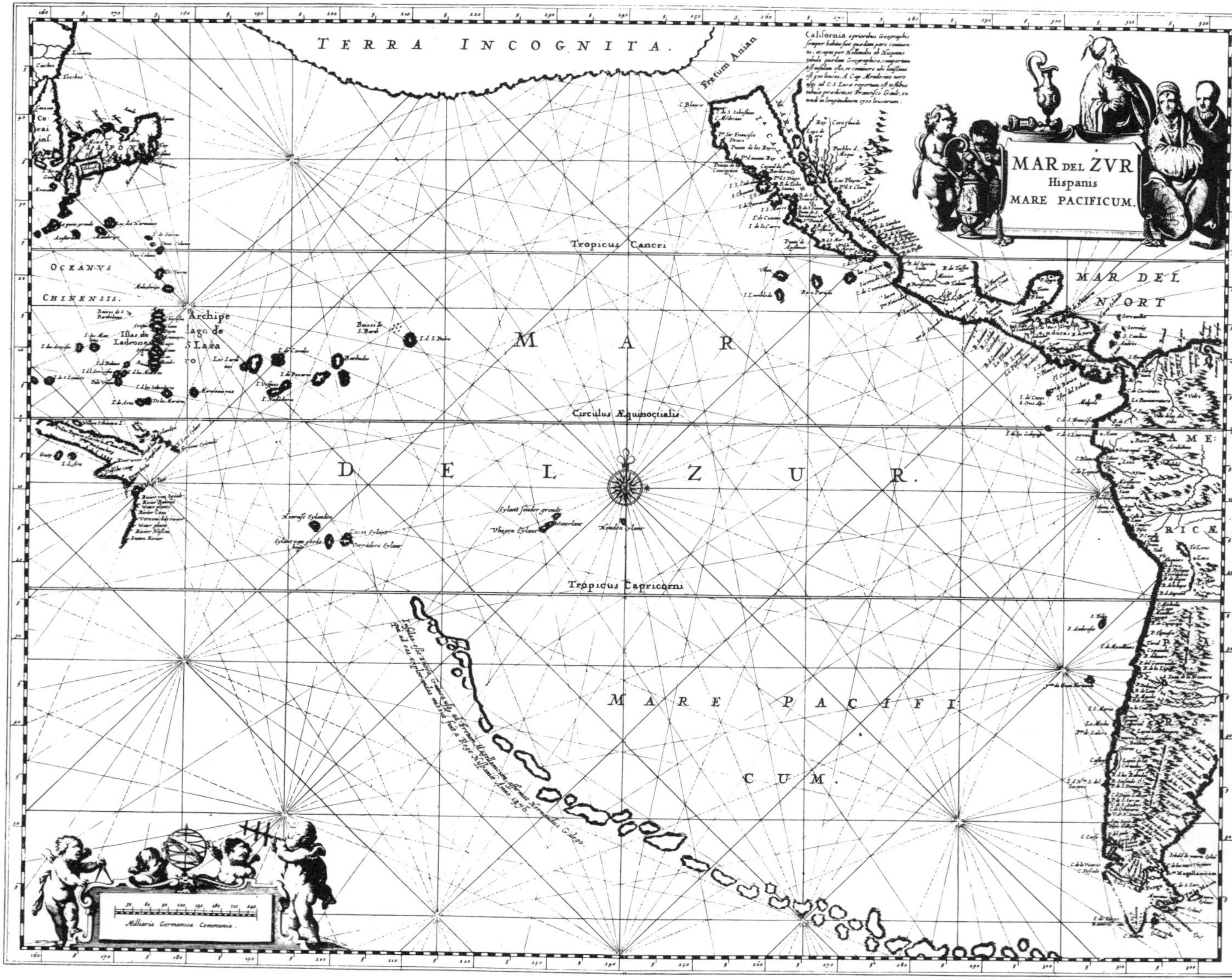

Plate 30 No. 10. Janson [1650].

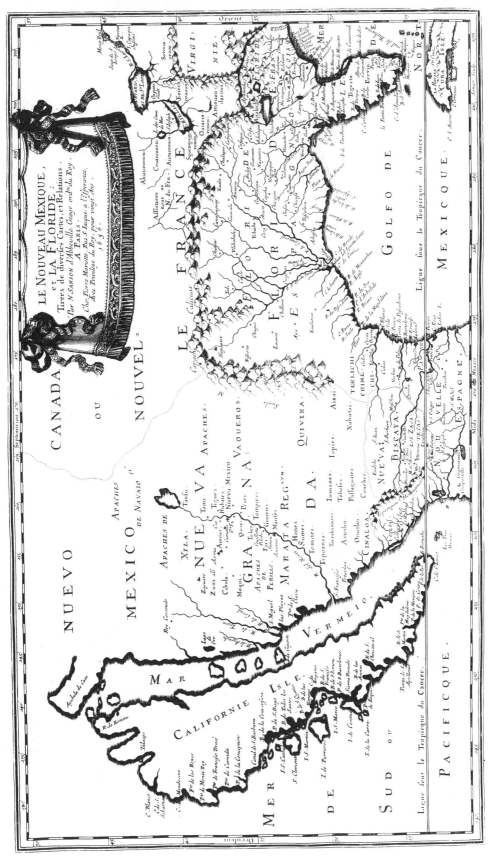

Plate 31   No. 14.   Sanson, 1656.

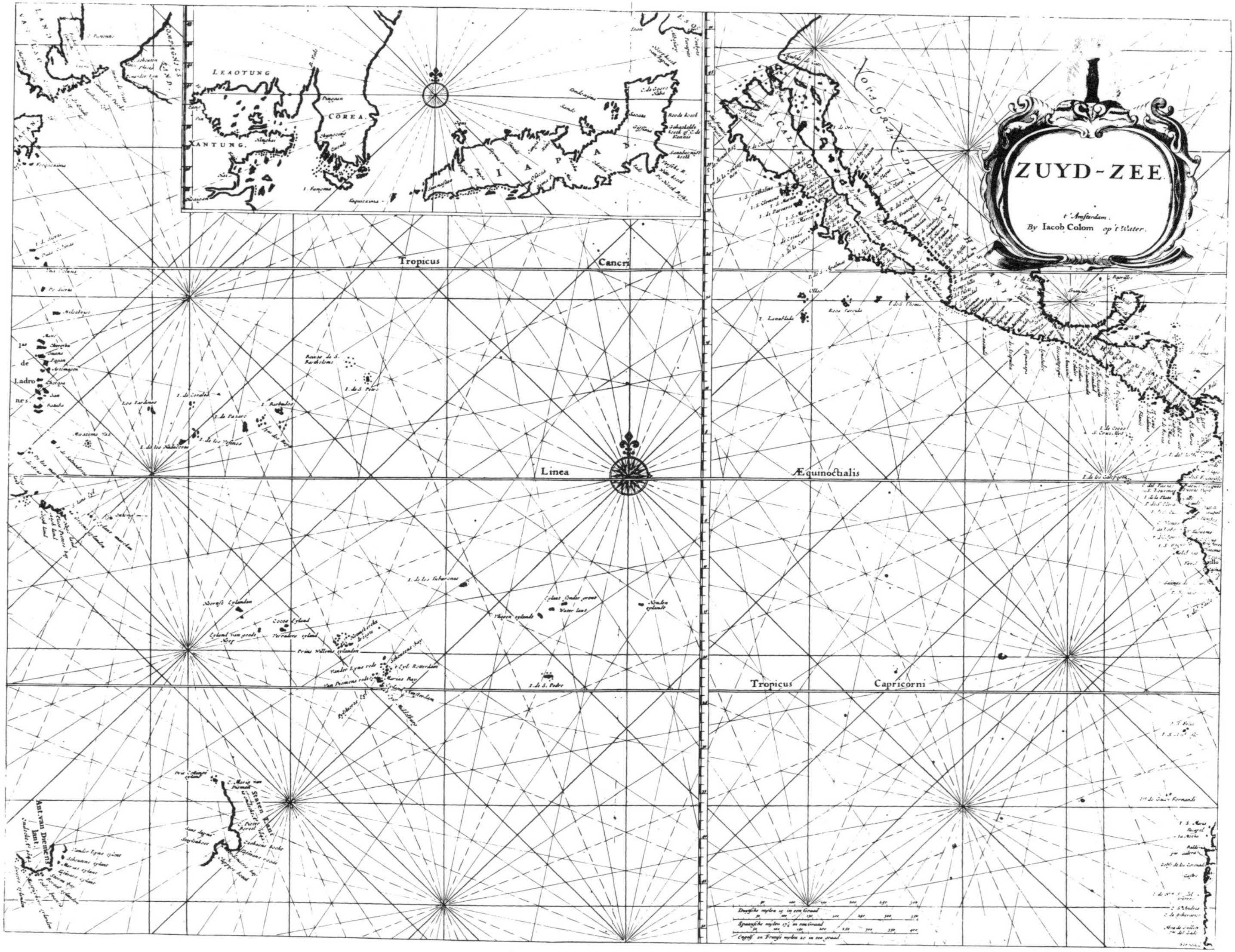

ZUYD-ZEE

t' Amsterdam
By Iacob Colom op t' Water.

Plate 32   No. 16.   Colom [1656]

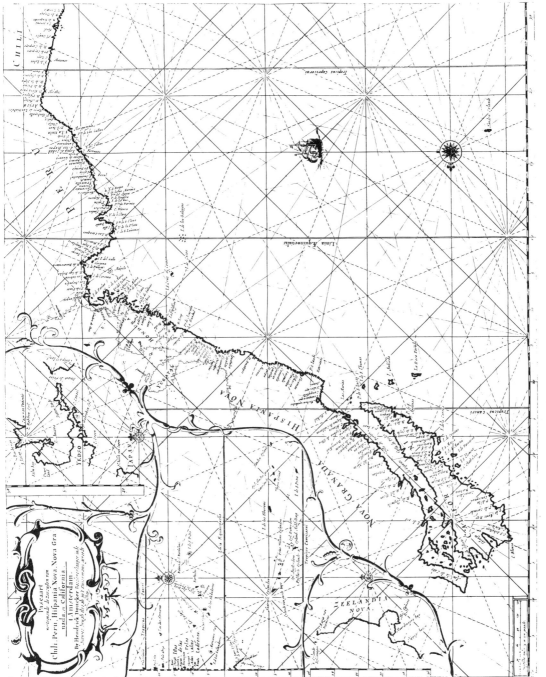

Plate 33   No. 17.   Doncker [1659].

Plate 34   No. 18.   Wit [1660].

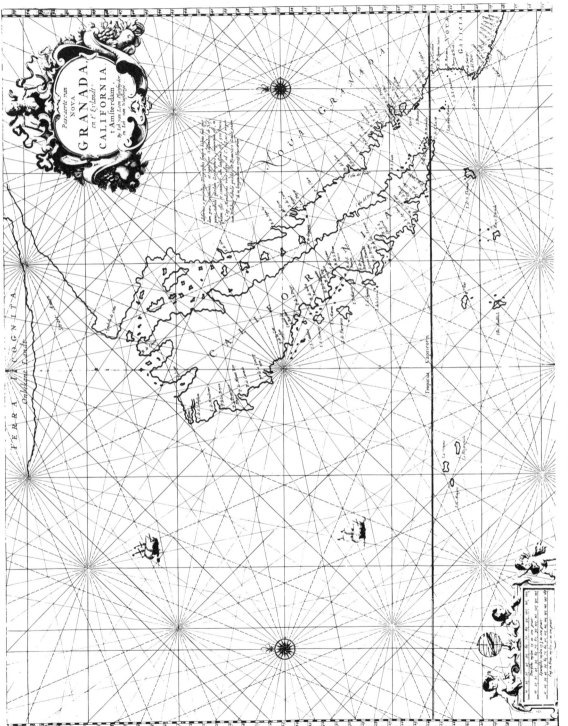

Plate 35   No. 19.   van Loon [1661].

Plate 36 No. 20. Du Val, 1664.

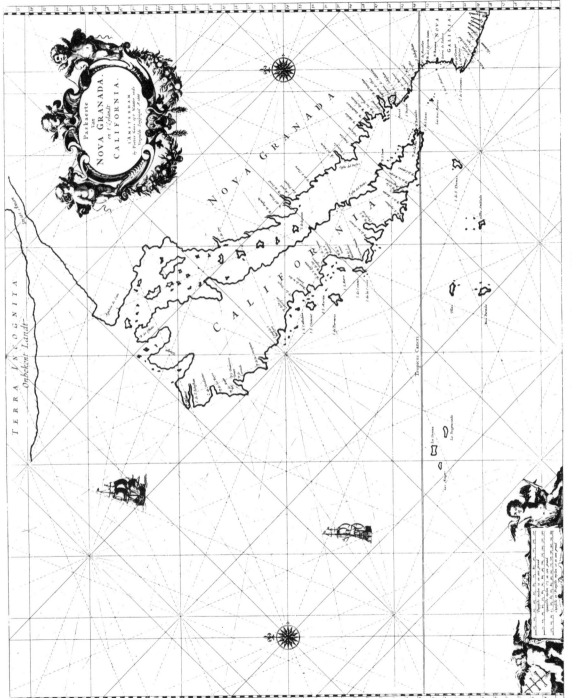

Plate 37   No. 22.   Goos, 1666.

Plate 38   No. 23.   Hollar, 1666.

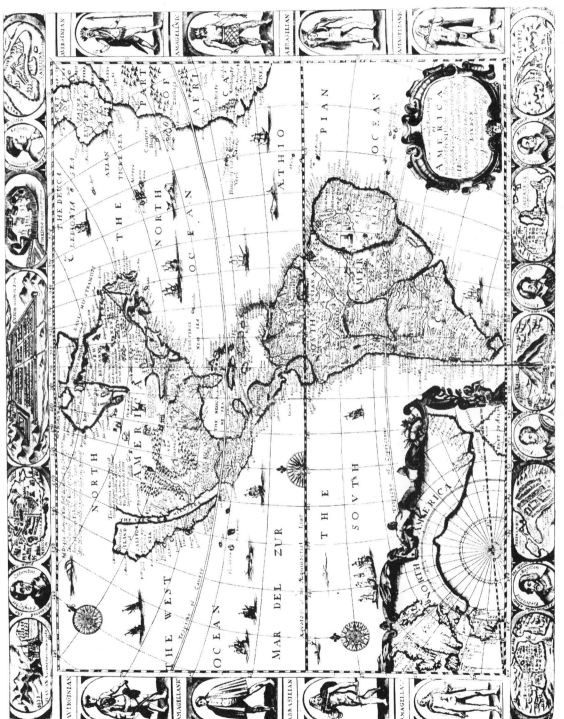

Plate 39   No. 24.   Overton, 1668.

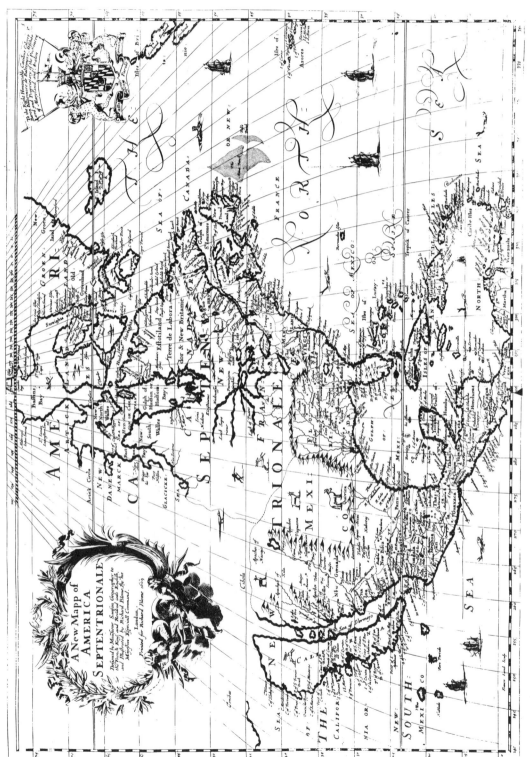

A New Mapp of AMERICA SEPTENTRIONALE

Plate 40   No. 26.   Blome, 1669.

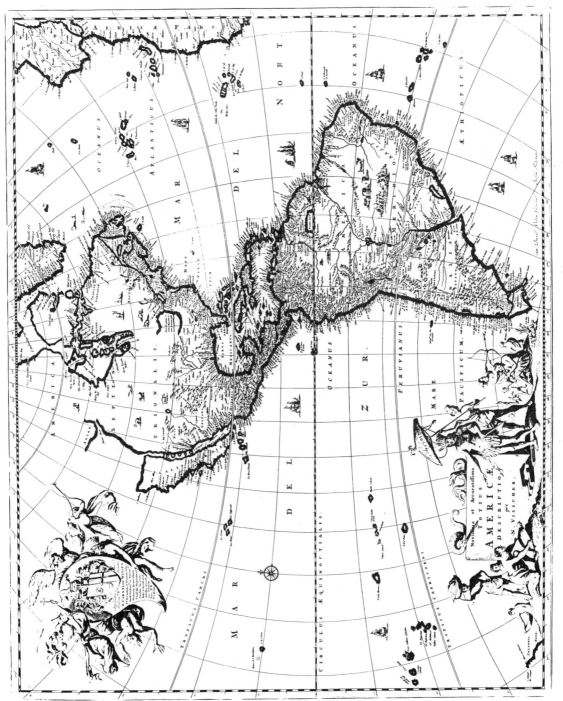

Plate 41   No. 29.   Visscher

Plate 42   No. 35.   Ogilby [1671].

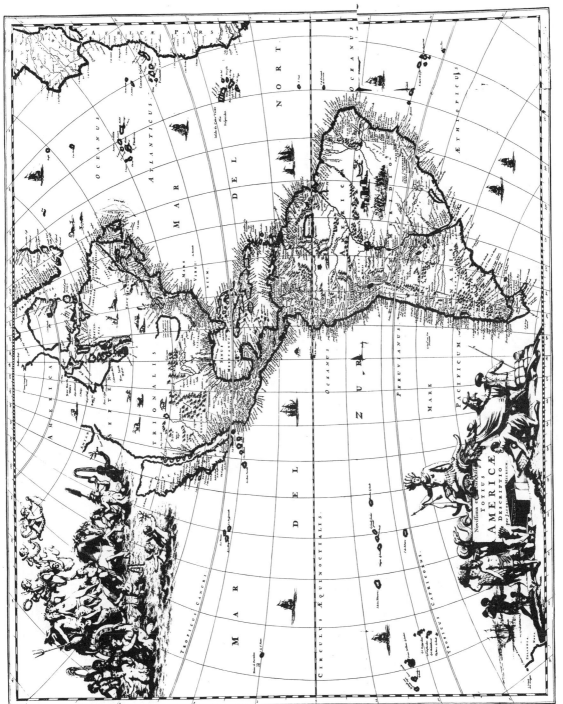

Plate 43   No. 36.   Meursius, 1671-73

L'AMERIQUE SEPTENTRIONALE DIVISÉE EN SES PRINCIPALES PARTIES, savoir: LES TERRES ARCTICQUES, LE CANADA, ou NOUVELLE FRANCE, LE MEXIQUE, ou NOUVELLE ESPAGNE, LE NOUVEAU MEXIQUE, LES ISLES DE TERRE NEUVE, DE CALIFORNIE, et ANTILLES ou SONT DISTINGUÉS LES UNS DES AUTRES LES ESTATS COMME ILS SONT POSSEDÉS PRESENTEMENT PAR LES FRANÇOIS, CASTILLANS, ANGLOIS, SUEDOIS, DANOIS, et PAR LES ESTATS GENERAUX DES PROVINCES VNIES ou HOLLANDOIS. Tiré des Relations de toutes ces Nations. Paris. Chez son Geographe ordinaire du Roy 1674.

OCEAN SEPTENTRIONAL

OCEAN ATLANTIQUE

MER DE NORT

TERRES ARCTIQUES

CANADA ou NOUVELLE FRANCE

MER DE CANADA ou MER GLACÉE

Baffins Bay

Hudson Bay

Nouveau Danemarca

MER GLACIALE

GRONELANDE

NOUVEAU GRONELANDE

ISLE DE ICARIE

ISLES BRITANNIQUE

Premier Meridien

ISLES AÇORES

Isles Bermudes

MER DE NORT

ISLES CARIBES

ISLES LUCAYES

MER ATLANTIQUE ou DE NOUVELLE ESPAGNE

MER DES ANTILLES

GOLFE DE MEXIQUE

FLORIDE

Cercle du Tropique du Cancer

NOUVEAU MEXIQUE

MEXIQUE

APACHES VAQUEROS

APACHES DE NAVAJO

NOUVELLE BISCAYE

MER VERMEIO ou MER ROUGE

ISLE DE CALIFORNIE

NOUVELLE ALBION

MER DE CALIFORNIE

MER DE SUD

AMERIQUE MERIDIONALE

TERRE DE IESSO

MER DE IESSO

Estotiland

Terre de Labrador ou Nouvelle Bretagne

Cercle du Pole Arctique

Orient

Occident

AMERIQUE SEPTENTRIONALE divisé en ses principales parties, ou sont distingués les vns des autres LES ESTATS suivant qu'ils appartienent presentement aux FRANÇOIS, CASTILLANS, ANGLOIS, SUEDOIS DANOIS HOLLANDOIS. Tiré des Relations de toutes ces Nations. Par le Sr Sanson Geographe ordinaire du Roy PRESENTÉ A MONSEIGNEUR LE DAUPHIN. Par une teuille de son Geographe et par Hubert Jaillot.

Plate 44   No. 37.   Sanson-Jaillot, 1674.

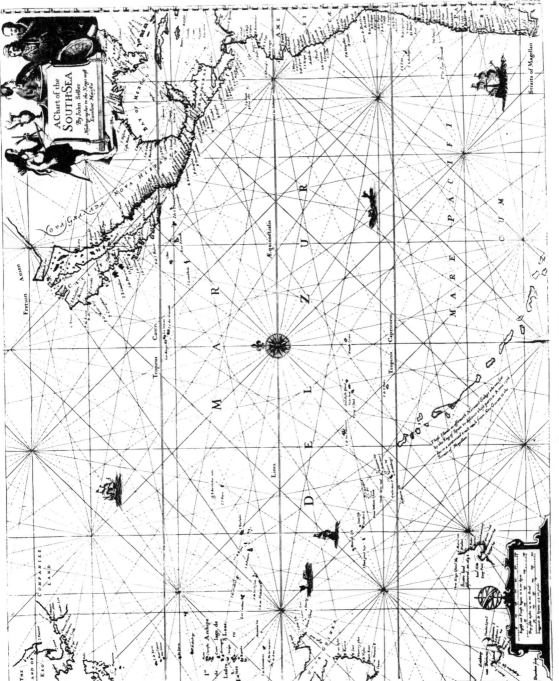

Plate 45   No. 38.   Seller, 1675.

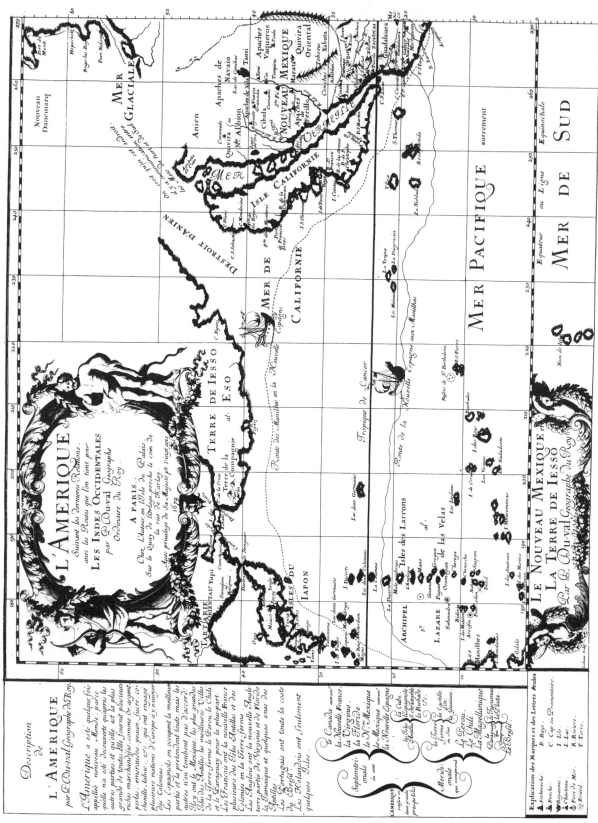

Plate 46   No. 43.   Du Val, 1679.

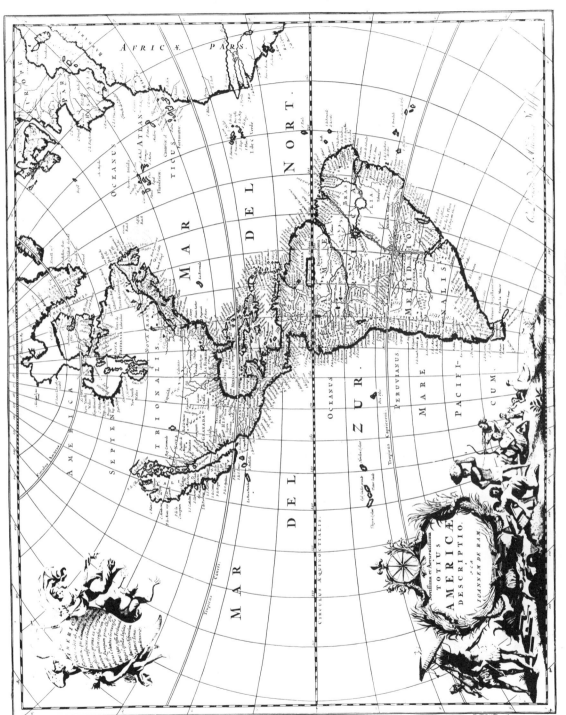

Plate 47   No. 47.   De Ram [1685].

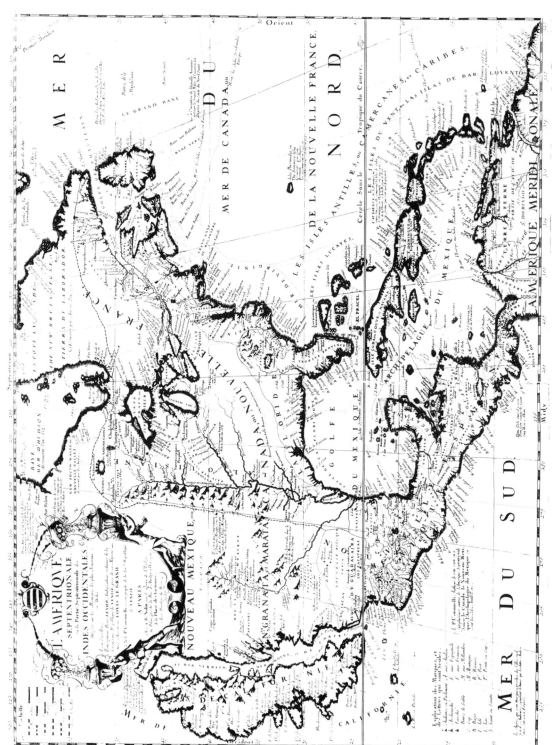

Plate 48   No. 49.   Coronelli, 1689.

NORTH AMERICA Divided into its III PRINCIPALL PARTS 1st ENGLISH EMPIRE continued Articklands 900 Hudsons Bay New North & Sou[th] Wales New Britain [...] Newfoundland Scotland N England N York Iarsies Pen[n]silvania Maryland Virginia Carolina Florida California Somer & Bahama Iarsies K. Charles I & Somers Pen. N Spa[...] Antilles & Panuco & Guaftica II [...]

Plate 49   No. 55.   [Lea, 1690].

Plate 50   No. 57.   Coronelli, 1696.

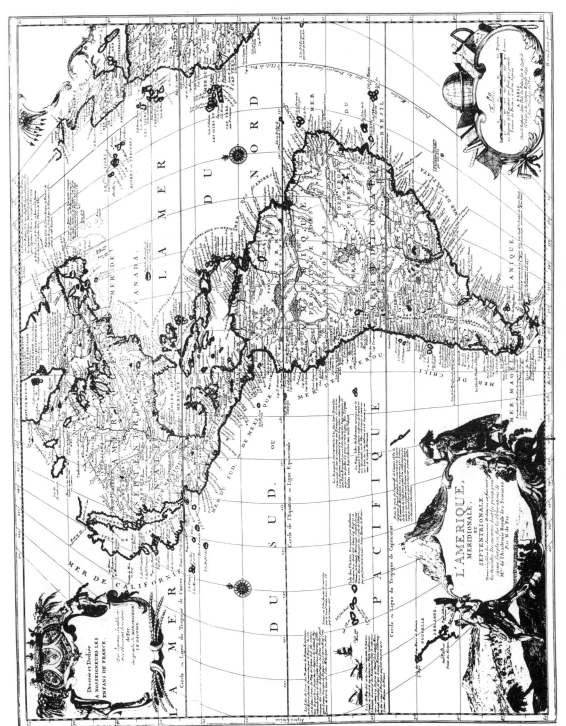

Plate 51   No. 60.   De Fer, 1699.

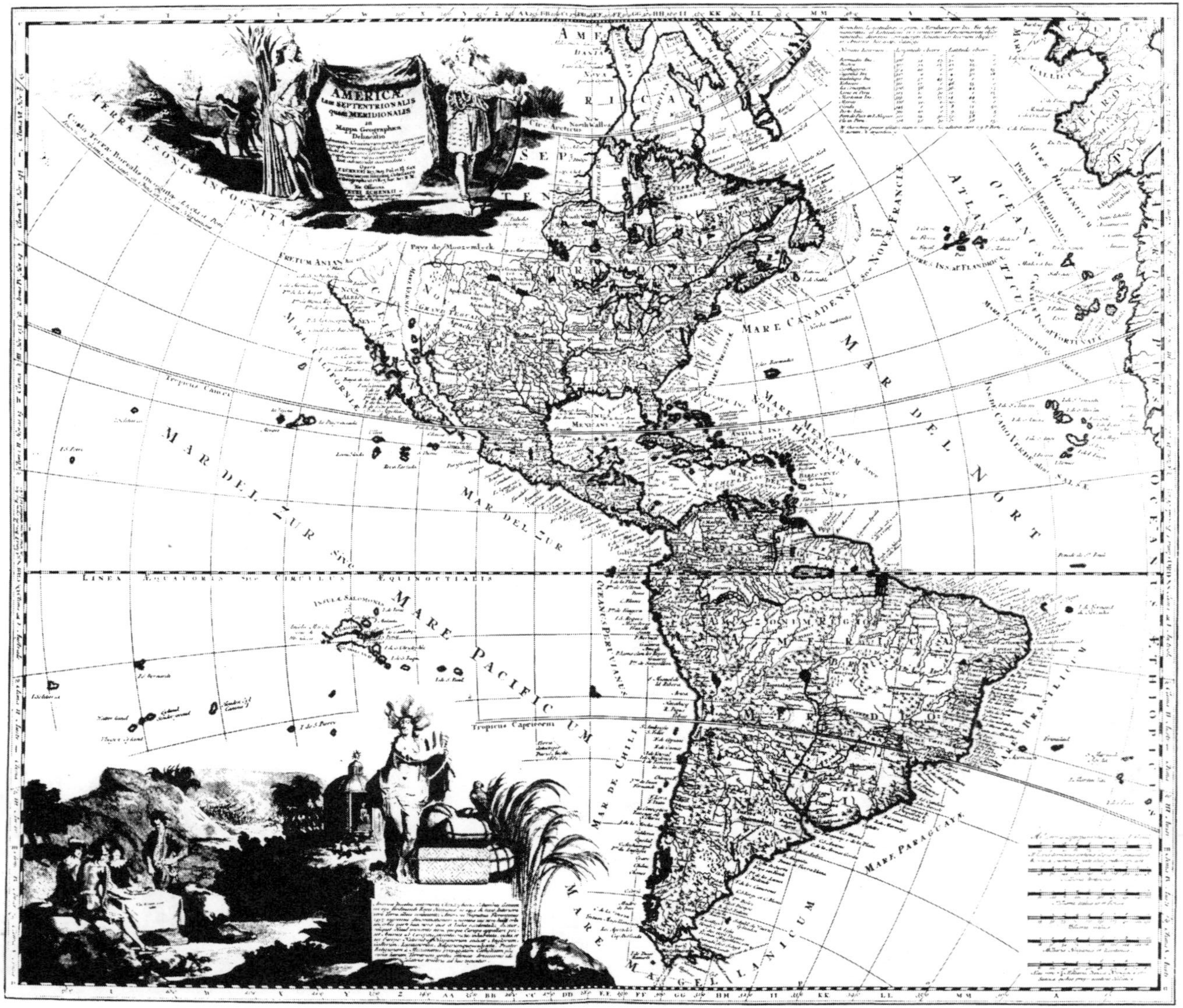

Plate 52   No. 67.   Schenk [1700].

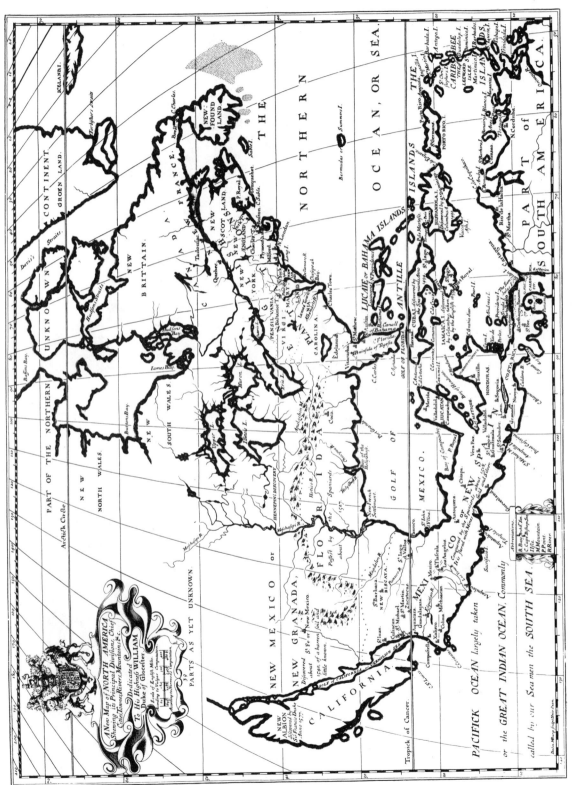

Plate 53   No. 68.   Wells [1700].

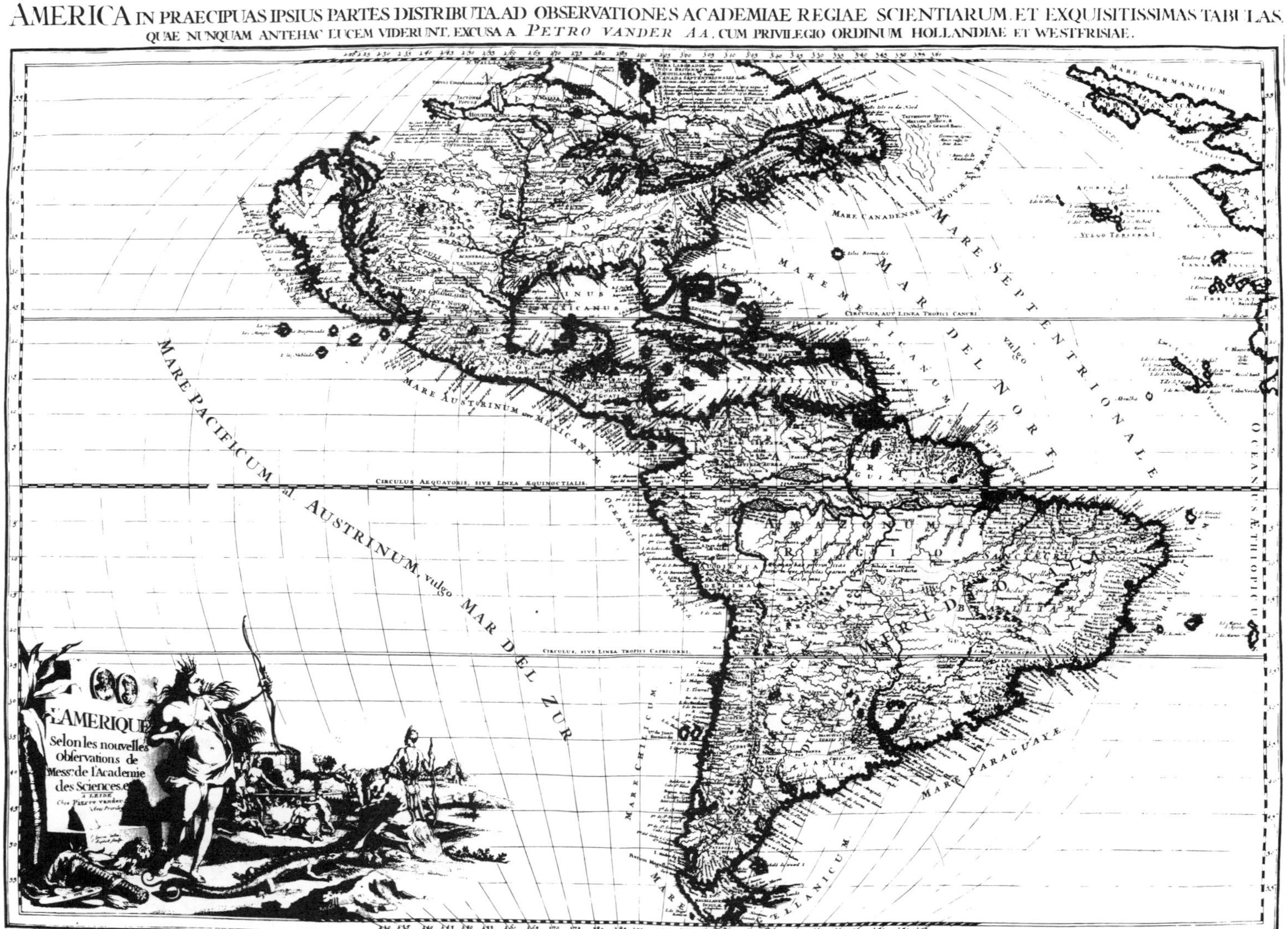

AMERICA IN PRAECIPUAS IPSIUS PARTES DISTRIBUTA AD OBSERVATIONES ACADEMIAE REGIAE SCIENTIARUM ET EXQUISITISSIMAS TABULAS QUAE NUNQUAM ANTEHAC LUCEM VIDERUNT, EXCUSA A *PETRO VANDER AA*, CUM PRIVILEGIO ORDINUM HOLLANDIAE ET WESTFRISIAE.

OCEANUS AETHIOPICUS

MARE SEPTENTRIONALE

MARE DEL NORT vulgo

MARE MEXICANUM

MARE ATLANTICUM

MARE PARAGUAYAE

MARE AUSTRINUM vel MEXILANUM

CIRCULUS AEQUATORIS SIVE LINEA AEQUINOCTIALIS

OCEANUS PERUVIANUS

MARE PACIFICUM al. AUSTRINUM, vulgo MAR DEL ZUR

MARE CHILICUM

MARE CALIFORNIÆ

AMERIQUE
Selon les nouvelles
observations de
Messrs de l'Academie
des Sciences

Plate 54   No. 71.   Aa [1706-1728].

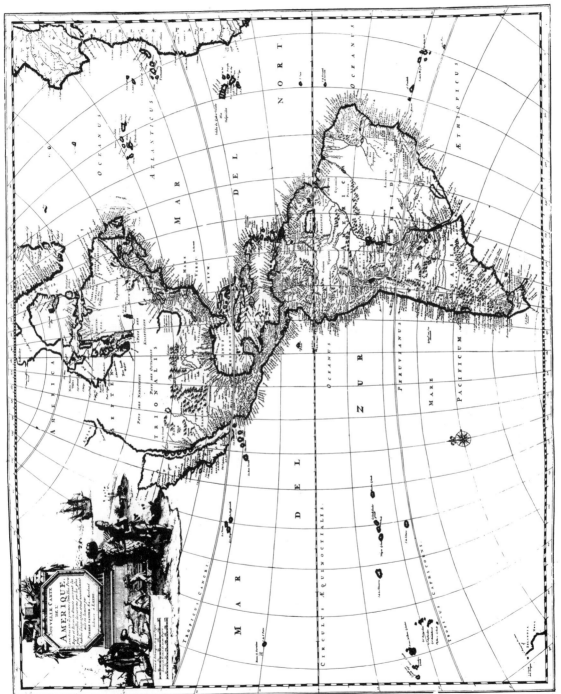

Plate 55 No. 72. Aa [1706-1728].

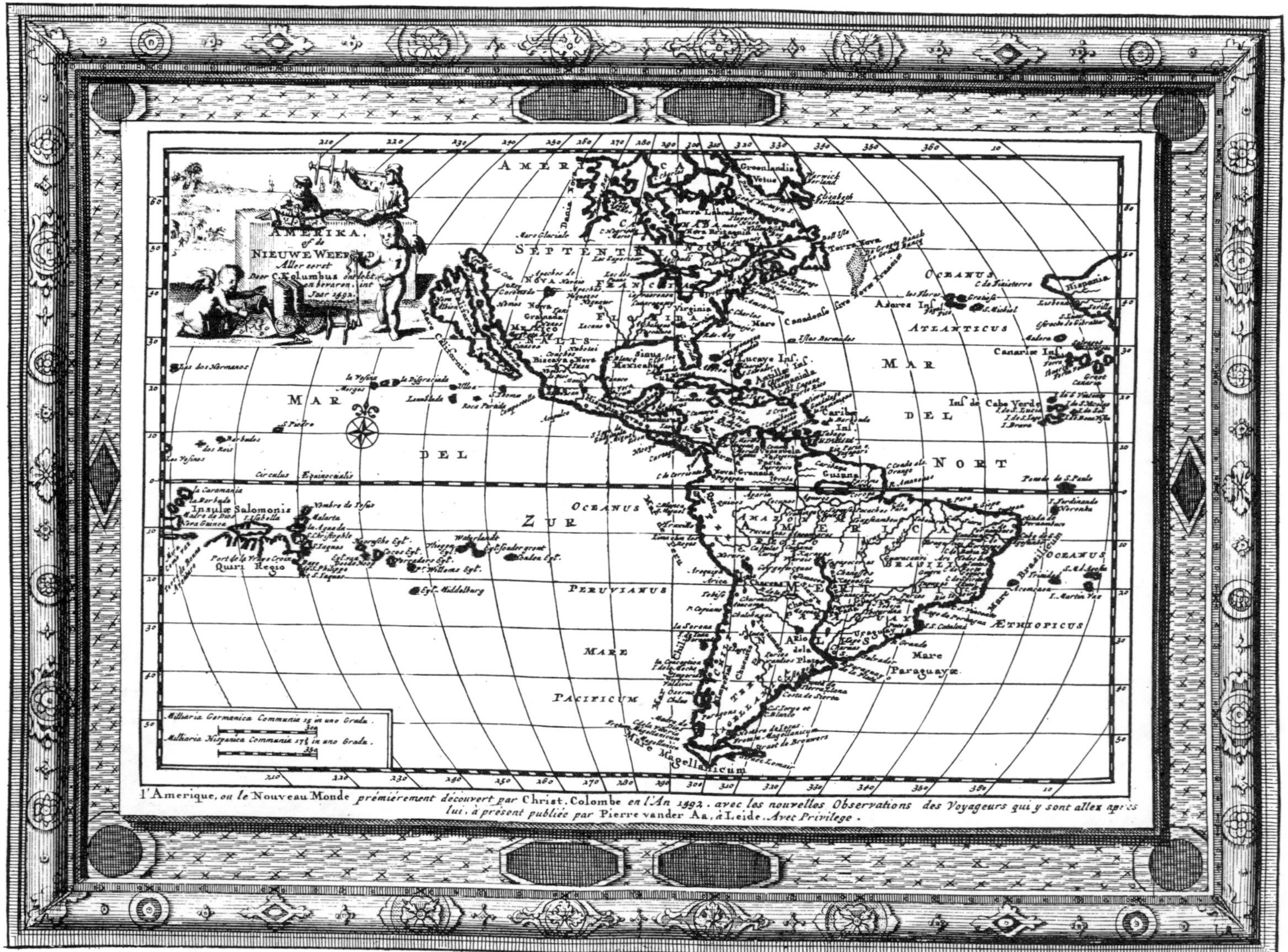

Plate 56   No. 74.   Aa [1706-1728].

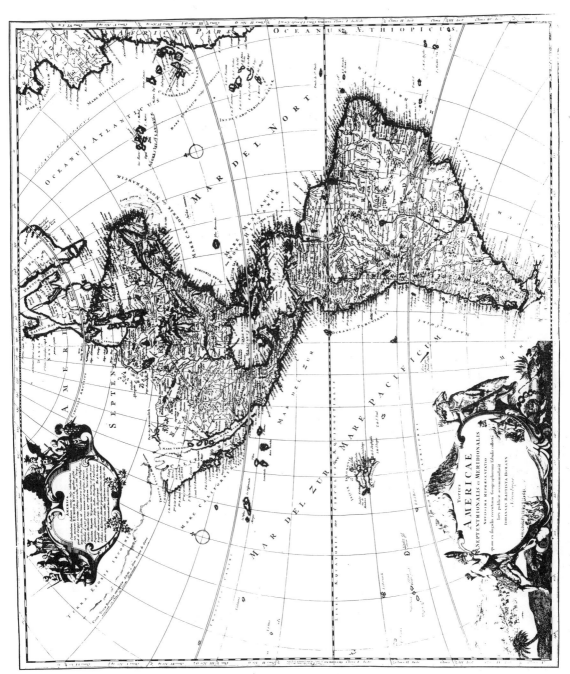

Plate 57　No. 79.　Homann [1710].

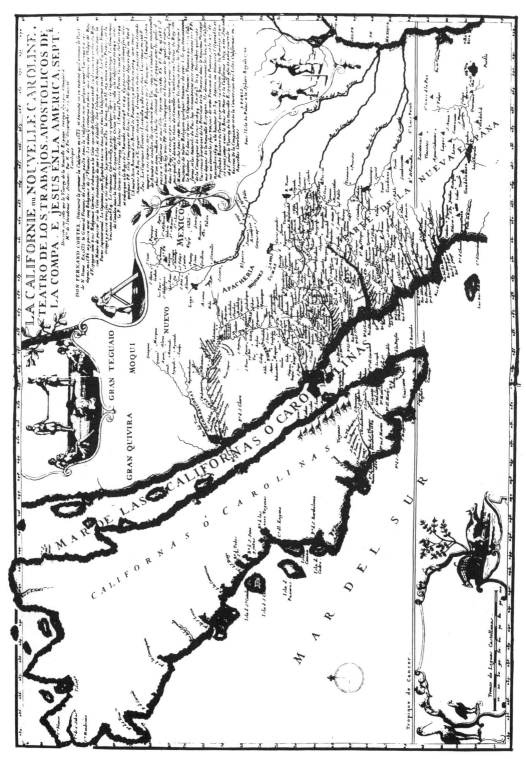

Plate 58   No. 83.   Fer, 1720.

Plate 59   No. 86.   Scherer [1720].

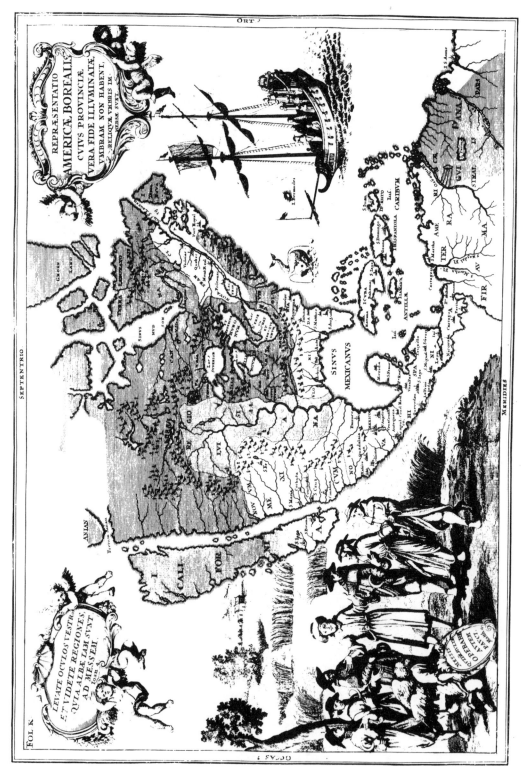

REPRÆSENTATIO
AMERICÆ BOREALIS
CVIVS PROVINCIÆ
VERA FIDE ILLVMINATÆ
VMBRAM NON HABENT.
RELIQVÆ VMBRIS IM-
JEREM. SVNT

SEPTENTRIO

FOL K

LEVATE OCVLOS VESTROS
ET VIDETE REGIONES,
QVIA ALBÆ IAM SVNT
AD MESSEM.
Joan. 4.

MERIDIES

Plate 60   No. 88.   Scherer [1720].

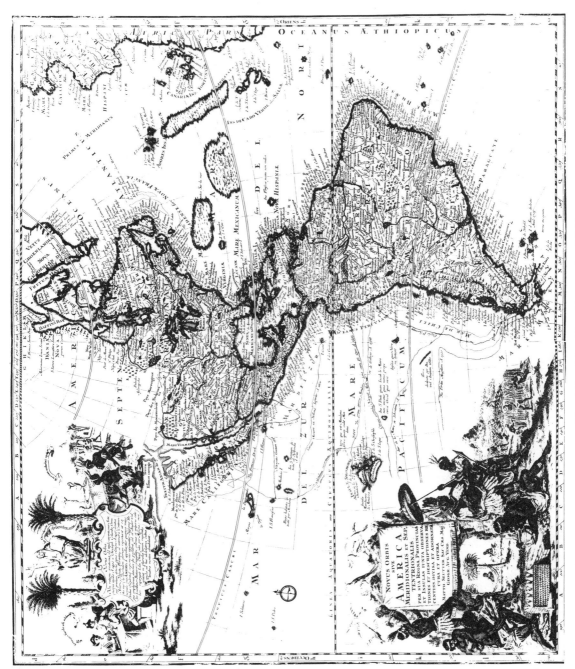

Plate 61   No. 91.   Seutter [c. 1730].

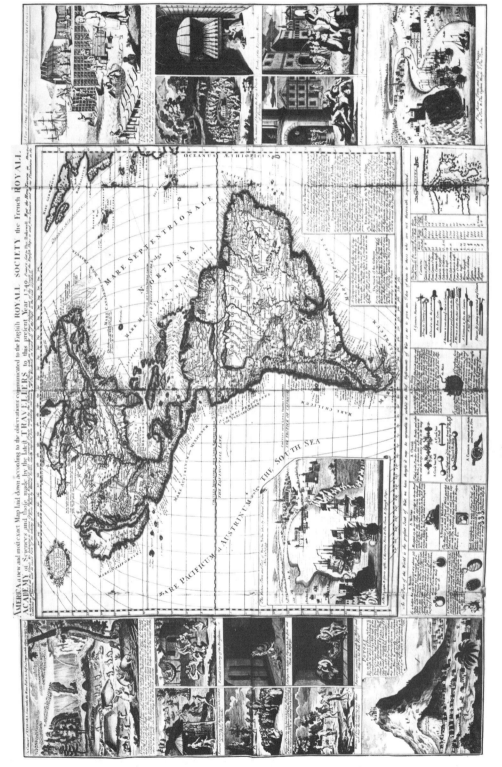

Plate 62   No. 93.   Bakewell, 1740.

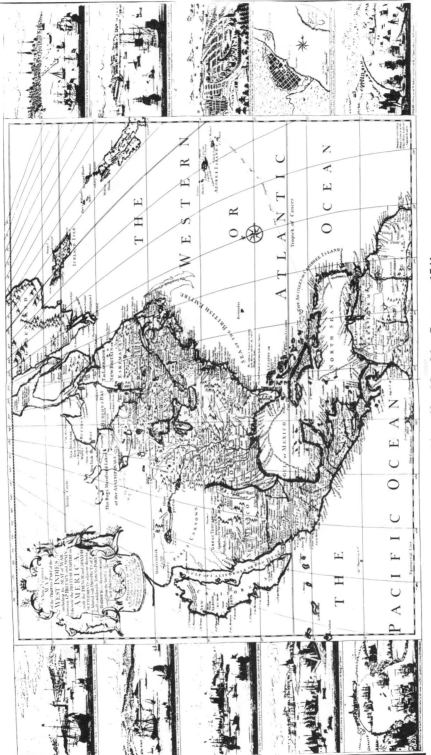

Plate 63   No. 96.   Overton, 1741.

Plate 64   No. 98.   Kitchin [1740–60]

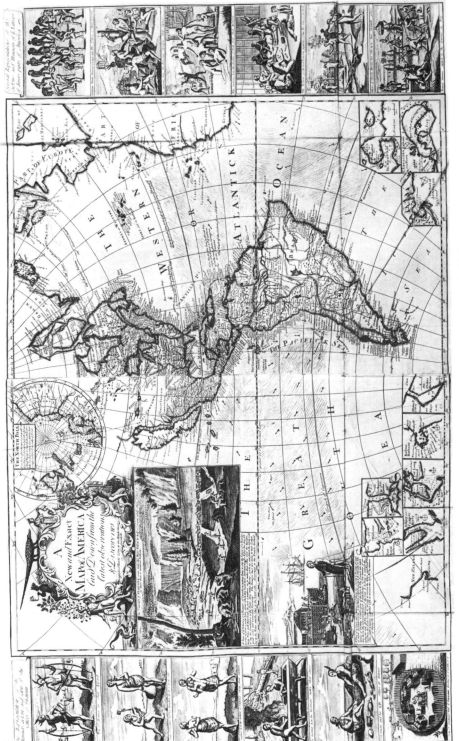

Plate 65   No. 99.   Bowles & Son [1754].

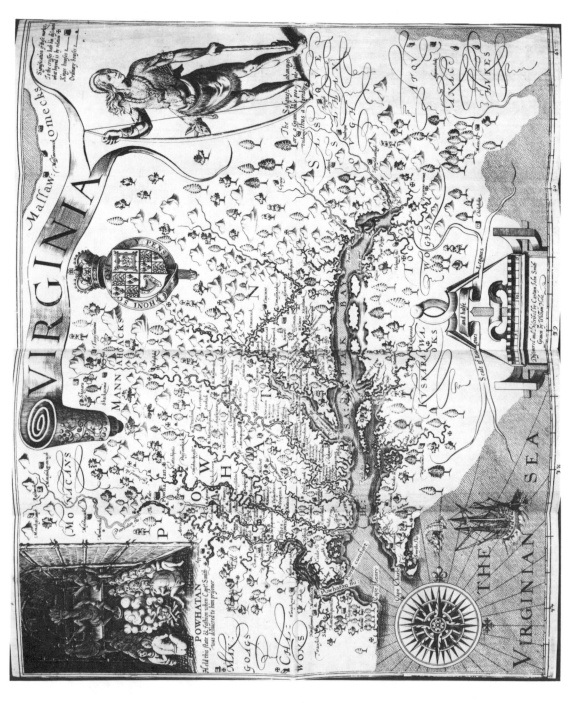

Plate 66   Smith [1612] (state 1)

Smith, 1607-[25] (state 12)

Plate 67

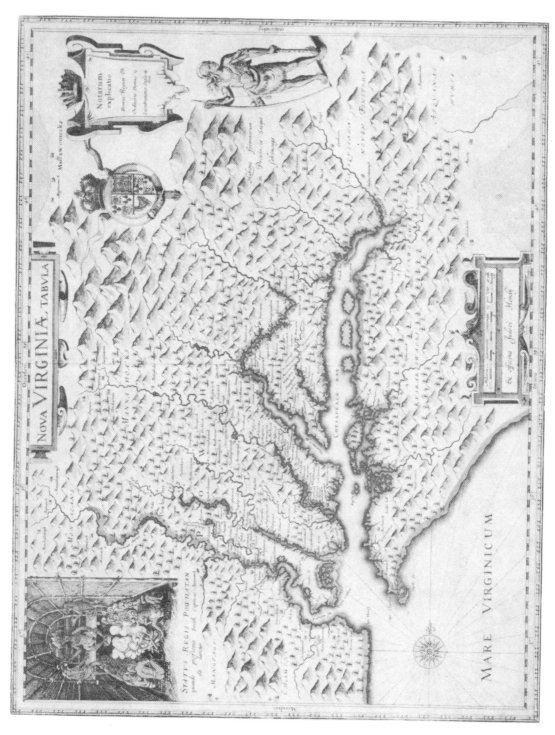

Plate 68   J. Hondius [1618] *derivative* 1, *state* 1

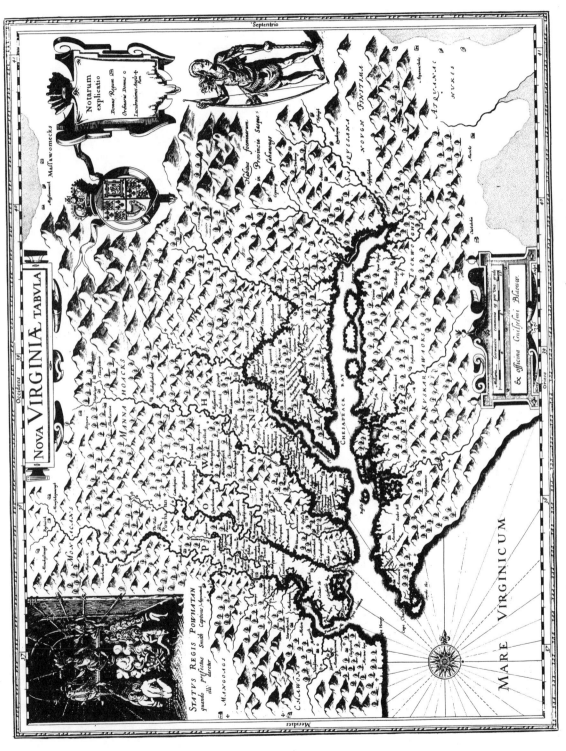

Blaeu [1630] *derivative 1, state 2*

Plate 69

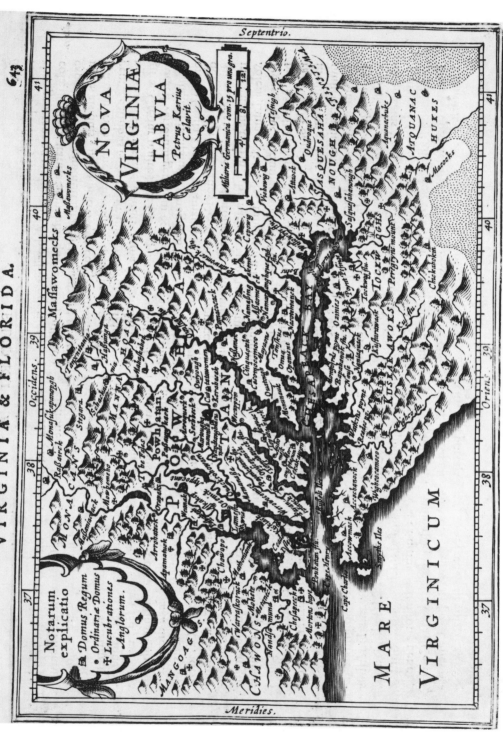

Plate 70   Minor-Mercator [1628] *derivative 2*

Plate 71   De Bry [1628] *derivative 3*

Plate 72

Mercator-Kaerius [1734] *derivative 4, state 3*

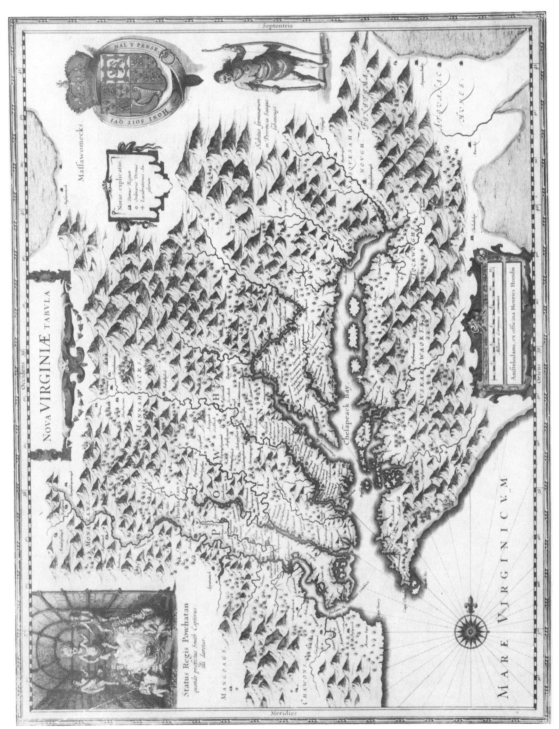

H. Hondius [1633] *derivative 5, state* 1

Plate 74   Hall, 1636, *derivative 6*

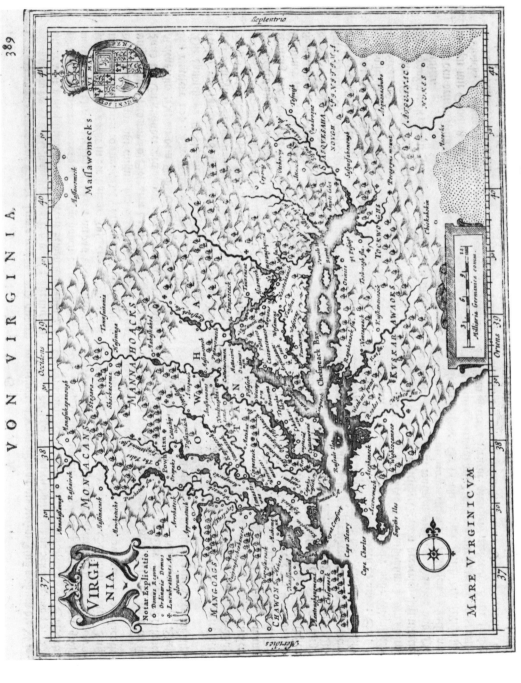

Minor-Mercator [1648] *derivative 7*

Plate 75

Plate 76   Montanus-Ogilby [1671] *derivative 8, state 1*

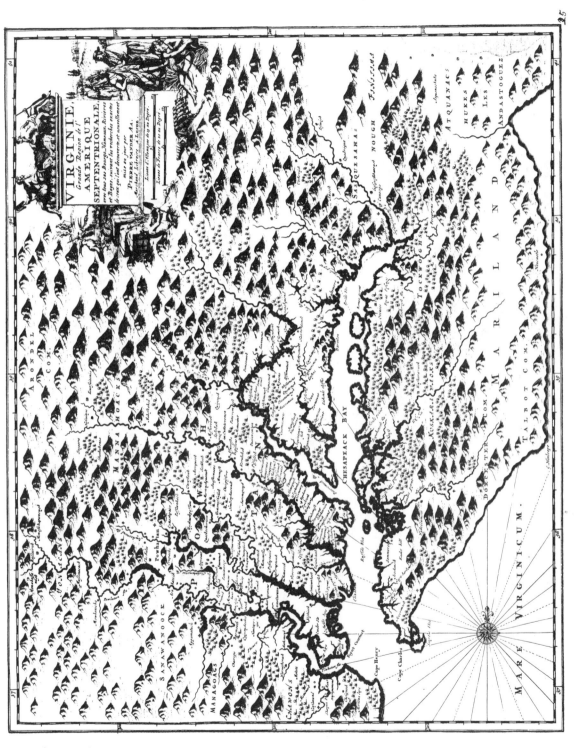

Plate 77   Vander Aa [1729] *derivative 8, state 2*

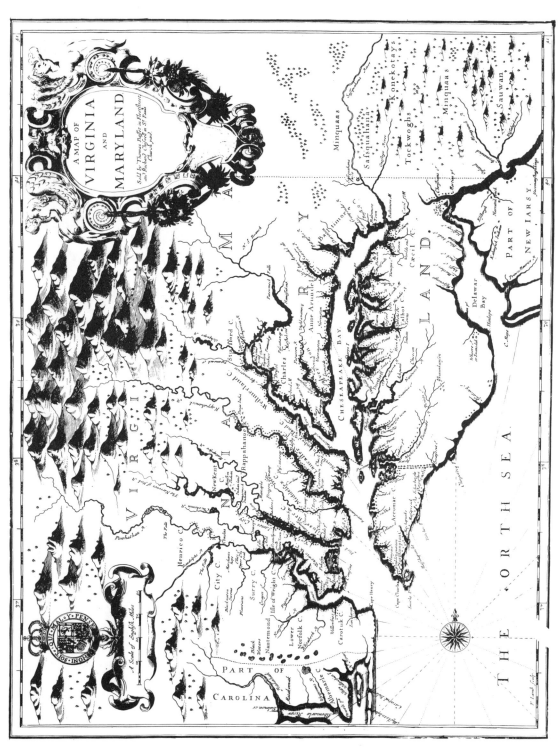

Plate 78   Speed [1676] *derivative 9, state 1*

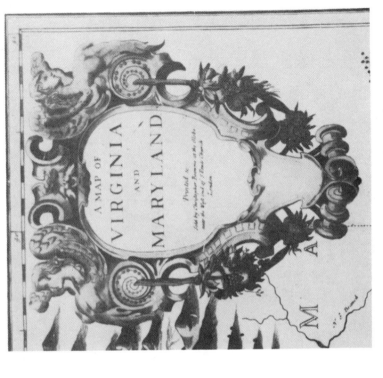

Basset & Chiswell [1676] *state* 1

Browne [c. 1685] *state* 3

derivative 9

Plate 79   Speed,

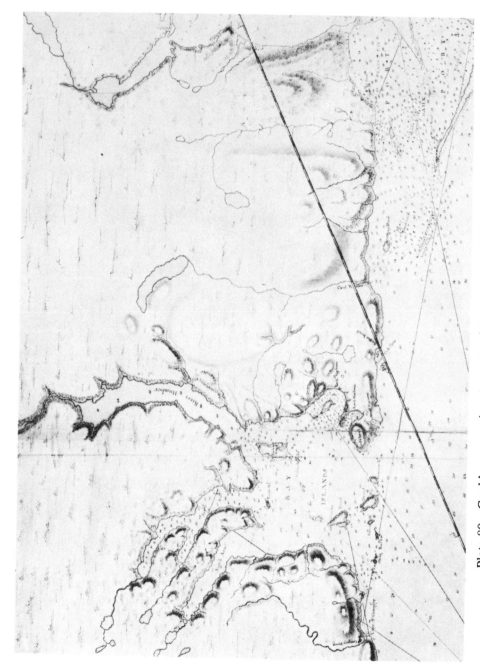

Plate 80 Cook's manuscript chart of the West Coast of Newfoundland: detail, showing the Bay of Islands, July 1767. (B.M., Add MS. 17,963 d).

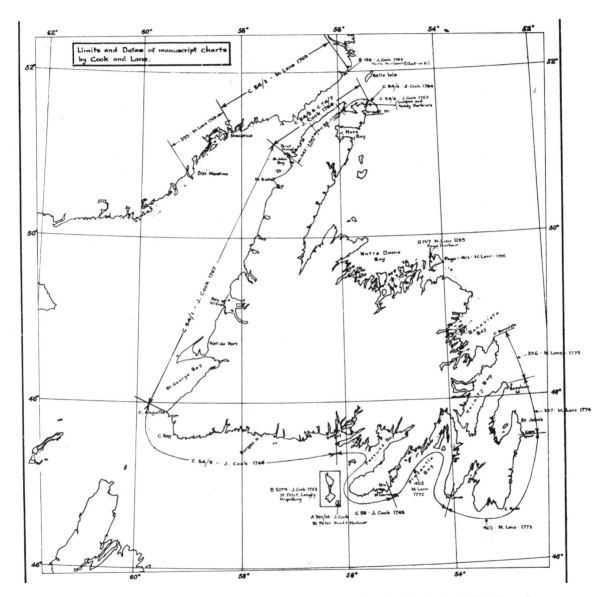

Plate 81 The surveys of Newfoundland and Labrador by Cook (1763-67) and
Lane (1768-73): limits and dates.

Jefferies . Map & Printseller. bottom of St Martin's Lane.

Plate 83 Thomas Jefferys asleep in his shop. Drawing by Paul Sandby
(Windsor Castle).

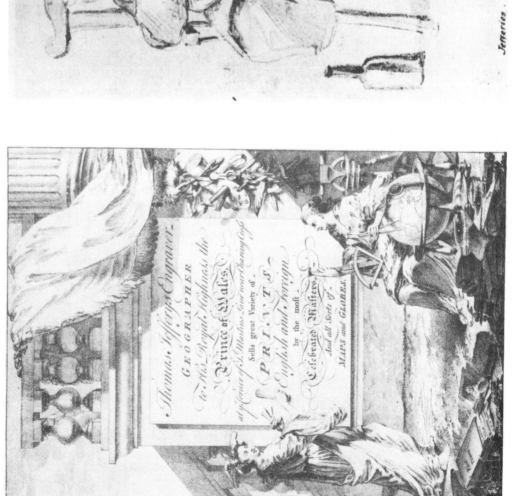

Plate 82 Thomas Jefferys' trade card.

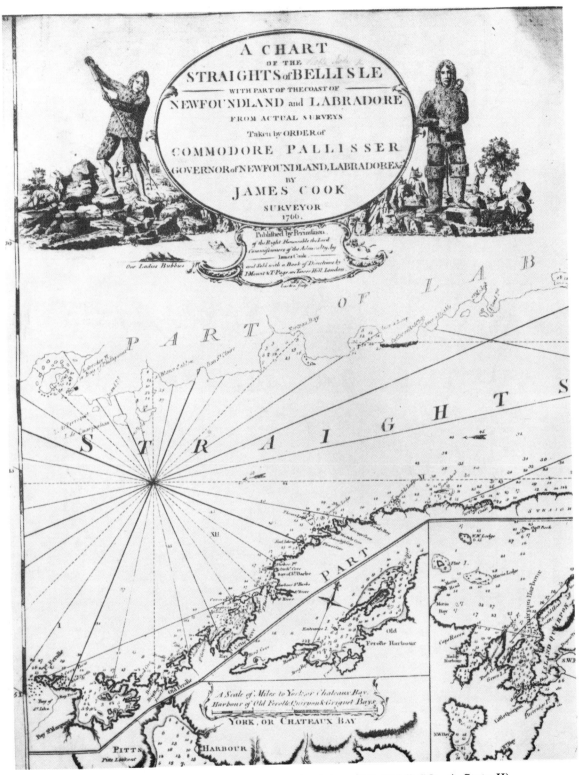

Plate 85 Detail of "A Chart of the Straights of Bellisle" (No. 4, State II), published separately by Cook in 1766.

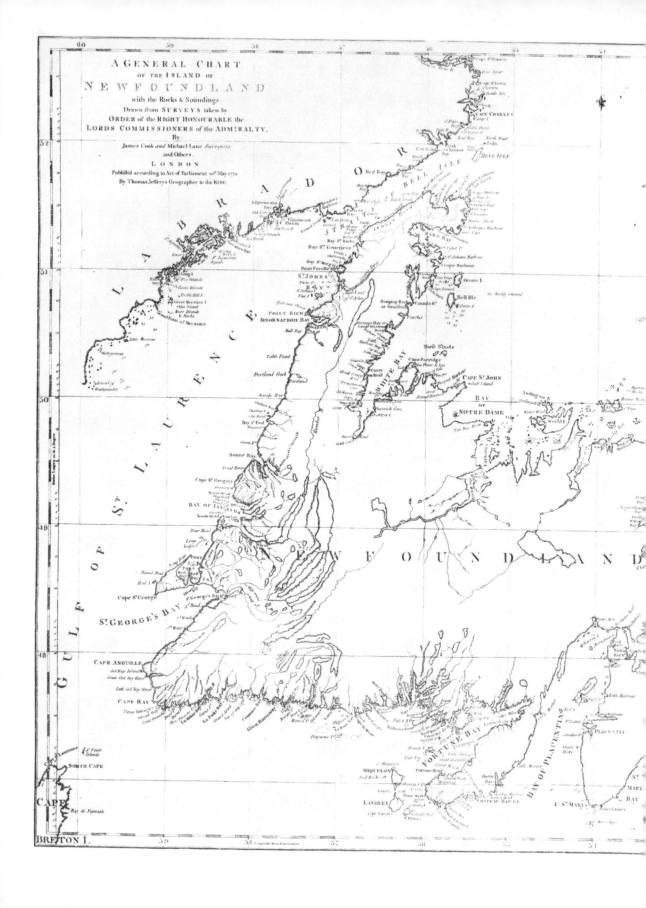

A GENERAL CHART
OF THE ISLAND OF
NEWFOUNDLAND
with the Rocks & Soundings.
Drawn from SURVEYS taken by
ORDER of the RIGHT HONOURABLE the
LORDS COMMISSIONERS of the ADMIRALTY.
By
James Cook and Michael Lane Surveyors
and Others.
LONDON
Publish'd according to Act of Parliament 10th May 1770
By Thomas Jefferys Geographer to the KING.

Plate 84 "A General Chart of the Island of Newfoundland" (No. 11 (1) State I), as published by Jefferys in the later issue (1770) of *A Collection of Charts* . . .

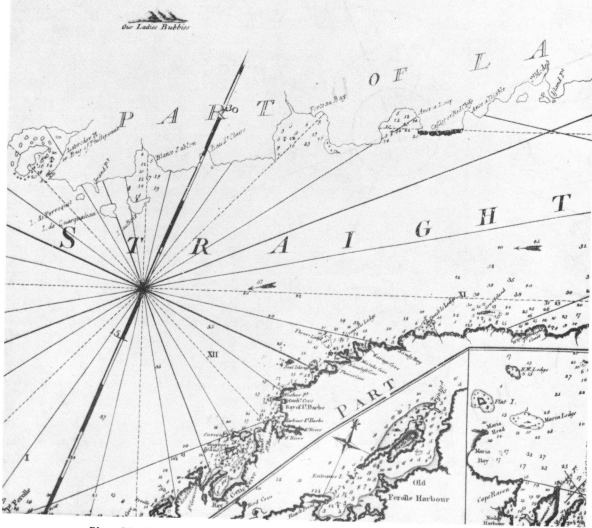

Plate 86   Detail of "A Chart of the Straights of Bellisle" (No. 4, State III),
as published by Jefferys in the earlier issue (1769) of *A Collection of Charts . . .*

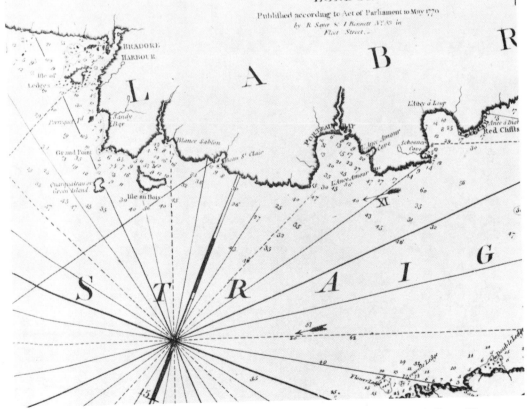

Plate 87   Detail of "A Chart of the Straights of Bellisle" (No. 4, State V), as published in the later issue (1770) of *A Collection of Charts . . .*   Incorporating Lane's surveys of 1768-9.

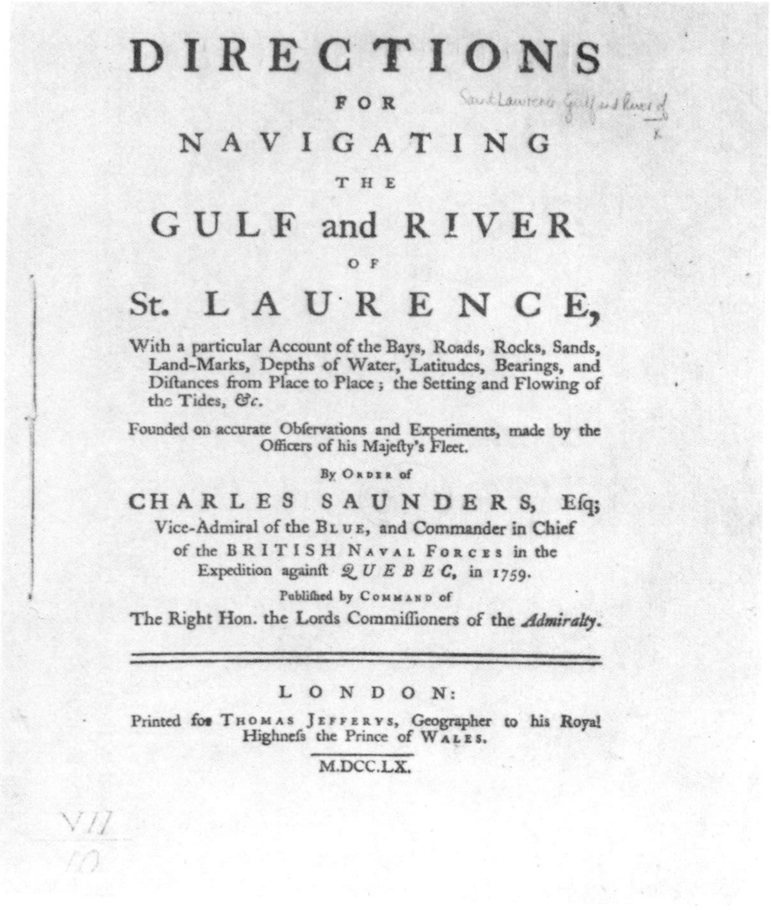

DIRECTIONS

For Navigating on Part of the

North East Side of Newfoundland,

And in the STREIGHTS of

BELL-ISLE,

WITH

A CHART thereof,

And a particular ACCOUNT of the

Bays, Harbours, Rocks, Land-Marks, Depths of Water,
Latitudes, Bearings, and Diſtances from Place to Place,
the Setting and Flowing of the Tides, &c.

Founded on actual SURVEYS, taken by Order of

Commodore PALLISSER, Governor of *Newfoundland*, *Labradore*, &c.

By JAMES COOK,
Surveyor of *Newfoundland.*

LONDON:

Printed for the AUTHOR and Sold by J. MOUNT and T. PAGE on
Tower-Hill, M.DCC.LXVI.

Plate 89   Bibliography, No. 5: titlepage.

DIRECTIONS

FOR

NAVIGATING

THE

GULF and RIVER

OF

St. LAURENCE,

With a particular Account of the Bays, Roads, Rocks, Sands,
Land-Marks, Depths of Water, Latitudes, Bearings, and
Diſtances from Place to Place ; the Setting and Flowing of
the Tides, &c.

Founded on accurate Obſervations and Experiments, made by the
Officers of his Majeſty's Fleet.

By ORDER of

CHARLES SAUNDERS, Esq;

Vice-Admiral of the BLUE, and Commander in Chief
of the BRITISH NAVAL FORCES in the
Expedition againſt QUEBEC, in 1759.

Publiſhed by COMMAND of

The Right Hon. the Lords Commiſſioners of the *Admiralty.*

LONDON:

Printed for THOMAS JEFFERYS, Geographer to his Royal
Highneſs the Prince of WALES.
M.DCC.LX.

Plate 88   Bibliography, No. 3: titlepage.

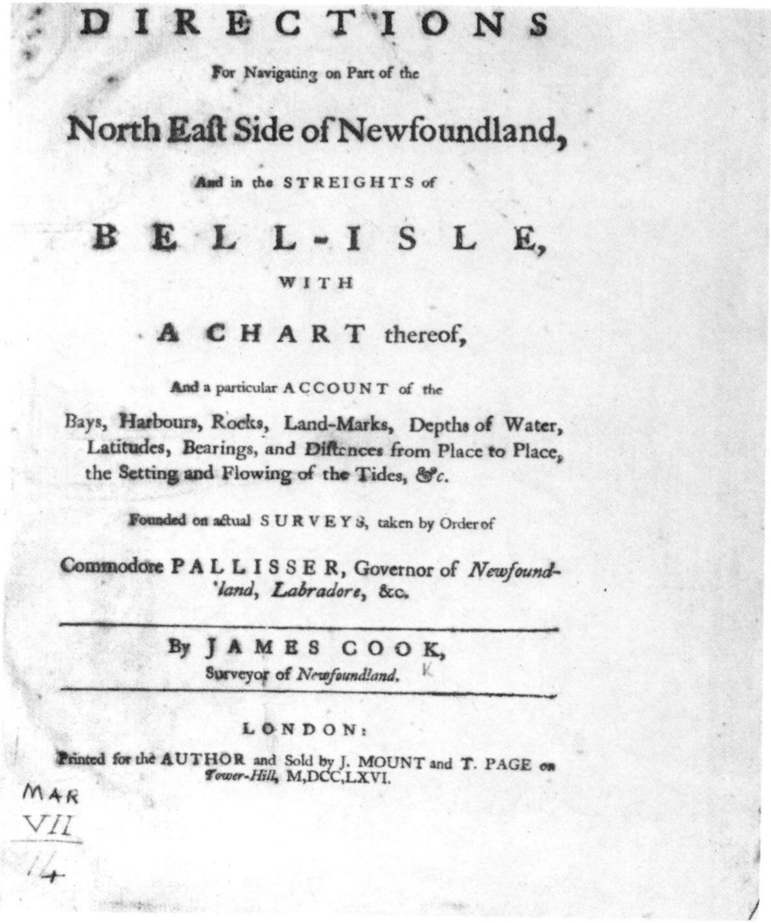

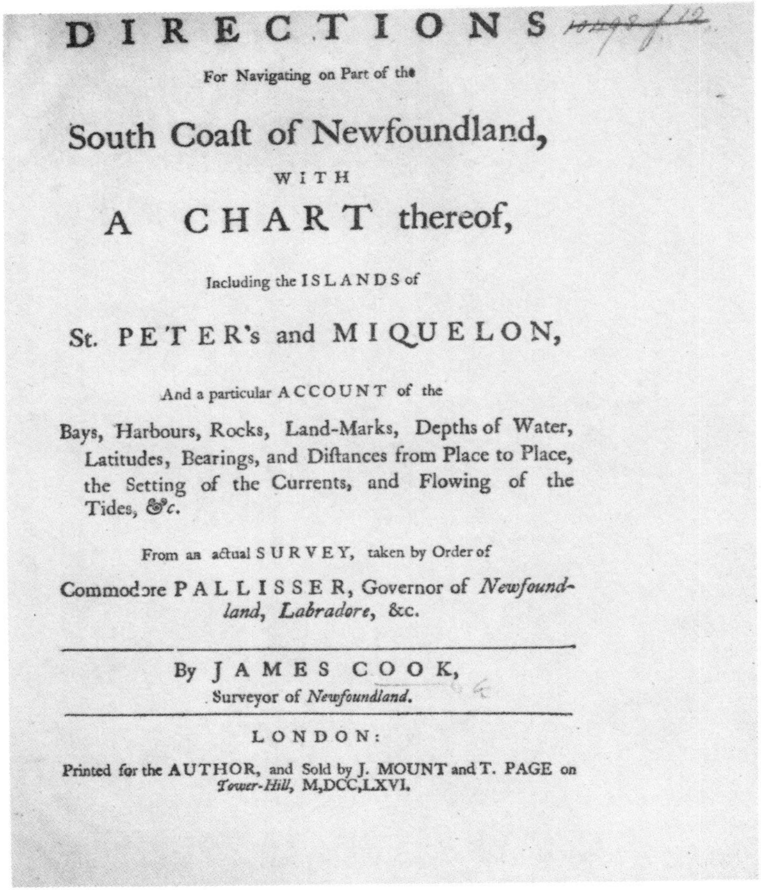

DIRECTIONS

For Navigating the

West - Coast of Newfoundland,

WITH

A CHART thereof,

And a particular ACCOUNT of the

Bays, Harbours, Rocks, Sands, Depths of Water, Latitudes, Bearings and Distances from Place to Place, the Flowing of the Tides, &c.

From an actual SURVEY, taken by Order of

Commodore PALLISSER, Governor of *Newfoundland, Labradore*, &c.

By JAMES COOK,

Appointed by the Admiralty to Survey the Coast of *Newfoundland*.

LONDON:

Printed for the AUTHOR, and Sold by J. MOUNT and T. PAGE, on *Tower-Hill*; A. DURY, in *Duke's-Court*, near St. *Martin's* Church; and T. JEFFERY's, the Corner of St. *Martin's-Lane*, and N. GILL, Naval Officer in St. *John's Newfoundland*, M,DCC,LXVIII.

Plate 91 Bibliography, No. 10: titlepage.

DIRECTIONS

For Navigating on Part of the

South Coast of Newfoundland,

WITH

A CHART thereof,

Including the ISLANDS of

St. PETER's and MIQUELON,

And a particular ACCOUNT of the

Bays, Harbours, Rocks, Land-Marks, Depths of Water, Latitudes, Bearings, and Distances from Place to Place, the Setting of the Currents, and Flowing of the Tides, &c.

From an actual SURVEY, taken by Order of

Commodore PALLISSER, Governor of *Newfoundland, Labradore*, &c.

By JAMES COOK,

Surveyor of *Newfoundland*.

LONDON:

Printed for the AUTHOR, and Sold by J. MOUNT and T. PAGE on *Tower-Hill*, M,DCC,LXVI.

Plate 90 Bibliography, No. 7: titlepage.

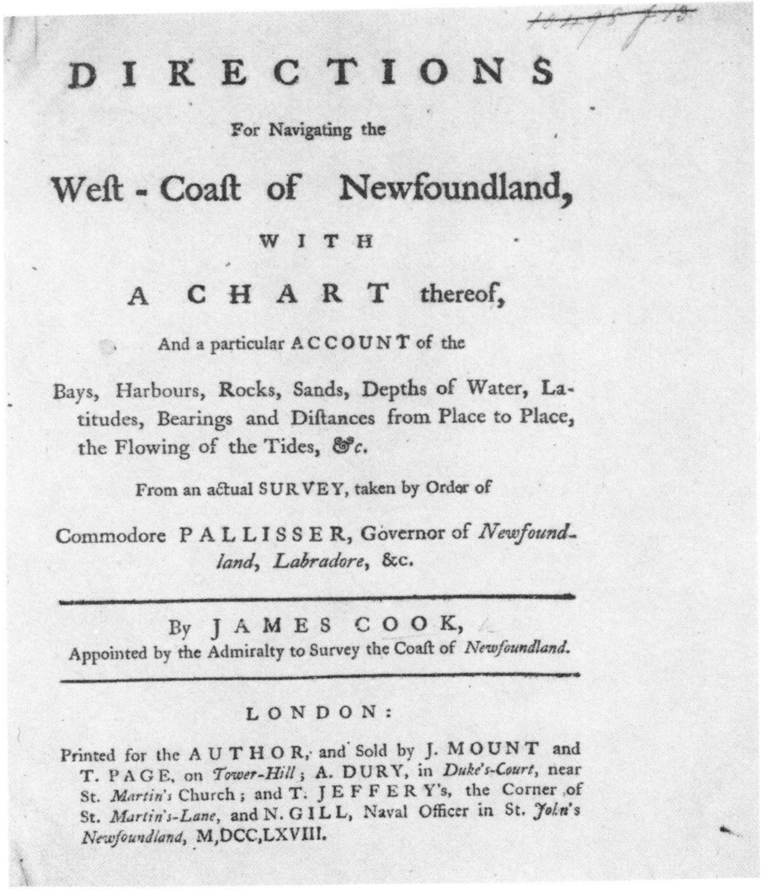

A
COLLECTION of CHARTS
Of the Coasts of
NEWFOUNDLAND
AND
LABRADORE, &c.

CONTAINING

1. A general Chart of Newfoundland.

2. The South Coast of Newfoundland, including the Islands of St. Peter's and Miquelon.

3. The W. Coast of Newfoundland.

4. The North Coast of Newfoundland, including the Streights of Bell-Isle and Part of the Coast of Labradore.

5. A Chart of the Coast of Labradore within the Streights of Bell-Isle, from Grand Point to Shecatica Island.

6. A Chart of the Coast of Labradore without the Streights of Bell-Isle, from the Entrance of the Streights to Cape Bluff.

7. A Chart of the Magdalen Islands in the Gulf of St. Lawrence.

8. A Chart of Sable Island, with Instructions for navigating about the same.

With particular PLANS of the principal Harbours, as follows:

In NEWFOUNDLAND.

Great and Little Harbours of St. Lawrence
Harbour Briton
Great Jervis Harbour
Port aux Basque
Old Ferolle
Harbour and Island of Quirpon
Griguet Bays
Croque Harbour

Trinity Harbour
Carboniere and Harbour Grace
St. John's Harbour
The Harbours of Ferryland, Aquafort and Caplin Bay
Trepassey Harbour, with Mutton & Biscay Bays
St. Mary's Harbour
Placentia

In LABRADORE.

Mecatina Harbour
St. Augustine's Harbour
Cumberland Harbour
Red Bay
Chateau or York Bay, with its contained

Harbours, viz. Pitt's Harbour, Temple Bay, Grenville and Henley Harbours
Petty Harbour, and the
Three Harbours of Sophia, Charlotte, and Mecklenburg

Drawn from ORIGINAL SURVEYS taken by

JAMES COOK and MICHAEL LANE, Surveyors,

JOSEPH GILBERT, and other Officers in the King's Service.

Published by Permission of the

Right Honourable the LORDS COMMISSIONERS of the ADMIRALTY.

Chiefly engraved by THOMAS JEFFERYS, Geographer to the King.

LONDON:

Printed according to the Act of Parliament; and sold by THOMAS JEFFERYS, in the Strand.

N. B. Of whom may be had the Newfoundland Pilot, containing a Collection of Directions for each of the above Charts.

Plate 92   Bibliography, No. 11: titlepage.

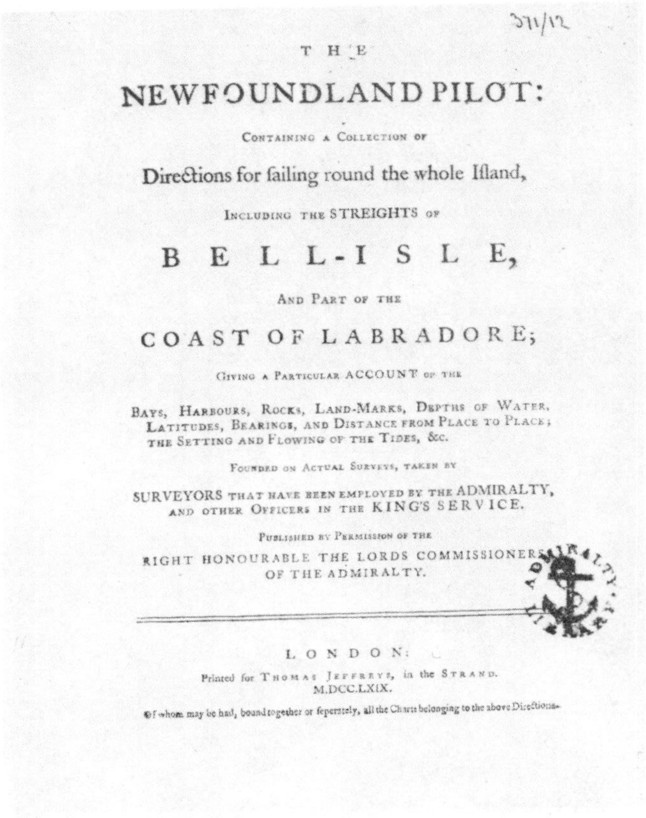

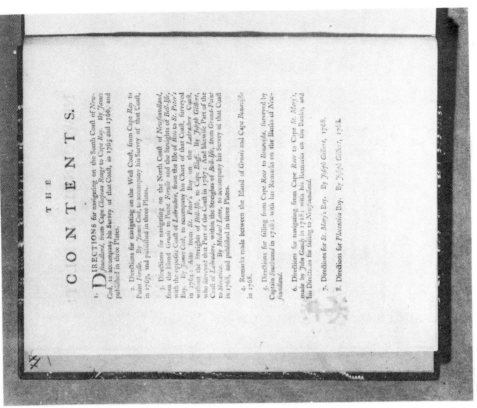

THE

CONTENTS.

1. Directions for navigating on the South Coast of Newfoundland, from Cape Chapeau Rouge to Cape Ray. By James Cook, to accompany his Survey of that Coast, in 1765 and 1766, and published in three Plates.

2. Directions for navigating on the West Coast, from Cape Ray to Point Ferolle. By James Cook, to accompany his Survey of that Coast, in 1767, and published in three Plates.

3. Directions for navigating on the North Coast of Newfoundland, from the Island Groais to Point Ferolle and the Streights of Bell-Isle, with the opposite Coast of Labradore, from the Isle of Bois to St. Peter's Bay. By James Cook, to accompany his Chart of that Coast, surveyed in 1764: Also from St. Peter's Bay on the Labradore Coast, without the Streights of Bell-Isle, to Cape Bluff. By Joseph Gilbert, who surveyed that Part of the Coast in 1767: And likewise Part of the Coast of Labradore, within the Streights of Bell-Isle, from Grand-Point to Senaclose. By Michael Lane, to accompany his Survey of that Coast in 1768, and published in three Plates.

4. Remarks made between the Island of Groais and Cape Bonavista in 1768.

5. Directions for sailing from Cape Race to Bonavista, surveyed by Captain Southwood in 1718: with his Remarks on the Banks of Newfoundland.

6. Directions for sailing from Cape Race to Cape St. Mary's, made by John Gaudy in 1718: with his Remarks on the Banks, and his Directions for sailing to Newfoundland.

7. Directions for St. Mary's Bay. By Joseph Gilbert, 1768.

8. Directions for Placentia Bay. By Joseph Gilbert, 1768.

Plate 94   Bibliography, No. 12: contents list on verso of titlepage.

THE

NEWFOUNDLAND PILOT:

CONTAINING A COLLECTION OF

Directions for sailing round the whole island,

INCLUDING THE STREIGHTS OF

BELL-ISLE,

AND PART OF THE

COAST OF LABRADORE;

GIVING A PARTICULAR ACCOUNT OF THE

BAYS, HARBOURS, ROCKS, LAND-MARKS, DEPTHS OF WATER, LATITUDES, BEARINGS, AND DISTANCE FROM PLACE TO PLACE; THE SETTING AND FLOWING OF THE TIDES, &c.

FOUNDED ON ACTUAL SURVEYS, TAKEN BY

SURVEYORS THAT HAVE BEEN EMPLOYED BY THE ADMIRALTY, AND OTHER OFFICERS IN THE KINGS SERVICE.

PUBLISHED BY PERMISSION OF THE

RIGHT HONOURABLE THE LORDS COMMISSIONERS OF THE ADMIRALTY.

LONDON:

Printed for Thomas Jefferys, in the Strand. M.DCC.LXIX.

Of whom may be had, bound together or separately, all the Charts belonging to the above Directions.

Plate 93   Bibliography, No. 12: titlepage.

THE

NORTH-AMERICAN PILOT

FOR

NEWFOUNDLAND, LABRADORE,

THE

GULF AND RIVER St. LAURENCE:

BEING A COLLECTION OF

SIXTY ACCURATE CHARTS AND PLANS,

DRAWN FROM ORIGINAL SURVEYS:

TAKEN BY

JAMES COOK and MICHAEL LANE, SURVEYORS,

AND

JOSEPH GILBERT, and other Officers in the KING's Service.

Published by PERMISSION of the

Right Hon. the LORDS COMMISSIONERS of the ADMIRALTY.

CHIEFLY ENGRAVED BY

The Late Mr. THOMAS JEFFERYS, GEOGRAPHER to the KING.

ON THIRTY-SIX LARGE COPPER-PLATES.

———————

LONDON:

Printed according to Act of Parliament, and sold by R. SAYER and J. BENNETT, No. 53, in FLEET-STREET.

M.DCC.LXXV.

N. B. Of whom may be had, the Sailing Directions for the above Charts.

Plate 95   Bibliography, No. 13: titlepage.

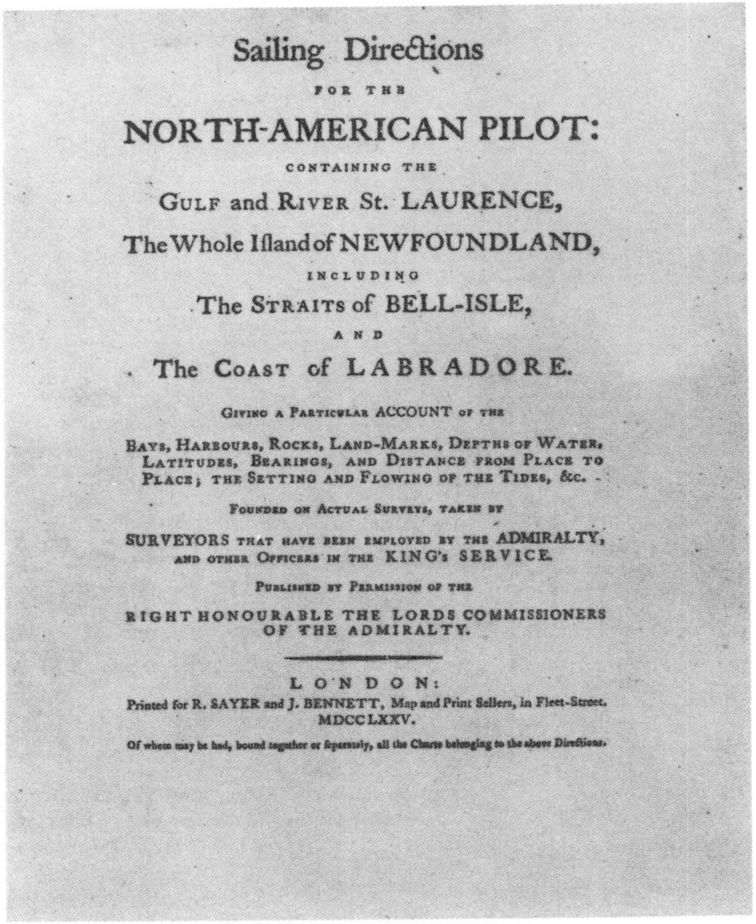

Plate 96 (titlepage):

Sailing Directions

FOR THE

NORTH-AMERICAN PILOT:

CONTAINING THE

GULF and RIVER St. LAURENCE,

The Whole Island of NEWFOUNDLAND,

INCLUDING

The STRAITS of BELL-ISLE,

AND

The COAST of LABRADORE.

GIVING A PARTICULAR ACCOUNT OF THE

BAYS, HARBOURS, ROCKS, LAND-MARKS, DEPTHS OF WATER, LATITUDES, BEARINGS, AND DISTANCE FROM PLACE TO PLACE; THE SETTING AND FLOWING OF THE TIDES, &c.

FOUNDED ON ACTUAL SURVEYS, TAKEN BY

SURVEYORS THAT HAVE BEEN EMPLOYED BY THE ADMIRALTY, AND OTHER OFFICERS IN THE KING'S SERVICE.

PUBLISHED BY PERMISSION OF THE

RIGHT HONOURABLE THE LORDS COMMISSIONERS OF THE ADMIRALTY.

LONDON:

Printed for R. SAYER and J. BENNETT, Map and Print Sellers, in Fleet-Street. MDCCLXXV.

Of whom may be had, bound together or separately, all the Charts belonging to the above Directions.

Plate 97 (page 6):

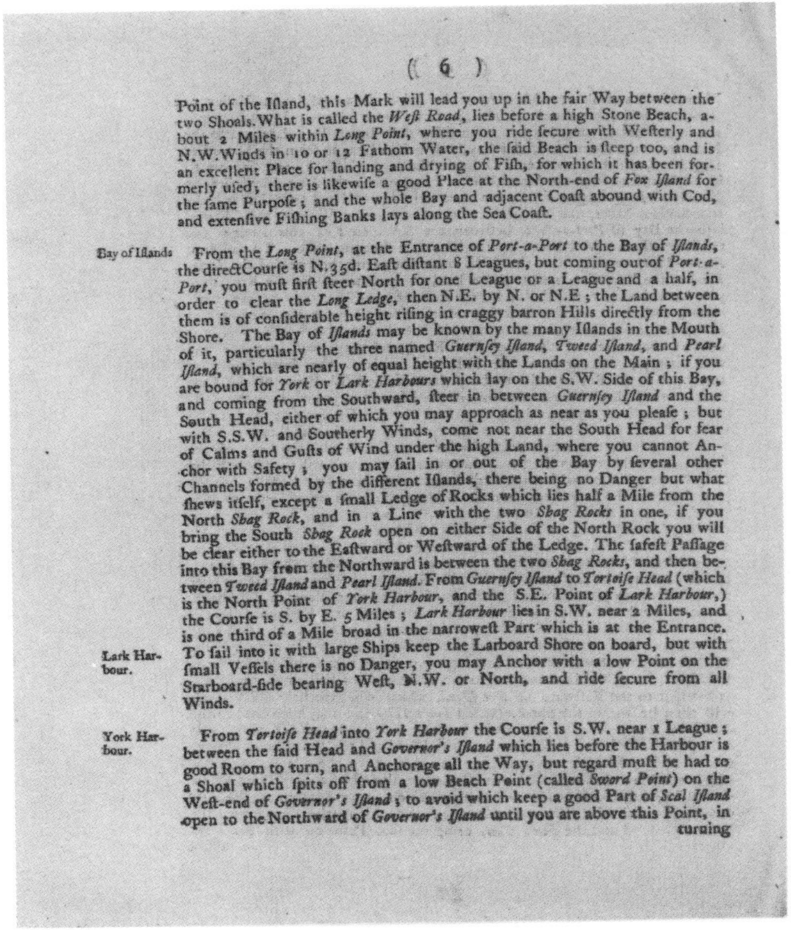

(6)

Point of the Island, this Mark will lead you up in the fair Way between the two Shoals. What is called the *West Head*, lies before a high Stone Beach, about 2 Miles within *Long Point*, where you ride secure with Westerly and N.W. Winds in 10 or 12 Fathom Water, the said Beach in steep too, and is an excellent Place for landing and drying of Fish, for which it has been formerly used; there is likewise a good Place at the North-end of *Fox Island* for the same Purpose; and the whole Bay and adjacent Coast abound with Cod, and extensive Fishing Banks lays along the Sea Coast.

Bay of Islands. From the *Long Point*, at the Entrance of *Port-a-Port* to the Bay of *Islands*, the direct Course is N.35d. East distant 8 Leagues, but coming out of *Port-a-Port*, you must first steer North for one League or a League and a half, in order to clear the *Long Ledge*, then N.E. by N. or N.E.; the Land between them is of considerable height riding in craggy barren Hills directly from the Shore. The Bay of *Island* may be known by the many Islands in the Mouth of it, particularly the three named *Guernsey Island, Tweed Island,* and *Pearl Island,* which are nearly of equal height with the Lands on the Main; if you are bound for *York* or *Lark Harbours* which lay on the S.W. Side of this Bay, and coming from the Southward, steer in between *Guernsey Island* and the South Head, either of which you may approach as near as you please; but with S.S.W. and Southerly Winds, come not near the South Head for fear of Calms and Gusts of Wind under the high Land, where you cannot Anchor with Safety, you may fail in or out of the Bay by several other Channels formed by the different Islands, there being no Danger but what shews itself, except a small Ledge of Rocks which lies half a Mile from the North *Slug Rock,* and in a Line with the two *Slug Rocks* in one, if you bring the South *Slug Rock* open on either Side of the North Rock you will be clear either to the Eastward or Westward of the Ledge. The safest Passage into this Bay from the Northward is between the two *Slug Rocks,* and then between *Tweed Island* and *Pearl Island.* From *Guernsey Island* to *Tweed Head* (which is the North Point of *York Harbour*), and the S.E. Point of *Lark Harbour,* the Course is S. by E. 5 Miles; *Lark Harbour* lies in S.W. near 2 Miles, and is one third of a Mile broad in the narrowest Part which is at the Entrance. To fail into it with large Ships keep the Larboard Shore on board, but with small Vessels there is no Danger, you may Anchor with a low Point on the Starboard-side bearing West, N.W. or North, and ride secure from all Winds.

Lark Harbour.

York Harbour. From *Tweese Head* into *York Harbour* the Course is S.W. near 1 League; between the said Head and *Governor's Island* which lies before the Harbour is good Room to turn, and Anchorage all the Way; but regard must be had to a Shoal which spits off from a low Beach Point (called *Sword Point*) on the West-end of *Governor's Island;* to avoid which keep a good Part of *Seal Island* open to the Northward of *Governor's Island* until you are above this Point, in curning

---

Plate 97 A page of Cook's printed sailing-directions, for the Bay of Islands. (Bibliography, No. 10).

Plate 96 Bibliography, No. 14: titlepage.

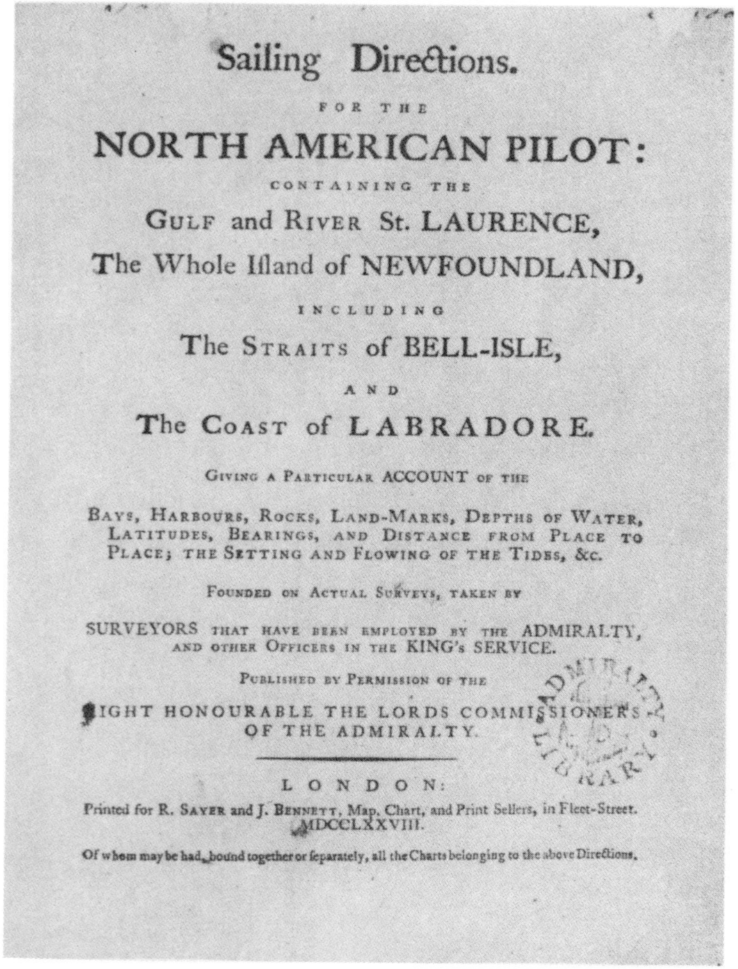

Sailing Directions

FOR THE

NORTH AMERICAN PILOT:

CONTAINING THE

Gulph and River St. LAURENCE,

The Whole Ifland of NEWFOUNDLAND,

INCLUDING

The Straits of BELL-ISLE,

AND

The Coast of LABRADORE:

GIVING A PARTICULAR ACCOUNT OF THE

BAYS, HARBOURS, ROCKS, LAND-MARKS, DEPTHS OF WATER,
LATITUDES, BEARINGS, AND DISTANCE FROM PLACE TO
PLACE; THE SETTING AND FLOWING OF THE TIDES, &c.

FOUNDED ON ACTUAL SURVEYS, TAKEN BY

SURVEYORS THAT HAVE BEEN EMPLOYED BY THE ADMIRALTY,
AND OTHER OFFICERS IN THE KING's SERVICE.

PUBLISHED BY PERMISSION OF

THE RIGHT HONOURABLE THE LORDS COMMISSIONERS
OF THE ADMIRALTY.

L'ONDON:

Printed for R. SAYER and J. BENNETT, Map, Chart, and Print-Sellers, in Fleet-Street.
MDCCLXXXII.

Or them may be had, bound together or feparately, all the Charts belonging to the above Direct...

Plate 99   Bibliography, No. 18: titlepage.

Sailing Directions.

FOR THE

NORTH AMERICAN PILOT:

CONTAINING THE

Gulf and River St. LAURENCE,

The Whole Ifland of NEWFOUNDLAND,

INCLUDING

The Straits of BELL-ISLE,

AND

The Coast of LABRADORE.

GIVING A PARTICULAR ACCOUNT OF THE

BAYS, HARBOURS, ROCKS, LAND-MARKS, DEPTHS OF WATER,
LATITUDES, BEARINGS, AND DISTANCE FROM PLACE TO
PLACE; THE SETTING AND FLOWING OF THE TIDES, &c.

FOUNDED ON ACTUAL SURVEYS, TAKEN BY

SURVEYORS THAT HAVE BEEN EMPLOYED BY THE ADMIRALTY,
AND OTHER OFFICERS IN THE KING's SERVICE.

PUBLISHED BY PERMISSION OF THE

...IGHT HONOURABLE THE LORDS COMMISSIONERS
OF THE ADMIRALTY.

LONDON:

Printed for R. SAYER and J. BENNETT, Map, Chart, and Print Sellers, in Fleet-Street.
MDCCLXXVIII.

Of whom may be had, bound together or feparately, all the Charts belonging to the above Directions.

Plate 98   Bibliography, No. 16: titlepage.

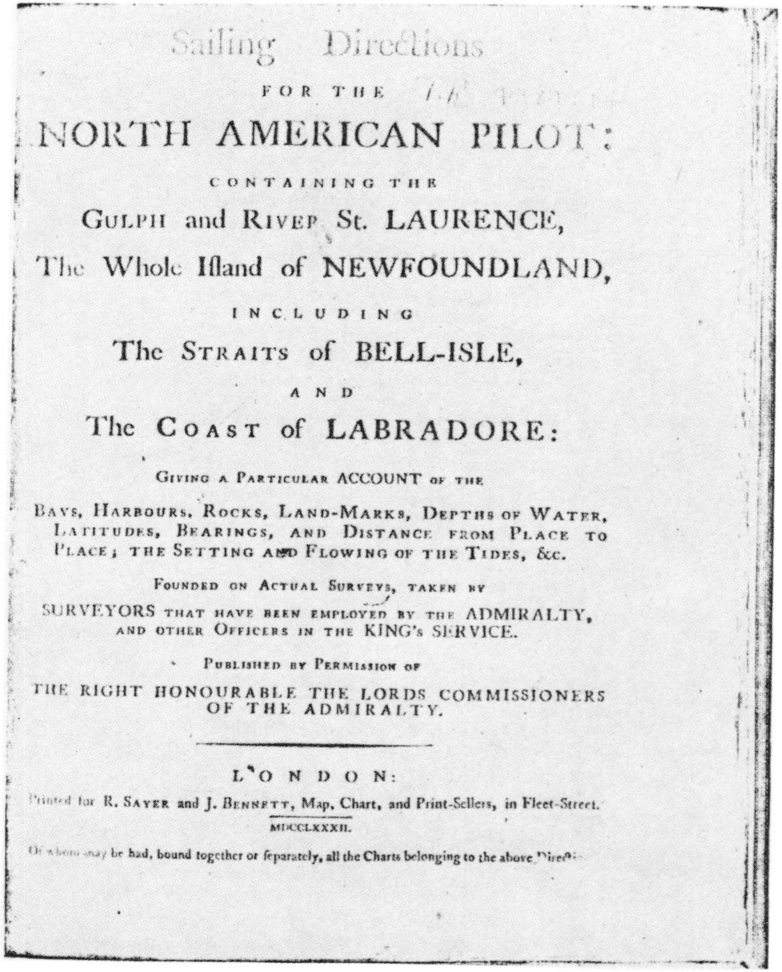

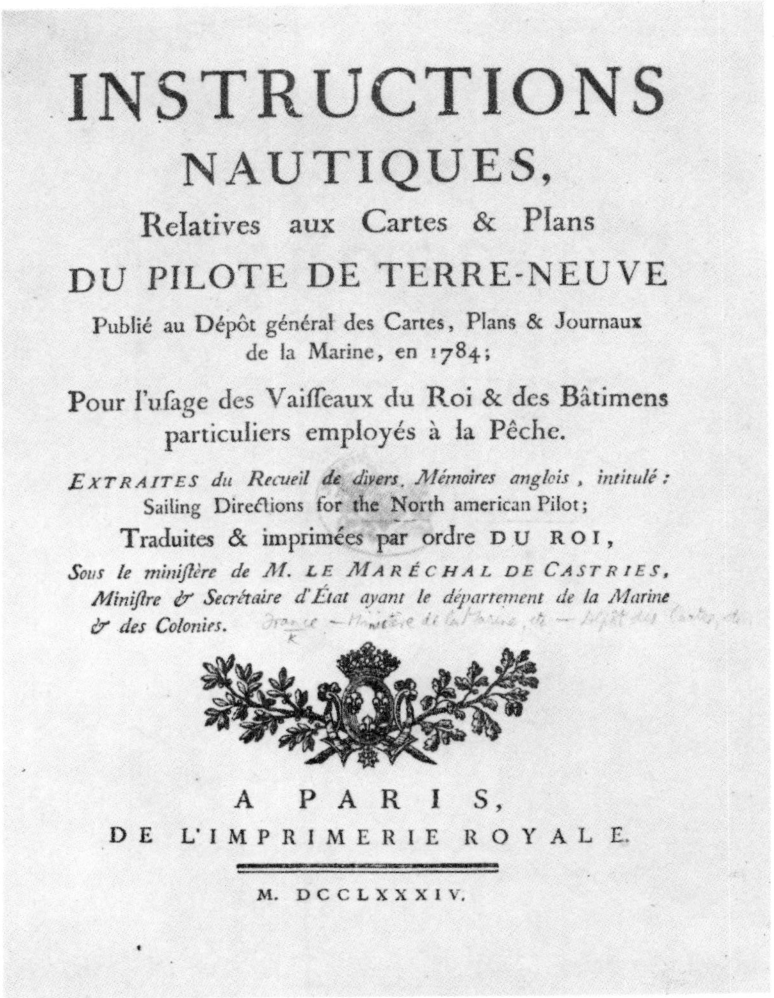

SAILING DIRECTIONS

FOR THE

FIRST PART

OF THE

NORTH AMERICAN PILOT:

CONTAINING THE

GULF AND RIVER ST. LAWRENCE,

THE WHOLE ISLAND OF

NEWFOUNDLAND,

INCLUDING THE

STRAITS OF BELLE-ISLE,

AND THE

COAST OF LABRADORE

GIVING

A PARTICULAR ACCOUNT

OF THE

BAYS, HARBOURS, ROCKS, LAND-MARKS, DEPTHS OF WATER, LATITUDES,
BEARINGS, AND DISTANCE FROM PLACE TO PLACE; THE SETTING
AND FLOWING OF THE TIDES, &c.

FOUNDED ON ACTUAL SURVEYS, TAKEN BY

CAPT. JAMES COOK, MICHAEL LANE,

AND OTHER OFFICERS AND SURVEYORS THAT HAVE BEEN EMPLOYED BY THE
ADMIRALTY, AND IN THE KING'S SERVICE:

PUBLISHED BY PERMISSION OF

THE RIGHT HONOURABLE

THE LORDS COMMISSIONERS OF THE ADMIRALTY.

A NEW EDITION.

London:

PRINTED FOR ROBERT LAURIE AND JAMES WHITTLE,

No. 53, FLEET STREET,

(SUCCESSORS TO THE LATE MR. ROBERT SAYER.)

1794.

N. B. This Book of Directions is sold only with the Pilot, but any of the Charts may be had separate.

Plate 101   Bibliography, No. 21: titlepage.

INSTRUCTIONS
NAUTIQUES,

Relatives aux Cartes & Plans

DU PILOTE DE TERRE-NEUVE

Publié au Dépôt général des Cartes, Plans & Journaux
de la Marine, en 1784;

Pour l'ufage des Vaiffeaux du Roi & des Bâtimens
particuliers employés à la Pêche.

EXTRAITS du Recueil de divers Mémoires anglois, intitulé :
Sailing Directions for the North american Pilot;
Traduits & imprimées par ordre DU ROI,

Sous le miniftre de *M. LE MARÉCHAL DE CASTRIES,*
Miniftre & Secrétaire d'État ayant le département de la Marine
& des Colonies.

A PARIS,

DE L'IMPRIMERIE ROYALE.

M. DCCLXXXIV.

Plate 100   Bibliography, No. 20: titlepage.

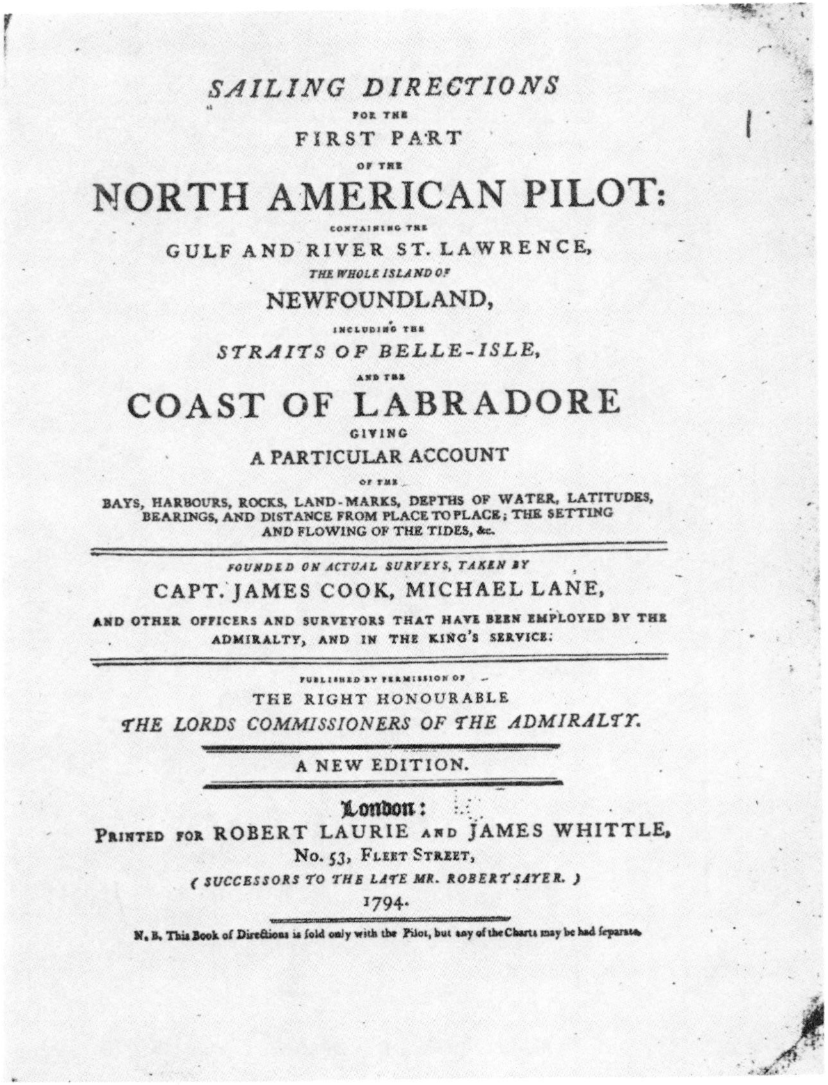

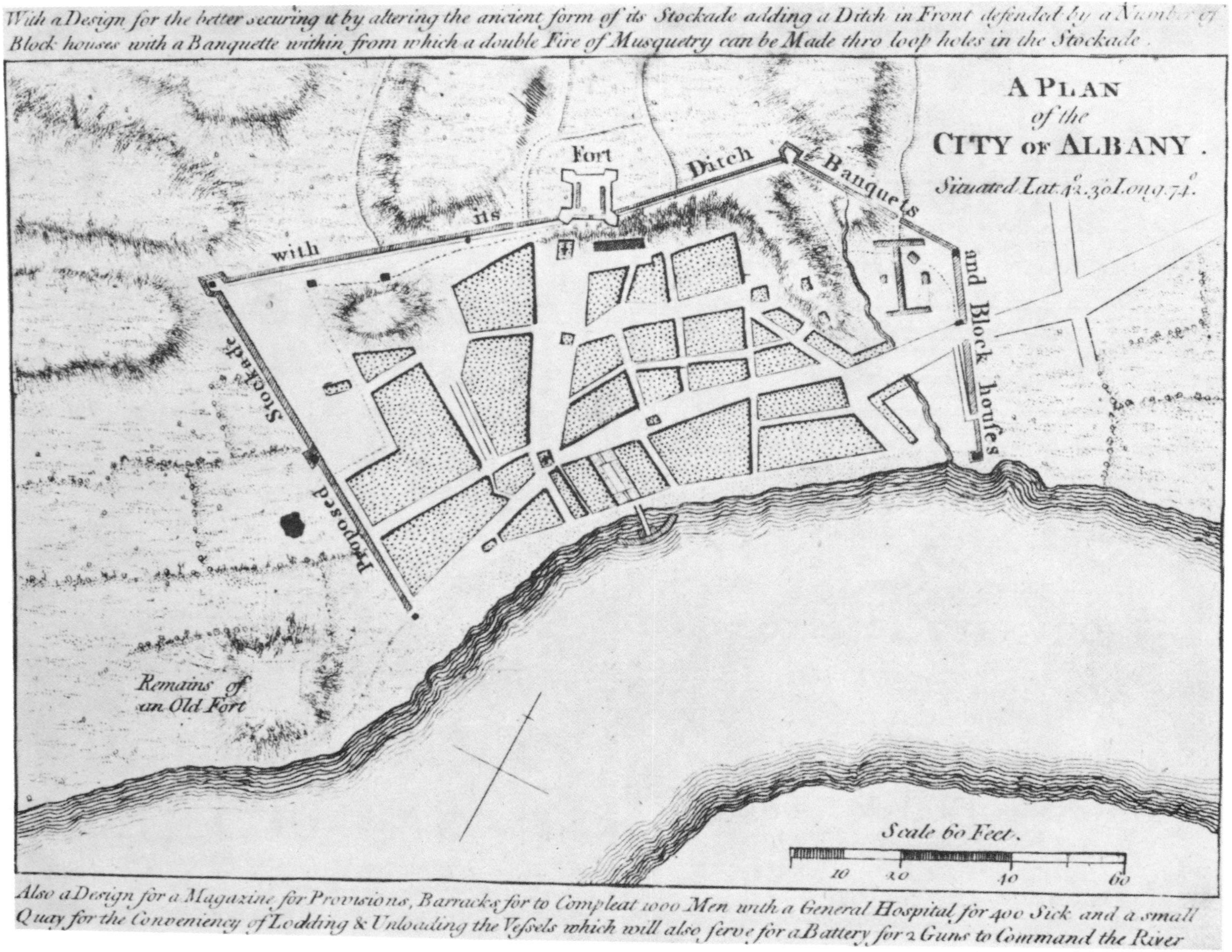

A PLAN
of the
CITY of ALBANY.
Situated Latt.42.30 long.174.

With a Design for the better securing it by altering the ancient form of its Stockade adding a Ditch in Front defended by a Number of Block houses with a Banquette within, from which a double Fire of Musquetry can be Made thro loop holes in the Stockade.

and Block houses

Banquets

Ditch

Fort

with

Stockade

Proposed

Remains of an Old Fort

Scale 60 Feet.

Also a Design for a Magazine for Provisions, Barracks for to Compleat 2000 Men with a General Hospital for 400 Sick and a small Quay for the Conveniency of Loading & Unloading the Vessels which will also serve for a Battery for 2 Guns to Command the River

Plate 102   Albany, 1765.

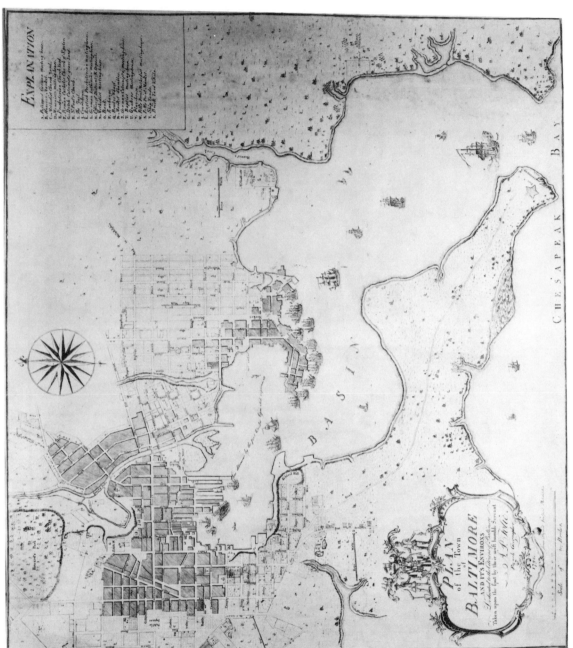

Plate 103   Baltimore (Maryland), 1792.

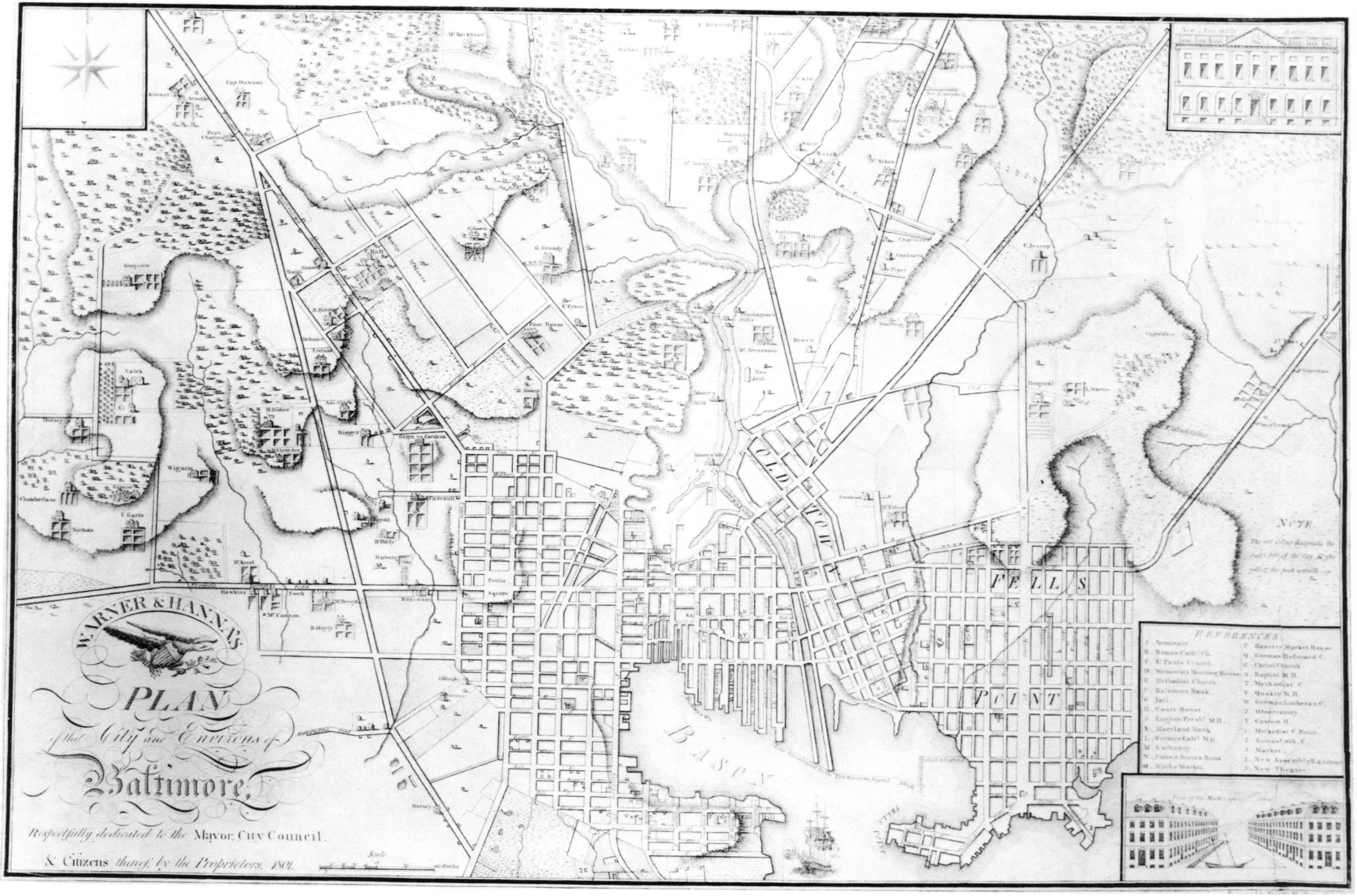

Plate 104   Baltimore (Maryland), 1801.

PLAN DE LA VILLE DE BOSTON

A. Batt.ᵉ de 25 Pieces de C.ⁿ
B. Batt. de 16.Pieces de Can.ⁿ
C. Batt. de 25 Pieces
D. Temple des Présbiteriens
E. Temple des Quaquers
F. Maison de Ville

G. Temple des Anabaptistes
H. Place d'Armes
J. Fanal
K. Guerite elevée et Sentinelle
L. Magasin a Poudre

M. Moulin et Digue
N. Bassin qui asseche
O. Prisons
P. Autre Temple des Presbiteriens
Q. Porte de Terre

Echelle de deux Mille Toises.

500   1000   2000 Toises

Batterie

Charles Town

VILLE DE

BOSTON

Isle Ronde

Moulin

Rade

Brod

Chenal

Roches trés Dangereuses

Ance ou peuvent mouiller des Barques et des Chaloupes

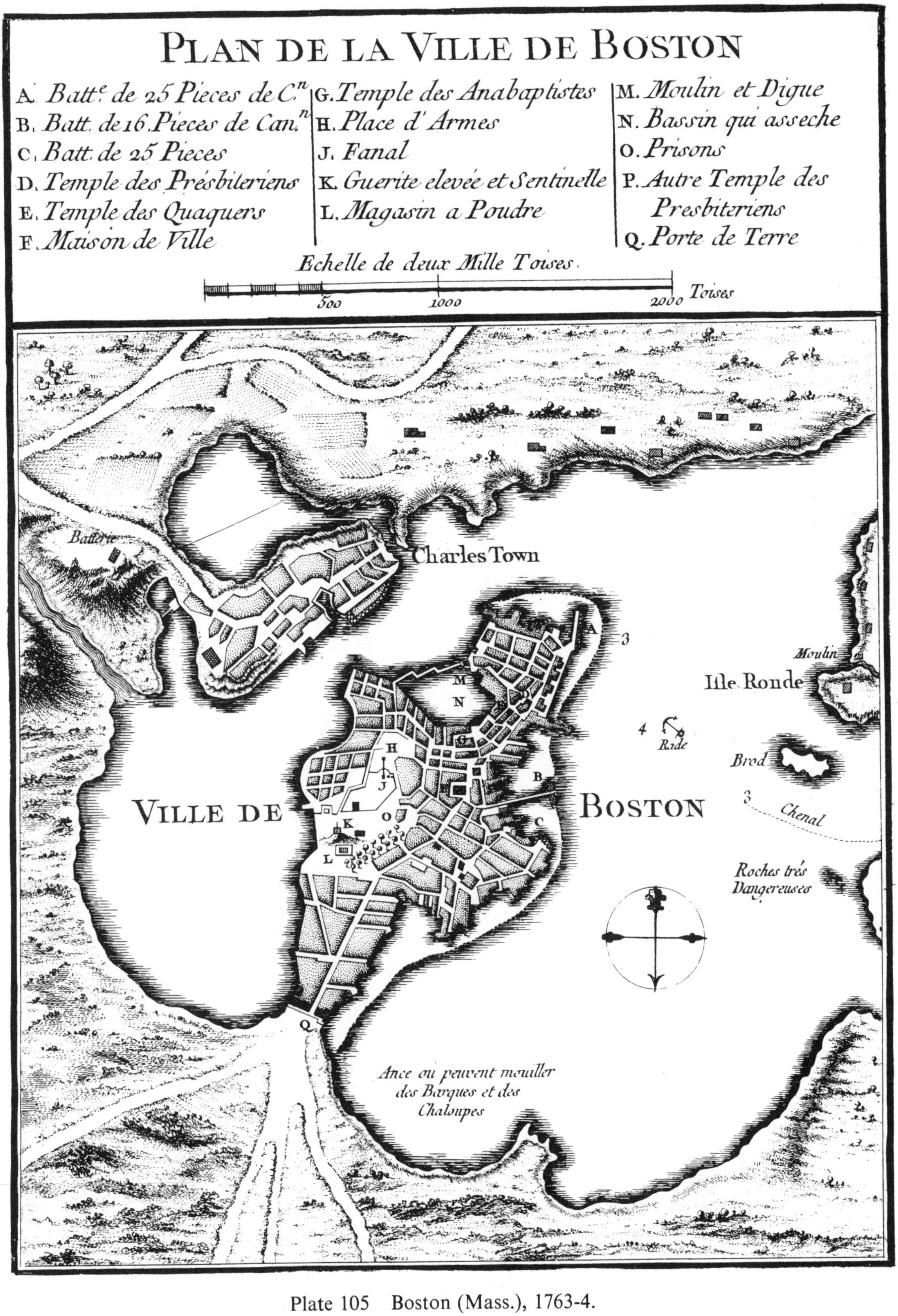

Plate 105   Boston (Mass.), 1763-4.

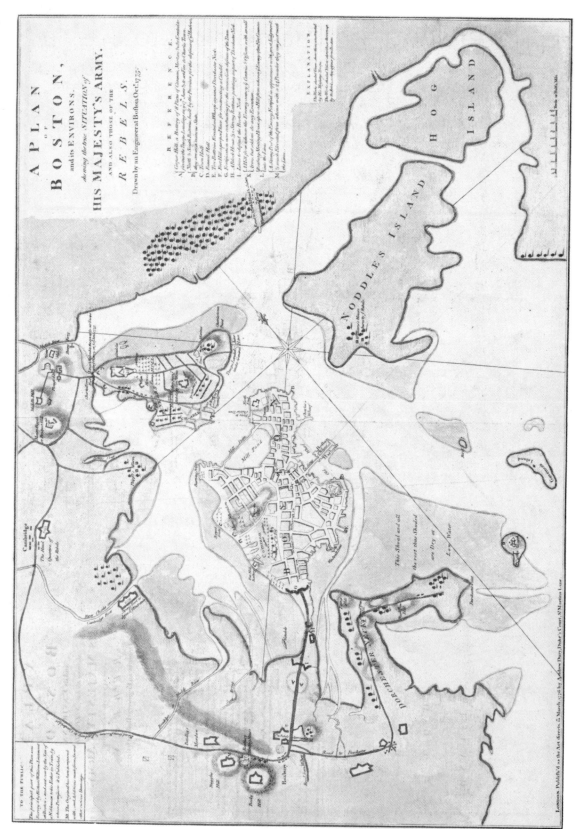

Plate 106   Boston (Mass.), 1775.

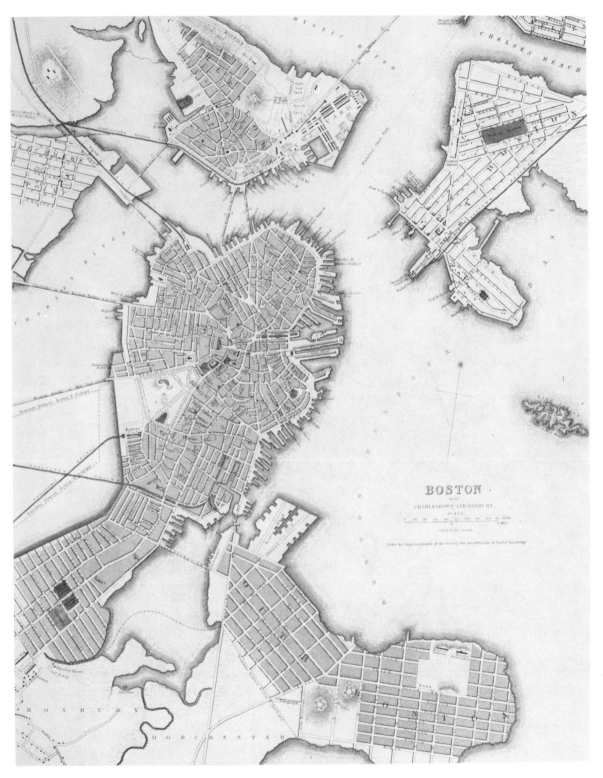

Plate 107   Boston (Mass.), 1842.

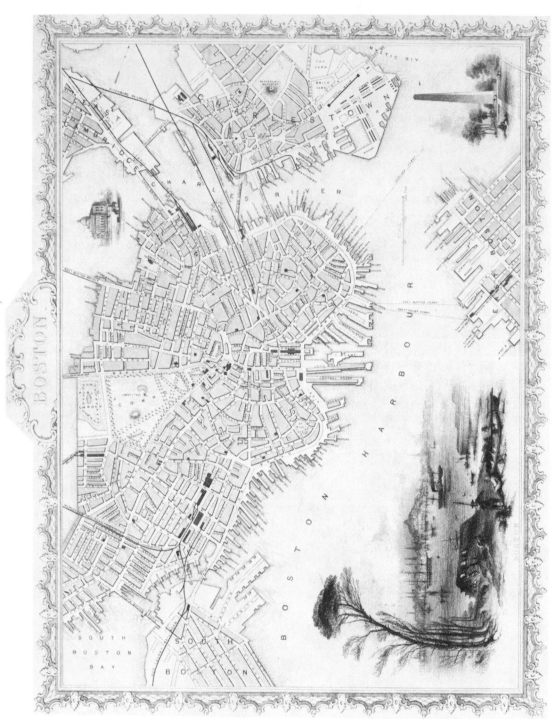

Plate 108   Boston (Mass.), 1851.

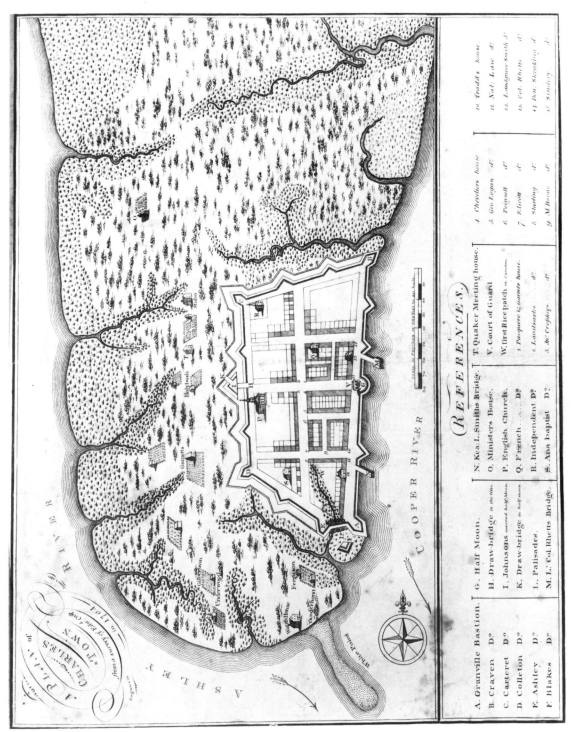

A PLAN of CHARLES TOWN in 1704

ASHLEY RIVER

COOPER RIVER

White point

(REFERENCES.)

A. Granville Bastion.	G. Half Moon.	N. Kea:I. Smiths Bridge.	T. Quaker Meeting house.	4 Chevrs house	10 Tredd's house
B. Craven Dº.	H. Draw-bridge on the tine.	O. Ministers House.	V. Court of Guard	5 Geo Logan dº	11 Nat: Law dº
C. Carteret Dº.	I. Johnsons corner half Moon	P. English Church.	W. first Rice patch in Carolina	6 Poinsett dº	12 Landgrave Smith dº
D. Colleton Dº.	K. Draw-bridge in half moon	Q. French Dº.	1 Pasquero & Garrets house.	7 Elicott dº	13 Col. Rhets dº
E. Ashley Dº.	L. Palisades.	R. Independent Dº.	2 Landsacks dº	8 Starling dº	14 Ben Skenking dº
F. Blakes Dº.	M.I. Col.Rhets Bridge.	S. Ana baptist Dº.	3 Mr Croksleys dº	9 Mr Boone dº	15 Simleys dº

Plate 109 Charles Town (Carolina), 1704.

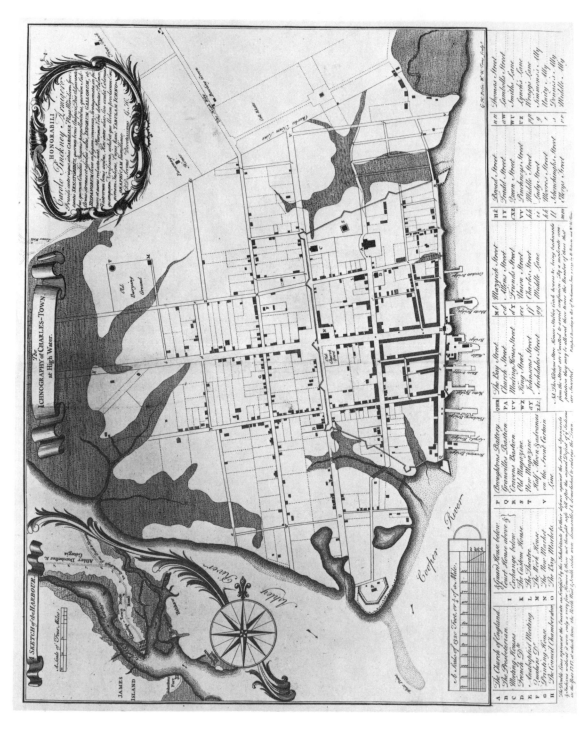

Plate 110 Charles Town (Carolina), 1739.

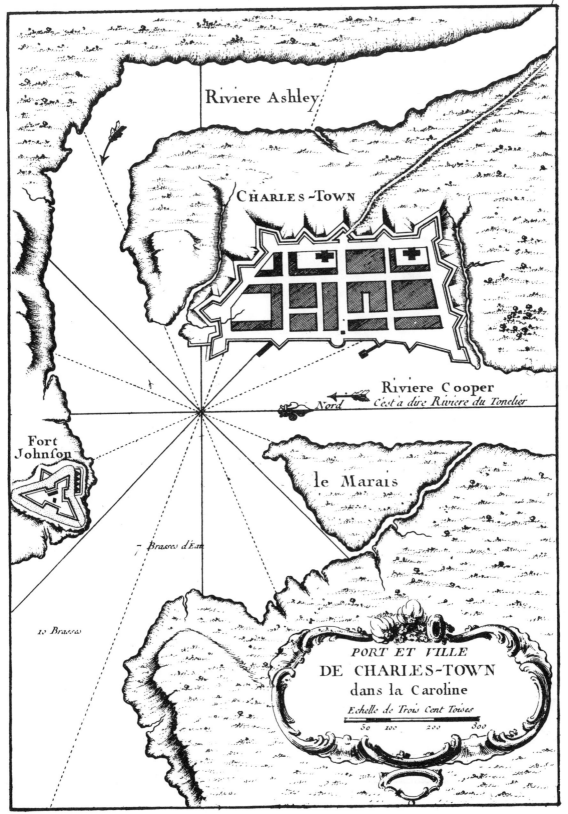

Riviere Ashley

CHARLES~TOWN

Riviere Cooper
Nord   C'est a dire Riviere du Tonelier

Fort Johnfon

le Marais

Braſſes d'Eau

10 Braſſes

PORT ET VILLE
DE CHARLES~TOWN
dans la Caroline
Echelle de Trois Cent Toiſes
50   100   200   300

Plate 111   Charles Town (Carolina), 1763-4.

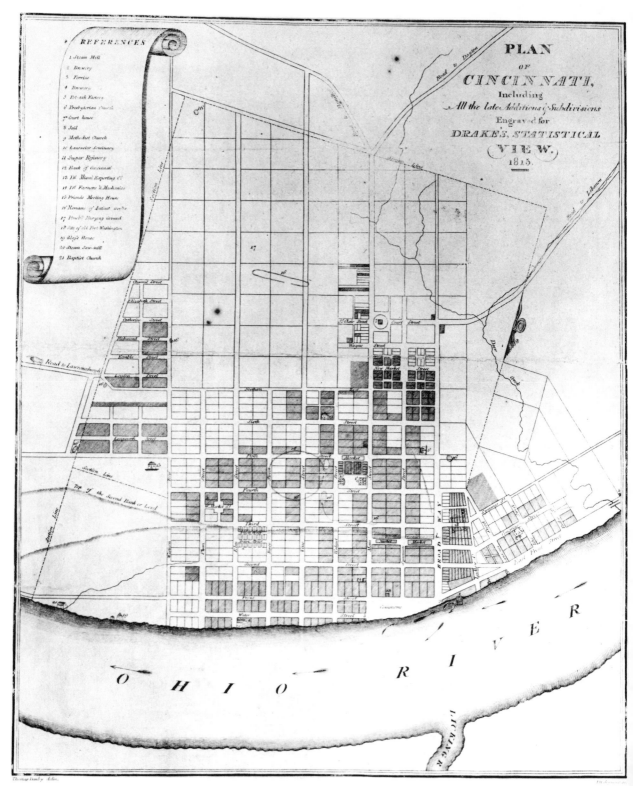

Plate 112   Cincinnati, 1815.

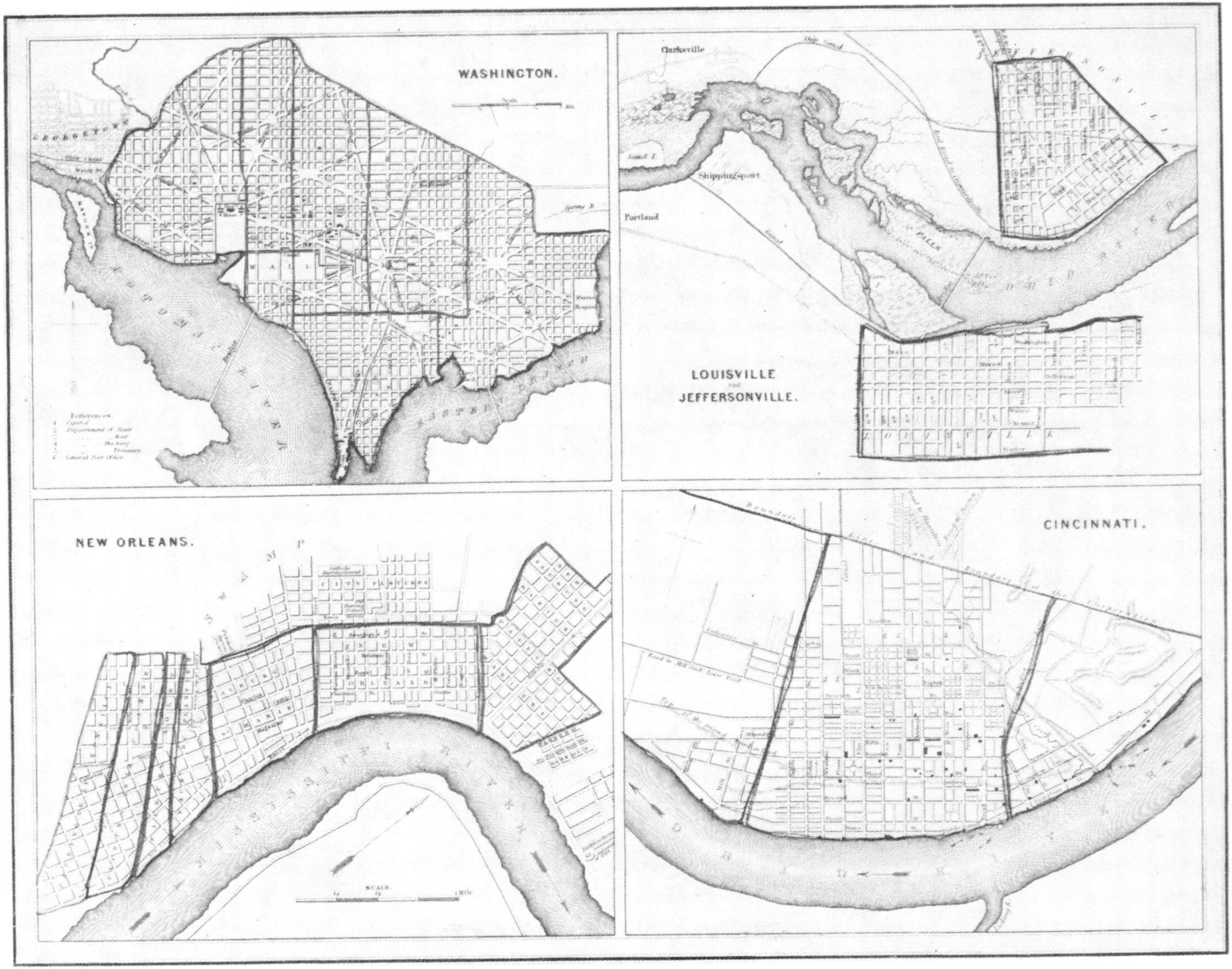
WASHINGTON.
GEORGETOWN
MALL
POTOMAC RIVER
LOUISVILLE and JEFFERSONVILLE.
Clarksville
Shippingsport
Portland
JEFFERSONVILLE
LOUISVILLE
OHIO RIVER
NEW ORLEANS.
SWAMP
NEW ORLEANS
MISSISSIPPI RIVER
CINCINNATI.
OHIO RIVER

Plate 113 Cincinnati, 1838.

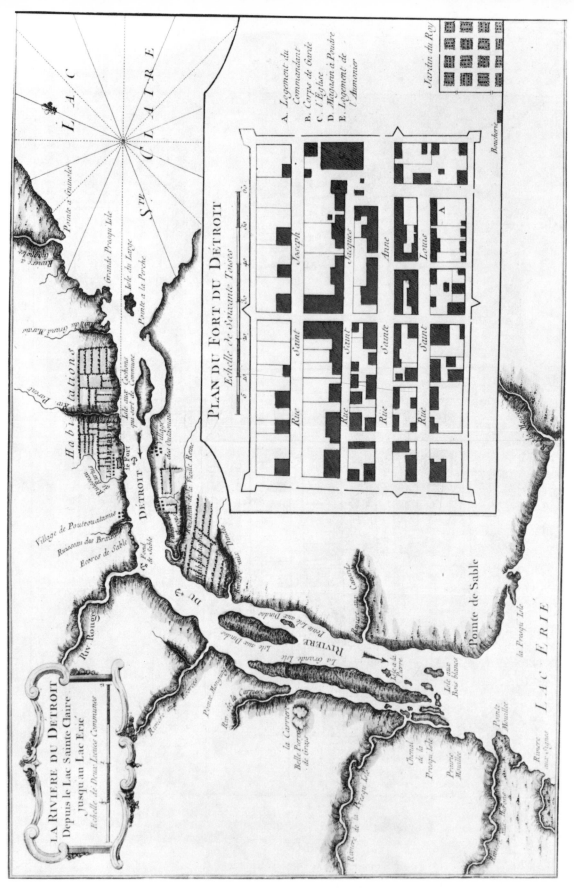

Plate 114   Detroit, 1763-4.

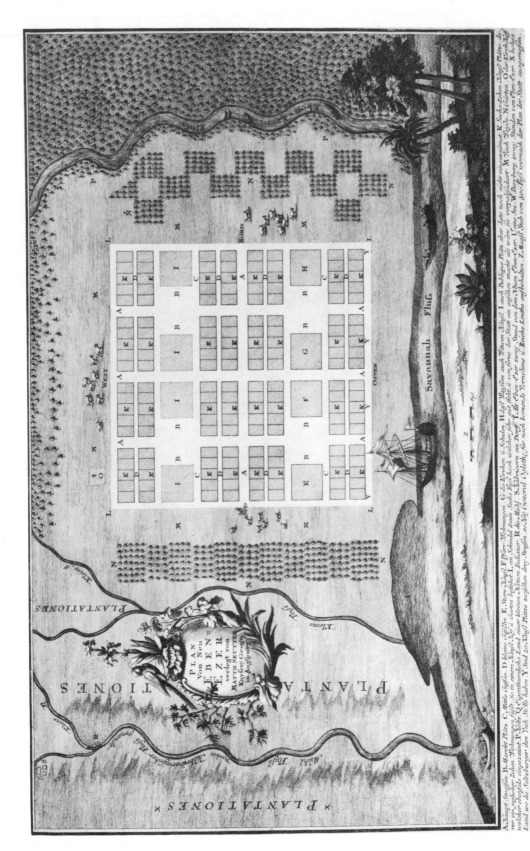

Plate 115 Ebenezer (Georgia), [1747].

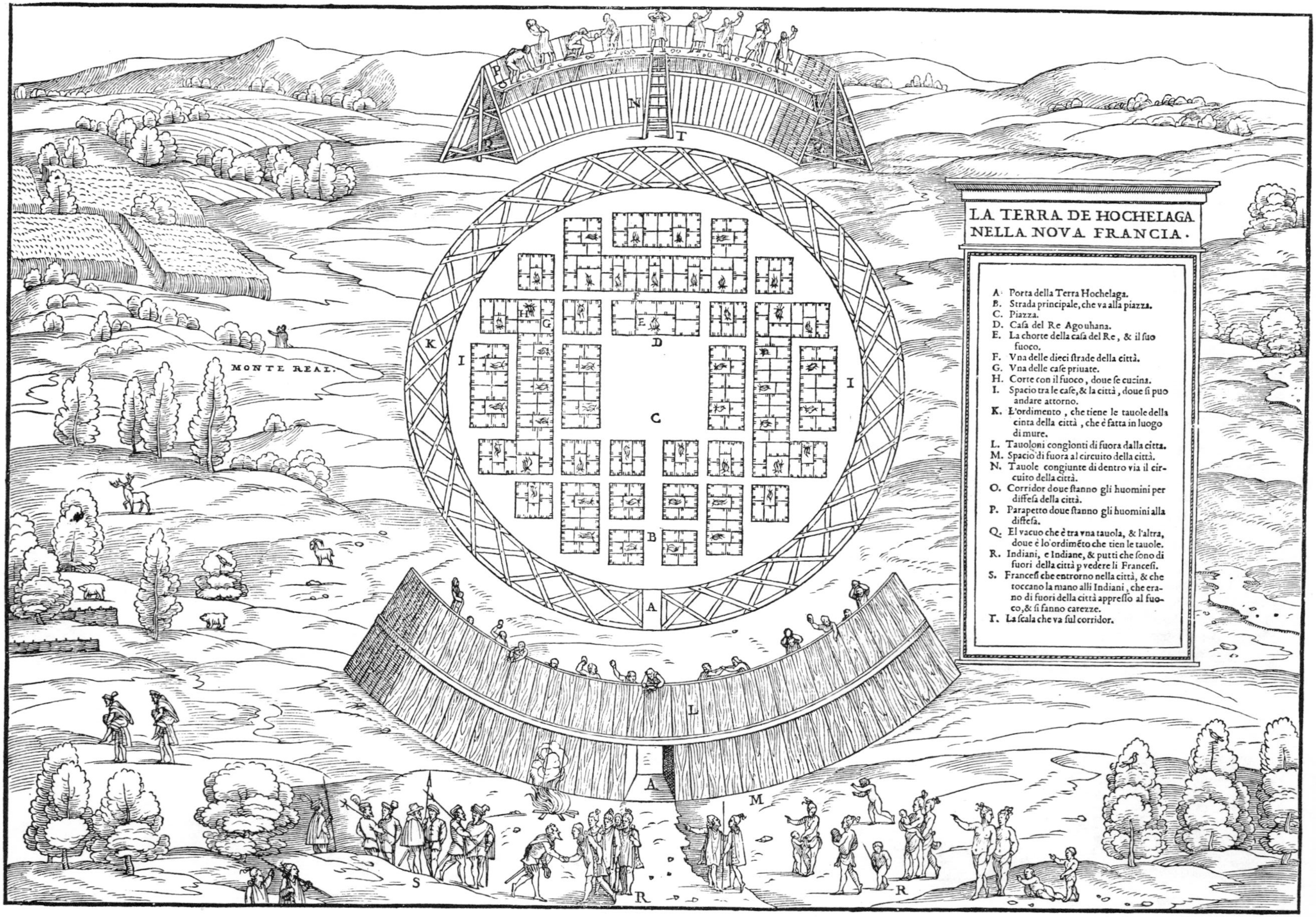

Plate 116 Montreal (Canada), 1556.

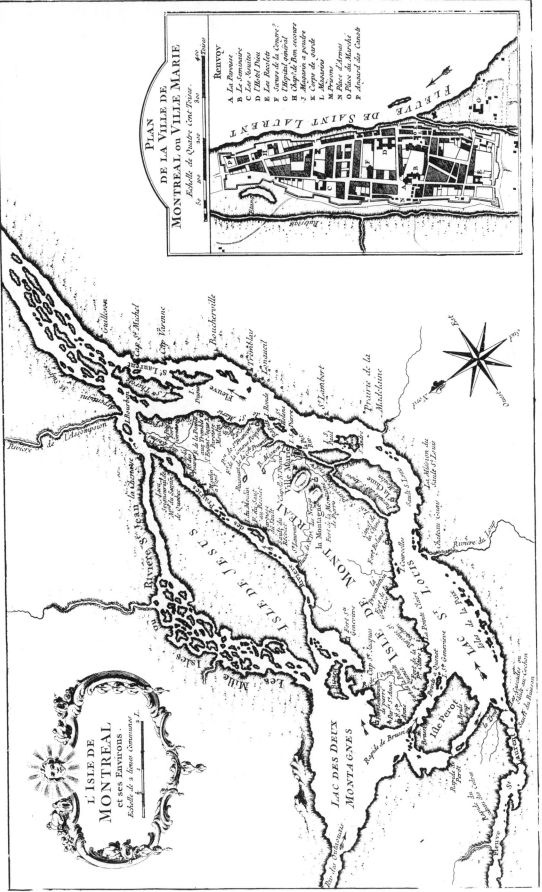

Plate 117 Montreal, 1763-4.

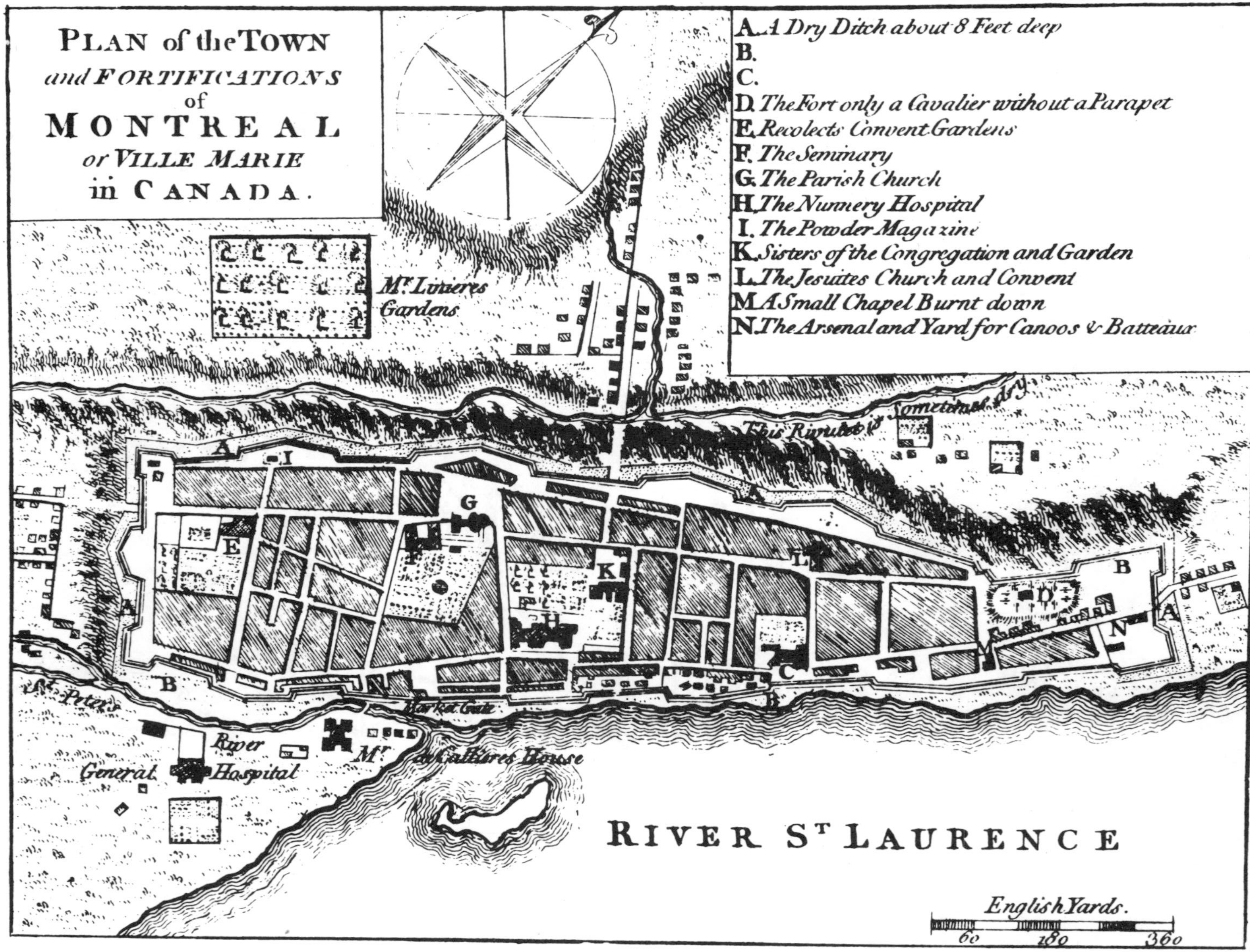
PLAN of the TOWN
and FORTIFICATIONS
of
MONTREAL
or VILLE MARIE
in CANADA.
A. A Dry Ditch about 8 Feet deep
B.
C.
D. The Fort only a Cavalier without a Parapet
E. Recolects Convent Gardens
F. The Seminary
G. The Parish Church
H. The Nunnery Hospital
I. The Powder Magazine
K. Sisters of the Congregation and Garden
L. The Jesuites Church and Convent
M. A Small Chapel Burnt down
N. The Arsenal and Yard for Canoos & Batteaux
Mr. Lineres Gardens
This Rivulet is Sometimes dry
Market Gate
River
General Hospital
RIVER ST LAURENCE
English Yards.
60
180
360

Plate 118 Montreal, 1765.

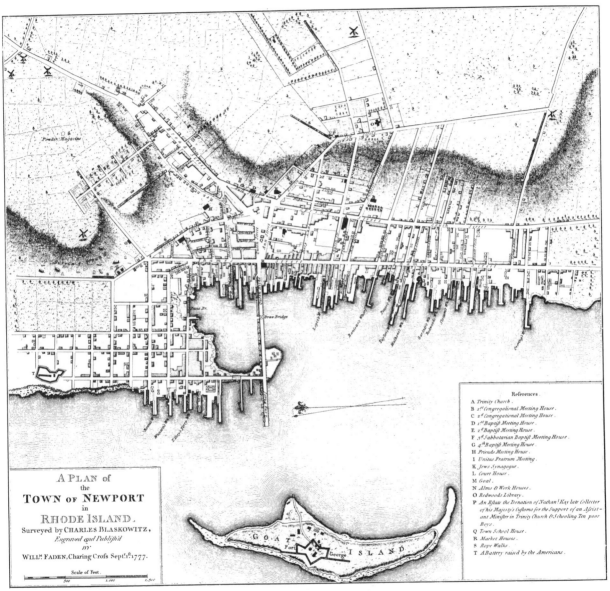

A PLAN of
the
TOWN OF NEWPORT
in
RHODE ISLAND.
Surveyed by CHARLES BLASKOWITZ,
Engraved and Publish'd
BY
WILL.^M FADEN, Charing Crofs Septr 1.st 1777.

Scale of Feet.

References.

A *Trinity Church*.
B *1st Congregational Meeting House*.
C *2^d Congregational Meeting House*.
D *1st Baptist Meeting House*.
E *2^d Baptist Meeting House*.
F *3^d Sabbatarian Baptist Meeting House*.
G *4th Baptist Meeting House*.
H *Friends Meeting House*.
I *Unitas Fratrum Meeting*.
K *Jews Synagogue*.
L *Court House*.
M *Goal*.
N *Alms & Work Houses*.
O *Redwoods Library*.
P *An Estate the Donation of Nathan.^l Kay late Collector
   of his Majesty's Customs for the Support of an Assist-
   ant Minister in Trinity Church & Schooling Ten poor
   Boys*.
Q *Town School House*.
R *Market Houses*.
S *Rope Walks*.
T *A Battery raised by the Americans*.

Plate 119   Newport (Rhode Is.), 1777.

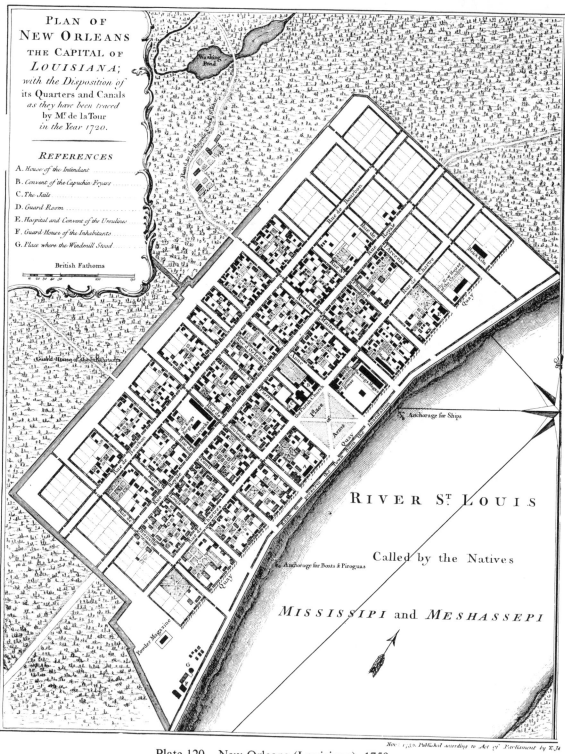

Nov. 1759. Published according to Act of Parliament by T. Je

Plate 120   New Orleans (Louisiana), 1759.

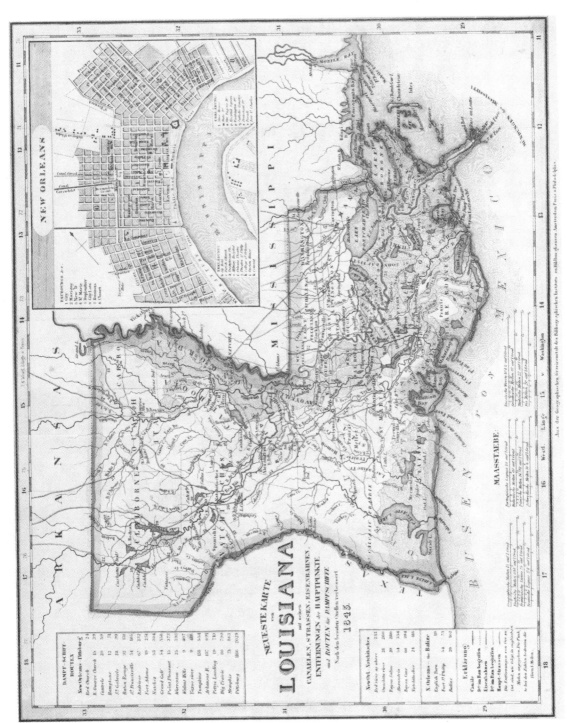

Plate 121   New Orleans (Louisiana), 1845.

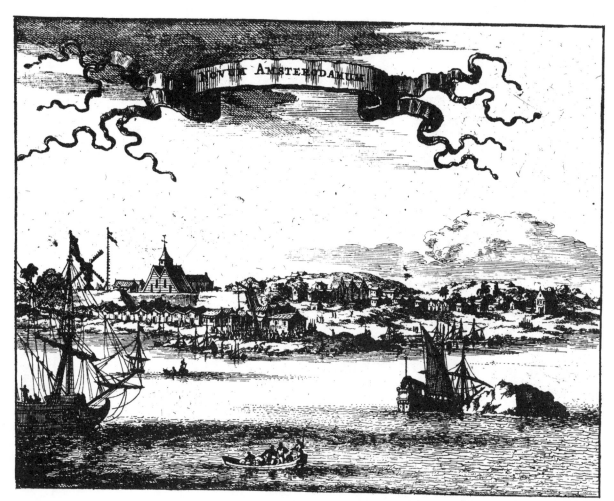

Plate 122   New York, 1670.

NEU AMSTERDAM al NEW YOR

Carolus a Allard excudit cum Privilegio ordinum Hollandiæ & Westfrisiæ.

Plate 123 New York, 1698.

VILLE DE MANATHE ou NOUVELLE-YORC

A. *Le Port des Barques*
B. *Pont pour décharger les Barques*
C. *Fontaines ou Puids*
D. *Maison du Gouverneur*

E. *Le Temple*
F. *Place d'Armes*
G. *Boucherie a debiter*
H. *Boucherie a tuer*

J. *la Basse Ville*
K. *Maison de Ville*
L. *Douane et Magasins*
M. *Magasins a Poudre*

Echelle de Cent Toises

5 10 15 20 25   50   100 *Toises*

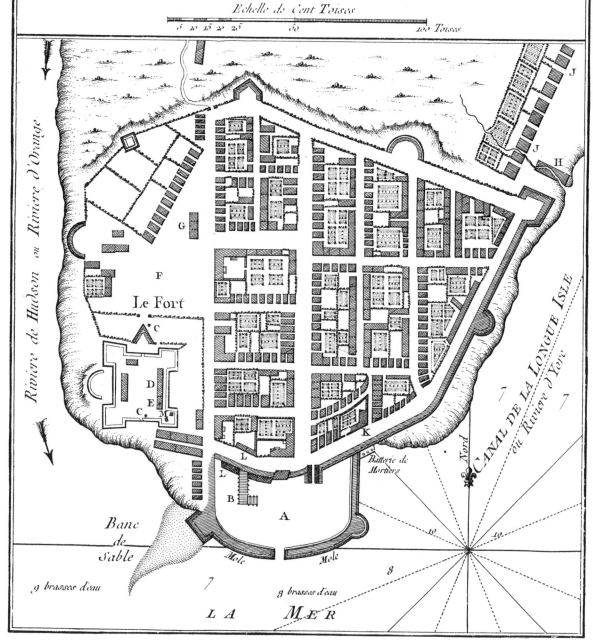

Plate 124   New York, 1763-4.

Plate 125   New York, 1763-5.

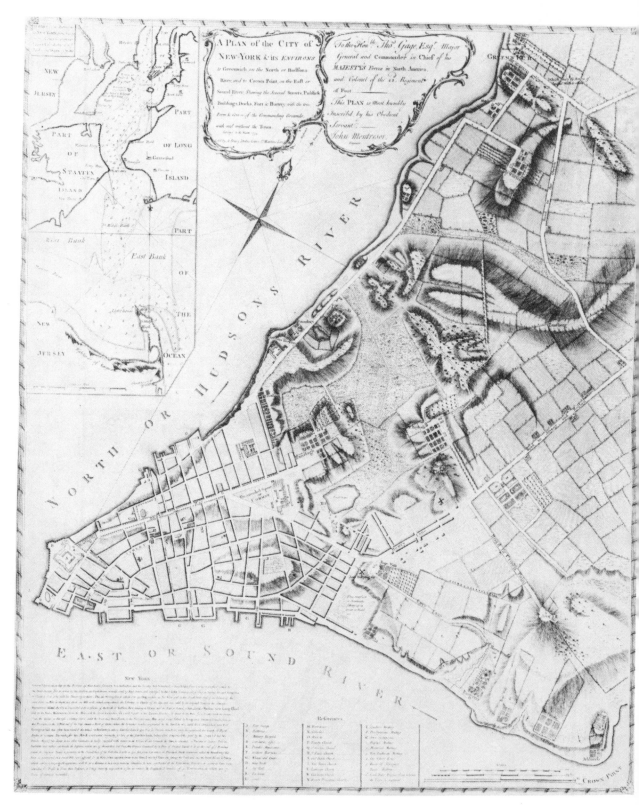

Plate 126　New York, 1775.

Plate 127   New York, 1776.

Plate 128   New York, 1840.

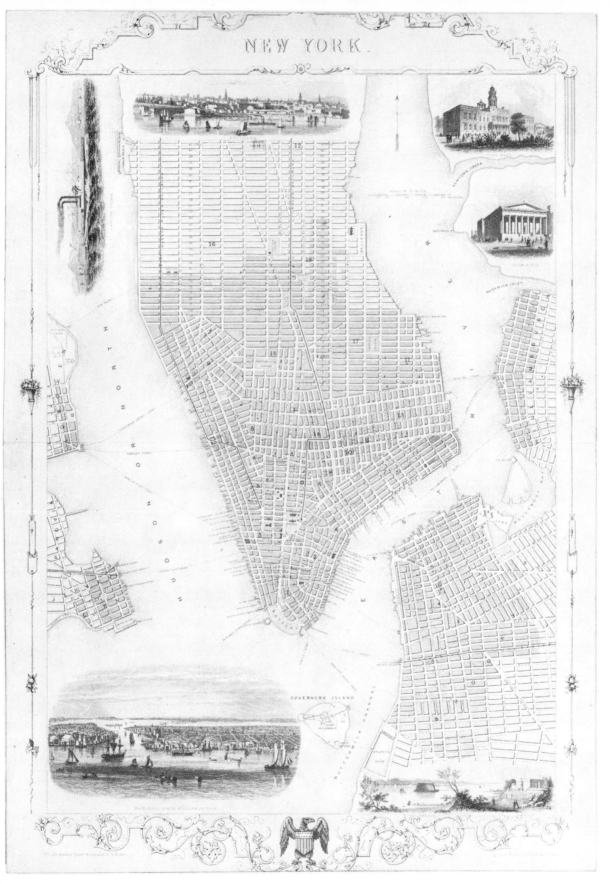

NEW YORK.

Plate 129   New York, 1851.

A MAPP OF Yᵉ IMPROVED PART OF PENSILVANIA IN AMERICA, DIVIDED INTO COUNTIES, TOWNSHIPS AND LOTTS

Surveyed by Thoˢ Holme

To William Penn Esqʳ Proprietor & Governer of PENNSILVANIA This Mapp is humbly Dedicated by his Friend Ino Harris

The City PHILADELPHIA

Delaware River

Scale of English Miles

NEW JARSEY

PART OF WEST

Plate 130   Philadelphia (Penn.), [1687].

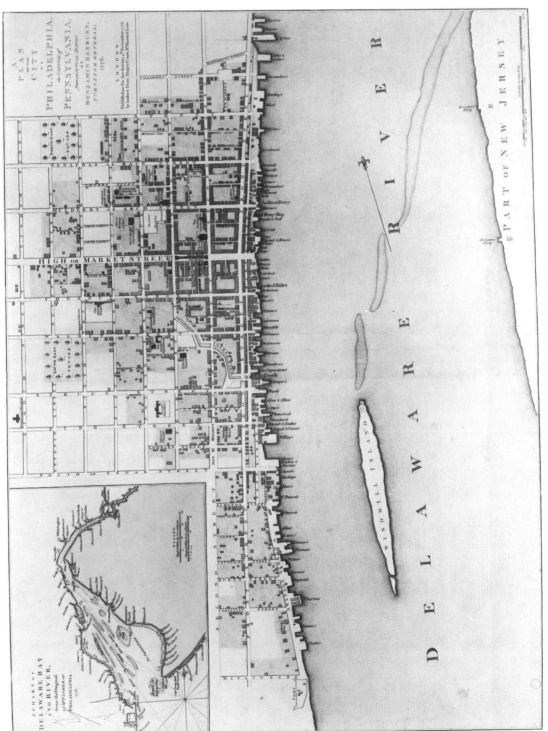

Plate 131 Philadelphia (Penn.), 1776.

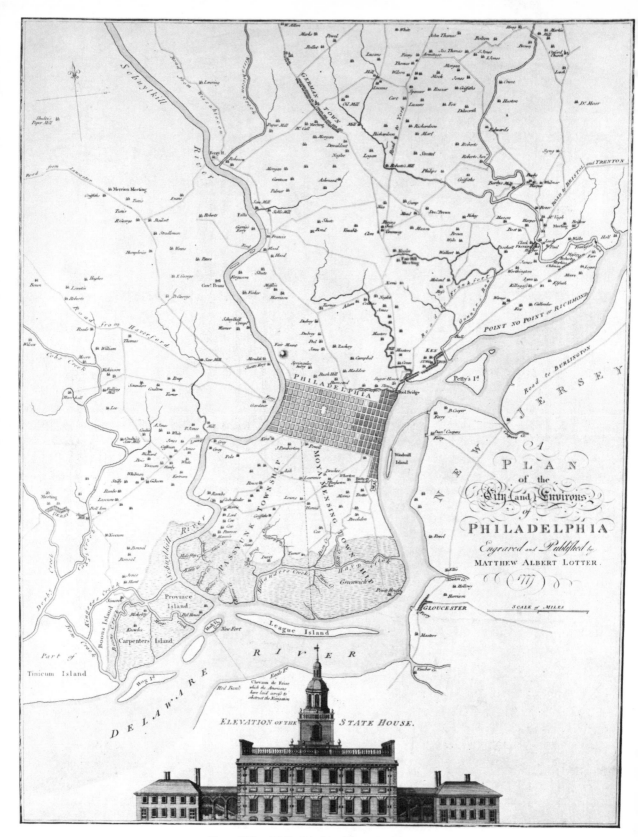

Plate 132   Philadelphia (Penn.), 1777.

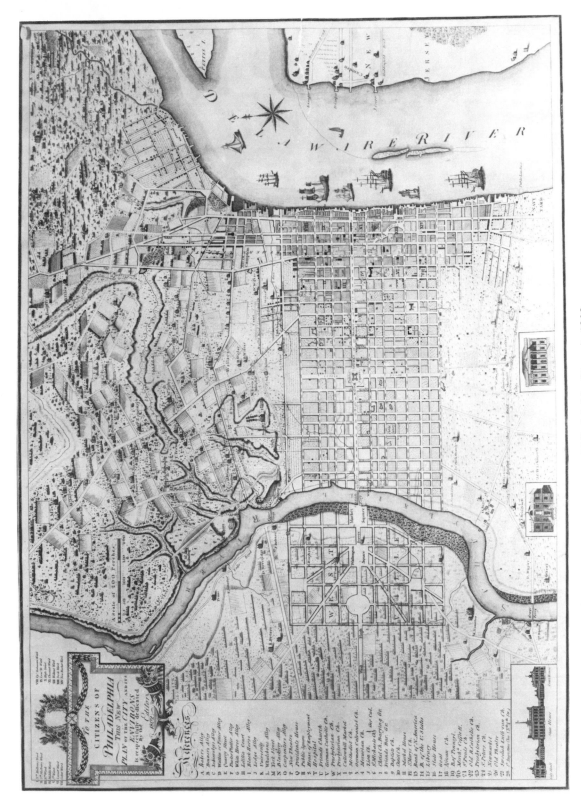

Plate 133   Philadelphia (Penn.), 1802.

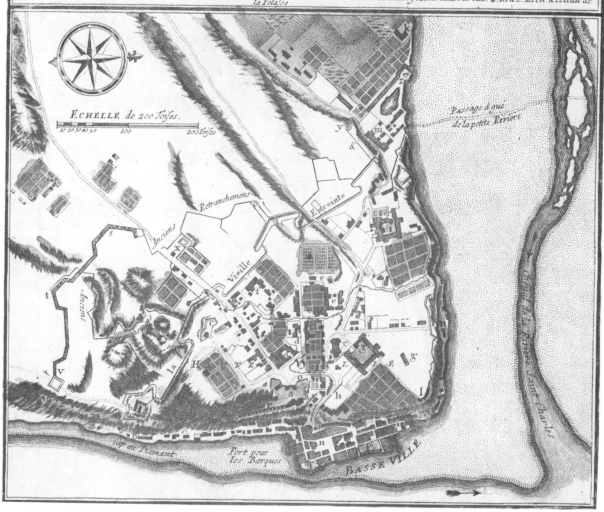

PLAN de la Ville de QUEBEC. a. *Fort St Louis.* b. *Redoute du Cap au Diamant.* c. *Cavalier du Moulin.* d. *Les Récolets.* e. *Les Jesuites et dépendances.* f. *Les Urselines.* g. *La Paroisse avec le Séminaire et dépendances.* h. *L'Evêché.* i. *L'Hôtel Dieu.* k. *St Roch.* l. *Le Sault au Matelot.* m. *L'Intendance.* n. *Eglise de la basse Ville.* o. *Batt. de Vaudreuil.* p. *Batt. Dauphine.* q. *Batt. Royale.* r. *Batt. du Château.* s. *Bast. St Louis* t. *Bast. de la Glaciere.* v. *Demi Bast. de Joubert.* x. *Red. St Ursule* y. *Red. au Boureau.* z. *Red. St Roch.* &. *Coteau de la Potasse.*

Plate 134   Quebec, 1756.

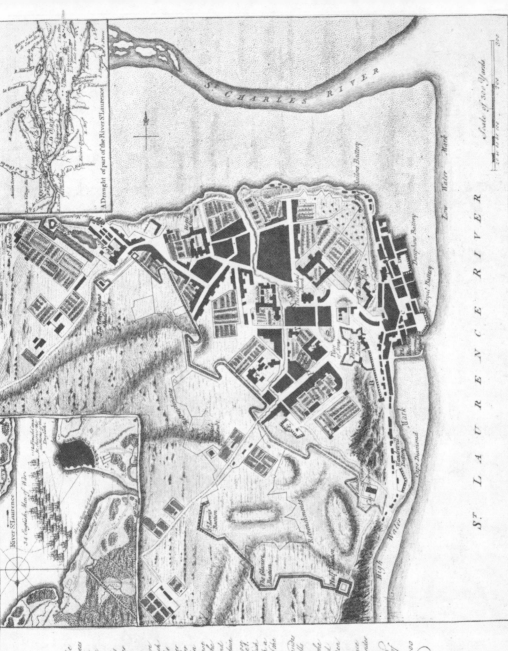

Published according to Act of Parliament Octr 1759 by T. Iefferys & fold by A. Rogers near Round Court in the Strand

Plate 135 Quebec, 1759.

A PLAN of QUEBEC.

The Capital of New France or Canada in America is situated upon the River St. Laurence in ye deg 19m. North latitude Longitude 32 degrees 30m West from the Island of Fero its distance from the Mouth of the River is about 90 Miles an extent Navigable for ships of most Burthen. the Harbour of Quebec being safe and spacious it accommodates East by North East by the Islands of Orleans. the City is pretty large and by far the greatest and most flourishing of all towns in the City which is built upon a Rock has several publick buildings as the Cathedral the Episcopal Palace built by the Bishop of St. Valier & Rising Quebec by the time...

REFERENCES.

A. Residence of the Governor General.
B. Battery of the Shore.
C. Notre Dame de la Victoire.
D. The Arms of the Congregation.
E. Cavalier of the Wind Mill.
F. Ursulines Convent. G. Jesuits.

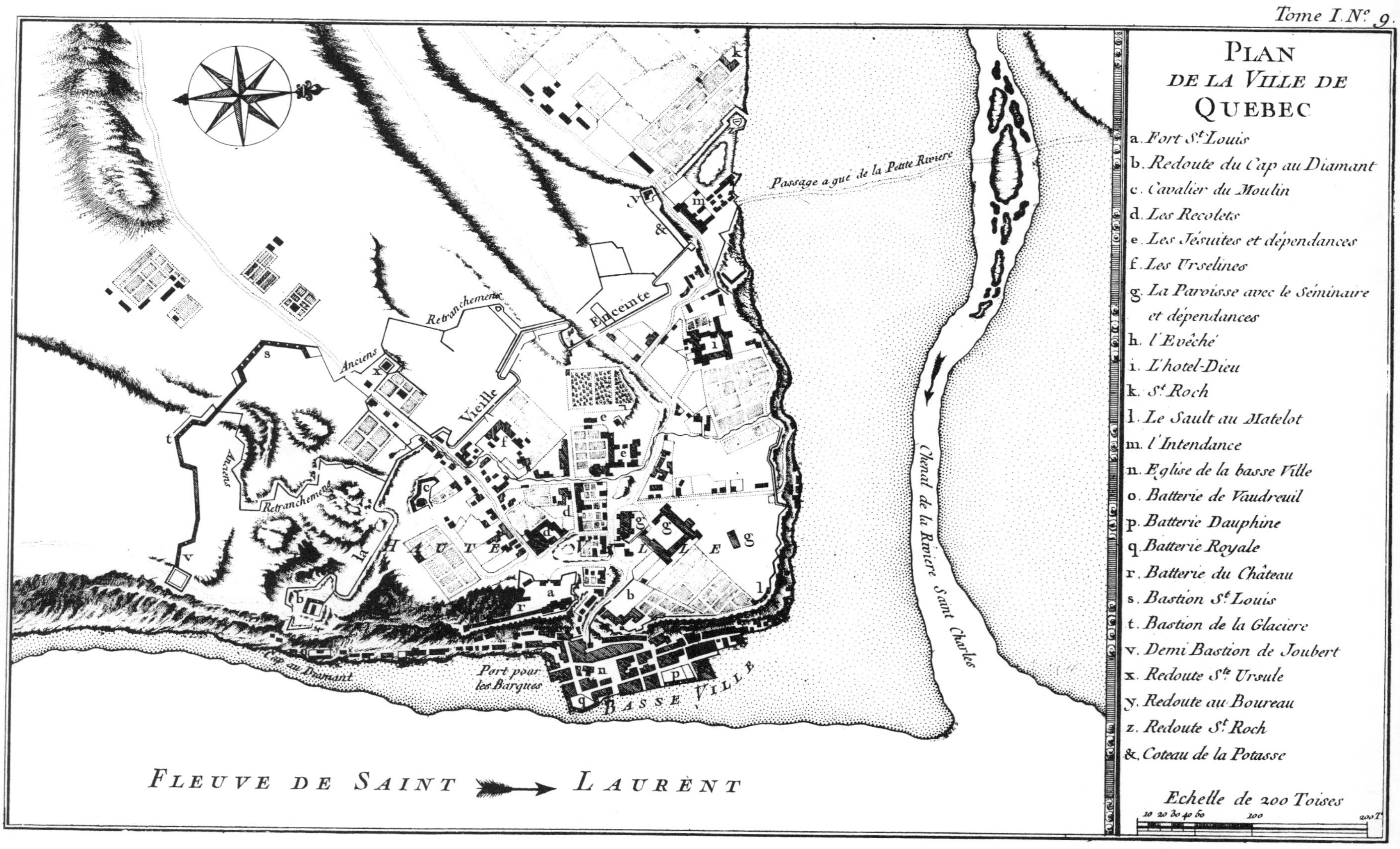
Tome I. N°. 9.
PLAN
DE LA VILLE DE
QUEBEC
a. Fort St. Louis
b. Redoute du Cap au Diamant
c. Cavalier du Moulin
d. Les Recolets
e. Les Jésuites et dépendances
f. Les Urselines
g. La Paroisse avec le Séminaire et dépendances
h. l'Evêché
i. L'hotel-Dieu
k. St. Roch
l. Le Sault au Matelot
m. l'Intendance
n. Eglise de la basse Ville
o. Batterie de Vaudreuil
p. Batterie Dauphine
q. Batterie Royale
r. Batterie du Château
s. Bastion St. Louis
t. Bastion de la Glaciere
v. Demi Bastion de Joubert
x. Redoute Ste. Ursule
y. Redoute au Boureau
z. Redoute St. Roch
&. Coteau de la Potasse
Echelle de 200 Toises
10 20 30 40 60
200
200 T.
Passage a gué de la Petite Riviere
Chenal de la Riviere Saint Charles
Enceinte
Vieille
Retranchement
Anciens
Retranchement
Anciens
Anciens
HAUTE VILLE
BASSE VILLE
Port pour les Barques
Cap au Diamant
FLEUVE DE SAINT LAURÈNT

Plate 136 Quebec, 1763-4.

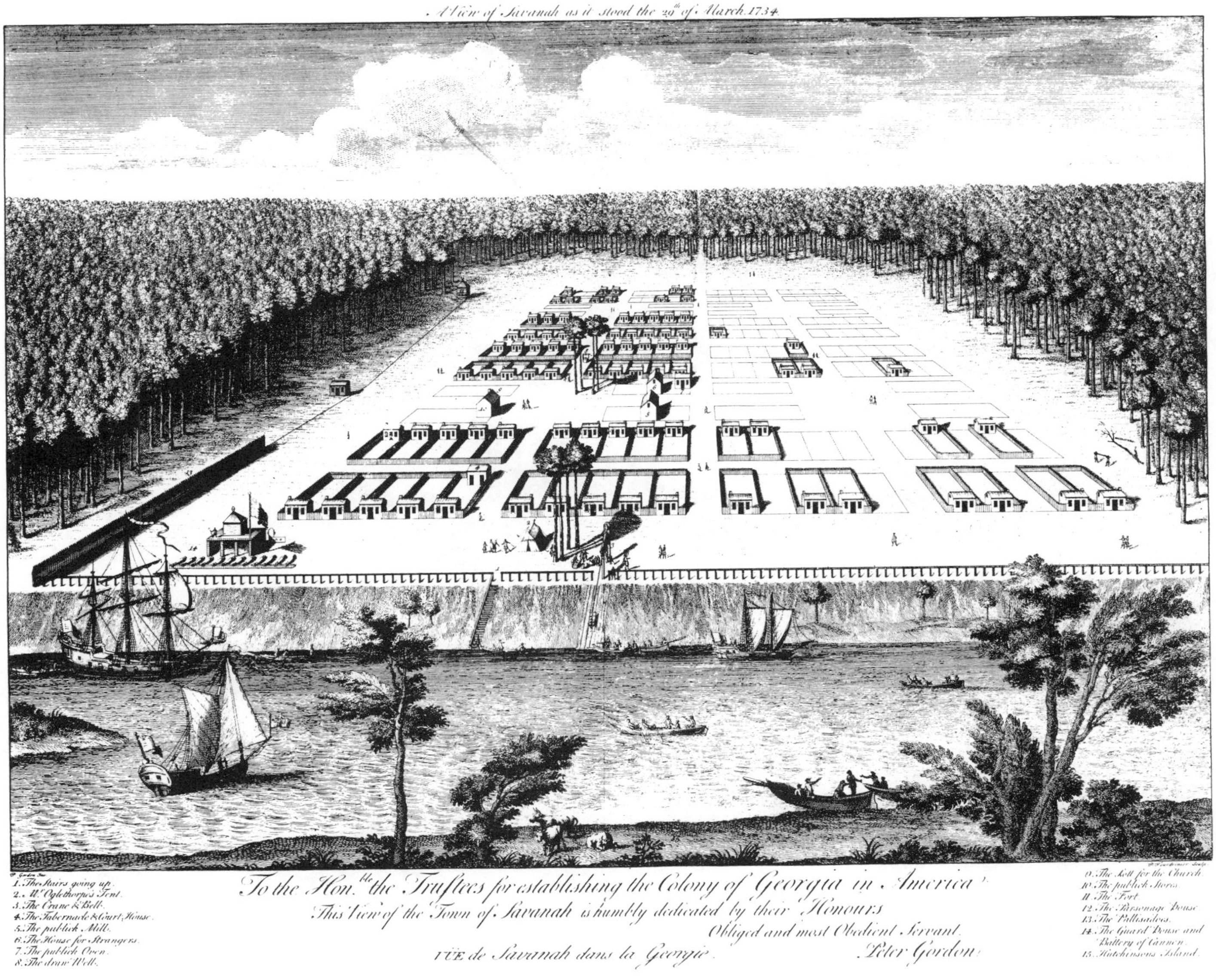

Plate 137   Savannah (Georgia), 1734.

PAGUS HISPANORUM in Florida

Plate 138 St. Augustine (Florida), 1670.

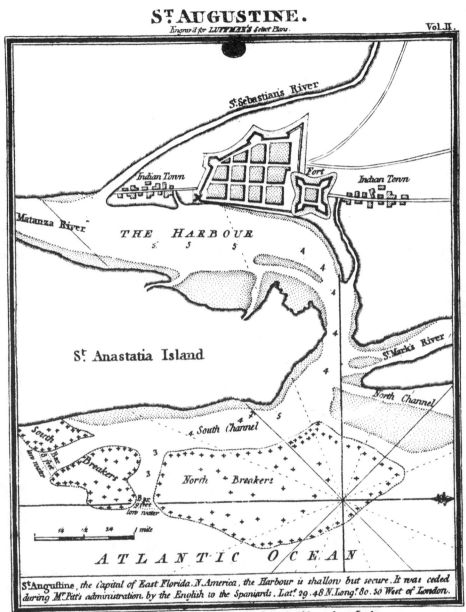

ST. AUGUSTINE.

Engrav'd for LUFFMAN'S Select Plans.

Vol. II.

St Sebastians River

Indian Town

Fort

Indian Town

Matanza River

THE HARBOUR

St. Anastatia Island

St Mark's River

North Channel

South Bar low water

South Channel

North Breakers

Breakers

Bar low water

14   ¼   34   1 mile

ATLANTIC OCEAN

St Auguftine, the Capital of East Florida, N America, the Harbour is shallow but secure. It was ceded during Mr Pitt's administration. by the English to the Spaniards. Latt: 29.48 N. Long: 80.50 West of London.

Engrav'd & Publish'd Jan.y 1. 1802. by J. Luffman. Little Bell Alley, Coleman Street, London.

Plate 139   St. Augustine (Florida), 1802.

FLORIDA ORIENTAL

Nº 37.

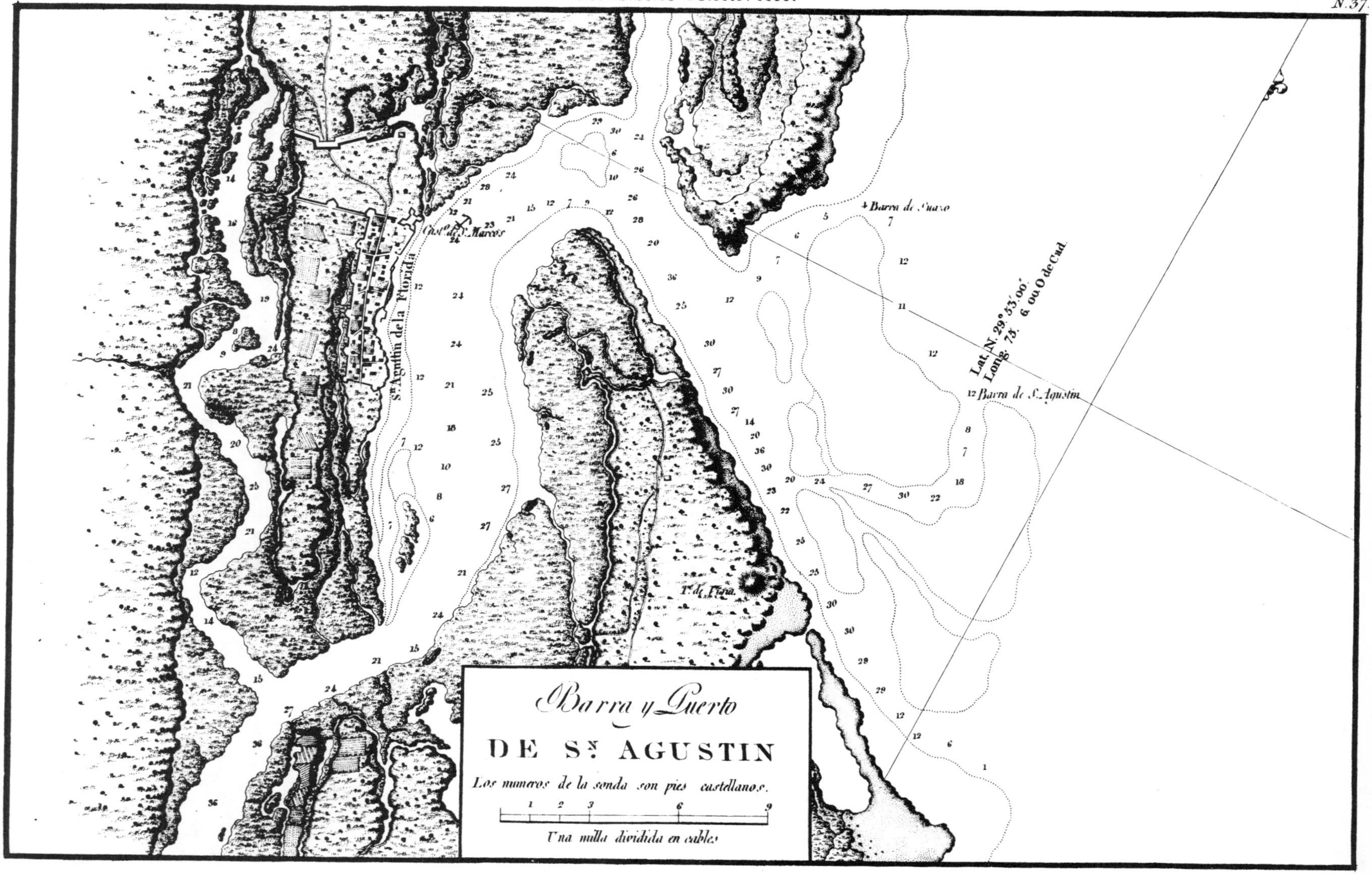
Barra y Puerto
DE Sn. AGUSTIN
Los numeros de la sonda son pies castellanos.
1 2 3 6 9
Una milla dividida en cables
Lat. N. 29° 53'. 00"
Long. 75. 6. 00 O de Cad.
Barra de S. Agustin
Barra de Suaxo
Stn. Agustin de la Florida
Castº de Sn. Marcos
Tª de Vigia

Plate 140 St. Augustine (Florida), 1818.

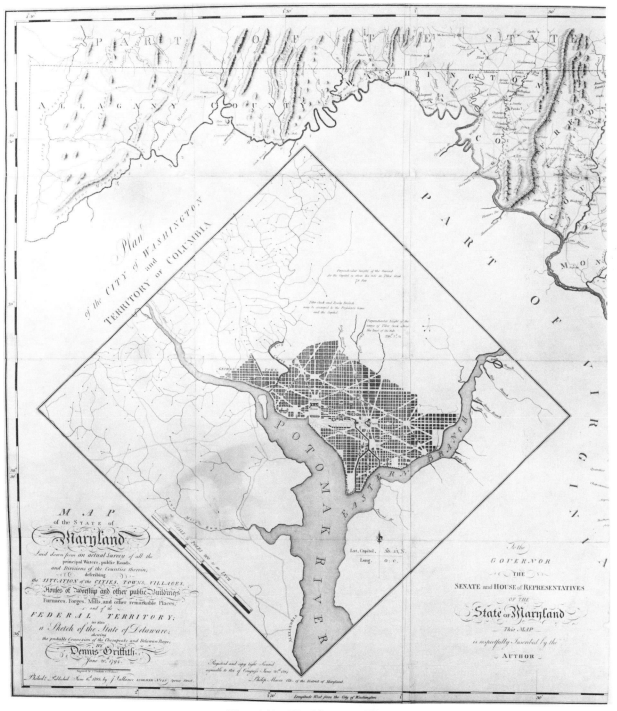

Plate 141   Washington, 1794.

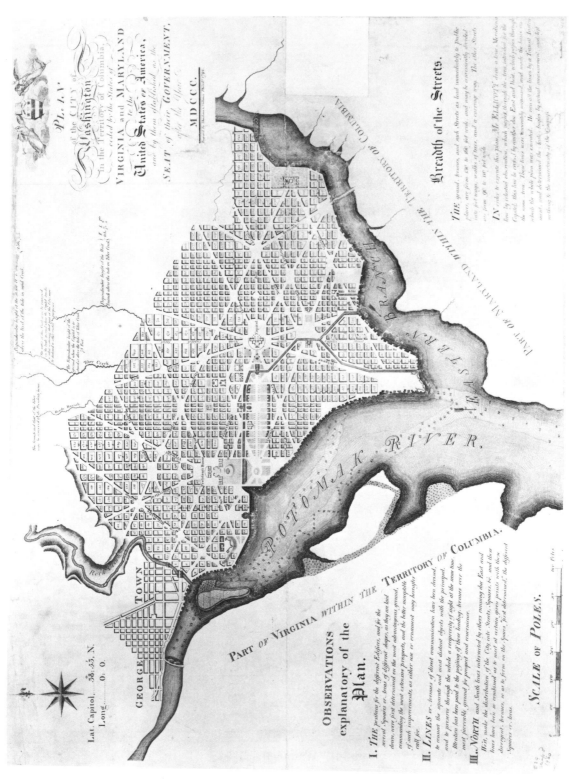

Plate 142 Washington, 1800.

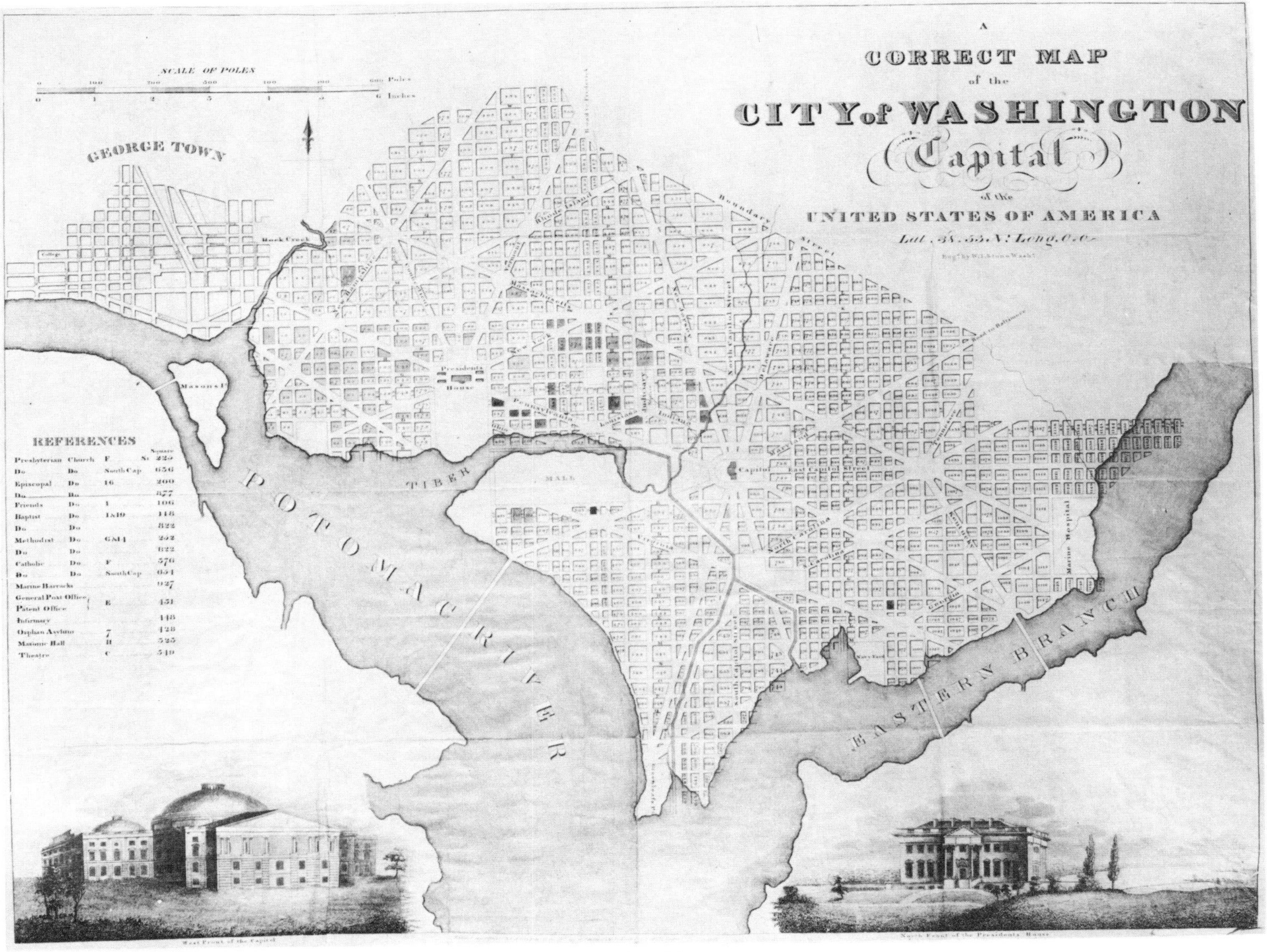

A

CORRECT MAP
of the
CITY of WASHINGTON
Capital
of the
UNITED STATES OF AMERICA

REFERENCES

		Squares
Presbyterian Church	F	456
Do.	Bo.	Southcap	656
Episcopal	Bo.	260
Do.	Bo.	627
French	Bo.	1046
Baptist	Bo.	532
Do.	Bo.	353
Methodist	Bo.	651	653
Do.	Bo.	570
Catholic	Bo.	664
Do.	Bo.	Southcap	627
Marine Barracks	E	851
General Post Office		146
Patent Office		120
Infirmary		525
Orphan Asylum	Z	
Masonic Hall	C	549
Theatre		

SCALE OF POLES

GEORGE TOWN

POTOMAC RIVER

EASTERN BRANCH

Plate 143   Washington.

Plate 144   No. 1.   Jansson, First state.

Plate 145   No. 2.   Jansson, Second state.

Plate 146   No. 3.   Jansson [Schenk & Valk], Third state.

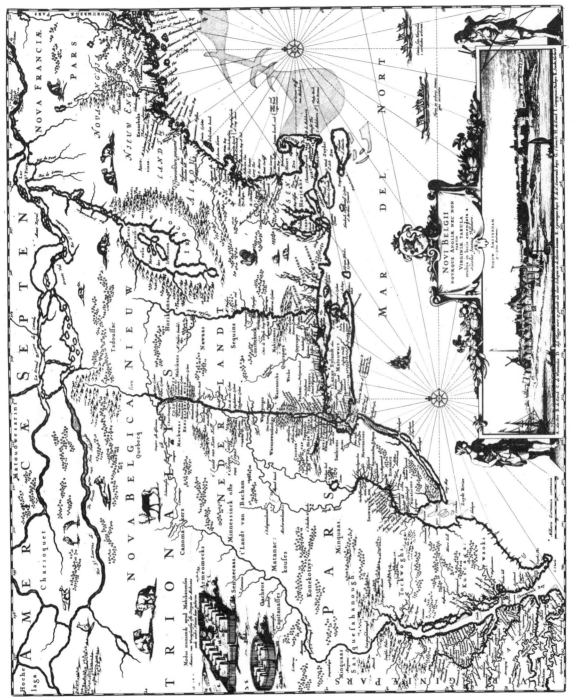

Plate 147 No. 5. Visscher (N. J.), Second state.

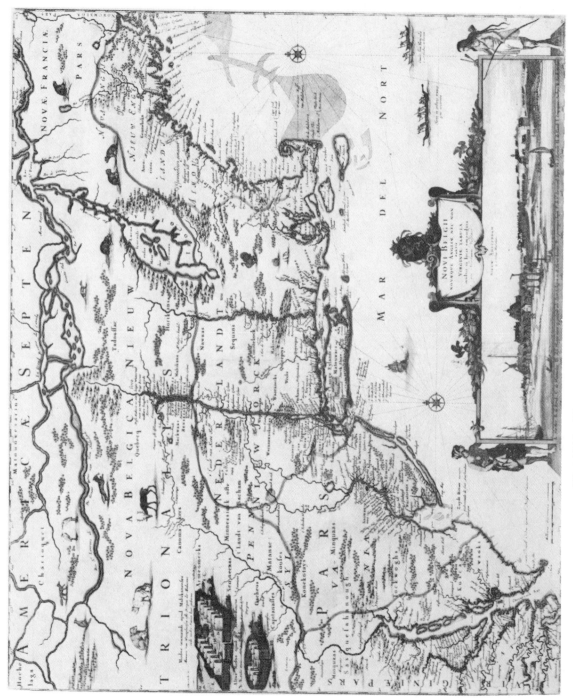

Plate 148   No. 6.   Visscher (N.), Fourth state.

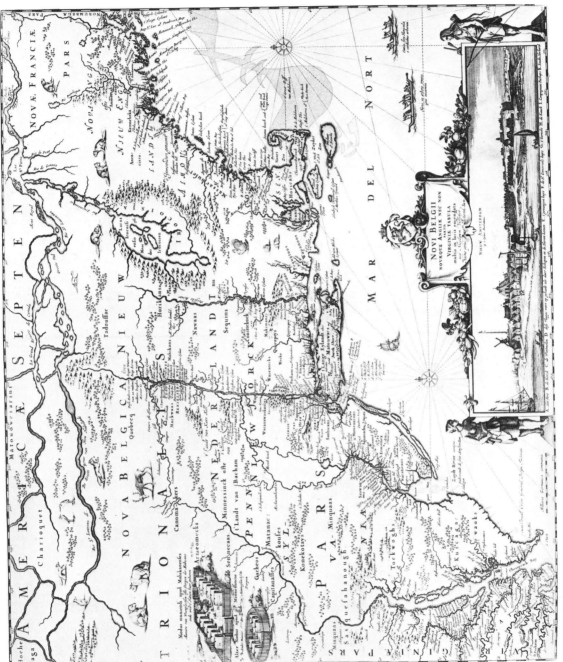

Plate 149   No. 7.   Visscher (Schenk junior), Fifth state.

Plates 150   No. 9.   Danckers, Second state.

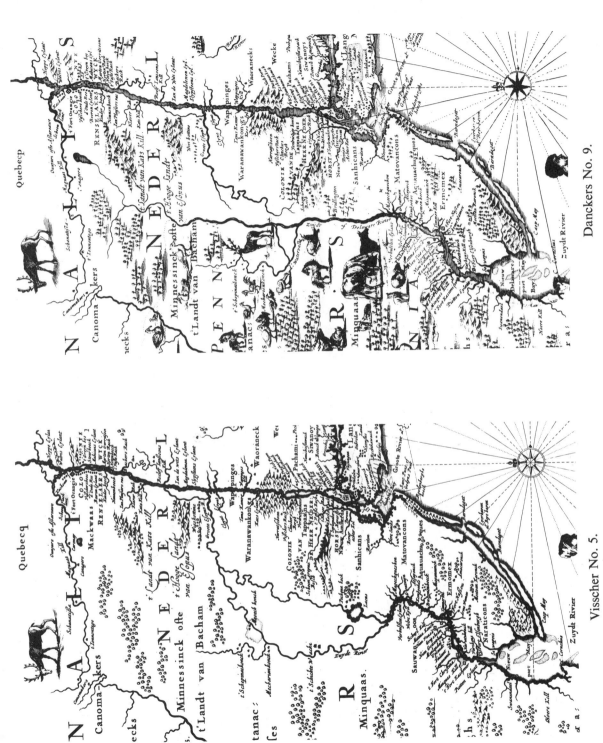

Quebecp

Danckers No. 9.

Quebecq

Visscher No. 5.

Plate 151   Details showing the Delaware River.

Plate 152   No. 11.   vander Donck, Second state.

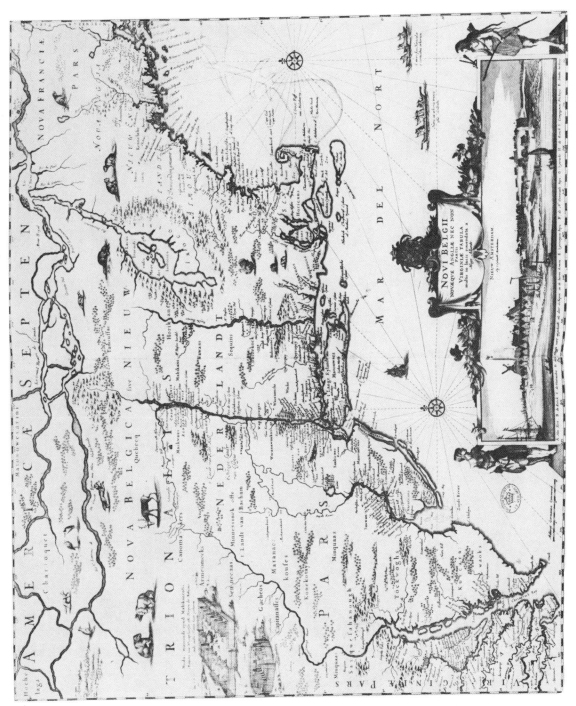

Plate 153   No. 14.   Allard (H.), First state.

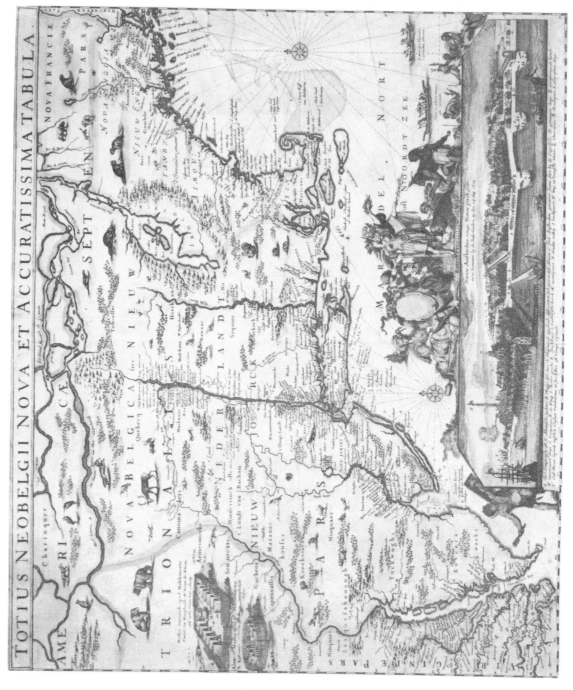

Plate 154   No. 15.   Allard (H.), Second state.

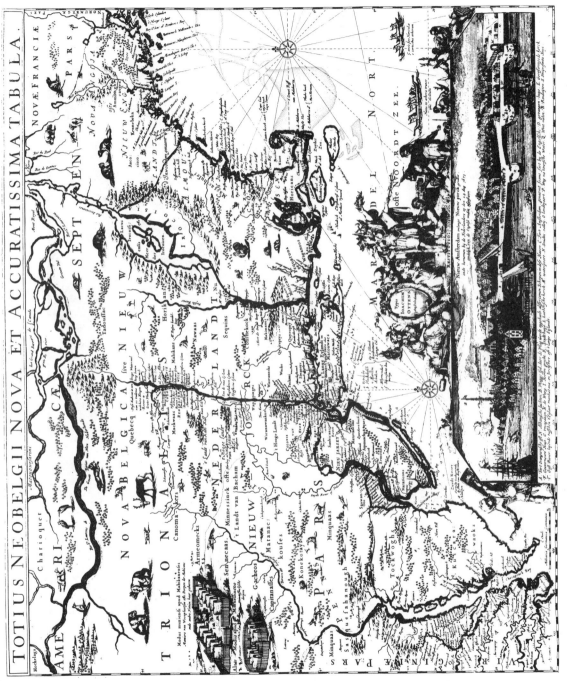

Plate 155   No. 19.   Allard [Ottens, J.], Sixth state.

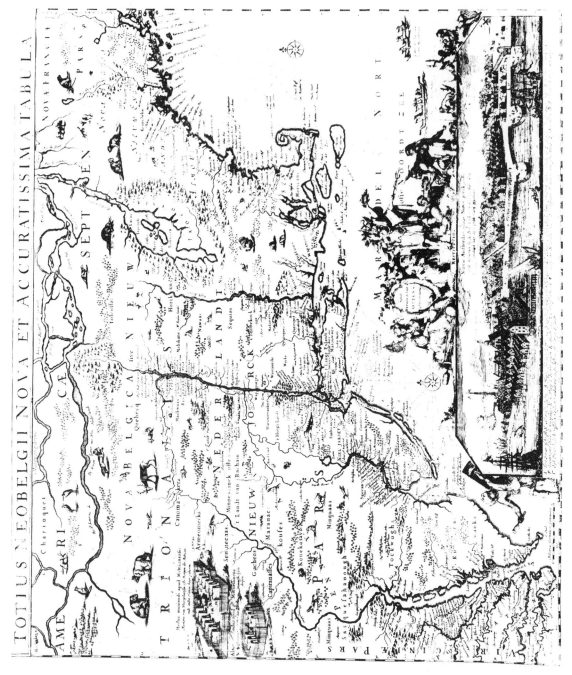

Plate 156   No. 20.   Allard [Ottens, R. & J.], Seventh state.

Plate 157   No. 21.   Ogilby-Montanus, First state.

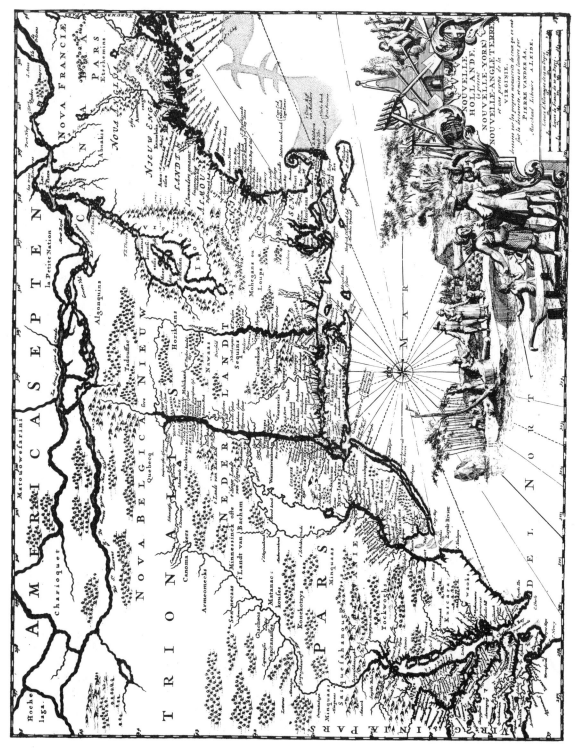

Plate 158   No. 22.   Ogilby-Montanus [vander Aa], Second state.

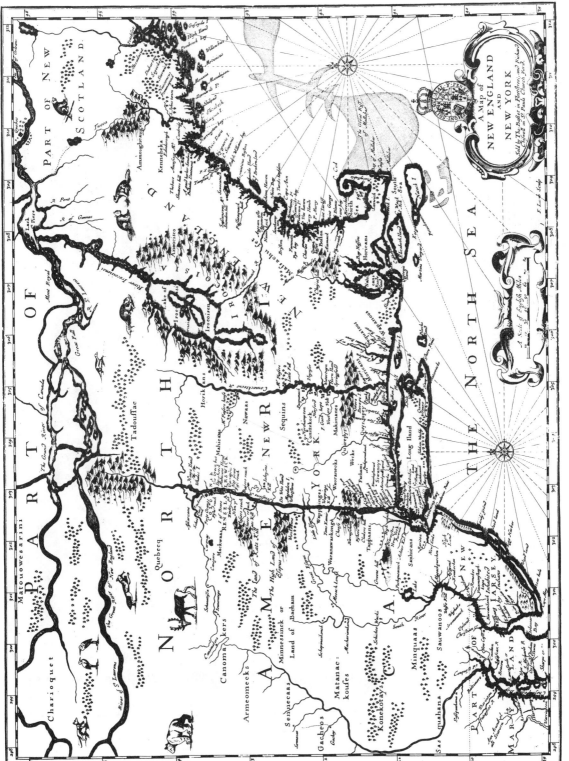

Plate 159   No. 23.   Speed.

Plate 160   No. 25.   Seutter, Second state.

RECENS EDITA
totius
NOV.I BELGII,
in
AMERICA SEPTENTRIONALI
fiti,
delineatio
cura et fumtibus
MATTHÆI SEUTTERI,
Chalcographi Auguftani.

No. 24.

RECENS EDITA
totius
NOV.I BELGII,
in
AMERICA SEPTENTRIONALI
fiti,
delineatio
cura et fumtibus
MATTHÆI SEUTTERI,
Sac.Cæs.Maj.Geographí
August.Vind.

No. 25.

RECENS EDITA
totius
NOVI BELGII,
in
AMERICA SEPTENTRIONALI
fiti,
delineatio
cura et fumtibus
MATTHÆI SEUTTERI,
Sac.Cæs.Maj.Geographí
August.Vind.

No. 26.

RECENS EDITA
totius
NOVI BELGII,
in
AMERICA SEPTENTRIONALI
fiti,
delineatio
cura et fumtibus
TOB.CONR LOTTERI,
Sac.Cæs.Maj.Geographí
August.Vind.

No. 27.

Plate 161   Details of the Seutter & Lotter imprints.

Lotter No. 27.

Speed No. 23.

Jansson No. 1.

Plate 162   Details showing Boston.

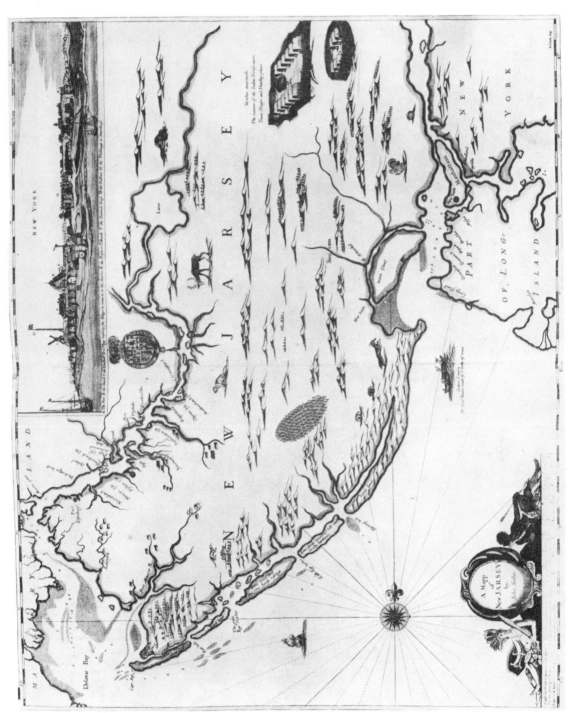

Plate 163   Addenda A.   Seller, First state.

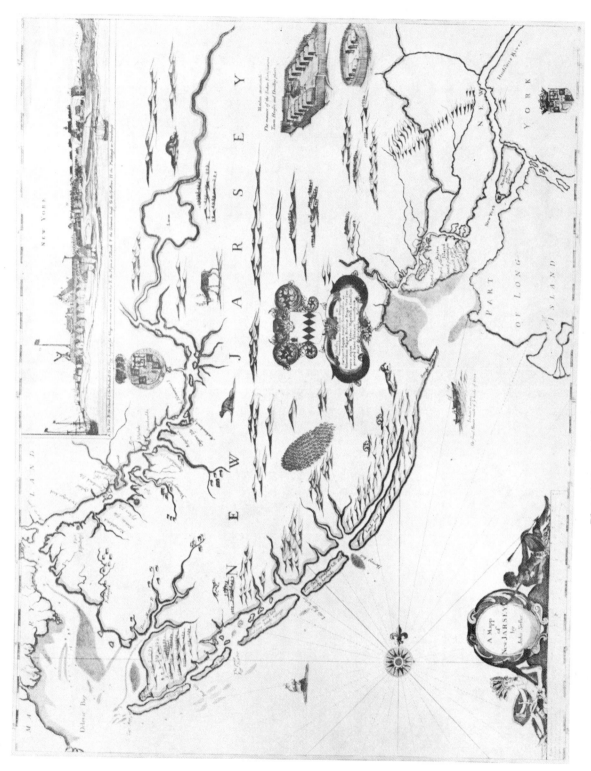

Plate 164   Addenda B.   Seller, Second state.

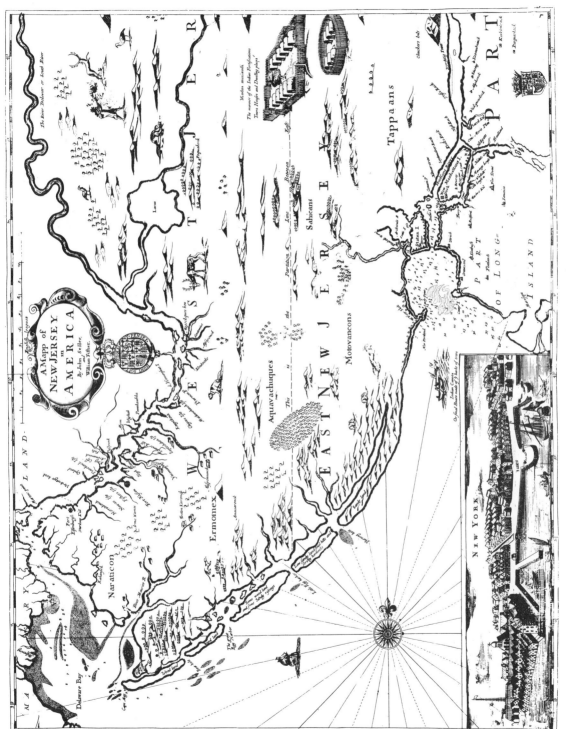

Plate 165   Addenda C.   Seller, Third state [centre sheet].

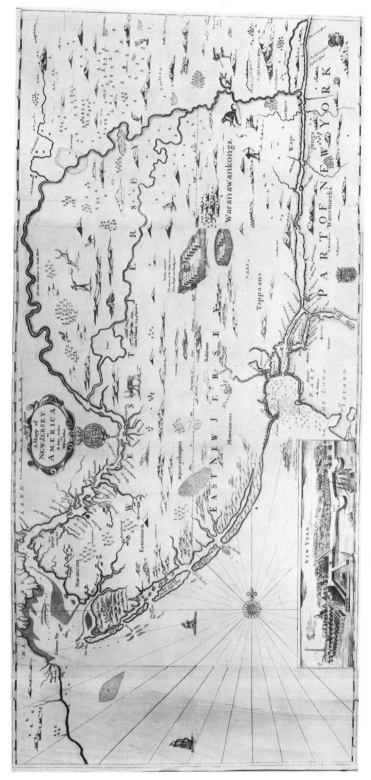

Plate 166   Addenda C.   Seller, Third state [with side panels].

NIEUW AMSTERDAM
op t Eylant Manhattans.

A. Het Fort B. de Kerck C. de Windmolen D. dese Vlagge wert op gehaelt als daer Schepen in de Haven komen. E. tgevangen huys F. de H. Generaels huys G. t Gerecht H. de Kaeck I. Compagnies Pachuys K. Stads Herbergh

Visscher view

Nieuw-Amsterdam onlangs Nieuw jorck genaemt ende hernomen by de Nederlanders op den 24 Aug. 1673.

A. Fort Orangie ofte Ø N. Alhingske hachten. B. Wolffs spil daer die Vlag werde opgehaelt alsser eenen Schepen in de Haven. C. Fort Amsterdam, genaemt Iaems fort by de Engelsche. D. gevangen-huys. E. Gereformeerde kerck. F. Gouverneurs Huys. G. t magazyn. H. de Waeg. I. Stveren gracht. K. Stadthuys. L. Luthersche kerck. M. waterpoort. N. Smales-valley. O. landtpoort. P. Weg na twveesche water. Q. Wint-molen. R. Rondajers. S. Schuijnesants huys T. Oost-Rivier, loopende tusschen t Eylant manhattans, en fort essare oft t litige Eylandt.

Restitutio view, c.1674.

Plate 167
The alternative views of New York.

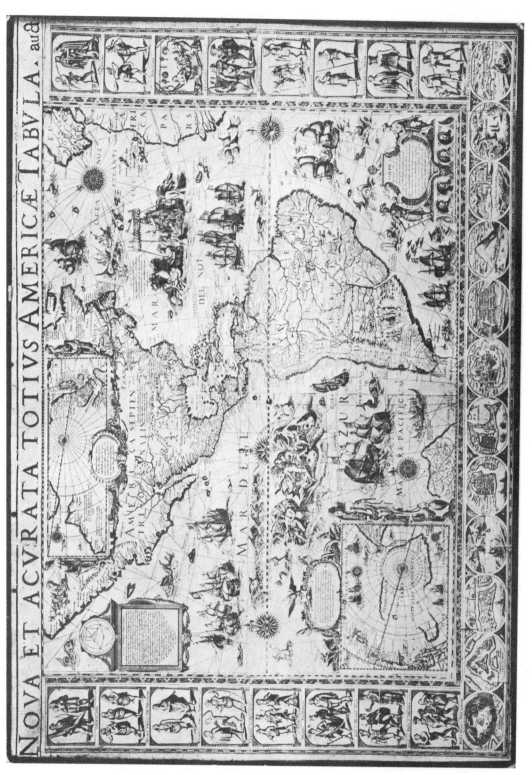

Plate 168   Blaeu, W.   [1673]

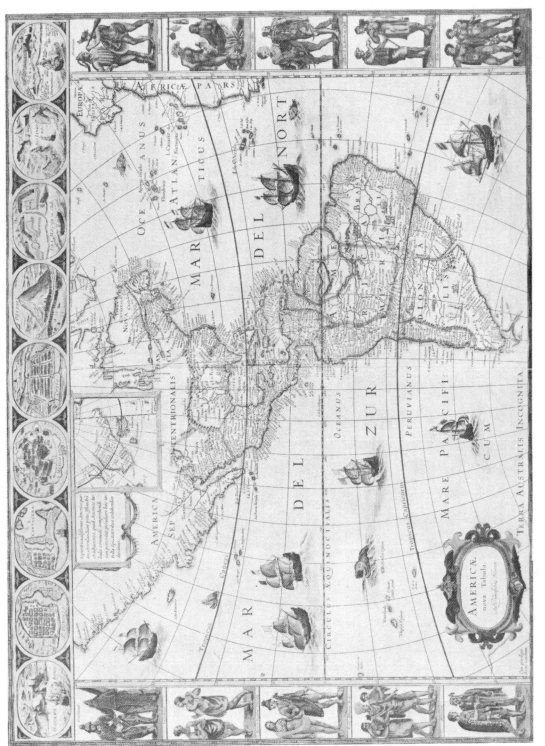

Plate 169   Blaeu, W.   [1630]

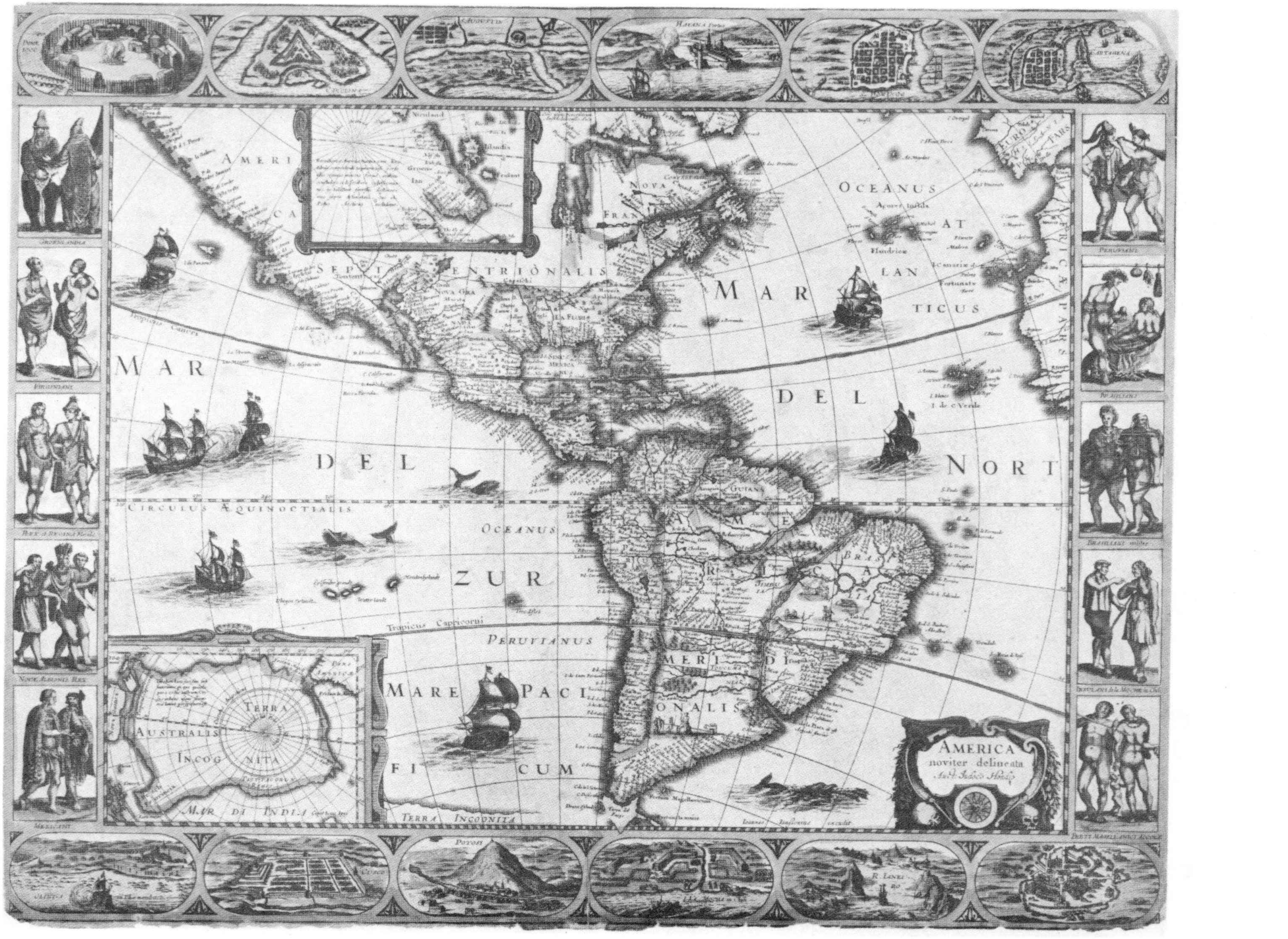

Plate 170   Hondius, J.   [1630]

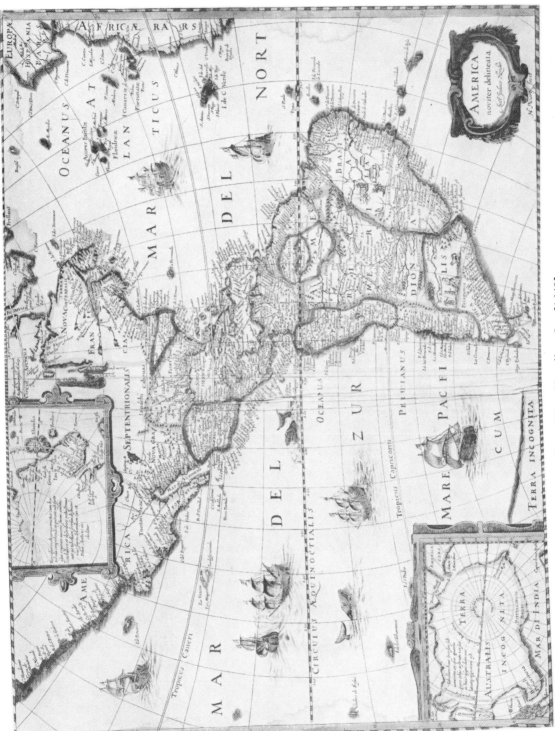

Plate 171   Hondius, J.   [1648]

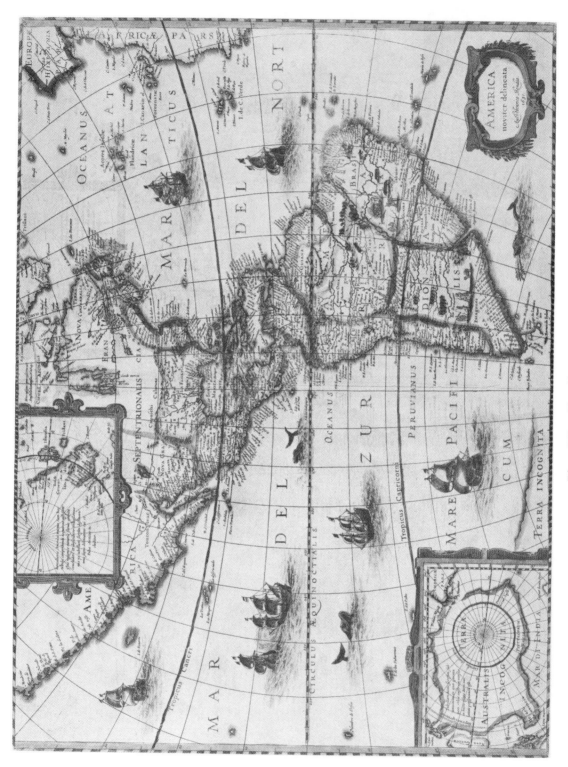

Plate 172   Hondius, H.   1631

Plate 173 Bertius, P. [1648]

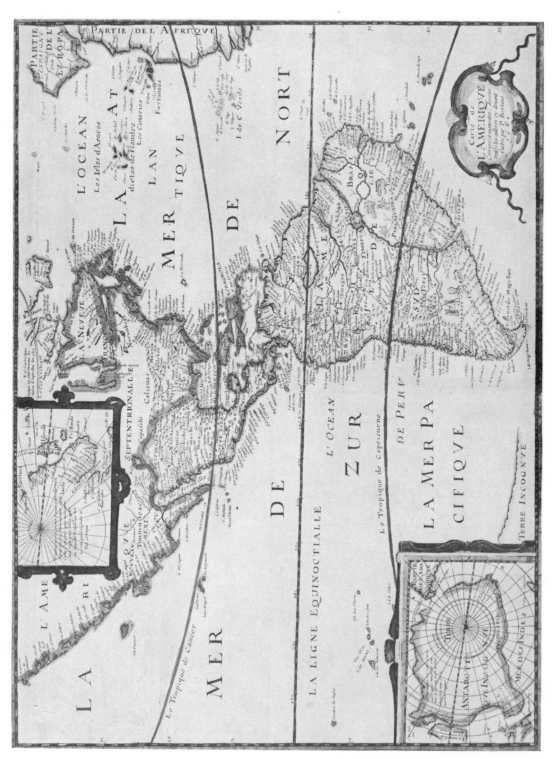

Plate 174   Bertius, P.   1661

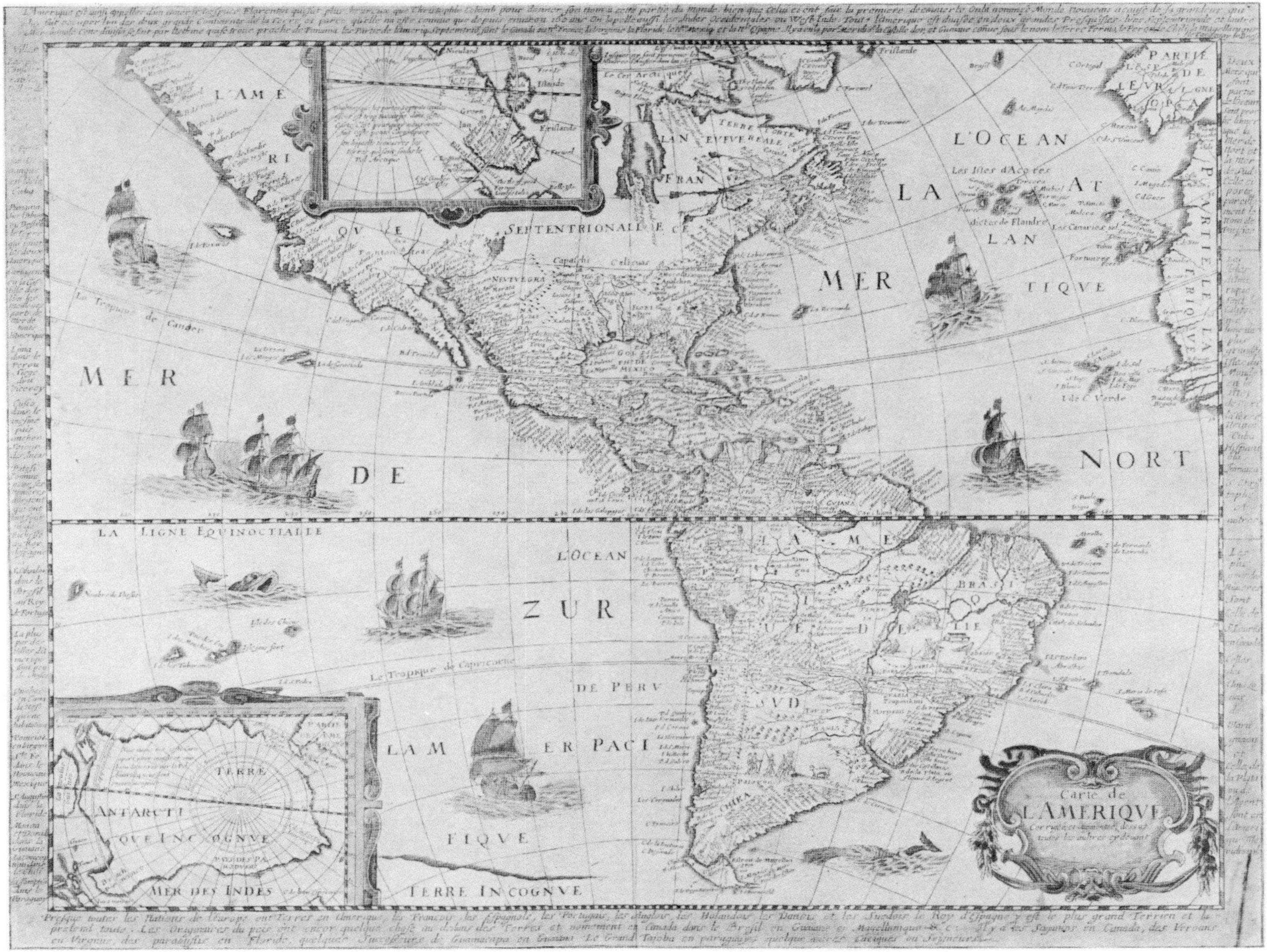

Plate 175   Bertius, P.   [1671]

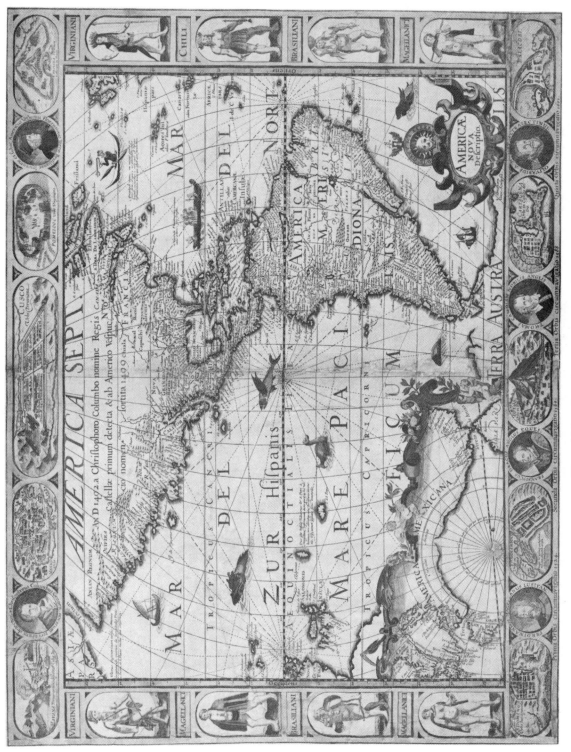

Plate 176   Kaerius, P.   1614 [16]

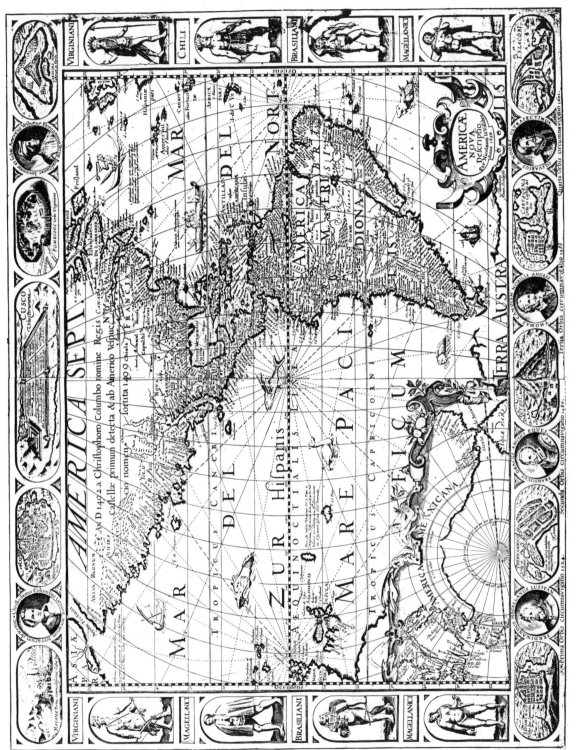

Plate 177   Visscher, N.   1652

Plate 178   Speed, J.   [1676]

Plate 179   Walton, R.   [1670]

INDEX

512

514